CMT LEVEL II

Theory and Analysis

Readings Selected by

The Market Technicians Association

WILEY

CONTENTS

iii

The Market Technicians Association is a not-for-profit professional regulatory organization servicing over 4,500 market analysis professionals in over 85 countries around the globe. The MTA's main objectives involve the education of the public, the investment community, and its membership in the theory, practice, and application of technical analysis.

The MTA has the following stated mission:

- Attract and retain a membership of professionals devoting their efforts to using and expanding the field of technical analysis and sharing their body of knowledge with their fellow members.

- Establish, maintain, and encourage the highest standards of professional competence and ethics among technical analysts.

- Educate the public and the investment community of the value and universality of technical analysis.

The MTA mission is accomplished through the effective execution of a wide variety of professional services including, but not limited to, regional seminars, local chapter meetings, the maintenance of an extensive library of technical analysis material, and the regular publication of newsletters and journals.

MTA members and affiliates include technical analysts, portfolio managers, investment advisors, market letter writers, and others involved in the technical aspects of equities, futures, options, fixed income securities, currencies, international markets, derivatives, etc.

Services provided to our members and affiliates are performed by a small NYC-based Headquarter staff, an active Board of Directors, Committee Chairs, and an extensive cadre of volunteers located in both U.S. and non-U.S. markets.

The Chartered Market Technician® (CMT) credential is the global standard for practitioners of technical analysis and technical risk management. It is a FINRA-recognized designation which sets apart CMT charterholders as specialists and value-generators among active investment professionals.

The designation is awarded to those who demonstrate mastery of a core body of knowledge in risk management and portfolio management settings. The advanced technical expertise represented by the CMT charter immediately communicates to clients and employers the disciplined approach, academic rigor, and unique professional skill set which CMT charterholders possess.

The objectives of the CMT Program are:

- To promote high ethical standards of education, integrity, and professional excellence

- To guide candidates in mastering a professional body of knowledge

- To professionalize the discipline of technical analysis

Those candidates who successfully complete all three levels of the CMT examination and agree to abide by the MTA Code of Ethics are granted the right to use the CMT credential.

■ What Will You Learn?

The CMT Program is offered in a self-study format. There are three levels of exams, each one building on the previous. The levels progressively narrow in focus while increasing the emphasis on higher-order reasoning.

The final exam requires candidates to implement critical analysis to arrive at well-supported recommendations in a professional investing/trading context.

The curriculum is organized into exam-specific knowledge domains that provide a framework for recognizing and implementing investment and trading opportunity.

Level I	Level II	Level III
I. Theory & History	I. Theory & History	I. Risk Management
II. Markets	II. Market Indicators	II. Asset Relationships
III. Market Indicators	III. Construction	III. Portfolio Management
IV. Construction	IV. Trend Analysis	IV. Classical Methods
V. Trend Analysis	V. Chart & Pattern Analysis	V. Behavioral Finance
VI. Chart & Pattern Analysis	VI. Confirmation	VI. Volatility Analysis
VII. Confirmation	VII. Cycles	VII. Ethics
VIII. Cycles	VIII. Selection & Decision	
IX. Selection & Decision	IX. System Testing	
X. System Testing	X. Risk Management	
XI. Statistical Analysis	XI. Statistical Analysis	
XII. Ethics	XII. Ethics	

The curriculum for the Market Technician Association's CMT exam level II is comprised of selected readings in the areas of technical analysis and other financial disciplines. The MTA curates each level of the 3-volume curriculum, reviewing the available academic literature as well as practitioner scholarship. The process distills the best readings from all available and applicable works into a concise study tool for CMT Candidates to gain broad understanding of the core body of knowledge and best practice in active money management. The MTA is indebted to the fine work of each author whose work is included in the curriculum.

PREFACE

Congratulations on qualifying yourself for the CMT Level II Exam. This exam will further extend your ability to produce uncommon insight in research and analysis. Completion of the Level II exam allows you to apply for a FINRA Series 86 license, with which you can become a FINRA-licensed technical analyst. Being a technical analyst is not the only job function that makes use of the CMT designation. More and more Chartered Market Technicians are found in a variety of roles around the industry. The Level II exam shows that you have sufficient depth of understanding about technical analysis to be among them. The exam is also a necessary stepping stone for the third and final level of exams.

The CMT Level II exam measures the candidates' competency in the **application** of concepts, theory, and techniques covered by the required readings. CMT Level II candidates must demonstrate their ability to apply concepts identified in their Level I studies to relevant conditions or scenarios.

Exam time length: 4 hours, 15 minutes

Exam format: Multiple Choice

The curriculum is organized into exam-specific knowledge domains that provide a framework for recognizing and implementing investment/trading decisions. The CMT Level II exam tests the candidate's knowledge in 12 domains:

1. Theory and History
2. Market Indicators
3. Construction
4. Trend Analysis
5. Chart and Pattern Analysis
6. Confirmation
7. Cycles
8. Selection and Decision
9. System Testing
10. Risk Management
11. Statistical Analysis
12. Ethics

■ Exam Topics & Question Weightings

1. Theory and History	a. behavioral finance	5%	7
	b. Adaptive Market Hypothesis		
2. Market Indicators	a. breadth indicators	8%	13
	b. sentiment measures		
	c. volatility		
3. Construction	a. volume	3%	4
4. Trend Analysis	a. trendlines	15%	23
	b. multiple time frame analysis		
	c. breakouts		
	d. moving averages		
	e. trend strength indicators		
5. Chart and Pattern Analysis	a. gap analysis	15%	23
	b. support and resistance		
6. Confirmation	a. oscillators and divergence	6%	9
	b. sector rotation		
	c. intermarket signals		
7. Cycles	a. seasonal cycles	3%	4
8. Selection and Decision	a. uncorrelated assets	10%	15
	b. relative strength		
	c. forecasting techniques		
9. System Testing	a. algorithmic development	10%	15
	b. objective analysis of rules		
	c. performance measures		
10. Risk Management	a. absolute and relative risk	15%	22
	b. risk modeling		
	c. value at risk		
	d. volatility risk		
	e. liquidity risk		
	f. diversification		
	g. leverage risk		
	h. portfolio risk management		
	i. risk-based performance measures		
11. Statistical Analysis	a. inferential statistics	7%	11
12. Ethics	a. standards and practices	3%	4

CHAPTER 1

Charting

From Perry J. Kaufman, *Trading Systems and Methods + Website,* 5th Edition (Hoboken, New Jersey: John Wiley & Sons, 2013), Chapter 3.

It is very likely that all trading systems began with a price chart, and we come back to a chart whenever we want a clear view of where the market is going. Nowhere can a picture be more valuable than in price forecasting. Elaborate theories and complex formulas may ultimately be successful, but the loss of perspective is easily corrected with a simple chart. We should remember the investor who, anxious after a long technical presentation by a research analyst, could only blurt out, "But is it going up or down?" Even with the most sophisticated market strategies, the past buy and sell signals should be seen on a chart. The appearance of an odd trade can save you a lot of aggravation and money.

Through the mid-1980s technical analysis was considered only as chart interpretation. In the equities industry, that perception is still strong. Most traders begin as chartists, and many return to it or use it even while using other methods. William L. Jiler, a great trader and founder of Commodity Research Bureau, wrote:

> One of the most significant and intriguing concepts derived from intensive chart studies by this writer is that of characterization, or habit. Generally speaking, charts of the same commodity tend to have similar pattern sequences which may be different from those of another commodity. In other words, charts of one particular commodity may appear to have an identity or a character peculiar to that commodity. For example, cotton charts display many round tops and bottoms, and even a series of these constructions, which are seldom observed in soybeans and wheat. The examination of soybean charts over the years reveals that triangles are especially favored. Head and shoulders formations abound throughout the wheat charts. All commodities seem to favor certain behavior patterns.[1]

---

[1] William L. Jiler, "How Charts Are Used in Commodity Price Forecasting," *Commodity Research Publications* (New York, 1977).

In addition to Jiler's observation, the cattle futures market is recognized as also having the unusual occurrence of "V" bottoms. Until recently, both the silver and pork belly markets have tendencies to look very similar, with long periods of sideways movement and short-lived but violent *price shocks,* where prices leap rather than trend to a new level. The financial markets have equally unique personalities. The S&P traditionally makes new highs, then immediately falls back; it has fast, short-lived drops and slower, steadier gains. Currencies show intermediate trends bounded by noticeable major stopping levels while interest rates and bonds have long-term trends.

Charting remains the most popular and practical form for evaluating price movement, and numerous works have been written on methods of interpretation. This chapter will summarize some of the accepted approaches to charting and the trading rules normally associated with these patterns. Some conclusions are drawn as to what is most likely to work and why.

■ Finding Consistent Patterns

A price chart is often considered a representation of human behavior. The goal of any chart analyst is to find consistent, reliable, and logical patterns that can be used to predict price movement. In the classic approaches to charting, there are consolidations, trend channels, top-and-bottom formations, and a multitude of other patterns that are created by the repeated action of large groups of people in similar circumstances or with similar objectives. The most important of all the chart patterns is the *trendline*.

Only recently have computer programs been able to interpret chart patterns; and only one book, Bulkowski's *Encyclopedia of Chart Patterns*[2] has managed to show a comprehensive analysis of chart formations. In all fairness, there can be numerous valid interpretations of the same chart. In order to identify a chart price formation, it is first necessary to select the data frequency (for example, daily or weekly), then the starting date and a time horizon (long-term or short-term), before a chart interpretation can begin. Given the wide range of choices, it should be surprising that any two analysts see the same patterns at the same time.

Chart analyses, frequently published in magazines, may themselves be the cause of the repeated patterns. Novice speculators approach the problem with great enthusiasm and often some rigidity in an effort to follow the rules. They will sell double and triple tops, buy breakouts, and generally do everything to propagate the survival of standard chart formations. Because of their following, it is wise to know the most popular techniques, if only as a defensive measure.

What Causes Chart Patterns?

Speculators have many habits, which, taken in large numbers, cause recognizable chart patterns. The typical screen trader (not on the exchange floor), or an investor

---

[2] Thomas N. Bulkowski, *Encyclopedia of Chart Patterns* (New York: John Wiley & Sons, 2000).

placing his or her own orders, will usually choose an even number—for example, buy Microsoft at $26.00, rather than at $26.15. If even dollar values are not used, then 50¢ and 25¢ are the next most likely increments, in that order. And, as the share prices get higher, the increments get farther apart. With Berkshire Hathaway (BKA) trading at $125,000 per share, placing an order at a $10 increment would seem very precise. In futures trading, the same is true. There are far more orders placed in the S&P Index at 1310.00 than at 1306.50, or 10-year Treasury notes at $115\,^{16}\!/_{32}$ instead of $115\,^{19}\!/_{32}$.

The public is also said to always enter into the bull markets at the wrong time. When the television financial news, syndicated newspapers, and radio carry stories of dangerously low oil supplies, a new cancer treatment drug, or the devastation of the nation's wheat crop, the infrequent speculator enters in what W. D. Gann calls the *grand rush,* causing the final runaway move before the collapse or the final sell-off before the rally; this behavior is easily identifiable on a chart. Gann also talks of *lost motion,* the effect of momentum that carries prices slightly past its goal. Professional traders recognize that a fast, volatile price may move as much as 10% farther than its objective. A downward swing in the U.S. dollar/Japanese yen from par at 1.0000 to a support level of 0.8000 could overshoot the bottom by 0.0100 without being considered significant.

The behavioral aspects of prices appear rational. In the great bull markets, the repeated price patterns and divergence from chance movement are indications of the effects of mass psychology. The classic source of information on this topic is Mackay's *Extraordinary Popular Delusions and the Madness of Crowds* originally published in 1841.[3] In the preface to the 1852 edition the author says:

> We find that whole communities suddenly fix their minds on one ob-
> ject, and go mad in its pursuit; that millions of people become simulta-
> neously impressed with one delusion. . . .

In 1975, sugar was being rationed in supermarkets at the highest price ever known, 50¢ per pound. The public was so concerned that there would not be enough at any price that they bought and horded as much as possible. This extreme case of public demand coincided with the price peak, and shortly afterwards the public found itself with an abundant supply of high-priced sugar in a rapidly declining market. The world stock markets are often the target of acts of mass psychology. While U.S. traders watched at a distance the collapse of the Japanese stock market from its heights of 38,957 at the end of December 1989 to its lows of 7,750 in 2003, a drop of 80%, they were able to experience their own *South Sea Bubble* when the NASDAQ 100 fell 83.5% from its highs of 4,816 in March 2000 to 795 in October 2002. And, while the subprime crisis has taken years to play out, the unparalleled drop in value of nearly all investments at the same time, September 2008, was clearly an act of investor panic. Prices seem to drop suddenly at the time when buyers are most confident, then start the long climb up

---

[3] Reprinted in 1995 by John Wiley & Sons.

again. It should not be difficult to understand why contrary thinking has developed a strong following.

Charting is a broad topic to be studied in detail; the chart paper itself and its scaling are sources of controversy. A standard bar chart (or line chart) representing highs and lows can be plotted for daily, weekly, or monthly intervals in order to smooth out the price movement over time. Bar charts have been drawn on semilog and exponential scales,4 where the significance of greater volatility at higher price levels is put into proportion with the quieter movement in the low ranges by using percentage changes. Each variation gives the chartist a unique representation of price action. The shape of the chart box and its ratio of height/width will alter interpretations that are based on angles. Standard charting techniques may draw trendlines at 45° or 30° angles across the chart; therefore, expanding or compressing a chart on a screen will change the angles. This chapter uses traditional daily price charts and square boxes.

It may be a concern to today's chartist that the principles and rules that govern chart interpretation were based on the early stock market, using averages instead of individual stocks or futures contracts. This is discussed in the next section. For now, refer to Edwards and Magee, who removed this problem by stating that "anything whose market value is determined solely by the free interplay of supply and demand" will form the same graphic representation. They continued to say that the aims and psychology of speculators in either a stock or commodity environment would be essentially the same, that the effect of postwar government regulations have caused a "more orderly" market in which these same charting techniques can be used.[5]

■ What Causes the Major Price Moves and Trends?

Prices can move higher for many months or even years, creating a *bull market*. They can also move down, creating a *bear market*. Although price moves can be as short as a few minutes or as long as decades (as happened with interest rates and gold), it is how each chartist defines a "trend" that is most important. Once recognized, the price trend forms a bias for trading decisions that can make the difference between success and failure. The long-term direction of prices is driven by four primary factors:

1. *Government policy.* When economic policy targets a growth rate of 4%, and the current growth rate is 1%, the Federal Reserve (the "Fed" or any central bank) lowers interest rates to encourage growth. Lowering rates stimulates business activity. The Fed raises interest rates and dampens economic activity to control inflation. Changing interest rates has a profound impact on the flow of investment money between countries, on international trade, on the value of currencies, and on business activity.

---

[4] R. W. Schabacker, *Stock Market Theory and Practice*, Forbes (New York, 1930), 595–600.
[5] Robert D. Edwards and John Magee, *Technical Analysis of Stock Trends* (Springfield, MA: John Magee, 1948), Chapter 16.

2. *International trade.* When the United States imports goods, it pays for it in dollars. That is the same as *selling* the dollar. It weakens the currency. A country that continually imports more than it exports increases its trade deficit and weakens its currency. A country that increases its exports strengthens its currency and its economy.

3. *Expectation.* If investors think that stock prices will rise, they buy, causing prices to rise. Expectations can lead an economic recovery although there is no statistical data to support a recovery. *Consumer confidence* is a good measure of how the public feels about spending. The economy is active when consumer confidence is high. A lack of public confidence following the subprime collapse dampened all economic activity and delayed the recovery for years.

4. *Supply and demand.* A shortage, or anticipated shortage, of any product causes its price to rise. An oversupply of a product results in declining prices. These trends develop as news makes the public aware of the situation. A shortage of a product that cannot be replaced causes a prolonged effect on its price, although the jump to a higher price may happen quickly.

■ The Bar Chart and Its Interpretation by Charles Dow

The *bar chart*, also called the *line chart,* became known through the theories of Charles H. Dow, who expressed them in the editorials of the *Wall Street Journal*. Dow first formulated his ideas in 1897 when he created the stock averages in order to have a more consistent measure of price movement for stock groups. After Dow's death in 1902, William P. Hamilton succeeded him and continued the development of his work into the theory that is known today. Those who have used charts extensively and understand their weak and strong points might be interested in just how far our acceptance has come. In the 1920s, a New York newspaper was reported to have written:

> One leading banker deplores the growing use of charts by professional stock traders and customers' men, who, he says, are causing unwarranted market declines by purely mechanical interpretation of a meaningless set of lines. It is impossible, he contends, to figure values by plotting prices actually based on supply and demand; but, he adds, if too many persons play with the same set of charts, they tend to create the very unbalanced supply and demand which upsets market trends. In his opinion, all charts should be confiscated, piled at the intersection of Broad and Wall and burned with much shouting and rejoicing.[6]

This attitude seems remarkably similar to the comments about program trading that followed the stock market plunge in October 1987, where it was condemned as the cause of the crash. In 2011 we again had comments about high frequency trading "manipulating" the markets, and in Europe they have banned short sales to stem volatility in the equity index markets. Of course, volatility continued to be high, but liquidity dropped. It's politics, not logic.

---

[6] Richard D. Wyckoff, *Stock Market Technique, Number One* (New York: Wyckoff, 1933), 105.

Charting has become an integral part of trading. The earliest authoritative works on chart analysis are long out of print, but the essential material has been recounted in newer publications. If, however, a copy should cross your path, read the original *Dow Theory* by Robert Rhea;[7] most of all, read Richard W. Schabacker's outstanding work *Stock Market Theory and Practice*, which is probably the basis for most subsequent texts on the use of the stock market for investment or speculation. The most available book that is both comprehensive and well written is *Technical Analysis of Stock Trends* by Edwards and Magee, now in its ninth edition.[8] It is focused on chart analysis with related management implications and a small section on commodities. For the reader who prefers concise information with few examples, the monograph by W. L. Jiler, *Forecasting Commodity Prices with Vertical Line Charts,* and a complementary piece, *Volume and Open Interest: A Key to Commodity Price Forecasting,* can still be found.[9] Two more recent publications that are widely read are John Murphy's *Technical Analysis of the Financial Markets* and Jack Schwager's *Schwager on Futures: Technical Analysis*, part of a two-volume set.

The Dow Theory

The Dow Theory[10] is still the foundation of chart interpretation and applies equally to stocks, financial markets, commodities, and the wide variety of investment vehicles used to trade them. It is part investor psychology supported by chart analysis. It is impressive that it has withstood the tests of more than 100 years. Charles Dow was the first to create an index of similar stocks—the Industrials and the Railroads, although today's components are very different from those in 1897. The purpose of the index was to smooth out erratic price movement and find consistency by combining less active stocks. Thin trading causes unreliable price patterns.

Dow's work can be viewed in two parts: his theory of price movement and his method of implementation. Both are inseparable to its success. Dow determined that the stock market moved as the ocean, in three waves, called *primary, secondary,* and *daily fluctuations.* The major advances and declines, lasting for extended periods, were compared to the tides. These tides were subject to secondary reactions called *waves,* and the waves were comprised of *ripples.* Readers familiar with other charting methods will recognize these patterns as the foundation of Elliott Wave analysis. In 1897, Dow published two sets of averages in the *Wall Street Journal*, the *Industrials* and the *Railroads,* in order to advance his ideas. These are now the *Dow Jones Industrial Average*

---

[7] Arthur Sklarew, *Techniques of a Professional Chart Analyst* (Commodity Research Bureau, 1980).

[8] Robert D. Edwards and John Magee, *Technical Analysis of Stock Trends*, 9th ed. (Snowball Publishing, 2010).

[9] Two other works worth studying are Gerald Appel, *Winning Market Systems: 83 Ways to Beat the Market* (Great Neck, NY: Signalert, 1974); and Gerald Appel and Martin E. Zweig, *New Directions in Technical Analysis* (Great Neck, NY: Signalert, 1976).

[10] The rules of the Dow Theory in this section are based on a fine article by Ralph Acampora and Rosemarie Pavlick, "A Dow Theory Update," originally published in the *MTA Journal* (January 1978, reprinted in the *MTA Journal*, Fall–Winter 2001). Other parts of this section are drawn from Kaufman, *A Short Course in Technical Trading* (Hoboken, NJ: John Wiley & Sons, 2003).

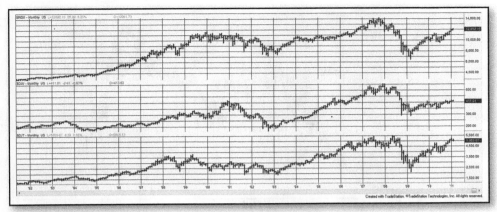

FIGURE 1.1 Dow Industrial, Utilities, and Transportation Indexes, 1991–2010. Dow originally created the industrial and railway averages to hide the large, erratic price moves caused by price manipulation and lack of liquidity. Dow Theory has been adapted to use the current versions of the major indexes, the Industrials (top panel), the Utilities (center panel), and the Transportation Index (bottom panel). Although these indexes represent different aspects of the economy, they have become highly correlated.

and the *Transportation Index*. Figure 1.1 shows more than 20 years of history for the three most important averages the Industrials, the Transportation, and the Utilities.

The Basic Tenets of the Dow Theory

There are six fundamental principles of the Dow Theory that fully explain its operation.

1. The Averages Discount Everything (except "acts of God") At the turn of the twentieth century there was considerably less liquidity and regulation in the market; therefore, manipulation was common. By creating averages, Dow could reduce the frequency of "unusual" moves in a single stock, that is, those moves that seemed unreasonably large or out of character with the rest of the market. Dow's Industrials average the share value of 30 companies (adjusted for splits); therefore, an odd move in one of those prices would only be $\frac{1}{30}$ of the total, reducing its importance so that it would not distort the results. The average also represented far greater combined liquidity than a single stock. The only large moves that would appear on a chart of the average price were price shocks, or "acts of God."

2. Classifications of Trends There are three classifications of trends: primary trends, secondary swings, and minor day-to-day fluctuations. The primary trend, also called the *wave,* is the trend on a grand scale. When there is a wave of rising prices we have a *bull market*; when prices are declining there is a *bear market*. A wave is a major move over an extended period of time, generally measured in years. A clear bull market can be seen in the previous Dow charts (Figure 1.1) throughout all of the 1990s ending at the beginning of 2000, and again from 2003 through mid-2007.

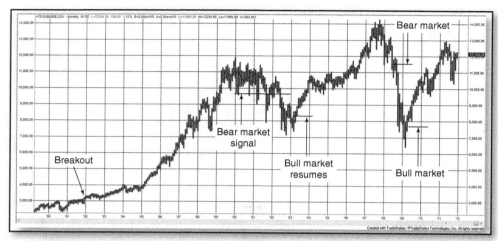

FIGURE 1.2 Bull and Bear Market Signals Are Traditional Breakout Signals, but on a Larger Scale.

Bull and Bear Market Formation (for Monthly or Weekly Prices)

The beginning of a bull or bear market is determined using a *breakout signal*, shown in Figure 1.2, based on large swings in the index value. The *bull market signal* occurs at the point where prices confirm the uptrend by moving above the high of the previous rally. The *bear market signal* occurs on a break below the low of the previous decline.

It is commonly accepted that a bull or bear market begins when prices reverse 20% from their lows or highs. In order to get an upwards breakout signal needed for a new bull market, we want to look at support and resistance levels (the previous intermediate high and low prices) separated by approximately a 10% price move based on the index value. This type of signal is called *swing trading*. At the top of Figure 1.2 the horizontal broken line should occur at about 20% below the absolute price highs, and the second peak should be approximately 10% higher than the previous swing low.

It is interesting to note that both bull and bear markets start with a price reversal of 20%. But 20% from the highs can be much greater than 20% from the lows. For example, in the sell-off in September 2008, the S&P was measured from its high of about 14,000 in late 2007. A decline to 11,200, or 2,800 points, triggered the bear market. In the first quarter of 2009, the S&P reached its lows of about 6,500. A new bull market began at 7,800, a rally of only 1,300 points. Thus the number of points needed to "officially" start a bull market was only 46% of the bear market trigger, showing a significant bias toward bull markets.

Bull and Bear Market Phases

In Dow Theory, the primary trends develop in three distinct phases, each characterized by investor action. These phases can be seen in the NASDAQ bull market of the late 1990s and the subsequent bear market (Figure 1.3).

The Bull Market

Phase 1: Accumulation. Cautious investors select only the safest and best-valued stocks to buy. They limit purchases to deeply discounted stocks at depressed

FIGURE 1.3 NASDAQ from April 1998 through June 2002. A clear example of a bull and bear market with a classic pattern of volume.

price levels and consider only primary services and industries, most often buying utilities and high yielding stocks.

Phase 2: Increasing volume. Greater investor participation causes increasing volume, rising prices, and an improving economic picture. A broader range of investors enters the market convinced that the market has seen its lowest prices. Secondary stocks become popular.

Phase 3: Final explosive move. Excessive speculation and an elated general population result in a final explosive move. Everyone is talking about the stock market; people who have never considered investing directly now enter the market. The public is convinced that profits will continue and buying becomes indiscriminate. Investors borrow to buy stocks. Value is unimportant because prices keep rising. Earnings and dividends are ignored.

The Bear Market

Phase 1: Distribution. Professionals begin selling while the public is in the final stages of buying. Stocks are distributed from stronger to weaker hands. The change of ownership is facilitated by less experienced investors who enter the bull market too late and pay what turn out to be unreasonably high prices.

Phase 2: Panic. Prices decline faster than at any time during the bull market and fail to rally. The news constantly talks about the end of the bull market. The public sees an urgency to liquidate. Investors who borrowed money to invest late in the bull market, trading on margin or leverage, now speed up the process. Some are forced to liquidate because their portfolio value has dropped below the critical point. The divesting of stocks takes on a sense of panic.

Phase 3: Lack of buying interest. The final phase in the sustained erosion of prices results from the lack of buying by the public. After taking losses, investors are not interested in buying even the strongest companies at extremely undervalued prices. All news is viewed as negative. Pessimism prevails. It is the summer of 2002.

Schabacker's Rules

Schabacker also had a simple guideline to identify the end of both a bull and a bear market.[11]

End of a Bull Market

1. Trading volume increases sharply.
2. Popular stocks advance significantly while some other companies collapse.
3. Interest rates are high.
4. Stocks become a popular topic of conversation.
5. Warnings about an overheated stock market appear on the news.

End of a Bear Market

1. Trading volume is low.
2. Commodity prices have declined.
3. Interest rates have declined.
4. Corporate earnings are low.
5. Stock prices have been steadily declining and bad news is everywhere.

Secondary Trends (Secondary Reactions Using Weekly or Daily Prices)

Secondary reactions are also called *corrections* or *recoveries* and can be identified using smaller swing values. Corrections in bull markets are attributed to the prudent investor taking profits. This profit phase can have an erratic start but is considered complete when prices rise above the previous secondary rally. The bull market is back in force when a new high occurs (see Figure 1.4), the point where a trader can enter a new long position. *Lines* may be substituted for secondary movements. In Dow Theory, a *line* is a sideways movement lasting from two to three weeks to months, trading in about a 5% range.

Characteristics of a Secondary Reaction

- There are a number of clear downswings.

- The movement is more rapid in the reversal (down during a bull market) than in the primary move.

- The reactions last from three weeks to three months.

- If the volume during the price drop is equal to or greater than the volume just prior to the decline, then a bear market is likely. If volume declines during the drop, then a reaction is confirmed.

- The atmosphere surrounding the decline is important. If there is a lot of speculation, then a bear market may develop.

---

[11] Adapted from James Maccaro, "The Early Chartists: Schabacker, Edwards, Magee," *Technical Analysis of Stocks & Commodities* (November 2002).

FIGURE 1.4 Secondary Trends and Reactions. A reaction is a smaller swing in prices that ends when a new high reinstates the bull market.

Minor Trends (Using Daily Prices)

In Dow Theory, minor trends are the only trends that can be manipulated. They are usually under six days in duration. Because they are considered market noise, not affecting the major price direction, they are seen as frequent up and down movements.

3. The Principle of Confirmation   For a bull or bear market to exist, two of the three major averages (the Industrials, the Transportation, and the Utilities) must confirm the direction. When first created, the Dow Theory required the confirmation on only the Utilities and the Railroads. Although much has changed since Dow devised this rule, the purpose is to assure that the bull or bear market is a widespread economic phenomenon and not a narrower industry-related event.

4. Volume Goes with the Trend   Volume confirms the price move. Volume must increase as the trend develops, whether it is a bull or bear market. It is greatest at the peak of a bull market or during the panic phase of a bear market.

5. Only Closing Prices Are Used   Dow had a strong belief that the closing price each day was the most important price. It was the point of evening-up. Not only do day traders liquidate all of their positions before the close of trading, reversing their earlier impact, but many investors and hedge funds execute at the close. Although liquidity was a problem during Dow's time, even actively traded stocks in today's market show increased price swings when a larger order is executed during a quiet period. There is always high volume at the close of trading, when investors with short and long time frames come together to decide the fair price.

Some traders believe that there is no closing price anymore, given the access to 24-hour trading; however, that is not yet true. Every market has a settlement price. This is usually at the end of the primary trading session (previously the *pit* or *open outcry session*). The settlement price is necessary to reconcile all accounts, post profits and losses, and trigger needed margin calls. Banks could not operate without an official closing time and settlement price.

6. The Trend Persists   *A trend should be assumed to continue in effect until its reversal has been signaled.* This rule forms the basis of all trend-following principles. It considers the trend as a long-term price move, and positions are entered only in the trend direction. The Dow Theory does not express expectations of how long a trend will continue. It simply follows the trend until a signal occurs that indicates a change of direction.

Interpreting Today's S&P Using Dow Theory

After 110 years, can the Dow Theory correctly interpret the major market index, the S&P? Figure 1.5 shows the S&P 500, using continuous, back-adjusted futures prices, from 1994 through the middle of 2003. The sustained bull market that began in 1987, or possibly 1984, peaks near the end of the first quarter of 2002. There is a steady increase in volume, as Dow had foreseen, although volume does not peak at the top of the market—it starts to decline noticeably about three months before the top. We will see in the study of volume that volume spikes occur at extremes, but a longer-term volume confirmation is very important. Declining volume at the beginning of 2003 signals a divergence in sentiment that foretells the end of the bull market. Volatility increases as prices move towards the end of the uptrend, another predictable pattern. The price move from 1994 through the peak in 2002 shows both Phase 2 and Phase 3 of the bull market.

The price decline in the third quarter of 1998 addresses the issue: Are there exceptions to the 20% rule that changes a bull market to a bear market? A 20% drop from a high of 1400 is 1120, very close to the point where prices stopped their decline and

FIGURE 1.5   Dow Theory Applied to the S&P. Most of Dow's principles apply to the current marketplace, but some experience and interpretation is necessary.

reversed. Dow never used the number 20%, and analysts would claim that, because of the speed of the decline and the quick recovery, this was not a bear market signal. Some of these decisions require judgment, some experience, and just a little bit of hindsight. Realistically, we cannot expect every Dow signal to always be correct, just as we cannot expect to be profitable on every trade. Long-term success is the real goal.

Transition from Bull to Bear in the S&P Looking again for a 20% reversal from the S&P highs of 1675, we target the price of 1340. This time, volume has declined into the highs and continues to decline quickly. From the second quarter of 2000 through the first quarter of 2001 prices fall sharply, giving back the gains from mid-1997, nearly three years. When prices break below 1300 they confirm the previous low at the end of 2000, making it clear that a bear market is underway.

During the subsequent decline, prices attempted to rally. There are four cases of a sharp "V" bottom followed by a significant move higher. After the low at 940 at the end of September 2001, prices move to about 1180, above the 20% reversal of 1128. However, after the first reversal to 1075 prices fail to move back above the highs, finally breaking below 1180 and continuing on to make new lows. Although the recovery exceeded 20%, the lack of a confirming breakout can be interpreted as a bull market failure. Not every pattern falls neatly into a rule.

We come to the last year of the S&P chart, where prices have resisted going below 850, and now appear to be moving above the level of 970 and about to confirm a bullish breakout. Is it the end of the bear market? Volume was the highest at the two lowest price spikes, and then declined. Many stocks are undervalued, according to experts, yet those same experts see no reason for the market to rally further because the recent rise has already reflected reasonable expectations for profits and growth in the next year. Who would be correct, Charles Dow or the talking heads of the financial news networks? It was Dow.

Dow Theory and Futures Markets

The principles of the Dow Theory are simple to understand. Major price moves are most important when they are confirmed by volume. They follow a pattern created by investor action that seems to be universal when seen from a distance. In order to implement his theory, Dow created an index that minimized the erratic moves in individual stocks due to lack of liquidity and price manipulation.

The primary features of the Dow Theory should hold for any highly liquid, actively traded market. This applies to index futures and most financial futures markets, as well as foreign exchange, which have enormous volume and reflect major economic trends. Because of the variety of products traded as futures and ETFs, an investor may be able to apply Dow's principle of confirmation using any two related financial markets, such as the S&P Index, 10-year Treasury notes, or the U.S. dollar index, in the same way that the Industrials, Utilities, and Transportation indexes were used for stocks. A strong economic trend often begins with interest rate policy and has a direct impact on the value of the currency, and a secondary effect on the stock market. Stock prices can be stimulated by lower rates or dampened by raising rates; therefore, confirmation from these three sectors is reasonable. When trading in futures, the nearby contract (the one closest to delivery) is most often used; however, the total volume of all futures contracts traded for each market must be used rather than volume for a single contract.

■ Chart Formations

While Dow Theory is a macro view of price movement, more often chart analysis deals with much shorter time periods. Most traders hold positions from a few days to a few weeks; however, they apply the same patterns to both shorter or longer intervals.

Chart analysis uses straight lines and geometric formations on price charts. It analyzes volume only in the most general terms of advancing and declining phases. Chart patterns can be classified into the broad groups of:

■ Trendlines and channels

■ One-day patterns

■ Continuation patterns

■ Accumulation and distribution (tops and bottoms)

■ Retracements

■ Other patterns

Of these, the most important is the *trendline*.

The Trend in Retrospect

It is easier to see the trend on a chart after it has occurred. Trying to identify the trend as it is developing is much more difficult. The monthly chart in Figure 1.6 shows a sustained

FIGURE 1.6 The Trend Is Easier to See after It Has Occurred. While the upwards trend is clear, are prices going to continue higher, or is this the end of the trend?

upwards trend, but there is a slowing of that trend toward the end. Will the upward trend continue? Will prices begin a downward trend? Will they move sideways? The purpose of charting is to apply tools that provide the best chance of identifying the future direction of prices. If wrong, these tools also control the size of the loss.

The time interval is a key element when identifying a trend. Weekly and monthly charts show the major trends more clearly than daily charts. Longer-term charts remove much of the noise that interferes with seeing the bigger picture. Many chartists start by evaluating a weekly or monthly chart, then apply the lines and values developed on those charts to a daily chart. The weekly chart provides direction or biases the direction of trades while the daily chart, or even a 15-minute chart, is used for timing entries and exits.

■ Trendlines

The trendline determines the current direction of price movement, and often identifies the specific point at which that direction will change. The trendline is the most popular and recognized tool of chart analysis. Most analysts will agree that *the trend is your friend*; that is, it is always safer to take a position in the direction of the trend.

■ An *upwards trendline* is drawn across the lowest prices in a rising market.

■ A *downwards trendline* is drawn across the highest prices in a declining market.

Figure 1.7 shows a classic downwards trendline, *A*, drawn on a chart of Intel. It connects the highest price of $22 with price peaks at 18.00, 16.75, and 16.15 before ending at 15.50. When prices move through the trendline heading higher, the downtrend has been *penetrated*. This may end the downtrend or cause a new downtrend line to be drawn. In this case it was the end of the downtrend.

FIGURE 1.7 Upwards and Downwards Trendlines Applied to Intel, November 2002 through May 2003.

Redrawing Trendlines

Most trendlines are not as long-lived or clear as the downtrend in Intel, which was drawn after the fact. Instead, we will treat the uptrend as it develops. The first uptrend line, *B*, is drawn when the first reversal shows a second low point. The upwards trendline *B* is drawn across the lows of points 1 and 2. Although prices do not decline through trendline *B*, rising prices pull back to points 3 and 4, well above the trendline. At that point, we choose to redraw the upwards trendline connecting point 2 with 3 and 4, forming what appears to be a stronger trendline. Trendlines are considered more important when they touch more points. However, prices move up quickly, and we decide to redraw the trendline connecting points 4 and 5. It is very common to redraw trendlines as price patterns develop. Care must be taken to draw the lines in a way that touches the most points, although some chart analysts would draw a line that connects points 1 and 5, crossing through points 2, 3, and 4, because the final picture seems to represent the dominant upwards price pattern. This can be seen as the broken line in Figure 1.7.

Support and Resistance Lines

Price movement creates patterns that reflect the combined perception that all investors have of the current economic situation. Trends result from confidence or concern about the health of business or the supply and demand of a product. When there is no dominant opinion, prices move sideways in a price range determined by current volatility levels—sometimes wide, sometimes narrow. Because there are always buyers and sellers, prices do not stand still. Investment funds continue to add and withdraw money from the market.

Periods of uncertainty form a sideways price pattern. The top of this pattern is called the *resistance level,* and the bottom is the *support level.* Once established, the support and resistance levels become key to identifying whether a trend is still in force.

A *horizontal support line* is drawn horizontally to the right of the lowest price in a sideways pattern. It is best when drawn through two or more points and may cross above the lowest price if it makes the pattern clear. It represents a firm price level that has withheld market penetration (or allowed minor penetration). It may be the most significant of all chart lines. In the chart of gold futures prices (Figure 1.8), the support line is drawn across the bottom of a sideways period, beginning at the first low price on the left but crossing slightly above the next lowest point. The support line could have been drawn at $280.50 to include the first cluster of low prices and crossing above the lows bars but representing a clear support level.

A *horizontal resistance line* serves the same purpose as the support line and is drawn across the highest highs of the sideways interval. It represents the price that has resisted upwards movement. Resistance lines are not normally as clear as support lines because they are associated with higher volatility and erratic price movement. In Figure 1.8 there are two choices for the horizontal resistance line. The most common selection would be the line that begins at top 1 and crosses below the high of top 2. In the same spirit as the support line, a resistance line could have been drawn

FIGURE 1.8 Horizontal Support and Resistance Lines Shown on Gold Futures Prices.

much lower, beginning at top 3 and crossing above a cluster of highs while penetrating through the bars with tops 1 and 2.[12]

Note the Position of the Closing Price of the Bar A price bar that has the high price penetrating upwards through resistance but closes lower is considered a *failed breakout* and confirms the sideways pattern. The same is true for a failed penetration of the support level. You may choose to raise the resistance line to the high of that failed bar, but most chartists ignore it, keeping the resistance line at its original position. Then we can expect to see a number of high prices penetrate through the resistance lines as shown by the *breakout 2* line in Figure 1.8.

Resistance Becomes Support, and Support Becomes Resistance Horizontal support and resistance lines are strong indicators of change. If prices are moving sideways because investors are unsure of direction, then a move through either support or resistance is usually associated with new information that causes investors to act. Whatever the cause, the market interprets this as a new event. Having moved out of the sideways pattern, prices have a tendency to remain above resistance to confirm the change. If prices have moved higher, then the resistance line becomes a support line. If prices fall below the resistance line, the price move is considered a failed breakout. In the right part of Figure 1.8, prices break out above the resistance levels and then come back to test those levels. In this example, prices seem to confirm that the *breakout 2* line was the more realistic resistance line.

---

[12] In Carol Oster, "Support for Resistance: Technical Analysis and Intraday Exchange Rates," *FRBNY Economic Policy Review* (July 2000), the author shows that support and resistance levels specified by six trading firms over three years were successful in predicting intraday price interruptions. In addition, these levels were valid for about five days after they were noted.

A Trendline Is a Support or Resistance Line The angled trendlines in Figure 1.7 are also called support and resistance lines. An upwards trendline, drawn across the lows, is a *bullish support line* because it defines the lowest price allowed in order to maintain the upwards trend. The downward trendline, drawn across the highs, is a *bearish resistance line*. These angled trendlines are most reliable when used to identify major price trends. Horizontal lines work well for shorter time frames.

Back-Adjusted Data All traders use online services to display charts. They can draw support and resistance lines using various tools supplied by the service and can convert daily data to weekly or monthly with a single click. When looking at prices that go back many years, the analyst must be sure that the older data is not *back-adjusted* in any way. For example, futures trade in contracts of limited maturity, and are most liquid during the last few months before expiration. Long-term charts put contracts together by back-adjusting the prices, so that the older data does not give the actual price at that time, but is altered by accumulated roll difference. Using those older prices as a guide for support or resistance doesn't make any sense.

This same problem exists for stocks that have split. The old price that you see on the chart may not be the actual price traded at that time. Floor traders are good at remembering the last major high or low and will trade against those prices, or buy and sell breakouts. When plotting the support and resistance lines, look for the data option that creates a history of prices without back-adjusting.

Rules for Trading Using Trendlines

The simplest formations to recognize are the most commonly used and most important: horizontal support and resistance lines, bullish and bearish support and resistance lines, and channels created using those lines. Proper use of these basic lines is essential for identifying the overall direction of the market and understanding the patterns formed as prices move from one level to another. Many traders will generate their buy and sell orders directly from their chart analysis. Other, more computer-oriented analysts have automated the more important trendlines, particularly horizontal support and resistance, which has become the basic breakout system. Major chart patterns create the underlying profitability of chart trading; the more complex formations, as we will discuss further, may enhance good performance but rarely compensate for losses resulting from being on the wrong side of the trend.

Once the support and resistance lines have been drawn, a price penetration of those lines creates the basic trend signal (Figure 1.9). The bullish support line defines the upward trend, and the bearish resistance line denotes the downward one. For long-term charts and major trends, this is often sufficient. Some traders add the additional rule that once the price has penetrated a trendline, it must remain penetrated for some time period in order to confirm the new trend. Most false penetrations correct quickly.

FIGURE 1.9 Basic Sell and Buy Signals using Trendlines.

Confirming the New Trend Direction   In actual trading, the price crossing the trendline is not as clean as in Figure 1.8. Most often prices that have been moving higher will cross below the trendline, then recross moving higher, then move lower again. The trendline is an important turning point, and there may be indecision that is reflected in a sideways price movement before prices reestablish a trend. To deal with this situation, traders may:

■ *Wait a set time period* to confirm that prices remain on the new side of the trendline.

■ *Wait for a reversal* after the penetration, then enter a trade in the new direction even if the reversal crosses the trendline again.

■ *Create a small safety zone* (called a *band* or *channel*) around the trendline and enter the new trade if prices move through the trendline and through the safety zone.

Each of these techniques requires a delay before entering. A delay normally benefits the trader by giving a better entry price; however, if prices fall quickly through an upwards trendline and do not reverse or slow down, then any delay will result in a much worse entry price. Unfortunately, most of the biggest profits result from breakouts that never pull back. Catching only one of these breakouts can compensate for all the small losses due to false signals. Many professional traders wait for a better entry price. They may be steady winners, but they do not often profit from the biggest moves.

Trading Rules for Horizontal Support and Resistance Levels

As with angled trendlines, horizontal support and resistance lines show clear points for buying and selling. Also similar to angled trendlines, the horizontal lines become increasingly important when longer time intervals and more points are used to form the lines. The technique for entering trades using horizontal lines is similar to that using angled trendlines; however, the maximum risk of the trade is clearly defined.

■ *Buy* when prices move above the horizontal resistance line

■ *Sell* when prices move below the horizontal support line

FIGURE 1.10 Trading Rules for Horizontal Support and Resistance Lines.

Once a long position has been entered, it is not closed out until prices move below the support line. The maximum risk of the trade is the difference between the support and resistance lines. As prices move higher, each swing reversal forms a low from which a new horizontal support line is drawn. After the initial entry, single points are most often used to create the horizontal support and raise the level at which the trade will be closed out. Figure 1.10 shows the pattern of horizontal support and resistance lines as the trade develops. For a swing low to form, prices must reverse by more than some threshold number of points or percentage. Not every small reversal qualifies as a swing low.

Note that the first pullback in Figure 1.10 shows prices crossing below the original resistance line. This is a common occurrence, but the original line no longer holds the importance it had before it was broken. While it should provide support for the pullback (a resistance, once broken, becomes a support), it is more important to record the bottom of the new pullback as the support level. These new support levels need only one price point. After the third support level is drawn, prices rally but then fall back through the third level, at which point the long position is closed out. A short position, if any, is not entered until a new sideways price pattern is established and horizontal support and resistance lines can be drawn across more than one point.

Identifying Direction from Consolidation Patterns It is said that markets move sideways about 80% of the time, which means that sustained directional breakouts do not occur often, or that most breakouts are false and fail to identify a new market direction. Classic accumulation and distribution formations, which occur at long-term lows and highs, attempt to find evolving changes in market sentiment. Because these formations occur only at extremes, and may extend for a long time, they represent the most obvious consolidation of price movement. Even a rounded or saucer-shaped bottom may have a number of false starts; it may seem to turn up in a uniform pattern, then fall back and begin another slow move up. In the long run, the pattern looks as if it is a somewhat irregular, extended rounded bottom; however, using this pattern to enter a trade in a timely fashion can be disappointing. It is easier to average *in*, where smaller positions are entered at fixed intervals as long as the developing formation remains intact.

Most other consolidation formations are best viewed in the same way as a simple horizontal sideways pattern, bounded above by a resistance line and below by a support line. If this pattern occurs at reasonably low prices, we can eventually expect a breakout upwards when the fundamentals change. Occasionally, prices seem to become less volatile within the sideways pattern, and chartists take this opportunity to redefine the support and resistance levels so that they are narrower. Breakouts based on these more sensitive lines tend to be less reliable because they represent a temporary quiet period inside the larger, normal level of market noise; however, there are two distinct camps, one that believes that breakouts are more reliable after a period of low volatility and the other that prefers breakouts associated with high volatility.

Creating a Channel with Trendlines

A *channel* is formed by a trendline and another line drawn parallel to the trendline enclosing a sustained price move. The purpose of the channel is to define the volatility of the price move and establish reasonable entry and exit points. Up to now, the trendline has only been used to identify the major price direction. A long position is entered when the price crosses a downward trendline moving higher. The trade is held until the price moves below the upwards trendline. However, it is more common to have a series of shorter trades. While the biggest profits come from holding one position throughout a sustained trend, a series of shorter trades each has far less risk and is preferred by the active trader. Be aware that trendlines using very little data are essentially analyzing noise and have limited value.

Before a channel can be formed, the bullish or bearish trendline must be drawn. A clear uptrend line requires at least two, and preferably three or more major low points on the chart, as shown in Figure 1.11, where points 1, 2, and 3 are used. These points do not have to fall exactly on the line. Once the trendline is drawn, the highest high, point *B,* can be used to draw another line parallel to the upwards trendline. The area in between the two parallel lines is the *channel*.

In theory, trading a channel is a simple process. We buy as prices approach the support line (in this case the upwards trendline), and we sell as prices near the resistance line. These buy and sell zones should be approximately the bottom and top 20% of the channel. Because the channel line is used to determine price targets, you might choose to draw the broken line across point *A*. The use of point *A* creates a channel that is narrower than the one formed using the higher point *B* and recognizes the variability of price movement. This allows you to take profits sooner.

If prices continue through the lower trendline after a long position has been set, the trade is exited. The trend direction has changed, and a new bearish resistance

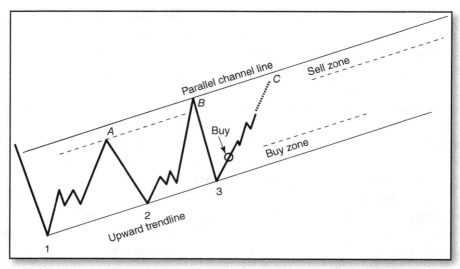

FIGURE 1.11 Trading a Price Channel. Once the channel has been drawn, buying is done near the support line and selling near the resistance line.

line, the downward trendline, needs to be drawn using points *B* and *C*, shown in Figure 1.12. Once the first pull-back occurs leaving a low at point 4, a parallel line is drawn crossing point 4, forming the downward channel. In a downward trending channel, it is best to sell short in the upper zone and cover the short in the lower zone. Buying in the lower zone is not recommended; trades are safest when they are entered in the direction of the trend.

When the support and resistance lines are relatively horizontal, or sideways, the channel is called a *trading range*. There is no directional bias in a trading range; therefore, you can enter new long positions in the support zone and enter new shorts in the sell zone. In both cases, penetration of either the support or resistance lines forces liquidation of the trade and establishes a new trend direction.

FIGURE 1.12 Turning from an Upward to a Downward Channel. Trades are always entered in the direction of the trend.

■ One-Day Patterns

The easiest of all chart patterns to recognize occur in one day. They include gaps, spikes, island reversals, reversal days, inside days, outside days, wide-ranging days, and, to a lesser extent, thrust days. Some of these patterns are important at the moment they occur, and others must be confirmed by other factors.

Gaps

Price *gaps* occur when important news influences the market at a time when the exchange is closed. Orders accumulate to be executed on the next open. An *upwards gap* exists when the low of the current day is higher than the high of the previous day. If all trading were 24 hours, then we would see a fast, volatile move, but not a gap. For example, there are three popular ways to trade the S&P 500 index,

1. Futures, traded in the Chicago Mercantile Exchange pit from 8:30 a.m. to 3:15 p.m. (Central time)
2. Spyders (SPY) on the AMEX during the same hours
3. The electronic S&P mini-futures contract which trades nonstop from Sunday evening at 6 p.m. until Friday afternoon at 3:15 p.m. on the Globex platform

Gaps only exist when using the primary trading session (the *pit* session). Most afterhours trading is on light volume and may be ignored for charting purposes. An exception is in Europe where they have an extended session from the original 4 p.m. close (European time) to 10 p.m. or 10:30 p.m. to allow trading at the same time the U.S. markets are open. The markets then close and reopen when the normal European business day begins. For European markets it is best to use the combined sessions that start at about 9 a.m. and continue until about 10 p.m.

Economic reports are released by the U.S. government at 7:30 a.m. (Central time); therefore, they occur before the S&P pit trading and the SPDRs begin trading, but during the electronic emini S&P session. There is no gap in electronic trading, but the other markets will open sharply higher or lower to adjust to the current emini price. When the financial news shows give the expected open of the stock market, they are using the difference between the previous NYSE closing price and the current price of the electronic session. This creates frequent opening gaps in those markets.

Gaps can also occur because of a large cluster of orders placed at the point where the stock or futures market penetrates support or resistance. It is possible to have a gap during the trading session, immediately following bullish economic report, or concurrent with an anticipated news release of consequence, when there are a large number of buyers and few sellers. There is also the rarer case of an event shock such as September 11, 2001.

In charting, gaps are interpreted differently based on where they occur in the current price pattern. In some cases, a gap signals a continued move and in other situations it is expected to be the end of a price move. The four primary gap formations are shown on a chart of Amazon.com in Figure 1.13. They are:

FIGURE 1.13 Price Gaps Shown on a Chart of Amazon.com.

1. The *common gap*, which appears as a space on a chart and has no particular attributes—that is, it does not occur at a point associated with any particular significance. A common gap appears in May 1999 during a downward move.

2. A *breakaway gap* occurs at a point of clear resistance or support. It occurs when there are a large number of buy orders just above a major resistance line, or sell orders below a support line. Most often this is seen after a prolonged period of sideways price movement when most chartists can draw the same horizontal support and resistance lines. The clearer the formation, and the longer the sideways period, the more likely there will be a large breakaway gap. The term *breakaway* requires some hindsight because it is applied only when the gap is followed by a sustained price move.

   There are two breakaway gaps in Figure 1.13, the first shortly after prices make a new high, the second in the middle of the chart when prices break upwards through a steep downward trendline, and the last near the right of the chart when prices gap through a clear downwards trendline.

   In order to trade a gap, a position must be entered in advance of the gap, as prices approach the support or resistance level. Once a long position is set and prices *gap up* you gain *free exposure,* which is the profit caused by the gap or by a fast market move in your favor. If prices do not gap up, they most often drift lower. The position can be exited with a small loss and reentered later.

3. An *exhaustion gap* occurs at the end of a sustained and volatile price move and confirms the reversal. Exhaustion gaps usually occur on the day after the highest price of the upwards move; however, in the Amazon chart, it is one day later. Because it signifies a clustering of orders anxious to exit the long side, it has all the signs associated with an exhaustion gap.

4. A *runaway gap* occurs at different points during a clear trend and confirms the trend. It does not appear to have any practical use because the trend can stop and reverse just after a runaway gap and it will be renamed an *island top,* or some other formation. When holding a long position, an upwards runaway gap quickly adds profits, but also signifies extreme risk.

Gaps can also be a hindrance to trading. A long position held when a downward breakaway gap occurs guarantees that any stop-loss order is executed far away from the order price. If the upwards breakaway gap occurs on light volume, it may be a false breakout. If a short is held, and if you are lucky, prices will fall back to the breakout level and then continue lower. If unlucky, you will be executed at the high of the move. In the final analysis, if the gap breakout represents a major change, a trade should be entered immediately *at the market.* The poor executions will be offset by the one time when prices move quickly and no pullback occurs. A breakaway gap on high volume is usually indicative of a strong move and a sustained change.

Filling the Gap Tradition states that prices will retrace to *fill the gap* that occurred sometime earlier. Naturally, given enough time, prices will return to most levels; therefore, nearly all gaps will eventually be filled. The most important gaps are not filled for some time.

The gap represents an important point at which prices move out of their previous pattern and begin a new phase. The breakaway gap will often occur just above the previous normal, or established, price level. With commodities, once the short-term demand imbalance has passed, prices should return to near-normal (perhaps slightly above the old prices given inflation), but also slightly below the gap. When a stock price gaps higher based on earnings, a new product announcement, or a rumor of an acquisition, the price may not return to the previous level.

Trading Rules for Gaps

- A *common gap* is small and occurs with low volume and for no specific reason; that is, it is not the result of an obvious, surprising news release. Active traders will take a position counter to the direction of the gap, expecting the move to reverse and fill the gap, at which point they will take profits. If the gap is not filled within a few days, the trade is liquidated.

- A *breakaway gap* is the result of bunched orders at an obvious support or resistance area. When a clear sideways pattern has developed, place a buy order just under the resistance level in order to benefit from the jump in prices (free exposure) when the breakout occurs. If a gap occurs on the breakout, then prices should continue higher.

- A *runaway gap* is often found in the middle of a significant move. It is considered a good point to add to your position because the runaway gap confirms the move and offers additional potential profits.

- An *exhaustion gap* is best traded as it is being filled, and, even at that stage, it is highly risky. Sell during the move upwards, placing a stop above the previous high

TABLE 1.1	Percentage of Time Gaps Are Closed within One Week, Based on a Sample of 100 Stocks	
Gap Type	Uptrends	Downtrends
Breakaway	1	6
Continuation	11	10
Exhaustion	58	72

of the move. If this pattern fails, prices could move higher in an explosive pattern. If you are successive, profits could also be large.

Bulkowski on Gaps   Bulkowski includes an extensive study of breakaway, continuation, and exhaustion gaps. The statistics developed for these three cases all conform to the expected patterns, as shown in Table 1.1. Almost by definition, we expect a breakaway gap, one that occurs when prices move out of a sideways range, to mark the beginning of a new trend, and the exhaustion gap (which actually can't be seen until it reverses) to be the end of a trend. The continuation gap is somewhere in between and is only defined within the context of an existing trend.

The results of the breakaway gap, only 1% and 6% retracements, confirm that the breakouts often continue the trend direction. Strategies that take advantage of this are the *N*-day breakout, swing trading, and pivot point breakouts, providing that the observation period is greater than 40 days, the minimum considered to be a macrotrend.

Spikes

A *spike* is a single, highly volatile day where the price moves much higher or lower than it has in the recent past. A spike can only be recognized one day later because trading range of the following day must be much lower. It is easiest to show spikes in markets, such as U.S. 30-year Treasury bonds, that react to frequent economic reports. In Figure 1.14 there is a series of three spikes about four weeks apart.

An upward spike, as shown in Figure 1.14, is always a *local top* because a spike is a day with above-average volatility and must be bracketed by two lower days. In all three cases shown, the spike represented the high price for at least one week. Because the spike is a clear top, when prices begin to rise again, they usually meet resistance at the top of the spike. Chartists draw a horizontal resistance line using the high price of the spike, which encourages selling at that level. After each spike the chart is marked with "failed test," showing the price level where resistance, based on the previous spike, slowed the advance. The spike did not stop the trend, but it did cause a unique pattern.

Quantifying Spikes   A spike has only one dominant feature: a price high or low much higher or lower than recent prices. It must therefore also have high volatility. The easiest way to identify an upside spike is to compare the trading range on the day

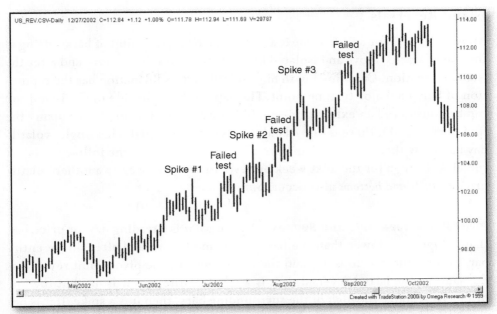

US_REV.CSV-Daily 12/27/2002 C=112.84 +1.12 +1.00% O=111.78 H=112.94 L=111.69 V=29787

Created with TradeStation 2000i by Omega Research © 1999

FIGURE 1.14 A Series of Spikes in Bonds. From June through October 2002, U.S. bonds show three spikes that represent local tops. The spikes represent clear resistance levels that cause a unique pattern in the upwards move.

of the spike to previous ranges and to the subsequent day. This can be programmed in TradeStation by using the *true range* function and satisfying the conditions that the high on the day of the spike is greater than the previous and subsequent highs by the amount of $k \times$ *average true range* over n days,

```
Spike = high[1] - highest(high,n)[2] > k*average(truerange,n)[2]
                          and
          high[1] - high > k*average(truerange,n)[2]
```

In this code, *spike* is a logical variable (true-false). A spike that occurs yesterday (where [1] indicates yesterday and [2] two days ago) is tested to see that the high of the spike is greater than the high of the previous n days, greater than the average true range of the same n days by a factor of k, and also greater than the high of today by the same factor k. Note that the use of [2] ends the true range calculation on the day before the spike. The value of k should be greater than 0.75. Spikes satisfying $k > 1$ are more desirable but less frequent.

In Excel, the true range is

```
TRn = Max(Hn - Ln,Hn - Cm,Cm - Ln)
```

where n is the current row, m is the previous row ($n - 1$), and the high, low, and close (H, L, can C) are in columns B, C, and D.

Island Reversals

An *island reversal* or an *island top* is a single price bar, or group of bars, sitting at the top of a price move and isolated by a gap on both sides, before and after the island formation. Combined with high volatility, this formation has the reputation of being a major turning point. The gap on the right side of the island top can be considered an exhaustion gap. In Figure 1.15, showing AMR during the first part of 2003, there is one island reversal in mid-April. This single, volatile day has a low that is higher than both the previous day and the following day. It remains the high for the next week but eventually gives way to another volatile price rise. *Island bottoms* also occur, but are less frequent.

Pivot Point Reversals and Swings A *pivot point* is a trading day, or price bar, that is higher or lower than the bars that come before and after. If the entire bar is above the previous day and the following day, the pivot point reversal is the same as the island reversal. If it is a very volatile upwards day but the low price is not above the high of the surrounding bars, then it is a spike. If it is not a volatile day, then it is a weaker form of a spike. If you were plotting swing highs and lows, the high of an upwards pivot point reversal day would often become the swing high. It is common to locate a *swing high* by comparing the high of any day with two or more days before and after. The patterns of the days on either side of the high bar are not important as long as the middle bar has the highest high. When more days are used to identify pivot points, these reversals are expected to be more significant; however, they take longer to identify.

FIGURE 1.15 AMR in Early 2003 Showing a Classic Island Reversal with Examples of Other One-Day Patterns.

According to tests by Colby and Meyers,[13] entries that occur based on a breakout of the highs or lows of the pivot points, called *pivot point channels,* are much more reliable than simply entering in the direction of the reversal based on the close of the last bar of the pivot point formation. For traders not interested in this very short-term strategy, a pivot point may help entry timing for any longer term method.

More recently, Colby[14] tested a *Pivot Point Reverse Trading System,* using the following rules:

- *Buy* (and close out short positions) when a pivot point bottom occurs and the close is higher than the previous close.

- *Sell* (and close out long positions) when a pivot point top occurs and the close is lower than the previous close.

Applying these rules to the Dow Jones Industrials (DJIA) for 101 years ending December 2000 showed nearly 7,000 trades (70 per year) with significant profits.

Cups and Caps   Another name given to the pivot point reversals are *cups* and *caps,* each determined by only three price bars, although another formation with the same name, *cup with handle*, is similar to a longer-term rounded bottom followed by a sideways or slight downward trend and a breakout to the upside. These two short-term formations are associated with trading rules that are identical to pivot point channels applied to the shortest time frame. Although some literature uses these formations backwards, a cap formation identifies a sell signal when the trend is up, while a cup is a setup for a buy signal in a downtrend. Once an uptrend is clear, a cap formation is found using either the daily closes or daily lows. For any three consecutive days, the middle day must have the highest close or the highest low. In a cup pattern, the middle day must have the lowest low or the lowest close of the three-day cluster. In both cases, the positioning of the highs and lows of the other two days are not important as long as the middle day is lower for the cup and higher for the cap.

The cup will generate a buy signal if:

- The cup formation is the lowest point of the downtrend

- The buy signal occurs within three days of the cup formation

- The current price closes above the highest high (middle bar) of the cup formation

The signal is false if prices reverse and close below the low of the cup formation, resuming the previous downtrend. This pattern is only expected to forecast a downward price move of two days; however, every change of direction must start somewhere, and this formation could offer an edge. A cap formation is traded with the opposite rules.

---

[13] Tests of pivot point reversals and pivot point channels can be found in Robert W. Colby and Thomas A. Meyers, *The Encyclopedia of Technical Market Indicators* (Homewood, IL: Dow Jones-Irwin, 1988).

[14] Robert W. Colby, *The Encyclopedia of Technical Market Indicators* (New York: McGraw-Hill, 2003), 510–514.

FIGURE 1.16 Russell 2000 during the Last Half of 2002 Showing Reversal Days, Key Reversal Days, Inside Days, and Outside Days.

Reversal Days and Key Reversal Days

A day in which there is a new high followed by a lower close is a *downwards reversal day*. An *upwards reversal day* is a new low followed by a higher close. A reversal day is a common formation, as seen in Figure 1.16, the Russell 2000 futures. Some of these days are identified; however, you can find many other examples in Figures 1.13 through 1.16. There have been many studies to determine the importance of reversal days for trading, but these are inconclusive. A reversal day by itself is not significant unless it can be put into context with a larger price pattern, such as a clear trend with sharply increasing volatility, or a reversal that occurs at the highest or lowest price of the past few weeks.

Key Reversals A *key reversal day* is a more selective pattern, and has been endowed with great forecasting power. It is also called an *outside reversal day,* and is a weaker form of an island reversal. A *bearish key reversal* is formed in one day by first making a new high in an upward trend, reversing to make a low that is lower than the previous low, and then closing below the previous close. It should be associated with higher volatility. Examples of key reversal days can be seen in Figures 1.14 and 1.15. It is considered more reliable when the trend is well-established.

As with reversal days, studies have shown mixed results using the key reversal as a sole trading indicator. The most complete analysis,[15] similar to others, concluded that the performance was "strikingly unimpressive." Even though tests

---

[15] Eric Evans, "Why You Can't Rely on 'Key Reversal Days,'" *Futures* (March 1985).

have not proved its importance, traders still pay close attention to key reversals. Because this pattern has kept its importance, we can conclude that other factors unconsciously enter into the selection of key reversal days for trading. A successful trader's senses should not be underestimated; the extent and speed of the prior trend, a change in liquidity, a quieter market *tone,* or some external news may be essential in confirming the important reversals. The job of a system developer is to find those factors that will turn this pattern into a successful indicator. The best place to start is by assuming the attitude of those traders who see a reversal day as an important pattern.

Figure 1.16 shows a number of reversal days during the rapid drop of the Russell 2000 in January 2002. Three patterns of particular interest are the reversal days at the two extreme lows in July and October 2002, and the high in between, during August. Although there are many other reversal days embedded within other parts of the price move, the reversals off the lows are clearly at higher volatility than most other days, and follow very sharp, accelerating price drops. The reversal day that ends the intermediate high during August does not share these attributes; however, it tops a pattern that is not the dominant trend, but an upwards reaction within a previous sustained downtrend. If we focus on the characteristics of those reversal days that mark price extremes, rather than all reversal days, we should expect successful results.

Programming Key Reversal Days   A key reversal day can be recognized and tested using a computer program. In TradeStation's *EasyLanguage* the instructions for downward key reversal are

```
KeyReversalDown = 0;
if close[1] > average(close[1],n) and high >= highest(high[1],n) and
    low < low[1] and close < close[1] then KeyReversalDown = 1;
```

where the first term tests for an uptrend over *n*-days, the second term tests that the current day is the highest price of the same *n*-days, the third term verifies that a lower low has occurred, and the last term tests for a lower close. This can be done in Excel by using the *max* and *min* functions instead of *highest* and *lowest*. A TradeStation function to identify key reversals is *TSM Key Reversals* and can be found on the Companion Website along with an Excel spreadsheet of the same name.

Adding a volatility factor, so that the key reversal day has noticeably higher volatility than the previous days seems to select more significant patterns. In the spreadsheet, which uses heating oil from 2005 through 2011 as an example, the basic rules gave marginal gains, but a filter that took only trades where today's true range was greater than 1.5 × *average prior 20-day true range* was much better.

2-Bar Reversal Patterns   Martin Pring[16] has called attention to a special 2-bar reversal pattern that frequently precedes a strong directional change. This pattern consists of two days that are essentially the mirror image of one another. Consider a

---

[16] Martin Pring, "Twice as Nice: The Two-Bar Reversal Pattern," *Active Trader* (March 2003).

market in which prices have been moving steadily higher. The first day of the pattern shows a volatile upwards move with prices opening near the lows and closing near the highs. On the following day, prices open where they had closed, trade slightly higher (nearly matching the previous day's highs), then fall sharply to close near the lows, giving back all of the previous day's move.

Following the 2-bar reversal to the downside, the next few days should not trade above the midpoint of the 2-bar reversal pattern. The smaller the retracement, the more likely there will be a good sell-off.

It is easy to explain the psychology of this pattern. The first bar represents the strong bullish feeling of the buyers, while the second bar is seen as complete discouragement at the inability to follow through to even higher levels. It will take some days before traders are willing to test the highs again. More traders may view this as a potential major reversal. High volume can confirm the reversal. The nature of the move to follow depends on the extent of the previous trend and the volatility. Four key factors in predicting a strong reversal are:

1. Stronger preceding trends
2. Wider, more volatile 2-bar patterns
3. Greater volume than in previous days
4. Smaller retracements following the 2-bar pattern

Wide-Ranging Days, Inside Days, and Outside Days

A *wide-ranging day* is a day of much higher volatility than recent days, but no requirement that it is higher or lower than other days. An *outside day* must have both a higher high and lower low than the previous day. *Inside days* are an example of *volatility compression*. All three patterns are very common but indicate that something special has happened. Examples of these patterns are shown in Figure 1.17, a one-year, active trading period for Tyco ending in July 2000, before any accounting scandal surfaced.

FIGURE 1.17 Wide-Ranging Days, Outside Days, and Inside Days for Tyco.

Wide-Ranging Days   A *wide-ranging day* is likely to be the result of a price shock, unexpected news, or a breakout in which many orders trigger one another, causing a large increase in volatility. A wide-ranging day could turn out to be a spike or an island reversal. Because very high volatility cannot be sustained, we can expect that a wide-ranging day will be followed by a reversal, or at least a pause. When a wide-ranging day occurs, the direction of the close (if the close is near the high or low) is a strong indication of the continued direction.

A wide-ranging day is easily seen on a chart because it has at least twice, or three times the volatility of the previous trading days. There is no requirement that it makes a new high or low relative to a recent move, or that it closes higher or lower. It is simply a very volatile day.

Outside Days   An *outside day* often precedes a reversal. An outside day can also be a wide-ranging day if the volatility is high, but when volatility is low and the size of the bar is slightly longer than the previous bar, it is a weak signal. As with so many other chart patterns, if one day has an unusually small trading range, followed by an outside day of normal volatility, there is very little information in the pattern. Selection is important.

Inside Days   An *inside day* is one where the high is lower than the previous high and the low is higher than the previous low. That is, an inside day is one where both the highs and lows are inside the previous day's trading range.

An inside day represents consolidation and lower volatility. In turn, lower volatility is most often associated with the end of a price move. After a burst of activity and a surge of upward direction, prices have reached a point where the buyers are already in and the price has moved too far to attract more buyers. Volume drops, volatility drops, and we get an inside day. An inside day is often followed by a change of direction, but that is not guaranteed. We only know that the event that drove prices up is now over. If more news surfaces to ignite prices, the next move could just as easily be up as down

In Figure 1.17 there are two inside days at the price peak on the top left of the Tyco chart. The first inside day is followed by a small move lower, then a small move higher, followed by another inside day. This last inside day precedes a major sell-off. On the right top of the chart there are two inside days immediately before another sharp drop.

Some analysts believe that a breakout from low volatility is more reliable than one following high volatility.

Some Notes about 1-Day Patterns   One-day patterns are very common; therefore, traders tend to be selective about when they are used. Taken as a group, patterns that are repeated frequently are less reliable and need to be combined with other patterns. Those that occur during periods of high or low volatility or volume may also be less dependable.

While a reversal day is clearly a 1-day formation and can be identified at the end of the trading day, and an opening gap is recognized instantly, most other 1-day patterns are not clear until the day after. An upwards spike and a downwards pivot point reversal both require the high of the next day to be much lower than the high of the spike or pivot day; and the island reversal must show a gap on the following day. Although they cannot be used at the end of the day on which they occur, these formations are reasonably timely for an active trader.

■ Continuation Patterns

Continuation patterns occur during a trend and help to explain the stage of development of that trend. A continuation pattern that occurs within a long-term trend is expected to be resolved by continuing in the direction of the trend. If prices fail to move in the direction of the trend following a major continuation pattern, then the trend is considered over. The primary continuation patterns are triangles, flags, pennants, and wedges. The larger formations of these patterns are more important than the smaller ones.

Symmetric, Descending, and Ascending Triangles

Triangles tend to be larger formations that occur throughout a trend. A *symmetric triangle* is most likely to occur at the beginning of a trend when there is greater uncertainty about direction. A symmetric triangle is formed by a price consolidation, where uncertainty of buyers and sellers results in decreasing volatility in such a way that prices narrow to the center of the previous trading range. In Figure 1.18 the symmetric triangle is formed at about the level of the previous support. The breakout from a symmetric triangle often marks the beginning of a longer-term trend.

FIGURE 1.18 Symmetric and Descending Triangles and a Developing Bear Market in Gold Futures.

Formation of a Descending Triangle

Even during a clear downward trend, prices will rally. Because the trend is clear, sellers are anxious to step in and sell these upwards moves, looking for the trend to continue. The top of this mid-trend rally is likely to be the last support point where prices broke out of a previous pattern. In Figure 1.18, the top of the first descending triangle comes very close to the breakout level of the symmetric triangle, and the larger descending triangle towards the lower right of the chart has its high point at the breakout of another descending triangle.

The recent lows of the new trend form a temporary support level, and prices may bounce off that level while short-term traders play for small profits. This action forms a *descending triangle*. As more traders are convinced that prices are still heading lower, rallies off the support level are sold sooner, causing a narrower pattern, until prices finally break below support. The descending triangle is complete. In an upwards trend an *ascending triangle* would be formed.

Size of the Triangles   A triangle should take no less than two weeks to form; however, they can span a much longer period, occasionally up to three months. Larger formations represent periods of greater uncertainty. They may be followed by another symmetric triangle, again indicating that traders are undecided about direction. If the symmetric triangle is resolved in the current trend direction, the trend is in full force, and a large price move is expected.

Triangles can be consistent indicators of investor confidence. Because they reflect human behavior, they are not always perfect in appearance and not always consistent in pattern. It takes experience to identify the formation in a timely manner.

Flags

A *flag* is a smaller pattern than a triangle, generally less than three months for the long-term trader, and is formed by a correction in a bull market or a rally in a bear market. A flag is a congestion area that leans away from the direction of the trend and typically can be isolated by drawing parallel lines across the top and bottom of the formation. At the beginning of a trend, the flags may not lean away from the direction of the new trend as clearly as during a well-established trend. If the first flag after an upwards breakout leans down, it confirms the new upwards trend.

Figure 1.19 shows an assortment of triangles, flags, and pennants. There are two small flags, one in the middle of the chart and one in the lower right, each leaning upwards as expected in a downtrend. A larger flag slightly below center could also have been a symmetric triangle. Both patterns are resolved by a continuation of the trend.

Pennants

Pennants are irregular triangles normally leaning toward the trend, similar to a descending triangle in a downtrend but without a horizontal support line. A typical pennant can be seen in the middle of Figure 1.19. During a sustained trend, triangles

FIGURE 1.19 An Assortment of Continuation Patterns. These patterns are all resolved by prices moving lower. A downward pennant can be found in the middle of the chart.

are large, clear formations, with horizontal support or resistance lines, while pennants are consolidation formations requiring only that the lines converge. They usually lean in the direction of the trend, but that is not a requirement. A larger pennant should lean in the direction of the trend in a manner similar to a descending triangle; however, a small pennant may serve the same purpose as a flag and lean away from the trend.

Wedges

A pattern that looks as if it is a large pennant, with both sides angling in the same direction, but does not come to a point, is a *wedge*. In an upwards-trending market, the wedge should be rising as shown on the right side of the General Electric chart, Figure 1.20, near the end of 1999. The earlier wedge has nearly a horizontal upper line, bridging the pattern between a wedge and a rising triangle. A rising wedge is formed in the same way as an ascending triangle. Investors, convinced that the share price will rise, will buy smaller and smaller reversals even as prices make new highs. In the end, prices continue in the direction of the trend. In a typical rising wedge the lower line has a steeper angle than the upper line.

The angle of the wedge should be steeper as the trend becomes clear. The earlier wedge formation shown in Figure 1.20 is nearly symmetric. If we study the bigger picture, we can see that the uncertainty at the beginning of the trend is reflected in the symmetric formation, while the rising wedge occurs after the trend is well established and investors anticipate a continuation.

GE LAST-Daily 01/31/2001 C=45.980 -72.583 -61.22% O=46.750 H=46.950 L=45.560 V=21346100

Created with TradeStation 2000i by Omega Research © 1999

FIGURE 1.20 Wedge. A weaker wedge formation is followed by a strong rising wedge near the end of 1999 in this chart of General Electric.

Run Days

Triangles, flags, pennants, and wedges represent the best of the continuation patterns. They can be identified clearly while they are still being formed and the direction of the breakout can be anticipated and traded. Other formations, such as *run days,* are not as timely. A run day occurs when the low of that day is higher than the previous *n* days, and the high of the day is lower than the subsequent *n* highs. When it occurs, this pattern confirms that a trend is in effect. The more days used to define the run day, the stronger the pattern. Therefore, a 5-day run day requires 11 days to identify, 5 before the run day and 5 after. Unlike the other continuation patterns, which have a breakout level that can be used as a trading signal, entering a long position after 11 days of a strong upwards move is not likely to be a good entry point. There are no trading rules or trading action associated with run days. They simply confirm what you have already seen on charts—that prices have been trending.

■ Basic Concepts in Chart Trading

Having covered the fundamental chart patterns, there are some additional concepts that should be discussed in order to keep the proper perspective. Charting involves a great deal of subjective pattern identification; therefore, there may be a choice of patterns within the same time interval. There are also many cases where prices nearly form a pattern, but the shape does not fit perfectly into the classic definition.

Major and Minor Formations

In the study of charting, the same patterns will appear in short- as well as long-term charts. An upwards trendline can be drawn across the bottom of a price move that only began last week, or it can identify a sustained 3-year trend in the financial markets, or a 6-month move in Amazon.com. In general, formations that occur over longer time intervals are more significant. All-time highs and lows, well-defined trading ranges, trendlines based on weekly charts, and head-and-shoulder formations are carefully watched by traders. Obscure patterns and new formations are not of interest to most chartists, and cannot be resolved consistently unless traders buy and sell at the right points. Charting is most successful when formations are easy to see; therefore, the most obvious buy and sell points are likely to attract a large number of orders.

Market Noise

All markets have a normal level of noise. The stock index markets have the greatest amount of irregular movement due their extensive participation, the high level of anticipation built into the prices, the uncertain way in which economic reports and news will impact prices, and because it is an index. This is contrasted to short-term interest rates, such as Eurodollars, which have large participation but little anticipation because it has strong ties to the underlying cash market, governed by the central bank. The normal level of noise can be seen in the consistency of the daily or weekly trading range on a chart of the Dow or S&P. When volatility declines below the normal level of noise, the market is experiencing short-term inactivity. An increase in volatility back to normal levels of noise should not be confused with a breakout.

This same situation can be applied to a triangular formation, which has traditionally been interpreted as a consolidation, or a pause, within a trend. This pattern often follows a fast price change and represents a short period of declining volatility. If volatility declines in a consistent fashion, it appears as a triangle; however, if the point of the triangle is smaller than the normal level of market noise, then a breakout from this point is likely to restore price movement to a range typical of noise, resulting in a flag or pennant formation. Both of these latter patterns have uniform height that can include a normal level of noise, but they would not be reliable signals.

◼ Accumulation and Distribution—Bottoms and Tops

Most of the effort in charting, and the largest payout in trading, goes into the identification of tops and bottoms. For long-term traders, those trying to take advantage of major bull and bear markets, these formations can unfold over fairly long periods. These prolonged phases, which represent the cyclic movement in the economy, are called *accumulation* when prices are low and investors slowly buy into their position, and *distribution* at the top, where the invested positions are sold off.

The same formations can occur over shorter periods and are very popular among all traders; however, they are not as reliable. There are many top and bottom formations that are popular and easily recognized. In order of increasing complexity, they are the *V*-top or *V*-bottom, the double or triple top or bottom, the common rounded top or bottom, the broadening top or bottom, the head-and-shoulders formation, and the complex top or bottom.

V-Tops and V-Bottoms

The *V-top* (actually an inverted "V"), which may also have a spike on the final day, is the easiest pattern to see afterwards, but the most difficult top formation to anticipate and trade. There have been times, such as in 1974, 1980, and 2000, when the frequency of *V*-tops were deceiving. *V*-tops are preceded by critical shortage and demand, and magnified by constant news coverage. In 1974, it was a combination of domestic crop shortage, severe pressure on the U.S. dollar abroad, and foreign purchases of U.S. grain that combined to draw public attention to a potential shortage in wheat. The news was so well publicized that novice commodity traders withdrew their funds from their declining stock portfolios and bought any commodity available as a hedge against inflation.

It could not continue for long. When the top came in soybeans, silver, and most other commodities, there was no trading for days in locked-limit markets; paper profits dwindled faster than they were made, and the latecomers found their investments unrecoverable. The public often seems to enter at the wrong time.

The most dramatic of all price moves was the technology bubble of the 1990s, ending with a peak in the NASDAQ index during March 2000. As you can see in Figure 1.21, prices rose faster near the end of the bull market, then collapsed just as quickly. It would have been reasonable to expect the move up to end any time after prices penetrated through 3,000, and difficult to expect them to reach 5,000.

FIGURE 1.21   A V-top in the NASDAQ Index, March 2000.

FIGURE 1.22 Cash Cotton Prices Showing V-Top in Early 2011.

Recently, there have been runs in many commodities, but cotton stands out as exceptional. Flooding in both Pakistan and Egypt has greatly reduced the supply causing prices to soar. Figure 1.22 shows prices in February 2011 at levels four times the normal price and a top has not yet formed. Normally, supply shortages in agricultural markets correct by the next season, but the current run has been so extensive that it may take more time to resolve. Inevitably, it will be solved in the same way, over one or two crop years.

The psychology of the runaway market is fascinating. In some ways, every *V*-top shares a similarity with the examples in Mackay's *Extraordinary Popular Delusions and the Madness of Crowds*. When beef is in short supply, the result of higher feed costs, the consumers do not tend to consider pork, fowl, or fish as an adequate substitute and will accept increased costs longer than expected. This is called *inelastic demand*. As prices near the top, the following changes occur:

- The cost becomes an increasing factor in the standard household budget.

- Rising prices receive more publicity.

- Movements for public beef boycotts begin.

- Grain prices decline due to the new harvest.

This becomes a matter explained by the *Theory of Elasticity*. It can be applied to the 1973 soybean, 1980 silver, and the recent cotton markets. The theory is based on the principle that when prices get high enough, four phenomena occur:

1. Previously higher-priced substitutes become practical (synthetics for cotton, reclaimed silver).
2. Competition becomes more feasible (corn sweetener as a sugar substitute, alternate energy).
3. Inactive operations start up (Southwest gold mines, marginal production of oil).
4. Consumers avoid the products (beef, bacon, silver, cotton).

Consequently, the demand suddenly disappears (the same conclusion arrived at by economists).

Announcements of additional production, more acreage, new products, boycotts, and a cancellation of orders all coming at once cause highly inflated prices to reverse sharply. These factors form a *V*-top that is impossible to anticipate with reasonable risk. There is a natural reluctance to cash in on profits while they are still increasing every day. The situation becomes even more perilous at the end of the move when more investors join the party. These latecomers who entered their most recent positions near the top will show a loss immediately and will need to get out of the trade first; they cannot afford a continued adverse move. Once a reversal day is recognized, there is a mad rush to liquidate. The large number of investors and speculators trying to exit at the same time causes the sharpness in the *V*-top and extends the drop in prices. There is a liquidity void at many points during the decline where there are no buyers and a long line of sellers. A *V*-top or *V*-bottom is always accompanied by high volatility and usually high volume. When the *V*-top is particularly extreme, it is commonly called a *blow-off*. A true *V*-top or *V*-bottom will become an important medium- or long-term high or low for that market.

Two V-Tops in Amazon.com   There is a classic *V*-top in Amazon.com during January 1999, shown in Figure 1.23, and another potential, smaller formation in April. This second one looked as though it was a *V*-top for two days, then quickly disappeared into a broader formation of no particular pattern. A *V*-top cannot be recognized after only a 1-day downturn. The final peak seen in Amazon in late April 1999 is broader than a classic *V*-top but could still be labeled the same.

When trading, you would expect rising prices to fail when they approach the level of a previous clear *V*-top, which forms significant resistance. In Figure 1.23, where

FIGURE 1.23   Classic V-Top in Amazon, January 1999, and Two Other Tops.

prices began the second *V*-top, declined for two days, rallied for the next three days, then dropped sharply for two days, we would normally expect a further decline. In this case, prices made another attempt to break the highs, succeeded, then collapsed. After the last peak, it will be necessary to wait until the price falls below the support level at $75 in order to confirm the downward break, having been fooled on the previous move.

V-Bottoms   *V-bottoms* are much less common than their upside counterparts. They occur more often in commodity markets where supply and demand can change dramatically and leverage causes surges of buying and selling. Both *V*-tops and *V*-bottoms should be read as a sign that prices have gone too far, too fast. Both buyers and sellers need time to reevaluate the fundamentals to decide where prices should be. *V*-bottoms are usually followed by a rebound and then a period of sideways movement. Two good examples can be found in the crude oil chart, Figure 1.24, and in the stock market crash of October 1987.

Double and Triple Tops and Bottoms

The experienced trader is most successful when prices are testing a major support or resistance level, especially an all-time high in a stock or a contract or seasonal high or low in futures. The more often those levels are tested, the clearer they become and the less likely prices will break through to a new level without additional fuel. This fuel comes in the form of higher earnings or a change in the fundamental supply and demand factors.

A *double top* is a price peak followed, a few days or weeks later, by another peak, and stopping very close to the same level. A *double bottom*, more common than a double

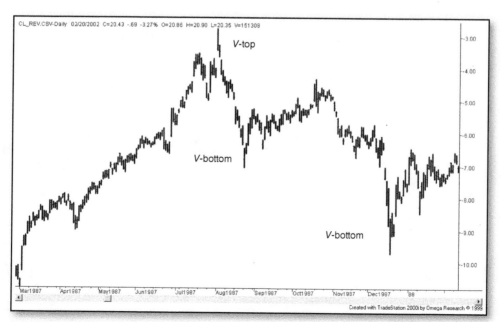

FIGURE 1.24   Two V-Bottoms in Crude Oil.

top, occurs when two price valleys show lows at nearly the same level. Because prices are more likely to settle for awhile at a lower price than a high one, prices often test a previous support level causing a double bottom.

Tops and bottoms occur at the same level because traders believe that the same reason that caused prices to fail to go higher the first time will be the reason they fail the second time. The exceptionally high or low prices are the result of speculation rather than fundamentals. In the same way that some stocks will trade at price/earnings ratios far above any rational assessment of business prospects in the near future, commodity prices can be pushed to extremes by crowd psychology without regard to value. Traders, looking for a place to sell an unreasonably high price, target the previous point where prices failed. Although a classic double top is thought to peak at exactly the same price, selling in anticipation of the test of the top may cause the second peak to be lower than the first. Figure 1.25 shows one type of double top in crude oil. While some double tops are two sharp peaks, this one looks as though it was gathering energy. It penetrated slightly above the previous high, but could not sustain higher prices. Double tops are rarely perfect.

Double Bottoms Bottoms are more orderly than tops. They should be quiet rather than volatile. They are caused by prices reaching a level that is low enough for the normal investor to recognize that there is little additional downside potential. Economists might call this the *point of equilibrium*. Neither buyers nor sellers are convinced that prices will continue to move lower. They wait for further news.

Double bottoms will often test the same price level because large-position traders and commercial users of commodities accumulate more physical inventory, or increase their futures position, each time the price falls to their target level. Once

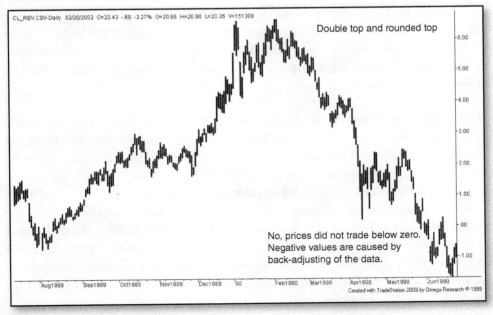

FIGURE 1.25 **A Double Top in Crude Oil.**

Double bottom confirmed

Double bottom

Created with TradeStation 2000i by Omega Research © 1999

FIGURE 1.26   A Double Bottom in Cisco.

prices are low, there is less chance of absolute loss. Selling a double top can be very risky. The greatest risk when buying a double bottom is that your timing is wrong. If prices do not rally soon, you have used your capital poorly.

Cisco shows a double bottom in Figure 1.26, although it lacks the clear decline in volatility that we would like to see, and which accompanies commodities when they reach a price level near the cost of production. The small spikes down show four attempts to go lower, followed by a faster move up. When prices cross above the highs formed between the two bottom patterns, we have a completion, or *confirmation,* of the double bottom.

Traders will start to buy a double bottom when prices slow near previous low levels. They will also look for declining volume or confirmation in the stock price of another related company or a related sector ETF. Waiting for the breakout above the highs of the bottom formation is a safer signal for a conservative trader, but lost opportunity for a more active one.

Triple Tops and Bottoms   *Triple tops* and *triple bottoms* are considerably less common than double tops and bottoms; however, of the two, bottoms can be found more readily. Figure 1.27 shows a classic triple top in natural gas. A triple top can be formed from a *V*-top, but in this case, the first peak is an island reversal, the second is a spike, and the third an extended top that ends the move.

If we did not have the advantage of seeing the triple top afterwards, each of the individual tops would look as if it were the end of the move. After the first island reversal prices dropped $2; after the second peak there was another large gap down and a 1-day loss of more than $1. High volatility is normally associated with an extreme top. By waiting for a confirmation of a decline after the single or double top, the trade would have been entered $1.50 to $2.50 below the top, and that position would be held while prices reversed to test the highs. Selling tops is risky business.

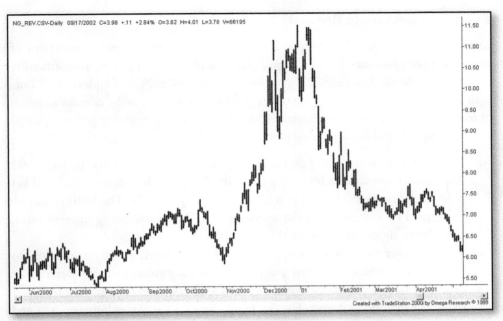

FIGURE 1.27   Natural Gas Shows a Classic Triple Top.

A triple bottom that can be traded is most likely to occur at low prices and low volatility, much the same as a double bottom. They show an inability to go lower because investors are willing to accumulate a position at a good value. For commodities, it is a good place for a processor to accumulate inventory.

The Danger of Trading Double and Triple Tops   There are many examples of double tops and a smaller number of triple tops. Ideally, there is a lot of money to be made by selling tops at the right place. However, the likelihood of this good fortune happening is less than it appears. Consider why a triple top is so rare. It is because prices continue higher and the potential triple top disappears into a strong bull market pattern.

This happens even more often with double tops. Every time a price pulls back from new highs, then starts moving up again, there is a potential double top. In a prolonged bull market, many double tops disappear in the move higher. Selection of the double top becomes important. This is done using volume, volatility, support, and resistance, and sometimes common sense. These confirming indicators are discussed throughout this book. Until then, it is important to recognize the difficulty of deciding whether the current pattern will be a single, double, or triple top, or simply a pause in a bull market. Although we would all like to be a seller at the highs, these tops are best sold after they are confirmed, that is, after a decline proves that the top has occurred. Even then, a new high should cause a fast exit from the trade.

As with other chart patterns, declining volume would be a welcome confirmation after the formation of the first top and would accompany each additional test of the top.

Extended Rectangle Bottom

Many of the important chart formations can be traded using a penetration of one of the support or resistance lines as a signal. Those with the most potential profitability occur on breakouts from major top or bottom formations. The simplest of all bottom formations, as well as one that offers great opportunities, is the *extended rectangle* at long-term low price levels. Fortunes have been made by applying patience, some available capital, and the following plan:

1. Find a market with a long consolidating base and low volatility. In July 2002 Amazon.com reaches a low with volatility declining. In futures, crude oil remained at low prices for 13 years, as seen in Figure 1.28. The bottom can be confirmed by a decrease in the open interest. When evaluating interest rates, consider using the yield rather than the price.

2. *Buy* whenever there is a test of its major support level, placing a stop-loss to liquidate all positions on a new low price. Increasing volume should confirm the buying, and with futures markets the upside breakout should be accompanied by increasing open interest. For crude oil, the resistance was between $21 and $22 because OPEC had set its OGSP (*Official Government Selling Price*) between $18 and $22.

3. After the initial breakout, buy again when prices pull back to the original resistance line (now a support level). Crude rallied from the lows to just under $40 before pulling back to the old resistance level at $19. Close out all positions if prices penetrate back into the consolidation area and start again at Step 2.

4. Buy whenever there is a major price correction in the bull move. These adjustments, or pullbacks, will become shorter and less frequent as the move

FIGURE 1.28 An Extended Rectangular Bottom in Crude Oil from 1986 through 1999.

develops. They will usually be proportional to current volatility or the extent of the price move as measured from the original breakout.

5. Liquidate all positions at a prior major resistance point, a top formation, or the breaking of a major bullish support line.

Building positions in this way can be done with a relatively small amount of capital and risk. The closer the price comes to major support, the shorter the distance from the stop-loss; however, fewer positions can be placed. In his book *The Professional Commodity Trader*, Stanley Kroll discussed "The Copper Caper—How We're Going to Make a Million," using a similar technique for building positions. It can be done, but it requires patience, planning, and capital. The opportunities continue to be there.

This example of patiently building a large position does not usually apply to bear markets. Although there is a great deal of money to be made on the short side of the market, prices move faster and may not permit the accumulation of a large position. There can also be exceptionally high risk caused by greater volatility. The only pattern that allows for the accumulation of a large short position is the rounded top, discussed in the next section. Within consolidation areas for commodities at low levels, there are a number of factors working in your favor: the underlying demand for a product, the cost of production, government price support (for agricultural products), and low volatility itself. There is also a clear support level that may have been tested many times. A careful position trader will not enter a large short-sale position at an anticipated top when volatility is high, but instead will join the buyers who contribute to the growing volume and open interest at a well-defined major support level.

Rounded Tops and Bottoms

When prices change direction over a longer time period they can create a rounded top or bottom pattern. A *rounded top* reflects a gradual change in market forces from buyers to sellers. In the stock market it is also called *distribution*. It is a clear sign that any attempt to move prices higher has been abandoned. Rounded tops often lead to faster and faster price drops as more investors liquidate their long positions or initiate shorts.

In Figure 1.29 we see two classic rounded tops in the German DAX stock index. The first is an example of gathering downside momentum as more investors become aware of the decline. Prices drop faster after a break of the double bottom. The rounded top offers a rare opportunity to accumulate a short position with relatively low volatility.

Rounded Bottom   A rounded bottom, similar to a rounded top, is an extended formation where prices gradually turn from down to up. In Figure 1.30 we see a rounded bottom in the Japanese yen followed by a breakaway gap. Similar to the extended rectangle, the rounded bottom offers traders an opportunity to accumulate a large long position. In this case, the sharp rally as prices move through the high of the rounded bottom, followed by a runaway gap, clearly marks the end of

FIGURE 1.29 Two Rounded Tops in the German DAX Stock Index.

the rounded bottom. The breakout can be interpreted as a change in the supply and demand balance. A breakout, whether in stocks or futures, indicates that something new has entered the picture.

FIGURE 1.30 A Classic Rounded Bottom in the Japanese Yen.

Wedge Top and Bottom Patterns

We have seen a wedge formation as a continuation pattern in Figure 1.20, but a large ascending wedge can mark the top of a move and a large descending wedge the bottom. The dominant characteristic of the wedge is that volatility is declining towards the end. In Figure 1.31 there is a declining wedge in the Japanese yen. Volatility compresses until a breakout is inevitable. If the breakout had been to the downside, this wedge would have been interpreted as a continuation pattern. In this example, a breakout in the opposite direction is a strong indicator of a major reversal.

Head-and-Shoulders Formation

The classic top and bottom formation is the *head and shoulders,* accepted as a major reversal indicator. This pattern, well known to chartists, appears as a left shoulder, a head, and a right shoulder, seen in Figure 1.32. The head-and-shoulders top is developed with the following five characteristics:

1. A strong upward breakout reaching new highs on increasing volume. The pattern appears to be the continuation of a long-term bull move.
2. A consolidation area formed with declining volume. This can look much like a descending flag predicting an upwards breakout, or a descending triangle indicating a downwards breakout.
3. Another upwards breakout on continued reduced volume forms the head. This is the key point of the formation. The new high is not confirmed by increased volume, and prices drop quickly.

FIGURE 1.31   A Large Declining Wedge Followed by an Upside Breakout in the Japanese Yen.

FIGURE 1.32 Head-and-Shoulders Top Pattern in the Japanese Nikkei Index.

4. Another descending flag or triangle is formed on further reduced volume, followed by a minor breakout without increased volume. This last move forms the right shoulder and is the third attempt at new highs for the move.

5. The lowest points of the two flags, pennants, or triangles become the *neckline* of the formation. A short sale is indicated when this neckline is broken.

Trading Rules for Head and Shoulders There are three approaches to trading a head-and-shoulders top formation involving increasing degrees of anticipation:

1. *Wait for a confirmation.*
   a. Sell when the final dip of the right shoulder penetrates the neckline. This represents the completion of the head-and-shoulders formation. Place a stop-loss just above the entry if the trade is to be held only for a fast profit, or place the stop-loss above the right shoulder or above the head in order to liquidate on new strength, allowing a longer holding period.
   b. Sell on the first rally after the neckline is broken. (Although more conservative, the lost opportunities may outweigh the improved entry prices.) Use the same stops as in Step 1a.

2. *Anticipation of the final shoulder.*
   a. Sell when the right shoulder is being formed. A likely place would be when prices have retraced their way half the distance to the head. A stop-loss can be placed above the top of the head.
   b. Wait until the top of the right shoulder is formed and prices appear to be declining. Sell and place a stop either above the high of the right shoulder or above the high of the head.

Both steps 2a and 2b allow positions to be taken well in advance of the neck-line penetration with logical stop-loss points. Using the high of the head for a protective stop is considered a conservative approach because it allows the integrity of the pattern to be tested before the position is exited.

3. *Early anticipation of the head.*
   Sell when the right part of the head is forming, on the downwards price move, with a stop-loss at about the high of the move. Although this represents a small risk, it has less chance of success. This approach is for traders who prefer to anticipate tops and are willing to suffer frequent small losses to do it. Even if the current prices become the head of the formation, there may be numerous small corrections that will look like the market top to an anxious seller.

Volume was a recognized part of the classic definition of the head-and-shoulders formation and appeared in Robert D. Edwards and John Magee's *Technical Analysis of Stock Trends,* published in 1948. This is no longer considered as important. There are many examples of successful head-and-shoulders formations that do not satisfy the volume criterion. Nevertheless, declining volume on the head or the right shoulder of a top formation must be seen as a strong confirmation of a failing upwards move, and is consistent with the normal interpretation of volume.

■ Episodic Patterns

There is little argument that all prices change quickly in response to unexpected news. The transition from one major level to another is termed an *episodic pattern*; when these transitions are violent, they are called *price shocks*. Until the late 1990s, there were very few price shocks in the stock market, the greatest being the one resulting from the terrorist attacks of September 11, 2001. Otherwise, price shocks can be caused by a surprising election result, the unexpected raising of interest rates by the Federal Reserve, the devaluation of a currency by an important Third World nation, sudden crop loss or natural disaster, or an assassination (or what we now call a *geopolitical event*). While price shocks are most common in futures markets, all markets are continually adjusting to new price levels, and all experience occasional surprises. Each news article, government economic release, or earnings report can be considered a mini-shock. A common price shock occurs when a pharmaceutical company's application for a new drug is unexpectedly rejected by the U.S. Department of Agriculture (USDA).

The pattern that results from episodic movement is exactly what one might expect. Following the sharp price movement, there is a period when volatility declines from its highs, narrowing until a normal volatility level is found and remaining at that level. In the Raytheon reaction to 9/11, the upwards price shock, shown in Figure 1.33 is followed by a volatile, unstable few days and then a steady decline in volatility as some level of equilibrium is found. The Raytheon price reacted opposite to most other stocks because it is a defense contractor, and a terrorist attack implies an increased amount of business from the government.

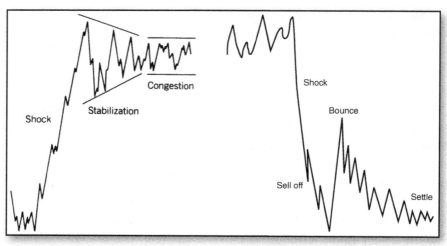

FIGURE 1.33 Episodic Pattern Shown in an Upward Price Shock in Raytheon Following 9/11/2001.

Unless the news that caused the price shock was an error, in which case prices immediately move back to levels prior to the news, prices will settle in a new trading range near the extreme highs or lows. It will take time for the market to absorb the consequences of the news, and many traders will find the risk too high to participate.

Price shocks have become the focus of much analytic work. Because a price shock is an unpredictable event, it cannot be forecast. This has a critical effect on the way in which systems are developed, especially with regard to the testing procedures. We understand at the time of the price shock that the event was entirely unexpected. However, years later, when the same prices are analyzed using a computer program, you might find that a trend or charting pattern *predicted* this move. The analysis records the profits as though they were predictable and you are now basing your conclusions on a false premise.

■ Price Objectives for Bar Charting

Most traders set price objectives and use them to assess the risk and reward of a potential trade. Objectives are most reasonable for short-term trading and successful objectives are based on straightforward concepts and not complex calculations. There is also a noticeable similarity between the price objectives for different chart patterns.

The simplest and most logical price objective is a major support or resistance level established by previous trading. When entering a long position, look at the most well-defined resistance levels above the entry point. These have been discussed in previous sections of this chapter. When those prior levels are tested, there is generally a technical adjustment or a reversal. The more well-established the support or resistance level, the more likely prices will stop. In the case of a strong upwards move, volatility often causes a small penetration before the setback occurs. A penetration of support or resistance, followed by a return to the previous trading range is considered a confirmation of the old range and a false breakout. Placing the price objective for a long position below the identifiable major resistance level will always be safe. The downside objective can be identified in a similar manner: Find the major support level and exit just above it.

When trading with chart patterns, it pays to be flexible. Regardless of which method you use to identify a profit target, be prepared to take profits sooner if the market changes. For example, you have entered a long in IBM at $160 and set your profit objective at $200. Prices move as predicted and reach $195 when volume starts to drop and the price pattern seems to move sideways. An experienced trader will say "close enough" and take the profit. Profit objectives are not perfect, only good guidelines. If you have set a single price target for a long position, and it falls slightly above a resistance level, then the lower resistance level should be used as the price objective.

Rather than rely on a single point, traders will fan out their target points around the most likely objective, dividing their goal into three or five levels. As each profit-target is reached the risk of the current trade is reduced as is the likelihood of turning a profit into a loss.

While waiting for prices to reach the objective, remember to watch for a violation of the current trend; trend changes take priority over profit objectives. If the trade is successful, and the goal is reached as expected, watch for a new pattern. If prices decline after the trade is closed out, then reverse and break through the previous highs or lows, the position may be reentered on the breakout and a new price objective calculated.

Common Elements of Profit Objectives

Most chart formations have a price objective associated with them. The common ground for all of them is volatility. Each chart pattern is larger or smaller because of the current price volatility; therefore, the price targets derived from these formations are also based on volatility. In general, the *price objective reflects the same volatility as the chart formation* and is measured from the point where prices break out of the pattern.

Profit Targets for Consolidation Areas and Channels

The most basic of all formations is the horizontal consolidation area, bounded on the top and bottom by a horizontal resistance and support lines. There are two possible profit targets, shown in Figure 1.34.

1. For any *horizontal consolidation pattern,* the target is above the breakout of the resistance line at a point equal to the height of the consolidation area (the resistance level minus the support level added to the resistance level). That makes the expected move equal to the extreme volatility of the consolidation area.
2. With *extended rectangular formations,* the upwards profit target is calculated as the width of the consolidation pattern added to the support level.

FIGURE 1.34 Price Objectives for Consolidation Patterns and Channels. (a) Two objectives for consolidation patterns. (b) Price objective for a channel.

Although price objective (2) is a well-known and popular calculation, it is unrealistic when the extended formation is very prolonged. The standard calculation, given in (1), is more reasonable. A third objective is more conservative but even more practical:

3. Use the average volatility of the consolidation formation, or reduce the target in (1) above by 20% to remove the extremes from influencing the objectives. A closer price target will be reached more often.

The price objective for a channel is the same as the traditional objective for a horizontal consolidation pattern. Because the channel is at an angle, it is necessary to measure the width of the channel as perpendicular to the angled support and resistance channel lines; then project that width upwards from the point of breakout.

The length of the channel does not change the profit target. Again, you may want to make the target slightly smaller than the original channel.

Changing Price Objectives Using Channels Price objectives can be found as trends change and new channels are formed. Figure 1.35 shows the change from an upwards to a downwards trend. Once a breakout of an upwards channel has occurred (marked "First point of reversal"), we wait until the low is reached at *a*, followed by the reaction back up to *b*. A resistance line, 1*R*, can be drawn from the prior high *h* to the top of the latest move *b*. A line, 1*S*, can be constructed parallel to 1*R* passing through point *a*, forming the initial downward channel. Price objective 1 is on line 1*S* of the new channel and is used once the top at point *b* is determined. Price objective 1 cannot be expected to be too precise due to the early development of the channel. If prices continue to point *c* and then rally to *d*, a more reasonable channel can now be defined using trendlines 2*R* and 2*S*. The support line will again become the point where the new price objective is placed. The upper and lower trendlines can be further refined as the new high and low reactions occur. The primary trendline is always drawn first; then the new price objective becomes a point on the parallel trendline.

Targeting Profits after Tops and Bottoms

Because profit targets are based on the volatility of the underlying pattern, the profit targets for all top and bottom formations will seem very much the same. Looking back at Figure 1.27, natural gas, there is a triple top formation. Between each top is a reversal marking an important support level. The first pullback after the island reversal brought prices to 8.20, followed by a test of the top that formed the second peak. The second retracement stopped at 9.00 and was followed by the third peak. When prices finally drop through the highest support level at 9.00, we can treat it as a breakout and sell short.

If this chart showed a double top, then the point where prices fall below the support between two tops *confirms the top*. Breaking this support level indicates that the topping formation is completed. But this was not a double top; therefore, we

FIGURE 1.35 **Forming New Channels to Determine Objectives.**

can take the lower of the two support levels between the three tops as the major confirmation of the pattern. In the natural gas chart, the lower support was at 8.20. Using either support level gives a measurement of the triple top pattern based on the volatility of prices.

Calculating the Profit Target for a Top Formation

The profit target is found by measuring the height of the top formation and projecting it downwards from the point where the top is confirmed, that is, the break of the support level. For this example, profit targets will be calculated based on each of the support levels. The highest price of the move is 10.75. Let's examine two profit targets:

1. Using the support level of 9.00, the height of the top is 10.75 – 9.00, or 1.75. Projecting that downwards from the breakout point of 9.00 gives a profit objective of 7.25. The first major pause in the price drop stopped at about 7.00, still showing high volatility.
2. Based on the second support level of 8.20, the height of the top is 2.65, and the profit objective, measured from the break at 8.20, is 5.55. Prices reach 5.55, but only after stalling at about 6.50.

The first target is very achievable and realistic. Prices are very volatile, and a drop of 1.75 could occur very quickly. The second target is less realistic. When targeting a much larger decline, and beginning at a much lower point, it is unrealistic to expect volatility to continue at the same high level. In the decline of natural gas from January through March, volatility also declines, so that by March it appears as though the move is over. Although price targets can often be correct, those that are far away will be less reliable.

Profit Targets after a Bottom Formation   The same principle can be applied to calculate the profit target for bottom formations. The distance from the lowest price of the bottom to the confirmation point is projected upwards from the breakout. This method can be applied to any type of bottom formation. In Figure 1.26, the double bottom in Cisco spanned the price range from about 5.00 to 6.25. The volatility of the bottom pattern, 1.25, is projected upwards from the breakout at 6.25 to get the target of 7.50. Because volatility should expand as prices rise, the exact volatility calculation can be used as a conservative measure.

The Head-and-Shoulders Price Objective   In keeping with other price targets, the head-and-shoulders top has a downside objective, which is also based on its volatility. This objective is measured from the point where the right shoulder penetrates the neckline and is equal to the distance from the top of the head to the neckline (Figure 1.36). For a major top, this goal seems modest, but it will be a good measure of the initial reaction and is generally safe, even if a new high price is reached later.

A very similar example can be found in the Japanese yen (Figure 1.30). The neckline also angles up and to the right, and the price target finds the bottom of the first major support level following the break of the right shoulder. The position of the price objective is so significant that the subsequent drop in prices creates a breakaway gap.

FIGURE 1.36 Head-and-Shoulders Top Price Objective.

Triangles and Flags   *Triangles* and *flags* have objectives based on volatility in a manner consistent with other patterns. The triangle objective is equal in size to the initial reaction, which formed the largest end of the triangle (Figure 1.37a). It may also be viewed as a developing channel rather than a triangle, with the ascending leg of the triangle forming the primary bullish trendline. The price objective then becomes the same as those used for channels.

The flag is assumed to occur midway in a price move; therefore, the objective of a new breakout must be equal to the size of the move preceding the flag (Figure 1.37b). Recalling the comments on the problems associated with the

FIGURE 1.37   Triangle and Flag Objectives. (a) Triangle objective is based on the width of the initial sides. (b) Flag objective is equal to the move prior to the flag formation.

decreasing volatility of the triangular formation, the use of the first reaction as a measure of volatility is a safe way to avoid problems. Using this technique with subsequent flags in a bull move will cause objectives to move farther away, becoming unrealistic.

The Rule of Seven   Another measurement of price objectives, the *Rule of Seven*, is credited to Arthur Sklarew.[17] It is based on the volatility of the prior consolidation formation and computes three successive price objectives in proportion to one another. The Rule of Seven is not symmetric for both uptrends and downtrends. Sklarew believes that, after the initial leg of a move, the downtrend reactions are closer together than the reactions in a rising market. Because the downside of a major bear market is limited, it is usually characterized by consolidation. Major bull markets tend to expand as they develop.

To calculate the objectives using the Rule of Seven, first measure the length L of the initial leg of a price move (from the previous high or low, the most extreme point before the first pullback). The objectives are:

1. In an *uptrend*:
   Upwards objective 1 = prior low + $(L \times 7/4)$
   Upwards objective 2 = prior low + $(L \times 7/3)$
   Upwards objective 3 = prior low + $(L \times 7/2)$
2. In a *downtrend*:
   Downwards objective 1 = prior high − $(L \times 7/5)$
   Downwards objective 2 = prior high − $(L \times 7/4)$
   Downwards objective 3 = prior high − $(L \times 7/3)$

The three objectives apply most clearly to major moves. During minor price swings, it is likely that the first two objectives will be bypassed. In Sklarew's experience, regardless of whether any one objective is missed, the others still remain intact.

■ Implied Strategies in Candlestick Charts

For a technique that is reported to have been used as early as the mid-1600s, Japanese candle charts were slow to find their way into the western method of analysis. Candle charts can be related to bar charts but offer additional visual interpretation. The *candles* are created simply by *shading* the piece of the bar between the opening and closing prices: white if the close is higher than the open and black if the close is lower than the open. The shaded area is called the *body* and the extended lines above and below the body are the *shadows*. With this simple change, we get an entirely new way of looking at and interpreting charts. The patterns become much clearer than the Western style of line chart.

---

[17] Arthur Sklarew, *Techniques of a Professional Chart Analyst* (Commodity Research Bureau, 1980).

Although many candlestick patterns have equivalent bar chart formations, there is an implied strategy in many of them. The following summary uses the traditional candlestick names representing the significance of the formation (see Figure 1.38):

- *Doji,* in which the opening and closing prices are the same. This represents indecision, a temporary balancing point. It is neither bullish nor bearish. A *double doji,* where two dojis occur successively, implies that a significant breakout will follow.

- *Engulfing patterns* seem at first to be the same as outside days in bar charting, but the pattern only refers to the part of the bar between the opening and closing prices. Engulfing patterns are considered exceptionally strong signals of price change. A *bullish engulfing pattern* has a black candle followed by a white, indicating a wide range with a higher close. The *bearish engulfing pattern* is white followed by black, showing a lower close on the engulfing day.

FIGURE 1.38 Popular Candle Formations.

- *Morning star* and *evening star* are 3-day patterns that show a similarity to an island reversal, but are more specific. In the morning star, a bullish reversal pattern, the first day has a lower close than the open, the second day (called the *star,* similar to the island bottom) has a higher close, and the final reversal day has an even higher close. The bearish reversal is just the opposite, with two higher closes followed by a reversal day with a lower close. If the star is also a doji, then the pattern has more significance.

- *Piercing line* and *dark cloud cover* are bullish and bearish reversals. The piercing line, a bullish reversal, begins with a black candle (a lower close) and is followed by a white candle in which the open is below the previous day's low and the close is above the midpoint of the previous day's body (the open-close range). The dark cloud cover is a bearish formation, the opposite of the piercing line.

- *Hammer*, a bullish reversal signal, showing the bottom of a swing, where the body is at the top of the candle, indicating an upwards change of direction, and the shadow is below the body. The body may be black or white.

- *Hanging man*, a bearish reversal pattern where the body of the candle represents the high of a swing, and the shadow lies below in the direction of the reversal. The body may be black or white.

- *Shooting star*, a bearish signal, also occurs at the top of a swing and has its body at the bottom of the candle with the shadow above. The body may be black or white.

Although these patterns are similar to Western bar chart formations, none of them are exactly the same. The hammer, hanging man, and shooting star are reversal patterns but can only be compared to the simple pivot point where the middle day is higher or lower than the bars on either side. None of these candle formations is exactly the same as a key reversal day or island reversal. The engulfing pattern is stronger than the typical outside day because the spanning of the prior day's range must be done only by the current day's open-close range.

The analysis of candle charts is a skill involving the understanding of many complex and interrelated patterns. For full coverage, Steve Nison's, *Japanese Candlestick Charting Techniques,* second edition, is recommended, as well as a selection of newer books, which can be found on Amazon.

Quantifying Candle Formations

The preciseness of the candle formations allow some patterns to be tested. The popular engulfing patterns can be defined exactly for a computer program as

Bullish engulfing pattern = Previous open > previous close and today's
open < previous close and today's close > previous open

Bearish engulfing pattern = Previous close > previous open and today's
open > previous close and today's close < previous open

Another technique uses the shadows as confirmation of direction. We can interpret an increase in the size of the upper shadows as strengthening resistance (prices are closing lower each day); an increase in the size of the lower shadows represents more support. One way to look at this is by defining

Upper shadow (white) = high − close   Lower shadow (white) = open − low
Upper shadow (black) = high − open   Lower shadow (black) = close − low

The sequences of upper and lower shadows can be smoothed separately using a moving average to find out whether they are rising or falling.[18]

A method for determining whether black or white candles dominate recent price movement is to use only the body of the candle, $B = close − open$, and apply a momentum calculation:

$$Body\ momentum = \frac{B_{up}}{B_{up} + B_{down}}$$

where
B_{up} = the sum of the days where $B > 0$ (body is white)
B_{down} = the sum of the days where $B < 0$ (body is black)
14 = the recommended number of days

When the body momentum is greater than 70, the whites dominate; when the value is below 20 the blacks dominate. These thresholds indicate a built-in upwards bias.

Morning Star and Evening Star   Two formations that are easily programmed are the *morning star* (a bullish signal) and *evening star* (a bearish signal). Using the morning star as an example, the rules call for a long downward (black) candle followed by a lower (the open of the next bar less than the close of the previous long bar), less volatile white candle, and finally an upward thrust shown as a gap up body with the close higher than the open (another white candle).

When programmed (see *TSM Morning Star* and *TSM Evening Star* in the Companion Website), there are very few signals when we put restriction on the size of the bodies of the three days. Instead, we only required that the body of the first day be greater than the 20-day average, the second day less, and the third day greater. While there are still only a modest number of trades, the S&P performs well on the day following both patterns.

Qstick

As a way of quantifying the Candle formations, Tuschar Chande[19] created *Qstick*, a moving average of the body of the candle. It is intended to be an aid interpreting the charts but has simple trading rules as well.

$$If\ Body_t = Close_t − Open_t$$

and

$Q_t = average(period1,body)$, where *period1* is suggested as 8 days
$AvgQ_t = average(period2,Q)$, where *period2* is also 8 days

[18] Both "shadow trends" and "body momentum" are adapted from Tushar Chande and Stanley Kroll, *The New Technical Trader* (New York: John Wiley & Sons, 1994).

[19] Tushar Chande and Stanley Kroll, *The New Technical Trader* (New York: John Wiley & Sons, 1994).

Then the trading rules are

$$Buy \text{ when } Q_t \text{ moves above } AvgQ_t$$
$$Sell \text{ when } Q_t \text{ moves below } AvgQ_t$$

Pivot Points and Candle Charts

John L. Person suggests that the strategies inherent in candle formations can be combined with support and resistance levels derived from pivot points.[20] He uses the following calculations:

1. Pivot point, $P = (high + low + close)/3$
2. First resistance level, $R1 = (P \times 2) - low$
3. Second resistance level, $R2 = P + high - low$
4. First support level, $S1 = (P + 2) - high$
5. Second support level, $S2 = P - high + low$

Once a key formation for a top or bottom is recognized using candle charts, support and resistance levels calculated based on pivot points can be a strong indication of the extent of the following price move. Person used Dow futures to support his study.

The Best of the Candles

Bulkowski has summarized his own research in the success of various candles[21] as

- The best-performing candles had closing prices within $\frac{1}{3}$ of the bar low, followed by the middle and high, respectively.

- Candle patterns in a bear market outperform other markets, regardless of the breakout direction.

- Most candles perform best on days with higher volume.

- Candles with unusually long wicks outperform.

- Unusually tall candles outperform.

■ Practical Use of the Bar Chart

Trends Are Easier to See in Retrospect

As important as it is to identify the direction of price movement, it is much easier to see the trend afterward than at the moment it is needed. There is no doubt that all stocks and futures markets have short-term swings and longer-term bull and bear markets. Unfortunately, at the time you are ready to trade, it is not going to be clear

---

[20] John L. Person, "Pivot Points and Candles," *Futures* (February 2003).
[21] Thomas Bulkowski, "What You Don't Know About Candlesticks," *Technical Analysis of Stocks & Commodities* (March 2011).

whether the current price trend is a short-term pattern that is about to change or long-term persistent trend experiencing a temporary reversal.

The ease of seeing charts on a screen has made the past patterns clear. It seems natural to expect prices to trend in the future as clearly as they appear on a chart; however, it is not easy to do it in a timely fashion. The eye has a remarkable way of simplifying the chart patterns. The purpose of drawing a trendline is to recognize the direction even though prices can swing violently up and down during that trending interval. A new trend signal to buy or sell always occurs as the trend is changing; therefore, it is at the point of greatest uncertainty.

Success in systematic trading, whether using charts or mathematics, relies on consistency. In the long run, it comes down to probabilities. Success can be achieved by recognizing the trend in 60% of the cases. In a typical trend-following system, because individual profits are much larger than losses, it is only necessary to be correct 30% or 35% of the time.

Long-Term Trends Are More Reliable than Short-Term Trends

Charting is not precise, and the construction of the trendlines, other geometric formations, and their interpretation can be performed with some liberties. When using the simplest trendline analysis, it often happens that there is a small penetration of the channel or trendline followed by a movement back into the channel. Some think that this inaccuracy with respect to the rules makes charting useless; however, many experienced analysts interpret this action as confirmation of the trend. The trendline is not redrawn so that the penetration becomes the new high or low of the trend; it is left in its original position.

We must always step back and look for the underlying purpose in each method of analysis, whether interpretive or fully systematic. The trendline is an attempt to identify the direction of prices over some time period. Chartists can use a simple straight line to visualize the direction; they draw the uptrend by connecting the lowest prices in a rising market, even though each point used may represent varying levels of volatility and unique conditions. The chance of these points aligning perfectly, or forecasting the exact price support level, is small. A trendline is simply a guide; it may be too conservative at one time and too aggressive at another; and you won't know until after the trade is completed. Applied rigorously, charting rules should produce many incorrect signals but be profitable in the most important cases. The challenge of the chartist is to interpret the pattern of prices in context with the bigger picture.

Many price moves are called trends, but the most important and sustained trends are those resulting from government policy, in particular those that affect interest rates. Therefore, the most reliable trends are long-term phenomena because government policy develops slowly and is often long-term. During a period of recession, as we saw in 2001 and 2002, the Federal Reserve continued to lower interest rates incrementally, causing a major bull market in all fixed-income maturities. It is easiest to see this trend by looking at a weekly chart of the 10-year Treasury note, rather than an intraday, 1-hour chart. The more detail there is, the more difficult it is to see the long-term trend. Following the subprime collapse of 2008, the Fed and other central banks decided to lower rates to the absolute minimum and keep them there as long as necessary to stimulate the economy. Ultimately, this will result in a protracted bull market in both stocks and commodities.

The average daily impact of the long-term trend on prices is very small. For example, if yields were to drop a staggering 2% in one year, a rise of approximately 16 full points in price, the net effect each day would be a change of .064%, or $\frac{2}{32}$ in price. If prices move nearly one full point, $\frac{2}{32}$ or 1%, each day, that upwards bias would be overwhelmed by the daily market noise. It would be difficult to draw a trendline on a daily price chart until prices had drifted higher for a few months. Using a weekly chart removes much of this noise and makes the trend easier to see.

Multiple Signals

Some of the impreciseness of charting can be offset with confirming signals. A simultaneous breakout of a short-term trendline and a long-term trendline is a much stronger signal than either one occurring at different times. The break of a head-and-shoulders neckline that corresponds to a previous channel support line is likely to receive much attention. Whenever there are multiple signals converging at, or near, a single price, whether based on moving averages, Gann lines, cycles, or phases of the moon, that point gains significance. In chart analysis, the occurrence of multiple signals at one point can compensate for the quality of the interpretation.

Pattern Failures

The failure to adhere to a pattern is equally as important as the continuation of that pattern. Although a trader might anticipate a reversal as prices near a major support line, a break of that trendline is significant in continuing the downward move. A failure to stop at the support line should result in setting short positions and abandoning plans for higher prices.

A head-and-shoulders formation that breaks the neckline, declines for a day or two, then reverses and moves above the neckline is another pattern failure. *Postpattern activity* must confirm the pattern. Failure to do so means that the market refused to follow through; therefore, it should be traded in the opposite direction. This is not a case of identifying the wrong pattern; instead, price action actively opposed the completion of the pattern. Wyckoff calls this "effort and results," referring to the effort expended by the market to produce a pattern that explains the price direction. If this pattern is not followed by results that confirm the effort, the opposite position is the best option.

Change of Character   Thompson[22] discusses the completion of a pattern or price trend by identifying a *change of character* in the movement. As a trend develops, the reactions, or pullbacks, tend to become smaller. Traders looking to enter the trend wait for reactions to place their orders; as the move becomes more obvious, these reactions get smaller, and the increments of trend movement become larger. When the reaction suddenly is larger, the move is ending; the change in the character of the move signals a prudent exit, even if prices continue erratically in the direction of the trend.

---

[22] Jesse H. Thompson, "What Textbooks Never Tell You," *Technical Analysis of Stocks & Commodities* (November/December 1983).

A similar example occurs in the way that prices react to economic reports or government action. The first time the Federal Reserve acts to raise rates after a prolonged decline, the market is not prepared, and interest rate prices react sharply lower. Before the next meeting of the Fed, the market may be more apprehensive, but is likely to be neutral with regard to expectation of policy. However, once there is a pattern of increasing rates following signs of inflation, the market begins to anticipate the action of the Fed. A sharp move in the opposite direction occurs when the government fails to take the expected action.

Bull and Bear Traps   While it is not much of a consolation to those who have gotten caught, a failed downside breakout is called a *bear trap,* and a failed upwards breakout is a *bull trap.* A bear trap occurs when prices fall below a clear support line, generating sell signals. After a few days, prices move back above the support line, often accelerating upwards. A bull trap is a failed breakout of a resistance level. In both cases, prices appear to be continuing in the trend direction, but the final picture is a reversal. Although there is no advice on how to avoid bull and bear traps, the failed reversal should be recognized as soon as possible and the position should be reversed. Bull and bear traps often precede significant price reversals.

As with other top and bottom patterns, a confirmation of the bear trap is complete when prices move above the next higher resistance level. In the case of a failed flag formation in a downward trend, prices break lower, as expected, then reverse. The confirmation occurs when prices move above the top of the failed flag pattern. The same principle would be true of other failed chart formations; the failure is confirmed when prices retrace the entire pattern.[23]

Testing Your Skill

Recognizing a pattern is both an art and science. Not everyone has an eye for patterns; others see formations where no one else does. The first decision may be the most important: How much of the chart do you use? It is perfectly normal for different time intervals to show different trends. In some cases, arbitrarily cutting the chart at some previous date might cause a clear trend to disappear. The price scale (the vertical axis) of the chart is another variable not considered by some chartists. When applying methods requiring specific angles, the chart paper is expected to have square boxes. Because of the shape of the box, the formations may appear different from one piece of chart paper, or computer screen, to another.

The timeliness of the pattern identification is the most serious problem. Can the formation be interpreted in time to act on a breakout, or is the pattern only seen afterwards? At different stages of development, the lines may appear to form different patterns. Before using your charting skills to trade, practice simulating the day-to-day development of prices using the following steps:

---

[23] See Christopher Narcouzi, "Winning with Failures," *Technical Analysis of Stocks & Commodities* (November 2001).

1. Hold a piece of the paper over the right side of the chart, covering the most recent months, or better still, have someone else give you the partial chart.
2. Analyze the formations.
3. Determine what action will be based on your interpretation. Be specific.
4. Move the paper one day to the right, or have someone else give you the next day's price.
5. Record any orders that would have been filled based on the prior day's analysis. Don't cheat.
6. Determine whether the new day's price would have altered your interpretation and trade.
7. Return to Step 3 until finished.

This simple exercise might save a lot of money but may be discouraging. With practice you will become better at finding and using formations and will learn to select the ones that work best. Very few traders base their trading decisions entirely on bar charts. Many refer to charts for confirmation of separate technical or fundamental analysis; others use only the most obvious major trendlines, looking for points at which multiple indicators converge. The general acceptance of bar charting analysis makes it a lasting tool.

■ Evolution in Price Patterns

A change has occurred in the stock market because of the S&P 500 index, SPDRs, and other index markets. If you think that stock prices are about to fall because of a pending interest rate announcement by the Fed, you can protect your portfolio by selling an equivalent amount of S&P futures. Afterwards, when you have decided that prices have stabilized, you can lift your hedge and profit from rising prices. It is an easy and inexpensive way to achieve portfolio insurance. You can also speculate in the S&P, NASDAQ, Dow, or sectors, rather than trade individual stocks.

When institutions and traders buy or sell large quantities of S&P futures, the futures price will drift away from the S&P cash index, which represents the weighted average of the actual component stock prices. *Program trading* is the process that keeps the price of futures and ETFs aligned with the cash price of the stocks that comprise those index markets. If you have enough capital, and the difference between the S&P futures price and the S&P cash index is sufficiently large, with the futures higher than the cash, you can sell the S&P futures and buy all of the stocks in the S&P 500 cash index. It is a classic arbitrage that brings prices back together. It is all done electronically in seconds.

But the ability to buy or sell all the stocks in the S&P at the same time has changed the patterns of individual stocks that are part of the S&P index. While at one time these stocks moved largely due to their own fundamentals, they now all move together. It no longer matters that IBM is fundamentally stronger than GE, or that Xerox is at a resistance level and Ford is at support, or even if a company is under investigation. When you buy the S&P futures, you buy all of the stocks at the same time.

Today's technical trader must keep one eye on the individual stock and the other eye on the index. Apple may have moved above its recent resistance level but stopped because

FIGURE 1.39 Similar Patterns in the S&P, GE, and Exxon.

the S&P Index is at its own resistance level, and there are more traders watching the S&P than even Apple. In today's market, you can anticipate when a stock will find support and resistance by looking at the S&P chart rather than at the individual stock chart.

Figure 1.39 shows the S&P 500 index, GE, and Exxon (prior to its collapse) over the same period from October 1999 through December 2000. Fundamentally, these three markets have little in common; however, the overall pattern of the three markets is remarkably similar, with most tops and bottoms occurring at nearly the same time. Because it is unlikely that the fundamentals of each company would result in such a similar price pattern, we can conclude that the S&P futures, combined with program trading, forces the patterns to be materially the same. This change in the way stocks are traded reduces the ability to get diversification by trading across sectors and increases risk.

Globalization: The Similarity of Asian Markets

There has been a noticeable and justifiable shift to Asian markets during the past five years. Their economies are booming while the United States and Europe are still trying to recover from the financial crisis. Although not all of the Asian stock markets are open to foreign investors, globalization has not passed them by. Figure 1.40 shows the equity index markets for Hong Kong (HSI), Singapore (SSG), Taiwan (STW), the Philippines (PHI), and Malaysia (KLI) as downloaded from Bloomberg. The patterns seem similar but the price levels are very different, making a comparison difficult.

By volatility-adjusting each price series and starting each at 100 on the first date (January 1, 2005), the five series look remarkably the same, as shown in Figure 1.41. It is understandable that, as trading partners, these countries are somewhat dependent upon one another, yet the similarity is surprisingly close. One possible explanation would be the traders. If traders believe that a poor economic sign in one

FIGURE 1.40 Equity Index Prices for Five Asian Countries.
Data from Bloomberg.

country means that others will also share in bad times, then they sell the equity index markets, or individual stocks, in each country. That would be similar to Hewlett-Packard announcing worse than expected earnings and having traders sell Dell expecting the same. Often the closer relationships caused by traders show that the movement of money is more important than the fundamentals. This was clearly the case for the subprime collapse in September 2008, when all markets moved the same way as investors withdrew their funds as quickly as possible.

FIGURE 1.41 Asian Equity Index Markets Adjusted to the Same Volatility Level and Started at the Value 100.
Data from Bloomberg.

CHAPTER 2

Understanding Implied Volatility

From Russell Rhoads, *Trading VIX Derivatives: Trading and Hedging Strategies Using VIX Futures, Options, and Exchange Traded Notes* (Hoboken, New Jersey: John Wiley & Sons, 2007), Chapter 1.

In this book, we will discuss the ins and outs of a popular market indicator, or index, that is based on implied volatility. The indicator is the CBOE Volatility Index®, widely known by its ticker symbol, VIX. It should come as no surprise that a solid understanding of the index must begin with a solid understanding of what implied volatility is and how it works.

Implied volatility is ultimately determined by the price of option contracts. Since option prices are the result of market forces, or increased levels of buying or selling, implied volatility is determined by the market. An index based on implied volatility of option prices is displaying the market's estimation of volatility of the underlying security in the future.

More advanced option traders who feel they have a solid understanding of implied volatility may consider moving to Chapter 3. That chapter introduces the actual method for determining the VIX. However, as implied volatility is one of the more advanced option pricing concepts, a quick review before diving into the VIX and volatility-related trading vehicles would be worthwhile for most traders.

■ Historical Versus Forward-Looking Volatility

There are two main types of volatility discussed relative to securities prices. The first is historical volatility, which may be calculated using recent trading activity for a stock or other security. The historical volatility of a stock is factual and known. Also, the historical volatility does not give any indication about the future movement of a stock. The forwardlooking volatility is what is referred to as the implied volatility. This type of volatility results from the market price of options that trade on a stock.

The implied volatility component of option prices is the factor that can give all option traders, novice to expert, the most difficulty. This occurs because the implied volatility of an option may change while all other pricing factors impacting the price of an option remain unchanged. This change may occur as the order flow for options is biased more to buying or selling. A result of increased buying of options by market participants is higher implied volatility. Conversely, when there is net selling of options, the implied volatility indicated by option prices moves lower.

Basically, the nature of order flow dictates the direction of implied volatility. Again, more option buying increases the option price and the result is higher implied volatility. Going back to Economics 101, implied volatility reacts to the supply and demand of the marketplace. Buying pushes it higher, and selling pushes it lower.

The implied volatility of an option is also considered an indication of the risk associated with the underlying security. The risk may be thought of as how much movement may be expected from the underlying stock over the life of an option. This is not the potential direction of the stock price move, just the magnitude of the move. Generally, when thinking of risk, traders think of a stock losing value or the price moving lower. Using implied volatility as a risk measure results in an estimation of a price move in either direction. When the market anticipates that a stock may soon move dramatically, the price of option contracts, both puts and calls, will move higher.

A common example of a known event in the future that may dramatically influence the price of a stock is a company's quarterly earnings report. Four times a year a company will release information to the investing public in the form of its recent earnings results. This earnings release may also include statements regarding business prospects for the company. This information may have a dramatic impact on the share price. As this price move will also impact option prices, the option contracts usually react in advance. Due to the anticipation that will work into option prices, they are generally more expensive as traders and investors buy options before seeing the report.

This increased buying of options results in higher option prices. There are two ways to think about this: the higher price of the option contracts results in higher implied volatility, or because of higher implied volatility option prices are higher. After the earnings report, there is less risk of a big move in the underlying stock and the options become less expensive. This drop in price is due to lower implied volatility levels; implied volatility is now lower due to lower option prices.

A good non-option-oriented example of how implied volatility works may be summed up through this illustration. If you live in Florida, you are familiar with hurricane season. The path of hurricanes can be unpredictable, and at times homeowners have little time to prepare for a storm. Using homeowners insurance as a substitute for an option contract, consider the following situation.

You wake to find out that an evacuation is planned due to a potential hurricane. Before leaving the area, you check whether your homeowners insurance is current. You find you have allowed your coverage to lapse, and so you run down to your agent's office. As he boards up windows and prepares to evacuate inland, he informs you that you may renew, but the cost is going to be $50,000 instead of the $2,000 annual rate you have paid for years. After hearing your objections, he is steadfast. The higher price, he explains, is due to the higher risk associated with the coming storm.

You decide that $50,000 is too much to pay, and you return home to ride out the storm. Fortunately, the storm takes a left turn and misses your neighborhood altogether. Realizing that you have experienced a near miss, you run down to your agent's office with a $50,000 check in hand. Being an honest guy, he tells you the rate is back down to $2,000. Why is this?

The imminent risk level for replacing your home has decreased as there is no known threat bearing down on your property. As the immediate risk of loss or damage has decreased tremendously, so has the cost of protection against loss. When applying this to the option market, risk is actually risk of movement of the underlying security, either higher or lower. This risk is the magnitude of expected movement of the underlying security over the life of an option.

When market participants are expecting a big price move to the upside in the underlying security, there will be net buying of call options in anticipation of this move. As this buying occurs, the price of the call options will increase. This price rise in the options is associated with an increase risk of a large price move, and this increase in risk translates to higher implied volatility.

Also, if there is an expectation of a lower price move, the marketplace may see an increase in put buying. With higher demand for put contracts, the price of puts may increase resulting in higher implied volatility for those options. Finally, if put prices increase, the result is corresponding call prices rising due to a concept known as put-call parity, which will be discussed in the next section.

■ Put-Call Parity

Put and call prices are linked to each other through the price of the underlying stock through put-call parity. This link exists because combining a stock and put position can result in the same payoff as a position in a call option with the same strike price as the put. If this relationship gets out of line or not in parity, an arbitrage opportunity exits. When one of these opportunities arises, there are trading firms that will quickly buy and sell the securities to attempt to take advantage of this mispricing. This market activity will push the put and call prices back in line with each other.

Put and call prices should remain within a certain price range of each other or arbitragers will enter the market, which results in the prices coming back into parity. Parity between the two also results in a similar implied volatility output resulting from using these prices in a model to determine the implied volatility of the market.

TABLE 2.1	Put, Call, and Stock Pricing to Illustrate Put-Call Parity
Stock/Option	Price
XYZ Stock	$50.00
XYZ 50 Call	$1.00
XYZ 50 Put	$2.00

Stated differently, increased demand for a call option will raise the price of that call. As the price of the call moves higher, the corresponding put price should also rise, or the result will be an arbitrage trade that will push the options into line. As the pricing of the option contracts are tied to each other, they will share similar implied volatility levels also.

For a quick and very simple example of how put-call parity works, consider the options and stock in Table 2.1.

Using the XYZ 50 Put combined with XYZ stock, a payout that replicates being long the XYZ 50 Call may be created. The combination of owning stock and owning a put has the same payout structure as a long call option position. With the XYZ 50 Call trading at 1.00 and the XYZ 50 Put priced at 2.00, there may be a mispricing scenario. Table 2.2 compares a long XYZ 50 Call trade with a combined position of long XYZ stock and long a XYZ 50 Put.

The final two columns compare a payout of owning XYZ stock from 50.00 and buying the XYZ 50 Put at 2.00 versus buying an XYZ 50 Call for 1.00. Note that at any price at expiration, the long call position is worth 1.00 more than the combined stock and put position. With this pricing difference, there is the ability to take a short position in the strategy that will be worth less and buy the strategy that will be worth more at expiration. The payout diagram in Figure 2.1 shows how the two positions compare at a variety of prices at expiration.

The lines are parallel throughout this diagram. The higher line represents the profit or loss based on buying the 50 call. The lower line represents the payout for the spread combining a long stock position and a long 50 put position. At any price at expiration, the combined position has less value than the long 50 call. Knowing this outcome, it is possible to benefit from the 1.00 spread, which will exist at any price at expiration for two positions that are basically the same.

Due to put-call parity and the mispricing between the 50 Call and 50 Put, the call may be purchased combined with a short position in the stock and put option. A quick

TABLE 2.2	Payout Comparison for Long Call and Long Stock + Long Put Trade			
XYZ at Expiration	Long XYZ Stock	Long XYZ 50 Put	Long Stock + Long Put	Long XYZ 50 Call
45.00	−5.00	3.00	−2.00	−1.00
50.00	0.00	−2.00	−2.00	−1.00
55.00	5.00	−2.00	3.00	4.00

FIGURE 2.1 Payout Diagram Comparison.

transaction using the prices in the example would result in a profit of 1.00 upon options expiration. This 1.00 profit would be realized regardless of the price of the stock at expiration. Firms would attempt to take advantage of this opportunity through buying the cheaper call option and selling the comparable more expensive put option. The market activity of these participants is what keeps put and call option prices in line with each other and the implied volatility of both put and call contracts at the same level.

■ Estimating Price Movement

What the implied volatility of an option projects onto the underlying security is the expected range of price movement over a certain period of time. This estimation of price movement is based on statistics and the bell curve. The implied volatility of an option is the projection of an annualized one standard deviation move in the underlying stock over the life of the option. According to statistics and using implied volatility as a guide, the price of a stock should land between up and down one standard deviation at option expiration. The closing price should land in this range 68.2 percent of the time.

This 68.2 percent comes from statistics and what is referred to as a normal distribution. Statistics like this reveal that 68.2 percent of the time a stock should be between up one standard deviation and down one standard deviation a year from today. A formula may also be used to take this annualized number and narrow down the projection to a single day. The normal distribution also indicates that there is a 95.4 percent expectation of the stock landing between up two standard deviations and down two standard deviations. Finally, at three standard deviations, the probability reaches 99.7 percent.

With a stock trading at $50 and the underlying option prices indicating 20 percent implied volatility, the result is a one standard deviation price move equal to $10 (20 percent of $50). In other words, the stock is expected to close between $40 (down $10) and $60 (up $10) with 68.2 percent certainty a year from today. A two standard deviation price move would be equal to $20. This is calculated by simply multiplying 2 times a single standard deviation. Using two standard deviations, it can be projected out that the stock should land between $30 and up $70, with a confidence of 95.4 percent. At three standard deviations, there is a 99.7 percent chance of the stock closing between $20 and $80 a year from the date of the calculation.

■ Valuing Options: Pricing Calculators and Other Tools

An option pricing calculator is a tool that allows a user the ability to input the pricing variables that determine the value of an option with the result being a theoretical option price. Ultimately the market determines the price of an option through buying and selling forces. However when analyzing and investigating option trades, using an option pricing calculator with certain assumptions gives an idea where an option may be trading in the future. Also, using an option pricing calculator is an excellent way to become familiar with the price action of option contracts. The CBOE has a free option calculator available on its website at www.cboe.com/tradtool; it is a valuable tool for option pricing.

The value of an option contract is derived from a variety of inputs. Inputs into an option pricing model include the price of the underlying security, the strike price of the option, the type of option, dividends, interest rates, and time to option expiration. The final input into an option pricing model is the implied volatility of the option. These inputs may be used in a model to determine the value of an option.

Table 2.3 demonstrates how an option pricing model is used to determine the value of an option. The inputs are at the top of the table, with the value of the option showing up as the only output. Option pricing models calculate a variety of pieces of useful information, such as the impact of changes in pricing factors. These outputs are known as the option Greeks. However, to keep focus on the topic at hand, implied volatility, only the necessary outputs are going to be demonstrated in this example of an option calculator.

TABLE 2.3	Option Pricing Calculator–Option Value Output
Factor	**Input**
Call/Put	Call
Underlying Price	44.75
Strike Price	45.00
Implied Volatility	30%
Days to Expiration	30
Interest Rate	1.00%
Dividends	0.00%
Output	**Result**
Option Value	1.45

The option price in the model is determined from a stock trading at 44.75 with implied volatility of 30 percent and a risk-free interest rate of 1.00 percent. The result is a call option value with a strike price of 45 and 30 days to expiration would be valued at 1.45 based on the inputs used in this model. Keep in mind that this is a pricing model, not the actual market trading price of the option. Again, the inputs in the model are assumptions, not just the market price. Just because using these inputs results in a value of 1.45 for this 45 Call does not mean it can be traded at this level. In fact, the market price of this option will vary if the market consensus differs from the inputs used in this model.

The real value of an option at any given time is actually determined by the price that it may be bought or sold in the market. In the case of this 45 Call, even though the inputs into the model result in a 1.45 value, when checking market quotes for this option we find that the current trading price is 1.70. The reason for the difference between our model's value and the market price is the result of different implied volatility levels being used. The previous model, in Table 2.3, takes inputs and the result in a difference in option values based on the inputs.

The pricing factors in an option pricing model are for the most part set in stone. The exception of this is the implied volatility input. For the model, the assumption of 30 percent implied volatility was used. However, the market is pricing in a higher implied volatility level. This is determined before any numbers or formulas have been run just by comparing the option market price and the option value assumption that resulted from the model. The market price of the option is higher than the pricing model output. Seeing this, it is pretty certain that the implied volatility based on market prices is higher than what was entered into the model. There is a direct correlation between high and low relative option prices and higher or lower implied volatility.

Table 2.4 is an option pricing model that uses the market price as an input with the sole output being implied volatility. This implied volatility level is being indicated by the 1.70 market price of the 45 Call. The higher option price here is a higher implied volatility than what was used in the first pricing model. As the option price in this model is higher than the option value that resulted from a 30 percent implied

TABLE 2.4 **Option Pricing Calculator—Implied Volatility Output**

Factor	Input
Call/Put	Call
Underlying Price	44.75
Strike Price	45.00
Option Price	1.70
Days to Expiration	30
Interest Rate	1.00%
Dividends	0.00%
Output	**Result**
Implied Volatility	35%

TABLE 2.5	Impact of a 5 Percent Increase in Implied Volatility	
Implied Volatility	30%	35%
Option Price	1.45	1.70

volatility, the expectation would be a higher implied volatility result. Using 1.70 as the price of the option actually results in the implied volatility that is being projected by this option price to be 35 percent. Professional traders generally start with the market price of an option to calculate implied volatility as that is where the implied volatility of an option is ultimately determined.

Another method of demonstrating the impact of different implied volatility levels on option prices appears in Table 2.5. Instead of a comparison of what the model output was versus the option price based on model outputs, consider the previous option prices in a different way. Consider the two option prices and implied volatility differences as changes based on an increase in demand for the option. Both prices represent the market and the option price increases from 1.45 to 1.70. This option price rise occurs due to an increase in buying of the call option while all other factors that influence the option price stay the same.

Since the price of the option contract has increased, the resulting implied volatility output from an option model has also increased. Higher option prices, whether put or call prices, will result in a higher implied volatility output with no changes in any of the other option pricing factors.

To recap, there is a direct link between the demand for option contracts and their prices in the marketplace. This is regardless of changes occurring in the underlying stock price. With demand in the form of buying pressure pushing option prices higher or an increase in selling occurring due to market participants pushing option prices lower, the implied volatility of an option is dictated by market forces.

■ Fluctuations Based on Supply and Demand

As mentioned in the first section of this chapter, implied volatility does fluctuate based on supply and demand for options. This leads to the question, "What exactly causes the supply and demand for options to fluctuate?" The short answer is the near-term expected price changes that may occur in the underlying stock. These moves are usually the result of information that has influenced the fundamental outlook for a stock. The best example of this type of information would be a company's quarterly earnings reports.

Every publicly traded company in the United States reports its earnings results four times a year. The date and timing (generally before the market open or after the market close) are usually known well in advance of the actual announcement. Along with the earnings results, other information is disseminated, such as the company's revenues and the source of those revenues. Many companies offer a possible outlook regarding the prospects for their business conditions, and most will hold a public conference call to answer professional investors' questions. These events often have a dramatic impact, either positive or negative, on the price of a stock.

Again, the date that these results are announced is public knowledge and often widely anticipated by analysts and traders. As the date draws near, there is usually trading in the stock and stock options that is based on the anticipated stock price reaction to the earnings announcement. The result is usually net buying of options as there is speculation regarding the potential move of the underlying stock. The net option buying results in higher option prices and an increase in the implied volatility projected by the options that trade on this stock. Usually this increase impacts only the options with the closest expiration and strike prices that are close to where the stock is trading. An excellent example of this can be seen in the option prices and resulting implied volatility levels for Amazon stock shown in Table 2.6.

These are market prices from just before the close of trading on July 22, 2010. Amazon's earnings were reported after the market close on the 22nd with weekly options that expire on the 23rd having only one trading day until expiration after the news was released. The difference in implied volatility between the options that have one trading day left and those that have just under a month left is pretty significant.

This difference stems from the options that market participants would use as a short-term trading vehicle related to Amazon's earnings announcement. This would be the same for hedgers and speculators alike. Both would focus on the strike prices that are closest to the trading price of the stock as well as the options with the least amount of time to expiration.

Option contracts that have the closest expiration to a known event that occurs after the event are the contracts that will have the most price reaction before and after the event occurs. With Amazon reporting earnings the evening of July 22 and an option series expiring on July 23, the July 23 options are the contracts that will see the most price action based on the stock price reaction to the earnings release.

TABLE 2.6 Amazon Option Implied Volatility and Option Prices Minutes Prior to an Earnings Announcement

	AMZN @ 120.07			
Call Strike	July 23 Call	July 23 Call IV	Aug 21 Call	Aug 21 Call IV
115	7.00	163%	9.25	48%
120	3.92	156%	6.25	45%
125	1.82	148%	4.05	45%
Put Strike	July 23 Put	July 23 Put IV	Aug 21 Put	Aug 21 Put IV
115	1.92	159%	4.05	48%
120	3.82	155%	6.20	47%
125	6.75	148%	8.90	45%

The stock price is very close to the 120 strike price when the option first listed and just before the earnings announcement. Using the 120 strike options, implied volatility for both the put and call options that expire the following day is around 155 percent. This indicates that on an annualized basis the option market is pricing in a 155 percent price move over a single day. This is much more dramatic sounding that it is in reality. Annualized implied volatility of 155 percent for an option with a single trading day left translates to a one-day move of around 9.76 percent. The math behind this is (see the following feature on calculating single day implied volatility):

$$9.76\% = 155\%/15.87$$

This single-day implied volatility can be interpreted as being a single standard deviation range of expected price movement of the stock on that day.

CALCULATING SINGLE-DAY IMPLIED VOLATILITY

Assuming there are 252 trading days in a year, the denominator of this formula turns out to be the square root of the number of trading days for the year.

1 Day Movement = Implied Volatility/Square Root of 252

Amazon did report its earnings, and the initial price reaction was pretty close to what the option market was pricing in. The NASDAQ opening price the day after the company reported earnings was down 11.76 percent from the previous day's close. The market was forecasting a 9.76 percent move based on option pricing.

As a refresher from college statistics: One standard deviation in statistics indicates there is a 68.2 percent chance that an outcome is going to land between up and down one standard deviation. So this single-day implied volatility indicates the market is expecting Amazon's stock to trade within up or down 9.76 percent with a 68.2 percent level of confidence in the next day.

Table 2.7 shows the increase in the implied volatility of the 120 Call projected by Amazon option prices as the earnings announcement approaches. Implied volatility for other options rises in the same way, since 120 is the closest strike to the stock price when the option started trading and just before earnings were announced. Also, the options contract is a weekly expiration option that begins trading on a

TABLE 2.7	Implied Volatility Changes Approaching Amazon Earnings		
Date	AMZN	120 Call	120 Call IV
July 15	120.13	4.80	71%
July 15	122.06	5.92	78%
July 16	118.49	4.00	84%
July 19	119.94	4.33	87%
July 20	120.10	3.95	90%
July 21	117.43	2.73	111%
July 22	120.07	3.92	155%

Thursday morning and expires on the following week's Friday close. This particular option started trading on July 15 with the last trading day being July 23 or is what is called a weekly option that has only eight trading days from listing to expiration.

The first row is the opening price for the weekly option and underlying price for the option. When the option first traded it had an implied volatility level of 71 percent. This compares to non-earnings-period implied volatility levels, which are usually in the mid 30 percent range for Amazon options.

Over the next few days, the earnings announcement draws closer and the stock stays in a fairly tight range. The implied volatility of the option contracts continues to rise as time passes. By the time the announcement is imminent, the implied volatility of the 120 Call has more than doubled.

This illustration of how implied volatility climbs in front of a potentially market-moving event is a bit magnified by the options only having one day of time value remaining before the announcement. However, it is a good illustration of how option prices, through the implied volatility component, discount a potential market-moving event when the timing of this event is a known entity.

■ The Impact on Option Prices

Implied volatility is commonly considered an indication as to whether an option is cheap or expensive. This determination may be made through examining past implied volatility levels for the options of a particular stock or index and comparing present values.

Demand for options pushes up the price of an option contract and results in higher implied volatility. However, other factors such as the underlying price, time to expiration, and interest-rate levels also determine the price of an option. These other factors are not impacted through the buying and selling pressure on option contracts. Only implied volatility will fluctuate based on market buying and selling pressure.

The goal of any directional trading strategy should be to buy low and sell high. If themarket considers any trading vehicle inexpensive, there will be participants that take advantage of this through purchasing the instrument. On the other hand, if something appears expensive it may be sold. Implied volatility is a measure that option traders use to define whether options are overvalued or undervalued.

As a simple example, take the option prices and implied volatility levels in Table 2.8. The data in this table represent a stock trading at 24.00 per share, and the value of a 25 Call with 90 days until expiration. The different option prices are based on various implied volatility levels. Note that as the option price increases so does the implied volatility of the 25 Call.

TABLE 2.8	Implied Volatility Levels and Option Prices	
Stock Price	**25 Call**	**Implied Volatility**
24.00	0.80	20%
24.00	1.05	25%
24.00	1.30	30%

If options for the underlying stock usually trade with an implied volatility of 25 percent, then when the option could be purchased for 0.80 it may be considered undervalued or inexpensive. At 0.80 the option had an implied volatility level of 20 percent. When implied volatility rose to 30 percent and the option was trading for 1.30, the option may be considered expensive. At 1.05 with an implied volatility of 25 percent, the historical norm, the 25 Call may be considered fairly valued.

Of course, using implied volatility as a measure of how expensive or cheap an option is must be done in the context of some external factors. Remember, if the company is preparing to announce quarterly earnings, the implied volatility would be expected to be high relative to other periods of time. In that case, a comparison to implied volatility behavior around previous earnings announcements would be a more accurate analysis of whether the options appear cheap or expensive.

■ Implied Volatility and the VIX

The VIX will be further defined in the next chapter, but the concepts in this chapter should be tied to the VIX before moving forward. The VIX is a measure of the implied volatility being projected through the prices of S&P 500 index options. The VIX can be used to indicate what type of market movement option prices are projecting on the S&P 500 over the next 30 days or even a shorter time. Since the VIX is measuring implied volatility of S&P 500 index options and since implied volatility is a measure of risk projected by option pricing, the VIX is considered a gauge of fear in the overall market.

The remainder of this book explores the VIX index which is based on the concept of implied volatility. With a solid understanding of implied volatility, exploration of the VIX index, methods of using the VIX for market analysis, and ways to directly trade volatility should be easier to comprehend.

CHAPTER 3

About the VIX Index

From Russell Rhoads, *Trading VIX Derivatives: Trading and Hedging Strategies Using VIX Futures, Options, and Exchange Traded Notes* (Hoboken, New Jersey: John Wiley & Sons, 2007), Chapter 2.

Officially known as the CBOE Volatility Index, the VIX is considered by many to be a gauge of fear and greed in the stock market. A more accurate description of what the VIX measures is the implied volatility that is being priced into S&P 500 index options. Through the use of a wide variety of option prices, the index offers an indication of 30-day implied volatility as priced by the S&P 500 index option market.

Before diving further into the calculation that results in the VIX, this chapter will cover the history of exactly how this index was developed followed by an overview of how the VIX is determined. Then for interested parties there is a more in-depth discussion of how the VIX is calculated. The VIX index has historically had an inverse relationship to performance of the S&P 500, and this often results in questions from traders who are new to the VIX. This relationship will be discussed in the context of putcall parity, which was mentioned in Chapter 1.

Finally, there are a handful of VIX-related indexes based on other equity-market indexes. The S&P 100–related VIX is still calculated using the old method to maintain some continuity for historical comparisons. Finally, there are also VIX indexes calculated on options based on the Nasdaq 100, Russell 2000, and Dow Jones Industrial Average, which are discussed toward the end of the chapter.

■ History of the VIX

The concept behind the VIX index was developed by Dr. Robert Whaley of Vanderbilt University in 1993. His paper "Derivatives on Market Volatility: Hedging Tools Long Overdue," which appeared in the *Journal of Derivatives*, laid the groundwork for the index. The original VIX was based on pricing of S&P 100 (OEX) options and used only eight option contracts to determine a volatility measure.

TABLE 3.1	S&P 500 Industry Weightings
Industry	**Weighting**
Consumer discretionary	9.10%
Consumer staples	11.70%
Energy	11.40%
Financials	15.40%
Health care	13.40%
Industrials	10.00%
Information technology	18.50%
Materials	3.40%
Telecom services	3.30%
Utilities	3.80%

At the time, OEX options were the most heavily traded index option series that reflected performance of the stock market in the United States. This volatility index was based on a limited number of options and was slightly disconnected from the overall stock market due to the narrower focus of the S&P 100 versus the S&P 500.

In 2003 there was a new methodology for calculation of the VIX index that was developed through work done by the CBOE and Goldman Sachs. Although the calculation was altered, the most important aspect to this change for individuals is that the underlying options changed from the OEX to options trading on the S&P 500. Another significant change was an increase in the number of options that were used in the index calculation. Through a wider number of option contract prices feeding the formula to calculate the VIX, a true 30-day implied volatility level that is being projected on the S&P 500 by the options market is realized.

The S&P 500 index is considered by professional investors to be the benchmark for the performance of the stock market in the United States. The members of the index are 500 of the largest domestic companies in the United States that meet criteria based on market capitalization, public float, financial viability, liquidity, type of company, and industry sector. Companies are usually dropped from the index when they have violated membership criteria or have ceased to operate due to a merger or acquisition.

The industry representation of the S&P 500 index appears in Table 3.1. With a broad distribution of companies in the index, there is no industry that dominates the index's performance. This diversification across industries is a major reason the S&P 500 is considered a performance benchmark by most professional investors.

■ Calculating the VIX

After the VIX index was introduced, the CBOE moved forward with the first exchange listed volatility derivative instruments. Through the CBOE Futures Exchange (CFE®), the CBOE introduced futures contracts based on the VIX. Other instruments have followed, and more are in development.

There are two ways to explain how the VIX is determined. First, it can be explained using simple nonmathematical terms. Then, for those interested in an in-depth discussion of the formula and calculation, a more detailed overview will follow. Having a basic understanding of how the VIX is determined is more than enough to move forward with trading. However, for those with more interest in the VIX calculation, the more comprehensive description is included.

The Nonmathematical Approach

The VIX is an indicator of 30-day implied volatility determined through the use of S&P 500 index option prices. The option price used in the formula is actually the midpoint of the bid-ask spread of relevant at and out of the money actively traded S&P 500 index options. Using the midpoint of the spread is a more accurate price description than the last price for an option contract. Also, the contracts used are the S&P 500 index options that trade to the next two standard expirations with at least eight days to expiration. When a series reaches this eight-day point, it is not used anymore in the calculation and the options that expire farther in the future then start to contribute to the VIX calculation.

All of these S&P 500 options are then used to create a synthetic at the money option that expires exactly 30 days from the very moment of the calculation. This time variable to the formula is constantly being updated to weight the balance of the two expiration series in the formula. Using a wide number of actively quoted S&P 500 index options, a synthetic 30-day option is created and the VIX is the implied volatility of that option. This results in implied volatility of the synthetic option contract, which is then reported as the VIX.

The Formula and Calculations

It is possible to trade the VIX with a cursory understanding of how the index is determined. Those who are satisfied with their understanding of the VIX and what it represents may skip ahead. However, readers who are more interested in how the VIX is calculated should be interested in the remainder of this section.

The input for calculating the VIX index comes from all actively quoted S&P 500 index options for the next two standard option expirations that have at least eight days remaining until expiration. Eliminating the nearer term expiration options that have only a week to expiration takes out some of the end-of-contract volatility that can occur in the market.

The option contracts from these two expiration series are the at and out of the money put and call options. The series of options used extends out of the money until there are two consecutive option strikes that have no bid-ask market posted. Again, the midpoint of the bid-ask spread for the options is used in the calculation.

The time to expiration part of the calculation is very specific, down to the second. This is constantly being updated to change the weighting between the two series of options feeding into the calculation. Although S&P 500 index options cease trading on a Thursday for Friday morning settlement, the time to expiration is based on the market opening time, 8:30 A.M. central time, on the Friday of expiration.

There is also a forward price for the S&P 500 that is calculated using the closest at the money options in conjunction with put-call parity. This S&P 500 forward price is the underlying security price and strike price used to price the synthetic option used in the calculation. The implied volatility of that option is what is quoted at the VIX. that option is what is quoted at the VIX.

Finally if there is interest in using Microsoft Excel© to replicate calculating the VIX, a paper produced by Tom Arnold and John H. Earl Jr. of the University of Richmond is useful. In a very short study, 10 pages, they lay out the groundwork for using Excel to replicate the calculation of the VIX (to read the full paper, go to http://papers.ssrn.com/sol3/papers.cfm?abstract id=1103971). Also, once the template has been set up, changing the time frame and underlying instrument is simple. Using the template, the VIX methodology may be applied to a variety of instruments or time frames with little effort.

■ The VIX and Put-Call Parity

Many traders and investors often ask why there appears to be an inverse relationship between the direction of stock prices and the VIX. The relationship may be broken down to the nature of purchasing options. When the market is under pressure, there is a net buying of put options, which will result in higher implied volatility. This rapid increase in demand for put options pushes the implied volatility for both put and call contracts higher; the reason behind this is called put-call parity.

Put-call parity states that the prices of put and call options that have the same strike price and expiration are related. This relationship exists due to the ability to create synthetic positions in one option through combining the other option with the underlying stock. With this possibility, if the price of one option differs enough from the price of the other, an arbitrage opportunity may present itself.

For instance, in a zero-interest-rate environment, a put and call price should have the same value if the stock is trading at the strike price. As the options are related in price, the implied volatility of these options is also related. This is unrealistic, but it is a good method of demonstrating putcall parity. The prices in Table 3.2 may be used to demonstrate what can happen when put-call parity breaks down.

It is possible to replicate the payout of a long call through combining a put option and a stock position. Stated another way, a long stock position along with owning a put will result in the same payout structure as being long a call option. So, if the same payout may be created in two methods, the pricing of these two should be equivalent. If they are not equal, the lower priced one may be bought

TABLE 3.2 Prices to Demonstrate Put-Call Parity	
Security	Price
XYZ Stock	45.00
XYZ 45 Call	2.50
XYZ 45 Put	2.00

TABLE 3.3	Long XYZ 45 Call versus Long XYZ 45 Put + Long XYZ at Expiration			
XYZ	Long XYZ Stock	Long XYZ 45 Put	Long Stock + Long Put	Long XYZ 45 Call
35	−10.00	8.00	−2.00	−2.50
40	−5.00	3.00	−2.00	−2.50
45	0.00	−2.00	−2.00	−2.50
50	5.00	−2.00	3.00	2.50
55	10.00	−2.00	8.00	7.50

while the higher priced one is simultaneously sold. This is known as an arbitrage trade, in which an instant profit may be realized through a pricing difference in two equivalent securities.

If the XYZ 45 Put is purchased and shares of XYZ stock are also bought, the resulting position at expiration will be the same as owning the XYZ 45 Call. Above 45.00, the call option would result in a long position in XYZ; below 45.00, the call would not be exercised and there would be no position in XYZ. With a long 45 put position combined with a long position in the stock, if the stock is below 45.00 at expiration the put option will be exercised and the stock sold. The result would be no position in XYZ. Above 45.00, the stock would still be owned, as the XYZ 45 Put would not be exercised. Regardless of the stock price at expiration, the resulting position in XYZ will be the same. Due to the different prices between the 45 Call and 45 Put, there is a difference in profit or loss of the position at expiration. Table 3.3 demonstrates this at a variety of price points at expiration.

The column Long Stock + Long Put represents the position payout at expiration of the combined long stock–long put position. Note at all price levels the combined long stock and long put position is worth 0.50 more than the long call position. If at all price levels at expiration the long call position will be worth less than stock plus put position, then an arbitrage opportunity exists.

The arbitrage trade would be to purchase the stock and put option while taking a short position in the call option. At any price level for XYZ at expiration, this trade would result in a profit of 0.50. Table 3.4 displays the outcome through buying XYZ at 45.00 and purchasing the XYZ 45 Put for 2.00 along with selling the XYZ 45 Call at 2.50.

TABLE 3.4	Long XYZ Stock + versus Long XYZ 45 Put + Short XYZ 45 Call at Expiration			
XYZ	Long XYZ Stock	Long XYZ 45 Put	Short XYZ 45 Call	Combined Profit/Loss
35	−10.00	8.00	2.50	0.50
40	−5.00	3.00	2.50	0.50
45	0.00	−2.00	2.50	0.50
50	5.00	−2.00	−2.50	0.50
55	10.00	−2.00	−7.50	0.50

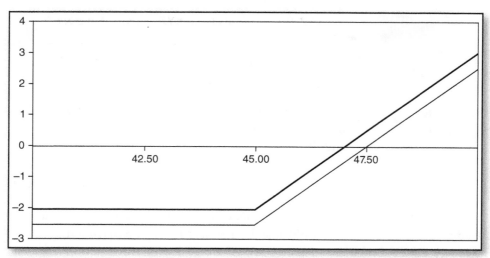

FIGURE 3.1 Payoff Comparison.

Admittedly this is an overly simplistic example, but the hope here is to get across the idea of put-call parity and what happens when put and call prices get out of line relative to each other. Execution of this combined position with the result of a riskless profit would involve transaction costs and a cost of capital. For individuals this might be prohibitive, but for professional trading firms this is an opportunity. When option prices get out of line to a point where a professional firm may take advantage through placing orders to buy and sell the instrument that are mispriced, then orders to take advantage of this mispricing will be executed. These trades will quickly push markets back into line and eliminate the arbitrage profit.

Figure 3.1 is a payoff diagram that compares the payout of the long call and combined long put–long stock position. The higher line represents the combined long put–long stock position. The lower line shows the profit or loss for the long call position. Note the lines are parallel—the only difference is the profit or loss. This difference shows an arbitrage profit that may be realized by shorting the long call and buying the other two instruments, then holding the positions to expiration.

The put-call parity formula has many components and is beyond the scope of this book. However, the formulas in Table 3.5 illustrate on a position basis what the equivalent single-position result is from different combinations of a put, call, or stock.

TABLE 3.5	Variety of Positions Created through Put-Call Parity
Position	**Combination**
Long call	Long stock + long put
Short call	Short stock + short put
Long put	Short stock + long call
Short put	Long stock + short call
Long stock	Long call + short put
Short stock	Short call + long put

A comparable payout of any single long or short position with a put, call, or stock may be created using a combination of the other two securities. Although it may seem like this does not relate to the VIX, there is a point to this exercise.

The relationship between put and call prices that results in put-call parity does have an impact on the VIX index. The level of the VIX is based on the implied volatility of a variety of both put and call options. The indicated implied volatility of option contracts rises and falls based on market forces. The specific market force that impacts implied volatility is the net buying or selling of options. This increase in demand is not necessarily purchase of either all call or all put options buy just net buying of option contracts. Since strong demand for call options will result in higher put prices and demand for puts will result in higher call prices, higher demand for either type of contract results in higher implied volatility for both put and call contracts.

The VIX has historically had an inverse relationship with the S&P 500 index. The reason behind this inverse relationship relates to the type of option activity that occurs during bullish markets versus bearish markets. When markets rally, there is rarely a rush by investors to purchase call options. Therefore when the market is rising, there is rarely dramatically higher option purchasing versus options selling.

When the S&P 500 comes under pressure, especially in very turbulent times, there is often a panic-like demand for put options. This demand for protection results in increased purchasing of put options. The result is a fast move higher in implied volatility for both S&P 500 put and call options. This higher demand then results in an increase in implied volatility and finally a move higher in the VIX index.

In summary, the VIX moves higher when there is more demand for S&P 500 options, this demand tends to increase when there is nervousness about the overall market. This concern about the market will result in increased demand for put options. Put-call parity is the reason the implied volatility of both types of options moves together. The result of this increased demand for puts is higher implied volatility indicated by the pricing of S&P 500 options and a move higher in the VIX.

■ The VIX and Market Movement

Again, the VIX is a measure of 30-day implied volatility as indicated by the pricing of S&P 500 index options. The VIX is expressed as an annualized volatility measure, but it may actually be used to determined shorter-term market-price movements. Recall the example with Amazon reporting earnings in the previous chapter. The implied volatility of the at the money options that only had a day left to expiration could be used to determine the magnitude of movement expected from Amazon stock the day following the company's earnings release. The implied volatility of those options was expressed as an annualized number.

The VIX is the 30-day implied volatility of the S&P 500, but it is also expressed as an annual figure. When the VIX is quoted at 20, this can be interpreted as SPX options pricing in an annualized move, up or down, of 20 percent in the S&P 500 index over the next 30 days. Using the VIX index, the anticipated movement of the underlying market may also be interpreted. The formula for determining the expected magnitude of market movements based on the VIX index is shown in the section following.

CALCULATING EXPECTED 30-DAY MARKET MOVEMENT

The formula for determining expected 30-day market movement is simple:

30-Day Movement = VIX/Square Root of 12

To determine the anticipated 30-day movement of the stock market as defined by the VIX involves dividing the VIX by the square root of 12. In the previous chapter the implied volatility for a stock was used to interpret the expected one-day move for the stock. The square root of 12 is a convenient number as 30 days is the average month and there are 12 months in the year. In a similar manner to breaking down what implied volatility was indicating about movement in Amazon stock, the VIX may be used to determine the anticipated 30-day move for the S&P 500.

If the VIX is quoted at 20, the result would be the market expecting movement of about 5.77 percent over the next 30 days. Following the formula for determining 30-day market movement, the math would be:

$$5.77\% = 20/3.46$$

At times the VIX has reached some extreme points with the index actually reaching over 100 intraday. Table 3.6 shows what different VIX levels indicate about anticipated stock market movement.

The VIX may also be used as an indication of what magnitude of daily price movement is being expected for the S&P 500. Much like the formula used in Chapter 1 for Amazon stock, the VIX can be taken down to a single-day estimate of market movement. Instead of repeating the formula from the previous chapter, a trader's rule of thumb about the VIX will be discussed.

TABLE 3.6	VIX and Expected 30-DayMovement of the S&P 500
VIX	**Expected 30-Day Move**
3.46	1%
6.92	2%
10.40	3%
13.85	4%
17.32	5%
20.78	6%
24.25	7%
27.71	8%
31.18	9%
34.64	10%

In the VIX trading arena, the option and futures traders take the level for the VIX and divide it by 16 to get a rough estimate of what sort of daily move is expected in the stock market based on the level of the VIX. Remember, the denominator of the formula in Chapter 1 was the square root of 252 or about 15.87. The traders round this up to 16 to get their denominator. So the VIX at 16 would indicate S&P 500 index options are anticipating daily pricemovement of 1 percent (16/16). A VIX of 32 would be interpreted as the S&P 500 option market anticipating a daily price move of 2 percent (32/16).

The math behind this method is not exact, but this is a pretty good rule of thumb. In 2008 when the VIX was trading in the mid-60s, this may be taken as the option market expecting a daily price move of 4 percent. Using a more common stock market index, this translates to the Dow Jones Industrial Average (DJIA) at 10,000 points being expected to trade in a 400-point range on a daily basis. Four-hundred-point days in the DJIA usually result in the stock market getting more than just professional investor's attention during the day. Those sort of moves generally grab headlines.

■ Equity Market Volatility Indexes

In addition to an index based on S&P 500 volatility, the CBOE has developed a handful of other volatility measures based on other common stock market indexes. Table 3.7 is a list of indexes based on index volatility that the CBOE has developed. There are also some quotes and strategybased and alternative-asset-based volatility indexes the CBOE has developed.

CBOE DJIA Volatility Index

The CBOE DJIA Volatility Index is calculated in a similar fashion as the VIX. Quotes for this index are disseminated using the symbol VXD. The index was created in 2005, and the index was introduced on March 18 of that year. The index indicates the market's expectation of 30-day implied volatility based on index option prices on the Dow Jones Industrial Average (DJX).

The DJX is one of the oldest stock indexes and is one of the most commonly quoted indicators of the overall stock market. Charles Dow, the publisher of the *Wall Street Journal*, created the index in order to bring more attention to his newspaper. The DJIA was first quoted on May 26, 1896. On days the stock market is open, at some point on the national

TABLE 3.7	CBOE Equity Market Volatility Indexes		
Index	Ticker	Underlying	Website
CBOE Volatility Index	VIX	SPX	www.cboe.com/vix
CBOE DJIA Volatility Index	VXD	DJX	www.cboe.com/vxd
CBOE NADSAQ-100 Volatility Index	VXN	NDX	www.cboe.com/vxn
CBOE Russell 2000 Volatility Index	RVX	RUT	www.cboe.com/rvx
CBOE S&P 100 Volatility Index	VXO	OEX	www.cboe.com/vxo
Amex QQQ Volatility Index	QQV	QQQ	www.nyse.com

Sources: www.cboe.com and www.nyse.com.

news how the DJX did on the day will be mentioned. Some other common names for the DJX are the DJIA, Dow Jones, or just the Dow. For a person who pays little attention to the stock market or even for most investors, the Dow Jones Industrial Average is what they think of when they think of the stock market.

The DJX is composed of 30 stocks that represent a wide variety of industries and some of the largest companies in the United States. The stocks appear in Table 3.8. The small concentration of companies does take something away from the index being representative of the overall economy, but it continues to be the most commonly quoted index.

TABLE 3.8 Members of the Dow Jones Industrial Average	
Company	**Symbol**
Alcoa Inc.	AA
American Express Company	AXP
AT&T Corp.	T
Bank of America Corp.	BAC
Boeing Co.	BA
Caterpillar Inc.	CAT
Chevron Corp.	CVX
Cisco Systems	CSCO
Coca-Cola Co.	KO
E.I. Du Pont de Nemours	DD
Exxon Mobil Corp.	XOM
General Electric Company	GE
Hewlett-Packard Co.	HPQ
Home Depot Inc	HD
Intel Corp.	INTC
International Business Machines Corp.	IBM
Johnson & Johnson	JNJ
J. P. Morgan Chase Company	JPM
Kraft Foods Inc.	KFT
McDonald's Corp.	MCD
Merck & Co. Inc.	MRK
Microsoft Corp.	MSFT
Minnesota Mining & Mfg. Co.	MMM
Pfizer Inc.	PFE
Procter & Gamble Co.	PG
The Travelers Companies	TRV
United Technologies Corp.	UTX
Verizon Communications Inc.	VZ
Wal-Mart Stores Inc.	WMT
Walt Disney Co.	DIS

TABLE 3.9	Dow Jones Industrial Average Industry Weightings
Sector	**Weighting**
Basic materials	3.75%
Consumer goods	10.52%
Consumer services	13.24%
Financials	10.80%
Health care	7.78%
Industrials	22.46%
Oil and gas	9.83%
Technology	17.64%
Telecommunications	3.98%

Note that although the index is referred to as an industrial index, a variety of industries are represented by the DJX. For example, Wal-Mart and Home Depot are major retailers, Pfizer is a pharmaceutical company, and The Travelers Companies specializes in financial services. The industry weightings for the DJX appear in Table 3.9.

The highest weighting of stocks in the DJX is represented by industrial companies, but only about a quarter of the performance of the index will be attributed to this market sector. A variety of other industries contribute to the DJX, which does result in an index that is representative of the overall economy in the United States. For instance, when consumer goods and services are combined, this area of the market represents about another quarter of the index's performance.

Finally, the CFE does not currently trade futures based on the VXD. However, from April 2005 to the middle of 2009 futures contracts based on this index did trade at the exchange.

CBOE NASDAQ-100 Volatility Index

Using quotes for options that trade on the NASDAQ-100 Index (NDX), the CBOE NASDAQ-100 Volatility Index is an indication of implied volatility on the NAS-DAQ-100 index. Trading with the symbol VXN, the index displays 30-day implied volatility for the NDX.

The NASDAQ-100 is an index composed of the 100 largest companies not involved in the financial sector that trade on the NASDAQ. The NASDAQ marketplace opened in 1971 as an alternative exchange to the traditional floor-based exchanges like the New York Stock Exchange. In 1985 the NASDAQ developed two market indexes to promote their exchange, one of which is the NASDAQ-100.

Table 3.10 shows the industry sector weightings that comprise the NDX. What is unique regarding this market index is the lack of financial and health care stocks in the index. The result is a focus on other industries with a very large weighting in the technology sector. In fact, the index is dominated by technology- and communications-oriented stocks, which when combined make up almost 75 percent of the index. Also, the SPX has approximately a 20 percent weighting in the financial sector, which results in the NDX and SPX having disparate performance at times.

TABLE 3.10	NASDAQ-100 Sector Weightings
Sector	Weighting
Basic materials	0.40%
Consumer cyclical	8.40%
Communications	24.40%
Consumer noncyclical	16.80%
Energy	0.50%
Industrial	3.10%
Technology	46.40%

Futures were also traded on the VXN from 2007 to 2009. As this index may experience higher volatility than some other market indexes, the demand for a return of these contracts may result in them being relisted at some point.

CBOE Russell 2000 Volatility Index

The Russell 2000 Index is composed of the 2,000 smallest companies that are in the Russell 3000 Index. Although representing two-thirds of the companies in the Russell 3000, which is composed of 3,000 of the largest publicly traded companies in the United States, the Russell 2000 only represents about 8 percent of the market capitalization of the Russell 3000. The Russell 2000 index is composed of small-cap companies, which mostly focus on domestic markets. This index has a great niche as a representation of domestic economic trends in the United States.

Russell Investments also calculates the Russell 1000 index, which consists of the 1,000 largest companies in the Russell 3000. The top third of those companies represents 92 percent of the market capitalization of the Russell 3000.

The ticker symbol RUT represents option trading on the index and, like the previous volatility related indexes, the Russell 2000 Volatility Index (RVX) attempts to show what the market is pricing in 30-day implied volatility for the index. At times the Russell 1000, Russell 2000, and Russell 3000 names are not entirely accurate. When, due to an acquisition, merger, or dissolution, a company ceases to exist as it had in the past, it may be replaced by a new company in a market index. These Russell indexes are actually reconfigured once a year at the end of June, with the number of stocks in each index taken back to the proper number.

Also, there is a minimum capitalization level for a company to be a member of the Russell 1000. When the indexes are rebalanced, the number of stocks in the Russell 1000 and Russell 2000 is very close to their respective numbers, but it may not be equal to the expected number of stocks in each index. For instance, after the 2010 rebalance the Russell 1000 consisted of 988 stocks and the Russell 2000 consisted of 2,012 stocks. The total of the two indexes results in all the stocks that make up the Russell 3000. The Russell 3000 makes up 99 percent of the market capitalization of the U.S. stock market.

Between the index restructuring dates, companies that cease to exist will be deleted from the indexes, but no replacement will necessarily be put in their place.

However, company spinoffs and initial public offerings may be added between the June reconstruction dates. Those stocks are added on a quarterly basis.

RVX futures traded at the CBOE from 2007 through early 2010.

CBOE S&P 100 Volatility Index

When the VIX was originally quoted by the CBOE, the calculation was based on the implied volatility of the S&P 100 Index (OEX), not the S&P 500. When the calculation was altered in 2003, it was done so with part of the revision resulting in a focus on the S&P 500 as opposed to the S&P 100 index.

The CBOE S&P 100 Volatility Index (VXO) is actually the original VIX index, which was created in 1993. It continues to be calculated using the original methodology based on OEX options. Introduced in 1983 by the CBOE, OEX was the first equity index option product. Originally the index name was the CBOE 100 Index. Loosely translated, OEX could mean Option Exchange 100. The OEX and options listed on the index were so innovative that entire books were written on trading OEX options.

The OEX represents 100 of the largest companies in the United States. This results in the combined components of the OEX being close to 45 percent of the total market capitalization of publicly traded stocks in the United States. Also, almost 60 percent of the S&P 500 market capitalization is represented by the 100 stocks in the OEX.

Even with just 100 names, the OEX is a diversified index with all industry sectors being covered. Table 3.11 is a summary of the industry weightings of the OEX. Note the industry weightings of the OEX are as diversified as the S&P 500 even though there are fewer stocks in the index.

■ Amex QQQ Volatility Index

The Amex QQQ Volatility index is another measure of implied volatility of the Nadsaq market. The method behind this index is similar to the original volatility index calculation used for the VXO. The index indicates the forward-looking volatility for

TABLE 3.11	S&P 100 Index Industry Weightings
Industry	Weighting
Consumer discretionary	6.25%
Consumer staples	15.32%
Energy	15.86%
Financials	11.06%
Health Care	15.40%
Industrials	10.59%
Information technology	17.35%
Materials	1.03%
Telecom services	5.30%
Utilities	1.86%

the QQQ based on option prices. To get a true option contract value, the midpoint of the bid-ask spread is used as the option price input for the calculation.

The CBOE and CFE currently trade options and futures only on the VIX index. However, these alternate VIX indexes may be used to gain insight into market activity. The VIX and other index-related volatility indexes are excellent representations of what sort of near-term volatility is expected from the overall stock market according to the implied volatility of index options. Each of the indexes that have VIX representation have slightly different components and may indicate that there is higher expected volatility in one sector as opposed to others.

CHAPTER 4

Intermarket Analysis

From Markos Katsanos, *Intermarket Trading Strategies* (Hoboken, New Jersey: John Wiley & Sons, 2008), Chapter 3.

It's not that I am so smart; it's just that I stay with the problems longer.

–Albert Einstein

The basic premise of intermarket analysis is that there is both a cause and effect to the movement of money from one area to another. Consider, for example, the price of gold and the dollar. Because gold is denominated in US dollars, any significant fluctuation of the dollar will have an impact on the price of gold, which in turn will affect the price of gold mining stocks.

The strength and direction of the relationship between two markets is measured by the correlation coefficient which reflects the simultaneous change in value of a pair of numeric series over time.

Highly positively correlated markets can be expected to move in similar ways and highly negatively correlated markets are likely to move in opposite directions. Knowing which markets are positively or negatively correlated with a given market is very important for gaining an understanding of the future directional movement of the market you propose to trade.

Advancements in telecommunications have contributed to the integration of international markets. Sophisticated traders are starting to incorporate intermarket analysis in their trading decisions through a variety of means ranging from simple chart analysis to correlation analysis. Yet the intermarket relationships hidden in this data are often quite complex and not readily apparent, while the scope of analysis is virtually unlimited.

But what is intermarket analysis?

The financial markets comprise more than 500 000 securities, derivatives, currencies, bonds, and other financial instruments – the size of a small city. All interact with each other to some extent and a seemingly unimportant event can cause a chain of reactions causing a landslide of large-scale changes to the financial markets.

Consider the following example: Let's suppose that the Bank of Japan dcides to buy dollars in order to push the yen down. As a result Japanese stock prices will go up as a weak yen will help boost profits for exporters. A sharp rise of the Nikkei will in turn have a positive effect on all other Asian markets. The next morning European markets, in view of higher Asian markets and in the absence of other overnight news, will open higher. This will in turn drive US index futures higher and boost US markets at open. In addition lower yen prices will encourage the "yen carry trade", i.e. borrowing yen at lower or near zero interest rates and buying higher yielding assets such as US bonds or even emerging market equities, which in turn will push bonds and equities higher. On the other hand, a scenario for disaster will develop if the opposite happens and the yen rises sharply against the dollar. This will cause a sharp unwinding of the "yen carry trade", triggering an avalanche of sharp declines in all financial markets.

But what might cause the yen to rise? The following is a possible scenario: As we head into the economic slowdown, the carry trade money that has flowed into risky cyclical assets is likely to fall in value. As a result, speculators in these assets will cut their losses, bail out and repay their yen debts. This is a scenario for disaster because when the yen rebounds against the dollar, it often snaps back very fast and carry trades can go from profit to loss with almost no warning.

A popular chaos theory axiom (known as the "butterfly effect" because of the title of a paper given by the mathematician Edward Lorenz in 1972 to the American Association for the Advancement of Science in Washington, D.C. entitled "Predictability: Does the Flap of a Butterfly's Wings in Brazil Set Off a Tornado in Texas?") stipulates that a small change in the initial condition of the system (the flapping of the wing) causes a chain of events leading to large-scale phenomena. Had the butterfly not flapped its wings, the trajectory of the system might have been vastly different.

A financial series would appear to be chaotic in nature, but its statistics are not because, as well as being orderly in the sense of being deterministic, chaotic systems usually have well defined statistics.

The rapid progress of global communications has contributed to the integration of all international financial markets as the world has gotten smaller due to the ability to communicate almost instantaneously. Relationships that were dismissed as irrelevant in the past cannot be ignored any more as the globalization of the markets contributes to a convergence of formerly unrelated markets.

Take a look at the comparison chart in Figure 4.1. The S&P 500 is depicted with a bold thick line. The second one however is not even a stock index. It is the Japanese yen exchange rate (USD/JPY).

The next composite chart in Figure 4.2 is of three stock indices. The first two (depicted with a bar chart and thick line) are of the S&P 500 and the Nasdaq Composite respectively. The third chart (thin line) is the Athens General Index which, surprisingly, correlates better with the S&P 500 than its compatriot, the Nasdaq Composite.

FIGURE 4.1 Comparison Chart of the S&P 500 (in Bold with the Scale on the Right Y-axis) and the Yen (USD/JPY) (with the Scale on the Left Axis) from June 2006 to January 2008.

FIGURE 4.2 Weekly Comparison Chart of the S&P 500 (Thick Line with the Scale on the Right Y-axis), the Nasdaq (in Bold with the Scale on the Left Axis) and the Greek Athens General Index (ATG) from 1999 to 2008.

The above examples are included to illustrate that the integration of global markets can extend beyond the obvious relations.

I often hear CNBC guests suggesting investing in international markets as a means of diversifying one's portfolio away from the US equity markets. Although some emerging markets may have relatively medium to low correlation with US markets, one important question to ask is whether diversification works when it is needed most. Evidence from stock market history suggests that periods of negative shocks and poor market performance were associated with high, rather than low, correlations. The events of 21 January 2008 are still fresh in my mind, when a 2.9% correction in the S&P 500 was followed the next day by a devastating 7.2% drop in the German DAX, wiping out nine months of profits in a day. Emerging markets sunk even more with the Jakarta Composite falling more than 12% in two days while Brazil's Bovespa lost more than 8.5%. Indeed, investors who have apparently relied upon diversification in the past to protect them against corrections of the market have been frequently disappointed.

The only effective method of diversifying one's portfolio is by including asset classes with low or negative correlation to stocks such as cash, foreign exchange or commodities. Whatever the relationship is – leading, lagging, or divergent responses to economic conditions – a strong negative correlation coefficient between two markets is a suggestion that these markets will move against each other sometime in the future. And, of course, the higher the absolute value of the coefficient of correlation, the higher the diversity of their performances.

Although intermarket analysis has been classified as a branch of technical analysis, it has not been embraced fully by analysts. The majority of traders continue to focus on only one market at a time and they tend to miss the forest for the trees. No market exists in a vacuum, and traders who focus on the bigger picture portrayed through all international markets tend to be the ones that deliver better performance.

Traditional technical analysis indicators such as moving averages are lagging indicators calculated from past data and are limited in assessing the current trend. Regardless of the hours spent in back-testing, there is a limit beyond which a system based on a lagging indicator can be improved further. Thus the addition of leading indicators that anticipate reversals in trend direction is essential and beneficial to the system's performance. These can only be created by taking into consideration directional movements of correlated markets.

The use of intermarket correlation analysis can help you improve on your trading system by avoiding trades against the prevailing direction of correlated markets, but can also be used on its own to develop a complete system based on divergences between two or more highly correlated markets. Knowing the correlation of the market you propose to trade with other markets is very important for predicting its future direction. In addition, short-term traders can take advantage of the time difference between world markets and anticipate the next day's movement. Asian markets are the first to start trading, followed by the European markets. For a US trader the insight gained from all preceding markets is a valuable tool in predicting at least the opening in his local market.

I have found that the most accurate economist is the market itself. It is far easier to forecast economic activity from the behavior of markets themselves than it is to forecast the capital markets from lagging economic statistics such as the unemployment index. The market is a discounting mechanism. It interprets the impact of economic news some time in the future. Of course, this is only a guess and guesses are not always right. But the truth is that the market is a much better guesser than any of us are, as it represents the average opinion of all the economists in the world.

There appears to be no end to the conclusions that can be drawn if a little understanding, imagination, and pure common sense are applied. Major changes in commodity prices affect the bond markets of different countries in different ways, depending upon their economic structure.

What sectors are affected first? Which asset class will provide the best potential profits? If opportunities dry up in one sector, where is the money heading to take advantage of the next cycle? This is what intermarket analysis can tell you if you learn what to look for, which makes it a grand endeavor and a continuing challenge but always worth the effort.

Intermarket analysis can also be useful in estimating the duration and state of the business cycle by watching the historic relationship between bonds, stocks and commodities as economic slowing favors bonds over stocks and commodities.

Near the end of an economic expansion bonds usually turn down before stocks and commodities and the reverse is true during an economic expansion. Bonds are usually the first to peak and the first to bottom and can therefore provide ample warning of the start or the end of a recession. Bonds have an impressive record as a leading indicator for the stock market, although this information cannot be used in constructing a trading system as the lead times can be quite long, ranging from one to two years.

You can see in Figure 4.3 that bonds peaked in October 1998, 18 months before stocks peaked in March 2000 and 29 months before the official start of the recession in March 2001. The Commodity Research Bureau (CRB) index was the last to peak, making a complex triple top formation with the last peak coinciding with the start of the recession.

Bonds were also the first to bottom in anticipation of the recovery, followed by commodities and then stocks. From the beginning of 2003 until the middle of 2005 all three were rising together. Commodities are usually the last to bottom during a recovery but this was not the case here as they were boosted by the weakness in the dollar. The dollar made a final peak in January 2002 and reversed direction, dropping like a rock against the euro and other major currencies. This triggered a secular bull market in gold which spread to the rest of the commodities and has continued until the end of June 2008, almost nine months after stocks peaked in September 2007.

More information on the business cycle, including sector rotation during economic cycles, can be found in John Murphy's excellent book *Intermarket Analysis: Profiting from Global Market Relationships* (see Bibliography).

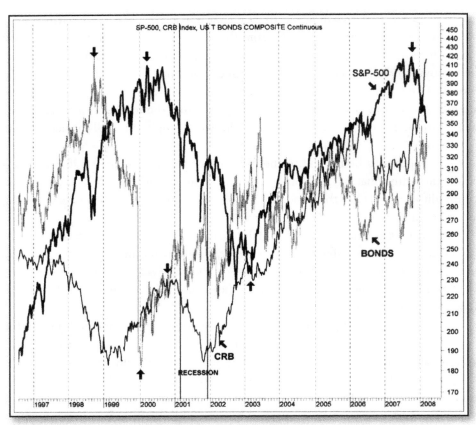

FIGURE 4.3 Weekly Composite Chart of the S&P 500 (Thick Line), the CRB Index (Thin Line with the Scale on the Right Y-axis) and US Treasury Bonds (Grey Bar Chart) from 1997 to 2008. Down arrows indicate major tops in stocks and bonds and up arrows bottoms.

■ 4.1 Determining Intermarket Relations

The simplest and easiest method of intermarket analysis is a visual inspection of a comparison chart of one security superimposed on the chart of another. A custom indicator can also be calculated from the ratio of prices, to help assess their past relation and anticipate future direction. Both of the above methods, however, are limited to two markets and the use of the correlation coefficient is essential for an analysis of multiple markets. For predictive purposes, we wish to detect correlations that are significantly different from zero. Such relationships can then be used to predict the future course of events in trading systems or forecasting models.

In addition, linear regression can be used to predict the future price trend of a market based on its correlation with multiple related markets.

When assessing intermarket relations you should always keep in mind that these are neither fixed nor static in time. Instead they fluctuate continuously in strength and time. It is usually very difficult to determine which market is leading or lagging. A lead can shift over time and become a lag, with the markets switching positions as follower and leader. In addition, a weak positive correlation can sometimes become negative and vice versa. For this reason it is always prudent to look at the prevailing rate of change of the correlation between two related markets before reaching any important conclusions or trading decisions.

The variability of the correlation over time is more evident in Figure 4.4, where yearly correlations between the S&P 500 and four major international indices are plotted against time from 1992 up to the end of 2007. You can see that correlations before 1996 were inconsistent and unpredictable but started to converge during the last ten year period. The most incongruous relationship is that between the S&P 500 and Japan's Nikkei (in white) as it fluctuated from negative to positive values over time.

The recent integration of global markets has also been accelerated by a flurry of mergers, acquisitions and alliances between international exchanges, the most important being the merger between the New York Stock Exchange and Euronext, Europe's leading cross-border exchange, which includes French, Belgian, Dutch and Portuguese national markets. A few months later the Nasdaq, after a failed bid for the London Stock Exchange, announced a takeover of the OMX, which owns and operates stock exchanges in Stockholm, Helsinki, Copenhagen, Reykjavik (Iceland) and the Baltic states.

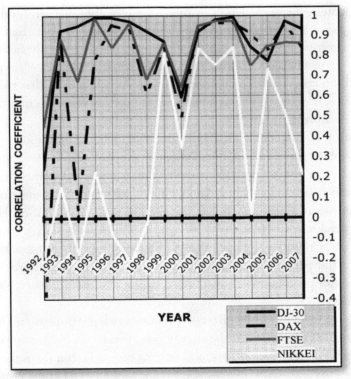

FIGURE 4.4 Yearly Correlation Variation Between the S&P 500 and Leading International Indices from 1992–2007. The correlation with the DJ-30 is depicted by a black line, with Germany's DAX by a dashed line, with the FTSE by a grey line, and with the Nikkei by a white line. Notice the correlation volatility, especially before 1996. The Nikkei had the weakest and most volatile correlation with the S&P 500.

◼ 4.2 Using Intermarket Correlations for Portfolio Diversification

The benefits of diversification are well known: most investment managers diversify by including international equities, bonds and cash in their US stock portfolio. Less common, however, is the diversification into other asset classes such as commodities or foreign currencies (forex).

There is a widely held belief that, because commodities and currencies are traded on very thin margins, they are just too risky and can lead to financial ruin. Visions of wheat being delivered to the trader's front yard, margin calls or stories of consecutive "limit down days" add fuel to the fire. Claims that "over 90% of all futures traders lose money over time" do not help either.

Because of their low correlation to equities, most commodities are attractive diversification candidates as they can lead to a large increase in returnwhile simultaneously reducing risk. Furthermore, futures diversification is particularly effective in declining stock markets, just where it is needed most.During periods of very lowor negative stock returns, commodities (except industrial metal futures) dominate the portfolio return, acting as a hedge, or buffer, in fallingmarkets. The benefit of including foreign stocks is not so clear as the world has gotten smaller due to the ability to communicate almost instantaneously.

Unfortunately, the approach of most novice investors or even fund managers is to have no risk management at all and it becomes obvious too late that this is an extremely dangerous omission. A fund or portfolio manager should not be evaluated only by the return he has achieved. Another important criterion of his performance is the portfolio risk exposure over time. A good benchmark of that risk is the standard deviation of returns. This is a measure of how far apart the monthly or yearly returns are scattered around the average.

Correlation is a relatively simple concept but absolutely mandatory in the use of investments. It basically refers to whether or not different investments or asset classes will move at the same time for the same reason and in the same direction. To be effective, diversification must involve asset classes that are not correlated (that is, they do not move in the same direction at the same time). High positive correlation reduces the benefits of diversification. On the other hand, selecting uncorrelated or negatively correlated asset classes not only reduces the downside volatility in the performance curve of the portfolio to a minimum but can also increase overall profitability as well. An example will help illustrate the basics of diversification.

Suppose you are considering diversifying your stock portfolio by adding an uncorrelated commodity future from the energy complex. If you invest your entire equity in either stocks or crude oil futures, and returns vary in the future as they have in the past, your equity line (in points) will be similar to the charts in the bottom window of Figure 4.5. If, however, you invest 70% of your initial capital in stocks and 30% in crude oil futures, your equity line will be similar to the top chart in Figure 4.5. You can clearly see that the portfolio's returns are not nearly as volatile as are those of the individual investments.

FIGURE 4.5 Monthly Comparison Chart of the S&P 500 (Bar Chart with the Scale on the Right Y-axis) and Light Sweet Crude Oil Futures Continuous Contract (NYMEX:CL) (Line Chart Below) from January of 1994 to January of 2008. The equity line of a composite portfolio consisting of 70% equities (represented by the S&P 500) and 30% oil futures is plotted in the top window. The composite portfolio produced better returns with less volatility.

The reason for the reduction in volatility is that stocks did not move in the same direction at the same time with crude oil futures. Thus, a crucial factor for constructing portfolios is the degree of correlation between investment returns. Diversification provides substantial risk reduction if the components of a portfolio are uncorrelated.

In fact, it is possible to reduce the overall risk of the portfolio to almost zero if enough investment opportunities having non-correlated returns are combined together!

Maximum return, however, is also proportional to risk. Low risk investments produce low returns and speculative or riskier investments can produce higher returns. Thus reducing risk can also reduce return. Like everything else in life, the best solution is a compromise between risk and return.

The problem is therefore reduced to finding an efficient portfolio that will maximize expected return according to one's individual risk preferences. The following example will help illustrate the basics of selecting an appropriate portfolio of securities or asset classes.

Let's suppose that we want to invest in international equities but also diversify into futures and forex. For simplicity's sake I include only one sample from each asset class, for example crude oil futures to represent commodities, gold to represent precious metals and the British pound to represent foreign exchange. International

TABLE 4.1	All Stock Index Returns Include Dividends. Also foreign index returns were converted to US dollars. The bond returns were obtained from the Lehman Brothers website (http://www.lehman.com/fi/indices/) and concerned aggregate returns of the US Bond Index. British pound (GBP/USD) returns include price appreciation versus the USD and also interest income. Oil returns were obtained from the historical continuous light sweet crude oil contract (NYMEX:CL).

Annual Returns

Year	S&P 500	FTSE	Hang Seng	Bonds	GBP	Gold	Crude Oil	Cash
1997	33.36	23.98	−17.3	9.65	2.31	−21.8	−31.9	5.25
1998	28.58	17.02	−2.15	8.69	6.47	−0.26	−31.7	5.06
1999	21.04	17.22	71.51	−0.82	2.37	0.00	112.4	4.74
2000	−9.10	−15.6	−8.96	11.63	−1.85	−5.55	4.69	5.95
2001	−11.9	−17.6	−22.0	8.44	1.39	2.48	−26.0	4.09
2002	−22.1	−8.79	−15.1	10.26	13.56	24.80	57.3	1.70
2003	28.68	27.60	38.55	4.10	14.35	19.09	4.23	1.07
2004	10.88	18.43	16.30	4.34	12.25	5.58	33.61	1.24
2005	4.91	9.70	7.82	2.43	−5.78	18.00	40.48	3.00
2006	15.79	27.77	37.35	4.33	18.85	23.17	0.02	4.76
Mean	10.02	9.97	10.61	6.31	6.39	6.55	16.31	3.69
St Dev	19.14	17.53	30.35	4.00	8.02	14.73	45.67	1.80

equities are represented by the S&P 500 (or a stock selection tracking the S&P), one European (the FTSE 100) and one Asian (the Hang Seng) index. In Table 4.1, I have prepared the average yearly percentage returns and standard deviation of returns. I have also calculated, at the bottom of the table, the total average 10-year return and the standard deviation of returns using Excel's STDEV function.

The correlation coefficients between the selected asset classes or indices are listed in Table 4.2. These coefficients are based on monthly percentage yields and are calculated, as part of this study, over the same 10-year period. As discussed later, the correlation coefficients play a role in selecting the asset class allocation.

TABLE 4.2	Pearson's Correlation of Monthly Percentage Yields for the 10-year Period from 1997 to 2006

Correlation of Monthly Returns

	S&P 500	FTSE	Hang Seng	Bonds	GBP	Gold	Crude Oil
S&P 500	1	0.81	0.57	−0.06	−0.09	−0.04	−0.03
FTSE	0.81	1	0.57	−0.02	−0.30	−0.06	0.03
Hang Seng	0.57	0.57	1	0.05	0.00	0.11	0.18
Bonds	−0.06	−0.02	0.05	1	0.10	0.08	0.11
GBP	−0.09	−0.30	0.00	0.10	1	0.36	0.00
Gold	−0.04	−0.06	0.11	0.08	0.36	1	0.18
Oil	−0.03	0.03	0.18	0.11	0.00	0.18	1

You can see from Table 4.2 that the S&P 500 is correlated only with international indices. Among the other asset classes, the British pound is weakly correlated with gold ($r = 0.36$) and negatively correlated with the FTSE ($r = -0.30$) so it might be beneficial to include the pound together with the FTSE but not with gold. Gold is also very weakly correlated with crude oil ($r = 0.18$). As you will see later, however, in the case of low correlations the volatility and not the correlation coefficient is the dominant factor to consider in reducing portfolio risk. Bonds had very low correlation with the British pound ($r = 0.10$) and crude oil ($r = 0.11$) but were not particularly correlated with the others.

A comparison of the returns, standard deviation and risk adjusted return of the four hypothetical passive portfolios shows the real effect of diversification (Table 4.3). The first portfolio (in the third column of Table 4.3) contained a typical allocation of asset classes found in an average US fund, i.e. 70% equities, 20% bonds and 10% money market. By including uncorrelated assets such as bonds and cash (with zero correlation with the S&P), a risk reduction of 31% was achieved with only 1.4% reduction in returns. A further 5% risk reduction was accomplished by including international equities (10% British and 10% Hong Kong equities). The main reason for including international equities was to improve on US equity returns, but this was not the case in the hypothetical portfolio as the Hang Seng underperformed the S&P 500 during the 1997–1998 Asian financial crisis. Commodities, however, were the real star of the show as they played an important role in significantly reducing risk and, at the same time, increasing return.

TABLE 4.3 Risk Reduction Associated with Asset Allocation and Correlations. The standard deviation of each portfolio was calculated in a separate spreadsheet by adding the annual returns of each asset class according to their percentage weights in the portfolio and then calculating the standard deviation of the annual returns for the entire 10-year period of the study.

Portfolio Allocation	US Stocks Only	Stocks & Bonds	International Stocks & Bonds	Stocks, Bonds & Futures	Minimum Risk	Maximum Return
S&P 500	100%	70%	50%	40%	10%	60%
Cash		10%	10%			
FTSE			10%			
Hang Seng			10%			10%
Bonds		20%	20%	40%		
GBP					55%	
Gold				10%		
CRB						
Oil				10%	15%	30%
Average % Return	10.0	8.64	8.69	8.81	8.92	11.96
Standard deviation	19.1	13.1	12.5	6.86	6.38	18.70
Risk adj. return	0.52	0.66	0.70	1.28	1.40	0.64

This is evident from the standard deviation of returns of the third hypothetical portfolio. A huge 64% reduction in risk was achieved by including gold (10%) and crude oil futures (10%), even though the standard deviation (and risk) of investing in crude oil alone was more than double that of the S&P.

The fourth portfolio was obtained by finding the best allocation (highest return) with the minimum risk. This produced a portfolio consisting of 30% US equities, 55% bonds and 15% oil futures. The relatively high percentage allocation of bonds was to be expected as their standard deviation was the lowest of the group. The presence of the highly volatile oil futures in the minimum risk portfolio, however, was certainly a surprise.

This portfolio reduced risk by an astonishing 64%, sacrificing only 1.2 percentage points in return compared to the equities only portfolio. The relatively low performance of this portfolio was no surprise as the standard deviation is proportional to returns: the smaller the standard deviation, the smaller the risk and, of course, the smaller the potential magnitude of the return. There is therefore a limit beyond which the expected return cannot be increased without increasing risk.

Finally I used Excel's Solver to maximize return without increasing the risk more than the first (equities) portfolio. This portfolio (last column in Table 4.3) included 60% US stocks, 10% international equities and 30% crude oil futures. It outperformed the S&P 500 by almost 2 percentage points with slightly less risk. Typically, futures can be added up to a maximum 30% allocation while maintaining a risk advantage over a portfolio without futures.

In maximizing the return I had to constrain the risk to lower than the first portfolio, otherwise the solver produced a portfolio consisting of 100% oil futures which is unacceptable. Similarly in minimizing risk (fourth portfolio) I had to specify a minimum return otherwise the solution also produced an unacceptable portfolio consistingmostly of cash and bonds. I also had to constrain the allocation percentages to positive values otherwise the solution occasionally included negative allocations indicating selling the asset short rather than buying.

Of course future performance rarely measures up fully to past results. While historical relations between asset classes may provide a reasonable guide, rates of return are often less predictable. In addition, as you can see from Figure 4.4, correlations can also change over time.

One solution is to rebalance the portfolio on a set time period to take into account the most recent correlations in order to maintain the desired level of risk exposure. This method of asset allocation, is not the only one, however.

A different, dynamic rather than static, approach would involve changing asset weights depending on market conditions. This can be accomplished by reducing the allotment of equities in favor of cash, precious metals or foreign exchange in a down market.

CHAPTER 5

Correlation

From Markos Katsanos, *Intermarket Trading Strategies* (Hoboken, New Jersey: John Wiley & Sons, 2008), Chapter 2.

Study the past if you would divine the future.
> —Confucius

■ 5.1 The Correlation Coefficient

5.1.1 Pearson's Correlation

The correlation coefficient measures the strength and direction of correlation or corelation between two variables.

There are several methods, depending on the nature of data being studied, for calculating the correlation coefficient, but the best known is Pearson's product-moment correlation coefficient, usually denoted by r, which is obtained by dividing the covariance of the two variables by the product of their standard deviations. The formula for calculating Pearson's r is:

$$r = \frac{\sigma_{XY}}{\sigma_X \sigma_Y} \tag{5.1}$$

where σ_{XY} is the covariance of variables X and Y and σ_X, σ_y are their standard deviations. The covariance is the cross product of the deviations from the mean and is calculated by the following formula:

$$\sigma_{XY} = \frac{\sum (x - \bar{x})(y - \bar{y})}{n - 1}. \tag{5.2}$$

Unfortunately the size of the covariance depends on the values of measurement of each variable and is not normalized between -1.0 and $+1.0$ as is the correlation coefficient.

Substituting for the covariance in (5.1) we get:

$$r = \frac{\sum Z_x Z_y}{\sigma_x \sigma_y (n-1)}$$ (5.3)

which is the average product of the z-scores, where $z_x = \sum (x_i \; \bar{x})$ and $z_y = \sum (y_i - \bar{y})$.

The correlation coefficient varies between -1 and 1. A value of $+1$ indicates a perfect linear relationshipwith positive slope between the two variables; a value of -1 indicates a perfect linear relationship with negative slope between the two variables and a correlation coefficient of 0means that there is no linear relationship between the variables. Values in between indicate the degree of correlation and their interpretation is subjective depending to some extent on the variables under consideration.

The interpretation is different for medical research, social, economic or financial time series data. In the case of financial time series the interpretation can again be different depending on whether we compare raw price data or percent changes (yields), as the direct calculation of the correlation based on absolute prices tends to overestimate the correlation coefficient as relations between financial price series are seldom linear. Correlations based on price percent changes, on the other hand, produce more realistic values for the correlation coefficient as they deviate less from linearity.

Therefore, although the correlation coefficient between two time series is unique, two different interpretations are included in Table 5.1, according to the method used

THEORY AND ANALYSIS

TABLE 5.1 Interpretation of Pearson's Correlation Coefficient. The second column applies to the correlation between raw price data and the last column to percent weekly changes or yields. The interpretation for negative values of Pearson's correlation is exactly the same.

Correlation Coefficient r	Interpretation	
Absolute Value	Price Comparison	Percent Changes
0.9 to 1	Extremely strong	Extremely strong
0.8 to 0.9	Very strong	Very strong
0.7 to 0.8	Strong	Very strong
0.6 to 0.7	Moderately strong	Strong
0.5 to 0.6	Moderate	Moderately strong
0.4 to 0.5	Meaningful	Moderate
0.3 to 0.4	Low	Meaningful
0.2 to 0.3	Very low	Low
0.1 to 0.2	Very slight	Very low
0 to 0.1	Non-existent	Non-existent

for the calculation, in order to take into account the error resulting from the violation of the linearity assumption.

A more precise interpretation arising from the correlation coefficient is recommended by some statisticians and requires one further calculation. If the correlation coefficient is squared, the result, commonly known as r^2 or r square or coefficient of determination (see also Section 5.1.2), will indicate approximately the percent of the "dependent" variable that is associated with the "independent" variable or the proportion of the variance in one variable associated with the variance of the other variable. For example, if we calculated that the correlation between the S&P 500 and the 10-year Treasury yield (TNX) is 0.50 then this correlation squared is 0.25, which means that 25% of the variance of the two indices is common. In thus squaring correlations and transforming the result to percentage terms we are in a better position to evaluate a particular correlation.

There is also another factor we must consider when we try to interpret the correlation coefficient—the number of points we have used.

If we plotted only two points, then we would be bound to get a straight line between them. With three points there is still a chance that the points will lie close to a straight line, purely by chance. Clearly, a high correlation coefficient on only a few points is not very meaningful.

Traders often need to know if time series of commodity or stock prices are cyclic and, if they are, the extent of the cycle. The correlation coefficient can also be used in this case by testing for auto-correlation at different lags (testing whether values in a given series are related to other values in the same series). By doing many correlations with differing lags, the extent or duration of the cycle can be determined.

5.1.2 Coefficient of determination

The coefficient of determination r^2 is the square of Pearson's correlation coefficient. It represents the percent of the data that is the closest to the line of best fit. For example, if $r = 0.922$, then $r^2 = 0.850$, which means that 85% of the total variation in y can be explained by the linear relationship between x and y (as described by the regression equation). The other 15% of the total variation in y remains unexplained and stems from other exogenous factors. In regression, the coefficient of determination is useful in determining how well the regression line approximates the real data points but it can also be used (as explained above) to interpret the correlation coefficient.

5.1.3 Spearman's ρ

The best known non-parametric correlation coefficient is Spearman's rank correlation coefficient, named after Charles Spearman and often denoted by the Greek letter ρ (rho). Unlike Pearson's correlation coefficient, it does not require the assumption that the variables are normally distributed but, like Pearson's correlation, linearity is still an assumption.

The main advantage of using the Spearman coefficient is that it is not sensitive to outliers because it looks at ranks as opposed to actual values.

The formula for calculating Spearman's correlation, ρ is:

$$\rho = 1 - \frac{6\sum d^2}{n(n^2 - 1)} \tag{5.4}$$

where d is the difference between paired ranks on the same row.

Similar to Pearson's correlation coefficient, Spearman's ρ takes values between -1 and $+1$. In calculating Spearman's coefficient some information is lost because the prices are converted to ranks. Therefore, when two variables appear to be normally distributed it is better to use Pearson's correlation coefficient.

The concept of correlation will be discussed extensively in the rest of the book and should be fully understood by the readers, so I have included an example of calculating both Pearson's and Spearman's correlation coefficients in the Excel worksheets in Tables 5.2 and 5.3 respectively.

■ 5.2 Assumptions

5.2.1 Linearity

The formula used when calculating the correlation coefficient between two variables makes the implicit assumption that a linear relationship exists between them. When this assumption is not true, the calculated value can be misleading. In practice this assumption can virtually never be confirmed; fortunately, the correlation coefficient is not greatly affected by minor deviations from linearity. However, it is always prudent to look at a scatterplot of the variables of interest before making important conclusions regarding the relation between two variables.

To understand what a linear relationship is, consider the scatterplots in Figures 5.1, 5.2 and 5.3.

The first scatterplot in Figure 5.1, between the S&P 500 and the British FTSE 100, illustrates an approximate linear relationship, as the points fall generally along a straight line. Keep in mind that in the financial markets there is no such thing as a perfect linear relationship. In contrast, the plot in Figure 5.2 between the S&P 500 and the Nasdaq 100 exhibits a curvilinear relationship. In this case increasingly greater values of the Nasdaq 100 are associated with increasingly greater values of the S&P 500 up to a certain value (approximately 1200 on the Nasdaq scale).

A statistician, not knowing what each variable represents, would try to fit a cubic line of the form

$$SP = a + b.NDX + c.NDX^2 + d.NDX^3$$

and predict future values of the S&P 500 using the cubic equation above.

A chart of the two indices in Figure 5.4, however, reveals the true reason of discontinuity of the linear relationship: a decoupling of the two indices which

TABLE 5.2 Example of Calculating Pearson's r in Excel. The Variables X and Y Are the Daily Percent Change in Gold and the Dollar Index Respectively from 8 December 2006 to 29 December 2006.

A	B	C	D	E	F	G	H	I
Date	X	Y	$X-\mu$	$(X-\mu)^2$	$Y-\mu$	$(Y-\mu)^2$	$(X-\mu)(Y-\mu)$	2
12-8-06	-1.344	0.640	-1.386	1.921	0.570	0.325	-0.790	3
12-11-06	0.929	-0.132	0.887	0.787	-0.202	0.041	-0.179	4
12-12-06	-0.008	-0.289	-0.050	0.003	-0.359	0.129	0.018	5
12-13-06	-0.325	0.470	-0.367	0.135	0.400	0.160	-0.147	6
12-14-06	-0.430	0.444	-0.472	0.223	0.374	0.140	-0.176	7
12-15-06	-1.664	0.406	-1.706	2.910	0.336	0.113	-0.573	8
12-18-06	0.163	-0.036	0.121	0.015	-0.106	0.011	-0.013	9
12-19-06	1.088	-0.667	1.046	1.094	-0.737	0.543	-0.771	10
12-20-06	-0.402	0.096	-0.444	0.197	0.026	0.001	-0.011	11
12-21-06	-0.250	0.072	-0.292	0.085	0.002	0.000	-0.001	12
12-22-06	0.332	0.263	0.290	0.084	0.193	0.037	0.056	13
12-26-06	0.613	0.298	0.571	0.326	0.228	0.052	0.130	14
12-27-06	0.401	-0.107	0.359	0.129	-0.177	0.031	-0.064	15
12-28-06	1.133	-0.179	1.091	1.190	-0.249	0.062	-0.272	16
12-29-06	0.394	-0.227	0.352	0.124	-0.297	0.088	-0.105	17
Σ	0.630	1.052		9.223		1.733	-2.897	18
N	15	15					-0.207	19
mean μ	0.042	0.070			Covariance σ_{xy} =		-0.725	20
σ	0.812	0.352			Pearson's Correlation **r**			21

Excel Formula

	19	20	21
		B18/B19	SQRT(E18/(B19−1))
		C18/C19	SQRT(G18/(C19−1))
	H18/(B19−1)		
		H19/B21/C21	

ROW 17

COLUMN
B B17−B$20
C D17*D17
D C17−C$20
E F17*F17
F F17*F17
G D17*F17
H D17*F17

TABLE 5.3 Example of Calculating Spearman's ρ in Excel. The Variables X and Y Are the Daily Percent Change in Gold and the Dollar Index Respectively from 8 December 2006 to 29 December 2006.

A	B	C	D	E	F	I
Date	X	Y	Rank	Rank	d^2	2
12-8-06	−1.344	0.640	14	1	169	3
12-11-06	0.929	−0.132	3	11	64	4
12-12-06	−0.008	−0.289	9	14	25	5
12-13-06	−0.325	0.470	11	2	81	6
12-14-06	−0.430	0.444	13	3	100	7
12-15-06	−1.664	0.406	15	4	121	8
12-18-06	0.163	−0.036	8	9	1	9
12-19-06	1.088	−0.667	2	15	169	10
12-20-06	−0.402	0.096	12	7	25	11
12-21-06	−0.250	0.072	10	8	4	12
12-22-06	0.332	0.263	7	6	1	13
12-26-06	0.613	0.298	4	5	1	14
12-27-06	0.401	−0.107	5	10	25	15
12-28-06	1.133	−0.179	1	12	121	16
12-29-06	0.394	−0.227	6	13	49	17
Σ	0.630	1.052				18
N	15					19
		Spearman's Correlation ρ=			−0.707	20

Excel Formula

ROW	17	18	20
COLUMN			
B		SUM(B3:B17)	
C		SUM(C3:C17)	
D	RANK(B17,B$3:B$17)		
E	RANK(C17,C$3:C$17)		
F	(D17−E17)^2		1-6*F18/B19/(B19^2-1)
H	D17*F17	SUM(F3:F17)	

started in the middle of 1998, with the Nasdaq outperforming the S&P until the bubble peak of March 2000, and its subsequent devastating collapse which happened to coincide for values of the Nasdaq greater than 1200. This is the reason for the breakout of the linear relationship as depicted in Figure 5.2 by the vertical line AB.

The third scatterplot in Figure 5.3 plots the S&P 500 vs. Japan's Nikkei 225.

Pearson's coefficient of correlation is −0.445 and Spearman's ρ is −0.4, suggesting a negative correlation for the period from 1 January 1992 to 13 December 2006. Both values are, however, meaningless for making any useful predictions for the Nikkei based on the S&P 500 as their relationship is not linear.

A closer examination of the scatterplot, however, reveals that the scatter is clustered around three distinct areas, each having completely different slopes: A rea A at the top left of the chart exhibits a distinct positive correlation with the S&P; area B in the center of the chart with a negative correlation; and area C at the bottom right with no correlation at all. The time period of the above different correlations can be identified more precisely by superimposing a chart of the Nikkei on the S&P (Figure 5.5). The period from 1992 to 2007 under study can be divided into six types.

FIGURE 5.1 Scatterplot of the S&P 500 and the British FTSE 100, for the Last 15-Year Period. The relationship is approximately linear, as the points fall generally along a straight line.

FIGURE 5.2 Scatterplot of the S&P 500 and the Nasdaq 100, for the Last 15-Year Period. The relationship is not linear, as the best fit line is curvilinear.

FIGURE 5.3 Scatterplot of the S&P 500 and the Nikkei, for the Last 15-Year Period. The relationship is not linear, as the points deviate significantly from the best fit line.

The first five from 1992 to 1999 (marked A, B, C, D and E) feature alternate positive and negative correlations and the last one (marked F in Figure 5.5) a distinct positive correlation for the period from 1999 to 2007. The positive correlation periods can be allocated to area A in Figure 5.3 and the negative correlated periods to area B.

Area C consists of smaller periods with zero or near zero correlation enclosed inside the longer periods.

In view of the above, it is evident that neither Pearson's nor Spearman's correlation coefficients are appropriate for analyzing nonlinear relationships. In these cases, mathematicians use the so-called coefficient of nonlinear correlation or Eta (denoted by the Greek letter η) which is computed by splitting one of the variables into groups of equal width according to their rank. Eta is then calculated by dividing the group by the total variance. Eta can be used to measure the degree of linearity of a relationship, as the extent to which Eta is greater than r is an estimate of the extent to which the data relationship is nonlinear. Unfortunately, Eta is not particularly useful for analyzing financial markets because, in the case of time series, the groups should be categorized according to time and not rank.

In cases of minor deviations from linearity (for example the relation between the FTSE and the S&P 500), transforming raw prices into percentage yields usually enhances the linear relationship between two variables, resulting in a more reliable correlation and regression analysis.

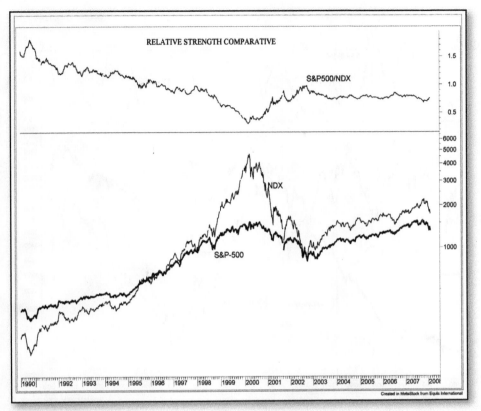

FIGURE 5.4 Weekly Chart of the S&P 500 (Thick Line) with the Nasdaq 100 Superimposed (Thin Black Line) from 1990 to 2007. The relative strength between the S&P 500 and the NDX is plotted in the top window.

Fortunately there are methods more appropriate for analyzing the nonlinear nature of the financial markets: artificial neural networks and kernel regression. Neural networks are nonparametric models which are inherently nonlinear in their computational elements and provide potentially the greatest opportunity for exploiting time series with low correlation dimension estimates by analyzing complex nonlinear relationships without making prior assumptions about the data distribution.

5.2.2 Normality

A correlation coefficient derived using Pearson's formula makes the implicit assumption that the two variables are jointly normally distributed. In the case of most financial series this assumption is not justified, and a nonparametric measure such as the Spearman rank correlation coefficient might be more appropriate.

Consider the histogram of 15-year S&P daily changes in Figure 5.6. Overlaying the normal (Gaussian) distribution we notice that these are not fully described by the Gaussian model. There are two problems with approximating S&P returns with the normal distribution model. The first is that the vast majority of the returns tend to be located near the center of the distribution and the second—and

FIGURE 5.5 Weekly Composite Chart of the S&P 500 (Thick Line) with Japan's Nikkei Superimposed (Thin Black Line) from 1990 to 2007. The 52-Week Pearson's correlation strength between the S&P 500 and the Nikkei is plotted in the top window.

FIGURE 5.6 Distribution of S&P 500 Daily % Returns for the 15-Year Period from 1992–2006.

most important—is that the actual distribution has fatter and longer tails. This means that the probability of a larger movement in the index is much higher than that predicted by the normal distribution. The Gaussian model predicted a virtually nil (0.000027) probability of a one day 4% decline in the index whereas such events occurred six times during the period from 1 January 1992 to 31 December 2006. This is more obvious in the normal plot in Figure 5.8 where it can be seen that for daily changes greater than 2% or less than −2% the distribution deviates significantly from normality. The volatility and hence the deviation from the normal curve has been exacerbated since the "uptick rule" (a regulation that prohibited short selling following downticks) was abolished by the SEC on 6 July 2007. The effect of the abolition of the uptick rule can be seen graphically in Figure 5.9 which has "fatter" tails (that is, higher frequency at extreme values) than the distribution in Figure 5.6. In addition, the standard deviation of daily changes, which was only 1.0 before the uptick was abolished, increased by more than 30% to 1.3 after the uptick rule was eliminated. It is not certain, however, that the increased volatility can be wholly contributed to the repeal of the uptick rule as it coincided with the sub prime mortgage financial upheaval and the collapse of Bear Stearns. At the time of writing, the situation with the financials has not yet normalized but it would be interesting to see the net effect of this rule on the distribution of daily changes of the S&P 500 as soon as enough data are available for such a study.

In any case, if we have to use statistical metrics that assume normality, it is preferable to use daily or weekly changes instead of raw index values. A comparison of the distribution of raw S&P values in Figure 5.7 with that of daily returns in Figure 5.6 will make this more obvious. In fact, Figure 5.7 bears no resemblance to a normal distribution at all.

FIGURE 5.7 Distribution of S&P 500 Daily Prices for the 15-Year Period from 1992–2006.

FIGURE 5.8 Normality Plot of the S&P 500 15-Year Daily % Returns.

FIGURE 5.9 Distribution of S&P 500 Daily % Returns since the Elimination of the Uptick Rule (from 9 July 2007 Until 5 May 2008). Notice the unusually high frequency of more than −2.5% daily declines during the relatively short period of 210 trading days. the standard deviation also increased by more than 30% and the Kurtosis (which is the variance due to infrequent extreme deviations) increased by more than 700% from 0.43 to 3.77.

FIGURE 5.10 Six Month Scatterplot of the Amex Oil Index (XOI) vs. Nymex Oil Futures. By removing just one outlier (enclosed in the square on the far right of the graph), the correlation improved from 0.523 to 0.568.

■ 5.3 Outliers

Because of the way in which the regression line is determined (especially the fact that it is based on minimizing the sum of the *squares* of distances of data points from the line and not the sum of simple distances) outliers have a significant influence on the slope of the regression line and, consequently, on the value of the correlation coefficient. This is more of a problem when working with financial series with small samples (less than a year's data).

A single outlier is capable of changing the slope of the regression line considerably and, consequently, the value of the correlation, as demonstrated in the following example in Figure 5.10 of the six month scatterplot of the Amex oil index (XOI) vs. the Nymex oil futures daily changes. By removing just one outlier (on the far right of the graph), the correlation improved from 0.523 to 0.568 and the coefficient of determination (r^2) from 0.283 to 0.323.

■ 5.4 Homoscedasticity

In calculating Pearson's correlation coefficient or the regression coefficients, the variance is assumed to be the same at any point along the linear relationship. Otherwise the correlation coefficient is a misleading average of points of higher and lower correlation. A set of random variables having the same variance is called homoscedastic.

FIGURE 5.11 Fifteen Year Scatterplot of the S&P 500 vs. Canada's TSX Composite Index. The plot shows a violation of the assumption of homoscedasticity. For lower values on the TSX-Axis, the points are all very near the regression line, while for higher values the variability around the regression line increases dramatically.

Serious violations in homoscedasticity (assuming a distribution of data is homoscedastic when in actuality it is heteroscedastic) result in underemphasizing the Pearson coefficient. Heteroscedasticity does not invalidate the analysis and can be usually rectified by transforming the price data to yields or logarithms. An example of heteroscedasticity is depicted in Figure 5.11 of the scatterplot of the S&P vs. Canada's TSX index, where the variance is greater for larger values of the indices at the top right of the graph.

CHAPTER 6

Regression

From Markos Katsanos, *Intermarket Trading Strategies* (Hoboken, New Jersey: John Wiley & Sons, 2009), Chapter 3.

Man loves company, even if only that of a small burning candle.
–Georg Christoph Lichtenberg

Regression involves the use of the concept of correlation in predicting future values of one security (dependent variable), in terms of another (independent or predictor variable). For example, if there is high correlation between the S&P 500 and the Euro Stoxx 50 index we can use the linear regression equation to predict future values of the S&P by extending the least squares or linear regression line into the future (Figure 6.1).

The mere fact that we use our knowledge of the relationship between the two indices to predict values of the S&P 500 from the Euro Stoxx doesn't imply that changes in the Euro Stoxx cause changes in the S&P. These could be caused by a number of economic or geopolitical reasons which affect both indices.

■ 6.1 The Regression Equation

The general form of a simple linear regression is:

$$y = bx + a \tag{6.1}$$

where a (regression constant) is the intercept and b (regression coefficient) is the slope of the line, y is the dependent variable and x is the independent variable. Estimates for the values of a and b can be derived by the method of ordinary least squares. The method is called "least squares" because estimates of a and b minimize the sum of squared error estimates for the given data set. The regression constant a and the coefficient b are calculated using the following formulae:

$$b = \frac{\Sigma(x_i - \overline{x})(y_i - \overline{y})}{\Sigma(x_i - \overline{x})^2} = \frac{n\Sigma(xy - \Sigma x \Sigma y}{n\Sigma x^2 - (\Sigma x)^2} \qquad (6.2)$$

$$a = \frac{\Sigma y - b\Sigma x}{n} = \overline{y} - b\overline{x} \qquad (6.3)$$

where $\overline{x}$ is the mean of the x values, and $\overline{y}$ is the mean of the y values.

The formula for the regression coefficient b can be alternatively expressed in terms of Pearson's correlation coefficient r:

$$b = r\frac{s_y}{s_x} \qquad (6.4)$$

where s_x is the standard deviation of the predictor variable x and s_y is the standard deviation of the dependent variable y.

Table 6.1 shows an Excel sheet of one day changes between gold and the dollar index, illustrating the calculation of the regression coefficient and the constant.

Thus the regression equation to predict the dollar index in terms of gold is
Y (dollar) $= -0.314 * X$ (gold) $+ 0.083$

In the following example only 15 data sets were used but in practice more than two years' data need to be taken into account for a reliable prediction.

6.2 Multiple Regression

The concept of linear regression with a single predictor variable can be extended for more than one variable combined into the following equation:

$$y = b_1x_1 + b_1x_1 + \ldots + b_k x_k + a \qquad (6.5)$$

In single regression we fitted a straight line to the scatterplot of points in a two dimensional graph. Extending this concept, the geometry of multiple regression (where two or more predictor variables are involved), would involve fitting a plane in multi-dimensional space.

However, since we live in a three-dimensional world, we cannot visualize the geometry when more than two independent variables are involved. We can extend, however, the same method only mathematically.

The practical problem in multiple linear regression is to select an effective set of predictor variables which will maximize the coefficient of determination, r squared, which is the proportion of variance in the dependent variable that can be explained by the variance of the predictor variables. Therefore, we want to include predictor variables that are highly correlated with the dependent variable but have low correlations among themselves.

As a rule of thumb, intercorrelation among the independents above 0.80 signals a possible problem and may cause the system to become unstable. The statistically

TABLE 6.1 Example of calculating the regression coefficient b and the intercept a using Excel. The Greek letter μ depicts the mean for both the X and Y variables. The variables X and Y are the one day percentage change of gold (spot) and the dollar index respectively from 8 December 2006 to 29 December 2006.

A Date	B X	C Y	D $X - \mu$	E $(X - \mu)^2$	F $X - \mu$	G $(Y - \mu)^2$	H $(X - \mu)(Y - \mu)$	
12/8/06	-1.344	0.60	-1.386	1.921	0.570	0.325	-0.790	3
12/11/06	0.929	-0.132	0.887	0.787	-0.202	0.041	-0.179	4
12/12/06	-0.008	-0.289	-0.050	0.003	-0.359	0.129	0.018	5
12/13/06	-0.325	0.470	-0.367	0.135	0.400	0.160	-0.147	6
12/14/06	-0.430	0.444	-0.472	0.223	0.374	0.140	-0.176	7
12/15/06	-1.664	0.406	-1.706	2.910	0.336	0.113	-0.573	8
12/18/06	0.163	-0.036	0.121	0.015	-0.106	0.011	-0.013	9
12/19/06	1.088	-0.667	1.046	1.094	-0.737	0.543	-0.771	10
12/20/06	-0.402	0.096	-0.444	0.197	0.026	0.001	-0.011	11
12/21/06	-0.250	0.072	-0.292	0.085	0.002	0.000	-0.001	12
12/22/06	0.332	0.263	0.290	0.084	0.193	0.037	0.056	13
12/26/06	0.613	0.298	0.571	0.326	0.228	0.052	0.130	14
12/27/06	0.401	-0.107	0.359	0.129	-0.177	0.031	-0.064	15
12/28/06	1.133	-0.179	1.091	1.190	-0.249	0.062	-0.272	16
12/29/06	0.394	-0.227	0.352	0.124	-0.297	0.088	-0.105	17
Σ	0.630	1.052		9.223		1.733	-2.897	18
n	15	15			Covariance $\sigma_{xy} =$		-0.207	19
mean μ	0.042	0.070			Pearson's Correlation **r**		-0.725	20
σ	0.812	0.352			Regression Coef. b (formula 6.2)		-0.314	21
					Regression Coef. b (formula 6.4)		-0.314	22
					Regression Constant a =		0.083	23
					Regression Constant a =		0.083	24

Formula for Column H

Row	
21	H18/E18
22	H20*C21/B21
23	(C18-H21*B18)/B19
24	(C18-H21*B18)/B19

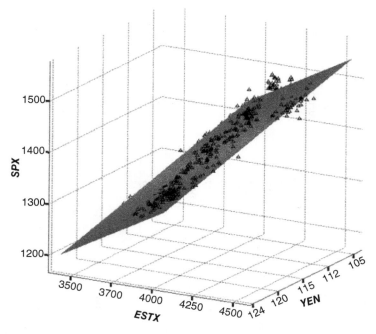

FIGURE 6.1 Three-dimensional scatterplot visualizing the relationship between the S&P 500 (on the *Y*-axis) vs. the Euro Stoxx 50 (on the *X*-axis) and the yen (on the *Z*-axis) for the 2-year period from 1 January 2006 to 31 December 2007. The more points fall inside the regression plane the better the predictive power of the regression model.

preferred method of assessing multicollinearity is to calculate the tolerance coefficient for each independent variable.

Tolerance is $1 - r^2$ (one minus the coefficient of determination) for the regression of each independent variable on all the other independents, ignoring the dependent. There will be as many tolerance coefficients as there are independents. The higher the intercorrelation of the independents, the more the tolerance will approach zero. As a rule of thumb, if tolerance is less than 0.20, a problem with multicollinearity is indicated.

High multicollinearity can be ignored when two or more independents are components of an index, and high intercorrelation among them is intentional and desirable. These are usually combined in an index prior to running regression, but when this is not practically possible they can be entered individually. For example, if data for an obscure index are not readily available some of the component stocks can be used instead of the index itself.

Perhaps this is better understood with an example. Let's say that we want to design an intermarket system to trade the S&P 500. The first step is to calculate the correlation between the S&P 500 with major international equity, commodity and financial indices.

Because of normality and linearity problems associated with raw index prices, these are converted to weekly percentage yields and the correlation matrix is calculated (depicted in Table 6.2). The next step is to add to the regression equation

TABLE 6.2 Correlation matrix of weekly % yields of major international indices, the CBOE volatility index (VIX,) the Utility Index (UTY) and the 10-year Treasury yield (TNX) with the S&P 500 for the 5-year period from 1 January 2001 to 31 December 2006.

	S&P 500	ESTX	DAX	CAC 40	FTSE	Nikkei	VIX	UTY	TNX
S&P 500	1	0.81	0.80	0.80	0.74	0.42	−0.72	0.60	0.39
ESTX	0.81	1	0.94	0.97	0.88	0.49	−0.57	0.43	0.45
DAX	0.80	0.94	1	0.92	0.82	0.51	−0.56	0.39	0.49
CAC 40	0.80	0.97	0.92	1	0.89	0.49	−0.56	0.43	0.46
FTSE	0.74	0.88	0.82	0.89	1	0.45	−0.54	0.40	0.42
Nikkei	0.42	0.49	0.51	0.49	0.45	1	−0.36	0.21	0.29
VIX	−0.72	−0.57	−0.56	−0.56	−0.54	−0.36	1	−0.43	−0.25
UTY	0.60	0.43	0.39	0.43	0.40	0.21	−0.43	1	0.04
TNX	0.39	0.45	0.49	0.46	0.42	0.29	−0.25	0.04	1

the predictor variables one at a time and calculate the coefficient of determination (r squared) and the tolerance for each variable. As you can see in Table 6.3, including more than three variables will only improve r squared marginally or not at all and the tolerance drops below 0.2 for a number of cross correlated variables. Thus the first step is to exclude the DAX, FTSE, and CAC 40 since they are highly correlated with the ESTX (Euro Stoxx). The Nikkei is then dropped from the analysis as it doesn't improve the r squared coefficient at all. The remaining variables are the ESTX, VIX, and UTY (model 3) and the regression equation becomes:

$$SP = 0.366 * ESTX - 0.067 * VIX + 0.206 * UTY + 0.045 \tag{6.6}$$

where SP, ESTX, VIX, TNX, and UTY are weekly percentage changes of the corresponding indices.

TABLE 6.3 The coefficient of determination (r^2), the r^2 change and the tolerance are depicted for each model. The first model includes only the Euro Stoxx, the second includes the Euro Stoxx and the VIX, and one more index is added for each subsequent model.

Model	r^2	r^2 change	Tolerance							
			ESTX	VIX	UTY	TNX	DAX	FTSE	CAC 40	Nikkei
1	0.65	0.65	1.00							
2	0.75	0.10	0.67	0.67						
3	**0.79**	**0.05**	**0.63**	**0.63**	**0.77**					
4	0.80	0.01	0.52	0.63	0.74	0.77				
5	0.81	0.01	0.12	0.62	0.74	0.74	0.12			
6	0.81	0.00	0.08	0.62	0.74	0.73	0.12	0.21		
7	0.81	0.00	0.05	0.62	0.73	0.73	0.11	0.19	0.05	
8	0.81	0.00	0.05	0.60	0.73	0.73	0.11	0.19	0.05	0.72

Substituting the values for ESTX, VIX, and UTY for 11/7/06 in (3.6):

$$SP = 0.366^* 1.7 - 0.067^* (-0.09) + 0.206^* (-1.6) + 0.045 = 0.343\% \text{vs } 0.36\%$$

the actual S&P 500 weekly change for the specific week.

■ 6.3 Assumptions

The correlation assumptions discussed in Chapter 5 are also valid for regression, since according to (6.4) regression is directly proportional to correlation.

The most important assumption is that of linearity. Checking that the linearity assumption is met is an essential task before using a regression model, as substantial violation of linearity means regression results may be more or less unusable.

Simple inspection of scatterplots is a common, if nonstatistical, method of determining if nonlinearity exists in a relationship. An alternative is to fit a preliminary linear regression and to use the appropriate diagnostic plots to detect departures from linearity. Transforming one of the variables (for example by taking differences or logs) can sometimes help linearize a nonlinear relationship between two financial series.

Normality is also a problem when considering raw stock or index prices but it is less of a problem when taking log differences or percentage yields. The problem of the longer tails can be partially overcome by removing some of the most extreme outliers.

Normality can be visually assessed by looking at a histogram of frequencies. Alternatively you can use a formal normality test such as the Shapiro-Wilks W test or the Kolmogorov-Smirnov D test.

■ 6.4 Nonparametric Regression

Nonparametric regression relaxes the usual assumption of linearity and makes no assumptions about the population distribution.

A more accurate estimate of the prediction is usually obtained by using nonparametric regression in cases of severe violations of linearity at the expense of much greater computation and a more difficult-to-understand result.

Two common methods of nonparametric regression are kernel regression and smoothing splines. The smoothing splines method minimizes the sum of squared residuals, adding a term which penalizes the roughness of the fit. The kernel regression algorithm falls into a class of algorithms called "SVMs" or "Support Vector Machines." SVM-based techniques typically use a kernel function to find an optimal separating hyperplane so as to separate two classes of patterns with maximal margin. SVM models are closely related to neural network models.

In recent years, SVMs have received considerable attention because of their superior performance in forecasting high noise and nonstationary financial time series. A major advantage of SVMs over other nonparametric methods is that they can have good performance even in problems with a large number of inputs. However, unlike other nonparametric methods the major difficulty of the SVM approach lies in the selection of its kernel, as choosing different kernel functions will produce different SVMs.

CHAPTER 7

Regression Analysis

From Perry J. Kaufman, *Trading Systems and Methods, +Website*, 5th Edition (Hoboken, New Jersey: John Wiley & Sons, 2013), Chapter 6.

ARIMA

An *Autoregressive Integrated Moving Average (ARIMA)* model is created by a process of repeated regression analysis over a moving time window, resulting in a forecast value based on the new fit. An ARIMA process automatically applies the most important features of regression analysis in a preset order and continues to reanalyze results until an optimum set of parameters or coefficients is found. In Level III, Chapter 10, the selection and testing of individual parameters within a trading strategy are discussed. This involves approximating their initial value and identifying a testing range. An ARIMA model does all of this as part of its special process. Because it is used to recalculate the *best fit* each time a new piece of data appears, it may be thought of as an *adaptive process.*

G. E. P. Box and G. M. Jenkins refined ARIMA at the University of Wisconsin,[1] and their procedures for solution have become the industry standard. This technique is often referred to as the *Box-Jenkins forecast.* The two important terms in ARIMA are *autoregression* and *moving average.* *Autoregression* refers to the use of the same data to self-predict, for example, using only gold prices to arrive at a gold price forecast. *Moving average* refers to the normal concept of smoothing price fluctuations, using a rolling average of the past *n* days. The moving average and popular variations are discussed thoroughly in Chapters 8 and 9. This process uses an exponential smoothing technique, which is convenient for computation.

In the ARIMA process, the autocorrelation is used to determine to what extent past prices will forecast future prices. In a *first-order autocorrelation*, only the prices on the previous day are used to determine the forecast. This would be expressed as

$$p_t = a \times p_{t-1} + e$$

[1] G.E.P. Box and G.M. Jenkins, *Time Series Analysis: Forecasting and Control,* 2nd ed. (San Francisco: Holden-Day, 1976).

where p_t = the price being forecast (dependent variable)
p_{t-1} = the price being used to forecast (independent variable)
a = the coefficient (constant factor)
e = the forecast error

In a *second-order autoregression*, the previous two prices are used,

$$p_t = a_1 \times p_{t-1} + a_2 \times p_{t-2} + e$$

where the current forecast p_t is based on the two previous prices p_{t-1} and p_{t-2}; there are two unique coefficients and a forecast error. The moving average is used to correct for the forecast error, e. There is also the choice of a first- or second-order moving average process,

First-order: $\qquad E_t = e_t - be_{t-1}$

Second-order: $\qquad E_t = e_t - b_1 e_{t-1} - b_2 e_{t-2}$

where $\qquad E_t$ = the approximated error term
e_t = today's forecast error
e_{t-1} and e_{t-2} = the two previous forecast errors
b_1 and b_2 = the two regression coefficients

Because the two constant coefficients, b_1 and b_2, can be considered percentages, the moving average process is similar to exponential smoothing.

The success of the ARIMA model is determined by two factors: high correlation in the autoregression and low variance in the final forecast errors. The determination of whether to use a first- or second-order autoregression is based on a comparison of the *correlation coefficients* of the two regressions. If there is little improvement using the second-order process, it is not used. The final forecast is constructed by adding the moving average term, which approximates the errors, back into the autoregressive process

$$p'_t = p_t + E_t + e'$$

where $\qquad P'_t$ = the new forecast
e' = the new forecast error

The moving average process is again repeated for the new errors e', added back into the forecast to get a new value p'' and another error e''. When the variance of the errors becomes sufficiently small, the ARIMA process is complete.

The contribution of Box and Jenkins was to stress the simplicity of the solution. They determined that the autoregression and moving average steps could be limited to first- or second-order processes. To do this, it was first necessary to *detrend* the data, thereby making it *stationary*. Detrending can be accomplished most easily by *differencing* the data, creating a new series by subtracting each previous term p_{t-1} from the next p_t. Of course, the ARIMA program must remember all of these changes, or *transformations,* in order to restore the final forecast to the proper price notation by applying these operations in reverse. If a satisfactory solution is not found in the Box-Jenkins process, it is usually because the data are still not stationary and further differencing is necessary.

With the three features just discussed, the Box-Jenkins forecast is usually shown as *ARIMA (p, d, q),* where *p* is the number of autoregressive terms, *d* is the number of differences, and *q* is the number of moving average terms. The expression *ARIMA* (0,1,1) is equivalent to simple exponential smoothing, a common technique discussed in the next chapter. In its normal form, the Box-Jenkins ARIMA process performs the following steps:

1. **Specification.** Preliminary steps for determining the order of the autoregression and moving average to be used:

   ■ *The variance must be stabilized.* In many price series, increased volatility is directly related to increased price. In stocks, the common assumption is that this relationship is *log-normal*, that increasing volatility takes the shape of a logarithmic curve. A simple test for variance stability, using the log function, is checked before more complex transformations are used.

   ■ *Prices are detrended.* This uses the technique of first differences; however, a second difference (or more) will be performed if it helps to remove further trending properties in the series (this is determined by later steps).

   ■ *Specify the order of the autoregressive and moving average components.* This fixes the number of prior terms to be used in these approximations (not necessarily the same number). In the Box-Jenkins approach, these numbers should be as small as possible; often one value is used for both. Large numbers require a rapidly expanding amount of calculation, even for a computer.

      The number of terms is a critical part of the ARIMA solution. The object of this last step is to find the fewest terms necessary to solve the problem. All ARIMA programs will print a *correlogram,* a display of the autocorrelation coefficients. The correlogram is used to find whether all the trends and well-defined periodic movements have been removed from the series by differencing. Figure 7.1 shows the output from ProStat for 15 lags using the first differences of 20 years of gold futures prices. If any of the correlations had been significant (for example, over 0.40), the data would be differenced again. The correlogram is one way of visualizing serial correlation, the dependence of current data on previous data. This same objective will be accomplished differently using a Monte Carlo process to estimate investment risk, discussed in Level III, Chapter 12.

2. **Estimation: determining the coefficients.** The previous step was used to reduce the number of autoregressive and moving average terms necessary to the estimation process. The ARIMA method of solution is one of minimizing the errors in the forecast. In minimization, it will perform a linear or nonlinear regression on price (depending on the number of coefficients selected),

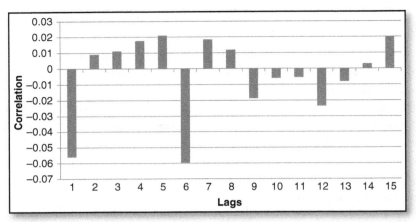

FIGURE 7.1 ARIMA Correlograms from Autocorrelations. Lags shown along the bottom give correlations at the left. None of them are significant (output from ProStat based on gold futures).

determine the errors in the estimation, and then approximate those errors using a moving average. It will next look at the resulting new error series, attempt to estimate and correct the errors in that one, and repeat the process until it cannot improve results further.

To determine when an ARIMA process is completed, three tests are performed at the end of each estimation pass:

1. *Compare the change in the coefficient value.* If the last estimation has caused little or no change in the value of the coefficient(s), the model has successfully converged to a solution.
2. *Compare the sum of the squares of the error.* If the error value is small or if it stays relatively unchanged, the process is completed.
3. *Perform a set number of estimations.* Unless a maximum number of estimations is set, an ARIMA process might continue indefinitely. This safety check is necessary in the event the model is not converging to a solution.

Once completed, the errors can be examined using an *O*-statistic to check for any trend. If one exists, an additional moving average term may be used to eliminate it.

Forecast Results

Once the coefficients have been determined, they are used to calculate the forecast value. These forecasts are most accurate for the next day and should be used with less confidence for subsequent days (see Figure 7.2).

What if the forecast does not work? First, the process should be checked to be certain that it was performed properly. Be sure that any data transformations were reversed. Pay particular attention to the removal of trends using the correlogram. Next, check the data used in the process. If the data sample is changing (which can be observed on a price chart), select either a shorter or longer period that contains more homogeneous data, that is, data similar to the current market period.

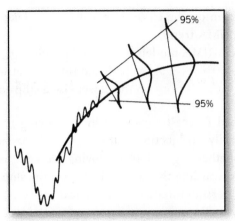

FIGURE 7.2   ARIMA Forecast Becomes Less Accurate as It Is Used Further Ahead.

ARIMA Trading Strategies

In the article that originally piqued the interest of traders,[2] Anon uses a 5-day-ahead forecast. If the ARIMA process forecasts an uptrend and prices fall below the forecast value, the market can be bought with added confidence (expecting lower risk and more profit by buying at a price that is below estimated value). This technique of selecting better entry points may compensate for some of the inaccuracies latent in any forecasting method. The danger of this approach is that prices may continue to move counter to the forecast.

Following the Trend   Use the 1-day-ahead forecast to determine the trend position. Hold a long position if the forecast is for higher prices, and take a short position if the process is expecting lower prices.

Mean-Reverting Indicator   Use the ARIMA confidence bands to determine overbought/oversold levels. Not only can a long position be entered when prices penetrate the *lowest* 95% confidence band, but they can be closed out when they return to the normal 50% level. Although mean reversion trades are tempting, they always carry more risk than trend trading. A conservative trader will enter the market only in the direction of the ARIMA trend forecast. As shown in Figure 7.2, if the trend is up, only the penetrations of a lower confidence band will be used to enter new long positions.

Use of Highs and Lows   The implied highs and lows, as well as the independently forecasted highs and lows, can be the basis for other interesting strategies.[3] The following two are used with intraday prices.

1. Using confidence bands based on the closing prices, buy an intraday penetration of the expected high or sell short a penetration of the expected low, and

[2] Louis J. Anon, "Catch Short-Term Profits with ARIMA," *Commodities Magazine* (December 1981).
[3] John F. Kepka, "Trading with ARIMA Forecasts," *Technical Analysis of Stocks & Commodities* (August 1985).

liquidate the position on the close. Use a stop-loss. Take positions only in the direction of the ARIMA trend.

2. Using the separate ARIMA models based on the daily high and low prices, buy a penetration of the 50% level of the high and sell a penetration of the 50% level of the lows. Liquidate positions on the close. Use a stop-loss.

Slope The 1-day-ahead forecast suggested in "Following the Trend" a few paragraphs earlier is essentially a projection of the slope of the trendline. The purpose of directional analysis, whether regression or moving averages, is to uncover the true direction of prices by discarding the noise. Therefore, the slope of the trendline, or the direction of the regression forecast, is the logical answer.

The popular alternate for triggering a new directional signal is a price penetration of an envelope or band value. Using regression analysis, that band can be replaced by a confidence level. While it is true that the number of random, or false, penetrations declines as the confidence band gets farther away from the trendline, so does the total number of penetrations. At any band distance, there are still a large number of erroneous signals. The slope itself should be viewed as the best approximation of direction.

Kalman Filters

Kalman offers an alternative approach to ARIMA, allowing an underlying forecasting model (*message model*) to be combined with other timely information (*observation model*). The message model may be any trading strategy, moving average, or regression approach. The observation model may be the specialist's or floor broker's opening calls, market liquidity, or earlier trading activity in the same stock or index market on a foreign exchange—all of which have been determined to good candidate inputs for forecasting.

Assume that the original forecast (message) model can be described as

$$M\left(P_t\right) = c_f P_{t-1} + me_t$$

and the observation model as

$$O\left(P_t\right) = c_0 P_t + oe_t$$

where *me* and *oe* are the message and observation model errors, respectively.

The combined forecast would then use the observation model error to modify the result

$$p'_{t+1} = c_f p'_t + K_{t+1} oe_t$$

where K is the Kalman gain coefficient,[4] a factor that adjusts the error term.

---

[4] For a more complete discussion, see Andrew D. Seidel and Philip D. Ginsberg, *Commodities Trading* (Englewood Cliffs, NJ: Prentice-Hall, 1983), or R. E. Kalman, "A New Approach to Linear Filtering and Prediction Problems," *Journal of Basic Engineering* (March 1960).

■ Basic Trading Signals Using a Linear Regression Model

A linear regression, or straight-line fit, could be the basis for a simple trading strategy similar to a moving average. For example, an n-day linear regression, applied to the closing prices, can produce a 1-day-ahead forecast price, F_{t+1}, a projection of the slope. We can use this with the following rules for trading:

- *Buy* when tomorrow's closing price (C_{t+1}) moves above the forecasted value of tomorrow's close (F_{t+1}).

- *Sell short* when tomorrow's closing price (C_{t+1}) moves below the forecasted value of tomorrow's close (F_{t+1}).[5]

Adding Confidence Bands

Because the linear regression line passes through the center of price movement during a steady period of rising or falling prices, these rules would produce a lot of buy and sell signals. To reduce the frequency of signals and avoid changes of direction due to market noise, confidence bands are drawn on either side of the regression line. A 90% confidence band is simply 1.65 times the standard deviation of the residuals (R_t, the difference between the actual prices and the corresponding value on the regression line as of time t, the most recent price). A 95% confidence band uses a multiplier of 1.96; however, most people use 2.0 simply for convenience. The new trading rules using a 95% confidence band would then become

- *Buy* when tomorrow's closing price (C_{t+1}) moves above the forecasted value of tomorrow's close (F_{t+1}) + ($2.0 \times R_t$).

- *Sell short* when tomorrow's closing price (C_{t+1}) moves below the forecasted value of tomorrow's close (F_{t+1}) − ($2.0 \times R_t$).

An important difference between a model based on linear regression and one founded on a moving average is the lag. Both methods assume that prices will continue to move according to the pattern identified using the last price data available. If prices continue higher at the same rate, a moving average system will initially lag behind, then increase at the same rate. The lag creates a safety zone to absorb some minor changes in the direction of prices without indicating that the trend has changed. (See Chapter 8 for a complete discussion of moving averages, and Chapter 9 for a comparison of a linear regression slope trading system with five other popular trending methods.)

A regression model, however, identifies a change of direction sooner by measuring tomorrow's actual price against the projected future price (a straight-line projection for a linear regression). Confidence bands around the straight-line projection will decide the size of the price move up or down needed to change the trend direction. Figure 7.3 shows the changing direction of a rolling linear regression at three points in time

---

[5] These rules were used by Frank Hochheimer and Richard Vaughn in *Computerized Trading Techniques 1982* (New York: Merrill Lynch Commodities, 1982).

FIGURE 7.3 Linear Regression Model. Penetration of the confidence band turns the trend from up to down. When prices move steadily up, the regression model will signal a change of direction faster than a moving average.

compared to a moving average. At the most recent period on the chart the reversal point for the trend direction is much closer using the confidence bands of the regression than the lagged moving average. This may not be the case during the intervals where price changes direction at the bottom of the chart. The Companion Website has a spreadsheet, *Bund regression with bands*, that produces trading signals and performance using regression bands. It also compares the results with the slope method described in the next section.

In general, the use of regression lines works well for finding the price trend, although actual trading signals differ from moving average and breakout strategies. As with most trending systems, performance tends to improve as the calculation period increases, capturing the largest economic trends.

Using the Linear Regression Slope

The slope of the linear regression line, the angle at which it is rising or falling, is an effective way to simplify the usefulness of the regression process. The slope shows how quickly prices are expected to change over a unit of time. The unit of time is the same as the period of data used to find the regression values. When you use a longer calculation period, the slope of the regression line changes slowly; when you use only a few days in your calculation, the slope changes quickly. Using only the slope, you can trade with the following rules:

- *Buy* when the value of the slope is positive (rising).

- *Sell* when the value of the slope is negative (falling).

When using the slope, there is less need for a confidence band because the longer calculation periods smooth out erratic price movement. The scale of the slope is

FIGURE 7.4   IBM Trend Using the Slope and R.

different from the prices; therefore it will be seen in a separate panel on a chart (the middle panel in Figure 7.4). The linear regression slope will be compared to other trending techniques in Chapter 9 and its performance is competitive.

Adding Correlations

The slope is a practical substitution for the regression line and confidence bands, but it can also be misleading. It is possible to have the same slope value while prices are moving higher in both a smooth pattern or in a very noisy, erratic one. Using the correlation coefficient, R^2, will provide a measurement of the consistency of the price movement.[6]

Instead of R^2, which is always positive, R will be used. And, instead of using the usual price differences (or return differences), the actual prices will be used and correlated against a series of sequential numbers. This should give us a better value for whether the prices are trending. If R becomes negative then prices are trending down. This can be seen in the bottom panel of Figure 7.4. A 60-day moving average of prices is shown at the top, a corresponding 60-day slope is in the middle, and a 60-day R is at the bottom along with a 30-day (R-period/2) trend of R.

The trading rules for the slope are normally the same as those for a moving average: a long position is entered when the trendline or slope turns up and a short sale begins when the trendline turns down; however, the slope today can be less than yesterday but still positive, which means that the trend is still up. Then another rule would be to buy when the slope turns positive and sell short when it turns negative.

Figure 7.4 shows that using the moving average trend is good, but has the greatest lag. The slope is much faster but less stable. Adding R gives a different view of where the trends change and can complement either method.

Forecast Oscillator

Tushar Chande used the regression forecast and its residuals to create trend-following signals called the *Forecast Oscillator*.[7] Using a 5-day regression, find the residuals and

---

[6] See Rudy Tesco, "LRS + R-Squared = the 95% Solution," *Technical Analysis of Stocks & Commodities* (February 2003).

[7] Tushar S. Chande and Stanley Kroll, *The New Technical Trader* (New York: John Wiley & Sons, 1994).

calculate the percentage variation from the regression line. A buy signal occurs when the 3-day average of the residuals crosses above the regression line; a short sale is when the 3-day average of the residuals crosses below the regression line. If

$$\%F_t = 100 \times \frac{y_t - \hat{y}_t}{y_t}$$

and $\%F_t(3)$ is the 3-day moving average of $\%F$, then

> *buy* when $\%F_t(3)$ crosses above $\hat{y}_t$
> *sell short* when $\%F_t(3)$ crosses below $\hat{y}_t$

This makes the assumption that the residuals have a trending quality.

◼ Measuring Market Strength

One of the natural applications of the linear regression is to measure and compare the strength of one market against another. For example, we might want to ask, "Which market is leading the other, Hewlett Packard or Dell? The slope of the linear regression, measured over the same calculation period, is the perfect tool for comparing, or *ranking*, a set of markets. Figure 7.5 shows the prices of four pharmaceutical companies, Amgen (AMGN), Johnson & Johnson (JNJ), Merck (MRK), and Pfizer (PFE). Which of them is the strongest during the last 60 days? No doubt it's PFE, the line at the bottom. But the weakest is not as clear.

FIGURE 7.5 Prices of Four Pharmaceutical Companies, 2010 through January 2011.

In order to rank these correctly, it is best to index the stock prices, starting at 100 on the same date. For only stocks, indexing is not necessary, but if you are mixing stocks and futures, or just using futures, indexing will be needed to put the trading units into the same notation. Figure 7.6 shows the indexed stocks beginning at the value of 100.

FIGURE 7.6 Indexed Stocks beginning at 100 Give a Better View of Relative Performance.

Once indexed, apply a rolling linear regression slope to each market using the same calculation period, 60 days in this example. Figure 7.7 shows that that PFE was the most volatile because the slope varied from much higher to much lower than the others, while each stock had its turn at being the strongest and weakest. At the right side of the chart, PFE finishes the strongest followed by AMGN, MRK, and JNJ. In Level III, Chapter 2 this technique will be used to create a classic market neutral strategy. The basis of the strategy is to either buy the strongest stocks and sell short the weakest, or sell short the strongest and buy the weakest. In either case, strongest and weakest are determined by the slope of the regression rather than a moving average trend.

FIGURE 7.7 Rolling Linear Regression Slope, Using a 60-day Calculation Period, Shows That Each Market Changes from Stronger to Weaker over the 1-Year Period.

CHAPTER 8

Time-Based Trend Calculations

From Perry J. Kaufman, *Trading Systems and Methods, + Website*, 5th Edition (Hoboken, New Jersey: John Wiley & Sons, 2013), Chapter 7.

The purpose of all trend identification methods is to remove the underlying noise in the market, those erratic moves that seem to be meaningless, and find the current direction of prices. But trends are somewhat dependent upon your time horizon. There may be more than one trend at any one time, caused by short-term events and long-term policy, and it is likely that one trader will search for the strongest, or most dominant trend, while another will seek a series of shorter-term moves. There is no "right" or "wrong" trend but a choice of benefits and compromises.

The technique that is used to uncover a particular trend can depend upon whether any of the underlying trend characteristics are known. Does the stock or futures market have a clear seasonal or cyclic component, such as the travel industry or coffee prices; or does it respond to long-term monetary policy based on the cost of servicing debt or interest income? If you know more about the reasons why prices trend, you will be able to choose the best method of finding the trend and the calculation period.

Chapter 7 used regression to find the direction of a single price series (based on one market and time), the relationship between two markets, and the ranking of both similar and diverse markets. Once you know that there is a fundamental relationship between data, a formula can be found that expresses one price movement in terms of the other prices and economic data. The predictive qualities of these methods are best when applied to data that have been seen before, that is, prices that are within the range of historic data. Forecasting reliability decreases when values are extrapolated outside the previous range of value. The most popular trend models, discussed in this chapter, ignore the reasons why trends exist and generalize the process of smoothing prices in order to find a trend's direction.

■ Forecasting and Following

There is a clear distinction between forecasting the trend and finding the current trend. Forecasting, predicting the future price, is much more desirable but very complex. As shown in the Chapter 7, it involves combining those data that are most important to price change and assigning a value to each one. The results are always expressed with a confidence level, the level of uncertainty in the forecast. There is always lower confidence as you try to forecast further into the future.

The techniques most commonly used for evaluating the direction or tendency of prices both within prior ranges or at new levels are called *autoregressive* functions. Unlike forecasting models, they are only concerned with evaluating the current price direction. This analysis concludes that prices are moving in an upward, downward, or sideways direction, with no indication of confidence. From this simple basis, it is possible to form rules of action and develop complex trading strategies.

All of these techniques make the assumptions that past data can be used to predict future price movement, and that the direction of prices today is the most likely forecast of the direction of prices tomorrow. For the most part, these assumptions have proved to be true. From a practical viewpoint, these trending methods are more flexible than the traditional regression models, but to achieve success they introduce a lag. A *lag* is a delay in the identification of the trend. Great effort has been spent trying to reduce this lag in an attempt to identify the trend sooner; however, the lag is the zone of uncertainty that allows the technique to ignore most of the market noise.

In an autoregressive model, one or more previous prices determine the next sequential price. If p_t represents today's price, p_{t-1} yesterday's price, and so on, then tomorrow's expected price will be

$$p_{t+1} = a_0 + a_1 p_t + a_2 p_{t-1} + \cdots + a_t p_1 + e$$

where each price is given a corresponding weight a_i and then combined to give the resultant price for tomorrow $p_{t+1} + e$ (where e represents an error factor, usually ignored). The simplest example is the use of yesterday's price alone to generate tomorrow's price:

$$p_{t+1} = a_0 + a_1 p_{t-1} + e$$

which you may also recognize as the formula for a straight line, $y = a + bx$, plus an error factor.

The autoregressive model does not have to be linear; each prior day can have a nonlinear predictive quality. Then each expected price p_{t+1}, could be represented by a curvilinear expression, $p_{t+1} = a_0 + a_1 p_t + a_2 p^2_{t-1} + e$, or by an exponential or logarithmic formula, $\ln p_{t+1} = a_0 + a_1 \ln p_t + a_2 \ln p_{t-1} + e$, which is commonly used in equity analysis. Any of these expressions could then be combined to form an autoregressive forecasting model for p_{t+1}. In going from the simple to the complex, it is natural to want to know which of these choices will perform best. Theoretically, the best method will be the one that, when used in a strategy, yields the highest return for the lowest risk; however, every investor has a personal risk preference. The answer can only be found by applying and comparing different methods, and experiencing how they perform when actually traded. It turns out that the best historic result often comes from *overfitting* the data, and is a poor choice for trading. At the end of Chapter 9 there is a comparison of popular trending systems, and Level III, Chapter 10 will show testing methods that are most likely to lead to robust results. Throughout the book there will be comparisons of systems and methods that are similar.

Least-Squares Model

The least-squares regression model is the same technique that was used in the previous chapter to find the relationship between two markets—Barrick Gold and cash gold, corn and soybeans—or to find how price movement could be explained by the main factors influencing them, supply and demand. Most trading systems depend only on price; therefore, we will look again using the least-squares model with time as the independent variable and price as the dependent variable. The regression results will be used in an autoregressive way to forecast the price n-days ahead, and we will look at the accuracy of those predictions. The slope of the resulting straight line or curvilinear fit will determine the direction of the trend.

Error Analysis

A simple error analysis can be used to show how time works against the predictive qualities of regression, or any forecasting method. Using 10 years of General Electric (GE) prices, ending February 15, 2010, the slope and y-intercept are calculated for a rolling 20 days. The 1-, 2-, 3-, 5-, and 10-day ahead forecast is found by projecting the slope by that number of days. The forecast error is the difference between the projected price and the actual price. Figure 8.1 shows the price for GE from December 31, 2010, through February 15, 2011, along with the five forecast prices. Even though the price move seems to be increasing steadily, the forecasts get farther away as the days ahead become larger. This result is typical of forecasting error, regardless of the method, and argues that the smallest forecast interval is the best.

The method of finding the forecast error is shown in Table 8.1 (the full spreadsheet can be found on the Companion Website as *TSM General Electric regression error forecast*). Only the closing prices are needed, and they appear in column 3. The slope and

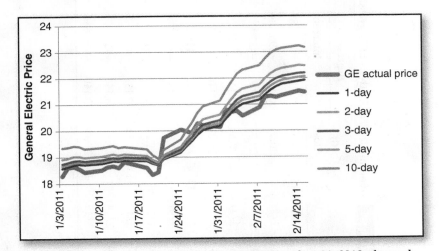

FIGURE 8.1 General Electric Price from December 31, 2010, through February 15, 2011. Forecast accuracy decreases as the forecast period increases.

TABLE 8.1   General Electric Analysis of Regression Error Based on a 20-Day Rolling Calculation Period

Seq	Date	GE Close	Regression		Forecast					Forecast error				
			Slope	Intercept	1-day	2-day	3-day	5-day	10-day	1-day	2-day	3-day	5-day	10-day
n	2/1/2011	20.80	0.118	−351.689	20.438	20.556	20.675	20.911	21.502	−0.616	−0.669	−0.769	−1.128	−1.404
$n+1$	2/2/2011	20.71	0.131	−390.484	20.673	20.804	20.934	21.195	21.848	−0.272	−0.420	−0.478	−0.791	−1.406
$n+2$	2/3/2011	20.75	0.141	−422.673	20.886	21.027	21.168	21.449	22.154	−0.077	−0.194	−0.354	−0.535	−1.657
$n+3$	2/4/2011	20.56	0.144	−432.439	21.019	21.162	21.306	21.594	22.314	0.326	0.244	0.115	−0.128	−1.616
$n+4$	2/7/2011	20.87	0.146	−440.206	21.166	21.313	21.459	21.752	22.484	0.149	0.157	0.064	−0.262	−1.588
$n+5$	2/8/2011	21.28	0.152	−458.803	21.367	21.519	21.672	21.976	22.738	−0.114	−0.118	−0.112	−0.369	−1.615
$n+6$	2/9/2011	21.31	0.156	−471.628	21.544	21.700	21.857	22.169	22.952	0.057	0.003	−0.004	−0.115	−1.301
$n+7$	2/10/2011	21.27	0.157	−471.985	21.675	21.831	21.988	22.301	23.084	0.274	0.249	0.189	0.179	−0.957
$n+8$	2/11/2011	21.33	0.152	−459.262	21.769	21.921	22.074	22.379	23.141	0.345	0.370	0.342	0.264	−0.654
$n+9$	2/14/2011	21.50	0.150	−452.185	21.879	22.029	22.180	22.480	23.231	0.269	0.331	0.357	0.252	−0.566
$n+10$	2/15/2011	21.46	0.140	−419.686	21.914	22.054	22.193	22.473	23.173	0.419	0.461	0.528	0.516	−0.322

TABLE 8.2 **The Standard Deviation of Errors for Different "Days Ahead" Forecasts**

Days Ahead	1	2	3	5	10
Stdev of Errors	1.137	1.336	1.519	1.860	2.672

intercept use the sequential numbers in column 1 for X, and the GE prices for Y. The n-day ahead forecast is

$$y_{t+n} = Intercept_t + Slope_t \times Price_t + n \times Slope_t$$

The standard deviations of the five forecast errors (Table 8.2), taken over the entire 10 years, shows the error increasing as the days-ahead increase. This confirms the expectation that forecasting accuracy decreases with time and that confidence bands will get wider with time. For this reason, any forecasts used in strategies will be 1-day ahead.

Limiting the Forecast to Direction

To be profitable trading a trending system, it is only necessary to be correct in one of the following two cases:

1. In more than 50% of the days you are correct in predicting whether prices will go up or down and the average up move is equal to the average down move.
2. Your forecast accuracy is less than 50% but the size of the correct moves is greater than the size of the incorrect moves.

Unfortunately, there is no way to prove that a particular method of forecasting, moving average, regression, or other techniques will be accurate over all calculation periods. The fact is that some calculation periods are profitable and others are not. Those that are profitable must satisfy one of the two conditions stated above. Therefore, the answer is *it's true when it works and not true when it doesn't work.*

Experience shows that the best choice of trending method will be the one that is profitable over most markets and most calculation periods. Even then, shorter calculation periods have no trend, so we need to restrict our statement to longer periods.

The methods discussed in the remainder of this chapter are all intended to identify the direction of prices based on past data. The trading systems that use them all assume that there is a better chance of prices continuing in that direction the next day. If the systems are profitable then the assumption was correct. There is sufficient performance history for macrotrend funds that justify this conclusion. These systems will be discussed in the next chapter.

■ Price Change over Time

The most basic of all trend indicators is the change of price over some period of time. This is written as

$$M_t = p_t - p_{t-n}$$

where M is called *momentum*, t is today, and n is the number of days. Sometimes this is called *rate of change*, but both momentum and rate of change are incorrect names. In mathematics, this is the *first difference*, and in physics it is *speed* (distance covered over time). The next chapter will discuss this and many variations of momentum.

If the change in price is positive, we can say that the trend is up, and if negative, the trend is down. Of course, this decision is based only on two data points, but if those points are far enough away from each other, that is, if n is large, then the trend as determined by this method will be very similar to a simple moving average, discussed in the next section. The simplest method can often be the most robust; therefore, as you read about many other approaches to analyzing price, keep asking, "Is it better than the simple change in price?"

■ The Moving Average

The most well-known of all smoothing techniques, used to remove market noise and find the direction of prices, is the *moving average (MA)*. Using this method, the number of elements to be averaged remains the same, but the time interval advances. This is also referred to as a *rolling calculation period*. Using a series of prices, $p_0, p_1, p_2, \ldots, p_t$, a moving average measured over the most recent n of these prices, or data points, at time t would be

$$MA_t = \frac{P_{t-n+1} + P_{t-n+2} + \cdots + P_t}{n} = \frac{1}{n}\sum_{i=t-n+1}^{t} P_i \, , \, n \le t$$

Then today's moving average value is the average (arithmetic mean) of the most recent n data points. For example, using three points $(n = 3)$ to generate a moving average starting at the beginning of the data:

$$MA_3 = (p_1 + p_2 + p_3)/3$$

$$MA_4 = (p_2 + p_3 + p_4)/3$$

$$\vdots$$

$$MA_t = (P_{t-2} + P_{t-1} + P_t)/3$$

If p_t represents a price at a specific time t, the moving average would smooth the price changes. When more prices, n, are used in the average, each price will be a smaller part of the average and have less effect on the final value. Using five successive prices is called a *5-day moving average*. When the next sequential price is added and the oldest is dropped off, the prior average is changed by $\frac{1}{5}$ of the difference between the old and the new values. If

$$MA_5 = (p_1 + p_2 + p_3 + p_4 + p_5)/5$$

and

$$MA_6 = (p_2 + p_3 + p_4 + p_5 + p_6)/5$$

then $c = p_2 + p_3 + p_4 + p_5$ can be substituted for the common part of the moving average. MA_6, the most recent value, can be solved in terms of MA_5, the previous value, to get

$$MA_6 = MA_5 + (p_t - p_{t-n})/5$$

This also gives a faster way to calculate a moving average. It can be seen that the more terms in the moving average, the less effect the addition of a new term will have:

$$MA_t = MA_{t-1} + (p_t - p_{t-n})/n$$

The selection of the number of terms, called the *calculation period*, is based on both the predictive quality of the choice (measured by the error but more often by the profitability) or the need to determine price trends over specific time periods, such as a season. For outright trading, the calculation period is chosen for its accuracy in identifying trend and the risk tolerance of the trader. Slower trends, using longer calculation periods, are usually better indicators of price direction, but involve larger risk. The stock market has adopted the 200-day moving average as its benchmark for direction; however, traders find this much too slow for timing buy and sell signals.

The length of a moving average can be tailored to specific needs. A 63-day moving average, ¼ of 252 business days in the year, would reflect quarterly changes in stock price, minimizing the significance of price fluctuations within a calendar quarter. A simple yearly calculation period, 252 days, would ignore all seasonality and emphasize the annual growth of the stock. Any periodic cycle that is the same length as the moving average length is lost; therefore, if a monthly cycle has been identified, then a moving average of less than 10 days (half the cycle length) would be best for letting the moving average show that cycle. Using a moving average to find seasonal and cyclic patterns is covered in Chapters 11 and 12. At this point it is sufficient to remember that if there is a possibility of a cyclic or seasonal pattern within the data, care should be taken to select a moving average that is out of phase with that pattern (that is, not equal to the cycle period).

The length of the moving average may also relate to its commercial use. A jeweler may purchase silver each week to produce bracelets. Frequent purchases of small amounts keeps the company's cash outlay small. The purchaser can wait a few extra days during a week while prices continue to trend downward but will buy immediately when prices turn up. A 6-month trend cannot help him because it gives a long-term answer to a short-term problem; however, a 5-day moving average may give the trend direction within the jeweler's time frame.

User-Friendly Software

Fortunately, we have reached a time when it is not necessary to perform these calculations the long way. Spreadsheet programs and specialized testing software provide simple tools for performing trend calculations as well as many other more complex functions discussed in this book. The notation for many of the different spreadsheets and software is very similar and self-explanatory:

Function	Spreadsheet Notation	TradeStation Notation
Sum	=sum (list)	summation (value, period)
Moving average	=average (list)	average (value, period)
Standard deviation	=stdev (list)	stddev (value, period)
Maximum value	=max (list)	highest (value, period)
Minimum value	=min (list)	lowest (value, period)

In the spreadsheet notation, *list* is a series of rows. For example, (D11:D30) would be 20 rows in column D, and in *TradeStation* notation, *period* is the calculation period and *value* is the closing daily price series, *close* or C.

What Do You Average?

The closing or daily settlement is the most common price applied to a moving average. It is generally accepted as the "true" price of the day and is used by many analysts for calculation of trends. It is the price used to reconcile brokerage accounts at the end of the day, create the *Net Asset Value* (NAV) for funds, and for futures trading it is called *marked-to-market accounting*. A popular alternative is to use the average of the high, low, and closing prices, representing some sort of center of gravity. You may also try the average of the high and low prices, ignoring the closing price entirely.

Another valid component of a moving average can be other averages. For example, if p_1 through p_t are prices, and MA_t is a 3-day moving average on day t, then

$$MA_3 = (p_1 + p_2 + p_3)/3$$
$$MA_4 = (p_2 + p_3 + p_4)/3$$
$$MA_5 = (p_3 + p_4 + p_5)/3$$

and

$$MA'_5 = (MA_3 + MA_4 + MA_5)/3$$

where MA'_5 is a *double-smoothed* moving average, which gives added weight to the center points. Double smoothing can be very effective and is discussed later in this chapter. Smoothing the highs and lows independently is another technique that creates a representation of the daily trading range, or volatility. This has been used to identify normal and extreme moves, and is also discussed in Chapter 9.

Types of Moving Averages

Besides varying the length of the moving average and the elements that are to be averaged, there are a great number of variations on the simple moving average. In the methods that follow, the notation assumes that the most recent day is t and the average is found over the past n days.

The Simple Moving Average The simple moving average is the average (mean) of the most recent n days. It has also been called a *truncated moving average,* and it is the most well-known and commonly used of all the methods. Repeating the formula from earlier in this chapter,

$$MA_t = \frac{P_{t-n+1} + P_{t-n+2} + \cdots + P_t}{n} = \frac{1}{n}\sum_{i=t-n+1}^{t} P_i \ , \ n \leq t$$

The main objection to the simple moving average is its abrupt change in value when an important old piece of data is dropped off, especially if only a few days are used in the calculation. We also know that, if the new data, p_t, is greater than the oldest data item that will be dropped off, p_{t-n}, then the new average, MA_t will be greater than the previous average, MA_{t-1}.

Average-Modified or Average-Off Method To avoid the end-off problem of the simple moving average, each time a new piece of data is added the previous average can be dropped off. This is called an *average-modified* or *average-off* method. It is computationally convenient because you only need to keep the old average value rather than all the data that was used to find the average. In general, the average-off method is

$$AvgOff_t = \frac{(n-1)\times AvgOff_{t-1} + P_t}{n}$$

The substitution of the moving average value for the oldest data item tends to smooth the results even more than a simple moving average and dampens the end-off impact.

Weighted Moving Average The *weighted moving average* opens many possibilities. It allows the significance of individual or groups of data to be changed. It may restore perceived value to parts of a data sample, or it may incorrectly bias the data. A weighted moving average is expressed in its general form as

$$W_t = \frac{w_1 P_{t-n+1} + w_2 P_{t-n+2} + \cdots + w_{n-1} P_{t-1} + w_n P_t}{w_1 + w_2 + \cdots + w_n} = \frac{\sum_{i=1}^{n} w_i P_{t-i+1}}{\sum_{i=1}^{n} w_i}$$

The weighted moving average at time t is the average of the previous n prices, each price having its own weighting factor w_i. There is no restriction on the values used as weighting factors; that is, they do not have to be percentages that all total to 1. The most popular form of this technique is called *front-loaded* because it gives more weight to the most recent data (n) and reduces the significance of the older elements. For the frontloaded weighted moving average (see Figure 8.2)

$$w_1 \leq w_2 \leq \cdots \leq w_n$$

The weighting factors w_i may also be determined by regression analysis, but then they may not necessarily be front-loaded. A common modification to front-loading is called *step-weighting* in which each successive w_i differs from the previous weighting factor w_{i-1} by a fixed increment

$$c = w_i - w_{i-1}$$

FIGURE 8.2 A Comparison of Moving Averages. The simple moving average, linearly weighted average, triangular weighted, and average off methods are applied to the S&P, April through December 2010.

The most common 5-day front-loaded, step-weighted average would have weighting factors increasing by $c = 1$ each day, $w_1 = 1$, $w_2 = 2$, $w_3 = 3$, $w_4 = 4$, and $w_5 = 5$. In general, for an n-day frontloaded step-weighted moving average:

$$w_{t-n+1} = 1$$

$$\vdots$$

$$w_{t-1} = n - 1$$

$$w_t = n$$

A TradeStation program for calculating an n-day, front-loaded, linearly weighted moving average is called *waverage*.

If simple linear step-weighting is not what you want, then a percentage relationship a between w_i elements can be used,

$$w_{i-1} = a \times w_i$$

If $a = 0.90$ and $w_5 = 5$, then $w_4 = 4.5$, $w_3 = 4.05$, $w_2 = 3.645$, and $w_1 = 3.2805$. Each older data item is given a weight of 90% of the more recent value. This is similar to *exponential smoothing* which will be discussed later in this chapter.

Weighting by Group   Prices may also be weighted in groups. If every two consecutive data elements have the same weighting factor, and p_t is the most recent price, n is the calculation period (preferably an even number), and there are $n/2$ number of weights, then

$$W_t = \frac{w_1 P_{t-n+1} + w_1 P_{t-n+2} + w_2 P_{t-n+3} + w_2 P_{t-n+4} + \cdots + w_{n/2} P_{t-1} + w_{n/2} P_t}{2 \times (w_1 + w_2 + \cdots + w_{n/2})}$$

For two or more data points using the same weighting, this formula can be regrouped as

$$W_t = \frac{w_1(P_{t-n+1} + P_{t-n+2}) + w_2(P_{t-n+3} + P_{t-n+4}) + \cdots + w_{n/2}(P_{t-1} + P_t)}{2 \times (w_1 + w_2 + \cdots + w_{n/2})}$$

Any number of consecutive data elements can be grouped for a step-weighted moving average.

If the purpose of weighting is to reproduce a pattern that is intrinsic to price movement, then either the *geometric average*, $G = (p_1 \times p_2 \times p_3 \ldots p_n)^{1/n}$ or *exponential smoothing*, explained later in this chapter, may be a better tool.

Triangular Weighting

While the simple moving average or linear regression treats each price equally, exponential smoothing and linear step-weighting put greater emphasis on the most recent data. There is an entire area of study in which the period of the dominant cycle is the basis for determining the best trend period. *Triangular weighting or triangular filtering*[1] attempts to uncover the trend by reducing the noise in both the front and back of the calculation window, where it is expected to have the greatest interference. Therefore, if a 20-day triangular weighting is used, the 10th day will have the greatest weight, while days 1 and 20 will have the smallest.

To implement triangular weighting, begin with the standard formula for a weighted average, calculated for n days as of the current day t,

$$W_t = \frac{\sum_{i=1}^{n} w_i P_{t-n+1}}{\sum_{i=1}^{n} w_i}$$

where n is also called the size, or width, of the window. For triangular weighting, the weighting factors w_i will increase linearly from 1 to the middle of the window, at $n/2$, then decrease to the end at n. This has a slightly different form when the period is odd or even,

$$w_i = i, \quad \text{for } i = 1 \text{ to } int((n+2)/2)$$
$$n - i + 1, \quad \text{for } i = int((n+2)/2) + 1 \text{ to } n \text{ (even values of } n)$$
$$n - i, \quad \text{for } i = int((n+2)/2) + 1 \text{ to } n \text{ (odd values of } n)$$

where *int* is a function that returns the integer portion by truncation. For odd values of n, the weighting factor has the value i, where i ranges from 1 to $n/2$ (rounded up with the help of the function *int*) and the value of $n - i$ from $n/2$ to n. Instead of a triangular filter, which climbs in equal steps to a peak at the middle value, a *Gaussian filter* can be used, which weights the data in a form similar to a bell curve. Here, the weighting factors are more complex, but the shape of the curve may be more appealing,

---

[1] J. J. Payne, "A Better Way to Smooth Data," *Technical Analysis of Stocks & Commodities* (October 1989).

$$w_i = 10^x \quad and \quad x = \frac{3}{2} \times \left(1 - \frac{2i}{n}\right)^2$$

Triangular weighting is often used for cycle analysis. Two techniques that use this method successfully, Hilbert and Fischer transforms, can be found in Chapter 12.

Pivot-Point Weighting

Too often we limit ourselves by our perception of the past. When a weighted moving average is used, it is normal to assume that all the weighting factors should be positive; however, that is not a requirement. The *pivot-point moving average* uses reverse linear weights (e.g., 5, 4, 3, . . .) that begin with a positive value and continue to decline even when they become negative.[2] In the following formula, the *pivot point*, where the weight is zero, is reached about ⅔ through the data interval. For a pivot-point moving average of 11 values, the eighth data point is given the weight of 0:

$$PPMA_t(11) = (-3p_{t-10} - 2p_{t-9} - 1p_{t-8} + 0p_{t-7} + 1p_{t-6} + 2p_{t-5}$$
$$+ 3p_{t-4} + 4p_{t-3} + 5p_{t-2} + 6p_{t-1} + 7p_t)/22$$

The intent of this pattern is to reduce the lag by front-loading the prices. The divisor is smaller than the usual linear weighted average (where the sum of 1 through 11 is 66) because it includes negative values. The general formula for an *n*-day pivot-point moving average is[3]

$$PPMA_t(n) = \frac{2}{n(n+1)} \sum_{i=1}^{n} (3i - n - 1)P_i$$

A computer program and indicator that calculates and displays the pivot-point moving average, both called *TSM Pivot Point Average*, are available on the Companion Website. The negative weighting factors actually reverse the impact of the price move for the oldest data points rather than just give them less importance. For a short interval this can cause the trendline to be out of phase with prices. This method seems best when used for longer-term cyclic markets, where the inflection point, at which the weighting factor becomes zero, is aligned with the cyclic turn or can be fixed at the point of the last trend change.

Standard Deviation Moving Average

A unique trend calculation technique uses the standard deviation of prices.[4] This method creates a comparatively smooth trendline, *StdAvg*, by modifying the moving average value with a percentage of the standard deviation of prices. The following instructions are from the program *TSM Stdev Mvg Avg*, available on the Companion Website. It uses 5% of a 30-period standard deviation, and a 15-period moving average; however, each of these values can be changed. The result is shown for S&P futures in Figure 8.3.

---

[2] Patrick E. Lafferty, "End-Point Moving Average," *Technical Analysis of Stocks & Commodities* (October 1995).
[3] Don Kraska, "Letters to S&C," *Technical Analysis of Stocks & Commodities* (February 1996), 12.
[4] Robert T. H. Lee, *Power Tools for Traders* (Hong Kong: MegaCapital Limited, 1997).

FIGURE 8.3 S&P Continuous Futures, April through December 2010, with Examples of the Simple Moving Average, Standard Deviation Average, Geometric Average, and Exponential Smoothing, All with Calculation Periods of 40 Days.

```
      SD = StdDev(close,30);
     SDV = (SD - SD[1]) / SD;
  StdAvg = Average(close,15) + .05*SDV;
```

■ Geometric Moving Average

The *geometric mean* is a growth function that is very applicable to long-term price movement. It is especially useful for calculating the components of an index. The geometric mean can also be applied to the most recent n points at time t to get a *geometric average* similar in function to a moving average

$$G_t = \left(p_{t-n+1} \times p_{t-n+2} \times \cdots \times p_{t-1} \times p_t\right)^{(1/n)} = \left(\prod_{i=1}^{n} p_{t-i+1}\right)^{(1/n)}$$

The daily calculation is more complicated but could be rewritten as

$$\ln G_t = \frac{\ln p_{t-n+1} + \ln p_{t-n+2} + \cdots + \ln p_{t-1} + \ln p_t}{n}$$

$$= \frac{1}{n}\left(\sum_{i=1}^{n} \ln p_{t-i+1}\right)$$

This is similar in form to the standard moving average based on the arithmetic mean and can be written in either spreadsheet or program code as

```
GA = average(log(price),n)
```

Note that some software will use the function *log* although the calculation is actually the *natural log*, ln. Other programs will allow the choice of *log(value)* or *ln(value)*. A weighted geometric moving average, for n days ending at the current day t, would have the form

$$\ln G_t = \frac{w_1 \ln p_{t-n+1} + w_2 \ln p_{t-n+2} + \cdots + w_{n-1} \ln p_{t-1} + w_n \ln p_t}{w_1 + w_2 + \cdots + w_n}$$

$$= \frac{\sum_{i=1}^{n} w_i \ln p_{t-i+1}}{\sum_{i=1}^{n} w_i}$$

The geometric moving average itself would give greater weight to lower values without the need for a discrete weighting function. This is most applicable to long data intervals where prices had a wide range of values. In applying the technique to recent index or stock prices, this distinction is not as apparent. For example, if the historical index values vary from 10 to 1000, the simple average of those two values is 505, and the geometric average is 100, but for the three sequential prices of 56.20, 58.30, and 57.15, the arithmetic mean is 57.2166, and the geometric is 57.1871. A 5-, 10-, or 20-day moving average of stock prices, compared to geometric averages of the same intervals, show negligible differences. The geometric moving average is best applied to long-term historic data with wide variance, using yearly or quarterly average prices.

■ Accumulative Average *not good for trend following*

An *accumulative average* is simply the long-term average of all data, but it is not practical for trend following. One drawback is that the final value is dependent upon the start date. If the data have varied around the same price for the entire data series, then the result would be good. It would also be useful if you are looking for the average of a ratio over a long period. Experience shows that price levels have changed because of inflation or a structural shift in supply and/or demand, and that progressive values fit the situation best.

■ Reset Accumulative Average

A *reset accumulative average* is a modification of the accumulative average and attempts to correct for the loss of sensitivity as the number of trading days becomes large. This alternative allows you to reset or restart the average whenever a new trend begins, a significant event occurs, or at some specified time interval, for example, at the time of quarterly earnings reports or at the end of the current crop year.

■ Drop-Off Effect

Many *rolling trend calculations* are distinguished by the *drop-off effect*, a common way of expressing the abrupt change in the current value when a significant older value is dropped from the calculation. Simple moving averages, linear regressions, and weighted averages all use a fixed period, or window, and are subject to this. For an *n*-period moving average, the importance of the oldest value being dropped off is measured by the difference between the new price being added to the calculation, *t*, and the one being removed, *t–n*, divided by the number of periods,

$$\text{Drop-off effect} = (p_t - p_{t-n})/n$$

A front-weighted average, in which the oldest values have less importance, reduces this effect because older, high volatility data slowly become a smaller part of the result before being dropped off. Exponential smoothing, discussed next, is by nature a front-loaded trend that minimizes the drop-off effect as does the average-off method.

CHAPTER 9

Trend Systems (Part 1)

From Perry J. Kaufman, *Trading Systems and Methods, +Website*, 5th Edition (Hoboken, New Jersey: John Wiley & Sons, 2013), Chapter 8.

The previous chapters developed the tools for calculating trends—a tradition-al moving average, various weighted averages, exponential smoothing, and regression. To profit from identifying the trend requires the use of trading rules and the selection of specific parameters that define the trend speed and an acceptable level of risk, among other factors. This chapter first discusses those rules that are necessary to all trading strategies and then gives examples of actual systems. The selection of trend speed is handled only briefly here but is continued with a detailed analysis of these and other systems throughout the book, and especially in Level III, Chapter 10. It is most important to find trends that are robust, that is, that work across many markets and under varied economic conditions. At the same time they must satisfy an investor's risk tolerance. It is a difficult balance.

Trend systems are the preferred choice of Commodity Trading Advisors (CTAs). Some advisors are reported to be using the same systems devised in 1980. Barclay Hedge (BarclayHedge.com) reports that hedge funds had a total of $1,762.9 billion under management as of the first quarter of 2012, and managed futures totaling $328.9 billion. Investments from both institutions and individuals have been flowing into the industry at an increasing rate, up almost 500% since 2002.

■ Why Trend Systems Work

Trend analysis is the basis for many successful trading programs, some with audited performance published for more than 30 years. Being able to identify the trend is also important if you are a discretionary trader looking to increase your chances for success by trading on "the right side of the market." Trend systems work because

■ *Long-term trends capture large price moves caused by fundamental factors*. Economic trends are most often based on government interest rate policy, which is both slow to develop and persistent. In turn, interest rates directly affect foreign exchange, the trade balance, mortgage rates, carrying charges, and the stock market.

■ *Prices are not normally distributed but have a fat tail.* The fat tail means that there is an unusually large number of directional price moves that are longer than would be expected if prices were randomly distributed. The fat tail will generate exceptional trend profits, which are essential to a trend system's long-term success.

■ *Money moves the markets.* Most trends are supported by the flow of investor funds. While this causes short-term noise, it also delivers the long-term trends. As trends become clearer to the general public, additional money flows in to continue the trend.

Trend trading works when the market is trending. It doesn't work in markets that are not trending. There is no magic solution that will generate profits for trending strategies when prices are moving sideways, and there is no one trending technique that is always best. You'll find that most trending methods have about the same returns over time but with different risk profiles. It is the risk profile and the trading frequency that distinguish one method from another, and those features will be discussed throughout this chapter.

How Often Do Markets Trend?

Is there a way to measure how often markets trend? One analyst defines a trend as 10 consecutive closes in the same direction, but that seems arbitrary and a small window. What if there were nine days up and one small down day?

A trend is a relative concept. It is relative to the trader's time horizon, and it is relative to the amount of noise and price swings that are acceptable within the trending period. Ultimately, a trend exists if you can profit from the price moves using a trending strategy.

The Fat Tail

The *fat tail* is a statistical phenomenon caused by a combination of market fundamentals and supported by human behavior. The net effect is that prices move in one direction much longer than can be explained by a random distribution. As a simple example, consider coin flipping as a classic way to produce a random distribution. In 100 coin tosses,

■ 50 will be a head or a tail followed by the opposite head or tail.

■ 25 will be two heads or two tails in a row.

■ 12½ (if we could have halves tosses) will be three heads or three tails in a row.

■ About 6 will be four heads or four tails in a row.

■ About 3 will be five in a row.

■ 1 or 2 will be six in a row of either heads or tails.

If price moves are substituted for coin flips, then heads would be a move up and tails a move down. If the pattern of up and down price moves follows a random distribution (and the up and down moves were of the same amount), then it would not be possible to profit from a trend system. But prices are not normally distributed. Price runs have a fat tail, which means that, instead of one run of 6 out of 100 days of trading, we may see a run of 12, or 3 runs of 6. That distribution is enough to make trend trading profitable.

Another factor is that these long runs translate into very large trading profits. It is not necessary to have every day go in the same direction in order to profit, only that the downward reversals during an uptrend not be large enough to change the direction of the trend and end the trade. The more tolerance for the size of the interim reversals, the more likely the fat tail can be captured.

If there are more runs of longer duration for every 100 daily price moves, what is the shape of the rest of the distribution? Figure 9.1 gives a theoretical representation of an actual price distribution compared to a random distribution. The extra movement that goes into creating the fat tail comes from the frequency of short runs. There are fewer runs of 1 and 2 and more runs greater than 6. The total remains the same. Readers interested in this subject should read the section "Gambling Techniques—The Theory of Runs" in Level III, Chapter 11. *fewer short losses more large profits.*

Distribution of Profits and Losses

As a trader, you would want to know "How often is there a profit from a fat tail?" To find the answer, we'll apply the most basic trending system, a simple moving average that buys when the trendline turns up and sells short when it turns down. This will be

FIGURE 9.1 Distribution of Runs. The shaded area shows the normal distribution of random runs. The solid dark line represents the distribution when there is a fat tail. In the fat tail distribution, there are fewer short runs and an unusually large number of longer runs or a single exceptionally long run.

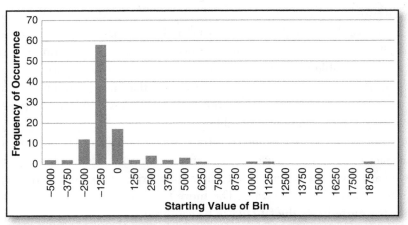

FIGURE 9.2 Frequency Distribution of Returns for S&P Futures Using a 40-Day Simple Moving Average Strategy. Results show a fat tail to the right.

discussed in more detail in the next sections. For now we need to know that results depend on both the market and the calculation period. Applying a simple 40-day moving average strategy to five diverse futures markets, 30-year bonds, the S&P, the euro currency, crude oil, and gold, the results of individual trades can be collected and displayed as a histogram (frequency distribution). The results of the S&P are shown in Figure 9.2.

In the frequency distribution, the bottom axis shows the starting value of the bins that hold the size of the profitable or losing trades, and the left scale shows the number of trades that fall into that bin. If the distribution was normal, then the shape would be a bell curve. This distribution is clearly extended far to the right, with one very large profit showing in the $18750 bin. That one profit offsets more than 30 losses in the largest bar marked −$1250. But the S&P is not the only market with this distribution; actually, the S&P has relatively smaller fat tails than other markets. Figure 9.1 shows the distribution sample. The tails to the right are very long and those to the left very short. It is important to remember that a pure trend strategy needs this distribution to be profitable.

Time Intervals, Market Maturity, and Trends

Trends are most easily seen using long-term charts, weekly rather than daily data, or daily rather than hourly data. The farther you step back from a chart, the clearer the

TABLE 9.1																				
			Frequency Distribution for a Sample of Five Diverse Markets, Showing the Fat Tail to the Right and a Short Tail to the Left																
Bin	1	2	3	4	5	6	7	8	9	10	11	12	13	14	15	16	17	18	19	20
Bonds	0	2	8	17	53	27	6	3	2	3	1	0	0	1	1	0	0	0	1	0
S&P	2	2	12	58	17	2	4	2	3	1	0	0	1	1	0	0	0	0	0	1
Euro	1	0	4	7	26	75	20	2	2	3	1	0	2	1	1	0	0	2	0	0
Crude	0	3	22	92	2	0	4	0	1	0	0	0	0	0	0	0	0	1	0	0
Gold	0	1	4	8	20	70	16	4	0	2	0	3	0	0	0	0	0	1	0	0

trend. If you display a daily chart, there will be some obvious trending periods and some equally clear sideways moves. Change that to a weekly chart, and the trends will seem much clearer. Change that to an hourly chart, and you'll see mostly noise. Lower frequency data translate into better performance when using longer-term trends. While there are always fast trends that show profits in backtesting, they tend to be less stable and inconsistent in their returns. Trends using longer calculation periods are more likely to track economic policy, such as the progressive lowering of interest rates by the central bank or a plan to allow the currency to weaken in order to stimulate exports and reduce debt.

Diverse markets may have very different trending qualities. Interest rate futures, money markets, and utility stocks are among the many investment vehicles closely tied to government rate policy and reflect the same long-term trend; this trend can persist for years. Foreign exchange is more complex and is constrained by monetary policy. Governments are more accepting of changes in the exchange rates if they occur slowly, but they will work hard to keep them within a target range. Most foreign exchange markets show clear but shorter trends compared to interest rates.

The stock market presents another level of difficulty. Individual stocks are driven by many factors, including earnings, competition, government regulation, management competence, and consumer confidence. Because the volume of trading in individual shares may vary considerably from day to day, these factors do not often net out as a clear trend. Stock prices may run up sharply on anticipation of better earnings or approval of a new drug, and reverse just as quickly within a few days. Liquidity, or volume, is an important element in the existence of a steady trend.

Individual stocks are also affected by concurrent trading in the index markets. When the S&P futures or the ETF SPY is bought and sold, all stocks within that index are bought and sold. If one company in the S&P 500 has just announced the loss of a major contract, but the overall market is strong, the share price of the suffering company may be dragged higher by arbitrage due to massive buying of the S&P index. This behavior makes for erratic price patterns in individual stocks.

Emerging markets are the exception. The introduction of a new market, such as the fictitious East European Stock Index, would be lightly traded but may be very trending. Initial activity would be dominated by commercials, such as banks, all of which would have a similar opinion on the economy of Eastern Europe. A small number of traders with the same opinion will cause very clear trends in the price. As the general public starts to participate, it adds liquidity while it also introduces noise, which in turn makes the trends less clear. Finding the trend then requires a longer time interval.

When using a trending strategy, select both the markets and the time frame that work with you. Longer calculation periods, lower frequency data, and markets that are more closely linked to their underlying fundamentals will all perform better.

■ Basic Buy and Sell Signals

Trends are based on the average always lagging price movement. It is the advantage and the disadvantage of the method. As the calculation period gets larger, the average lags further. Figure 9.3 shows Amazon prices from April 2010 through February 2011 with a 40-day moving average. Clearly, the moving average smoothes prices.

FIGURE 9.3 Amazon (AMZN) with a 40-Day Moving Average.

The basic idea behind using the moving average as a trend signal is to be long when prices are above the average and short when below. The rules are stated as

- *Buy* when prices cross above the trendline.

- *Sell short* when prices cross below the trendline.

Even with these simple rules, there are important choices to be made. Do you buy at the moment rising prices cross the trendline during the trading session, or do you wait for the price to close above the trendline? As seen in Figure 9.3, prices may cross back and forth through the trendline before settling on a final direction. If you subscribe to the belief that the closing price of the day is the most reliable price, then the number of trading signals can be reduced by using the rules:

- *Buy* when prices close above the trendline.

- *Sell short* when prices close below the trend line.

Another school of thought prefers the average of high and low prices, or the average of the high, low, and closing prices. A buy or short sale signal occurs when the (high + low)/2 or (high + low + *close*)/3 crosses above or below the current trendline value. In both of these cases, the averages could not be calculated until the end of the trading session because none of the three component values would be known until then.

Using the Trendline for Signals

The trendline represents the netting of all prices. Its purpose is to remove the price noise and show you the underlying price direction. Then it seems more reasonable to use the trendline to generate the trading signal. The change in the value of the trendline from the previous calculation to the current one is its direction—up, down, or unchanged. The direction of the trendline is a candidate for generating trading signals.

- *Buy* when the change in the trendline is up.

- *Sell short* when the change in the trendline is down.

The penalty for using the trendline as a trading signal is its lag. Figure 9.3 shows that, using a 40-day moving average, prices cross above the trendline during July a few days ahead of the point where the trendline turns up. The benefit using the trendline signal is that the trend turn is clear and more stable. During July and November, prices crossed back and forth through the trendline, but the trendline did not change direction; therefore, the trading signal remained the same.

Comparing Basic Trading Signals

The main differences between using a price penetration or the trendline to generate signals is that the trendline produces fewer trading signals, and those signals are delayed. If Amazon prices are used as an example, both methods of entry can be compared for a sample of calculation periods to see if one approach is consistently better than the other. Although this is a single example, it represents the general case.

As shown in Table 9.2, five calculation periods are used beginning with 5 days and doubling the period for each test. This maintains the percentage change in the calculation period and gives a better distribution sample (this is discussed further in Level III, Chapter 10). The two columns headed *Number of Trades* show that the trendline method has from 26% to 37% fewer trades and, for the most part, better performance. The *Profit Factor* is the performance ratio used by TradeStation equal to the gross profits divided by the gross losses. While not as good as the *information ratio* or *Sharpe ratio*, the results allow you to compare performance.

It appears that using the trendline signals is always better, but that is not necessarily the case. To be certain, you would need to compare a wide range of diverse markets rather than just Amazon. Even if these results seem compelling, it is always necessary to confirm the numbers to be confident of the answers and to be sure that you understand the process.

While it seems convincing that the trendline is best for the slower trends, it is not as clear for faster trading. For the case using a 5-day moving average, both methods netted a loss, but the price penetration shows a smaller loss. It is very possible that,

TABLE 9.2 Comparison of Entry Methods for 10 Years of Amazon (AMZN)

Signals using the trendline direction are shown on the left, and price penetration on the right.

| Trend Calculation Period | Signal Using Trendline | | | Signal Using Price Cross | | | Increase in Trades |
	Total Profit/ Loss	Profit Factor	Number of Trades	Total Profit/ Loss	Profit Factor	Number of Trades	
80	48.24	1.34	84	57.16	1.31	106	26%
40	94.42	1.46	120	32.21	1.12	164	37%
20	111.97	1.45	196	(7.31)	0.98	252	29%
10	(87.67)	0.81	292	(90.82)	0.82	370	27%
5	(90.31)	0.84	439	(49.15)	0.92	597	36%

for faster trading, the lag in the trendline is too much of a burden to overcome and the price penetration is better. This will be discussed further in Level III, Chapter 5, "Day Trading."

Anticipating the Trend Signal

Consistency is important. The system that is tested and the one that is traded should be the same. In this book, the closing price is used for most of the calculations; however, any combination of open, high, low, and close could be substituted. The normal process for generating a trading signal is to wait until prices close, then calculate the new moving average or trendline value, then see whether a crossing occurred or the direction of the trendline changed according to the basic buy and sell rules. But using the closing price for the calculation of the entry signal implies that you could enter on the close.

The process of waiting for the close price to perform the necessary calculations and generate a signal requires that orders be placed in the after-hours market or on the next open. While the trading system is indicating a new buy or sell signal as of the close of trading, you are entering the market significantly late. You are not following the system as it was tested. A practical solution to this dilemma is to record the prices shortly before the close, generate the trading signals, then enter the buy and sell orders for execution on the close. Occasionally, the order will be wrong because prices changed direction in the last few minutes of trading, but the cost of exiting the trade will usually be small compared to the improvement in overall execution.

The other alternative is to calculate, in advance, the closing price that will generate a signal using either the trendline method or the price crossing method. For an n-day moving average the calculation is simple—the new moving average value will be greater than the previous value if today's price is greater than the price dropped off n-days ago. Because all of the other values in the average remain the same except for the first and last, the answer only needs those two values. If a 40-day average is used and the oldest price p_{t-0} was 30.25, then any price greater than 30.25 today would cause the trendline to move up, and any price greater than 30.25 would also cause an upwards price penetration. Then an order can be placed in advance to *buy at 30.26 stop*.

How important is this? A lot depends on the trending nature of the market. In other books, our discussion of market noise showed that the short-term interest rates had the lowest amount of noise, and the equity index markets had the most noise. Using the Eurodollar interest rates and the S&P 500 futures as the extremes, the method that enters using the trendline was compared when entries were taken on the current close, the next open, and the next close to assess the sensitivity of the total profits to entry delays. Table 9.3 shows the results.

All Eurodollar results show a profit for trades entered on the close of the day that a signal occurred. Longer trend periods were generally more profitable, confirming the premise that trends are more dominant in the long term due to government policy. When entries were delayed to the next open or next close, the results

TABLE 9.3 Comparison of Entries on the Close, Next Open, and Next Close

Results vary with the trending nature of the market. Analysis uses 10 years of S&P and Eurodollar interest rate futures, back-adjusted, ending in February 2011.

| | Eurodollar Interest Rates | | | | | | S&P 500 | | | | | |
| | Today's Close | | Next Open | | Next Close | | Today's Close | | Next Open | | Next Close | |
Calculation Period	Total Profit or Loss	Profit Factor	Total Profit or Loss	Profit Factor	Total Profit or Loss	Profit Factor	Total Profit or Loss	Profit Factor	Total Profit or Loss	Profit Factor	Total Profit or Loss	Profit Factor
80	16150	2.87	16325	2.89	15630	2.75	(12325)	0.87	(10463)	0.89	16363	1.20
40	9603	1.61	9050	1.55	9383	1.61	(29138)	0.75	(26013)	0.78	5013	1.05
20	7745	1.37	6258	1.29	3850	1.16	13088	1.12	13900	1.13	22738	1.20
10	10773	1.40	8765	1.31	1165	1.04	(27925)	0.83	(22738)	0.86	(12550)	0.93
5	3368	1.09	(1715)	0.96	(870)	0.98	(21725)	0.90	(19588)	0.91	(56350)	−0.76

were worse. This is best seen in the profit factors, which measure reward to risk rather than only total profits.

The S&P is also clear but not as clean as Eurodollars. Equity index markets are noisy; that is, prices moving up are not expected to continue up for any sustained number of days. A new buy signal will usually happen on a day when prices are moving higher, but waiting until the next open or the next close could be better because of the noise. This was true for all calculation periods except 5 days. As for the calculation period, there was no particular pattern, although absolute losses were smaller as the trend period got longer, a modest confirmation that longer trends are better. We know from other tests and other markets that this limited example is generally true, but market characteristics always create exceptions.

Profile of a Simple Moving Average System

Using the moving average trendline as the basis for system signals, we chose a 40-day calculation period because it tends to be the fastest one that also identifies the major price trends. The profile of results is typical of any moving average system. Figure 9.4 shows the NASDAQ 100 for one year, ending February 2011. Buy and sell signals are generated from the direction of the trendline; there were no transaction fees.

The trading signals in Figure 9.4 show that the major upwards move is captured, but not before there are a number of false signals due to the trendline changes during sideways price periods. However, given enough tries, the trend surfaces, and the system gains a large profit, similar to the fat tail discussed at the beginning of this chapter. The profile of this NASDAQ example, shown in Table 9.4, is typical of longer-term trend-following systems. Of the 150 trades over 10 years, only 52 of them were profitable, about 35%. However, the average winning trade was much larger than the average losing trade, with a ratio of 2.22, and winning trades were held much longer than losing trades, supporting the adage "cut your losses and let your profits run." Finally, there were more consecutive losses than consecutive profits, but that follows because there are

FIGURE 9.4 A Trend System for NASDAQ 100. Applying a 40-day moving average and taking the trading signals from the direction of trendline results gives a typical trend system profile.

TABLE 9.4	Performance Statistics for NASDAQ Futures, 10 Years Ending February 2011	
Total profit		$1,880
Number of trades		150
Number of winning trades		52
Percentage of winning trades		34.7%
Average winning trade		1424.71
Average losing trade		−41.28
Win/loss ratio		2.22
Average bars in winners		31.65
Average bars in losers		6.64
Consecutive winner		6
Consecutive losses		10

many more losses. The performance picture is that trend following gets in and out quickly when it has a loss but holds the trade whenever trends and profits develop. This category of strategy is called *conservation of capital*, referring to the feature that cuts losses quickly.

We can generalize the trend-following profile as:

- The percentage of profitable trades is low—often less than 30%.

- The average winning trade must be significantly larger than the average losing trade; actually, given only 30% profitable trades, the ratio must be greater than 100:30 to be profitable.

- The average winning trades are held much longer than losses.

- There is a high frequency of losing trades; therefore, there are also long sequences of losing trades.

There are many analysts that have a lifetime goal of improving these statistics, that is, capturing the long-term trend but improving the percentage of profitable trades. Some small amount of success is possible but not without changing the risk characteristics of trend-following systems. For example, if you add profit-taking (discussed throughout the book) or stop-losses (Level III, Chapter 12), then you reduce or eliminate the chance of capturing the fat tail, which has been shown to be necessary for a long-term profit. Still, many traders do not like the idea of holding the trades for such a long time and giving back so much of the unrealized profits when the major trend changes direction. Different traders make different choices. A program to test the entry rules and execution options, including *long-only*, is *TSM Moving Average*, available on the Companion Website.

Bands and Channels

A good way to improve the reliability of signals without altering the overall trend profile is by constructing a *band*, or *channel*, around the trendline. It can be used to effectively slow down trading without sacrificing the biggest profits. If we accept the premise that the point of trend change is also the time of greatest indecision, then a simple way to avoid frequent false signals is by using a band.

Bands Formed by Highs and Lows

The most natural band is one formed from the daily high and low prices. Instead of applying the *n*-day moving average to the closing prices, it is applied separately to the highs and lows. Long positions are entered when today's high crosses the average of the highs and short sales when today's low crosses the average of the lows. To get a broad view of whether this is an improvement to entry points, the two most extreme markets (the Eurodollar considered the trendiest and the S&P the noisiest) are tested for 10 years with the five calculation periods used in an earlier example. Results are shown in Table 9.5.

For a highly trending market, such as the Eurodollar interest rates, entering later, on a penetration of either the highs or lows, is not as good as entering on a price penetration of the close. If this had not been determined from our study of noise in other works, these results would cause us to draw the same conclusion. Just the opposite is seen in the S&P results. Waiting longer to enter improves results noticeably, and, in the case of the 40-day trend, it turns a loss into a profit.

We can conclude that a band can be a profitable variation to a simple trend system, but not for all markets. The next question is "Are there other bands that work better?"

Keltner Channels

One of the original band calculations was by Keltner,[1] which goes as follows:

$$\text{(Average daily price)} \qquad AP_t = (H_t + L_t + C_t)/3$$

	TABLE 9.5	**Results of Using a Moving Average of the Highs and Lows, Compared to the Closes**						
	Eurodollar Interest Rates				S&P 500			
	Close Crossing		High-Low		Close Crossing		High-Low	
Calculation Period	Total Profit or Loss	Profit Factor	Total Profit or Loss	Profit Factor	Total Profit or Loss	Profit Factor	Total Profit or Loss	Profit Factor
80	16320	2.94	13842	2.18	30027	1.54	36443	1.74
40	16035	2.18	15000	2.02	(10337)	0.91	12402	1.14
20	10172	1.44	5167	1.20	5987	1.05	16512	1.15
10	2727	1.08	3667	1.11	(49000)	0.76	(33751)	0.82
5	7812	1.20	(337)	0.99	(106950)	0.64	(43760)	0.81

[1] Chester W. Keltner, *How to Make Money in Commodities* (Kansas City, MO: The Keltner Statistical Service, 1960).

(10-day moving average)	$MA_t = average(C_t, 10)$
(Upper band)	$UB_t = MA_t + AP_t$
(Lower band)	$LB_t = MA_t + AP_t$

These days we would tend to use true range, rather than the high-low range as a better representation of volatility.

Percentage Bands

Another simple construction is a percentage band, formed by adding and subtracting the same percentage of price from the trendline based on the closing prices. If c is the percentage to be used (where $c = 0.03$ means 3%), then

$$
\begin{aligned}
\text{(Upper band)} \quad B_U &= (1 + c) \times MA_t \\
\text{(Lower band)} \quad B_L &= (1 - c) \times MA_t
\end{aligned}
$$

where MA_t = today's moving average value

Therefore, if the moving average value for Merck (MRK) is $33, and the band is 3%, then the upper band is 33.99 and the lower band is 32.01. Because the moving average is much smoother than the price series, the band will be uniform around the moving average, narrowing and widening slightly as prices decline and rise.

The band can be more sensitive to change if the current price p_t is used to calculate the band instead of the moving average trendline. The bands are then

$$
\begin{aligned}
\text{(Upper band)} \quad B_U &= (1 + c) \times p_{t-1} + MA_t \\
\text{(Lower band)} \quad B_L &= (1 - c) \times p_{t-1} + MA_t
\end{aligned}
$$

The band is still oriented around the moving average trendline to prevent it from jumping up and down too often. Using the price to generate the band also requires that yesterday's price be used; otherwise the band would never be penetrated. Using a percentage band would work for stocks but not for futures. Most futures analysis uses back-adjusted data, and if the carry is mostly negative, then the oldest back-adjusted data could actually become negative. That doesn't affect a moving average trading signal, but it does make any percentage price calculation wrong. Back-adjusted historic prices are simply not correct.

If only a small buffer zone is needed, rather than one that adjusts over time, then a band based on absolute point value could be used. For example, stocks trading between $20 and $40 could have a $1 band. If your goal is to avoid a few very small variations around the time of trend change, then an absolute point value band may be a simple alternative solution.

Volatility Bands

To the degree that volatility increases as prices increase, the percentage band is a volatility band; however, that relationship is both long term and not as good as actually measuring the individual volatility for many stocks and futures markets. Regardless of the method, creating a band that is responsive to volatility may improve the reliability of trend signals. The independent smoothing of the high and low prices over any calculation period forms a natural volatility band. Although it may be practical to use the same smoothing technique or the same calculation period as the underlying trend (e.g., 10-day or 10% smoothing constant) for the high, low, and closing prices, it is not a requirement. If the same smoothing criterion is used, the band will be uniform with respect to the moving average of the closing price; if not, all three trendlines may weave around one another, which creates some practical problems.

There are many choices for measuring volatility and creating a band around the trendline. All of the methods of forming bands are subject to scaling. Scaling is accomplished by using a constant value as a multiplier or scaling factor; it increases or reduces the sensitivity of the band. If s is a scaling factor and c is a fixed percentage, then the following bands can be constructed:

$$B_t = MA_t \pm s \times c \times MA_t \qquad \text{(Percentage of trendline)}$$

$$B_t = MA_t \pm s \times c \times p_t \qquad \text{(Percentage of price)}$$

$$B_t = MA_t \pm s \times ATR_{t-1} \times MA_t \qquad \text{(Average true range)}$$

$$B_t = MA_t \pm s \times stdev_{t-1} \times MA_t \qquad \text{(Standard deviation)}$$

When $s = 1$, the scaling effect is nullified; for $s > 1$, the width of the band is increased; and for $s < 1$, the band width is reduced. In the choices above, MA was used to indicate a moving average, but any method of calculating the trend can be substituted, such as an exponential smoothing or a regression. Figure 9.5 shows the four types of bands applied to the S&P futures. All use a scaling factor of 2, which may be too close for some methods and too far for others. The purpose of the chart is to show the relative shape of the bands and distance from the prices.

In Figure 9.5 the center line is a 20-day moving average. The first two methods of calculating bands, the percentage of trendline and percentage of price, are almost

FIGURE 9.5 Four Volatility Bands around a 20-Day Moving Average, Based on (a) 2% of Trendline, (b) 2% of Price, (c) 2 × Average True Range, and (d) Annualized 20-Day Volatility.

168

THEORY AND ANALYSIS

identical, very smooth, and are the farthest from the center. The next band closer to the moving average is the average true range. It moves slightly farther apart when prices are more volatile. The band closest to the trendline is the annualized volatility, which is most sensitive to price changes.

Because the same scaling factor produces bands that are different for each method, it is difficult to compare them without finding the scaling factors that come closest to average band width for each technique. The bigger decision is whether it is more sensible to use a very smooth band or one that reacts to changes in price volatility. That decision is up to each trader.

It may be convenient to have separate exit and entry bands, the entries less sensitive than the exits so that the strategy exits quickly but enters slowly. Or, if the entry occurs on a penetration of the band, but the exit is based on the trendline, then trades are not reversed from long to short. That improves slippage because only half the number of shares or contracts are traded on each order, and may avoid some false signals.

Bollinger Bands

Perhaps the simplest and most robust measurement of price volatility is the standard deviation of the prices themselves, calculated over recent price history. This was the last method listed in the previous section. John Bollinger has popularized the combination of a 20-day moving average with bands formed using 2 standard deviations of the price changes over the same 20-day period. They are now frequently called *Bollinger bands*.[2] Because the standard deviation represents a confidence level, and prices are not normally distributed, the choice of two standard deviations equates to an 87% confidence band (if prices were normally distributed, two standard deviations would contain 95.4% of the data). In their normal use, Bollinger bands are combined with other techniques to identify extreme price levels. These are discussed later in this section.

Figure 9.6 shows Ford (F) plotted with a traditional Bollinger band. One of the characteristics of this band is that, once the price moves outside either the upper or lower band, it remains outside for a number of days in a row. This type of pattern

FIGURE 9.6 Bollinger Bands Applied to Ford.

[2] John A. Bollinger, Bollinger Capital Management, Inc. P.O. Box 3358, Manhattan Beach, CA 90266, www.bollingerbands.com. Also *Bollinger on Bollinger Bands* (New York: McGraw-Hill, 2001).

FIGURE 9.7 Combining Daily and Weekly Bollinger Bands.

Source: Chart created using The Fibonacci Trader by Robert Krausz. Used with permission from Fibonacci Trader Corporation, St. Augustine, FL. www.fibonaccitrader.com.

was typical of what used to be called *high momentum*. Note that the width of the band varies considerably with the volatility of prices and that a period of high volatility causes a "bubble," which extends past the period where volatility declines. These features and more about volatility will be discussed in Level III, Chapter 9.

Figure 9.6 was created using the TradeStation indicator *Bollinger Bands*, which lets you vary both the calculation period for the trend and the number of standard deviations. But then, if it's not a 20-day average and 2 standard deviations, it's not a Bollinger band.

Bollinger bands can also be applied effectively to multiple time frames. An excellent example that uses a combination of weekly and daily data applied to the S&P 500 is seen in Figure 9.7. The price pattern follows the weekly Bollinger band higher, where the daily and weekly prices come together during the week of July 14.

Modified Bollinger Bands   One of the significant problems with Bollinger bands, as well as any volatility measure based on historic data, is that the bands will expand after increasing volatility but are slow to narrow as volatility declines. An excellent correction[3] for this requires the following calculations for the center line, *D*,

$$M_t = \alpha \times C_t + (1 - \alpha) \times M_{t-1}$$
$$U_t = \alpha \times M_t + (1 - \alpha) \times U_{t-1}$$

[3] Dennis McNicholl, "Better Bollinger Bands," *Futures* (October 1998).

THEORY AND ANALYSIS

$$D_t = \frac{(2-\alpha) \times \dot{M}_t - U_t}{1-\alpha}$$

where C is the closing price and α is the smoothing constant, set to 0.15 to approximate a 20-day moving average. In order to correct the bulge in the bands following a volatile period, the upper and lower bands (BU and BL) are calculated as

$$m_t = \alpha \times \left| C_t - D_t \right| + (1-\alpha) \times m_{t-1}$$

$$u_t = \alpha \times m_t + (1-\alpha) \times u_{t-1}$$

$$d_t = \frac{(2-\alpha) \times m_t - u_t}{1-\alpha}$$

$$BU_t = D_t + f \times d_t$$

$$BL_t = D_t - f \times d_t$$

where f is the multiplier for the width of the band, suggested at 2.5 compared to Bollinger's 2.0. Figure 9.8 shows the modified Bollinger bands along with the original (lighter lines) for gold futures during the first part of 2009. While the new bands do not remove the bulge, they are faster to correct and more uniform in the way they envelop prices. Programs to calculate and display the original and modified bands are *TSM Bollinger bands* and *TSM Bollinger Modified*, available on the Companion Website.

Rules for Using Bands

Regardless of the type of band that is constructed, rules for using bands to generate trading signals are limited. The first decision to be made is whether the trading strategy is one that is always in the market (a reversal strategy), changing from long to short and back again as the bands are penetrated. If so, the following rules apply:

- *Buy* (close out shorts and go long) when the prices close above the upper band.
- *Sell short* (close out longs and go short) when the prices close below the lower band.

FIGURE 9.8 Modified Bollinger Bands Shown with Original Bands (Lighter Lines), Applied to Gold Futures, February–August 2009.

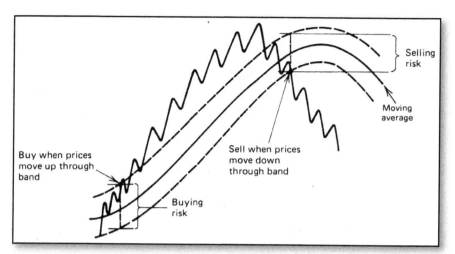

FIGURE 9.9   Simple Reversal Rules for Using Bands.

This technique is always in the market with a maximum risk (without execution costs) equal to the width of the band, which changes each day (see Figure 9.9). Alternately, you may prefer to exit from each trade when prices move into the zone between the bands or when prices cross the original trendline.

- *Buy* (go long) when prices close above the upper band. Close out longs when prices reverse and close below the moving average value (the center of the band).

- *Sell short* when prices close below the lower band. Cover your shorts when prices close above the moving average value.

The band is then used to enter into new long or short trades, and the actual trendline at the center of the band is used for liquidation. If prices are not strong enough to penetrate the opposite band on the close of the same day, the trade is closed out but not reversed. The next day, penetration of either the upper or lower band will signal a new long or short trade, respectively.

This technique allows a trade to be reentered in the same direction in the event of a false trend change. If a pullback occurs after a close-out while no position is being held (as shown in Figure 9.10), an entry at a later date might be at a better price. It also reduces the order size by 50%, which is likely to improve the execution price and add liquidity for large traders. The disadvantage is when the price changes direction and moves so fast that both the close-out and the new signal occur on the same day. Reversing the position immediately would be better in a fast market.

The high and low of the day may also be used as penetration criteria. Again using the outer bands for entry and the moving average for exit, apply the following rules:

- *Buy* when the high of the day penetrates the upper band, and close out longs when the low of the day penetrates the moving average.

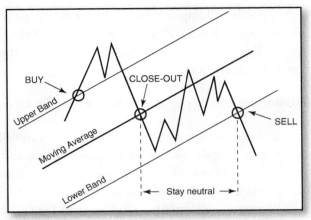

FIGURE 9.10 Basic Rules for Using Bands.

- *Sell short* when the low of the day penetrates the lower band, and cover shorts when the high penetrates the moving average.

Using the trendline as an exit, risk is limited to half of the full band width. If the bands are narrow, there is a greater chance that an entry on an intraday high might also see an exit below the trendline on the close of the same day.

Timing the Order

The type of execution order placed when following a system will affect its results over the long term. The use of a moving average band identifies a change of trend when a breakout occurs. Buying at the point of the upside breakout or selling during a downside breakout often results in poor entry prices, and has been known to place the trader in a new trend at the point where prices are ready for a technical correction. In an attempt to overcome these problems, a number of rules can be used:

- *Buy* (or *sell*) on the close after an entry (intraday) signal has been indicated.

- *Buy* (or *sell*) on the next day's open following a signal.

- *Buy* (or *sell*) with a delay of 1, 2, or 3 days after the signal.

- *Buy* (or *sell*) after a price retracement of 50% (or some other value) following a signal.

- *Buy* (or *sell*) when prices move to within a specified risk level relative to a reversal or exit point.

The object is to enter a new position and see an immediate profit, or reduce risk. Some of these rules can be categorized as timing and others as risk management. If intraday prices are used to signal new entries and exits, a rule may be added that states:

> Only one order can be executed in one day; either the liquidation of a current position or an entry into a new position.

While better entry points will improve overall performance, an entry rule that is contingent on price action, such as a pullback, risks the possibility of not entering at all. A contingent order that is missed is guaranteed to be a profit. It might be better to combine the entry order, for example,

Buy (or sell) after prices reverse by 0.50 × ATR or enter on the next close.

Once you have decided on a timing rule, you must test it carefully. The perception of improvement does not always live up to expectations. In tests on trend-following systems conducted over many years, positions calculated on the close but delayed until the next open improved execution prices about 75% of the time but resulted in smaller overall total profits. Why? Fast breakouts that never retrace result in missed trades. Therefore, while three out of four executions returned a better price by a small amount, those improvements were often offset by the profitable breakouts that were never entered.

The Compromise between Reliability and Delay

As with most trading techniques, the benefits of one approach can also have negative factors. The use of a band around a trendline improves the reliability of the trading signal and reduces the total number of signals. The wider the band, the fewer signals. Both of these characteristics are significant benefits. But wider bands mean delayed entries; therefore, you cannot capture as much of the trend, and the average profits will be smaller. If the bands are too wide, then the average profits can decline to zero. The use of wider bands also means greater risk on each trade. It will be necessary to trade smaller positions or capitalize the account with a larger investment.

These are serious choices that must be made with every trading program. Although there are classic solutions to this problem discussed in Level III, Chapter 12, traders must choose the methods that complement their risk preference.

Bollinger on Bollinger Bands

While most trading strategies buy when there is an upwards penetration of the top band and sell when prices move below the lower band, the use of Bollinger bands is usually mean-reverting, or counter to the price direction. However, this can be unnecessarily risky, especially when prices are volatile. Bollinger recommends confirming a downside penetration using other indicators, primarily those based on volume and market breadth. If prices are moving lower but volume is not increasing and negative breadth is not confirming the downward move, then a buy signal is realistic.[4]

Bollinger uses the concept that volatility is cyclic, but without a regular period. He sees very low volatility as a forecast for high volatility and very high volatility forecasting low volatility, similar to the way traders use the CME Volatility Index

---

[4] John Bollinger, "John Bollinger of Bollinger Bands Fame," *Technical Analysis of Stocks & Commodities* (May 2002).

(VIX). Based on this, a major price rally with dramatically higher volatility, that expands the bandwidth to extremes, should be sold when the bandwidth begins to narrow. This only applies to upwards price moves.

Combining Bollinger with Other Indicators

Williams[5] suggests that a number of indicators can be combined to capture volatile moves after a price contraction, using:

1. A standard 20-day, 2-standard deviation Bollinger band
2. A 20-day Keltner Channel
3. A 21-day Chaikin Oscillator to monitor the flow of funds

To enter a long position, the following conditions must be satisfied:

- The Bollinger bands constrict to inside the Keltner Channel while the Chaikin Oscillator is below zero.

- The Chaikin Oscillator crosses above the zero line.

For shorts,

- The Bollinger bands constrict to inside the Keltner Channel while the Chaikin Oscillator is above zero.

- The Chaikin Oscillator crosses below the zero line.

■ Applications of a Single Trend

For any trend technique, the selection of the calculation period—the interval over which you will define the trend—is the most important decision in the ultimate success of the trading system. Entry rules and timing improve performance but are considered refinements. The calculation period determines the frequency of trading and the nature of the underlying trend that will be targeted. Deciding the calculation period is more important than the method of identifying the trend. You can be profitable using a simple moving average, regression, breakout, or any other technique—if you can settle on the right time interval.

The previous sections have used examples of calculation periods without any claim that one time interval was better than another. We have discussed that the long-term trend mimics government policy of interest rates or economic growth; therefore, there is good reason to choose a longer calculation period. We also saw that the trends were clearer when looking at a weekly chart rather than at a daily, and it was not clear that an intraday chart had any persistent trends. But for most traders, the risk of using this long time frame is unacceptable; they prefer smaller profits and smaller losses associated with faster trading. There is now strategy development software that makes it easy to test a range of calculation periods to find the one that

---

[5] Billy Williams, "Biting Off Profits with the Rattlesnake Breakout Method," *Futures* (October 2010).

performed best in the past. This technique is called optimization and is discussed in Level III, Chapter 10. But the power of the computer is not always as good as simple human reasoning and common sense. The computer is best for validating an idea, not for discovering one.

Before the computer, analysts struggled with the same problem of finding the best calculation period. At first, the trend period was based on multiples of calendar periods, such as a week or a month, expressed as trading days. When these techniques were limited to a small group of analysts, these approaches were very successful. Many traders still subscribe to the idea that certain time intervals have value. The most popular calculation periods have been: 3 days, the expected duration of a short price move; 5 days, a trading week; 20 to 23 days, a trading month; 63 days, a calendar quarter; and of course, 252 days, a calendar year. Implied volatility calculations traditionally use 20 days. It is not clear where the 200-day moving average, used for stocks, came from.

More recently, a class of adaptive trends has appeared. These techniques attempt to change the speed of the trend based on a characteristic of price movement, such as volatility or noise. These techniques are another alternative to optimization and are discussed in Level III, Chapter 6.

The following sections include classic examples of well-known systems that use one trend, as well as a comparison of trading performance of the most popular single-trend techniques over a broad range of calculation periods.

A Simple Momentum System

In Chapter 8 the *n-day momentum* was defined as the change in price over *n* days. It's not actually "momentum" but that is the term commonly used by the industry. The simplest trend system is the one that buys when the *n*-day change is positive and sells when the *n*-day change is negative. For large values of *n,* the results will be surprisingly similar to a simple moving average system; therefore we will not give examples here. Keep in mind that momentum can be very effective even as it is very simple.

A Step-Weighted Moving Average

In 1972, Robert Joel Taylor published the "Major Price Trend Directional Indicator" (MPTDI), which was reprinted in summary form in the September 1973 *Commodities Magazine* (now *Futures*). The system was promoted and implemented through Enterex Commodities in Dallas and was tested in 1972 on historical data provided by Dunn and Hargitt Financial Services in West Lafayette, Indiana. It was one of the few well-defined published systems and served as the basis for much experimentation for current technicians and aspiring analysts.

MPTDI is a moving average with a band. Its unique feature is that the calculation period and band width change based on price volatility, the current trading range. Because the method has distinct trading range thresholds (called steps), the method is called a *step-weighted moving average*. It is unique in its complete dependence on incremental values for all aspects of the system: the moving average, entry, and stop-loss points. For example, Table 9.6 shows what conditions might be assigned to gold.

TABLE 9.6 | MPTDI Variables for Gold*

Average Trading Range	Number of Days in Calculation	Weighting-Factors Progression	Entry Signal Penetration	Approximate Stop-Loss Point
50–150	2–5 days	TYPE A	100 pts	150 pts
150–250	20 days	TYPE B	200 pts	300 pts
250–350	15 days	TYPE C	250 pts	350 pts
350–450	10 days	TYPE D	350 pts	450 pts
450+	5 days	TYPE E	450 pts	550 pts

*100 points = $1 per ounce.

If gold were trading in an average range of 250 to 350 points each day ($2.50 to $3.50 per ounce, but remember this was 1972), the weighting factor for the moving average would be TYPE C, indicating medium volatility (TYPE A is lowest). Using TYPE C with a 15-day moving average, the most recent 5 days are given the weight 3, the next 5 days 2, and the last 5 days are weighted by 1. The entry signals use the corresponding penetration of 250 points above the moving average for a buy and 250 below for a sell. The intraday highs or lows are used to trigger the entry based on values calculated after the close of trading on the prior day. A stop-loss is fixed at the time of entry equal to the value on the same line as the selected volatility. The penetration of the stop-loss will cause the liquidation of the current trade. A new signal in the reverse direction will serve as both the exit for the current trade and the entry for a new trade.

There is a lot to say in favor of the principles of MPTDI. It is individualized with respect to markets and self-adjusting to changing volatility. The stop-loss serves to limit the initial risk of the trade and allow the coordination of a money management approach. The fixed risk differs from moving averages using standard bands because a moving average and its band can back away from system entry points if there is a gradual reversal of the price trend. But there are some rough edges to the system. The incremental ranges for volatility, entry points, and stops seem to be a crude measure. Even if they are accurate in the center of the range, they must get less accurate at the extremes where volatility causes an abrupt change in parameter values when it moves from one range to another.

MPTDI sets the groundwork for a smoother, more adaptive process. Before such a process can be developed, however, it is necessary to study price movement at discrete levels, such as those shown in MPTDI. From discrete relationships it is possible to generalize a continuous relationship. These methods are covered in Level III, Chapter 6.

The Volatility System

Another method that includes volatility and is computationally simple is the *Volatility System*.[6] Signals are generated when a price change is accompanied by an unusually

---

[6] Richard Bookstaber, *The Complete Investment Book* (Glenview, IL: Scott, Foresman, 1984), 231.

large move relative to average volatility. If the average volatility measured over n days is

$$V_t = \frac{1}{n} \sum_{i=t-n+1}^{t} TR_i$$

where TR_i is the *true range* on day i and V_t is the called the *average true range* on day t.

Trading rules are given as

- *Sell* if the close drops by more than $k \times V(n)_{t-1}$ from the previous close.

- *Buy* if the close rises by more than $k \times V(n)_{t-1}$ from the previous close.

The value of k is generally about 3.0. Note that the current price change is always compared to the previous volatility calculation.

The 10-Day Moving Average Rule

The most basic application of a moving average system was proposed by Keltner in his 1960 publication, *How to Make Money in Commodities*. Of three mechanical systems presented by Keltner, his choice of a moving average was based on performance and experience. The system itself is quite simple, a 10-day moving average using the average of the daily high, low, and closing prices, with a band on each side formed from the 10-day moving average of the high-low range (similar to a 10-day average true range). A buy signal occurs on penetration of the upper band and a sell signal when the lower band is broken; positions are always reversed.

The *10-Day Moving Average Rule* is basic, but it does apply the fundamental volatility principle by using the high-low range as a band, and serves as an early example of moving averages. Keltner expresses his preference for this particular technique because of its identification of minor rather than medium- or long-term trends, and there are some performance figures that substantiate his conclusion. As an experienced trader, he prefers the speed of the 10-day moving average, which follows the market prices with more reasonable risk than slower methods. A side benefit to the selection is that the usual division required by a moving average calculation can be substituted by a simple shift of the decimal place; in an era before the pocket calculator, who knows how much impact that convenience had on Keltner's choice.

The history of prices now shows us that price movement was much smoother up to the end of the 1970s and has been getting noisier ever since. A 10-day moving average, supplemented by a volatility band, was truly the state-of-the-art technology. While the shorter calculation periods are not generally successful for current price moves, the use of volatility to create bands has held up well over time.

---

[7] Jack K. Hutson, "Good TRIX," *Technical Analysis of Stocks & Commodities* (July 1983).

CHAPTER 10

Trend Systems (Part 2)

From Perry J. Kaufman, *Trading Systems and Methods, +Website*, 5th Edition (Hoboken, New Jersey: John Wiley & Sons, 2013), Chapter 8.

■ Techniques Using Two Trendlines

There are many situations where two trends of different calculation periods can solve a problem better than one. It is often the case that there is a dominant, long-term trend driven by government interest rate policy. Trends based on fiscal policy can last for years and can be very successful. Most traders, however, are not likely to hold a single long-term trade for the full period of its move. Even if convinced of the ultimate outcome of the trade, there can be very large price swings along the way. Most traders would rather enter and exit the market many times, in the direction of the longer-term trend, each time taking a small profit but with much smaller risk. The final result may be lower total profits, but a much more comfortable risk level for each trade.

This problem can be solved with two simple moving averages or a combination of any two trendlines of different speeds. The slower trendline, using a longer calculation period, identifies the primary trend. The faster trendline is used for timing. The faster signal does not have to be a trend at all; it can be pattern recognition or any timing method. In this section, we will use the same trending techniques previously discussed to create a system. The longer calculation period will represent the major trend and the shorter period will be used for timing. Consider the idea that a good entry point is when there is a recent short-term surge of prices in the direction of the major trend. To implement this plan, select two moving averages, one noticeably faster than the other, and apply one of the following sets of rules (also shown in Figure 10.1).

1. *Buy* when the faster moving average crosses the slower moving average going up. *Sell short* when the faster moving average crosses the slower moving average going down.

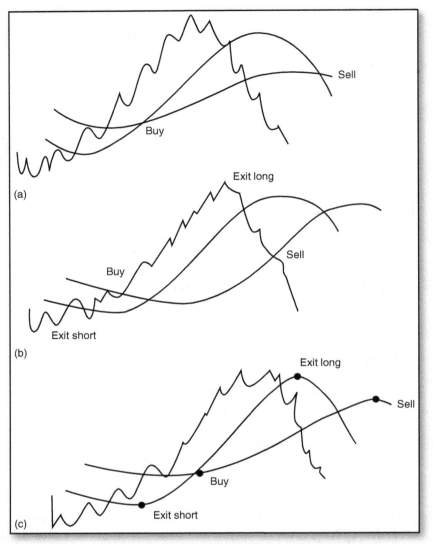

FIGURE 10.1 Three Ways to Trade Systems Using Two Moving Averages.
(a) Enter and exit when the trendlines cross. (b) Buy and sell when the
price crosses the trendlines, staying out of the market when prices are
between the trendlines. (c) Enter when both trendlines are moving in
the same direction; exit when they conflict.

2. *Buy* when the current price crosses above *both* moving averages and close out
   long positions when prices cross below *either* moving average. *Sell short* when
   the current price crosses below *both* moving averages, and close out short positions when prices cross above *either* moving average.
3. *Buy* when the faster trendline turns up and the slower trendline is up. *Sell short*
   when the faster trendline turns down and the slower trendline is down. *Exit* the
   trade when the two trendlines are moving in opposite directions.

The first set of rules always has a position in the market, going from long to short
and back again as the faster trend crosses the long-term trend. The second and third

sets of rules create a neutral zone, where no position is held. Rule 2 attempts to extract the stronger part of the price move based on price, while Rule 3 looks for both trends to provide confirmation. Exiting a trade, rather than reversing, adds liquidity by reducing the order size and allows you to enter the next trade in the same direction as the previous one, instead of always reversing.

To further reduce the problem of whipsaws caused by erratic penetration of the trendlines in Rule 2, yet maintain a faster response to price change than Rule 3, a small band can be placed around each of the trendlines. Prices must move higher through the upper band before a buy signal occurs and then back through the lower band before that signal is reversed. It is a small safety zone that can eliminate the frequency of bad trades in proportion to the size of the band. With this technique you would want the band to be small; otherwise, you will interfere with the natural process that is the benefit of the two trendlines.

Donchian's 5- and 20-Day Moving Average System

The method claiming one of the longest recorded trading histories, beginning January 1, 1961, is *Donchian's 5- and 20-Day Moving Average*.[1] In 1961, when moving averages were considered state-of-the-art, there was less noise, and agricultural markets were the most liquid. The equivalent of a 1- and 4-week moving average would have worked well. Even now, the use of calendar periods—such as 21 and 63 days for a month and a quarter, respectively—may pick up trends driven by the action of major fund managers as they rebalance their portfolio each month, and also respond to price direction resulting from quarterly earnings reports.

Donchian's idea was to use a volatility-penetration criterion relative to the 20-day moving average, but with some added complication. The current price penetration must not only cross the 20-day moving average but also exceed any previous 1-day penetration of a closing price by at least one volatility measure. In this way Donchian places a flexible band around the 20-day trendline. One volatility measure can be calculated as the average true range over one or more days.

The 5-day moving average serves as a liquidation criterion (along with others) and is also modified by prior penetration and volatility. These features tend to make Donchian's approach an early rendition of self-adjusting rules. To maintain a human element, Donchian requires execution of certain orders to be delayed a day if the signals occurred on specific weekdays or before a holiday. The combination of different factors was the result of refinement over years of actual operation.

Rather than try to implement Donchian's idea exactly, the program *TSM Donchian Moving Average System*, available on the Companion Website, uses the calculations:

1. A 5-day moving average
2. A 20-day moving average
3. The average true range based on the longer moving average

[1] Richard D. Donchian, "Donchian's 5- and 20-Day Moving Averages," *Commodities Magazine* (December 1974).

These three calculations are then used with the rules

- If position is not long and $Close_t > MA5_{t-1} + 1ATR_{t-1}$ and $close_t > MA20_{t-1} + 1ATR_{t-1}$ then *buy*

- If position is not short and $Close_t < MA5_{t-1} - 1ATR_{t-1}$ and $close_t < MA20_{t-1} - 1ATR_{t-1}$ then *sell short*

- If position is long and $(Close_t < MA5_{t-1} - 1ATR_{t-1}$ or $close_t < MA20_{t-1} - 1ATR_{t-1})$ then exit long position

- If position is short and $(Close_t > MA5_{t-1} + 1ATR_{t-1}$ or $close_t > MA20_{t-1} + 1ATR_{t-1})$ then cover short position

Because the price level and volatility of the market have changed dramatically since 1960, new positions should be sized according their volatility

$$Position\ size = Investment/(ATR \times Big\ Point\ Value)$$

Where ATR is calculated over the longer moving average period and the *Big Point Value* is the conversion factor for a futures contract, for example $50 for corn and $1000 for U.S. bonds.

How did this strategy perform? Applying these rules to corn, which would have been the primary market during the 1960s, and without costs (which were much higher until the mid-1990s), the cumulative profits are shown in Figure 10.2. Although the rate of return has slowed, it seems remarkable that a simple method could have been consistently profitable for 50 years. For those analysts who are interested, the program on the Companion Website allows the calculation periods to change as well as the penetration factor. Only corn was run for this example, and no parameters were tested or changed.

Donchian's 20- and 40-Day Breakout

One level slower than the 5- and 20-day average is Donchian's 20- and 40-Day Breakout. Instead of 1 week and 1 month, this looks at 1 month and 2 months. The

FIGURE 10.2 Donchian's 5- and 20-Day Moving Average System (somewhat modernized) Applied to Corn Futures from 1960.

method is far less complicated and only considers simple breakouts rather than using volatility bands. The rules are

> *Buy* when *today's high* > *high* of the past 40 days
>
> *Sell* short when *today's low* < *low* of the past 40 days
>
> *Exit* longs when *today's low* < *low* of the past 20 days
>
> *Exit* shorts when *today's high* > *high* of the past 20 days

Readers will recognize that this is the basis for the Turtle's trading method.

The Golden Cross and the Death Cross

The most popular stock market trending methods are the simplest, which does not mean they don't work. Of course, the 200-day moving average is shown as the key technical indicator on most financial networks, but 50, 100, and 200 days are equally popular. It is not clear how these began, but doubling the period is a simple way of keeping percentage changes the same and getting a good distribution of results over time.

The *Golden Cross* is the point at which the 50-day average crosses above the 200-day average indicating the beginning of a bullish move in the market. It has yielded very good results for the past 60 years and avoided the damaging declines of 2008. When the 50-day average crosses below the 200 day, it is ominously called the *Death Cross*.

In Figure 10.3, the results of Golden Cross are compared to the passive returns of the S&P index (SPX) and continuous futures, remembering that SPX cannot be traded. When the trend signal indicates a short sale, the 1-day returns of the 3-month T-bill rate are used for the daily returns. A spreadsheet named TSM Golden Cross can be found on the Companion Website.

For the 11 years beginning mid-1999, the passive return of the stock market was a loss of 7.8%. During the same period, the Golden Cross returned 66.7% using SPX and 36.7% using futures. While the cash index can be traded as the ETF SPY, the futures contract is reasonable alternative. In addition, futures can be leveraged considerably, increasing the returns (and the risk).

FIGURE 10.3 The Golden Cross Applied to the S&P Index (SPX) and

All the calculations are shown in the Golden Cross spreadsheet, but the way in which the returns of continuous futures are matched to SPX needs some explanation. While the daily returns of SPX are calculated as $\ln(p_t / p_{t-1})$, continuous futures are back adjusted and values can become negative. The annualized volatility of SPX was calculated in the classic way, but the annualized volatility of the futures was calculated based on the daily change in dollar value of the futures contract.

1. Begin with an arbitrary, but large, investment size
2. Calculate the daily returns based on the initial investment size
3. Calculate the rolling 20-day annualized volatility of the returns
4. Find the factor needed to make the annualized volatility 12%
5. Multiply the current returns by the previous volatility factor
6. Create the NAVs from the volatility-adjusted returns

In Figure 10.3 the annualized volatility of SPX is 11.5%, and the volatility of the futures returns is 10.9%. The process of adjusting the portfolio volatility is discussed in detail in Level III, Chapter 12.

ROC Method   Another classic method for trading the major index is *Woodshedder's long-term indicator.*[2] The rules are

- *Buy* when the 5-day ROC (rate-of-change) is below the 252-day ROC for two consecutive days.

- *Exit the long* when the 5-day ROC is above the 252-day ROC for two consecutive days.

- When there is no position, the system earns one-half of the cash 3-month T-bill rate.

In Figure 10.4, the results are compared to the Golden Cross, both using SPY as the basis for trading, from April 15, 1994 (the first available data for SPY plus the

FIGURE 10.4   Comparison of Golden Cross and ROC Method Using SPY.

---

[2] The *Woodshedder* blog can be found at www.ibankcoin.com/woodshedderblog and covers many other strategies. This method was reviewed by *MarketSci blog* on October 4, 2011, but used SPX (the cash index) rather than SPY.

252-day windup), through September 2011. No costs were charged although SPY has administrative cost included. The ROC method far outperformed the Golden Cross even with an annualized volatility of 14.1% compared to the Golden Cross volatility of 10.5%. Note that trading the SPY gave better returns than SP futures, shown in Figure 10.4.

Staying Ahead of the Crowd

There is always an attempt to find out where others are placing their orders and get ahead of them. For example, if you know that most trend-followers are using a 30-day calculation period, then using a 28-day average might edge them out. During the 1980s and 1990s there was a trend system that used 8 and 18 days to beat the 10 and 20 days that was most popular. The following calculations would use *fastperiod* = 8 and *slowperiod* = 18. The *differenceperiod* = 9.

$$FasterAverage = Average(close, fastperiod)$$
$$SlowerAverage = Average(close, slowperiod)$$
$$TrendDifference = FasterAverage - SlowerAverage$$
$$DifferenceAverage = Average(TrendDifference, differenceperiod)$$

The trading rules were

Buy when *today's TrendDifference* > *yesterday's DifferenceAverage*
Sell short when *today's TrendDifference* < *yesterday's DifferenceAverage*

Although these calculation periods may not be profitable in today's markets, the idea of being slightly ahead of the crowd can give you *free exposure*, a small jump in profits caused by many orders following yours. If you can figure out where the crowd is buying and selling, then this concept will give you an edge.

■ Multiple Trends and Common Sense

If two trendlines can improve trading, it should follow that three or more are even better—but there may be more problems than benefits. Many analysts subscribe to the idea that *simpler is better*. A single moving average may not have a high percentage of profitable trades but the longer-term periods work because they capture the fat tail.

With the use of two trends, the number of combinations expands rapidly. Is there a *best* relationship between the slower speed and the faster one, that is, should the faster trend period be ¼ of the slower? Certainly, a 38- and 40-day combination will not offer much value, but is a 10-day and 40-day the right combination?

Consider something else. If a 10-day trend is not profitable, and a 20-day trend is not profitable, each taken on their own, but the combination is profitable, would you trade it? These questions will be addressed in Level III, Chapter 10, but some of the concepts should be clear now. If, by computer testing, we were to "discover" that a combination of 2 or 3 trends was profitable, would you be convinced to trade

Trend	Number of Trades	Days Held	Total Profit	Ratio	Avg Trade Profit	%Prof Trades
60	164	31	16537	1.65	149	22.5
20	350	16	21737	1.44	62	31.0
Both	254	16	15310	1.50	92	34.6

it? Not likely, unless a very large percentage of the combinations were profitable or each trend served a particular purpose and had a calculation period that reflected that purpose.

For example, if longer-term trends are intended to track macro fundamental policy and were generally profitable, then that longer-term period would be a good candidate for one of the trends. But those trades can be held for months, and you don't like that profile, so you want a shorter trend to tell you when to get in and out of that trade, always holding a position in the direction of the long-term trend. Using Eurodollars with 60-day and 20-day trends over the past 20 years, with a $40 round-turn cost, Table 10.1 shows the change in performance. Both single trends do very well, but the 60-day holds trades for an average of 31 days, about 1½ months. The 20-day trend would be better, but the average profit per trade is only $62. By combining the two trends and trading only in the direction of the long-term trend, the profits per trade jump to $92, and the days held remain the same as the 20-day trend. Overall, you get slightly worse performance than the long-term trend but hold the trade for half the time. That makes sense because you are only trading the longs rather than both longs and shorts.

Another benefit of the two-trend method is that you are in the market only 50% of the time. That reduces your risk, especially the risk of a price shock. That is a benefit not to be taken lightly.

Three Trends

Is there a rationale for more than two trends? If the long-term trend is for market direction, and the shorter one is to reduce the length of the holding period, then the third could be using for entry timing. The third trend could be very fast, perhaps 3 days.

Gerald Appel[3] adds three rate-of-change (ROC) indicators together (actually momentum, the difference between the price today and the price *n* days ago), and applies the composite to the S&P index (SPX), all expressed in percent. He recommends buying when the composite crosses above 4% and exiting when it falls below 4%. If you consider the upwards bias in the S&P, the 4% threshold may not be arbitrary.

---

[3] Gerald Appel, *Technical Analysis: Power Tool for Active Traders* (Upper Saddle River, NJ: FT Prentice Hall, 2005), 59.

Modified 3-Crossover Model

The justification for using three trends is that one or more slower moving averages may result in a buy or sell signal at a time when the prices are actually moving opposite to the position that is about to be entered. This may happen if the trading signal is generated when the two moving average lines cross, rather than when price move through the averages. The slope of a third, faster moving average, $MA3_t - MA3_{t-1}$, can be used as a confirmation of direction to avoid entry into a trade that is going the wrong way. This filter can be added to any moving average or multiple moving average system with the following rule:

> Do not enter a new long (or short) position unless the slope of the confirming moving average (the change in the moving average value from the prior day to today) was up (or down).

The speed of this third, confirming moving average only makes sense if it is equal to or faster than the fastest of the trends used in the Crossover System. A program to test the three-trend model is TSM Modified 3MA Cross, available on the Companion Website.

In earlier tests of the 3-Crossover method compared to the 2-Crossover, results showed that the added timing in the 3-Crossover reduced the number of trades and increased the size of the returns per contract. Overall, the profitability remained about the same.

4-9-18 Crossover Model

During the late 1970s, the 4-9-18 Crossover model was very popular. It seems likely that the selection of 4, 9, and 18 days was a conscious effort to be slightly ahead of the 5, 10, and 20 days frequently used in moving average systems during that period. It is also likely to have been the outcome of the first computerized testing. Even now, high frequency traders continue to look for the smallest edge that keeps them ahead of the competition. In addition to the marginally faster calculation periods each moving average is (nearly) twice the speed of the prior, enhancing their uniqueness for recognizing different trends. Increasing the period in this way keeps a constant percentage difference.

To get an idea of how three trends compare to either one or two trends, a small test was run using Eurobund futures from 1990 to mid-2011. Granted this is a trending market, and one test does not reflect the big picture; nevertheless, the results, shown in Table 10.2, were unexpected. Because we already know that

TABLE 10.2	Comparison of Single Trend Results with a 2- and 3-Moving Average Crossover Strategies, Applied to Eurobunds, 1990 to Mid-2011			
Strategy	Net PL	Profit Factor	Trades	Profit/Contract
40-Day MA	13300	1.11	310	42
80-Day MA	55620	1.88	152	365
40-80 Crossover	35040	1.45	229	153
20-40-80 Crossover	61210	2.80	42	1457

faster trends are not performing as well in recent years as they did in the 1970s, the test of Eurobunds compared a 40-day and an 80-day calculation period with a 40-80-day crossover and a 20-40-80-day combination. The 3-crossover method outperformed all others but also reduced the number of trades by emphasizing the trend direction.

■ Comprehensive Studies

Because computerized testing platforms have made it easy for anyone to test any number of trends in combination, there have been very few comprehensive studies published since 1990. The exceptions are Colby's *The Encyclopedia of Technical Market Indicators* and Bulkowski's *Encyclopedia of Chart Patterns*, both of which show results in a standard form and make it easy to compare the differences between systems. But most traders seeking a strategy will need to test it themselves and add their own special features. Both Colby and Bulkowski will give you a good idea of which methods and patterns to avoid.

There is a great deal to learn from putting the results of various systems and markets side by side. Earlier in this chapter, there is an informative comparison of six major trending systems; in Level III, Chapter 10 tests of single-trend strategies are compared for a standard set of 17 futures markets. In addition, a 2-trend crossover strategy is compared to the single trend methods. An objective of the testing process is to find parameters that succeed over time; this discussion can also be found in Level III, Chapter 10.

■ Selecting the Right Trend Method and Speed

Up to now, the selection of the right moving average, the one that will work in the future, has only been discussed in general terms. The success of a single calculation period for a single trend strategy does not mean that it is the right choice for trading. In addition, the best moving average speed for institutional or commercial participants may be very different from that of an active trader.[4] For example, a mutual fund receives new investments that must be moved into the market, collectively, once or twice each month. In the same way, a cattle feed lot will choose one time each month to fix the price of new inventory. A 3-day moving average might generate 5 to 10 buy and sell signals in one month, each the result of a 2-day price move—an ineffective tool for either participant looking for just one place to enter the market. A calculation period of 10 days may come closer to generating the one buy signal needed for the fund or one sell signal that is best for the hedger. The noncommercial trader is not concerned about the frequency of trades, only the returns and risk.

[4] Perry J. Kaufman, "Moving Averages and Trends" in Todd Lofton, ed., *Trading Tactics: A Livestock Anthology* (Chicago: Chicago Mercantile Exchange, 1986).

For the trader or speculator, the right moving average speed is the one that produces the best performance profile. This profile could be simply maximum profits, or it could be a more complex combination of profits, risk, and time in the market. In Level III, Chapter 10, automated testing is used to find the combination of speed, stop-loss, and other rules that best satisfy an objective; a computer, however, is not always necessary.

Computer testing of a trend system or other trading strategies sometimes leads to solutions that are highly fitted. The computer may find that a 3-day moving average was slightly more profitable and had lower risk than a 20-day average. Our common sense tells us that the results of the 3-day system will be more difficult to attain in real trading because execution costs will have a larger impact. An occasional fast market may cause the execution price to be far off from the price indicated by the system signal. A slower trend selection with fewer trades is less affected by poor executions.

Dominant seasonal factors are an important influence on the calculation period of the trend. While some stocks, such as travel and leisure, can be highly seasonal, their seasonal price patterns can be overwhelmed by a strong trend in the overall market, as measured by the S&P 500. In fact, the arbitraging of the S&P 500 futures with the actual stocks has significantly changed the patterns of the many stocks, forcing many of them to have higher correlations. However, a grain trader knows that the price pattern has a clear cycle each year. At best, we can expect one long upwards move followed by a shorter, faster decline. Not all trend speeds can capture the profits in this pattern. For example, if the uptrend lasts for 6 months, a 6-month moving average will not see any of it; therefore, it is necessary to use a moving average with a period less than one quarter of the length of the trend. If computerized testing of a large range of moving average calculation periods results in a "best" moving average period of six months or more, that choice should be interpreted as a failure to capture the seasonal move.

We also discussed the "right" trend method earlier in this chapter. Tests over many years and many diverse markets will show that the differences in net returns using different trend strategies are small. Those differences will be larger when the trend speeds are faster. The most important differences are not in the profits but in the frequency of trades, the size of the individual returns, and the risk of each trade. Experience shows that the primary reason why trend-following systems work is because sustained price moves exist, driven mostly by government interest rate policy. Every trend-following system can capture these moves.

Selecting the Trend Speed

Level III, Chapter 10 will discuss the systematic ways to find the "best" trend, and that is the most likely way that traders make their choice. But you can find a reasonable choice by simply looking at a price chart. The trends that two traders see are often different. Some traders immediately focus on long-term price trends; others see much shorter movements. To find your own best trend speed without the use of a computer, mark on a chart the beginning and end of each price move that you would like to capture. These trends may occur every few days, or only three or four times each year.

FIGURE 10.5   Finding the Moving Average Calculation Period from the
Average Span of Peaks and Valleys.

Using a daily price chart of IBM from July 2000 through May 2002 (Figure 10.5), the tops and bottoms of the major price swings that we would like to capture were circled. Noting that each gridline on the chart represents one month, there were eight tops and bottoms over a total period of 22 months. The average price swing was then 2¾ months, nearly one calendar quarter. Because it is so close to a quarterly value, which is the period of earnings reports, we will choose three months as the average swing period. Applying the rule of thumb that the trend can be isolated using a calculation period of one-quarter of the swing period, the moving average period becomes 16 days.

Applying a 16-day moving average system to the two years of IBM price data, buying and selling whenever the trendline changes direction, the trade results are shown in Table 10.3. There are a total of 36 trades, of which 20 were profitable (no transaction costs were used)—a very high percentage for a trend-following system. Total profits were better than $114 per share, on an average share price of about $100, showing that it is not necessary to optimize using a computer to create a successful trading program. Of course, there is no assurance that this pattern of swings will continue, but basing the decision on quarterly swings, which corresponds to earnings reports, is a hopeful sign.

Another approach to finding the trend period is to consider the worst price retracement. In the IBM chart, the move from $87 to $105, beginning in November 2000 and lasting about two months, is the one to avoid. Remembering that a trend is neutralized with regard to a price move when the trend period is the same length as the total move, we apply a moving average of 42 days. This method successfully avoids the price correction and holds the downtrend, but the much

TABLE 10.3	Performance of 16-Day Moving Average Applied to IBM from July 2000 through May 2002							
Trade #	Entry Date	Entry Order	Entry Price	Exit Date	Exit Order	Exit Price	Profit/ Loss	Total P/L
1	6/29/2000	Sell	114.00	7/20/2000	SExit	117.25	−3.25	−3.25
2	7/20/2000	Buy	117.25	7/24/2000	LExit	112.50	−4.75	−8.00
3	7/24/2000	Sell	112.50	7/25/2000	SExit	112.00	0.50	−7.50
4	7/25/2000	Buy	112.00	9/18/2000	LExit	123.25	11.25	3.75
5	9/18/2000	Sell	123.25	11/9/2000	SExit	99.44	23.81	27.56
6	11/9/2000	Buy	99.44	11/10/2000	LExit	93.00	−6.44	21.12
7	11/10/2000	Sell	93.00	11/13/2000	SExit	97.44	−4.44	16.68
8	11/13/2000	Buy	97.44	11/27/2000	LExit	98.44	1.00	17.68
9	11/27/2000	Sell	98.44	12/5/2000	SExit	103.38	−4.94	12.74
10	12/5/2000	Buy	103.38	12/6/2000	LExit	96.75	−6.63	6.11
11	12/6/2000	Sell	96.75	1/5/2001	SExit	94.00	2.75	8.86
12	1/5/2001	Buy	94.00	2/20/2001	LExit	111.50	17.50	26.36
13	2/20/2001	Sell	111.50	4/5/2001	SExit	98.21	13.29	39.65
14	4/5/2001	Buy	98.21	5/11/2001	LExit	111.81	13.60	53.25
15	5/11/2001	Sell	111.81	5/15/2001	SExit	113.58	−1.77	51.48
16	5/15/2001	Buy	113.58	5/23/2001	LExit	117.40	3.82	55.30
17	5/23/2001	Sell	117.40	5/24/2001	SExit	119.60	−2.20	53.10
18	5/24/2001	Buy	119.60	5/29/2001	LExit	115.27	−4.33	48.77
19	5/29/2001	Sell	115.27	6/5/2001	SExit	116.97	−1.70	47.07
20	6/5/2001	Buy	116.97	6/12/2001	LExit	117.25	0.28	47.35
21	6/12/2001	Sell	117.25	6/22/2001	SExit	112.87	4.38	51.73
22	6/22/2001	Buy	112.87	6/25/2001	LExit	112.65	−0.22	51.51
23	6/25/2001	Sell	112.65	7/31/2001	SExit	105.21	7.44	58.95
24	7/31/2001	Buy	105.21	8/6/2001	LExit	106.51	1.30	60.25
25	8/6/2001	Sell	106.51	8/10/2001	SExit	104.95	1.56	61.81
26	8/10/2001	Buy	104.95	8/17/2001	LExit	104.59	−0.36	61.45
27	8/17/2001	Sell	104.59	10/5/2001	SExit	98.02	6.57	68.02
28	10/5/2001	Buy	98.02	1/11/2002	LExit	120.31	22.29	90.31
29	1/11/2002	Sell	120.31	3/4/2002	SExit	105.90	14.41	104.72
30	3/4/2002	Buy	105.90	3/6/2002	LExit	106.30	0.40	105.12
31	3/6/2002	Sell	106.30	3/12/2002	SExit	108.50	−2.20	102.92
32	3/12/2002	Buy	108.50	3/26/2002	LExit	102.90	−5.60	97.32
33	3/26/2002	Sell	102.90	5/22/2002	SExit	84.00	18.90	116.22
34	5/22/2002	Buy	84.00	5/24/2002	LExit	83.10	−0.90	115.32
35	5/24/2002	Sell	83.10	5/28/2002	SExit	82.08	1.02	116.34
36	5/28/2002	Buy	82.08	5/31/2002	LExit	80.45	−1.63	114.71

slower trend nets a significant loss over the 2-year period. It is best to accept the frequent small losses that are natural in a trend-following system than attempt to remove them.

■ Moving Average Sequences: Signal Progression

Consider the case where you have selected a 20-day moving average to trade. You enter the day long Biotech, and you get a sell signal. However, you are unaware that the 19-day and 21-day moving averages did not get sell signals. This means that the day that was dropped off the calculation 20 days ago caused a slight shift not seen by the other neighboring trends. This can be an important piece of information when assessing the reliability of the trend signal.

A moving average is simply a consensus of direction. It is an approximation of values intended to steer a trader to the right side of the market at the right time. It is most fallible when prices are changing direction or going sideways. Any information that clears up the problem is helpful. For any trend system, it is best to see a steady progression of trend changes from the short term to the long term. This is seen in the following tables, where *u* is an uptrend and *d* is a downtrend associated with the calculation period above those letters.

In Table 10.4, prices have turned up in such a way that the trend calculation periods 1 through 19 show uptrends, while calculation periods from 20 and higher have not yet turned. Unfortunately, normal price movement is not often as uniform as this example. The shorter-term trends can be very erratic, and often appear in smaller, alternating groups of up and down trends (see Table 10.5). This is easily explained because adding and subtracting one day when only two, three, or four days are used in the moving average calculation can quickly change the direction of the trend. As you get to longer intervals, such as 20, 30, and 50 days, this is not the case, and in reality, it does not happen often. Yet when it does, the trend change is not to be trusted.

There are also cases where the longer trend begins to reassert itself and the results appear the same as in Table 10.4; however, the trend change occurs from the longer-term down (from right to left instead of left to right). The case we must watch for satisfies neither of these, but occurs in an erratic pattern, such as in Table 10.6. Here we see a dominant long-term uptrend with the very short end

TABLE 10.4   Orderly Trend Change

	Moving Average Period in Days																								
	1	2	3	4	5	6	7	8	9	10	11	12	13	14	15	16	17	18	19	20	21	22	23	24	25
Trend	u	u	u	u	u	u	u	u	u	u	u	u	u	u	u	u	u	u	u	d	d	d	d	d	d

TABLE 10.5   Erratic Trend Change for the Short Calculation Periods

	Moving Average Period in Days																								
	1	2	3	4	5	6	7	8	9	10	11	12	13	14	15	16	17	18	19	20	21	22	23	24	25
Trend	u	u	d	d	u	d	u	d	u	u	u	u	u	u	u	u	u	u	u	d	d	d	d	d	d

TABLE 10.6   Progression of Trend Changes

	Moving Average Period in Days																								
	1	2	3	4	5	6	7	8	9	10	11	12	13	14	15	16	17	18	19	20	21	22	23	24	25
Trend	d	d	d	d	u	u	u	u	u	u	u	u	u	u	u	u	u	u	d	d	u	u	u	u	u
Trend	d	d	d	d	d	d	d	d	d	d	d	d	d	u	u	u	u	u	d	d	u	u	u	u	u

turning down. Because of another downturn a few days ago, which then disappeared, this most recent downturn also caused a shadow turn in the 20-day range. Is it a leading indicator or a false signal? All indications are that smooth changes in a trend are more reliable precursors of change. Another case is given in the second line of Table 10.6. Here, the smooth trend change from up to down is occurring from left to right; however, as it gets to 13 days, it also jumps ahead to 19 and 20 days, leaving days 14 through 18 still in an uptrend. For trends in this faster range, it appears best to wait for all fastest trends to change. As the calculation period becomes longer, it is unrealistic to expect all faster trends to be the same; therefore, you will need to settle for an orderly change in a group of trends faster than the target trend period.

An example of this process is shown in Figure 10.6. Moving average calculation periods of 5 to 50 days are shown in increments of five days for a total of 44 consecutive days. This illustration points out how the long-term uptrend (X) is breached by shorter-term, less consistent trends. Perhaps the best trend is the one with the majority of Xs or Os on the same line.

Averaging the Sequences

The idea of requiring consistency in a range of trends can be automated by selecting a range of calculation periods preceding a target period, finding the trend signal (an uptrend or downtrend), and then deciding according to one of two rules:

1. Average the final trend values to get the average trend result. Compare the previous average result with the current value to determine the direction of the trend.
2. Scan the trend directions for consistent progression.

When selecting the range of calculation periods, start from 1 if the target period is small (e.g., your intended trend is 15 days). If you are looking at an intermediate trend period, for example, 30 days, you may want to include the range from 20 to 30, or 20 to 32. A few up-and-down price moves that make the short-end erratic should not alter the medium-term trend direction. By extending the calculation periods slightly past the target period, you gain confirmation at the cost of a small lag.

The idea that trends are sensitive to small price changes and the drop-off effect is not a surprise. An alternative to examining sequences is simply to select a number of calculation periods and net out the trends looking for a consensus. That would remove any dependence on a single selection.

	Moving Average Period									
Day	5	10	15	20	25	30	35	40	45	50
1	X	X	X	X	X	X	X	X	X	X
2	O	O	X	X	X	X	X	X	X	X
3	O	X	X	X	X	X	X	X	X	X
4	X	X	X	X	X	X	X	X	X	X
5	X	X	X	X	X	X	X	X	X	X
6	X	X	X	X	X	X	X	X	X	X
7	X	X	X	X	X	X	X	X	X	X
8	O	X	X	X	X	X	X	X	X	X
9	X	O	O	O	X	X	X	X	X	X
10	O	O	O	O	O	X	X	X	X	X
11	O	O	O	O	X	X	X	X	X	X
12	O	O	O	O	O	O	O	X	X	X
13	O	O	O	O	X	X	X	X	X	X
14	X	O	O	O	O	O	X	X	X	X
15	O	O	O	O	O	O	O	O	O	X
16	O	O	O	O	O	O	O	O	O	O
17	O	O	O	O	O	O	O	O	O	O
18	O	O	O	O	O	O	O	O	O	O
19	X	O	O	O	O	O	O	O	O	O
20	X	O	O	O	O	O	O	O	O	O
21	X	X	X	O	O	O	O	X	X	X
22	X	X	X	X	O	X	X	X	X	X
23	X	X	X	O	O	O	O	X	X	X
24	X	X	X	X	O	O	O	X	X	X
25	X	X	X	X	O	O	O	X	X	X
26	O	X	X	O	O	O	O	O	O	X
27	O	O	O	O	O	O	O	O	O	O
28	O	O	O	O	O	O	O	O	O	O
29	O	X	X	X	O	O	O	O	O	X
30	X	X	X	X	X	O	O	O	X	X
31	X	X	X	X	X	O	O	O	O	X
32	X	X	X	X	X	X	X	X	X	X
33	X	X	X	X	X	X	X	X	X	X
34	X	X	X	X	X	X	X	X	X	X
35	X	X	X	X	X	X	X	X	X	X
36	X	X	X	X	X	X	X	X	X	X
37	X	X	X	X	X	X	X	X	X	X
38	O	X	X	X	X	X	X	X	X	X
39	O	O	X	X	X	X	X	X	X	X
40	O	O	X	X	X	X	X	X	X	X
41	O	X	X	X	X	X	X	X	X	X
42	X	X	X	X	X	X	X	X	X	X
43	X	X	X	X	X	X	X	X	X	X
44	X	X	X	X	X	X	X	X	X	X

FIGURE 10.6 Sequences of Moving Averages.

Early Exits from a Trend

By now we know that capturing the fat tail is necessary for the success of trend-following systems. However, there are always practical exceptions if you are allowed to add discretion to your trading decisions. One of the oldest truths for trend-following is "Take your losses and let your profits run." By imposing profit-taking, or even stop-losses, this can be changed to "Take your profits and let your losses run." There is a need to be very careful when making exceptions. But consider the following situation.

Interest rates have declined for nearly all of the 30 years from 1981 through 2011. For many traders, that's more than their entire professional career. To profit from this move, a slow trend system can track the 10-year Treasury note futures contract, a municipal or corporate bond index, or any number of varying maturity funds. If a 200-day trend were used, then there would be a lag of 100 days. That is, for a bond fund, the current value of the trendline would reflect the bond prices at the midpoint of the calculation period, 50 days. If the yield on interest rates had steadily dropped a total of 2% during the past year, then the trendline would be lagging about 1% behind current yields. That can translate into a large loss in unrealized gains.

One advantage of macrotrends is that they are based on a sustained economic policy. If that policy changes, then the trend is over, even if the trendline has not yet reversed direction. If the Fed were now to raise interest rates (or strongly hint that a rate hike is likely), it would signal a shift in policy. You can reasonably conclude that basis for the long-term uptrend in prices is over and that the trendline is due to turn down. A central bank rarely raises rates one month and lowers them the next. Because the very slow trend lags far behind the actual market price, it may be six months before the trendline actually signals a change of position. This will occur after a large part of your profits has been given back to the market. Exiting the trade when the fundamentals change would be a safe way of capturing more profits and being exposed to less market risk. Often, these decisions are clear only after the fact. In 2010 it seemed that Fed policy was going to change, yet 2011 was one of the strongest trend years in history, with yields reaching record lows.

Moving Average Projected Crossovers

If moving averages can successfully be used to identify the trend direction, it follows that a projection of the moving average will be valuable in anticipating when the trends will change. If a moving average trading strategy uses a single trend, the forecasted price ($CP1$) at which the standard n-day moving average line would cross is

$$CP1 = \frac{\text{Sum of last } N-1 \text{ prices}}{N-1} = \frac{\sum_{t-N+2}^{t} P_i}{(N-1)}$$

That is, an n-day moving average would cross the next price at the value equal to the $n-1$-day moving average.

The price ($CP2$) needed to cause two moving averages, of periods m and n, to cross is[5]

$$CP2 = m \times \left(\frac{\sum most\ recent\ m-1\ prices}{m} - \frac{\sum most\ recent\ n-1\ prices}{n} \right)$$

The projected crossover price is most useful when it is likely that a trend change will occur within a few days, that is, when the two moving averages begin converging and become close in value. Acting on the expected price would give the trader a great advantage in order execution. A chart of this, however, may not appear to be much different from a simple *relative strength* indicator. The difference between the price and the moving average line constitutes the relative strength.

The change in the projected crossover is considered a more valuable tool by Lambert.[6] He creates a *Market Direction Indicator* (MDI) with the following formula:

$$MDI = \frac{100 \times (Crossover\ price_{previous} - Crossover\ price_{today})}{Avera}$$

The point at which the MDI crosses the zero line moving higher is a buy signal, and the point where it crosses moving lower is a sell signal.

Forecasting When the Moving Average Will Turn   There are two basic rules for generating a moving average signal, when the price penetrates the moving average trendline and when the moving average trendline changes up or down. In the previous section, the forecast was based on when the price crosses the moving average, which is a very common way of generating a trading signal.

Tests often show that results are better when the trendline itself is used to generate the signal rather than the penetration. This was discussed earlier in the chapter, but the rationale goes that once prices have been included in the moving average, then it is the moving average that tells you the correct direction, and that the price penetration takes away from the value of the trendline. There are two reasons for this. The trendline is smoother than price movement, so the results are more uniform, and the price penetrations generate many more trades and additional costs.

Having decided to use the trendline, then how do you forecast when that line will change direction? It is simply whether today's price is greater or less than the price that is dropped off the end of the moving average period, n days ago. And, that being the case, using the moving average trendline is exactly the same as using the n-day momentum which states that you go long when today's price is greater than the price n days ago. It seems too simple, but in most cases the results are better than using the price penetration of a moving average.

[5] Calculation courtesy of Alexander Solodukhin, Mizuho Alternative Investments, New York.
[6] Donald R. Lambert, "The Market Directional Indicator," *Technical Analysis of Stocks & Commodities* (November/December 1983).

CHAPTER 11

Momentum and Oscillators

From Perry J. Kaufman, *Trading Systems and Methods, + Website*, 5th Edition (Hoboken, New Jersey: John Wiley & Sons, 2013), Chapter 9.

The study of momentum and oscillators is the analysis of price changes rather than price levels. Among technicians, momentum establishes the speed of price movement and the rate of ascent or descent. Analysts use *momentum* interchangeably with *slope*, the angle of inclination of price movement usually found with a simple least squares regression (Figure 11.1). In mathematics it is also the *first difference*, the difference between today's price and the previous day. Momentum is often considered using terms of Newton's Law, which can be restated loosely as *once started, prices tend to remain in motion in more-or-less the same direction.*

Indicators of change, such as momentum and oscillators, are used as leading indicators of price direction. They can identify when the current trend is no longer maintaining its same level of strength; that is, they show when an upwards move is decelerating. Prices are rising, but at a slower rate. This gives traders an opportunity to begin liquidating their open trend trades before prices actually reverse. As the time period for the momentum calculation shortens, this indicator becomes more sensitive to small changes in price. It is often used in a *countertrend,* or *mean reversion* strategy. The *change in momentum*, also called *rate of change, acceleration,* or *second difference*, is even more sensitive and anticipates change sooner.

Before beginning a discussion of various momentum calculations, a brief comment on terminology is necessary to understand how various techniques are grouped together. The use of a single price, such as Microsoft at $25.50 or gold at $1400, has no direction or movement implied. We are simply relating a price level and not indicating that prices are going up or down.

Next, we describe the speed at which prices are rising or falling. To know the speed, it is not enough to say that the S&P rose 3 points; you must specify the time interval over which this happened—"the S&P rose 3 points in 1 hour." When you say that you

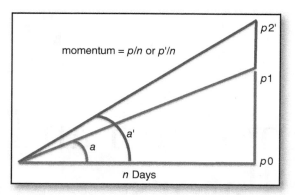

FIGURE 11.1

drove your car at 60, you really imply that you were going 60 miles per hour, or 60 kilometers per hour. This description of speed, or distance covered over time, is the same information that is given by a single momentum value. Then, if the *daily* momentum of the NASDAQ 100 is +10, it is rising at the rate of 10 points per day.

Having made a point of saying that momentum is change over time, which it is, the "industry" uses *momentum* to mean *price change* with the time implied (and often not even given) where *speed* is always the price change divided by the time interval. The same interpretation will be used here. The term *rate of change* (ROC) will also be used to describe *acceleration*, an increase or decrease in the speed; when the rate of change is zero, we are talking about speed and momentum.[1]

You will see in this chapter that acceleration is more sensitive than speed. We will begin with the least sensitive indicator, momentum, increase to acceleration, and then address the variations and applications, including *divergence,* the most popular use of momentum indicators.

■ Momentum

Momentum is the difference between two prices taken over a fixed interval. It is another word for *speed*, the distance covered over time; however, everyone uses it to mean *change*. For example, today's 5-day momentum value M would be the difference between today's price p_t and the price five days ago:

$$5\text{-day momentum, } M = p_t - p_{t-5}$$

Using notation familiar to many programmers:

$$5\text{-day momentum} = \text{price} - \text{price}[5]$$

---

[1] Be careful about terminology. Many books and software use rate of change (ROC) interchangeably with momentum, the change in price over n days, rather than the change in momentum. Also, momentum indicators can also be used for mean reversion and may be called *oscillators* because their values swing from positive to negative.

or

$$n\text{-day momentum} = \text{price} - \text{price}[n]$$

where the notation [n] refers to the price n days ago.

The momentum value M_t increases as the change in price increases over the same 5-day period. Figure 11.1 shows how the momentum changes as the price increases over the same time period. Over n days, the price moves from p_0 to p_1. It forms angle a and has a momentum of $p_1 - p_0$. If prices had increased to point p_2, then the momentum would have been greater, and the angle a' would have been larger. For example, if the 5-day change in price is an increase of 100, then the momentum is simply 100, but the speed is $100/5 = 20$. If prices increase by 100 points over a 10-day time interval, the momentum would still be 100, but the speed, or slope, would be $100/10 = 10$. When calculating momentum, the interval of the calculation must always be stated. To avoid confusion, we state that the *5-day momentum is 20* and the *10-day momentum is 10*.

Today's 5-day momentum, which we will now show as $M(5)_t$, can range in value from the maximum upwards move to the maximum downwards move that the price can make in five days; the momentum is zero if prices are unchanged after five days. For stocks, there is no actual limit on the maximum price range over any time interval. In cases such as Enron, prices could collapse to zero in short order. From a practical view, most stocks and futures markets have a history of volatility that relates to their price level. The higher the price, the greater the price moves. As the price of gold rose to $1000 per ounce, the 5-day momentum could have been as high as $100 per ounce ($20 per day). When it was at $250 and investors lost interest, it may have shown a $1 per ounce change over five days.

Momentum is not volatility. Gold can move from $1200 to $1250 in two days then back to $1200 over the next three days and the momentum would be zero but the volatility would be high.

Figure 11.2 shows a typical pattern of momentum. Smooth prices are used to make the relationship between price change and momentum clear. During the first 15-day cycle, prices rise steadily, peaking on day 9. As prices rise at a slower rate during days 5 through 9 the momentum declines but remains above zero. As long as the 5-day momentum is greater than zero, prices are rising. The highest momentum value occurs on day 3 when prices have the largest positive price change.

On day 10 the momentum value is zero. Looking at the price chart, this occurs when the 5-day change in price is zero. The lowest momentum value occurs on day 16 when the prices have declined the most. After prices reach their lowest point and begin up, the momentum is negative but rising.

If prices always moved in the smooth pattern shown in Figure 11.2, then momentum would be a perfect leading indicator. You could buy when momentum turned up and sell when it turned down, and be ahead of the change in price direction. Unfortunately, prices movement is irregular; consequently, momentum values are irregular. Because momentum contains valuable information, we will look at a number of systematic ways to evaluate momentum and improve trading. These focus on extreme momentum values and momentum patterns, all of which have proved to be valuable additions to trading strategies, in particular to the timing of entries and exits.

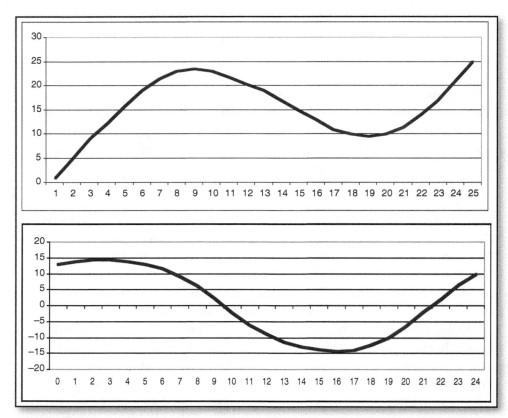

FIGURE 11.2

Characteristics of Momentum

Momentum is a way of smoothing price movement and can serve the same purpose as a trend. Although the momentum values are not as smooth as a moving average, larger momentum periods reduce the extremes seen in the price chart. One key advantage of momentum is that it does not have the lag that exists in a moving average.

The AOL chart (Figure 11.3) compares 20- and 40-day moving averages at the top with 20- and 40-day momentum along the bottom. The 40-day momentum (dark line) is smoother and peaks at about the same place as the price. The faster 20-day momentum is not as smooth but peaks sooner than the 40-day momentum and actually leads the price movement. The peaks of the faster momentum represent the maximum price change over a 20-day period. Had prices continued higher at the same rate—that is, if prices had increased $1 per day—the 20-day momentum would have turned sideways and become a horizontal line.

The 20-day and 40-day momentum lines both peak significantly sooner than their moving average equivalents, showing that the speed represented by momentum is a more sensitive measure than the direction of a trendline. The cost of this leading indicator is the increased noise seen in the erratic pattern of momentum compared to the smoothness of the trendline.

Momentum can be used as a trend indicator by selling when the momentum value crosses downward through the horizontal line at zero and buying when it crosses

FIGURE 11.3 20- and 40-Day Momentum (lower panel) Compared to a 20- and 40-Day Moving Average, Applied to AOL.

above the zero line. Because there is more noise in momentum than in the equivalent moving average, you would want to draw a small band around the zero line about the width of the small variations in momentum. A sell signal would be given when the momentum falls below the lower band and a buy when it moves upward through the upper band. However, the momentum crossing zero is essentially the same as the moving average turning up or down. It means that the price today is the same as the price n-days ago. Chapter 9 compared the performance of a trend and a momentum system over the same calculation periods.

Momentum as a Percentage

It is always convenient to express all markets in the same notation. It makes comparisons much easier. For the stock market, momentum can be expressed as a percentage where a 1-day momentum is equivalent to the 1-day return,

$$1\text{-day momentum in percent} = \frac{(P_t - P_{t-1})}{P_{t-1}} = \frac{P_t}{P_{t-1}} - 1$$

or, because they are returns, the alternative can be used, $\ln \frac{P_{t-1}}{P_t}$. But momentum is most often calculated over more than one day; therefore, the n-day momentum as a percentage is

$$M(n) = \frac{P_t}{P_{t-n}} - 1$$

Using percentages does not work for futures markets because most data used for analysis are continuous, back-adjusted prices. Back-adjusting over many years and many contracts will cause the oldest data to be very different from the actual prices that occurred on those dates; therefore, percentages are incorrect. When using momentum with back-adjusted futures prices, it is best to use the price differences.

Momentum as the Difference between Price and Trend

The term *momentum* is very flexible. It is common for it to refer to the difference between today's price and a corresponding moving average value, in a manner similar to *beta,* which indicates the relative strength of a stock compared to an index. The properties of this new value are the same as standard momentum. As the momentum becomes larger, prices are moving away from the moving average. As it moves towards zero, the prices are converging with the moving average.

The upper panel of Figure 11.4 shows a 20-period moving average plotted on a daily chart of Intel during the 14 months ending May 2003. The center panel shows the standard 20-period momentum, the difference between prices that are 20 days apart. The bottom panel is the difference between the price and the 20-day moving average. The range of values for the center panel is approximately +6 to −11, and the scale on the lower panel is +3 to −7. Because a trendline lags behind price movement, the difference between the price and trendline is smaller at points where there are larger price swings and typically larger momentum values.

A comparison of the two lower panels of Figure 11.4 also shows that there are differences in the small movements but the overall pattern is the same. When a price moves to an extreme, it is generally farthest from the moving average and farthest

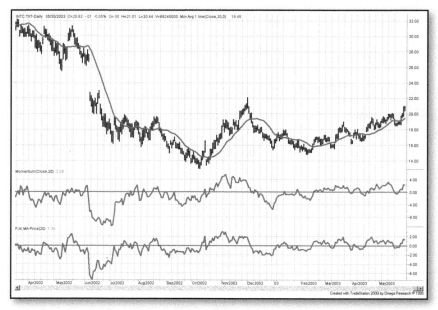

FIGURE 11.4 **Momentum Is Also Called** *Relative Strength*, **the Difference between Two Prices or a Price and a Moving Average (lower panel). The traditional momentum calculation is shown in the center panel.**

from the price *n*-days ago; therefore, the most extreme points occur at exactly the same place. This momentum calculation has also been called *relative strength* because it is measured relative to a previous price or relative to a trendline.

Momentum as a Trend Indicator

The momentum value is a smoothing of price changes and can serve the same purpose as a standard moving average. Many applications use momentum as a substitute for a price trend. By looking at the net change in price over the number of days designated by an *n*-day momentum indicator, intermediate fluctuations are ignored, and the pattern in price trend can be seen. The longer the span between the observed points, the momentum calculation period, the smoother the results. This is very similar to faster and slower moving averages.

To use momentum as a trend indicator, choose any calculation period. A *buy* signal occurs whenever the value of the momentum turns from negative to positive, and a *sell* signal is when the opposite occurs, as shown in Figure 11.5. If a band is used to establish a neutral position or a commitment zone, as discussed in the previous chapter, it should be drawn around the horizontal line representing the zero momentum value.

In order to find the best choice of a momentum span, a sampling of different values could be tested for optimum performance, or a chart could be examined for some natural price cycle. Identify the significant tops and bottoms of any bar chart, and average the number of days between these cycles, or find the number of days that would closely approximate the occurrences of these peaks and valleys. Then use ½ or ¼ the number of days from peak to peak or valley to valley. These natural cycles will often be the best choice of momentum calculation interval (Figure 11.6). Momentum and oscillators, however, are more often used to identify abnormal price movements and for timing of entries and exits in conjunction with a longer-term trend.

Timing an Entry

Momentum is a convenient way of identifying good entry points based on small price reversals within a trend that are not large enough to change the direction of the trend. By choosing a much shorter time period for the momentum calculation

FIGURE 11.5

FIGURE 11.6 Relationship of Momentum to Prices. (a) Tops and bottoms determine momentum value. (b) Corresponding momentum.

(for example, 6 days) to work in combination with a longer trend of 30 to 50 days, the momentum indicator will show frequent opportunities within the trend. The short time period for the momentum calculation assures you that there will be an entry opportunity within about three days of the entry signal; therefore, it becomes a practical timing tool. This is particularly useful when you view momentum as a countertrend signal, which will be discussed in the next section. Examples of using a momentum as entry timing can also be found in Level III, Chapter 8.

Identifying and Fading Price Extremes

An equally popular and more interesting use for momentum focuses on the analysis of relative tops and bottoms. All momentum values are bounded (although somewhat irregularly) in both directions by the maximum move possible during the time interval represented by the span of the momentum. The conditions at the points of high positive and negative momentum are called *overbought* and *oversold,* respectively.

A market is *overbought* when it can no longer sustain the strength of the current upwards trend and a downward price reaction is imminent; an *oversold* market is ready for an upward move. Faster momentum calculations (those using shorter calculation periods) will tend to fluctuate above and below the zero line based on small price changes. Longer calculation periods will take on the characteristics of a trend and stay above or below the zero line for the extent of the trend. In Figure 11.7, using S&P futures, the 20-day momentum in the center panel stays above zero for most of the period from September 2010 through

FIGURE 11.7 20-Day Momentum (center panel) and 3-Day Momentum (bottom panel) Applied to the S&P, June 2010 through February 2011.

February 2011. The very fast 3-day momentum in the bottom panel consistently penetrates the zero line, although the peaks on the upside are larger than those on the downside.

The values on the right scale of the two lower panels in Figure 11.7 show the range of price movement over the 20-day and 3-day periods. The 20-day scale goes from +100 to –60 while the 3-day scale is smaller, about +60 to –40. The 3-day momentum is not 3/20ths of the 20-day momentum because volatility does not increase linearly over time. That is, volatility can increase faster in a few days, but over longer periods it has up and down movement that limits the total move in one direction.

A system can take advantage of the momentum extremes by *fading the price movement* (selling rallies and buying declines). This is done by drawing two horizontal lines on the momentum chart (as shown in Figure 11.6b) above and below the zero line in such a way that the tops and bottoms of the major moves are isolated. These lines may be selected

- Visually, so that once the line is penetrated, prices reverse shortly afterwards.

- Based on a percentage of the maximum possible momentum value.

- A multiple of the standard deviation of momentum values. Using two standard deviations would position the lines so that only 5% of all momentum values penetrate above and below the two horizontal lines.

When positioning these bands, there is always a trade-off between finding more trading opportunities and entering the market too soon. This can be a complicated choice and is discussed in "System Trade-Offs" in Level III, Chapter 11. Once these lines have been drawn, the entry options will be one of the following basic trading rules:

- *Aggressive.* Enter a new long position when the momentum value penetrates the lower bound; enter a new short position when the value penetrates the upper bound.

- *Minor confirmation.* Enter a new short position on the first day the momentum value turns down after penetrating the upper bound (the opposite for longs).

- *Major confirmation.* Enter a new short position when the momentum value penetrates the upper bound moving lower (the opposite for longs).

- *Timing.* Enter a new short position after the momentum value has remained above the upper bound for *n* days (the opposite for longs).

To close out a profitable short or long position, there are the following alternatives (the rules are symmetrical for longs and shorts):

- *Most demanding.* Close out long positions or cover shorts when the momentum value satisfies the entry condition for a reverse position.

- *Moderately demanding.* Cover a short position when the momentum penetrates the zero line, minus one standard deviation (or some other target point partway between the zero line and the lower bound).

- *Basic exit.* Cover a short position when the momentum value becomes zero.

- *Allowing an extended move.* Cover a short position if the momentum crosses the zero line moving up *after* penetrating that line moving down.

The *basic exit*, removing your trade when the momentum reaches the zero line, is the benchmark case. It is based on the conservative assumption that prices will return to the center of the recent movement (in other words, *mean reverting*). It is less reasonable to assume that prices will continually move from overbought to oversold and back again. Most statisticians would agree that the mean is the best forecast of future prices, and the zero momentum value represents the mean. You may try to increase the profits by assuming that the momentum value will penetrate the zero line by a small amount because there is always some amount of noise. However, if you require a larger penetration of zero to cause an exit, many of the exit opportunities will be lost. You can be more conservative by exiting somewhat before the zero line is reached, but then you also reduce your average profit.

The same momentum calculations, viewed over a longer time period, show one of the problems with using momentum for timing. Figure 11.8 covers a critical period, from August 2005 through February 2011. Notice that the scale of the momentum values change dramatically from the beginning to the end of the chart. This is especially important for the 20-day momentum in the middle panel. For all of 2006, volatility was very low. Had we used momentum as an overbought/oversold indicator, the entry bands would have been at about ±30. For the 3-day momentum, it would have been closer to ±15. As we saw before, the faster momentum is more symmetric than the slower one. During 2006, there were more selling than buying opportunities.

Volatility increases in 2007. If buy entries were targeted as momentum values of −30 then traders would have held a 120 point loss as momentum dropped to −150. A similar pattern was repeated on the upside for sell signals. It would be necessary to increase the width of the buy and sell bands to ±75 and still hold larger losses

FIGURE 11.8 A Longer View of the 20- and 3-Day Momentum Applied to the S&P. The magnitude of the momentum values change over time.

waiting for a price reversal. But then comes 2008, and any countertrend entry, buying as prices fall, would have caused a complete loss of equity. However, let's say that we were able to avoid disaster and the entry-exit bands were at ±100 for the 20-day momentum and ±50 for the 3-day. Volatility finally declines and we get only the occasional entry signal. The bands need to be adjusted back down to a smaller range.

The problem with using momentum for timing is that the scale is unpredictable. Even if we waited for a reversal after penetrating the band there is no assurance that prices will not reverse and go to new extremes. Some risk protection is needed, a way of dynamically adjusting the bands (as discussed in Chapter 9), or a different way of measuring momentum.

Risk Protection A protective *stop-loss order* can be used whenever you trade against the current price momentum. A stop-loss is a specific order to exit if the price goes the wrong way (discussed in Level III, Chapter 12 but also throughout the book). This is most important with the *aggressive* entry, which advocates selling when the momentum value moves above the upper threshold line, regardless of how fast prices are rising. While the other entry options allow for a logic positioning of a stop-loss, the aggressive entry does not. You will simply need to decide, based on historic momentum values, where to limit your risk. With the other entry options, prices are no longer at their extremes, so that stops may be placed using one of the following techniques:

- Place a protective stop above or below the most extreme high or low momentum value.

- Follow a profitable move with a trailing, nonretreating stop based on fixed points or a percentage.

- Establish zones that act as levels of attainment (using horizontal lines of equal spacing), and do not permit reverse penetrations once a new zone is entered.

Risk protection must be flexible in the way it deals with volatility. As prices reach higher levels, increased volatility will cause momentum tops and bottoms to widen;

with low volatility, prices may not be active enough to penetrate the upper or lower bounds. This is shown in Figure 11.8. Therefore, both the profits and risk of a trade entered at extremes must increase with volatility and higher prices. Stops could be based on a percentage of price or a multiple of volatility.

The aggressive entry option remains the greatest problem for controlling risk, where a short signal is given when prices are very strong. If an immediate reversal does not occur, large open losses may accrue. To determine the proper stop-loss amount, a computer test was performed using an immediate entry based on penetration of an extreme boundary and with a stop-loss at the close of the day for risk protection. The first results were thought to have outstanding profits and consistency until it was discovered that the computer had done exactly the opposite of what was intended—it *bought* when the momentum crossed the upper bound and placed a close stop-loss *below* the entry. It did prove, for a good sampling of futures markets, that *high momentum* periods continued for enough time to capture small but consistent profits. It also showed that the aggressive entry trading rule, anticipating an early reversal, would be a losing strategy. One should never forget that declining momentum does not mean that prices are falling.

The Trend Provides Protection   In these examples, momentum is not a strategy itself, but a way of entering a trend trade. When a trend signal first occurs, it is not entered. If the signal was long, then the strategy waits until the 3-day momentum penetrates the lower band. If prices continue lower, then the trend will change from up to down, and the position will be exited. It would not be necessary to have a stop-loss.

Profit Targets for Fading Extreme Moves   When using momentum as a mean-reversion strategy, the most reasonable exit for a short entered at an extreme momentum high, or a long position entered at a low, is when the momentum returns to near zero. Prices do not have an obligation to go from extreme lows to extreme highs; however, any extreme can be expected to return to normal, which is where momentum is zero. Returning to zero does not mean that all trades will be profitable. If there has been a strong upwards move that lasted longer than the calculation period of the momentum, then prices will be higher when momentum finally returns to zero. The trend is not your friend if it fights with your mean-reversion position.

The number of profitable trades can be increased by targeting a momentum level that is more conservative than zero. That is, if a long was entered at an extreme low, a sell would be placed 5% or 10% below the zero momentum line, based on the distance between the buying threshold line and zero. Trades that *almost* return to normal would then be closed out with profits, although the average size of the profit would be smaller. To increase the size of the profits per trade, you would target the opposite side of the zero momentum line; therefore, if you held a long position, you would wait until the momentum value was greater than zero by 5% or 10% of the range. The success of taking profits early or late depends on the amount of noise in the momentum values as it fluctuates near the zero value. In many cases where extreme prices are followed by a sideways pattern, momentum will fluctuate around zero so that there is ample opportunity to exit the trade at a better price.

High-Momentum Trading

Some professional traders have made a business of trading in the direction of the price move only when momentum exceeds the *high threshold level* rather than anticipating a change of direction. There is a small window of opportunity when prices are moving fast. They will usually continue at the same, or greater, momentum for a short time, measured usually in minutes or hours, but occasionally a few days. There is a lot of money to be made in a short time—but at great risk if prices reverse direction sooner than expected.

Price patterns have changed. There are many more day traders. When one stock breaks out above a previous high, everyone sees it as an opportunity for profit. Buy orders start to flow, and volume increases. Stocks that are normally ignored can attract large volume when prices make a new high. Traders ride the rising prices for as long as possible, watching to see when volume begins to drop, then they exit. Some may just target a modest profit and get out when that target is reached.

High-momentum trading is a fast game that requires tools that allow you to scan a wide range of stocks. You are looking for one that has made a new high after a long, quiet period. You may also continually sort stocks by the highest momentum values. You need to stay glued to your screen, enter fast and exit fast. It is a full-time commitment.

Moving Average Convergence/Divergence (MACD)

Many of the practical problems of fading prices using momentum are solved with the *Moving Average Convergence/Divergence* (MACD),[2] developed by Gerald Appel. The MACD uses momentum calculated as the difference between two trendlines, produced using exponential smoothing. This momentum value is further smoothed to give a *signal line*. The most common form of MACD uses the difference between a 12-day and 26-day exponential smoothing. The signal line, used to produce trading recommendations, is a 9-day smoothing of the MACD. The MACD can be created as follows:

Step 1: Choose the two calculation periods for the trend, for example, 20 and 40. Convert to smoothing constants using $2/(n+1)$.

Step 2: Calculate the slow trendline, $E40$, using the smoothing value 0.0243.

Step 3: Calculate the fast trendline, $E20$, using the smoothing value 0.0476.

Step 4: The *MACD line,* the slower-responding line in the bottom panel of Figure 11.9, is $E20 - E40$. When the market is moving up quickly, the fast smoothing will be above the slow, and the difference will be positive. This is done so that the MACD line goes up when prices go up.

Step 5: The *signal line* is the 9-day smoothing (using a constant of 0.10) of the MACD line. The signal line is slower than the MACD; therefore, it can be seen in the bottom panel of Figure 11.9 as the lower line when prices are moving higher.

The 20- and 40-day momentum lines, corresponding to the MACD line and the histogram, are shown in the center panel of Figure 11.9. It is clear that the MACD process smoothes these values significantly; therefore, it makes trading signals easier to see.

---

[2] From John D. Becker, "Value of Oscillators in Determining Price Action," *Futures* (May 1994).

FIGURE 11.9   MACD for AOL. The MACD line is the faster of the two trendlines in the bottom panel; the signal line is the slower. The histogram is created by subtracting the slower signal line from the MACD line.

Reading the MACD Indicator   The MACD is normally seen as it appears at the bottom of Figure 11.9. The MACD line is higher in an uptrend and lower in a downtrend. The histogram is created by subtracting the slower signal line from the MACD line. When the histogram is above zero, it confirms the uptrend.

The 40/20 MACD line is similar to the 40-day momentum line. We can compare the MACD in the lower panel with the 20- and 40-day momentum in the center panel and see that the peaks and valleys are in about the same place, but the MACD line is much smoother because it is the difference between two trendlines rather than prices.

You should note the point at which the MACD and signal lines turn down in May 2001, compared to the corresponding moving averages that are shown with prices in the top panel of the chart. The MACD leads the moving averages in showing the downturn and has only slightly more up-and-down variation in its values. The signal line also leads the moving averages in the downturn and is equally smooth.

Trading the MACD   The most common use of the MACD is as a trend indicator. For this purpose, only the MACD and signal lines are used in the following way:

> *Buy* when the MACD line (faster) crosses upwards through the signal line (slower).
> *Sell* when the MACD line crosses from above to below the signal line.

In the bottom panel of Figure 11.9, the buy signals that occur right after an extreme low in April and October of 2001 generated large gains. Unfortunately, there were many other crossings that generated losses; therefore, it is necessary to select which trades to enter. To accomplish that, the MACD uses thresholds similar to those shown for momentum, but in the opposite way. The MACD must first penetrate the lower band; then it must signal a new uptrend before a long position can be entered. In this way, it removes some of the whipsaws that might occur in a sideways market. Threshold levels were established by observing the historically high and low momentum values, shown as horizontal lines at the +2.00 and −2.00 levels in Figure 11.9. Sell signals would have been taken only after the MACD value had been above +2.00, and buy signals only when the MACD value had fallen below −2.00. The trading signals that satisfy these conditions are the *buy* signal in April, a *sell* in May, and a *buy* in October. However, fitting the threshold lines make them unreliable values for trading. One solution can be found in "An RSI Version of MACD" in the next section.

Appel has written extensively on the MACD, and many variations can be found in his book, *Technical Analysis*.[3] Many of the examples are interpretive, similar to the way we look at chart patterns. Appel also preferred using trends of 19 and 39 days for the NASDAQ composite. An equally important use of MACD is for divergence signals. *Bearish divergence* occurs when prices are rising but the MACD values are falling. Because this technique applies to many indicators in addition to the MACD, it is covered in detail in the section "Momentum Divergence" toward the end of this chapter.

■ Divergence Index

A method similar to MACD but one that uses an interesting combination of generalized techniques is the *divergence index*, the volatility-adjusted difference between two moving averages, for example, 10 and 40 days. Using general notation:

1. *Slow average$_t$* = 40-day average of the most recent prices
2. *Fast average$_t$* = 10-day average of the most recent prices
3. *Difference$_t$* = *price$_t$* − *price$_{t-1}$*

Then the divergence index (DI),

$$DI_t = \frac{Fast\ average_t - Slow\ average_t}{StDev\,(Difference_t, slow\ perio)^2}$$

The standard deviation of the price differences, taken over the slow period of 40, volatility-adjusts the results. The trading rules require a band around zero to trigger entries.

$$Band_t = stdev(DI_t, slow\ period)$$
$$Upper\ band_t = factor \times Band_t$$
$$Lower\ band_t = -factor \times Band_t$$

where factor = 1.0. By using the standard deviation of DI, the band also adjusts to changes in volatility. In Figure 11.10 the index in the lower panel has high peaks followed by periods of low or varying volatility. The standard deviation allows the bands to widen or narrow according to the pattern of fluctuations. This example used the slow period for the standard deviation; however, the fast period would have caused more rapid changes to the band.

---

[3] Gerald Appel, *Technical Analysis, Power Tools for Active Investors* (Upper Saddle River, NJ: FT Prentice Hall, 2005).

FIGURE 11.10

The trading rules are

Buy when the DI moves below the lower band while in an uptrend
Sell when the DI moves above the upper band while in a downtrend
Exit longs and shorts when the DI crosses zero

Figure 11.10 shows the DI and the upper and lower bands in the bottom panel. The top panel shows the trading signals for the S&P 500 futures contract.

■ Oscillators

Because the representation of momentum is that of a line fluctuating above and below a zero value, it has often been termed an *oscillator*. Even though it does oscillate, the use of this word is confusing. In this presentation, the term *oscillator* will be restricted to a specific form of momentum that is *normalized* and expressed in terms of values that are limited to the ranges between +1 and −1 (or +100 to −100), +1 and 0, or +100 and 0 (as in a percent).

To transform a standard momentum calculation into the normalized form with a maximum value of +1 and a minimum value of −1, divide the momentum calculation by its maximum value over the same rolling time period. This allows the oscillator to self-adjust to changes in price or volatility. For example, in April 2006, Amazon was trading at about $34. During a 10-day period it had a high of $35.31 and a low of $31.52, a range of $3.79. During 10 days in February 2011, Amazon had a high of $191.40 and a low of $174.77, a range of $16.63. Therefore, a price move of $2 in 2006 would be the same as a move of $8.77 in 2011. By dividing $2 by $3.79 or $8.77 by $16.63 we get 0.52 in both cases. Hence, *normalization*, which is the basis for most momentum indicators, can be an excellent way to self-adjust to price changes.

The following sections show how a number of useful oscillators are calculated. In each case, the purpose is to have the indicator post high values when prices are at a peak and low values when they are in a valley. To be most useful, prices should reverse direction soon after the oscillator records values near its extremes.

Relative Strength Index

One of the most popular indicators for showing overbought and oversold conditions is the *Relative Strength Index* (RSI) developed by Welles Wilder.[4] It provides added value to the concept of momentum by scaling all values between 0 and 100. It is more stable than momentum because it uses all the values in the calculation period rather than just the first and last. It is a simple measurement that expresses the relative strength of the current price movement as increasing from 0 to 100. It is calculated as

$$RSI = 100 - \left(\frac{100}{1+RS} \right) = 100 \times \left(\frac{RS}{1+RS} \right)$$

where
$$RS = \frac{AU}{AD}$$

AU = the total of the upwards price changes during the past 14 days

AD = the total of the downwards price changes (used as positive numbers) during the past 14 days

Once the first calculation has been made, both the AU and AD values can be calculated daily using an *average-off* method:

$$AU_t = AU_{t-1} + \frac{AU_{t-1}}{14} + \max(p_t - p_{t-1}, 0)$$

$$AD_t = AD_{t-1} + \frac{AD_{t-1}}{14} + \max(p_{t-1} - p_t, 0)$$

This method essentially subtracts an average value and adds the new value, if any (see "Average-Off Method" in Chapter 8). All price changes are treated as positive numbers. The daily calculation of the RSI becomes a matter of simple arithmetic. Wilder has favored the use of 14 days because it represents one-half of a natural cycle, in this case, 1 month. He has set the significant threshold levels for the RSI at 30 and 70. Penetration of the lower level is indicative of an imminent upturn and penetration of the upper level, a pending downturn. A chart of an RSI is shown along with a comparable momentum and stochastic indicator in the next section, Figure 11.15.

Use of the RSI alone to generate trading signals often requires interpretation similar to standard chart analysis. Lines are drawn across the tops of the RSI values to indicate a downtrend. A head-and-shoulders formation can be used as the primary confirmation of a change in direction. Wilder himself used the RSI top and bottom formations shown in Figure 11.11. A break of the reaction bottom between the declining tops is a sell signal. In addition, the *failure swing*, or divergence (discussed later in this chapter), denotes an unsuccessful test of a recent high or low RSI value.

Wilder created other popular indicators. One of these is a momentum calculation called the *Average Directional Movement* (ADX). The ADX is a byproduct of the *Directional Movement* and is discussed in Level III, Chapter 22. All of these indicators are actively used by traders.

---

[4] J. Welles Wilder Jr., *New Concepts in Technical Trading Systems* (Greensboro, NC: Trend Research, 1978).

FIGURE 11.11

Modifying the RSI   An obvious objection to the RSI might be the selection of a 14-day *half-cycle*. Maximum divergence is achieved by using a moving average that is some fraction of the length of the dominant cycle, but 14 days may not be that value. If a 14-day calculation period is too short, then the RSI would remain outside the 70-30 zones for extended periods rather than signaling an immediate turn. In practical terms, a 14-day RSI means that a sustained move in one direction that lasts for more than 14 days will produce a very high RSI value. If prices continue higher for more than 14 days, then the RSI, as with other oscillators, will go sideways. The idea is to pick the calculation period for which there are very few larger sustained moves, and 14 may be that value. If more frequent overbought and oversold conditions are needed, then the period could be lowered to 10. At the same time, the zones could be increased to 80-20. Some combination of calculation period and zone will usually give the frequency of trades that is needed.

A study by Aan[5] on the distribution of the 14-day RSI showed that the average RSI top and bottom value consistently grouped near 72 and 32, respectively. Therefore, 50% of all RSI values fall between 72 and 32, which can be interpreted as *normally distributed*, and equivalent to about 0.675 standard deviations. This would suggest that the 70-30 levels proposed by Wilder are too close together to act as selective overbought/oversold values, but should be moved farther apart. The equivalent of 1.5 standard deviations is a comfortable trade-off between frequency of trades and risk. It is generally safer to err on the side of less risk. If there are too many trades being generated by the RSI, a combination of a longer interval and higher confidence bands will be an improvement.[6]

Further Smoothing with N-Day Ups and Downs   Instead of increasing the number of days in the RSI calculation period, a smoother indicator can be found by increasing the period over which each of the *up* and *down* values are determined. The original RSI method uses 14 individual days, where an *up day* is a day in which the price change was positive. Instead, we can replace each 1-day change with a 2-day change, or an *n*-day change. If we use 2-day changes, then a total of 28 days will be needed, so that each 2-day period does not overlap another; there will be 14 sets of two days each. Using 14 sets of 2 will give a smoother indicator than using 28 single-day changes.

THEORY AND ANALYSIS

---

[5] Peter W. Aan, "How RSI Behaves," *Futures* (January 1985).

[6] For another interesting approach to RSI optimization, see John F. Ehlers, "Optimizing RSI with Cycles," *Technical Analysis of Stocks & Commodities* (February 1986).

RSI Countertrend Trading Momentum indicators are used for timing and counter-trend trading. Normally, it is the absolute overbought or oversold level that is the trigger for a trade. However, either a very fast move in price or an extreme value for a momentum indicator could be a criterion for a reversal. When $RSI_t - RSI_{t-k} > a$, or when $RSI_t - RSI_{t-k} < -a$, where a is a threshold value, we could sell and buy, respectively. This also increases the number of trades because it does not require that $RSI_t > 0$, only that it has moved quickly. Exits can be taken when momentum returns to near zero, or after n days. A program to test this is *TSM RSI Countertrend*, available on the Companion Website.

Net Momentum Oscillator Another variation on the RSI is the use of the difference between the sum of the up days and the sum of the down days, called a *net momentum oscillator*.[7] If you consider the unsmoothed RSI $= 100 \times (S_u/(S_u + S_d))$ then the net momentum oscillator would be

$$CMO = 100 \times (S_u - S_d)/(S_u + S_d)$$

This method replaces some of the indicator movement lost to smoothing in the normal RSI, and shows more extremes. This may also be done by shortening the number of periods in the RSI calculation.

The 2-Day RSI Among the interesting information published on MarketSci Blog[8] is Michael Stokes's "favorite" indicator, the 2-day RSI, which replaces each 1-day closing price change with a 2-day change; otherwise, the calculations and the number of data points are the same. If you already have a program to calculate the RSI, you only need to change the statement $p_t - p_{t-1}$ with $p_t - p_{t-2}$ to get overlapping 2-day data. Or, to try an n-day RSI, replace the "2" with your choice of days. The effect of using combined 2 days instead of 1 is some smoothing and a general increase in volatility.

Stokes uses threshold levels of 10 and 90 for the S&P and the rules

Buy on the next close when the 2-day RSI penetrates the threshold of 10 moving lower
Sell short on the next close when the 2-day RSI penetrates the threshold of 90 moving higher
Exit one day later on the close

Figures 11.12a and b are from the MarketSci Blog on December 9, 2008. Figure 11.12a shows that the profitability of the RSI reversed in about 1998. From 1970 to 1998 it was a good trend indicator; that is, when the RSI moved above 90 the S&P continued up. After 1998 it has been a much better mean-reverting indicator. Figure 11.12b is the result of applying a method of scaling in to trades according to the following rules:

If the RSI < then *buy* this %		If the RSI > then *sell short* this %	
< 5	100%	> 95	100%
< 10	75%	> 90	75%
< 15	50%	> 85	50%
< 20	25%	> 80	25%

[7] Tushar S. Chande and Stanley Kroll, *The New Technical Trader* (New York: John Wiley & Sons, 1994).
[8] Free subscriptions are available at MarketSci Blog email@marketsci.com. The author, Michael Stokes, presents his own ideas and analysis of various systematic approaches.

FIGURE 11.12a Performance of the 2-Day RSI, MarketSci Blog's Favorite Oscillator, from the December 9, 2008, Posting, Simple Entries <10 and >90 Applied to the S&P, 1970 through 2008.

On day t the RSI was 14, and we entered 50%, but then on day $t + 1$ the RSI dropped to 8; it was not clear whether we added an extra 25%, but we assume that is the case. Then the trade is exited if we do not add on the next day. Because the RSI can stay above or below 50 for long periods of time, an exit rule that waits for the RSI to cross 50 is not likely to be successful. Stokes's approach of exiting after one day seems much safer. Figure 11.12b separates the longs and short sales from 2000 through 2008, showing that both sides performed well, a very desirable outcome. Having good performance for longs and shorts is not common because many markets have an upwards bias (especially the stock market). However, 1-day trades are sensitive to costs. Traders will need to see if the returns per share, or per contract, are sufficient to cover commissions and slippage.

FIGURE 11.12b A Breakdown of Longs and Short Sales Using the Scaling-in Method, S&P 2000 through 2008.

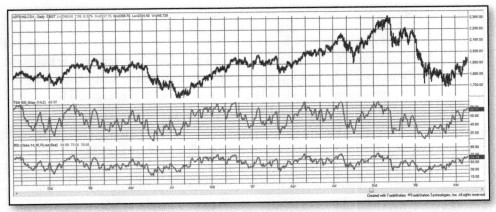

FIGURE 11.13 2-Period RSI (center panel) Compared with the Traditional 14-Day RSI (bottom panel), Applied to NASDAQ Futures, August 2005 through September 2008.

A Standard 2-Period RSI In Figure 11.13 a standard 2-period RSI is shown in the middle panel and the traditional 14-day RSI in the lower panel. Both are applied to NASDAQ futures, from August 2005 through September 2008, which appears at the top. The classic RSI penetrates the extremes of 30 and 70 but does not reach 20 or 80, while the 2-period RSI touches near 15 and 85 a number of times. We might expect a 2-period oscillator to jump between 0 and 100 every day that prices changed direction, but the average-off calculation slows down the process and makes the 2-period chart a somewhat more volatile version of the standard RSI.

An RSI Version of MACD While the MACD creates a histogram of the difference between two moving averages, we can make that pattern easier to interpret by applying the RSI to the spread of the moving averages. In Figure 11.14 a 5-day RSI is applied to the difference between the 10- and 40-week moving average for the emini-S&P futures. Using the standard 30-70 thresholds, this seems to find credible points where prices are overbought and oversold.

FIGURE 11.14 RSI Applied to the Spread between a 10-Week and 40-Week Moving Average of S&P Futures.

Stochastics

The *stochastic* indicator, created by George Lane, is an oscillator that measures the relative position of the closing price within a past high-low range. It is based on the commonly accepted observation that closing prices tend to resist penetrating the high prices of the past few days, the place where a horizontal resistance line would be drawn on a chart. Similarly, in a downtrend prices must be able to close below the lows of the past few days for the move to continue. When the market is about to turn from up to down, for instance, it is often the case that the highs are higher than previous days, but the closing price settles nearer the low of the day, failing to indicate a continuation of the uptrend. This makes the stochastic oscillator different from the MACD, which uses the difference between two trends, and the RSI which uses only the closing prices. The stochastic uses the high, low, and close and unlike the other oscillators, there does not have to be any smoothing to introduce a lag.

The three indicators that result from the stochastic measurement are called *%K*, *%D*, and *%D-slow*. These indicators show increasingly slower interpretation of price movement, with *%D* being the most popular as a single indicator; however, *%D* and *%D-slow* are often used together to produce a trading signal. Calculation of these indicators for today's value t over the past 5 days, are

$$Initial\ (raw)\ \%K_t = 100 \times \frac{C_t - L_t(5)}{R_t(5)}$$

$$\%D = \text{"%K-slow"} = \frac{\%K_t + \%K_{t-1} + \%K_{t-2}}{3} = \left(\frac{\sum_{i=t-2}^{t} \%K_i}{3} \right)$$

$$\%D_t\text{-slow} = \frac{\left(\sum_{i=t-2}^{t} \%D_i \right)}{3}$$

Where C_t = today's closing price
$L_t(5)$ = the low price of the last 5 days
$R_t(5)$ = the range of the last 5 days (highest high minus lowest low) as of today.[9]

Calculating the 10-Day Stochastic for Hewlett-Packard (HPQ) Using an Excel spreadsheet, each of the stochastic components can be calculated in only a few columns. In Table 11.1, the historic prices for Hewlett-Packard are imported into columns A–D. The 10-day stochastic calculations, columns E–J, are:

1. Column *E*, the 10-day high using the function *Max*.
2. Column *F*, the 10-day low using the function *Min*.

---

[9] Harry Schirding, "Stochastic Oscillator," *Technical Analysis of Stocks & Commodities* (May/June 1984).

TABLE 11.1

Row	Date	High	Low	Close	10-Day High	10-Day Low	10-Day Range	%K	%K-Slow	%D-Slow

TABLE 11.1   Excel Example of 10-Day Stochastic for Hewlett-Packard (HPQ)

	A	B	C	D	E	F	G	H	I	J
Row	Date	High	Low	Close	10-Day High	10-Day Low	10-Day Range	%K	%K-Slow	%D-Slow
1	1/3/2011	43.49	42.22	42.74						
2	1/4/2011	43.77	43.01	43.63						
3	1/5/2011	44.22	43.40	44.20						
4	1/6/2011	44.96	44.18	44.88						
5	1/7/2011	45.39	44.71	45.09						
6	1/10/2011	45.05	44.57	44.86						
7	1/11/2011	46.06	45.20	45.43						
8	1/12/2011	45.71	45.27	45.64						
9	1/13/2011	45.84	45.31	45.65						
10	1/14/2011	46.40	45.61	46.25	46.40	42.22	4.18	96.41		
11	1/18/2011	46.42	46.08	46.34	46.42	43.01	3.41	97.65		
12	1/19/2011	46.48	46.08	46.32	46.48	43.40	3.08	94.81	96.29	
13	1/20/2011	46.79	45.76	46.78	46.79	44.18	2.61	99.62	97.36	
14	1/21/2011	47.64	46.83	47.23	47.64	44.57	3.07	86.64	93.69	95.78
15	1/24/2011	47.59	46.66	47.55	47.64	44.57	3.07	97.07	94.44	95.16
16	1/25/2011	47.83	46.88	47.08	47.83	45.20	2.63	71.48	85.07	91.07
17	1/26/2011	47.28	46.57	46.88	47.83	45.27	2.56	62.89	77.15	85.55
18	1/27/2011	46.98	46.58	46.74	47.83	45.31	2.52	56.75	63.71	75.31
19	1/28/2011	46.69	45.36	45.51	47.83	45.36	2.47	6.07	41.90	60.92

3. Column *G,* calculate the high-low range by subtracting *F* from *E*.
4. Column *H*, row *n*, calculate the raw stochastic %K as (D*n*-F*n*)*100/G*n*.
5. Column *I*, the *%Kslow* is the 3-day average of %K, column *H*.
6. Column *J*, *%Dslow* is the 3-day average of *%K-slow*, column *I*.

The raw stochastic in column *H* of the spreadsheet shows that values start above 90% and drop to 6% in a few days. This happens when prices close near the highest or lowest prices of the past 10 days. When calculating the stochastic, today's close is always included in the *max, min,* and *range* calculations. If today's price is the highest or lowest of the calculation period, then the raw stochastic will have a value of 100 or 0. The full spreadsheet *TSM Stochastic calculation for HPQ,* can be found on the Companion Website.

Comparing the Stochastic to Momentum and the RSI   The calculations for momentum, RSI, and the stochastic are very different; therefore, we would expect a chart of these indicators to vary considerably from one another. However, there are surprising similarities among the three, even calculated over the same 14-day period, as shown in Figure 11.15. The momentum and stochastic both show how today's price relates to the prices over the calculation interval; therefore, we would expect

FIGURE 11.15 Comparison of Simple Momentum, RSI, and Stochastic, All for 14-Day Calculation Periods, General Electric, May 2008 through February 2011.

them to be most similar, and that appears to be true. Both have peaks at the same place, although the *%D-Slow* stochastic has a smoother overall line due to the two successive 3-day averages.

The RSI chart does not seem to be lagged, instead it is dampened, appearing to have less volatility. In fact, the highs and lows rarely touch 70 and 30, while the stochastic highs and lows often go above 90 and below 10, even though it is smoothed. The overall impression of the stochastic is that it moves faster and exaggerates the swings.

Trading the Stochastic   Traditionally, the stochastic can be traded by using a combination of a slower and faster calculation to give signals, or by combining extreme stochastic values for entry or exit timing with a trend. To use the stochastic by itself, *%D* and *%D-slow* can take on the role of the faster indicator and the slower signal line in the same way as the MACD and its signal line were used. The fastest calculation, *%K*, is not often used due to its instability.[10] Figure 11.16 shows the two 20-day calculations, *%D* and *%D-slow*, along the bottom of an S&P futures continuation chart from December 2001 through September 2002. A 60-day moving average is in the top panel.

The downtrend in the S&P during 2002 produces two good sell signals using the stochastics. In March and August, the slower *%D* penetrates above the 80% threshold and crosses the signal line moving down. A third peak in May touches near 70% and would produce an additional sell signal if the upper threshold were set lower. During a sustained downtrend, it is common for the indicator values to fall below the lower threshold and remain there for extended periods. Although the rolling calculation is intended to self-adjust, the most practical solution is to combine the stochastic signals with a trend.

---

[10] It is common practice to use the notation *%K* and *%D* to mean *%K*-slow and *%D*-slow, respectively. All writings on the stochastic use the smoothed values, rather than the initial *%K* calculation, regardless of the omission of "-slow." Any use of *%K* in this text also refers to *%K*-slow unless specifically stated.

FIGURE 11.16 20-Day Stochastic (bottom) and a 60-Day Moving Average for the S&P Futures Continuation Series.

The 60-day moving average, shown along with prices in the upper part of Figure 11.16, indicates a downtrend for the entire period of the chart. Using the relatively slow 20-day stochastic, the penetration of the upper 80% threshold gives very good timing for short sale entries, and avoids the problems of an unfavorable distribution of stochastic values. The 20-day stochastic does not indicate where to exit the downtrend. A faster stochastic can be used to produce more frequent sell signals that can be applied as follows

> *Enter a short sale* after the trend has turned down on the first stochastic sell signal (the stochastic crosses the signal line going down).
> *Enter a long* after the trend has turned up on the first stochastic buy signal.

The problem with all timing rules is that, if prices move higher and do not retrace, then there will not be a stochastic signal, or it will occur well after there would have been profits in the trade. Many of the lost opportunities can be eliminated by using a faster stochastic calculation period. It is particularly dangerous to use a timing rule for exiting a position. Delays in entering are lost opportunities, but delays exiting are real trading losses.

Left and Right Crossovers

The faster *%K-slow* will usually change direction sooner than the *%D-slow*, crossing the *%D-slow* line while it is still moving in the prior trend direction. The opposite case, when the *%D-slow* turns first, indicates a slow, stable change of direction and is a more favorable pattern (Figure 11.17a). Using the fast *%K-Slow* and the slower *%D-Slow*, the following patterns have been identified:

> *Hinge.* A reduction in the speed of either the *%K-slow* or *%D-slow* lines, shown as a flattening out, indicates a reversal on the next day (Figure 11.17b).

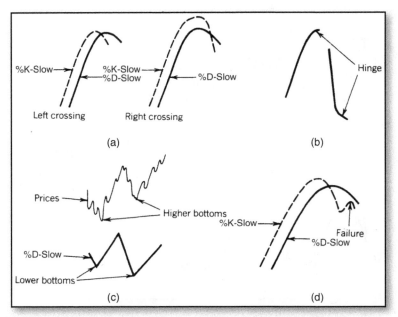

FIGURE 11.17 Lane's Patterns. (a) Left and right crossings. (b) Hinge. (c) Bear market set-up. (d) *%K-slow* failure.

Warning. An extreme turn in the faster *%K-slow* (from 2 to 12%) indicates at most two days remaining in the old trend.

Extremes. Reaching the extreme *%K-slow* values of 0 and 100 requires seven consecutive days of closes at the highs (or lows). The test of these extremes, following a pullback, is an excellent entry point.

Set-up. Although the line chart shows higher highs and lows, if the *%D-slow* line has lower lows, a *bear market set-up* has occurred. Look for a selling opportunity on the next rally (Figure 11.17c).

Failure. An excellent confirmation of a change in direction occurs when *%K-slow* crosses *%D-slow* (after penetrating the extreme level), then pulls back to the *%D-slow* line, but fails to cross it again (Figure 11.17d).

Creating a Stochastic from the RSI

Any series or indicator value can be converted to a raw stochastic, %K, without adding lag by replacing the closing price with the indicator value. This creates a measure of where that indicator lies in its high-low range over the calculation period and may simplify the generation of buy and sell signals. A stochastic created from an RSI would be[11]

$$n\text{-}day\ StochRSI = \frac{RSI_{today} - RSI_{n\text{-}day\ low}}{RSI_{n\text{-}day\ high} - RSI_{n\text{-}day\ low}}$$

---

[11]Tushar Chande and Stanley Kroll, *The New Technical Trader* (New York: John Wiley & Sons, 1994).

Williams's Oscillators

Larry Williams has been known for his development of trading methods based on oscillators since his publication of the *A/D Oscillator* in 1972. The three techniques described below have some similarities, even though the last one, the *Ultimate Oscillator*, was published 13 years later.

A/D Oscillator In 1972, Jim Waters and Larry Williams published a description of their *A/D Oscillator*. For their method, *A/D* means *accumulation/distribution* rather than the popular notation of advance/decline, a well-known indicator for stocks. They used a unique form of relative strength, defining *buying power* (BP) and *selling power* (SP) as

$$BP = high - open$$

$$SP = close - low$$

where the values used were today's open, high, low, and closing prices. The two values, BP and SP, show the additional buying strength (relative to the open) and selling strength (compared to the close) in an effort to measure the implied direction of the day's trading. This definition of buying and selling power is still used today. The combined measurement, called the *Daily Raw Figure* (DRF) is calculated as

$$DRF_t = \frac{BP_t + SP_t}{2 \times (H_t - L_t)}$$

The maximum value of 1 is reached when a market opens trading at the low and then closes at the high: $BP_t - SP_t = H_t - L_t$. When the opposite occurs and the market opens at the high and closes on the lows, the $DRF = 0$. Each price series develops its own patterns, which can be smoothed or traded in many ways similar to a momentum index. The Waters-Williams A/D Oscillator solves problems of volatility and limit moves (although there are very few markets with trading limits any more) in futures markets. *DRF* completely adjusts to higher or lower trading ranges because the divisor itself is a multiple of the day's range; because each day is treated independently, the cumulative values of the momentum index are not part of the results.

This day-to-day evaluation has no memory and causes DRF to be very volatile, yet it still takes on the pattern of the underlying market. If fewer trades are preferred, the DRF can be smoothed. In the example in Table 11.2, a 0.30 exponential smoothing was used (selected arbitrarily) and the entry bands narrowed from 80-20 to 70-30 to reflect fewer extreme prices. Because the 1973 examples used soybeans, this example will do the same, but for 2011 data. Table 11.2 shows the calculations for the DRF and the smoothed DRF. The DRF is plotted as bars on a scale of 0 to 1.00 in Figure 11.18 and is extremely erratic. The solid line is the smoothed DRF. Once plotted, two horizontal lines can be drawn to isolate the peaks and bottoms of DRF; the top part becomes a zone representing an overbought condition, and the bottom zone represents oversold. For this chart, the 80-20 levels were used, although we expect this to be consistent over time because the range used in the denominator normalizes volatility. Even though we do not claim that these thresholds are predictive, the original article by Waters and Williams had lines drawn in a similar place. The thresholds for the smoothed DRF were set at 70-30.

| TABLE 11.2 | A/D Oscillator and Trading Signals, Soybeans, January 1, 2011 through March 4, 2011 |

| | | | | | | Raw DRF | | | 30% DRF Smoothing | |
| | | | | | | 80-20 | Entry | | 70-30 | Entry |
Date	Open	High	Low	Close	DRF	Signal	(Lagged)	DRF	Signal	(Lagged)
1/3/2011	1409.00	1422.00	1388.00	1392.00	0.250			0.250		
1/4/2011	1391.25	1403.50	1370.50	1382.50	0.367			0.285		
1/5/2011	1385.00	1408.00	1375.00	1406.50	0.826	Sell ↘		0.447		
1/6/2011	1405.50	1411.75	1389.00	1391.00	0.181	Buy ↘	1405.50	0.368		
1/7/2011	1389.75	1395.50	1373.25	1378.00	0.236	Buy	1389.75	0.328		
1/10/2011	1381.00	1407.50	1379.00	1393.50	0.719	Buy		0.445		
1/11/2011	1395.00	1401.50	1368.25	1370.00	0.124	Buy		0.349		
1/12/2011	1372.50	1440.00	1372.00	1428.00	0.908	Sell ↘		0.517		
1/13/2011	1431.75	1445.50	1426.00	1429.00	0.429	Sell	1431.75	0.491		
1/14/2011	1431.50	1442.50	1418.00	1435.50	0.582	Sell		0.518		
1/18/2011	1425.25	1443.00	1421.25	1426.25	0.523	Sell		0.519		
1/19/2011	1429.50	1444.75	1415.25	1424.50	0.415	Sell		0.488		
1/20/2011	1426.00	1434.00	1396.50	1427.25	0.517	Sell		0.497		
1/21/2011	1428.75	1440.00	1418.00	1425.25	0.420	Sell		0.474		
1/24/2011	1425.50	1439.50	1409.75	1417.50	0.366	Sell		0.441		
1/25/2011	1417.25	1421.00	1383.25	1387.50	0.106	Buy ↘		0.341		
1/26/2011	1388.50	1404.00	1377.25	1398.50	0.687	Buy	1388.50	0.445		
1/27/2011	1402.25	1414.00	1391.00	1412.50	0.723	Buy		0.528		
1/28/2011	1414.50	1436.25	1405.50	1411.00	0.443	Buy		0.503		
1/31/2011	1408.25	1426.50	1407.50	1426.00	0.967	Sell ↘		0.642		
2/1/2011	1426.50	1453.50	1421.25	1451.00	0.880	Sell	1426.50	0.713	Sell ↘	
2/2/2011	1452.50	1465.00	1446.50	1457.00	0.622	Sell		0.686	Sell	1452.50
2/3/2011	1459.00	1465.50	1447.00	1448.50	0.216	Sell		0.545	Sell	
2/4/2011	1451.50	1455.75	1435.25	1446.50	0.378	Sell		0.495	Sell	
2/7/2011	1451.00	1456.75	1434.25	1437.50	0.200	Sell		0.406	Sell	
2/8/2011	1438.00	1450.00	1427.00	1447.25	0.701	Sell		0.495	Sell	
2/9/2011	1450.00	1468.75	1448.00	1464.00	0.837	Sell		0.598	Sell	
2/10/2011	1464.25	1468.00	1443.00	1446.00	0.135	Buy ↘		0.459	Sell	
2/11/2011	1444.75	1454.50	1423.00	1429.00	0.250	Buy	1444.75	0.396	Sell	
2/14/2011	1431.75	1438.00	1413.25	1416.00	0.182	Buy		0.332	Sell	
2/15/2011	1416.00	1422.00	1378.00	1381.25	0.105	Buy		0.264	Buy ↘	
2/16/2011	1382.25	1389.00	1370.00	1378.50	0.401	Buy		0.305	Buy	1382.25
2/17/2011	1378.50	1418.75	1378.50	1416.50	0.972	Sell ↘		0.505	Buy	
2/18/2011	1417.50	1421.25	1373.00	1381.00	0.122	Buy ↘	1417.50	0.390	Buy	
2/22/2011	1391.00	1397.50	1311.00	1311.00	0.038	Buy	1391.00	0.284	Buy	

TABLE 11.2 *Continued*

Date	Open	High	Low	Close	Raw DRF			30% DRF Smoothing		
					DRF	80-20 Signal	Entry (Lagged)	DRF	70-30 Signal	Entry (Lagged)
2/23/2011	1310.00	1335.00	1296.25	1331.50	0.777	Buy		0.432	Buy	
2/24/2011	1332.25	1336.75	1310.25	1329.25	0.443	Buy		0.436	Buy	
2/25/2011	1328.75	1399.25	1322.00	1375.00	0.799	Buy		0.545	Buy	
2/28/2011	1378.00	1380.25	1357.75	1364.75	0.206	Buy		0.443	Buy	
3/1/2011	1368.00	1376.50	1353.75	1375.25	0.659	Buy		0.508	Buy	
3/2/2011	1374.50	1399.00	1372.00	1394.25	0.866	Sell ↘		0.615	Buy	
3/3/2011	1390.50	1414.50	1384.50	1412.00	0.858	Sell	1390.50	0.688	Buy	
3/4/2011	1410.25	1424.50	1395.75	1414.00	0.565	Sell		0.651	Buy	

FIGURE 11.18 A/D Oscillator.

The rules for using the A/D Oscillator were not defined in the original article, but some simple rules could be:

- *Sell* when the DRF (or smoothed DRF) penetrates into the overbought zone. Close out all accumulated long positions (if any) and go short on the open of the next trading day.

- *Buy* and exit the short position when the opposite conditions occur.

- All positions are entered on the next open after a signal.

For risk control, positions could be exited if the DRF does not post a lower value (for shorts) within one or two days, and the opposite for longs. In Table 11.2 no stops were used. Long positions were held until a short signal occurred, and shorts until a long was signaled. If the DRF (or smoothed DRF) enters an overbought or oversold zone more than once without the opposite zone being entered, an additional position can be added, although that was not done in the example. Following these rules, the A/D Oscillator showed nine trades, six of them profitable. For the smoothed DRF there were only two trades, both profitable. The amount of smoothing can easily be changed. For more signals, increase the smoothing constant so that it's greater than 0.30. An Excel spreadsheet and a TradeStation program, both named *TSM AD Oscillator*, can be found on the Companion Website.

Although this example was very good, there are potential problems in the A/D Oscillator. The first happens on locked-limit days (where the market opens at the allowable limit and does not trade). In that case the open, high, low, and close are all the same and the DRF cannot be calculated because the divisor is zero. Fortunately, there are few markets in which that can happen, but it did recently in cotton. A more basic problem concerns gap openings. A much higher opening with a stronger close would also upset the resulting DRF value. Consider the following example:

	Open	High	Low	Close	DRF	ΔRFs	ΣΔDRF
Monday	43.00	44.00	40.00	41.00	0.25		
Tuesday	42.00	42.00	39.00	40.00	0.17	−0.17	−0.17
Wednesday	38.50	38.50	38.00	38.00	0.00	+0.17	0.00
Thursday	42.00	42.00	39.00	40.00	0.17	−0.33	−0.33
Friday	40.00	43.00	40.00	42.00	0.83	+0.50	+0.17

Note that on Wednesday, the DRF indicates that the momentum has reversed, but in fact the price is falling rapidly and gives no indication of recovering; it may actually be gaining momentum. On Thursday the price soars up and closes in the midrange, but the DRF shows a new downward momentum. The problem seems to be related to lack of association with the prior closing price. The daily movement can take on different appearances if the entire range was above or below the closing price. To form this link, replace the current high or low with the prior closing price, in the manner of the *true range* calculation, if that price was outside the current trading range. The following example shows that the results smoothed out and leaves the trend intact.

	Open	High	Low	Close	DRF	ΔDRF	ΣΔDRF
Monday	43.00	44.00	40.00	41.00	.25		
Tuesday	42.00	42.00	39.00	40.00	.17	−.17	−.17
Wednesday	38.50	(40.00)	38.00	38.00	.37	+.04	.13
Thursday	42.00	42.00	(38.00)	40.00	.25	−.12	−.25
Friday	40.00	43.00	40.00	42.00	.83	+.58	+.33

Linking the Current Day with the Prior Day   Another oscillator can be constructed using the highs and lows relative to the prior close:

$$O_t = \frac{H_t - C_{t-1}}{H_t - L_t}$$

The two days are linked together, and the ratio of the high price relative to the prior close is measured against the total range for the day. For the normal case, $H_t \geq C_{t-1} \geq L_t$; but if C_{t-1} replaces either H_t or L_t to extend the range, the value of O_t will be either 1 or 0 for these extreme cases. As with the A/D Oscillator, the values derived from this method may also be smoothed.

Oscillators are not the only tools for measuring momentum or for determining overbought or oversold conditions. Because momentum is very different from either a charting technique or a moving average, it is valuable either on its own or as a confirmation of another method.

A word of caution: Trading against the trend can be exciting and profitable, but at considerably greater risk than a trend-following system. The problem with selling an overbought condition is that it is much more difficult to hold losses to a minimum. A long position may be entered while prices are falling fast, and they may continue to fall at the same speed after you are long. Even a quick exit may sustain substantial losses.

%R Method   After the publication of Williams's *How I Made One Million Dollars . . . Last Year . . . Trading Commodities*, the %R oscillator became well known. It is a simple way of calculating where today's closing price fits into the recent trading range. Using the last 10 days, define

$$\%R = \frac{Buying\ power}{Range} = \frac{High_{10} - Close_{today}}{High_{10} - Low_{10}}$$

Williams's 10-day %R is different from a *10-day stochastic,* because it measures how strong the market closed today compared to the high of the past 10 days. It is also conceptually upside down; that is, as the close gets stronger the value of %R gets smaller. It may be intuitively easier to work with if you use $1.0 - \%R$. Williams viewed this as a timing device to add positions within a major technical or fundamental trend. This same approach was discussed with regard to the stochastic, and is shown in Figure 11.16. Trades were not entered if they contradicted the major market direction.

The Ultimate Oscillator   In the *Ultimate Oscillator,* Williams seems to combine his original idea of the A/D Oscillator with a great deal of Wilder's RSI.[12] He adds the unique feature of three concurrent time periods in order to offset the negative qualities of the short time period used for the %R, without slowing the system too much. The Ultimate Oscillator uses the following steps:

1. Calculate today's *buying pressure* BP_t by subtracting the *true low* from the closing price, $BP_t = C_t - TL_t$. The true low $TLt = \min(Lt, Ct{-}1)$.
2. Calculate today's *true range,* $TR_t = \max(H_t - L_t, H_t - C_{t-1}, C_{t-1} - L_t)$.
3. Total the buying pressure BP_t separately over the three intervals 7, 14, and 28 days, designated as SB_7, SB_{14}, and SB_{28}.

---

[12] Larry Williams, "The Ultimate Oscillator," *Technical Analysis of Stocks & Commodities* (August 1985).

FIGURE 11.19

4. Total the true range TR_t over the same three periods, SR_7, SR_{14}, and SR_{28}.
5. Divide the sum of the buying pressures by the corresponding true range, that is, SB_7/SR_7 and scale by multiplying the 7-day value by 4 and the 14-day value by 2. All three calculations are now in the same scale.

Notice that the nearest seven values for the buying pressure and the true range are each used seven times, that is, they are multiplied by both the scaling factors of 4 and 2, and used once more in the 28-day calculation. Williams has created a step-weighted momentum, assigning values of 7, 3, and 1 to the first 7 days, second 7 days, and last 14 days, respectively. The last 14 days account for only 10% of the total.

The rules for using this oscillator (Figure 11.19) are:

1. A *sell set-up* occurs when the oscillator moves above the 50% line, peaks at a high value, declines, and then moves higher. If the oscillator fails to move above the peak on the next rally, a *short sale* order can be placed when the oscillator fails on the right shoulder. This is a traditional top confirmation signal.
2. Short positions are closed out when a long signal occurs, when the 30% level is reached, or if the oscillator rises above 65% (the *stop-loss* point) after being below 50%.
3. A *buy* signal is given using the opposite formation as the short signal (rule 1).
4. Close out longs when a short signal occurs, when the 70% level is reached, or if the oscillator falls below 30% (after being above 50%).

Relative Vigor Index

John Ehlers, who has contributed extensively in the mathematical analysis of prices, in particular using cycles, has created the *Relative Vigor Index* (RVI), a very smoothed momentum indicator.[13] The basic form of RVI is

$$RVI = (Close - Open)/(High - Low)$$

However, the final RVI uses a 4-day symmetric weighting (similar to a triangular weighting) of the *close* − *open* in the numerator, and a similar symmetric weighting of the *high* − *low* in the denominator.

[13] John F. Ehlers, "Relative Vigor Index," *Technical Analysis of Stocks & Commodities* (January 2002).

RVI is conceptually similar to the A/D Oscillator; however, the RVI is smoothed in a special way that targets a particular price cycle and eliminates the 2-bar cycle and its associated unwanted frequencies. While it is preferable that the price series be analyzed for its cycle period, Ehlers suggests using 10 as the nominal value. The RVI is calculated as

$$N_t = [(C_t - O_t) + 2 \times (C_{t-1} - O_{t-1}) + 2 \times (C_{t-2} - O_{t-2}) + (C_{t-3} - O_{t-3})]/6$$

$$D_t = [(H_t - L_t) + 2 \times (H_{t-1} - L_{t-1}) + 2 \times (H_{t-2} - L_{t-2}) + (H_{t-3} - L_{t-3})]/6$$

$$Numerator_t = \Sigma N_i, \ i = t - n + 1, t$$

$$Denominator_t = \Sigma D_i, \ i = t - n + 1, t$$

$$RVI = Numerator_t / Denominator_t, \text{ while } Denominator_t \neq 0$$

$$RVI \ signal \ line_t = (RVI + 2 \times RVI_{t-1} + 2 \times RVI_{t-2} + RVI_{t-3})/6$$

where O_t, H_t, L_t, and C_t are today's open, high, low, and closing prices and n is the calculation period, nominally 10.

The RVI signal line is used in the same manner as the MACD signal line. After a peak in the RVI value, showing an overbought situation, the sell signal occurs the first time that the RVI crosses the RVI signal line moving lower.

■ Double-Smoothed Momentum

Important contributions to the study of momentum have been made by William Blau.[14] In addition to creating new momentum indicators, he has added substantial value to the old ones. Also refer to his work on double smoothing of momentum in Chapter 8.

True Strength Index

Much of Blau's work combines double smoothing of momentum values (1-period price differences) which has surprisingly little calculation *lag* given the amount of smoothing. By using the first differences, he has based the calculations on values more sensitive than price and then slowed them down by smoothing. In effect, he speeds up the price movement before slowing it down. The net result is that the final index value has less lag than we would normally expect, and the index line is much smoother than a standard moving average. Blau refers to this as *using momentum as a proxy for price*. One of Blau's most popular indicators is the *True Strength Index* (TSI) which combines these features:

$$TSI(close, r, s) = \frac{100 \times XAverage(XAverage(close - close[1], r)s)}{XAv}$$

---

[14] William Blau, *Momentum, Direction and Divergence* (New York: John Wiley & Sons, 1995).

Where r = the calculation period of the first momentum smoothing
        s = the calculation period of the second momentum smoothing
        $close - close[1]$ = the 1-day momentum
        $XAverage(close, period)$ = the TradeStation function for exponential smoothing
        $AbsValue$ = the TradeStation function for absolute value

A spreadsheet to calculate the True Strength Index for crude oil, *TSM True Strength Index*, and a program indicator, *TMS True Strength*, are available on the Companion Website. The spreadsheet code, which is easily entered, is set up as follows:

1. Column *B* is the closing prices
2. Column *C* is the 1-day difference in prices
3. Column *D* is the first smoothing, where D3 = C3 and D4 = D3 + H2*(C3-D3)
4. Column *E* is the second smoothing, E4 = D4, and E5 = E4 + H3*(D5-E4)

The smoothing constants in *H* are derived from the days in *G* using $2/(n+1)$. A sample of the spreadsheet appears in Table 11.3.

TABLE 11.3								
	A TSI Calculations Using Two 20-Day Smoothing Periods					G	H	
Column	Date	Crude	Diff	Smooth 1	Smooth 2			
2	1/3/2011	96.35				Smooth 1	20	0.0952
3	1/4/2011	94.18	−2.17	−2.170		Smooth 2	20	0.0952
4	1/5/2011	95.1	0.92	−1.876	−1.876			
5	1/6/2011	93.18	−1.92	−1.880	−1.876			
6	1/7/2011	92.83	−0.35	−1.734	−1.863			
7	1/10/2011	94.05	1.22	−1.453	−1.824			
8	1/11/2011	95.91	1.86	−1.137	−1.758			
9	1/12/2011	96.42	0.51	−0.980	−1.684			
10	1/13/2011	95.85	−0.57	−0.941	−1.613			

The numerator and denominator of the TSI differ only in that the denominator takes the absolute value of the price changes (the 1-day momentum). This guarantees that the denominator will be at least as large as the numerator. The 1-day differences are first smoothed over the period r, and then the result is smoothed over the period s. The relationship between the standard momentum (the difference in prices over r days) and the TSI can be seen in Figure 11.20 for Intel (INTC). The standard 20-day momentum indicator (second panel) has the typical erratic pattern of prices, and a slight lead identifying the peaks. The TSI is much smoother with peaks and valleys lagging prices slightly (third panel). If more smoothing is necessary to avoid false signals, a *signal line* can be created by smoothing the TSI using a 3-period moving average, then buying when the TSI crosses the signal line after a high or low value was reached. This can be a basic trend signal, or it can be applied in the manner of

FIGURE 11.20 Comparing the TSI with 10-20-20 Smoothing (bottom) to a Standard 20-Period Momentum (center) Using INTC from January 2001 through March 2002.

MACD. The slight lag in the TSI seems a small problem compared to the extreme noise of the momentum calculation.

Additional Smoothing without Adding Lag   In creating the TSI, Blau missed an opportunity to improve the smoothing with only a minor increase in the lag. Instead of taking the 1-day differences, substitute the *n*-day differences in the first step. This smoothes the trendline even more at the cost of a slight additional lag. Figure 11.20 shows the TSI with a 10-day difference followed by two 20-day exponential smoothings in the bottom panel.

Anticipating the Turn   When working with trendlines that are very smooth, such as the 10-20-20 TSI, you can anticipate the change in the trend direction most of the time. Instead of waiting for the smoothed trendline to change from up to down, you can sell when it gets to a "near-zero slope" and is continuing to flatten. This anticipation can greatly reduce the lag and improve performance even at the cost of a few false signals.

Double-Smoothed Stochastics

Because of Blau's great interest in double smoothing, he defines the general form of a *double-smoothed stochastic* as:

$$DS\,(q,r,s) = \frac{100 \times XAverage\,(XAverage\,(close - Lowest(low,q),r),s)}{XA}$$

Where $Close - Lowest(low,q)$ = the numerator of Lane's raw stochastic, the lowest low over the past *q* periods

$Highest(high,q) - Lowest(low,q)$ = the denominator of Lane's stochastic, the greatest high-low range over the past *q* periods

$XAverage((...,r),s)$ = an exponential smoothing of the numerator, first calculated over *r* periods, then over *s* periods

TRIX

Similar to Blau's double smoothing is *TRIX,* a triple-smoothed exponential that is most often used as an oscillator. Introduced by Jack Hutson,[15] it is created using steps similar to Blau except that there are three exponential smoothings and the differencing is done at the end. Typically, the same smoothing constants (calculation periods) are used for each smoothing. This method has been applied to daily, hourly, or even 1-minute price data.

1. Calculate the natural log (ln) of the closing prices (daily or intraday bars). This implicitly corrects for price volatility; however, it is commonly omitted from the calculation because back-adjusted data in futures will cause errors.
2. Calculate the *p*-period exponential smoothing of the closing prices, or the ln of the closing prices, to get *trend* 1.
3. Calculate the *q*-period exponential smoothing of *trend* 1 to get *trend* 2.
4. Calculate the *r*-period exponential smoothing of *trend* 2 to get *trend* 3.
5. Get the 1-period differences of *trend* 3 by subtracting each value from the previous value. As with the added smoothing of the TSI, the 1-period differences can be replaced with the *s*-period differences.
6. Scale the results by multiplying by 10,000. This is an attempt to get TRIX scaled to a positive integer value for charting and may also be omitted.

The resulting TRIX indicator acts as an oscillator due to Step 5. It can be very smooth when the calculation periods are larger; it also reduces the lag because of the differencing step. TRIX can be used as a trend indicator by buying when the value of TRIX crosses above zero and selling when it crosses below zero. It can produce buy and sell signals sooner by buying when the TRIX value is rising for two or three consecutive periods, and selling when TRIX is falling for two or three consecutive periods. Because the triple smoothing results in a very smooth TRIX value, trading signals can safely use the change in TRIX as an advance indicator of trend.

Figure 11.21 compares TRIX (center panel) with the TSI (lower panel), both based on first differences, but using the smoothing constant of 1.0 to negate one of the steps. The point is to show that TRIX is actually smoother because the differences are taken at the end rather than the beginning. The lag in TRIX is slightly more than the TSI, but it would be unnecessary to use *n*-day differences for TRIX to get further smoothing; therefore, TRIX may have less lag in its final form.

Changing the Divisor

All return calculations divide the price change from yesterday to today by the starting value, yesterday's price. There is no rule that says that you cannot divide the change by the current price,

$$r_t = \frac{Close_t - Close_{t-1}}{Close_t} - 1$$

---

[15] Referenced in Robert W. Colby, *The Encyclopedia of Technical Market Indicators* (New York: McGraw-Hill, 2003) as "Good Trix" by Jack K. Hutson, *Technical Analysis of Stocks & Commodities* 1, no. 5.

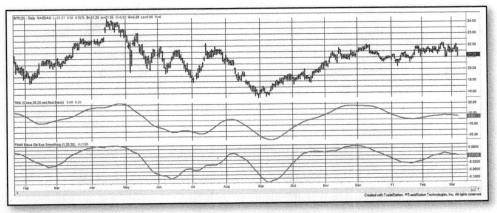

FIGURE 11.21 Comparison of TRIX (center panel) and TSI (lower panel) Using Two 20-Day Exponential Smoothings Applied to INTC.

While this would result in only small changes, the cumulative effect is said to add stability to an indicator that is based on returns.

An Oscillator to Distinguish between Trending and Sideways Markets

The lack of predictability of trending markets is the greatest problem for the analyst. The work found under the topics "Ranking of Markets for Selection" and "Directional Movement" in Level III, Chapter 12 discusses that issue. Based on the idea that the trend component is stronger when price is further from fair value, and the noise (sideways movement) is greater when price is near value, an oscillator can be created to show the strength of the trend component based on this concept,

$$Strength\,Oscillator_t = \frac{Average(Close_t - Close_{t-1}, n)}{Average(High_t - \quad_t, \quad)}$$

As the trend increases, the average change in closing prices becomes larger relative to the high-low range for the day. During an unusual period, when the market gaps open, it would be possible for the differences in the closing prices to become larger than the daily range. In a sideways market, both the change in the closes and daily range will get smaller, but the net price change over period n should be close to zero. This oscillator can be smoothed by taking the change in price over two or three days (for example, $close_t - close_{t-3}$), rather the most recent day, as well as taking the high-low range over the same number of days. The indicator and function, *TSM Strength Oscillator*, can be found on the Companion Website.

Adding Volume to Momentum

A momentum indicator can also incorporate volume by multiplying the price change over n periods by the total volume over that same period. The use of the cumulative volume over the period, or even better, the average volume, will help to stabilize the volume, which is often erratic when seen as only one day's activity. The *average volume* will appear to be the same magnitude as the volume and can be plotted along with it on a chart. That gives the *momentum-volume indicator (MV)*, shown mathematically and in programming notation:

$$MV_t = (p_t - p_{t-n}) \times \frac{\sum_{i=t-n+1}^{t} volume_i}{n}$$

```
MV = (close-close[n])*average(volume,n)
```

Alternately, the price change over *n* periods could have been divided by *n* to give a per unit value. The following sections will include those techniques that combine price change and volume or open interest; for methods that use volume but not price, see Chapter 13.

Scaling by a Percentage or Volatility

The same conversions can be applied to momentum with and without volume. Using a percentage rather than price will add some robustness over long test periods. Because volatility often increases faster than a fixed percentage of the price when prices rise, momentum can be scaled according to a shorter measure of true range. If the true range is averaged over 20 to 65 days, approximately one month to one quarter, then the 1-day change in price will become a relative momentum value. By using a much longer period for averaging the true range, you can create a stable profile of the volatility changes in the underlying market.

Percentage momentum with volume
```
%MV = (close − close[n]) / close[n] * average(volume,n)
```
Momentum with volume scaled by true range
```
TRMV = (close − close[n]) / average(truerange,p) * average(volume,n)
```
where *truerange* is always calculated for the most recent period (e.g., 1 day), and the average of the 1-day true ranges for the past *p* days is *average(truerange,p)*.

Volume-Weighted RSI

In the same way that the RSI accumulates the price changes for positive days and divides by the sum of the negative changes, it is possible to weight each day by its volume to add another factor, called *money flow*,[16] to the calculation. A positive or upwards day is when the average of today's high, low, and close is greater than the previous average. Each average is then multiplied by the volume, giving the daily money flow, and a ratio of the past 14 days is used to create a *money ratio* and finally a *money flow index,* both steps similar to Wilder's RSI.

$$Moneyflow_t = Volume_t \times \frac{High_t + Low_t + Close_t}{3}$$

---

[16] Gene Quong and Avrum Soudack, "Volume-Weighted RSI: Money Flow," *Technical Analysis of Stocks & Commodities* (March 1989).

$$Moneyratio_t = \frac{\sum_{i=t-13}^{t} Moneyflow_i \, if > 0}{\sum_{i=t-13}^{t} Moneyflow_i \, if < 0}$$

$$Moneyflowindex_t = 100 - \frac{100}{1 + Moneyratio_t}$$

Herrick Payoff Index

Using the change in the underlying value of the futures contract, rather than only the change in price, the *Herrick Payoff Index*[17] (HPI) combines volume and open interest to generate an indicator that is not bounded as is the basic momentum calculation. The daily value is:

$$HP_t = cf \times V_t \times (M_t - M_{t-1}) \times \left[1 + \left(\frac{M_t - M_{t-1}}{|M_t - M_{t-1}|} \right) \left(\frac{2 \times |OI_t - OI_{t-1}|}{\min(OI_t, OI_{t-1})} \right) \right]$$

Where $\quad t = $ today

$t - 1 = $ the previous day

$cf = $ the conversion factor (value of a one big point move)

$V_t = $ today's volume

$(M_t - M_{t-1}) = $ the difference in the mean values, $M = (high + low)/2$, where vertical bars denote absolute value

$|OI_t - OI_{t-1}| = $ the absolute value of the change in open interest (for futures)

$\min(OI_t, OI_{t-1}) = $ the smaller of the open interest for today or the previous day

The expression that divides the change in mean prices by the absolute value of the same change is used to create a value of +1 or −1. The index HP_t is then scaled down to a manageable value and smoothed using a 0.10 smoothing factor, s (about 19 days). This complex formula for HPI can also be written in programming code as

```
HP = BigPointValue*volume*((high-low)/2 - (high[1]-low[1])/2)*
        (1+(((high-low)/2 - (high[1]-low[1])/2) /
        absvalue((high-low)/2 - (high[1]-low[1])/2))*2*
        (absvalue(opint - opint[1])/lowest(opint,2)))

HPI = smoothedaverage(HP,19)
```

Most analysts who use the Herrick Payoff Index divide the HPI by 100,000 to scale the value to a more usable level (in the example below it is scaled by 1,000,000). The final series, when seen along with prices, may appear volatile and require interpretation, often using trendlines. This is due to the fluctuations in volume and open interest, which are smoothed over 20 days, rather than a longer period. The Herrick Payoff Index may be helpful, despite its volatility, because it is a combination of factors not included in most other indexes. It has patterns that appear to lead price

---

[17] From the original *CompuTrac* manual, which became the Dow Jones Telerate division, and finally just Dow Jones.

FIGURE 11.22 The Herrick Payoff Index Applied to the DAX, 2000 through February 2011.

change to compensate for its noisy behavior. A spreadsheet, *TSM Herrick Payoff Index for DAX*, and a program, *TSM Herrick Payoff*, can be found on the Companion Website.

Figure 11.22 gives an idea of how the HPI reacts to prices, in this case using the German DAX from 2000 through February 2011. It shows higher volatility at the turning points and very low volatility during the upwards trends from 2004 to 2006 and again in 2010. It turns out that volume is a good surrogate for volatility and might actually be a good forecaster of volatility. This is discussed in Chapter 13.

Comments on the Use of Volume

Volume is an important piece of information, but it can be difficult to interpret. It fluctuates in a much larger range than price, and may be 50% higher or lower from day to day. While it indicates market interest and potential volatility, there are many days for which a high or low volume does not have a consistent reaction.

In general, adding volume to an indicator results in a more volatile, erratic series. Therefore, the first steps in using volume are:

1. Create a long-term, smoothed volume series.
2. Locate days with extremely high volatility to identify only those exceptional days where continued high volatility should follow.
3. Low volume should not be determined by a single day, but by either a few unusually low days clustered together or by a decay in the smoothed volume over a modest time period.

Using volume to enhance trend signals as well as identifying important volume patterns is discussed in Chapter 13.

CHAPTER 12

Cycle Analysis

From Perry J. Kaufman, *Trading Systems and Methods, + Website,* 5th Edition (Hoboken, New Jersey: John Wiley & Sons, 2013), Chapter 11.

The cycle is another basic element of price movement, along with the trend and seasonality, but as a mathematical problem it can be more difficult to evaluate and is often avoided. But there are many different types of cycles, from agricultural to presidential election, and many of them are simple to evaluate and can improve trading.

Cycles come in many forms—seasonality, production startup and shutdown, inventory or stocks, behavioral, and even astronomical. Seasonality is a special case of a calendar or annual cycle. Seasonality was covered in the previous chapter, and its special features are not considered here. Some of the cycles are clearly *periodic,* having regular intervals between peaks and valleys; others are more uniform in their *amplitude* or height but irregular in period. The most definitive and regular cycle remains the seasonal, which is determined by periodic physical phenomena, the changing of the year.

This chapter will discuss the major commodity and financial cycles that most likely result from business decisions, government programs, and long-term market characteristics and phenomena. Short-term cycles are usually attributed to behavior and will be covered in Level III, Chapter 4, Pattern Recognition.

There are a few important ways to find the cycle, the most common being *trigonometric curve fitting* and *Fourier (spectral) analysis.* Both will require a computer and will be explained in the following sections. John Ehlers introduced *Maximum Entropy Spectral Analysis* (MESA), which finds price cycles based on small amounts of data, at the same time avoiding some of the problems inherent in other methods. Examples of solutions will be included in the explanation of the methods and applications that follows. Computer programs that solve the trigonometric problems can be found on the Companion Website as well as in Appendix 3, along with additional examples. Commercial software examples will also be used to show the classic solutions.

■ Cycle Basics

The cycle, along with the trend and seasonality, comprise the three orderly components of price movement. The fourth is noise, which includes everything not accounted for in the first three. To find any one component, we must remove the others. In earlier chapters we found that we can eliminate the trend by taking the first differences of the data; that is, subtracting the previous value from the current value. In the previous chapter on seasonality, we used the simple technique of subtracting a 1-year moving average (a 12-period average applied to monthly data) from the original price series to remove the seasonal pattern. Alternatively, statistical software will subtract this month's average price from that of 12 months ago, or today's daily price from that of 252 days ago in order to detrend the data. By finding the first differences and then subtracting the 1-year average, or by removing the 1-year differences, we are left with the cycle and the unaccountable price movement, which we call *noise*.

Even when the seasonal pattern is eliminated, most cycles are still based on the periodic effects in our Universe. After the 1-year orbit of our planet around the Sun, there is the 28-day lunar cycle; converted to business days, this gives the very familiar 20-day reference that remains overwhelmingly popular among all analysts (also corresponding to four weeks). Other planetary effects, which should by no means be discarded off-hand, can be found in Level III, Chapter 3 under the topic "Financial Astrology." The possibility cannot be eliminated that planetary motion may account for, besides seasonality, the effects of mass behavior, which can produce a consistent cycle that repeats with a fixed period.[1]

Cycles can be complex and difficult to see because there is often a combination of larger and smaller patterns, and cycles within cycles, all acting at the same time. Nevertheless, they exist, and they are real. The cycles that appear to be most important are either long-term or the sum of a number of subcycles that come together at peaks or valleys. This gives us a way to identify one point on a cycle; we must remember that, when the individual components are found, there may be a number of smaller patterns that cause this effect. Thinking about it as *harmonics*, just as in music, means that a smaller cycle is a fraction of the larger cycle, for example, its cycle length is ½, ⅓, ¼, . . . of the larger. When two cycles are *synchronized*, their peaks or valleys occur at the same time. Any price series can be decomposed into individual cycles, and represented as the sum of multiple cycles.

Observing the Cycle

Before selecting a market for cycle analysis, it is necessary to observe that a dominant cycle exists; it is also useful to know why it exists in order to avoid uncovering spurious patterns. This is most easily done for markets in which you can clearly identify the fundamental or industrial reasons for cycles. The basis for a cycle could be a pattern of holding inventory, the fixed time needed for breeding and feeding of livestock, seasonality, the time necessary for closing a mining operation then starting it up again, expansion or contraction of business based on disposable income, the effects of government interest rate policy, or other economic factors.

---

[1] See the section "The Moon," in Level III, Chapter 3.

The Cattle Cycle Using cattle as an example, Figure 12.1a shows a clear 9- to 11-month cycle in futures prices[2] over a 6-year period from 1980 through 1985. The peaks and valleys vary by up to one month, making the pattern reliable for use as part of a long-term trading strategy. Although feedlots in the Southwest have made the supply of cattle more evenly distributed throughout the year, there are still a large number of ranchers in the North who send their cattle to market in the early fall to avoid the difficulties of feeding during a harsh winter. This causes generally lower prices in the Fall and higher prices in the mid-Winter when supplies are low.

A similar pattern can be seen more recently in Figure 12.1b. During the past six years the peaks of the cycle are consistently 12 months apart, although the valleys are not as consistent, most often coming within a few months after the peaks. The overall picture shows that cattle prices continue to have a clear cycle, driven by the fundamentals of production.

The Swiss Franc Cycle The Swiss franc cycle (denominated as Swiss francs/U.S. dollars on Chicago's International Monetary Market) shown in Figure 12.2a is quite different.[3] There are two likely cycles: the primary one (shown using letters at the peaks and valleys) and a subcycle (marked with numbers). The subcycle ranges from 24 to 35 weeks with a 40% variance compared to 20% for cattle. Most important, the cycle in the Swiss franc cannot be attributed to any specific fundamental cause. There is certainly a long-term cycle based on the strength and weakness of the U.S. economy with respect to the Swiss economy, or the relative attractiveness of U.S. interest rates. There is also the general ebb and flow of the U.S. trade balance and, of course, investor behavior. Unlike cattle, these patterns do not need to be rigid.

Looking at Swiss franc prices from 1997 through 2002 there are obvious peaks and valleys that continue a cyclic pattern (see Figure 12.2b). Although they are crisp in appearance, the cycle now has an average period of about 38 weeks with a range from 30 to 52 weeks. The new cycle falls about midway between the periods of the previous primary and subcycles. Although the cycles seem clear, the change in period and the variance between cycle tops will make a systematic strategy difficult.

Basic Cycle Identification

A simple way to begin the search for major cycles is to look at a long-term chart, displayed as weekly rather than daily prices. The dominant half-cycle can be found by locating the obvious price peaks and valleys, then averaging the distance between them. A convenient tool for estimating the cycle length is the Ehrlich Cycle Finder.[4] Developed in 1978, it is an expanding device with evenly spaced points, allowing you to align the peaks and valleys and to observe the consistency in the cycle. For finding a single pattern, it is just as good as some of the mathematical methods that follow. It is best to have at least eight cycle repetitions before concluding that you have a valid cycle.

---

[2] Jacob Bernstein, "Cycle and Seasonal Price Tendencies in Meat and Livestock Markets," in Todd Lofton, ed., *Trading Tactics* (Chicago: Chicago Mercantile Exchange, 1986).

[3] Jacob Bernstein, *The Handbook of Commodity Cycles* (New York: John Wiley & Sons, 1982).

[4] More information and a cycle-finding tool can be found on www.stanehrlich.com.

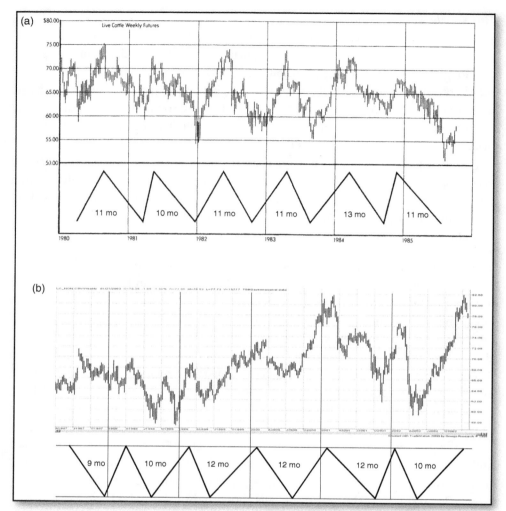

FIGURE 12.1 (a) 9- to 11-Month Cycle in Live Cattle, 1980–1985 Futures Prices. (b) The Cattle Cycle, 1997–2002.

Cycles can be obscured by other price patterns or market noise. Strong trends, such as the ones in Swiss francs (Figure 12.2a) or the seasonal movement of crops, may overwhelm a less pronounced cycle. Classic cycle identification requires that these noncycle factors first be removed by detrending and then by deseasonalizing. The resulting data will then be analyzed and the trend and seasonal factors added back once the cycle has been found. To find a subcycle, the primary cycle should be removed and a second cycle analysis performed on the data. This can be a tedious process. In order to bypass these steps, the methods that follow (trigonometric regression and spectral analysis) can locate the dominant cycle and subcycles at one time using an integrated process.

The Business Cycle

The global business cycle, as distinguished from industry cycles, is the result of macroeconomic events, such as recessions, inflation, and government economic policy.

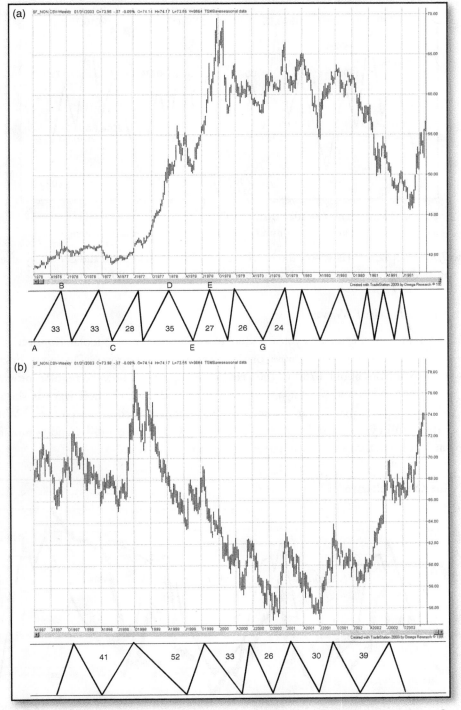

FIGURE 12.2 **(a) Cycle in Swiss franc futures, 1975–1979. The lettered peaks and valleys show the choice for a primary cycle; the numbered peaks and valleys show a likely subcycle. (b) Cycle in Swiss franc futures, 1997–2002.**

Figure 12.3, a product of the Princeton Economic Institute, shows that this cycle is about 8.6 years, or about 4 years from top to bottom in each cycle. Although this chart dates from 1997, it seems remarkably accurate in capturing the tech bubble that ended in 2000, the downturn that followed, ending in 2003, the rally preceding

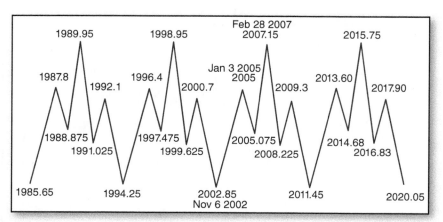

FIGURE 12.3 The 8.6-Year Business Cycle.

Source: The Princeton Economic Institute, available on www.financialsense.com.

the 2008 subprime crisis, and the extreme fall of the market and the economy afterward. It shows the bottom of this cycle in 2011, which we all hope is true.

The Kondratieff Wave

Much of the popularity of cycles is due to the publicity of Nicolai Kondratieff's 54-year cycle, known as the *K-wave*, or more recently, the *long wave*. During its documented span from about 1780 to the present, it appears to be very regular, moving from highs to lows and back again. In Figure 12.4 the Kondratieff wave is shown with major events (particularly wars) that have contributed to its pattern.[5] With only three full cycles completed, it is difficult to tell if the overall trend is moving upwards, or whether the entire pattern is just a coincidence.

FIGURE 12.4 The Kondradieff Wave.

Source: Walker, Jeff, "What K-Wave?" *Technical Analysis of Stocks & Commodities* (July 1990).

---

[5] Jeff Walker, "What K-Wave?" *Technical Analysis of Stocks & Commodities* (July 1990).

The forecast of the *K*-wave, shown in Figure 12.4, corresponds to a sharp decline in wholesale prices due at about the year 1990, the millennium's equivalent to the depression of the 1930s. In fact, the 1990s posted remarkable gains in the stock market, peaking at the beginning of 2000. According to the chart pattern, this peak should be followed by 10 to 20 years of downturn in the economy, in which case we are in the middle, having experienced a major correction in 2008. It should be noted that the peaks of the four waves are of different duration, 1870 being the shortest and the recent one in 2000 the longest.

Although we all accept the existence of an economic cycle, pinpointing the peaks and valleys is impractical. Even if the 54-year period varied only by 10%, we could be entering an investment position 5 years too soon or too late. Determining long-term cycles for any market has the same problem—the actual price pattern will never correspond exactly to the predicted peaks and valleys that most often come at regular intervals. Fortunately, there are other choices. Shorter-term cycles do not need to have the same constant period, and the way in which cycles interact with other strategy components will make them more flexible. However, some investors will want to keep this big picture concept, both the business cycle and the Kondratieff wave, as a general guide to investment timing.

Presidential Election Cycle

Of all the events that move the market, the presidential elections have been the most consistent. The patterns stem from the motivation of the incumbent party to provide good economic news to the voters prior to the election year, and as far into the election year as possible. Stock market action during the election year is always more erratic, as parties battle over the value of each other's actions.

Typically, the year preceding the election (year 3 in the president's term) posts the strongest gains for the market, followed by a reasonably strong election year. (See Table 12.1.) Some analysts have been more specific by starting on October 1 of the previous year. The two years after the election show returns below average as the reality of politics reasserts itself and the new administration tries to implement campaign promises that turn out to be unpopular. More recently, it is only in the first year that the president can push for serious reform. Beginning in the second year, the mid-term elections of members of Congress become more important.

There is the additional possibility that there is an eight-year cycle that should be watched;[6] however, the eight-year period should be most informative if it represented only those years in which the same president was in office. Actions by a president who cannot be reelected are likely to be different from one who seeks another term; therefore, we should expect a different pattern. This can be made more intricate by studying the patterns preceding and following a change of party, all of which have a fundamental basis in the behavior of the political parties and the voters.

---

[6] Articles by Adam White, "The Eight-Year Presidential Election Pattern," *Technical Analysis of Stocks & Commodities* (November 1994); Arthur Merrill, "The Presidential Election Cycle," *Technical Analysis of Stocks & Commodities* (March 1992); and Michael J. Carr, "Get out the Vote and into Stocks," *Futures* (February 1996), all show very similar results for the four-year election pattern.

TABLE 12.1	The Presidential Election Cycle, 1912–1992, Based on the Percentage Returns of the Dow Jones Industrial Averages	
Pre-election year		11.0%
Election year		7.0
Post-election year		4.7
Mid-term year		2.3
Average year		6.3%

Source: Adam White.

More sophisticated computer software, such as that provided by Logical Information Machines,[7] a Chicago firm, can produce a very interesting, closer view of how voters respond to election politics. Table 12.2 breaks the election year into seven periods between the key events for those years in which the stock market began the election year within 8% of its 2-year high price (*days* refer to business days):

1. The returns of the year preceding the election year.
2. The first 10 days of the new year, typically a strong period (days 0–10).
3. Through the State of the Union address and the primaries (days 10–83).
4. Waiting for the conventions (days 83–161).

TABLE 12.2	Election Year Analysis for Years in Which the Stock Market Began the Year within 8% of the Previous 2-Year Highs						
Year	1. Previous Year	2. First 2 weeks (1–10)	3. Primaries (10–83)	4. Pre-convention (83–161)	5. Pre-election (161–195)	6. Election to year-end (195–253)	7. (2) + (4) + (6)
1936	41.82	2.76	4.64	11.91	−0.62	5.85	20.52
1944	19.45	1.63	−0.84	9.27	−0.86	3.14	14.04
1952	16.15	1.60	−2.82	8.02	−2.49	5.47	15.10
1956	27.25	−1.78	5.42	3.16	−6.65	2.38	3.76
1960	8.48	−2.49	−5.75	2.94	−7.13	8.49	8.95
1964	18.89	1.79	4.44	3.03	2.52	0.06	4.88
1968	20.03	0.26	−0.10	1.44	4.39	4.25	5.95
1972	10.82	1.41	3.39	5.30	−1.78	4.88	11.59
1980	12.31	2.26	−5.42	18.57	−0.20	7.66	28.49
1984	17.53	1.27	−5.01	4.27	0.41	0.63	6.17
1992	26.30	0.80	−2.72	2.14	−0.23	5.87	8.82
Average	19.91	0.86	−0.44	6.37	−1.15	4.43	11.66

Source: Michael Carr, Logical Information Machines.

---

[7] See www.lim.com.

TABLE 12.3	Updated Presidential Election Cycle Based on S&P Futures	
Cycle	S&P Total Returns
Preelection	16.4
Election	69.5
1st year	(30.0)
2nd year	48.3

5. Preelection blahs: the actual campaign (days 161–195).
6. The election to year-end reaction (days 195–253).
7. Combined periods (2) + (4) + (6).

Combining the three periods (2), (4), and (6), which have strong upward biases, gives consistently positive results. Even if the newly elected party fails to deliver on its campaign promises, traders could have already converted those marketing gimmicks into stock market profits.

Presidential Cycle from 1983 to 2010 In our rapidly changing world, it is always interesting to see if the market reality continues to support expectations. In fact, using the S&P futures and calculating the year-end returns, the results (in Table 12.3) confirm our new expectations of the presidential cycle. There are moderately good returns in the preelection year, but excellent returns in the year of the election as all candidates and parties promise whatever is necessary to get elected.

Reality follows in the first year of office, when the president attempts to fulfill campaign promises but also takes this one opportunity for economic reforms that are likely to be unpopular, such as budget reductions and tax increases. A better year follows ahead of the mid-term elections, which have become a more important political event than in the past.[8]

■ Uncovering the Cycle

Before resorting to the highly mathematical methods for finding cycles, there are some simple approaches that may serve many traders. For example, if you believe that the dominant cycle has a 20-day period, then you simply create a new price series by subtracting the current data from a 20-day moving average. This removes the trend that may obscure the cycle. This is the same method used for removing seasonality, which subtracted the values of a one-year trend from the corresponding prices. Alternatively, you can take the 20-day differences ($pt - pt_{-20}$), which effectively removes the 20-day trend.

Most oscillators, such as a stochastic or RSI, can also serve to identify a price cycle; however, if you want to see the peaks and valleys of a 20-day cycle, you will need to use a calculation period for the oscillators that is no more than 10 days.

---

[8] Gerald Appel states, "There is a clear election-year cycle, where the election year is +10%, year after +4.5%, 2 years before next −1.25%, and the year before +20%." *Technical Analysis: Power Tool for Active Traders* (Upper Saddle River, NJ: FT Prentice Hall, 2005), 94.

Removing the Trend

The cycle can become more obvious by removing the price trend. While we traditionally only use one trendline to do this, the use of two trendlines seems to work very well in most cases.[9] First smooth the data using two exponential moving averages, where the longer average is half the period of the dominant cycle (using your best guess), and the shorter one is half the period of the longer one. Then create an MACD indicator by subtracting the value of one exponential trend from the other; the resulting *synthetic* series reduces the lag inherent in most methods while removing the trend.

Using Triangular Weighting   One method for enhancing the cycle is the use of *triangular weighting* instead of exponential smoothing. The weighting is *triangular* because it creates a set of weighting factors that are smallest at the ends and largest in the middle, and typically symmetric. You must first decide the calculation period and the weighting factor for the center price. For practical purposes, it is only necessary to give the center price the weight of 2.0. Because there needs to be a center price, the triangular weighting method will eliminate the oldest price if the calculation period is an even number.

The weighting factors begin with the value $2.0/(P/2)$, and increase by the same value. If the calculation period $P = 10$, the weighting begins at $t - P + 2$, or $t - 8$, eliminating the oldest value in order to have an odd number of prices. The weighting factors, w_i, are then 0.4, 0.8, 1.2, 1.6, 2.0, 1.6, 1.2, 0.8, and 0.4. The triangular average is

$$TMA_t = (w_1 \times P_{t-P+2} \times w_2 \times P_{t-P+3} + \cdots + w_{P-1} \times P_t) \, / \, P$$

Enhancing the cycle requires that you calculate two triangular averages, one of which is half the period of the other, then take the difference of the two. The smooth curve of the *triangular MACD* in Figure 12.5 shows the enhanced cyclic pattern of IBM (shown for one year) based on 63 days (about the number of days in a calendar quarter) under the assumption that cycles are likely to be related to periodic

FIGURE 12.5   A 20-10 Triangular MACD Applied to IBM.

[9] In his article "Finding Cycles in Time Series Data," *Technical Analysis of Stocks & Commodities* (August 1990), A. Bruce Johnson credits John Ehlers for his work in the use of two exponential trends. See John Ehlers, "Moving Averages, Part 1" and "Moving Averages, Part 2," *Technical Analysis of Stocks & Commodities* (1988).

FIGURE 12.6 A 252-126 Triangular MACD Applied to Back-Adjusted Corn Futures.

earnings releases. Figure 12.6 uses a full year, 252 days, as the primary cycle, with back-adjusted corn prices covering more than five years.

While this method creates a smooth representation of cyclic movement, it has the characteristics of a momentum indicator because the peaks and valleys are not quite evenly spaced and the amplitude of the cycles varies considerably. However, the smoothness of the indicator allows you to anticipate the major changes in the direction of prices. A program, *TSM Triangular MACD*, is available on the Companion Website.

Terminology

Before getting technical about the measurement and calculation of cycles, there are a few terms that describe most of the concepts discussed throughout this chapter. Note that the use of *wave* and *cycle* are interchangable.

> *Cycle or wave.* A recurring process that returns to its original state.
> *Amplitude (a).* The height of the wave from its horizontal midpoint (the *x*-axis).
> *Period (T).* The number of time units necessary to complete one wavelength (cycle).
> *Frequency (ω).* The number of wavelengths that repeat every 360°, calculated as
> $\omega = 1/T$.
> *Phase.* A measurement of the starting point or offset of the cycle relative to a benchmark wave.
> *Phase angle.* Locates the position within the cycle measured as the minute hand of a clock moving clockwise, where 0° is three o'clock.
> *Left and right translation.* The tendency for a cycle peak to fall to the left or right of the center of the cycle.

Finding the Cycle Using the Hilbert Transform

Ehlers is able to recognize the cyclic component of price movement using very little data as contrasted with the traditional regression methods. In one technique, using the *Hilbert Transform*,[10] only a small part of one cycle is needed to form a picture of the entire process, as little as 4 bars. This allows the cycle to be shown as an indicator with only a modest amount of lag.

---

[10] John F. Ehlers, *Rocket Science for Traders* (New York: John Wiley & Sons, 2001), Chapter 6.

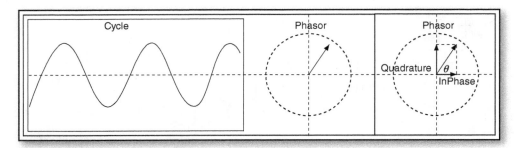

FIGURE 12.7 A Cycle with the Phasor and Phase Angle.
Source: Adapted from John F. Ehlers, *Rocket Science for Traders* (New York: John Wiley & Sons, 2001).

The Hilbert Transform is based on the separation of the cycle phase, represented by a *phasor,* into two components, the *Quadrature* and *InPhase,* shown in Figure 12.7. The left circle with a single arrow points to the current position of the cycle based on the phasor being straight up (270°) at the cycle peaks and straight down (90°) at the cycle valleys. The cycle begins when the phasor is pointing to the right (0°). The right circle separates the phasor into its horizontal and vertical components, InPhase and Quadrature, respectively. The *phase angle,* shown as θ (theta), is the arctangent of the ratio of the Quadrature and InPhase components. Ehlers reduces the equations for the Hilbert Transform to:

Quadrature
$$Q = 0.0962 \times price_t + 0.5769 \times price_{t-2} - 0.5769 \times price_{t-4} - 0.0962 \times price_{t-6}$$
InPhase
$$I = price_{t-3}$$

These equations make it possible to write simple program indicators (*TSM Hilbert Transformation* and *TSM Hilbert Transformation V2,* available on the Companion Website) to plot the results of the Hilbert Transform for any data series. Although there are some penalties for truncating the Hilbert Transform, which is an infinite series, those penalties should not affect the use of this method for trading.

Applying the Hilbert Transform to soybean monthly prices gives the results shown in Figure 12.8. The continuous, back-adjusted series is shown at the top of the chart. Continuous data is preferable in this case to avoid any odd jumps in prices when one contract is rolled to another at expiration.

The bottom panel in Figure 12.8 is the result of first detrending the monthly data (part of the calculation process), then applying the Hilbert Transform with *alpha* = 0.07. The Hilbert Transform creates sharp peaks and valleys at the points where the cycle is expected to be at maximum and minimum value. There is usually one peak and one valley each year, and the minimum level often coincides with late summer or early fall, when the harvest yield is known and there is usually a surplus (or anticipated surplus) of soybeans. Sharp peaks are particularly good for mean reversion trading compared to indicators that reach maximum or minimum values and stay there while prices continue in the same direction. However, as we saw when comparing the results of cash and back-adjusted futures, these extremes will vary due to forward discounting of prices. Peaks tend to be earlier in the year using futures data;

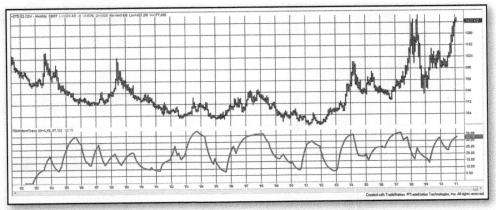

FIGURE 12.8 Back-Adjusted Soybean Futures from 1982 with the Hilbert Transform in the Lower Panel.

nevertheless, futures data are the only practical means of trading. In addition, geopolitical events have been much more influential in the past 10 years, and these are more likely to affect the high prices than the lows. A more thorough discussion can be found in Chapter 11. The same method can be applied to weekly data. If the obvious major cycle is yearly, then a 52-period average can be used to detrend the data.

The Hilbert Transform indicator does a very good job of locating relative peaks and the highest and lowest values of the indicator could be used for sell and buy signals. However, the chart of the indicator does show characteristics similar to momentum indicators; that is, larger peaks in the indicator follow periods of low volatility in prices because the subsequent peaks will be seen as *relative highs*. While the peak to valley might be an ideal trade, the net returns will vary due to individual market volatility.

The Fisher Transform

It is well known that prices are not normally distributed; that is, the distribution of price changes, or price minus a trendline (detrended prices), does not appear to be a bell-shaped, symmetric curve. We have already discussed some of the idiosyncrasies of price movement in earlier chapters, including the fat tail of trend-following performance, or the increase in volatility with price. The distribution of prices is called a *probability density function* (PDF), and the normal, bell-shaped curve is a *Gaussian PDF*.

The way in which prices move between two bands is very similar to the probability density function of a sine wave,[11] which spends more time in the vicinity of the peaks and valleys (where it changes direction) than in the middle (where it moves the fastest). Figure 12.9a shows two cycles of a sine wave with the PDF to the right (Figure 12.9b). Although the PDF is normally shown with the phasor angle along the bottom, as in (Figure 12.9c), this chart is drawn to represent a typical frequency distribution. The peaks of the sine wave occur when the phasor angle is 270° and the lowest points when the angle is 90°. The frequency of the peaks (the top of the

---

[11] This section is adapted from John Ehlers, *Cybernetic Analysis for Stocks & Commodities* (Hoboken, NJ: John Wiley & Sons, 2004), Chapter 1.

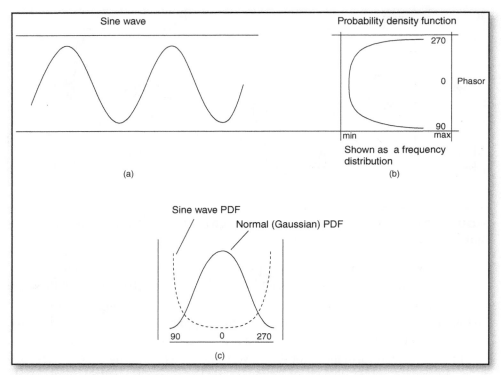

FIGURE 12.9 Probability Density Function (PDF) of a Sine Wave.

chart) and valleys (the bottom of the chart) are much greater than the frequency of the other angles, especially 0° and 180°.

The same PDF can be seen in price movement if we form a channel around the prices and measure the relative position of prices within that channel. The channel high (*MaxH*) is simply the maximum price during period *p*, and the channel low (*MinL*) is the minimum price during the same period *p*. The value used in the distribution is calculated

$$X_t = 0.5 \times 2 \times ((P_t - MinL)/(MaxH - MinL) - 0.5) + 0.5 \times x_{t-1}$$

The Fisher Transform takes this distribution and changes it to one that is approximately Gaussian with the following formula:

$$y = 0.5 \times \ln\left(\frac{1+x}{1-x}\right)$$

where x = the input

            y = the output

            $\ln$ = the natural log

The result of applying the Fischer Transform to AMR monthly data can be seen in the second panel of Figure 12.10. For comparison, the Hilbert Transformation is in the third panel. In this case, the period for the calculation of the bands was 12 months, in order to allow a better comparison with other methods. An alternate choice would be 3 months

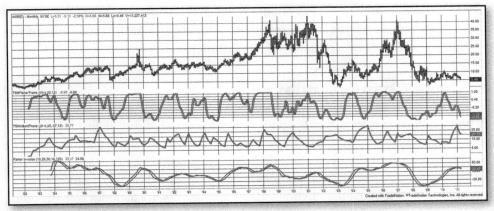

FIGURE 12.10 Monthly AMR (Top) Prices from 1982 with the Fisher Transform (2nd Panel), Hilbert Transform (3rd Panel), and Inverse Fisher Transform (Lower Panel).

to correspond to calendar quarters and earnings reports. Values for the Fisher Transform range from +1.0 to −1.0. The peaks of the Fisher Transformation are remarkably in line with the price peaks, and show very little lag compared to the Hilbert Transformation, although they occasionally peak out early and hold that level until prices reverse. The bottoms are also good, although there is an occasional lag. The Fisher Transform produces clearer, sharper turning points than a typical momentum-class indicator. A *trigger* is also included that corresponds to the MACD *signal line*. A sell signal occurs when the Fisher Transform value crosses the trigger moving lower. Experience shows that the best signals are those occurring just after an extreme high or low value and not after a turning point where the value is near zero, similar to MACD rules. Programs for creating the Hilbert, Fisher, and Inverse Fisher transforms are *TSM Hilbert Transform, TSM Fisher Transform,* and *TSM Fisher Inverse,* which can be found on the Companion Website.

Inverse Fisher Transform One more variation produces a very credible momentum indicator, the *Inverse Fisher Transform.*[12] While the Fisher Transform uses the price to solve for the distribution, the Inverse Fisher Transform does the opposite,

$$x = \frac{e^{2y} - 1}{e^{2y} + 1}$$

However, implementation of this is wrapped around the RSI indicator as follows (shown in TradeStation code):

```
series = close - close[mom];
x1 = 0.1*(RSI(series,RSIper) - 50);
x2 = WAVERAGE(x1,waper);
invfisher = 100*(EXPVALUE(2*x2) - 1.0)/(EXPVALUE(2*x2) + 1);
```

using the input values, *mom* = 10, *RSIper* = 20, and *waper* = 30. Note that *RSI* and *WAVERAGE* are the functions for the RSI and the linearly weighted average.

---

[12] See www.mesasoftware.com/papers/ and follow the link.

This process gives a bipolar distribution, where results are most likely to cluster near the extremes, +1 and −1. Based on monthly data of AMR, the results of the Inverse Fisher Transform are shown in the bottom panel of Figure 12.10.

■ Cycle Channel Index

A trend-following system that operates in a market with a well-defined cyclic pattern should have specific qualities that do not exist in a basic smoothing model. In order to confirm the cyclic turning points, which do not often occur precisely where they are expected, a simple moving average should be used, rather than an exponentially smoothed one. Exponential smoothing always includes some residual effect of older data, while the moving average uses a fixed period that accommodates the characteristics of a cycle. The cyclic turning point will use part of the data that represents about ¼ of the period, combined with a measure of the relative noise in the series which may obscure the turn.

These features have been combined by Lambert[13] into a *Commodity Cycle Index* (CCI), which is calculated as:

$$CCI_t = \frac{x_t - \overline{x}_t}{0.015 \times MD_t}$$

where $x_t = (H_t + L_t + C_t)/3$ is the average of the daily high, low, and close

$$\overline{x}_t = \sum_{i=1-N+1}^{t} x_i, \text{ the moving average over the past } N \text{ days}$$

$$MD_t = \sum_{i=1-N+1}^{t} |x_i - \overline{x}|, \text{ the mean deviation over the past } N \text{ days}$$

$N =$ the number of days selected (less than ¼ cycle)

Because all terms are divided by N, that value has been omitted in the final formula. In the CCI calculations, the use of $0.015 \times MD$ as a divisor scales the result so that 70% to 80% of the values fall within a +100 to −100 channel. The rules for using the CCI state that a value greater than +100 indicates a cyclic turn upward; a value lower than −100 defines a turn downward. Improvements in timing rest in the selection of N as short as possible but with a mean-deviation calculation that is a consistent representation of the noise. The CCI concept of identifying cyclic turns is good because it accounts for the substantial latitude in the variance of peaks and valleys, even with regular cycles.

---

[13] Donald R. Lambert, "Cycle Channel Index," *Commodities* (1980), reprinted in *Technical Analysis of Stocks & Commodities.*

■ Short Cycle Indicator

In an excellent article,[23] Francisco Lorca-Susino presents the *Short Cycle Indicator*. This method is expected to correct some of the difficulty in financial time series, which are said to have a *long memory*, obscuring some of the patterns. It is applied to intraday bars and is best interpreted over multiple time frames.

The formula is based on the squared difference of two exponential moving averages, and the relationship of those trendlines with the highest low and lowest high of the slower period, a form of stochastic indicator. The term $(XF - XS)/XF$ addresses the convergence of the two trends. The combination of squaring and the stochastic is intended to smooth while still retaining the most important aspects of sensitivity.

$Slow = 20$

$Fast = 8$

$XF =$ fast exponential smoothing (*Fast*)

$XS =$ slow exponential smoothing (*Slow*)

$LH =$ Lowest (*High, Slow*)

$HL =$ Highest (*Low, Slow*)

$SF_1 = 1,000,000$

$SF_2 = 100$

$SF_3 = 1000$

$$Lorca1 = \left(\frac{(XS - LH)^2 + (XS - HL)^2}{XS} \right) \times \frac{XF - XS}{XF} \times SF_1$$

$$Lorca2 = \frac{(XS - LH)^2 + (XS - HL)^2}{XS} \times SF_2 \times \frac{\dfrac{XF - XS}{XF} \times SF_3}{C^2} \times SF_1$$

As seen in Figure 12.11, the indicator tends to stay above or below the trigger line but reacts to changing volatility, recognized as divergence of the trendlines and the price extremes. These usually occur before prices change direction. It is interesting to note the multiple divergence signals that occur as prices rally on the first part of the chart, and that the indicator posts its lows in advance of the lows on April 5.

To generate a *sell* signal, Lorca looks for volatility to expand in a particular pattern. One of the three conditions must be satisfied:

1. $Lorca1_t > 0$ and $Lorca1_t < Lorca1_{t-12}$ and $Lorca1_t < Lorca1_{t-14}$ and $Lorca1_t < Lorca1_{t-16}$ and $H_t - L_t > H_{t-1} - L_{t-1}$ and $H_t =$ Highest$(H, 12)$

[14] Francisco J. Lorca [Susino], "Exploiting Stock Market Cycles," *Futures* (April 2009). The author appreciates the help of Mr. Lorca-Susino in this section. He can be reached at franlorcasusino@gmail.com.

FIGURE 12.11 The Short Cycle Indicator Applied to the emini S&P 30- and 60-Minute Bars, May 2011.

2. $Lorca1_t > 0$ and $H_t = \text{Highest}(H,16)$ and $Lorca1_t = \text{Lowest}(Lorca1,32)_{t-1}$
3. $Lorca1_t > 0$ and $H_t = \text{Highest}(H,16)$ and $Lorca1_{t-2} = \text{Lowest}(Lorca1,32)_{t-1}$

In case 1, the indicator is rising but it is lower than the interval from 12 to 14 bars ago. In addition, the trading range of the current bar must be greater than the range of the previous bar and confirmed by a new 12-bar high, both measures of expanding volatility.

Cases 2 and 3 are simpler, requiring that the indicator is rising and that this is a 16-bar high. Then a *sell* signal occurs if either the current indicator value is the lowest of the past 32 bars or the indicator 2 bars ago is the lowest of the past 32 bars.

■ Phasing

One of the most interesting applications of the cyclic element of a time series is presented by J. M. Hurst in *The Profit Magic of Stock Transaction Timing*.[15] He uses *phasing*, the synchronization of a moving average, to represent cycles. This section highlights some of the concepts and presents a simplified example of the method. It is already known that to isolate the cycle from the other elements, the trending and seasonal factors should be subtracted, reducing the resulting series to its cyclic and remaining noise parts. In many cases, the seasonal and cyclic components are similar but the trend is unique. Hurst treats the cyclic component as the dominant component of price movement and uses a moving average to identify the combined trend-cycle.

The system can be visualized as measuring the oscillation about a straight-line approximation of the trend (a best-fit centered line), anticipating equal moves above and below. Prices have many long- and short-term trends, depending on the interval of analysis. Because this technique was originally applied to stocks, most of the examples used by Hurst are long-term trends expressed in weeks. For futures the same technique could be used with continuous back-adjusted data.

---

[15] J. M. Hurst, *The Profit Magic of Stock Transaction Timing* (Upper Saddle River, NJ: Prentice Hall, 1970), reprinted in trade paper by Traders Press, 2000.

As a simple example of the concept, choose a moving average of medium length for the trending component. The *full-span* moving average period may be selected by averaging the distance between the tops on a price chart (a rough measure of the cycle). The *half-span* moving average is then equal to half the days used in the full-span average.

The problem with using moving averages is that they always lag. A 40-day moving average is considered to be 20 days behind the price movement. The current average is normally plotted under the most recent price, although it actually represents the average of the calculation period and could be lagged by one-half the period. Hurst's method applies a process called *phasing*, which aligns the tops and bottoms of the moving average with the corresponding tops and bottoms of the price movement. To phase the full- and half-span moving averages, lag each plot by half the days in the average; this causes the curve to overlay the prices (Figure 12.12). Then project the phased full- and half-span moving averages until they cross. A line or curve connecting two or more of the most recent intersections will be the major trendline. The more points used, the more complicated the regression formula for calculating the trend; Chapter 7 discusses a variety of linear and nonlinear techniques for finding the best fit for these intersections, although a basic least-squares solution might be best. Once the trendline is calculated, it is projected as the center of the next price cycle.

FIGURE 12.12 Hurst's Phasing.

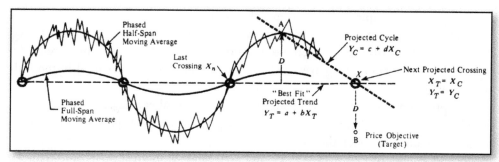

FIGURE 12.13 Finding the Target Price.

With the trend identified and projected, the next step is to reflect the cycle about the trend. When the phased half-span average turns down at point A (Figure 12.13), measure the greatest distance D of the actual prices above the projected trendline. The system then anticipates that prices will cross the trendline at point X and decline an equal distance D below the projected centered trendline. Once the projected crossing becomes an actual crossing, the distance D can be measured and the exact price objective specified. The rules for using this technique are:

1. Calculate the full-span moving average for the selected calculation period; lag the plot by half the days. If the full-span moving average uses F days, the value of the average is calculated at $t - F/2$, where t is the current day. Call this phased point PH_t.
2. The half-span moving average is calculated for H days and plotted at $t - H/2 + PH_t$.
3. Record the points where the two phased averages PH_i and PF_i cross and call these points $X_n, X_{n-1}, \ldots$.
4. Find the trend by performing a linear regression on the crossing points $X_n, X_{n-1},$ $\ldots$. For the straight line, $Y_T = a + bX_T$.
5. Record the highest (or lowest) values of the price since the last crossing, X_n.
6. Calculate the projection of the half-span by creating a straight line from the highest (or lowest) half-span value since the last crossing A to the last calculated half-span value. This equation will be $Y_c = c + dX_c$.
7. Find the point at which the projected trendline crosses the projected cyclic line by setting the equations equal to one another and solving for X and Y. At the point of crossing $(X_T, Y_T) = (X_c, Y_c)$, giving two equations in two unknowns, which is easily solvable (X is time in days; Y is price).
8. If the half-span is moving down, the maximum price reached since the last crossing is subtracted from the Y coordinate of the projected crossing to get D. This distance D is subtracted again from the Y coordinate to determine the price objective, equidistant below the best-fit line. If the half-span is moving up, the price objective uses the minimum price and reflects the distance above the projected crossing. It should be noted that this calculation of distance is simplified because the trend is established by a straight line; for nonlinear fits, the measurement of D will be more complicated.

9. Recalculate the moving averages (Step 1), the half-span projection (Step 6), the projected crossing (Step 7), and price objective (Step 8) each day until the actual crossing occurs. At that time D is fixed.

10. Follow the trading rules:

   a. *Enter a new long position* when the half-span moving average turns up; cover any existing short positions regardless of the price objective.

   b. *Enter a new short position* when the half-span moving average turns down; close out any long positions.

   c. *Close out both long and short positions* if the price objective is reached. An error factor of 10% of the height of the full cycle (lowest to highest point) should be allowed. Therefore, the price objective should be closer by 10%.

Hurst's approach is a good example of a complex problem solved using elementary mathematics. There are many techniques for determining trends and a number of seasonally oriented systems, but a cyclic approach is rare. Hurst's explanation is more complete and the interpretation presented in this section should be considered only as a reasonable approximation.

Patterns in volume have always been tied closely to chart analysis of both the stock and futures markets. Volume is a valuable piece of information that is not often used, and one of the few items, other than price, that is traditionally considered valid data for the technician. Nevertheless, there has been little research published that relates volume to futures markets; its popular use has assumed the same conclusions as in stock market analysis.

The stock and futures markets have two other measures of participation that are related. In equities, the large number shares being traded allow for measurements of *breadth*. In the same way that the stock index has become a popular measure of overall market trend, the *breadth of the market* is the total number of stocks that have risen or fallen during a specific period. When you have the ability to view the bigger picture of market movement, breadth seems to be a natural adjunct to the index. In addition, tallies of *new highs* and *new lows* may add value to a trading decision. This chapter will look at different way these statistics can complement other indicators.

In futures, *open interest* is the measurement of those participants with outstanding positions; it is the netting out of all open positions (longs and short sales) in any one market or delivery month, and gives an understanding of the depth of participation and anticipated volume. A market that trades only 10,000 contracts per day but has an open interest of 250,000 is telling the trader that there are many participants who will enter the market when the price is right. These are most likely to be commercial traders, using the futures markets for hedging. Unlike the stock market, which can only trade a fixed number of outstanding shares, the futures market can add net contracts for every new buyer and short seller and reduce the interest in the market when both buyers and sellers liquidate.

■ A Special Case for Futures Volume

In futures markets, where you trade contracts for delivery in specific months, the volume of each contract is available, along with the total volume of all contracts traded for that market. Spread transactions within that market, for example, buying the March delivery and selling June, are not included in the reported volume, a point that is inconsistent with stocks, which report both sides of a high frequency trade. In futures, volume data and open interest are officially posted one day late, but estimates are available for many markets during the day on services such as Bloomberg. Total volume of crude oil is estimated every hour; it is released to news services and is available on the Internet.

Individual contract volume is important to determine which delivery month is most active. Traders find that the best executions are where there is greatest liquidity. Analysts, however, have a difficult time assessing trends in volume because there is a natural increase in volume as a contract moves from deferred to delivery, from second month out to the nearby, and traders most often roll their positions to the closest delivery month. There is a corresponding decline in volume as a contract approaches its delivery date. Because spread volume is not posted, movement between delivery months does not affect the volume patterns.

Each futures market has its unique pattern of volume for individual contracts. Some, such as the interest rates, shift abruptly on the last day of the month prior to delivery, because the exchange raises margins dramatically for all traders holding positions in the delivery month. Currencies are very different and tend to trade actively in the nearest month up to one or two days before that contract goes *off the board*. While volume increases slightly in the next deferred contract, anyone trading sizable positions will need to stay with the nearby contract to just before the end.

Other than for determining which contract to trade, and perhaps the size of an order that the market can absorb, an analysis of volume as discussed in this chapter will use total volume (the aggregate of all contracts) in order to have a series that does not suffer the patterns of increasing and decreasing participation based on the coming and going of individual delivery months. When traders roll from the nearby to the next deferred contract, the transactions are usually executed as a spread, and those trades are not included in the volume figures. Because positions are closed out in one contract and opened in another there is no change in the open interest.

The stock market equivalent to using total volume would be to add the volume for all stocks in the same sector or industrial group. This would help to smooth over those periods when the volume is concentrated in a few stocks following a news or earnings release, only to switch the next week when other stocks in the same sector are noticed.

Tick Volume

The popularity of quote machines and fast trading requires a measurement of volume that can be used immediately to make decisions. Lacking a service such as Bloomberg with continually updated volume, *tick volume* can be substituted. Tick volume is the number of recorded price changes, regardless of volume or the size of the price change that occurs during any time interval. Tick volume relates directly to actual volume because, as the market becomes more active, prices move back and forth from bid to asked more often. If only two trades occur in a 5-minute period, then the market is not liquid. From an analytic view, tick volume gives a reasonable approximation of true volume and can be used as a substitute. From a practical view, it is the only choice. Higher-than-normal tick volume at the beginning of the day implies higher volume throughout the day. Tick volume patterns are discussed later in this chapter.

Variations from the Normal Patterns

The *W* Intraday Pattern

One note of warning when using intraday volume or volume indicators to confirm price direction: The patterns in volume have a dominant *W* pattern throughout the day. They begin high, drop quickly, increase modestly near midday, fall again, then increase significantly toward the close of trading. To decide that a buy signal is more important near the end of the trading day because volume was rising is not correct; volume is always higher at the beginning and end of the day. You may conclude, in general, that the beginning and end of the day, or higher-than-average volume produces more reliable trading signals; however, an intraday volume confirmation must be compared against the normal volume for that time of day.

Open interest and market breadth have seasonal patterns. In agricultural markets, farmers hedge in larger numbers during the growing season than in the winter, raising the open interest. In stocks, there is a lot of activity associated with the end-of-year positioning for tax purposes and traditional rallies during holiday seasons. Volume is low during the summer when many investors take their vacations. None of these changes indicate that something special is occurring. These variations are discussed in detail later in this chapter.

Variance in Volume

Nearly all volume analysis uses smoothed or averaged data because volume can vary substantially from one day to the next. As an example, Table 12.4 shows the breakdown of Microsoft (MSFT) volume for the five years from June 1998 through May 2003. While the volume was higher during the price peak of January 2000, the overall numbers show consistency at an average of 71 million shares per day.

Table 12.4 also shows the standard deviation of the daily volume changes, which is about 38% of the average volume. One standard deviation of this magnitude says that 68% of the days will show *changes* in daily volume ranging from 41 million to 101 million shares. Looking at it in reverse, 32% of the days will show changes in volume less than or greater than 41 million and 101 million shares. Compare that to the price of Microsoft during the same period, which ranged from $20 to $60 but had 1 standard deviation of $0.957—that is, the daily change in price was less than $1, or about 2.9% of the $33.38 average price. Keep in mind that this variation is the basis for most of the volume indicators and strategies.

TABLE 12.4	Microsoft Daily Volume by Year from June 1998 through May 2003	
Period	**Average**	**StDev**
Jun98–May99	62,861,035	21,511,856
Jun99–May00	64,512,077	34,741,178
Jun00–May01	83,915,101	35,621,716
Jun01–May02	64,638,359	21,125,063
Jun02–May03	79,584,139	22,129,923
Jun98–May03	*71,105,478*	*27,832,841*

Volume Spikes

> Madness is the exception in individuals but the rule in groups.
>
> —*Nietzsche*

A *volume spike* is a single day on which the volume was much higher than the previous day—at least twice as high, perhaps three or four times. A volume spike is a warning that something happened, most likely the result of a surprising news release or new economic data. It could be the crescendo of a few days of rising volume associated with sharply rising or falling prices.

A volume spike is a clear, positive action by investors. It implies that a very large number of investors, perhaps even the general public, all hold the same opinion on the direction of the market and feel compelled to act on that opinion at the same time. It is the result of mass behavior discussed by Mackay in his famous book, *Extraordinary Popular Delusions and the Madness of Crowds*. A volume spike means that everyone has jumped into the boat at the same time. Traditional interpretation of a volume spike is that it indicates the end of a price move, that is, the boat sinks.

AOL shows three good examples of volume spikes in Figure 12.14. The highest volume days in April, August, and September 1999, and in January 2000 all occur at the bottom of a price move. Prices reverse direction immediately after the spike, and usually that reversal is substantial. A volume spike does not indicate the strength of the price reversal, it simply tells you that the current move is exhausted. It may turn out to be a major top or bottom, or simply a local turning point.

Volume spikes are a good example of extremes and the clearest cases for trading. The theory of a spike is that, when everyone has entered the market, there is no one left to buy (or sell) and prices must reverse. The crowd is always wrong—at least their timing is always wrong.

Drop in Volume

Although a drop in volume is less impressive than a volume spike, it can be equally important. Volume can decline because there is little interest in a stock or futures market, which often happens when prices are very low. Volume can also drop when a price reaches *equilibrium*, the price at which buyers and sellers agree is *fair value*. Volume may also drop on the day before a holiday, or just by chance.

While there can be seasonal and other predictable patterns associated with a decline in volume, they all represent a lack of conviction, or a perceived lack of potential price movement, on the part of the traders. In Figure 12.14 there is a steady decline in the average volume from October 1999 through the end of 1999 while prices moved steadily higher. This period had only one-half the volume traded earlier in the year and is interpreted as a lack of investor support for higher prices. Having been hurt earlier in the year, more investors stood aside on the second rally and, while AOL prices did top the previous highs, another sell-off followed. This declining pattern fits the standard interpretation of volume.

FIGURE 12.14 AOL Price and Volume Showing Three Major Volume Spikes and Declining Volume while Prices Rise at the End of 1999.

■ Standard Interpretation

The interpretation of volume has been part of the trading culture from its beginning. Volume is always considered in combination with price movement:

Volume	Price	Interpretation
Rising	Rising	Volume confirms price rise
Rising	Falling	Volume confirms price drop
Falling	Rising	Volume indicates weak rally
Falling	Falling	Volume indicates weak pullback

This interpretation implies that *volume confirms direction*. When volume declines, it indicates that a change of direction should follow because there is no general support for the price move. Therefore, *volume normally leads price*. It has also been said that 1-week returns accompanied by declining volume tend to reverse the next week. Using weekly data would smooth the volume and may well add consistency.

The classic interpretation of volume was published in the monograph by W. L. Jiler, *Volume and Open Interest: A Key to Commodity Price Forecasting*, a companion piece to his most popular *Forecasting Commodity Prices with Vertical Line Charts*.

In both the futures and stock markets, volume has the same interpretation: When volume increases, it is said to confirm the direction of prices. Price changes that occur on very light volume are less dependable for indicating future direction than those changes associated with relatively heavy volume. An additional uncertainty exists for stocks that are not actively traded, and for low-priced shares where the total dollar volume can be small. In these cases, it might be best to look at the accumulated volume of similar companies or its sector.

Volume and Open Interest

Open interest is a concept unique to futures markets, but helps to explain the depth of the market as well as trader expectations. New *interest* in a market is the result of new buyers and sellers meeting, which increases the open interest, the net of all outstanding contracts being traded. The following table explains the combinations of buyers and sellers that changes open interest:

Buyer	Meets	Seller	Change in Open Interest
New		New	Increase in open interest
New		Old	No change in open interest
Old		New	No change in open interest
Old		Old	Decrease in open interest
Where		"New" buyer (seller) is a trader with no market position seeking to be long (short). "Old" buyer (seller) is a trader who had previously entered a short (long) position and seeks to exit.	

When the open interest increases while prices rise quickly, it is commonly interpreted as more traders entering long positions. This may seem strange because for every new buyer of a futures contract there must be a new seller; however, the seller is likely to be someone looking to hold a position for a few hours or days, looking to profit from the normal ups and downs of price movement. The position trader, who is willing to sit for much more time holding a long position, is the one who is attributed with the open interest. In reality, no one knows. However, if prices keep rising, the shorts are more likely to be forced out while the longs have staying power.

The traditional interpretation of changes in volume and open interest (for futures markets) can be summarized as:

Volume	Open Interest	Interpretation
Rising	Rising	Confirmation of trend
Rising	Falling	Position liquidation (at extremes)
Falling	Rising	Slow accumulation
Failing	Falling	Congestion phase

Three generally accepted notions for the use of volume and open interest are:

1. Open interest increases during a trending period.
2. Volume may decline but open interest builds during an accumulation phase. Volume occasionally spikes.

3. Rising prices and declining volume/open interest indicate a pending change of direction.

There is a traditional interpretation for the combined movement of price direction, volume, and open interest.

Prices	Volume	Open Interest	Interpretation
Rising	Rising	Rising	New buyers are entering the market.
Falling	Falling	Falling	Longs are being forced out; the downtrend will end when all sellers have liquidated their positions.
Rising	Falling	Falling	Short sellers are covering their positions causing a rally. Money is leaving the market.
Falling	Rising	Rising	New short selling. Bearish money is entering the market.

Exceptions

No method is without exceptions, including volume patterns in the stock market. There are days or periods when volume is expected to change, and must be considered in the analysis. For example, volume is expected to decline:

> On the first day of the week.
> On the day before a holiday.
> During the summer.

The most important exception to rising prices and rising volume is the volume spike, which signals a change of direction rather than a confirmation.

Volume is also higher on *triple witching day* (or *quadruple witching day*, if you include futures on stocks), when S&P futures, options on futures, and options on the individual stocks all expire at the same time.

In the futures markets, there are similar patterns. Lighter volume exists during holiday periods and summer months, but may be heavier on Fridays and Mondays during a trending market or a weather market for agricultural products (uncertainty over rain, drought, or frost over the weekend). Liquidation often occurs before the weekend and positions are reentered on the first day of the next week.

Richard Arms' Equivolume

Most of the techniques for using volume discussed in this chapter will multiply or accumulate volume, creating an index that rises faster as volume increases. *Equivolume*, a charting method introduced by Richard Arms,[16] takes the unique approach of substituting volume for time along the bottom scale of a chart. When volume increases, the price bar is elongated to the right; therefore, an upwards move on high volume will appear as a higher box that is also wider.

There are no systematic methods for using Equivolume included here and its applications parallel standard chart interpretations; however, analysts can represent

---

[16] See www.armsinsider.com/education/armsonthemarket/equiv_chart.asp for examples.

this type of chart by creating a new price series in which the daily closing price is repeated based on the relative volume. For example, if the normal volume day causes a closing price to be repeated 10 times, then a day with twice the volume will repeat that price 20 times, and a day with half the volume will show 5 prices. This approach may cause a short-term moving average trend to look strange; however, a linear regression or long-term trend should reflect the importance of varying time.

Herrick Payoff Index

The *Herrick Payoff Index* (HPI) is the most popular calculation that combines price, volume, and open interest. It is designed to gauge the strength of the current trend, and has been applied primarily to futures prices. Because it adds volume and open interest to a momentum calculation, it can be found in Chapter 10 along with some other indicators that use volume as an added feature.

Volume Is a Predictor of Volatility

Most often high volume and high volatility occur at the same time. It is easy to see on a chart that one confirms the other. However, not all days that have high volume also have high volatility. Even on days with high volume, the price can close nearly unchanged from the previous day. We need to look at those days as a sign of *potential volatility*—a large number of traders all with their own objectives somehow managed to offset each other. Tomorrow, if there is an imbalance in the buyers and sellers, and volume is still high, prices could break out in either direction. Therefore, *high volume means high risk*, even on those days when the risk does not materialize.

■ Volume Indicators

Both the stock and futures markets have numerous indicators that use only volume, or those that add volume, intending to make other calculations more robust. The following section gives the most popular of these indicators, most of which originate in the stock market; many use the number of advancing and declining stocks. Readers should note the way in which the data is used from one technique to another and consider the significance of these changes. They are discussed at the end of this section.

Average Volume

The most basic of all volume indicators is the *average*, and the calculation most commonly used for the equity markets is 50 days, although it may be reasonable to use the same period as the price average that is being used. Then, if you are tracking the 200-day moving average, a 200-day average of the volume would make sense. Anything less than 50 days is not likely to be smooth.

Normalizing the Volume

It is always convenient to normalize prices to view them compared to the recent average. This can also be done for volume. Letting the calculation period, N, be either 50 or 200 days, we can normalize the volume and represent the result as a percent,

$$NormVol_t = 100 \times \frac{V_t}{\left(\sum_{i=t-P+1}^{t} V_t\right) / N}$$

The normalized volume lets us say that "today's volume is 20% higher than the volume over the past 200 days." This can be seen in the third panel of Figure 12.15, showing Microsoft prices and volume.

Volume Momentum and Percentage Change

Two other basic volume indicators are *momentum* and *rate of change*. These techniques treat volume as they would price. For momentum, this means finding the change in volume over a specific time interval; percentage change measures the size of the volume change relative to the starting value. If t is today and n is the number of days back (the observation period), then

$$Volume\ momentum_t = Volume_t - Volume_{t-n}$$

$$Volume\%_t = \frac{Volume_t - Volume_{t-n}}{Volume_{t-n}}$$

Because of the high variance in volume from day to day, volume momentum tends to increase the erratic pattern. It will be necessary to smooth the volume momentum in order to have a useful indicator.

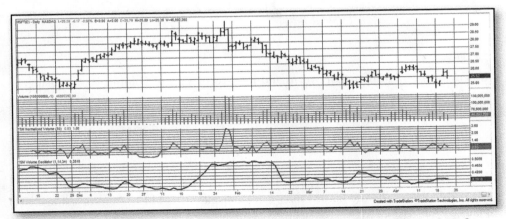

FIGURE 12.15 Microsoft Prices (Top), Volume (Second Panel), Normalized 50-day Volume (Third Panel), and Volume Oscillator from Ratio (Bottom), Based on 14- and 34-day Periods.

Force Index

Devised by Alex Elder, the *Force Index* is the change in price multiplied by the daily volume,

$$Force\ Index_t = (Close_t - Close_{t-1}) \times Volume_t$$

The Force Index will be positive or negative if the price change was higher or lower. It is also not limited to daily charts, but can be applied to weekly or monthly data, as can many of the other methods in this chapter. Once the daily Force Index is calculated, it should be smoothed. For timing entries and exits, it is suggested that a 2-day exponential moving average (EMA) with a smoothing constant 0.667 be used to avoid unnecessary noise in the indicator. For longer-term analysis, a 13-day EMA (smoothing constant 0.1428) should be used. Consistent with the idea of noise, the 2-day smoothed Force Index *buys* when the value is low and *sells short* when it's high; however, the 13-day value is treated as a trend, giving a buy signal when it crosses above zero and a sell when it crosses below zero. Signals remain in effect until the smoothed Force Index crosses the zero line in the other direction.

Volume Oscillator

Visualizing the pattern of volume can be very helpful, and the simplest way to do this is with a *volume oscillator,* which addresses the issue of erratic data by using two smoothed values. A volume oscillator is a two-step process and may use trends of any calculation period. Here, 14- and 34-day periods are used.

Method 1
Calculate the difference between a short-term and long-term average of volume. Using 14 and 34 days gives

$$VO(Diff)_t = \frac{\sum_{i=t-14+1}^{t} V_i}{14} - \frac{\sum_{i=t-34+1}^{t} V_i}{34}$$

Method 2
Calculate the ratio of a short-term and long-term sum of volume. Again, using 14 and 34 days,

$$VO(Ratio)_t = \frac{\sum_{i=t-14+1}^{t} V_i}{\sum_{i=t-34+1}^{t} V_i}$$

Once calculated, the oscillator values can be displayed as a histogram or a line chart. Figure 12.15 shows Microsoft from November 2010 through April 2011 in the top panel, volume in the second panel, the normalized 50-day volume in the third panel, and the volume oscillator using the ratio at the bottom. In this example, the volume oscillator does not confirm the upwards or downwards trends. Perhaps that is the correct interpretation because these trends were short lived.

On-Balance Volume

Made famous by Joseph Granville, *On-Balance Volume*[17] is now a byword in stock analyst circles. On days when prices close higher, it is assumed that all volume represents the buyers; on lower days, the volume is controlled by the sellers. The volume is then added or subtracted from a cumulative value, *OBV*, to get today's value.

IF *Today's price change* $(p_t > p_{t-1})$ then $OBV_t = OBV_{t-1} + Volume_t$

IF *Today's price change* $(p_t < p_{t-1})$ then $OBV_t = OBV_{t-1} - Volume_t$

The result is a volume-weighted series, which serves to smooth out the erratic nature of the data. In the following formula, the expression in parentheses simply uses the closing prices to produce a value of +1, 0, or −1, which then determines whether today's volume will be added or subtracted from the volume series:

$$OBV_t = OBV_{t-1} + \frac{Close_t - Close_{t-1}}{\left|Close_t - Close_{t-1}\right|} \times Volume_t$$

Determining the OBV manually is a simple accumulation process as shown in Table 12.5. On day 2 prices closed higher; therefore, the volume of 30 (assume thousands) is added to the starting volume of zero. On the next day, the price was again higher, and the volume is added to the total. On day 4 the price drops so that day's volume is subtracted from the total. In this example, volume was higher when price closed up and lower when prices closed down. This is the ideal pattern in a market with a clear uptrend. Traditionally, the advantage of recording the OBV is in observing when the trend of the prices diverges from the OBV values. The general interpretation of OBV is given in Table 12.6.

TABLE 12.5	Calculating On-Balance Volume		
Day	Closing Price	Daily Volume (in 1000s)	On-Balance Volume
1	310	25	0
2	315	30	30
3	318	27	57
4	316	15	42
5	314	12	30
6	320	28	58

[17] Robert W. Colby and Thomas A. Meyers, *The Encyclopedia of Technical Market Indicators* (New York: McGraw-Hill, 2003), is a comprehensive study of most market indicators, including On-Balance Volume and some other techniques in this section.

TABLE 12.6	Interpreting On-Balance Volume	
Price Direction	**OBV Direction**	**Interpretation**
Up	Up	Clear uptrend
	Sideways	Moderate uptrend
	Down	Weak uptrend near reversal
Sideways	Up	Accumulation period (bottom)
	Sideways	No determination
	Down	Distribution period (top)
Down	Up	Weak downtrend near reversal
	Sideways	Moderate downtrend
	Down	Clear downtrend

Because a volume series has many erratic qualities caused by large variations in volume from day to day, it is most often used with a moving average trend of up to 100 weeks, then identifying a simple volume direction when the OBV value crosses the trend. An upward trend in volume is interpreted as a confirmation of the current price direction, while a downturn in volume can be liquidation or uncertainty. It is intended that the OBV values be used instead of price for making trading decisions.

In Figure 12.16, the OBV is plotted along with the volume at the bottom of the GE chart, covering from December 2010 through April 2011. The pattern of the OBV is similar to the pattern of prices in the top panel even though it is created from volume. The primary difference between the price chart and the OBV line is that the peak in the center is flattening and the OBV does not decline as far. This divergence in the center of the chart, prices moving higher than the OBV, would be interpreted as a divergence in which prices will stop rising.

FIGURE 12.16 On-Balance Volume Applied to GE from December 2010 through April 2011. Volume is shown on the left lower scale and the OBV on the right lower scale.

FIGURE 12.17 S&P prices are shown with the volume, OBV, and a 40-day trend of the OBV in the bottom panel. Trading signals are derived from the OBV trendline. A corresponding 40-day moving average is shown in the top panel.

The spreadsheet code, *TSM OBV*, is available on the Companion Website.

Substituting the OBV for Price in a Moving Average   If the OBV systematically improves, then we can use the OBV instead of price to find trend signals. In Figure 12.17, the S&P emini prices are shown in the top panel with a 40-day moving average, and the volume, OBV, and a 40-day moving average of the OBV are in the bottom panel. The corresponding moving average trendlines are equally smooth, but slightly different on the far right where prices rise sooner than the OBV.

It would be necessary to do a comprehensive test on many markets to find out if the OBV produced better trend results than simply using the price. We already know that the S&P and stocks in general are not the best choice for trending; therefore, tests of interest rates would be more interesting. Volume indicators that combine the price move with volume are additional possibilities. An example of a strategy, *TSM OBV Trend*, that applies a trend to a volume indicator can be found on the Companion Website.

Money Flow Index   A simple variation of On-Balance Volume uses the average of the high, low, and closing prices instead of only the close. It is called the *Money Flow Index*, and has been compared to the RSI.

$$TP_t = (H_t + L_t + C_t)/3$$

$$\text{If } TP_t > TP_{t-1} \text{ then } MFP_t = MFP_{t-1} + TP_t \times V_t$$

$$\text{If } TP_t < TP_{t-1} \text{ then } MFN_t = MFN_{t-1} + TP_t \times V_t$$

$$MFI_t = 100 - \frac{100}{\left(\dfrac{1 + MFP_t}{MFN_t}\right)}$$

Volume Count Indicator An indicator that closely resembles On-Balance Volume is a running total of the days when volume increases minus the days when volume declines. That is, add 1 to the cumulative value on a day when today's volume is greater than the previous day; otherwise, subtract 1. This *Volume Count Indicator* (VCI) can be written as:

$$VCI_t = VCI_{t-1} + \frac{V_t - V_{t-1}}{|V_t - V_{t-1}|}$$

Volume Accumulator

A variation on Granville's OBV system is Mark Chaiken's *Volume Accumulator* (VA). Instead of assigning all the volume to either the buyers or the sellers, the Volume Accumulator uses a proportional amount of volume corresponding to the relationship of the closing price to the intraday mean price. If prices close at the high or low of the day, all volume is given to the buyers or sellers as in the OBV calculation.[18] If the close is at the midrange, no volume is added. This can be accomplished with the following calculation:

$$VA_t = VA_{t-1} + \left(\frac{Close_t - Low_t}{High_t - Low_t} - 0.50 \right) \times 2 \times V_t$$

Accumulation Distribution

Similar to the Volume Accumulator, and also developed by Mark Chaiken, the *Accumulation Distribution* indicator as well as the Intraday Intensity, the Price and Volume Trend, and the Positive and Negative Volume Indexes use a concept that relates to buying and selling pressure. This compares the strength of the close compared to the open divided by the trading range. It is also called *money flow* in some references. In the following formula, the previous close can be substituted for the open if the opening price is not available.

$$AD_t = AD_{t-1} + \frac{C_t - O_t}{H_t - L_t} \times V_t$$

Intraday Intensity

Intraday Intensity uses the distribution of daily trading range to create a new indicator. If the intraday low is further from the close than the intraday high, in other words, prices close nearer to the high, then the indicator increases in value.

$$II_t = II_{t-1} + \left(\frac{(C_t - L_t) - (H_t - C_t)}{H_t - L_t} \right) \times V_t$$

---

[18] Both OBV and the Volume Accumulator are characterized as "momentum" systems. See Chapter 10 for more information on similar techniques.

Price and Volume Trend, the Positive Volume Index, and the Negative Volume Index

The *Price and Volume Trend* (PVT)[19] applies volume to the daily percentage price change, which can be positive or negative. Note that this cannot be used for back-adjusted futures prices, only for cash markets, stock prices, and indexes.

$$VPT_t = VPT_{t-1} + \left(\frac{C_t}{C_{t-1}} - 1 \right) \times V_t$$

There are two variations on the *Positive Volume Index* (PVI) and *Negative Volume Index* (NVI). Both take the approach that a single indicator that adds and subtracts volume based on market direction is not as informative as two separate series that can be viewed at the same time. In the first variation, the direction of the closing price determines whether volume is added to the positive or negative index. In the second variation, higher or lower volume, compared to the previous day, is the basis for adding to the positive or negative index.

Variation 1, the close as the determining factor:

$$\text{If } C_t > C_{t-1} \text{ then } PVI_t = PVI_{t-1} + V_t$$

$$\text{If } C_t < C_{t-1} \text{ then } NVI_t = NVI_{t-1} + V_t$$

Variation 2, the volume as the determining factor:

$$\text{If } V_t > V_{t-1} \text{ then } PVI_t = PVI_{t-1} + \frac{C_t}{C_{t-1}} \times V_t$$

$$\text{If } V_t < V_{t-1} \text{ then } NVI_t = NVI_{t-1} + \frac{C_t}{C_{t-1}} \times V_t$$

In Norman Fosback's *Stock Market Logic*, the author studied stock trends from 1941 through 1975 based on variation 1 and concluded that:

■ If the *PVI* trend is *up* there is a 79% chance that a bull market exists.

■ If the *PVI* trend is *down* there is a 67% chance that a bear market exists.

■ If the *NVI* trend is *up* there is a 96% chance that a bull market exists.

■ If the *NVI* trend is *down* there is a 50% chance that a bear market exists.

In order to find the trend of either the *PVI* or *NVI*, a 6-month (127-day) or 1-year (255-day) moving average was applied to the individual index values.

---

[19] Dennis D. Peterson, "Positive Volume Index," *Technical Analysis of Stocks & Commodities* (April 2003). Also see Norman G. Fosback, *Stock Market Logic* (The Institute for Economic Research, 1985).

Aspray's Demand Oscillator

Using direction to separate volume into two series of *Buying Pressure* and *Selling Pressure*, Aspray then nets them into his own *Demand Oscillator*.[20] Note that during a rising market the Selling Pressure has been *divided* by a percentage of the volume, which has been scaled to be greater than 1. The following calculations show the separate steps needed to create Aspray's *Demand Oscillator*:

For rising prices:

$$\left(Buying\ Pressure \right) BP_t = V_t$$

$$\left(Selling\ Pressure \right) SP_t = \frac{V_t}{K \times \dfrac{C_t - C_{t-1}}{C_{t-1}}}$$

For declining prices:

$$BP_t = \frac{V_t}{K \times \dfrac{C_t - C_{t-1}}{C_{t-1}}}$$

$$SP_t = V_t$$

and where

$$K = \frac{3 \times C_t}{\left[\sum_{i=t-9}^{t} \left(\max\left(H_t, H_{t-1} \right) - \min\left(L_t, L_{t-1} \right) \right) \right] / 10}$$

and

$$Demand\ Oscillator_t = BP_t - SP_t$$

K is a volatility scaling factor that is 3 times the closing price divided by the 10-day moving average of the maximum 2-day high-low combined range, and has a value likely to be well over 100. For example, if the S&P is trading at 1,000 and the average volatility is 15 full points (which is very high for a 10-day average), then $K = 3000/15 = 200$.

Tick Volume Indicator

In a manner similar to Wilder's RSI, Blau double-smoothes the tick volume as a way of confirming price direction. The *TickVolume Indicator*, seen in Figure 12.18, is calculated as

$$TVI(r,s) = \frac{100 \times DEMA(upticks, r, s) - DEMA(downsticks, r, s)}{DEMA(upticks, r, s) + DEMA(downsticks, r, s)}$$

TVI ranges from -100 to $+100$ and *DEMA* (Double Exponential Moving Average) is the double smoothing of the downticks or upticks. The exponential smoothing is first

[20] Thomas Aspray, "Fine-Tuning the Demand Index," *Technical Analysis of Stocks & Commodities* (June 1986), and "Demand Oscillator Momentum," *Technical Analysis of Stocks & Commodities* (September 1989).

FIGURE 12.18 Blau's Tick Volume Indicator.

Source: William Blau, *Momentum, Direction, and Divergence* (New York: John Wiley & Sons, 1995), 45.

calculated over *r* bars, and the result of that smoothing is again smoothed over the past *s* bars. More about this double-smoothing technique can be found in Chapter 8. This technique differs from Blau's price smoothing because it does not first create a momentum series; therefore, the *TVI* will be lagged slightly less than half the sum of the two calculation periods.

Volume-Weighted MACD

The MACD is based on the difference between two moving averages (see Chapter 10). To add volume, the closing prices for each day are multiplied by the corresponding volume, and each moving average is normalized by the average volume over the same period. The recommended calculation periods are 12 and 26 days, the standard MACD values. A signal line, also the same as MACD, is the exponentially smoothed VWMACD line using a 0.20 smoothing constant, the equivalent of about 9 days.

$$VWMACD_t = \left(\frac{\sum_{t=t-12+1}^{t} C_i \times V_i}{\sum_{i=t-12+1}^{t} V_i} \right) - \left(\frac{\sum_{t=t-26+1}^{t} C_i \times V_i}{\sum_{i=t-26+1}^{t} V_i} \right)$$

Figure 12.19 uses a program *TSM Volume Weighted MACD*, available on the Companion Website, to plot the VWMACD for euro currency futures, which appears in the bottom panel. The heavier line is the VWMACD, and the thinner, smoother line is the signal. As with the MACD, the rules are to enter a new long position when the VWMACD crosses above the signal line, and the opposite for shorts. When compared to the MACD, this variation appears to make only small changes, yet a slight improvement in timing can be a great advantage in trading.

FIGURE 12.19 Volume-Weighted MACD Applied to Euro Currency Futures.

Variably Weighted Moving Average Using Volume

A unique approach taken by Christian Fries[21] uses the relationship between the number of outstanding shares, the current price, and the volume of the next period or the next trade, to create an *Elastic Volume-Weighted Moving Average (eVWMA)*. Using the difference between the number of outstanding shares and the number of shares being traded he creates a weighting factor. That weighting factor causes the previous trend value to have more importance when fewer shares are traded and less weight when relatively more shares are traded. The net effect is that the weighted average is more responsive to change when relatively more shares are traded.

$$eVWMA_t = \frac{(OS - V_t) \times eVWMA_{t-1} + V_t \times C_t}{OS}$$

where OS = the number of outstanding shares.

Using Merck (MRK) as an example, the total outstanding shares was set to 200 million, based on an observed maximum daily volume of approximately 150 million. By keeping the outstanding shares slightly bigger than the maximum volume, the indicator will vary across a wider range and show more of its characteristics. Figure 12.20 compares the eVWMA to a standard exponential smoothing of 0.10. The results are very similar although the eVWMA tracks closer to the price in the center of the chart.

Substituting Open Interest for Volume Using Futures

Futures volume can create very different results from volume for stocks. The markets themselves—energy, gold, and even interest rates—have been in an uptrend for years. This causes many of the indicators, especially OBV, to move steadily higher, while it appears to oscillate when applied to stocks over the past 10 years.

---

[21] Christian P. Fries, "Elastic Moving Averages," *Technical Analysis of Stocks & Commodities* (June 2001).

FIGURE 12.20 Elastic Volume-Weighted Moving Average Applied to Merck (MRK) Compared with a 0.10 Exponential Smoothing.

It has already been mentioned that futures volume comes in two parts, contract volume and total volume. Contract volume begins at zero, increases as the contract moves from deferred (many months away from delivery) to the nearby delivery, then back to zero as the contract expires. Open interest follows a similar pattern. To avoid this pattern, total volume is used instead of contract volume. In the same way, futures data shows contract open interest and total open interest. That data varies in the same pattern as volume; however, open interest is much more stable than volume. Similar to volume, open interest increases as market activity increases; therefore, it reflects the same fundamentals.

Total open interest can be a preferable substitute for volume in many of the indicators covered in the previous sections. It should be remembered that open interest, as well as volume, is usually available on downloaded data one day late. These numbers could be manually downloaded from Bloomberg, but it is safer to use them as a longer-term indicator, which best suits their purpose.

A spreadsheet example of applying OBV to S&P futures, using both total volume and total open interest, is available on the Companion Website as *TSM OBV*.

VWAP

As a note, order executions can be placed as a *VWAP*, a *volume-weighted average price*. For larger positions, this would return an average price representing how actively the market traded at different levels throughout the day. It is most convenient for hedge funds that do not want to force prices higher by placing an excessively large buy order at one point during the day, or even on the close. Equally spaced orders that ignore liquidity use *TWAP*, a *time-weighted average price*.

■ Breadth Indicators

Market breadth measures the imbalance between the number of advancing and declining stocks on a given day. It is the percentage of rising stocks to the total number of stocks traded. In general, more advancing issues should add confidence to an upwards price move in the same way that volume confirms price. A net increase in the S&P 500 while more issues are declining should generate concern that the upwards move is poorly supported.

The information for advances and declines is published along with stock prices each day. You may also want the volume of advancing issues and the volume of declining issues. Both of these values can be found in the *Wall Street Journal* under "Trading Activity." In this section, the CSI data series, UVDV, will be used. In addition, we will look at the new highs and new lows using CSI data MKST, to see if those numbers add value to price analysis.

To interpret the CSI data files, use the following guide. The normal field designation is in the heading and the actual content is below.

Series	Date	Open	High	Low	Close	Volume	OpInt
UVDV	Date	Total traded	Advanced	Declined	Unchanged	Up Volume	Down Volume
MKST	Date	Total traded	Advanced	Declined	Unchanged	52-Week Highs	52-Week Lows

Market breadth indicators are typically used as a confirmation of price direction. The table below shows that the interpretation of market breadth is the same as the relationship between volume and price.

Market Breadth	Price	Interpretation
Rising	Rising	Breadth confirms price rise
Falling	Falling	Breadth confirms price drop
Falling	Rising	Breadth does not confirm price rise
Rising	Falling	Breadth does not confirm price drop

The measurement of breadth must relate to what you are trading. If 75% of the stocks in the Dow rise, the S&P Small Cap Index can still be lackluster or declining. Investors shift from small-cap stocks to the S&P 500 and then to the Dow when they are looking for safety. The breadth of the overall market, or the breadth of large caps, is not enough to confirm an upwards trend in the small caps.

It is worth noting that Gerald Appel, a well-known market analyst and technician, points out that, when using market breadth, it is best if it is equally weighted (i.e., a simple count).

Separating Advancing from Declining Volume

The most basic of all techniques for determining market breadth is the *Advance-Decline Index*, which creates a new series by adding the net of the number of advancing and declining stocks each day. Unchanged issues are ignored.

$$Advance\text{-}Decline\ Oscillator_t = Advances_t - Declines_t$$

$$Advance\text{-}Decline\ Index_t = Advance\text{-}Decline\ Index_{t-1} - Advances_t - Declines_t$$

In some of the techniques that follow, only the oscillator, or single-period calculation, may be shown. An index can be created by accumulating these values.

Sibbett's Demand Index

One method that smoothes volume by using the total activity of the past 10 days is James Sibbett's *Demand Index*. The technique bears a resemblance to the approach used in Wilder's RSI. It can be used as an oscillator with individual daily values or accumulated into an index. Where $n = 10$, the individual days are calculated as the sum of the upside volume divided by the sum of the downside volume:

$$Demand\ Index_t = \frac{\sum_{i=t-n+1}^{t} upside\ volume_i}{\sum_{i=t-n+1}^{t} downside\ volume_t}$$

The values for upside and downside volume can also be found in the *Wall Street Journal* under the heading "Trading Activity." Arthur Merrill, another well-known stock analyst, has suggested using $n = 5$.

Bolton-Tremblay

Introducing the net advancing stocks compared to the number of stocks that were unchanged, the Bolton-Tremblay approach also includes a form of geometric weighting of the results. In the following calculation, *BT* is the daily Bolton-Tremblay value, and *BTI* is the index resulting from accumulating the individual daily values.

$$BT_t = \frac{Advancing_t - Declining_t}{Unchanged_t}$$

If $BT_t > 0$ then $BTI_t = BTI_{t-1} + \sqrt{BT_t}$

If $BT_t < 0$ then $BTI_t = BTI_{t-1} - \sqrt{BT_t}$

The Bolton-Tremblay calculation will have large spikes on days when the advancing or declining breadth is very strong, which make the unchanged number of stocks in the denominator very small.

Schultz

Schultz chose to look at the advancing stocks only as a percentage of the total stocks, which puts the results in the convenient range of 0 to 100:

$$Schultz\ A/T_t = \frac{Advancing_t}{Total\ stocks_t}$$

McClellan Oscillator

The *McClellan Oscillator* starts with the net advances (NA) and then creates an oscillator by subtracting two smoothed trends, 19 and 39 days, based on the net advances, in a manner similar to the MACD. Converting the 19- and 39-day calculation periods to smoothing constants using $2/(n+1)$ we (conveniently) get $s_1 = 0.10$ and $s_2 = 0.05$.

$$NA_t = Advances_t - Declines_t$$

$$E1_t = E1_{t-1} + s_1 \times \left(NA_t - E1_{t-1}\right)$$

$$E2_t = E2_{t-1} + s_2 \times \left(NA_t - E2_{t-1}\right)$$

$$McClellan\,Oscillator_t = E1_t - E2_t$$

Figure 12.21 compares Sibbett's Demand Index with the more complicated McClellan Oscillator. S&P futures prices are in the top panel, the Demand Index in the second panel, the up and down volume in the third panel, and the McClellan Oscillator at the bottom. The scales of the two indicators are very different. The Demand Index is a ratio; therefore, it varies above and below 1.0, and reflects the upside/downside volume over a rolling 10-day period. The McClellan Oscillator uses a longer calculation period and smoothes even further using exponential smoothing.

Both indicators stay slightly above neutral during the long upward move, but the most interesting feature would be the extreme highs and lows, which are clearer in the McClellan Oscillator, corresponding nicely to two price lows and one peak. The high point that ended the long upwards move shows as divergence in the two indicators, a pattern that is not as easy to identify at the time, but can be very useful.

Upside/Downside Ratio

A simple *Upside/Downside Ratio* (UDR) is similar to Sibbett's Demand Index but is not smoothed. With this ratio, it is easier to see the asymmetry of the calculation.

FIGURE 12.21 S&P Futures (Top Panel), Sibbett's Demand Index (Second Panel), the Up/Down Volume (Third Panel), and the McClellan Oscillator (Bottom Panel).

When the declining volume is very low, for example only 20% of the total volume, the UDR will have a value of 4.0. In contrast, if the advancing volume is low (20% of the declining volume), the ratio is 0.20. There is no upside limit when stocks are advancing but the downside ratio is limited to the range between 0 and 1. This is a familiar pattern for advancing and declining prices expressed as a percentage. High values of the UDR are expected to precede a bull market period.

$$UDR_t = \frac{Advancing\,Volume_t}{Declining\,Volume_t}$$

Arms Index (TRIN)

Richard Arms explains the relationship between the number of advancing and declining stocks, and the up and down volume, in the *Arms Index*, more popularly known as *TRIN*, the *Trader's Index*. It divides the ratio of the number of advancing and declining stocks by the ratio of the volume of the advancing and declining stocks.

$$TRIN_t = \frac{Advancing\,stocks_t\,/\,Declining\,stocks_t}{Advancing\,volume_t\,/\,Declining\,volume_t}$$

Thrust Oscillator

Tushar Chande's *Thrust Oscillator* (TO) uses the same values as *TRIN* but creates a bullish oscillator by multiplying the number of advancing stocks by the volume of the advancing stocks and subtracting the comparable declining values, then dividing by the sum of the two.

$$TO_t = 100 \times \frac{Adv\,stocks_t \times Vol\,of\,adv\,stocks_t - Decl\,stocks_t \times Vol\,of\,decl\,stocks_t}{Adv\,stocks_t \times Vol\,of\,adv\,stocks_t + Decl\,stocks_t \times Vol\,of\,decl\,stocks_t}$$

The Thrust Oscillator is used as an overbought/oversold indicator to complement another strategy that would decide on the major direction of the market. Values of ± 30 may be used to identify overbought and oversold levels, respectively. Whenever an indicator is not smoothed, the extremes become the most interest points of action.

Figure 12.22 shows the Thrust Oscillator (second panel) along with S&P futures (top panel). The bands of ± 30 give short-term indications of overbought and oversold days and occur more frequently during a sideways price move. For the 3-month period when the S&P was steadily rising, the indicator gave many more buy signals (penetration of the bottom band) than sell signals, a good outcome.

When studying both the Arms Index (TRIN) and the Thrust Oscillator (TO) it would seem sensible to express all the component values as percentages of the whole. That is, the number of advancing and declining stocks should each be divided by the total number of stocks, and the volume of the advancing and declining stocks should each be divided by the total volume of all shares traded. This would make those days with low relative volume less important. In the current calculations, inactive days might produce highly distorted values.

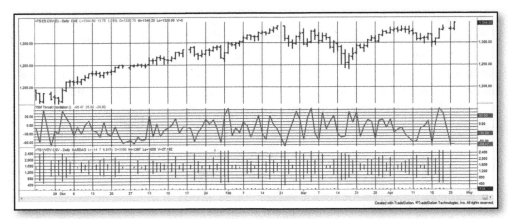

FIGURE 12.22 The Thrust Oscillator (Second Panel) Shown with S&P Futures (Top Panel).

New Highs and Lows

There is very little literature on the use of the number of new highs and lows that occur daily, yet the data are available and can be used in ways similar to market breadth. The most obvious way to represent this data is by creating a *High-Low Index* (HLX),

$$HLX_t = HLX_{t-1} + NH_t - NL_t$$

where *NH* are new 52-week highs and *NL* are new 52-week lows. Another approach would be a simple ratio of the new highs compared to the combined new highs and lows, over the past *n* days,

$$HLR_t = \frac{\sum_{i=t-n+1}^{t} NH_i}{\sum_{i=t-n+1}^{t} (NH_i + NL_i)}$$

Gerry Appel[22] uses this *High-Low Ratio*, smoothed over 10 days, and generates a buy signal when the ratio crosses above a threshold of, for example, 0.80 or 0.90, and a sell signal when it crosses back below that level. In Figure 12.23, the S&P futures are shown with the HLR in the middle panel, and the high-low data in the bottom panel. The top line of the middle panel is 0.90 and might serve as a threshold to extract high-momentum trades during the steady uptrend. It may also be useful to create a fast smoothing of the HLR to use as a signal line, in the same manner as MACD, which would avoid the need for a strict threshold entry and exit value.

Baskets of New Highs and Lows

Another method that will be discussed in more detail in Level III, Chapter 2 is buying a basket of stocks making new highs and selling a basket of stocks making new lows.

---

[22] Gerald Appel, *Power Tools for Active Traders* (Upper Saddle River, NJ: Financial Times Prentice Hall, 2005), 126.

FIGURE 12.23 S&P Futures (Top Panel) Shown with the High-Low Ratio (HLR) in the Second Panel, and the High-Low Data at the Bottom.

Naturally, this assumes that each stock making a new high will sustain that direction because there has been some fundamental change in its earnings or structure that the market sees as positive. Similarly, those stocks making new 52-week lows have negative fundamental changes. To avoid unnecessary risk, the long basket and short basket must have the same volatility.

Is One Volume or Breadth Indicator Better than Another?

The final test of a successful indicator is whether it adds value to your trading decisions. This can be determined by programming the indicator into a strategy and testing the rules over a reasonable historic time period. Before doing that, we should decide what an increase or decrease in volume or breadth is telling us, and how we will use that information for trading. Volume and breadth indicators are more difficult than those that use price because the values have greater variance. That makes translating a sound concept into a profitable strategy more difficult. If performance testing does not confirm our expectations, then the indicator needs to be applied differently. There seems no doubt that volume and breadth data are telling us something, and uncovering those messages would improve our trading performance.

Looking at the previous selection of indicators, we see that small net changes in price can result in all volume being designated to one market direction. This is the case with Granville's On-Balance Volume and in the Bolton-Tremblay method. Is it reasonable to add all volume to the accumulated index if the S&P gained only a fraction of one point? On a single day this may seem to be arbitrary, but just as in many basic systems, over a long period of time the net effect of this decision is sound.

The changes made by Mark Chaiken, which take a percentage of volume based on the relative close of prices within the daily range, seem very sensible and avoid the all-or-nothing technique used in On-Balance Volume. Sibbett's Demand Index, by using the sum of 10 days' volume, avoids this problem completely and smoothes out results, a situation often needed when using the highly variable values of volume and breadth.

FIGURE 12.24 Total PL Using the AD Ratio as a Countertrend Signal.

By seeing these indicators close together, they appear to be a collection of minor manipulation of data. Traditional technicians still advocate interpretation using trend lines, divergence, or new highs and lows. Instead of having to interpret only the difficult movements of prices, they have added an equally difficult series of volume or breadth. While it is clear that volume and breadth contribute to the understanding of a price move, you must first be able to test whether you can use that information profitably. To do that, some fully systematic method is needed to insure that any approach can be implemented and validated.

Breadth as a Countertrend Indicator

All the literature favors using breadth to confirm direction, but Connors argues the opposite.[23] He trades the advance/decline (*AD*) ratio as follows:

Sell the index when $AD > 2.0$
Buy the index when $AD < 0.50$
Exit the trade after 5 days unless a reverse signal occurs

Using the series UVDV-I or MKST-I defined earlier in this section, we added the SPX in column 2, then created the advance/decline ratio. The buy and sell rules were applied, but because there were very frequent signals, all trades were held until an opposite signal occurred, rather than for 5 days. The total PL (in percent) is shown in Figure 12.24. Complete calculations can be found in the Excel spreadsheet, *TSM MKST-I Market Breadth*, on the Companion Website.

■ Interpreting Volume and Breadth Systematically

Most systematic approaches to volume apply a long-term smoothing method to the data and then identify trend changes to confirm price direction. This can be implemented with any of the accumulation indexes, but not with single-day momentum or

---

[23] Larry Connors, "Fade the Breadth," *Futures* (January 2005).

oscillator values. For the oscillators, most analysts have taken the approach that high volume confirms a new price direction; extreme volume, on the other hand, is more likely to be a reversal signal. If volume and price peaks do not occur at the same time, a volume peak should precede a trend change. A decline in volume has also been used to confirm direction, but it is more likely to indicate that prices have reached equilibrium, and that a further advance or decline requires additional confirmation.

Identifying a Volume Spike

A *volume spike* is one of the clearest and best examples of useful volume information. In its most obvious form, a volume spike is a day when the volume is at least twice that of other days over a period generally longer than one month, most likely longer than three months. Volume spikes may come in clusters due to an unstable political or economic situation; however, it is normally associated with the end of a significant price move.

Figure 12.25 shows 12 years of Microsoft prices with volume along the bottom. There are a few dozen times when volume spikes. Just after 2000 there is a cluster of spikes that are associated with the end of the tech bubble, a price drop of 50% in just a few weeks. Most of the spikes on the chart fall on days with large price moves and precede reversals. While the reversals are not always large, the volatility spike marks the end of the current move.

A simple spike can be measured as exceeding a threshold, T, where T is a multiple of the average volume, $AV = average\ (volume,\ n)$, over the recent n days. Then a volume spike exists if today's volume is greater than the average volume on the previous day times its multiplier, $V_t > T \times AV_{t-1}$.

Most cases are not as clear as a 1-day spike following much lower volume. More likely, volume has increased significantly over the past two or three days, culminating in a spike that is much higher than the average volume, but may only be 25% higher than the previous day. The solution to this is to lag the average volume so that it does not reflect the increasing volume of the recent few days.

We will make the assumption that volume resulting in a spike takes no longer than three days to develop. We can safely say that the average volume, lagged five days,

FIGURE 12.25 Microsoft Prices with Volume Along the Bottom.

FIGURE 12.26 NASDAQ Prices and Volume Show Both High and Low Volume Associated with Price Reversals.

should not reflect the recent rise in volume. Then a volume spike would be identified when

$$V_t > \frac{\sum\limits_{i=t-n-5}^{t-5} V_i}{n}$$

The right part of this formula is the average volume over n days beginning $t - n - 5$ days ago and ending $t - 5$ days ago. If t is today, then the average volume stops five days ago; therefore, it is not influenced by recent volume data.

Volume spikes are not as extreme when dealing with futures markets and indexes. In Figure 12.26 NASDAQ futures are shown with total (all contracts) volume for a period in May 2010. Higher volume days correspond to two cases where prices reversed from lows, and the peak in the center of the chart is associated with low volume. Both situations offer an opportunity to improve trading.

In the crude oil chart, Figure 12.27, the spikes in volume can be seen as frequently occurring at price reversal points, while lower volume may be indicative of the continued price direction. Although there are no comprehensive tests available to confirm these observations, high volume seems to precede a price reversal, even if it lasts only one day.

Moving Average Approaches

Not all analysts agree that higher volume is a reversal signal. A straightforward way of using higher volume to confirm a trend is to calculate a 10-day moving average of the volume as a complement to a 20-day trend position.[24] By simply requiring the current volume to be greater than the average volume over those past 10 days, you introduce the idea of greater participation associated with the new trend. An

---

[24] Alex Saitta, "A Price and Volume-Based System," *Technical Analysis of Stocks & Commodities* (March 1996).

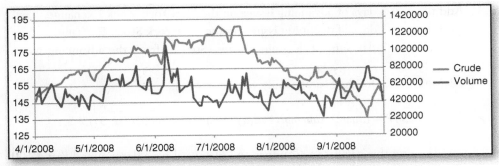

FIGURE 12.27 Crude Oil Futures (Back-Adjusted), with Total Volume Shown as a Line.

additional important benefit is that this volume condition acts as a filter, eliminating a substantial number of trades. If the net returns are the same, the volume-filtered approach is far better because you are out of the market more, reducing your risk and not reversing your position every time there is a new signal. That improves liquidity.

A similar method was proposed by Waxenberg.[25] A 10-day moving average of the volume is calculated as the normal level, and a change in trend must be confirmed by a 20% increase in volume above this norm. (The 20% threshold acts as an additional smoothing filter, but may be replaced by a longer trend and smaller threshold.) Extremes in a price move can be found at points that exceed approximately a 40% volume increase. Applied to the stock market, Waxenberg used the extreme volumes to indicate the end of a sell-off. To add more flexibility over longer test periods, and to adapt more quickly to volatility changes, Bollinger bands (based on 2 standard deviations, or 95% probability) can be substituted for the fixed percentage thresholds.

Alternately, using 13 days of volume, subtract the total down volume from the total up volume. A plot of the results will serve as a momentum indicator from which overbought and oversold levels can be identified. If these values are unstable due to lack of liquidity, they may be smoothed using a short-term moving average.

Advance-Decline System

Advance and decline values, as with most volume figures, can be more useful if they are smoothed. By combining peak values of the net of smoothed advancing and declining shares with a directional move in price, Connors and Hayward have created a basic system structure that they named CHADTP[26] (*Connors-Hayward Advance-Decline Trading Patterns*). This system tries to identify reversal patterns by applying the following steps:

---

[25] Howard K. Waxenberg, "Technical Analysis of Volume," *Technical Analysis of Stocks & Commodities* (March 1986).

[26] Laurence A. Connors and Blake E. Hayward, *Investment Secrets of a Hedge Fund Manager* (Chicago: Probus, 1995).

1. Add the past 5 days of advancing issues on the New York Stock Exchange.
2. Add the past 5 days of declining issues on the New York Stock Exchange.
3. Subtract the 5-day sum of declining issues (Step 2) from the advancing issues (Step 1).
4. Divide by 5 to get the average daily value.

$$CHADTP = (Sum(AdvancingNYSE, 5) - Sum(DecliningNYSE, 5)) / 5$$

To trade using this oscillator, Connors and Hayward have determined that ± 400 are the extreme levels where the values have been overbought and oversold. Based on this, we can apply the following rules to the S&P futures:

1. *Sell short* when CHADTP $> + 400$ and the S&P futures trade 10 basis points below the low of the previous day; *buy* when CHADTP $< - 400$ and the S&P futures trade 10 basis points above the high of the previous day.
2. Note that the oscillator does not have to exceed its recent extremes on the day of the buy or sell signal.
3. Timing is best if the signal occurs at the same time as a newspaper commentary indicating "depressed volume," or volume significantly below the 3-month average, which is seen as an excess of cash waiting to enter the market.

This system targets returns over a 5- to 7-day period. A drop in the oscillator, which results in values in the midrange, is an opportunity to exit. A standard price oscillator can be constructed to generate overbought and oversold signals within this time frame. An opposite entry signal would reverse the position.

We should be aware that this method was developed in 1995 when the S&P was lower and less volatile. As of 2011, the DJIA is about four times its 1995 value, while the S&P is only about one-third higher. However, the markets are more volatile now. A change of 10 basis points (0.10%) in the S&P is about 1.30 points, which is likely to happen every day. Raising the threshold to 50 or 100 basis points may make it easier to assess the value of this method.

Breadth as a Countertrend Indicator

Equities have a tendency to be mean reverting because they have more noise than most other sectors. That seems to hold true for market breadth. Larry Connors has shown that more declining stocks is an excellent leading indicator of a stock market advance.[27]

■ If declining NYSE stocks are greater than advancing NYSE stocks for at least three days in a row, then the S&P averaged a gain of 0.50% the following week.

■ If declining NASDAQ stocks are greater than advancing NASDAQ stocks for at least two days in a row, then the NASDAQ 100 index gained an average of 0.80% the next week.

[27] Larry Connors, "Fade the Breadth," *Futures* (January 2005).

- If declining NYSE stocks were at least twice the NYSE advancing stocks, then the S&P gained an average of 0.60% the following week.

In addition, when the opposite occurred, all three situations showed essentially no gain in the respective index during the following week. The observation period was 1996–2003, which contained extreme bull and bear markets.

■ An Integrated Probability Model

If there is a noticeable relationship between price, volume, and open interest (or market breadth), then a probability model can be constructed to test its importance.[28] To do this it is necessary to construct a 1-day-ahead forecast using a simple linear regression model and then backtest weighting factors for each element. Because of powerful software products, this has become a very manageable process. Using TradeStation's *EasyLanguage*, each 1-day-ahead forecast is determined using the previous n days:

Price forecast:	$Pf = Price + LinearRegSlope(close, n)$
Volume forecast:	$Vf = Volume + LinearRegSlope(volume, n)$
Open interest forecast:	$Of = Opint + LinearRegSlope(opint, n)$
On-Balance Volume forecast:	$OBVf = OBV + LinearRegSlope(OBV, n)$

The function *LinearRegSlope* returns the 1-period increase or decrease in the input value based on a straight-line fit of the past n days. That value can be added to the current price, volume, open interest, or On-Balance Volume to get the 1-day-ahead forecast. The calculation period n can be selected by subtracting the actual next-day value from the forecast and creating an error series that can be measured using a standard deviation. The number of days, n, that generates the smallest standard deviation is the best forecast period. It is possible that the optimal forecast period will differ for each of the four items above but a robust solution would seem to be the one period that minimized the errors across all the components. These and other testing issues are thoroughly discussed in Level III, Chapter 10.

Having found the four 1-day-ahead forecasts, an index can be created that gives one weight w_1 to the price forecast and the remaining weights, $1 - w_1$, to a combination of the other three factors. This assumes that price is the most important predictor of price. Then

$$Forecast\ index = w_1 Pf + (1 - w_1) \times (w_2 Vf + w_3 Of + w_4 OBVf)$$

This formula can be backtested for values of w_1, w_2, w_3, and w_4 where $\sum w = 1$. The final index can be used instead of price for determining the trend. It will still require a moving average, or some smoothed line, to signal new uptrends and

---

[28] Based on the May 1995 "CSI Technical Journal," Commodity Systems Inc., Boca Raton, Florida.

downtrends; however, the results, if successful, should be more reliable than using only price.

One advantage of testing the weighting factors is that, if one of the four elements is not helpful in predicting a trend, the weighting factor should be near zero. Another approach, that does not cluster the nonprice data together, would be to treat each item separately in the classic form:

$$Forecast\ index = w_1 Pf + w_2 Vf + w_3 Of + w_4 OBVf$$

CHAPTER 13

Volume, Open Interest, and Breadth

From Perry J. Kaufman, *Trading Systems and Methods, +Website*, 5th Edition (Hoboken, New Jersey: John Wiley & Sons, 2013), Chapter 12.

Patterns in volume have always been tied closely to chart analysis of both the stock and futures markets. Volume is a valuable piece of information that is not often used, and one of the few items, other than price, that is traditionally considered valid data for the technician. Nevertheless, there has been little research published that relates volume to futures markets; its popular use has assumed the same conclusions as in stock market analysis.

The stock and futures markets have two other measures of participation that are related. In equities, the large number shares being traded allow for measurements of *breadth*. In the same way that the stock index has become a popular measure of overall market trend, the *breadth of the market* is the total number of stocks that have risen or fallen during a specific period. When you have the ability to view the bigger picture of market movement, breadth seems to be a natural adjunct to the index. In addition, tallies of *new highs* and *new lows* may add value to a trading decision. This chapter will look at different way these statistics can complement other indicators.

In futures, *open interest* is the measurement of those participants with outstanding positions; it is the netting out of all open positions (longs and short sales) in any one market or delivery month, and gives an understanding of the depth of participation and anticipated volume. A market that trades only 10,000 contracts per day but has an open interest of 250,000 is telling the trader that there are many participants who will enter the market when the price is right. These are most likely to be commercial traders, using the futures markets for hedging. Unlike the stock market, which can only trade a fixed number of outstanding shares, the futures market can add net contracts for every new buyer and short seller and reduce the *interest* in the market when both buyers and sellers liquidate.

■ A Special Case for Futures Volume

In futures markets, where you trade contracts for delivery in specific months, the volume of each contract is available, along with the total volume of all contracts traded for that market. Spread transactions within that market, for example, buying the March delivery and selling June, are not included in the reported volume, a point that is inconsistent with stocks, which report both sides of a high frequency trade. In futures, volume data and open interest are officially posted one day late, but estimates are available for many markets during the day on services such as Bloomberg. Total volume of crude oil is estimated every hour; it is released to news services and is available on the Internet.

Individual contract volume is important to determine which delivery month is most active. Traders find that the best executions are where there is greatest liquidity. Analysts, however, have a difficult time assessing trends in volume because there is a natural increase in volume as a contract moves from deferred to delivery, from second month out to the nearby, and traders most often roll their positions to the closest delivery month. There is a corresponding decline in volume as a contract approaches its delivery date. Because spread volume is not posted, movement between delivery months does not affect the volume patterns.

Each futures market has its unique pattern of volume for individual contracts. Some, such as the interest rates, shift abruptly on the last day of the month prior to delivery, because the exchange raises margins dramatically for all traders holding positions in the delivery month. Currencies are very different and tend to trade actively in the nearest month up to one or two days before that contract goes *off the board*. While volume increases slightly in the next deferred contract, anyone trading sizable positions will need to stay with the nearby contract to just before the end.

Other than for determining which contract to trade, and perhaps the size of an order that the market can absorb, an analysis of volume as discussed in this chapter will use total volume (the aggregate of all contracts) in order to have a series that does not suffer the patterns of increasing and decreasing participation based on the coming and going of individual delivery months. When traders roll from the nearby to the next deferred contract, the transactions are usually executed as a spread, and those trades are not included in the volume figures. Because positions are closed out in one contract and opened in another there is no change in the open interest.

The stock market equivalent to using total volume would be to add the volume for all stocks in the same sector or industrial group. This would help to smooth over those periods when the volume is concentrated in a few stocks following a news or earnings release, only to switch the next week when other stocks in the same sector are noticed.

Tick Volume

The popularity of quote machines and fast trading requires a measurement of volume that can be used immediately to make decisions. Lacking a service such as Bloomberg with continually updated volume, *tick volume* can be substituted. Tick volume is the number of recorded price changes, regardless of volume or the size of the price change that occurs during any time interval. Tick volume relates directly to actual volume because, as the market becomes more active, prices move back and forth from bid to asked more often. If only two trades occur in a 5-minute period, then the market is not liquid. From an analytic view, tick volume gives a reasonable approximation of true volume and can be used as a substitute. From a practical view, it is the only choice. Higher-than-normal tick volume at the beginning of the day implies higher volume throughout the day. Tick volume patterns are discussed later in this chapter.

■ Variations from the Normal Patterns

The *W* Intraday Pattern

One note of warning when using intraday volume or volume indicators to confirm price direction: The patterns in volume have a dominant *W* pattern throughout the day. They begin high, drop quickly, increase modestly near midday, fall again, then increase significantly toward the close of trading. To decide that a buy signal is more important near the end of the trading day because volume was rising is not correct; volume is always higher at the beginning and end of the day. You may conclude, in general, that the beginning and end of the day, or higher-than-average volume produces more reliable trading signals; however, an intraday volume confirmation must be compared against the normal volume for that time of day.

Open interest and market breadth have seasonal patterns. In agricultural markets, farmers hedge in larger numbers during the growing season than in the winter, raising the open interest. In stocks, there is a lot of activity associated with the end-of-year positioning for tax purposes and traditional rallies during holiday seasons. Volume is low during the summer when many investors take their vacations. None of these changes indicate that something special is occurring. These variations are discussed in detail later in this chapter.

Variance in Volume

Nearly all volume analysis uses smoothed or averaged data because volume can vary substantially from one day to the next. As an example, Table 13.1 shows the breakdown of Microsoft (MSFT) volume for the five years from June 1998 through May 2003. While the volume was higher during the price peak of January 2000, the overall numbers show consistency at an average of 71 million shares per day.

Table 13.1 also shows the standard deviation of the daily volume changes, which is about 38% of the average volume. One standard deviation of this magnitude says that 68% of the days will show *changes* in daily volume ranging from 41 million to 101 million shares. Looking at it in reverse, 32% of the days will show changes in volume less than or greater than 41 million and 101 million shares. Compare that to the price of Microsoft during the same period, which ranged from $20 to $60 but had 1 standard deviation of $0.957—that is, the daily change in price was less than

TABLE 13.1	Microsoft Daily Volume by Year from June 1998 through May 2003	
Period	Average	StDev
Jun98–May99	62,861,035	21,511,856
Jun99–May00	64,512,077	34,741,178
Jun00–May01	83,915,101	35,621,716
Jun01–May02	64,638,359	21,125,063
Jun02–May03	79,584,139	22,129,923
Jun98–May03	*71,105,478*	*27,832,841*

$1, or about 2.9% of the $33.38 average price. Keep in mind that this variation is the basis for most of the volume indicators and strategies.

Volume Spikes

> Madness is the exception in individuals but the rule in groups.
>
> —*Nietzsche*

A *volume spike* is a single day on which the volume was much higher than the previous day—at least twice as high, perhaps three or four times. A volume spike is a warning that something happened, most likely the result of a surprising news release or new economic data. It could be the crescendo of a few days of rising volume associated with sharply rising or falling prices.

A volume spike is a clear, positive action by investors. It implies that a very large number of investors, perhaps even the general public, all hold the same opinion on the direction of the market and feel compelled to act on that opinion at the same time. It is the result of mass behavior discussed by Mackay in his famous book, *Extraordinary Popular Delusions and the Madness of Crowds*. A volume spike means that everyone has jumped into the boat at the same time. Traditional interpretation of a volume spike is that it indicates the end of a price move, that is, the boat sinks.

AOL shows three good examples of volume spikes in Figure 13.1. The highest volume days in April, August, and September 1999, and in January 2000 all occur at the bottom of a price move. Prices reverse direction immediately after the spike, and usually that reversal is substantial. A volume spike does not indicate the strength of the price reversal, it simply tells you that the current move is exhausted. It may turn out to be a major top or bottom, or simply a local turning point.

Volume spikes are a good example of extremes and the clearest cases for trading. The theory of a spike is that, when everyone has entered the market, there is no one left to buy (or sell) and prices must reverse. The crowd is always wrong—at least their timing is always wrong.

Drop in Volume

Although a drop in volume is less impressive than a volume spike, it can be equally important. Volume can decline because there is little interest in a stock or futures

FIGURE 13.1 AOL Price and Volume Showing Three Major Volume Spikes and Declining Volume while Prices Rise at the End of 1999.

market, which often happens when prices are very low. Volume can also drop when a price reaches *equilibrium*, the price at which buyers and sellers agree is *fair value*. Volume may also drop on the day before a holiday, or just by chance.

While there can be seasonal and other predictable patterns associated with a decline in volume, they all represent a lack of conviction, or a perceived lack of potential price movement, on the part of the traders. In Figure 13.1 there is a steady decline in the average volume from October 1999 through the end of 1999 while prices moved steadily higher. This period had only one-half the volume traded earlier in the year and is interpreted as a lack of investor support for higher prices. Having been hurt earlier in the year, more investors stood aside on the second rally and, while AOL prices did top the previous highs, another sell-off followed. This declining pattern fits the standard interpretation of volume.

■ Standard Interpretation

The interpretation of volume has been part of the trading culture from its beginning. Volume is always considered in combination with price movement:

Volume	Price	Interpretation
Rising	Rising	Volume confirms price rise
Rising	Falling	Volume confirms price drop
Falling	Rising	Volume indicates weak rally
Falling	Falling	Volume indicates weak pullback

This interpretation implies that *volume confirms direction*. When volume declines, it indicates that a change of direction should follow because there is no general support for the price move. Therefore, *volume normally leads price*. It has also been said that 1-week returns accompanied by declining volume tend to reverse the next week. Using weekly data would smooth the volume and may well add consistency.

The classic interpretation of volume was published in the monograph by W. L. Jiler, *Volume and Open Interest: A Key to Commodity Price Forecasting*, a companion piece to his most popular *Forecasting Commodity Prices with Vertical Line Charts*.

In both the futures and stock markets, volume has the same interpretation: When volume increases, it is said to confirm the direction of prices. Price changes that occur on very light volume are less dependable for indicating future direction than those changes associated with relatively heavy volume. An additional uncertainty exists for stocks that are not actively traded, and for low-priced shares where the total dollar volume can be small. In these cases, it might be best to look at the accumulated volume of similar companies or its sector.

Volume and Open Interest

Open interest is a concept unique to futures markets, but helps to explain the depth of the market as well as trader expectations. New *interest* in a market is the result of new buyers and sellers meeting, which increases the open interest, the net of all outstanding contracts being traded. The following table explains the combinations of buyers and sellers that changes open interest:

Buyer	Meets	Seller	Change in Open Interest
New		New	Increase in open interest
New		Old	No change in open interest
Old		New	No change in open interest
Old		Old	Decrease in open interest
Where		"New" buyer (seller) is a trader with no market position seeking to be long (short).	
		"Old" buyer (seller) is a trader who had previously entered a short (long) position and seeks to exit.	

When the open interest increases while prices rise quickly, it is commonly interpreted as more traders entering long positions. This may seem strange because for every new buyer of a futures contract there must be a new seller; however, the seller is likely to be someone looking to hold a position for a few hours or days, looking to profit from the normal ups and downs of price movement. The position trader, who is willing to sit for much more time holding a long position, is the one who is attributed with the open interest. In reality, no one knows. However, if prices keep rising, the shorts are more likely to be forced out while the longs have staying power.

The traditional interpretation of changes in volume and open interest (for futures markets) can be summarized as:

Volume	Open Interest	Interpretation
Rising	Rising	Confirmation of trend
Rising	Falling	Position liquidation (at extremes)
Falling	Rising	Slow accumulation
Failing	Falling	Congestion phase

Three generally accepted notions for the use of volume and open interest are:

1. Open interest increases during a trending period.
2. Volume may decline but open interest builds during an accumulation phase. Volume occasionally spikes.
3. Rising prices and declining volume/open interest indicate a pending change of direction.

There is a traditional interpretation for the combined movement of price direction, volume, and open interest.

Prices	Volume	Open Interest	Interpretation
Rising	Rising	Rising	New buyers are entering the market.
Falling	Falling	Falling	Longs are being forced out; the downtrend will end when all sellers have liquidated their positions.
Rising	Falling	Falling	Short sellers are covering their positions causing a rally. Money is leaving the market.
Falling	Rising	Rising	New short selling. Bearish money is entering the market.

Exceptions

No method is without exceptions, including volume patterns in the stock market. There are days or periods when volume is expected to change, and must be considered in the analysis. For example, volume is expected to decline:

On the first day of the week.
On the day before a holiday.
During the summer.

The most important exception to rising prices and rising volume is the volume spike, which signals a change of direction rather than a confirmation.

Volume is also higher on *triple witching day* (or *quadruple witching day*, if you include futures on stocks), when S&P futures, options on futures, and options on the individual stocks all expire at the same time.

In the futures markets, there are similar patterns. Lighter volume exists during holiday periods and summer months, but may be heavier on Fridays and Mondays during a trending market or a weather market for agricultural products (uncertainty over rain, drought, or frost over the weekend). Liquidation often occurs before the weekend and positions are reentered on the first day of the next week.

Richard Arms' Equivolume

Most of the techniques for using volume discussed in this chapter will multiply or accumulate volume, creating an index that rises faster as volume increases. *Equivolume*, a charting method introduced by Richard Arms,[1] takes the unique approach of substituting volume for time along the bottom scale of a chart. When volume increases, the price bar is elongated to the right; therefore, an upwards move on high volume will appear as a higher box that is also wider.

There are no systematic methods for using Equivolume included here and its applications parallel standard chart interpretations; however, analysts can represent this type of chart by creating a new price series in which the daily closing price is repeated based on the relative volume. For example, if the normal volume day causes a closing price to be repeated 10 times, then a day with twice the volume will repeat that price 20 times, and a day with half the volume will show 5 prices. This approach may cause a short-term moving average trend to look strange; however, a linear regression or long-term trend should reflect the importance of varying time.

Herrick Payoff Index

The *Herrick Payoff Index* (HPI) is the most popular calculation that combines price, volume, and open interest. It is designed to gauge the strength of the current trend, and has been applied primarily to futures prices. Because it adds volume and open interest to a momentum calculation, it can be found in Chapter 30 along with some other indicators that use volume as an added feature.

Volume Is a Predictor of Volatility

Most often high volume and high volatility occur at the same time. It is easy to see on a chart that one confirms the other. However, not all days that have high volume also have high volatility. Even on days with high volume, the price can close nearly unchanged from the previous day. We need to look at those days as a sign of *potential volatility*—a large number of traders all with their own objectives somehow managed to offset each other. Tomorrow, if there is an imbalance in the buyers and sellers, and volume is still high, prices could break out in either direction. Therefore, *high volume means high risk*, even on those days when the risk does not materialize.

■ Volume Indicators

Both the stock and futures markets have numerous indicators that use only volume, or those that add volume, intending to make other calculations more robust. The following section gives the most popular of these indicators, most of which

---

[1] See www.armsinsider.com/education/armsonthemarket/equiv_chart.asp for examples.

originate in the stock market; many use the number of advancing and declining stocks. Readers should note the way in which the data is used from one technique to another and consider the significance of these changes. They are discussed at the end of this section.

Average Volume

The most basic of all volume indicators is the *average*, and the calculation most commonly used for the equity markets is 50 days, although it may be reasonable to use the same period as the price average that is being used. Then, if you are tracking the 200-day moving average, a 200-day average of the volume would make sense. Anything less than 50 days is not likely to be smooth.

Normalizing the Volume

It is always convenient to normalize prices to view them compared to the recent average. This can also be done for volume. Letting the calculation period, N, be either 50 or 200 days, we can normalize the volume and represent the result as a percent,

$$NormVol_t = 100 \times \frac{V_t}{\left(\sum_{i=t-P+1}^{t} V_t \right) / N}$$

The normalized volume lets us say that "today's volume is 20% higher than the volume over the past 200 days." This can be seen in the third panel of Figure 13.2, showing Microsoft prices and volume.

Volume Momentum and Percentage Change

Two other basic volume indicators are *momentum* and *rate of change*. These techniques treat volume as they would price. For momentum, this means finding the change

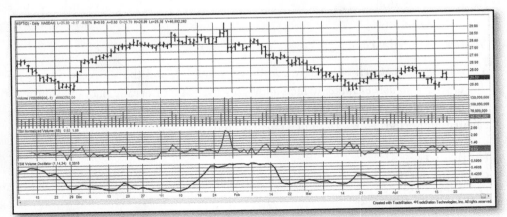

FIGURE 13.2 Microsoft Prices (Top), Volume (Second Panel), Normalized 50-Day Volume (Third Panel), and Volume Oscillator from Ratio (Bottom), Based on 14- and 34-Day Periods.

in volume over a specific time interval; percentage change measures the size of the volume change relative to the starting value. If t is today and n is the number of days back (the observation period), then

$$Volume\ momentum_t = Volume_t - Volume_{t-n}$$

$$Volume\%_t = \frac{Volume_t - Volume_{t-n}}{Volume_{t-n}}$$

Because of the high variance in volume from day to day, volume momentum tends to increase the erratic pattern. It will be necessary to smooth the volume momentum in order to have a useful indicator.

Force Index

Devised by Alex Elder, the *Force Index* is the change in price multiplied by the daily volume,

$$Force\ Index_t = (Close_t - Close_{t-1}) \times Volume_t$$

The Force Index will be positive or negative if the price change was higher or lower. It is also not limited to daily charts, but can be applied to weekly or monthly data, as can many of the other methods in this chapter. Once the daily Force Index is calculated, it should be smoothed. For timing entries and exits, it is suggested that a 2-day exponential moving average (EMA) with a smoothing constant 0.667 be used to avoid unnecessary noise in the indicator. For longer-term analysis, a 13-day EMA (smoothing constant 0.1428) should be used. Consistent with the idea of noise, the 2-day smoothed Force Index *buys* when the value is low and *sells short* when it's high; however, the 13-day value is treated as a trend, giving a buy signal when it crosses above zero and a sell when it crosses below zero. Signals remain in effect until the smoothed Force Index crosses the zero line in the other direction.

Volume Oscillator

Visualizing the pattern of volume can be very helpful, and the simplest way to do this is with a *volume oscillator,* which addresses the issue of erratic data by using two smoothed values. A volume oscillator is a two-step process and may use trends of any calculation period. Here, 14- and 34-day periods are used.

Method 1
Calculate the difference between a short-term and long-term average of volume. Using 14 and 34 days gives

$$VO(Diff)_t = \frac{\sum_{i=t-14+1}^{t} V_i}{14} - \frac{\sum_{i=t-34+1}^{t} V_i}{34}$$

Method 2

Calculate the ratio of a short-term and long-term sum of volume. Again, using 14 and 34 days,

$$VO(Ratio)_t = \frac{\sum_{i=t-14+1}^{t} V_i}{\sum_{i=t-34+1}^{t} V_i}$$

Once calculated, the oscillator values can be displayed as a histogram or a line chart. Figure 13.2 shows Microsoft from November 2010 through April 2011 in the top panel, volume in the second panel, the normalized 50-day volume in the third panel, and the volume oscillator using the ratio at the bottom. In this example, the volume oscillator does not confirm the upwards or downwards trends. Perhaps that is the correct interpretation because these trends were short lived.

On-Balance Volume

Made famous by Joseph Granville, *On-Balance Volume*[2] is now a byword in stock analyst circles. On days when prices close higher, it is assumed that all volume represents the buyers; on lower days, the volume is controlled by the sellers. The volume is then added or subtracted from a cumulative value, *OBV*, to get today's value.

IF *Today's price change* $(p_t > p_{t-1})$ then $OBV_t = OBV_{t-1} + Volume_t$

IF *Today's price change* $(p_t < p_{t-1})$ then $OBV_t = OBV_{t-1} - Volume_t$

The result is a volume-weighted series, which serves to smooth out the erratic nature of the data. In the following formula, the expression in parentheses simply uses the closing prices to produce a value of +1, 0, or −1, which then determines whether today's volume will be added or subtracted from the volume series:

$$OBV_t = OBV_{t-1} + \frac{Close_t - Close_{t-1}}{|Close_t - Close_{t-1}|} \times Volume_t$$

Determining the OBV manually is a simple accumulation process as shown in Table 13.2. On day 2 prices closed higher; therefore, the volume of 30 (assume thousands) is added to the starting volume of zero. On the next day, the price was again higher, and the volume is added to the total. On day 4 the price drops so that day's volume is subtracted from the total. In this example, volume was higher when

[2] Robert W. Colby and Thomas A. Meyers, *The Encyclopedia of Technical Market Indicators* (New York: McGraw-Hill, 2003), is a comprehensive study of most market indicators, including On-Balance Volume and some other techniques in this section.

TABLE 13.2 **Calculating On-Balance Volume**

Day	Closing Price	Daily Volume (in 1000s)	On-Balance Volume
1	310	25	0
2	315	30	30
3	318	27	57
4	316	15	42
5	314	12	30
6	320	28	58

price closed up and lower when prices closed down. This is the ideal pattern in a market with a clear uptrend. Traditionally, the advantage of recording the OBV is in observing when the trend of the prices diverges from the OBV values. The general interpretation of OBV is given in Table 13.3.

Because a volume series has many erratic qualities caused by large variations in volume from day to day, it is most often used with a moving average trend of up to 100 weeks, then identifying a simple volume direction when the OBV value crosses the trend. An upward trend in volume is interpreted as a confirmation of the current price direction, while a downturn in volume can be liquidation or uncertainty. It is intended that the OBV values be used instead of price for making trading decisions.

In Figure 13.3, the OBV is plotted along with the volume at the bottom of the GE chart, covering from December 2010 through April 2011. The pattern of the OBV is similar to the pattern of prices in the top panel even though it is created from volume. The primary difference between the price chart and the OBV line is that the peak in the center is flattening and the OBV does not decline as far. This divergence in the center of the chart, prices moving higher than the OBV, would be interpreted as a divergence in which prices will stop rising.

The spreadsheet code, *TSM OBV*, is available on the Companion Website.

TABLE 13.3 **Interpreting On-Balance Volume**

Price Direction	OBV Direction	Interpretation
Up	Up	Clear uptrend
	Sideways	Moderate uptrend
	Down	Weak uptrend near reversal
Sideways	Up	Accumulation period (bottom)
	Sideways	No determination
	Down	Distribution period (top)
Down	Up	Weak downtrend near reversal
	Sideways	Moderate downtrend
	Down	Clear downtrend

FIGURE 13.3 On-Balance Volume Applied to GE from December 2010 through April 2011. Volume is shown on the left lower scale and the OBV on the right lower scale.

Substituting the OBV for Price in a Moving Average If the OBV systematically improves, then we can use the OBV instead of price to find trend signals. In Figure 13.4, the S&P emini prices are shown in the top panel with a 40-day moving average, and the volume, OBV, and a 40-day moving average of the OBV are in the bottom panel. The corresponding moving average trendlines are equally smooth, but slightly different on the far right where prices rise sooner than the OBV.

It would be necessary to do a comprehensive test on many markets to find out if the OBV produced better trend results than simply using the price. We already know that the S&P and stocks in general are not the best choice for trending; therefore, tests of interest rates would be more interesting. Volume indicators that combine the price move with volume are additional possibilities. An example of a strategy, *TSM OBV Trend*, that applies a trend to a volume indicator can be found on the Companion Website.

FIGURE 13.4 S&P prices are shown with the volume, OBV, and a 40-day trend of the OBV in the bottom panel. Trading signals are derived from the OBV trendline. A corresponding 40-day moving average is shown in the top panel.

Money Flow Index A simple variation of On-Balance Volume uses the average of the high, low, and closing prices instead of only the close. It is called the *Money Flow Index*, and has been compared to the RSI.

$$TP_t = (H_t + L_t + C_t)/3$$

$$\text{If } TP_t > TP_{t-1} \text{ then } MFP_t = MFP_{t-1} + TP_t \times V_t$$

$$\text{If } TP_t < TP_{t-1} \text{ then } MFN_t = MFN_{t-1} + TP_t \times V_t$$

$$MFI_t = 100 - \frac{100}{\left(\dfrac{1 + MFP_t}{MFN_t}\right)}$$

Volume Count Indicator An indicator that closely resembles On-Balance Volume is a running total of the days when volume increases minus the days when volume declines. That is, add 1 to the cumulative value on a day when today's volume is greater than the previous day; otherwise, subtract 1. This *Volume Count Indicator* (VCI) can be written as:

$$VCI_t = VCI_{t-1} + \frac{V_t - V_{t-1}}{|V_t - V_{t-1}|}$$

Volume Accumulator

A variation on Granville's OBV system is Mark Chaiken's *Volume Accumulator* (VA). Instead of assigning all the volume to either the buyers or the sellers, the Volume Accumulator uses a proportional amount of volume corresponding to the relationship of the closing price to the intraday mean price. If prices close at the high or low of the day, all volume is given to the buyers or sellers as in the OBV calculation.[3] If the close is at the midrange, no volume is added. This can be accomplished with the following calculation:

$$VA_t = VA_{t-1} + \left(\frac{Close_t - Low_t}{High_t - Low_t} - 0.50\right) \times 2 \times V_t$$

Accumulation Distribution

Similar to the Volume Accumulator, and also developed by Mark Chaiken, the *Accumulation Distribution* indicator as well as the Intraday Intensity, the Price and Volume Trend, and the Positive and Negative Volume Indexes use a concept that relates to buying and selling pressure. This compares the strength of the close compared to the open divided by the trading range. It is also called *money flow* in some references. In the following formula, the previous close can be substituted for the open if the opening price is not available.

---

[3] Both OBV and the Volume Accumulator are characterized as "momentum" systems. See Chapter 30 for more information on similar techniques.

$$AD_t = AD_{t-1} + \frac{C_t - O_t}{H_t - L_t} \times V_t$$

Intraday Intensity

Intraday Intensity uses the distribution of daily trading range to create a new indicator. If the intraday low is further from the close than the intraday high, in other words, prices close nearer to the high, then the indicator increases in value.

$$II_t = II_{t-1} + \left(\frac{(C_t - L_t) - (H_t - C_t)}{H_t - L_t} \right) \times V_t$$

Price and Volume Trend, the Positive Volume Index, and the Negative Volume Index

The *Price and Volume Trend* (PVT)[4] applies volume to the daily percentage price change, which can be positive or negative. Note that this cannot be used for back-adjusted futures prices, only for cash markets, stock prices, and indexes.

$$VPT_t = VPT_{t-1} + \left(\frac{C_t}{C_{t-1}} - 1 \right) \times V_t$$

There are two variations on the *Positive Volume Index* (PVI) and *Negative Volume Index* (NVI). Both take the approach that a single indicator that adds and subtracts volume based on market direction is not as informative as two separate series that can be viewed at the same time. In the first variation, the direction of the closing price determines whether volume is added to the positive or negative index. In the second variation, higher or lower volume, compared to the previous day, is the basis for adding to the positive or negative index.

Variation 1, the close as the determining factor:

$$\text{If } C_t > C_{t-1} \text{ then } PVI_t = PVI_{t-1} + V_t$$

$$\text{If } C_t < C_{t-1} \text{ then } NVI_t = NVI_{t-1} + V_t$$

Variation 2, the volume as the determining factor:

$$\text{If } V_t > V_{t-1} \text{ then } PVI_t = PVI_{t-1} + \frac{C_t}{C_{t-1}} \times V_t$$

$$\text{If } V_t < V_{t-1} \text{ then } NVI_t = NVI_{t-1} + \frac{C_t}{C_{t-1}} \times V_t$$

---

[4] Dennis D. Peterson, "Positive Volume Index," *Technical Analysis of Stocks & Commodities* (April 2003). Also see Norman G. Fosback, *Stock Market Logic* (The Institute for Economic Research, 1985).

In Norman Fosback's *Stock Market Logic*, the author studied stock trends from 1941 through 1975 based on variation 1 and concluded that:

- If the *PVI* trend is *up* there is a 79% chance that a bull market exists.

- If the *PVI* trend is *down* there is a 67% chance that a bear market exists.

- If the *NVI* trend is *up* there is a 96% chance that a bull market exists.

- If the *NVI* trend is *down* there is a 50% chance that a bear market exists.

In order to find the trend of either the *PVI* or *NVI*, a 6-month (127-day) or 1-year (255-day) moving average was applied to the individual index values.

Aspray's Demand Oscillator

Using direction to separate volume into two series of *Buying Pressure* and *Selling Pressure*, Aspray then nets them into his own *Demand Oscillator*.[5] Note that during a rising market the Selling Pressure has been *divided* by a percentage of the volume, which has been scaled to be greater than 1. The following calculations show the separate steps needed to create Aspray's *Demand Oscillator*:

For rising prices:

$$\left(Buying\ Pressure \right) BP_t = V_t$$

$$\left(Selling\ Pressure \right) SP_t = \frac{V_t}{K \times \dfrac{C_t - C_{t-1}}{C_{t-1}}}$$

For declining prices:

$$BP_t = \frac{V_t}{K \times \dfrac{C_t - C_{t-1}}{C_{t-1}}}$$

$$SP_t = V_t$$

and where

$$K = \frac{3 \times C_t}{\left[\sum_{i=t-9}^{t} \left(\max\left(H_t, H_{t-1} \right) - \min\left(L_t, L_{t-1} \right) \right) \right] / 10}$$

and

$$Demand\ Oscillator_t = BP_t - SP_t$$

K is a volatility scaling factor that is 3 times the closing price divided by the 10-day moving average of the maximum 2-day high-low combined range, and has a value likely

[5] Thomas Aspray, "Fine-Tuning the Demand Index," *Technical Analysis of Stocks & Commodities* (June 1986), and "Demand Oscillator Momentum," *Technical Analysis of Stocks & Commodities* (September 1989).

to be well over 100. For example, if the S&P is trading at 1,000 and the average volatility is 15 full points (which is very high for a 10-day average), then $K = 3000/15 = 200$.

Tick Volume Indicator

In a manner similar to Wilder's RSI, Blau double-smoothes the tick volume as a way of confirming price direction. The *TickVolume Indicator*, seen in Figure 13.5, is calculated as

$$TVI(r,s) = \frac{100 \times DEMA(upticks, r, s) - DEMA(downsticks, r, s)}{DEMA(upticks, r, s) + DEMA(downsticks, r, s)}$$

TVI ranges from −100 to +100 and *DEMA* (Double Exponential Moving Average) is the double smoothing of the downticks or upticks. The exponential smoothing is first calculated over *r* bars, and the result of that smoothing is again smoothed over the past *s* bars. More about this double-smoothing technique can be found in Chapter 28. This technique differs from Blau's price smoothing because it does not first create a momentum series; therefore, the *TVI* will be lagged slightly less than half the sum of the two calculation periods.

Volume-Weighted MACD

The MACD is based on the difference between two moving averages (see Chapter 30). To add volume, the closing prices for each day are multiplied by the corresponding volume, and each moving average is normalized by the average volume over the same period. The recommended calculation periods are 12 and 26 days, the standard

FIGURE 13.5 Blau's Tick Volume Indicator.

Source: William Blau, *Momentum, Direction, and Divergence* (New York: John Wiley & Sons, 1995), 45.

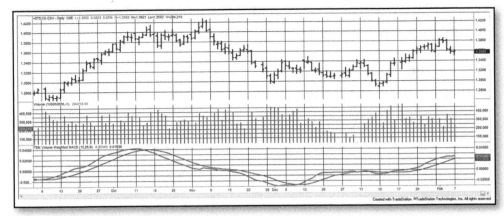

FIGURE 13.6 Volume-Weighted MACD Applied to Euro Currency Futures.

MACD values. A signal line, also the same as MACD, is the exponentially smoothed VWMACD line using a 0.20 smoothing constant, the equivalent of about 9 days.

$$VWMACD_t = \left(\frac{\sum_{t=t-12+1}^{t} C_i \times V_i}{\sum_{i=t-12+1}^{t} V_i} \right) - \left(\frac{\sum_{t=t-26+1}^{t} C_i \times V_i}{\sum_{i=t-26+1}^{t} V_i} \right)$$

Figure 13.6 uses a program *TSM Volume Weighted MACD*, available on the Companion Website, to plot the VWMACD for euro currency futures, which appears in the bottom panel. The heavier line is the VWMACD, and the thinner, smoother line is the signal. As with the MACD, the rules are to enter a new long position when the VWMACD crosses above the signal line, and the opposite for shorts. When compared to the MACD, this variation appears to make only small changes, yet a slight improvement in timing can be a great advantage in trading.

Variably Weighted Moving Average Using Volume

A unique approach taken by Christian Fries[6] uses the relationship between the number of outstanding shares, the current price, and the volume of the next period or the next trade, to create an *Elastic Volume-Weighted Moving Average (eVWMA)*. Using the difference between the number of outstanding shares and the number of shares being traded he creates a weighting factor. That weighting factor causes the previous trend value to have more importance when fewer shares are traded and less weight when relatively more shares are traded. The net effect is that the weighted average is more responsive to change when relatively more shares are traded.

$$eVWMA_t = \frac{(OS - V_t) \times eVWMA_{t-1} + V_t \times C_t}{OS}$$

where OS = the number of outstanding shares.

[6] Christian P. Fries, "Elastic Moving Averages," *Technical Analysis of Stocks & Commodities* (June 2001).

FIGURE 13.7 Elastic Volume-Weighted Moving Average Applied to Merck (MRK) Compared with a 0.10 Exponential Smoothing.

Using Merck (MRK) as an example, the total outstanding shares was set to 200 million, based on an observed maximum daily volume of approximately 150 million. By keeping the outstanding shares slightly bigger than the maximum volume, the indicator will vary across a wider range and show more of its characteristics. Figure 13.7 compares the eVWMA to a standard exponential smoothing of 0.10. The results are very similar although the eVWMA tracks closer to the price in the center of the chart.

Substituting Open Interest for Volume Using Futures

Futures volume can create very different results from volume for stocks. The markets themselves—energy, gold, and even interest rates—have been in an uptrend for years. This causes many of the indicators, especially OBV, to move steadily higher, while it appears to oscillate when applied to stocks over the past 10 years.

It has already been mentioned that futures volume comes in two parts, contract volume and total volume. Contract volume begins at zero, increases as the contract moves from deferred (many months away from delivery) to the nearby delivery, then back to zero as the contract expires. Open interest follows a similar pattern. To avoid this pattern, total volume is used instead of contract volume. In the same way, futures data shows contract open interest and total open interest. That data varies in the same pattern as volume; however, open interest is much more stable than volume. Similar to volume, open interest increases as market activity increases; therefore, it reflects the same fundamentals.

Total open interest can be a preferable substitute for volume in many of the indicators covered in the previous sections. It should be remembered that open interest, as well as volume, is usually available on downloaded data one day late. These numbers could be manually downloaded from Bloomberg, but it is safer to use them as a longer-term indicator, which best suits their purpose.

A spreadsheet example of applying OBV to S&P futures, using both total volume and total open interest, is available on the Companion Website as *TSM OBV*.

VWAP

As a note, order executions can be placed as a *VWAP*, a *volume-weighted average price*. For larger positions, this would return an average price representing how actively the market traded at different levels throughout the day. It is most convenient for hedge funds that do not want to force prices higher by placing an excessively large buy order at one point during the day, or even on the close. Equally spaced orders that ignore liquidity use *TWAP*, a *time-weighted average price*.

■ Breadth Indicators

Market breadth measures the imbalance between the number of advancing and declining stocks on a given day. It is the percentage of rising stocks to the total number of stocks traded. In general, more advancing issues should add confidence to an upwards price move in the same way that volume confirms price. A net increase in the S&P 500 while more issues are declining should generate concern that the upwards move is poorly supported.

The information for advances and declines is published along with stock prices each day. You may also want the volume of advancing issues and the volume of declining issues. Both of these values can be found in the *Wall Street Journal* under "Trading Activity." In this section, the CSI data series, UVDV, will be used. In addition, we will look at the new highs and new lows using CSI data MKST, to see if those numbers add value to price analysis.

To interpret the CSI data files, use the following guide. The normal field designation is in the heading and the actual content is below.

Series	Date	Open	High	Low	Close	Volume	OpInt
UVDV	Date	Total traded	Advanced	Declined	Unchanged	Up Volume	Down Volume
MKST	Date	Total traded	Advanced	Declined	Unchanged	52-Week Highs	52-Week Lows

Market breadth indicators are typically used as a confirmation of price direction. The table below shows that the interpretation of market breadth is the same as the relationship between volume and price.

Market Breadth	Price	Interpretation
Rising	Rising	Breadth confirms price rise
Falling	Falling	Breadth confirms price drop
Falling	Rising	Breadth does not confirm price rise
Rising	Falling	Breadth does not confirm price drop

The measurement of breadth must relate to what you are trading. If 75% of the stocks in the Dow rise, the S&P Small Cap Index can still be lackluster or declining. Investors shift from small-cap stocks to the S&P 500 and then to the Dow when they are looking for safety. The breadth of the overall market, or the breadth of large caps, is not enough to confirm an upwards trend in the small caps.

It is worth noting that Gerald Appel, a well-known market analyst and technician, points out that, when using market breadth, it is best if it is equally weighted (i.e., a simple count).

Separating Advancing from Declining Volume

The most basic of all techniques for determining market breadth is the *Advance-Decline Index*, which creates a new series by adding the net of the number of advancing and declining stocks each day. Unchanged issues are ignored.

$$Advance\text{-}Decline\ Oscillator_t = Advances_t - Declines_t$$

$$Advance\text{-}Decline\ Index_t = Advance\text{-}Decline\ Index_{t-1} - Advances_t - Declines_t$$

In some of the techniques that follow, only the oscillator, or single-period calculation, may be shown. An index can be created by accumulating these values.

Sibbett's Demand Index

One method that smoothes volume by using the total activity of the past 10 days is James Sibbett's *Demand Index*. The technique bears a resemblance to the approach used in Wilder's RSI. It can be used as an oscillator with individual daily values or accumulated into an index. Where $n = 10$, the individual days are calculated as the sum of the upside volume divided by the sum of the downside volume:

$$Demand\ Index_t = \frac{\sum_{i=t-n+1}^{t} upside\ volume_i}{\sum_{i=t-n+1}^{t} downside\ volu_t}$$

The values for upside and downside volume can also be found in the *Wall Street Journal* under the heading "Trading Activity." Arthur Merrill, another well-known stock analyst, has suggested using $n = 5$.

Bolton-Tremblay

Introducing the net advancing stocks compared to the number of stocks that were unchanged, the Bolton-Tremblay approach also includes a form of geometric weighting of the results. In the following calculation, BT is the daily Bolton-Tremblay value, and BTI is the index resulting from accumulating the individual daily values.

$$BT_t = \frac{Advancing_t - Declining_t}{Unchanged_t}$$

$$\text{If } BT_t > 0 \text{ then } BTI_t = BTI_{t-1} + \sqrt{BT_t}$$

$$\text{If } BT_t < 0 \text{ then } BTI_t = BTI_{t-1} - \sqrt{BT_t}$$

The Bolton-Tremblay calculation will have large spikes on days when the advancing or declining breadth is very strong, which make the unchanged number of stocks in the denominator very small.

Schultz

Schultz chose to look at the advancing stocks only as a percentage of the total stocks, which puts the results in the convenient range of 0 to 100:

$$Schultz\ A\ /\ T_t = \frac{Advancing_t}{Total\ stocks_t}$$

McClellan Oscillator

The *McClellan Oscillator* starts with the net advances (NA) and then creates an oscillator by subtracting two smoothed trends, 19 and 39 days, based on the net advances, in a manner similar to the MACD. Converting the 19- and 39-day calculation periods to smoothing constants using $2/(n+1)$ we (conveniently) get $s_1 = 0.10$ and $s_2 = 0.05$.

$$NA_t = Advances_t - Declines_t$$

$$E1_t = E1_{t-1} + s_1 \times \left(NA_t - E1_{t-1}\right)$$

$$E2_t = E2_{t-1} + s_2 \times \left(NA_t - E2_{t-1}\right)$$

$$McClellan\ Oscillator_t = E1_t - E2_t$$

Figure 13.8 compares Sibbett's Demand Index with the more complicated McClellan Oscillator. S&P futures prices are in the top panel, the Demand Index

FIGURE 13.8 S&P Futures (Top Panel), Sibbett's Demand Index (Second Panel), the Up/Down Volume (Third Panel), and the McClellan Oscillator (Bottom Panel).

in the second panel, the up and down volume in the third panel, and the McClellan Oscillator at the bottom. The scales of the two indicators are very different. The Demand Index is a ratio; therefore, it varies above and below 1.0, and reflects the upside/downside volume over a rolling 10-day period. The McClellan Oscillator uses a longer calculation period and smoothes even further using exponential smoothing.

Both indicators stay slightly above neutral during the long upward move, but the most interesting feature would be the extreme highs and lows, which are clearer in the McClellan Oscillator, corresponding nicely to two price lows and one peak. The high point that ended the long upwards move shows as divergence in the two indicators, a pattern that is not as easy to identify at the time, but can be very useful.

Upside/Downside Ratio

A simple *Upside/Downside Ratio* (UDR) is similar to Sibbett's Demand Index but is not smoothed. With this ratio, it is easier to see the asymmetry of the calculation. When the declining volume is very low, for example only 20% of the total volume, the UDR will have a value of 4.0. In contrast, if the advancing volume is low (20% of the declining volume), the ratio is 0.20. There is no upside limit when stocks are advancing but the downside ratio is limited to the range between 0 and 1. This is a familiar pattern for advancing and declining prices expressed as a percentage. High values of the UDR are expected to precede a bull market period.

$$UDR_t = \frac{Advancing\,Volume_t}{Declining\,Volume_t}$$

Arms Index (TRIN)

Richard Arms explains the relationship between the number of advancing and declining stocks, and the up and down volume, in the *Arms Index*, more popularly known as *TRIN*, the *Trader's Index*. It divides the ratio of the number of advancing and declining stocks by the ratio of the volume of the advancing and declining stocks.

$$TRIN_t = \frac{Advancing\,stocks_t\,/Declining\,stocks_t}{Advancing\,volume_t\,/}$$

Thrust Oscillator

Tushar Chande's *Thrust Oscillator* (TO) uses the same values as *TRIN* but creates a bullish oscillator by multiplying the number of advancing stocks by the volume of the advancing stocks and subtracting the comparable declining values, then dividing by the sum of the two.

$$TO_t = 100 \times \frac{Adv\,stocks_t \times Vol\,of\,adv\,stocks_t - Decl\,stocks_t \times Vol\,of\,decl\,stocks_t}{Adv\,stocks_t \times Vol\,of\,adv\,stocks_t + Decl\,stocks_t \times V}$$

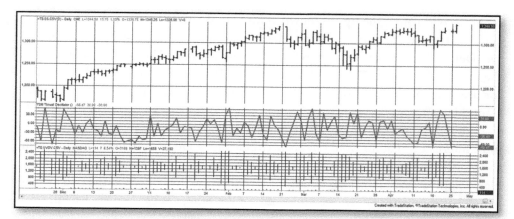

FIGURE 13.9 The Thrust Oscillator (Second Panel) Shown with S&P Futures (Top Panel).

The Thrust Oscillator is used as an overbought/oversold indicator to complement another strategy that would decide on the major direction of the market. Values of ±30 may be used to identify overbought and oversold levels, respectively. Whenever an indicator is not smoothed, the extremes become the most interest points of action.

Figure 13.9 shows the Thrust Oscillator (second panel) along with S&P futures (top panel). The bands of ±30 give short-term indications of overbought and oversold days and occur more frequently during a sideways price move. For the 3-month period when the S&P was steadily rising, the indicator gave many more buy signals (penetration of the bottom band) than sell signals, a good outcome.

When studying both the Arms Index (TRIN) and the Thrust Oscillator (TO) it would seem sensible to express all the component values as percentages of the whole. That is, the number of advancing and declining stocks should each be divided by the total number of stocks, and the volume of the advancing and declining stocks should each be divided by the total volume of all shares traded. This would make those days with low relative volume less important. In the current calculations, inactive days might produce highly distorted values.

New Highs and Lows

There is very little literature on the use of the number of new highs and lows that occur daily, yet the data are available and can be used in ways similar to market breadth. The most obvious way to represent this data is by creating a *High-Low Index* (HLX),

$$HLX_t = HLX_{t-1} + NH_t - NL_t$$

where *NH* are new 52-week highs and *NL* are new 52-week lows. Another approach would be a simple ratio of the new highs compared to the combined new highs and lows, over the past *n* days,

$$HLR_t = \frac{\sum_{i=t-n+1}^{t} NH_i}{\sum_{i=t-n+1}^{t} (NH_i + NL_i)}$$

FIGURE 13.10 S&P Futures (Top Panel) Shown with the High-Low Ratio (HLR) in the Second Panel, and the High-Low Data at the Bottom.

Gerry Appel[7] uses this *High-Low Ratio*, smoothed over 10 days, and generates a buy signal when the ratio crosses above a threshold of, for example, 0.80 or 0.90, and a sell signal when it crosses back below that level. In Figure 13.10, the S&P futures are shown with the HLR in the middle panel, and the high-low data in the bottom panel. The top line of the middle panel is 0.90 and might serve as a threshold to extract high-momentum trades during the steady uptrend. It may also be useful to create a fast smoothing of the HLR to use as a signal line, in the same manner as MACD, which would avoid the need for a strict threshold entry and exit value.

Baskets of New Highs and Lows

Another method that will be discussed in more detail in Level III, Chapter 2 is buying a basket of stocks making new highs and selling a basket of stocks making new lows. Naturally, this assumes that each stock making a new high will sustain that direction because there has been some fundamental change in its earnings or structure that the market sees as positive. Similarly, those stocks making new 52-week lows have negative fundamental changes. To avoid unnecessary risk, the long basket and short basket must have the same volatility.

Is One Volume or Breadth Indicator Better than Another?

The final test of a successful indicator is whether it adds value to your trading decisions. This can be determined by programming the indicator into a strategy and testing the rules over a reasonable historic time period. Before doing that, we should decide what an increase or decrease in volume or breadth is telling us, and how we will use that information for trading. Volume and breadth indicators are

---

[7] Gerald Appel, *Power Tools for Active Traders* (Upper Saddle River, NJ: Financial Times Prentice Hall, 2005), 126.

more difficult than those that use price because the values have greater variance. That makes translating a sound concept into a profitable strategy more difficult. If performance testing does not confirm our expectations, then the indicator needs to be applied differently. There seems no doubt that volume and breadth data are telling us something, and uncovering those messages would improve our trading performance.

Looking at the previous selection of indicators, we see that small net changes in price can result in all volume being designated to one market direction. This is the case with Granville's On-Balance Volume and in the Bolton-Tremblay method. Is it reasonable to add all volume to the accumulated index if the S&P gained only a fraction of one point? On a single day this may seem to be arbitrary, but just as in many basic systems, over a long period of time the net effect of this decision is sound.

The changes made by Mark Chaiken, which take a percentage of volume based on the relative close of prices within the daily range, seem very sensible and avoid the all-or-nothing technique used in On-Balance Volume. Sibbett's Demand Index, by using the sum of 10 days' volume, avoids this problem completely and smoothes out results, a situation often needed when using the highly variable values of volume and breadth.

By seeing these indicators close together, they appear to be a collection of minor manipulation of data. Traditional technicians still advocate interpretation using trend lines, divergence, or new highs and lows. Instead of having to interpret only the difficult movements of prices, they have added an equally difficult series of volume or breadth. While it is clear that volume and breadth contribute to the understanding of a price move, you must first be able to test whether you can use that information profitably. To do that, some fully systematic method is needed to insure that any approach can be implemented and validated.

Breadth as a Countertrend Indicator

All the literature favors using breadth to confirm direction, but Connors argues the opposite.[8] He trades the advance/decline (AD) ratio as follows:

Sell the index when $AD > 2.0$
Buy the index when $AD < 0.50$
Exit the trade after 5 days unless a reverse signal occurs

Using the series UVDV-I or MKST-I defined earlier in this section, we added the SPX in column 2, then created the advance/decline ratio. The buy and sell rules were applied, but because there were very frequent signals, all trades were held until an opposite signal occurred, rather than for 5 days. The total PL (in percent) is shown in Figure 13.11. Complete calculations can be found in the Excel spreadsheet, *TSM MKST-I Market Breadth*, on the Companion Website.

---

[8] Larry Connors, "Fade the Breadth," *Futures* (January 2005).

FIGURE 13.11   Total PL Using the AD Ratio as a Countertrend Signal.

Interpreting Volume and Breadth Systematically

Most systematic approaches to volume apply a long-term smoothing method to the data and then identify trend changes to confirm price direction. This can be implemented with any of the accumulation indexes, but not with single-day momentum or oscillator values. For the oscillators, most analysts have taken the approach that high volume confirms a new price direction; extreme volume, on the other hand, is more likely to be a reversal signal. If volume and price peaks do not occur at the same time, a volume peak should precede a trend change. A decline in volume has also been used to confirm direction, but it is more likely to indicate that prices have reached equilibrium, and that a further advance or decline requires additional confirmation.

Identifying a Volume Spike

A *volume spike* is one of the clearest and best examples of useful volume information. In its most obvious form, a volume spike is a day when the volume is at least twice that of other days over a period generally longer than one month, most likely longer than three months. Volume spikes may come in clusters due to an unstable political or economic situation; however, it is normally associated with the end of a significant price move.

Figure 13.12 shows 12 years of Microsoft prices with volume along the bottom. There are a few dozen times when volume spikes. Just after 2000 there is a cluster of spikes that are associated with the end of the tech bubble, a price drop of 50% in just a few weeks. Most of the spikes on the chart fall on days with large price moves and precede reversals. While the reversals are not always large, the volatility spike marks the end of the current move.

A simple spike can be measured as exceeding a threshold, T, where T is a multiple of the average volume, $AV = average\ (volume, n)$, over the recent n days. Then a volume spike exists if today's volume is greater than the average volume on the previous day times its multiplier, $V_t > T \times AV_{t-1}$.

Most cases are not as clear as a 1-day spike following much lower volume. More likely, volume has increased significantly over the past two or three days, culminating

FIGURE 13.12 Microsoft Prices with Volume Along the Bottom.

in a spike that is much higher than the average volume, but may only be 25% higher than the previous day. The solution to this is to lag the average volume so that it does not reflect the increasing volume of the recent few days.

We will make the assumption that volume resulting in a spike takes no longer than three days to develop. We can safely say that the average volume, lagged five days, should not reflect the recent rise in volume. Then a volume spike would be identified when

$$V_t > \frac{\sum_{i=t-n-5}^{t-5} V_i}{n}$$

The right part of this formula is the average volume over n days beginning $t - n - 5$ days ago and ending $t - 5$ days ago. If t is today, then the average volume stops five days ago; therefore, it is not influenced by recent volume data.

Volume spikes are not as extreme when dealing with futures markets and indexes. In Figure 13.13 NASDAQ futures are shown with total (all contracts) volume for a period in May 2010. Higher volume days correspond to two cases where prices

FIGURE 13.13 NASDAQ Prices and Volume Show Both High and Low Volume Associated with Price Reversals.

FIGURE 13.14 Crude Oil Futures (Back-Adjusted), with Total Volume Shown as a Line.

reversed from lows, and the peak in the center of the chart is associated with low volume. Both situations offer an opportunity to improve trading.

In the crude oil chart, Figure 13.14, the spikes in volume can be seen as frequently occurring at price reversal points, while lower volume may be indicative of the continued price direction. Although there are no comprehensive tests available to confirm these observations, high volume seems to precede a price reversal, even if it lasts only one day.

Moving Average Approaches

Not all analysts agree that higher volume is a reversal signal. A straightforward way of using higher volume to confirm a trend is to calculate a 10-day moving average of the volume as a complement to a 20-day trend position.[9] By simply requiring the current volume to be greater than the average volume over those past 10 days, you introduce the idea of greater participation associated with the new trend. An additional important benefit is that this volume condition acts as a filter, eliminating a substantial number of trades. If the net returns are the same, the volume-filtered approach is far better because you are out of the market more, reducing your risk and not reversing your position every time there is a new signal. That improves liquidity.

A similar method was proposed by Waxenberg.[10] A 10-day moving average of the volume is calculated as the normal level, and a change in trend must be confirmed by a 20% increase in volume above this norm. (The 20% threshold acts as an additional smoothing filter, but may be replaced by a longer trend and smaller threshold.) Extremes in a price move can be found at points that exceed approximately a 40% volume increase. Applied to the stock market, Waxenberg used the extreme volumes to indicate the end of a sell-off. To add more flexibility over longer test periods, and to adapt more quickly to volatility changes, Bollinger bands (based on 2 standard deviations, or 95% probability) can be substituted for the fixed percentage thresholds.

---

[9] Alex Saitta, "A Price and Volume-Based System," *Technical Analysis of Stocks & Commodities* (March 1996).

[10] Howard K. Waxenberg, "Technical Analysis of Volume," *Technical Analysis of Stocks & Commodities* (March 1986).

Alternately, using 13 days of volume, subtract the total down volume from the total up volume. A plot of the results will serve as a momentum indicator from which overbought and oversold levels can be identified. If these values are unstable due to lack of liquidity, they may be smoothed using a short-term moving average.

Advance-Decline System

Advance and decline values, as with most volume figures, can be more useful if they are smoothed. By combining peak values of the net of smoothed advancing and declining shares with a directional move in price, Connors and Hayward have created a basic system structure that they named CHADTP[11] (*Connors-Hayward Advance-Decline Trading Patterns*). This system tries to identify reversal patterns by applying the following steps:

1. Add the past 5 days of advancing issues on the New York Stock Exchange.
2. Add the past 5 days of declining issues on the New York Stock Exchange.
3. Subtract the 5-day sum of declining issues (Step 2) from the advancing issues (Step 1).
4. Divide by 5 to get the average daily value.

$$CHADTP = (Sum(AdvancingNYSE, 5) - Sum(DecliningNYSE, 5)) / 5$$

To trade using this oscillator, Connors and Hayward have determined that ±400 are the extreme levels where the values have been overbought and oversold. Based on this, we can apply the following rules to the S&P futures:

1. *Sell short* when CHADTP $> +400$ and the S&P futures trade 10 basis points below the low of the previous day; *buy* when CHADTP < -400 and the S&P futures trade 10 basis points above the high of the previous day.
2. Note that the oscillator does not have to exceed its recent extremes on the day of the buy or sell signal.
3. Timing is best if the signal occurs at the same time as a newspaper commentary indicating "depressed volume," or volume significantly below the 3-month average, which is seen as an excess of cash waiting to enter the market.

This system targets returns over a 5- to 7-day period. A drop in the oscillator, which results in values in the midrange, is an opportunity to exit. A standard price oscillator can be constructed to generate overbought and oversold signals within this time frame. An opposite entry signal would reverse the position.

We should be aware that this method was developed in 1995 when the S&P was lower and less volatile. As of 2011, the DJIA is about four times its 1995 value, while the S&P is only about one-third higher. However, the markets are more volatile now. A change of 10 basis points (0.10%) in the S&P is about 1.30 points, which is likely

---

[11] Laurence A. Connors and Blake E. Hayward, *Investment Secrets of a Hedge Fund Manager* (Chicago: Probus, 1995).

to happen every day. Raising the threshold to 50 or 100 basis points may make it easier to assess the value of this method.

Breadth as a Countertrend Indicator

Equities have a tendency to be mean reverting because they have more noise than most other sectors. That seems to hold true for market breadth. Larry Connors has shown that more declining stocks is an excellent leading indicator of a stock market advance.[12]

- If declining NYSE stocks are greater than advancing NYSE stocks for at least three days in a row, then the S&P averaged a gain of 0.50% the following week.

- If declining NASDAQ stocks are greater than advancing NASDAQ stocks for at least two days in a row, then the NASDAQ 100 index gained an average of 0.80% the next week.

- If declining NYSE stocks were at least twice the NYSE advancing stocks, then the S&P gained an average of 0.60% the following week.

In addition, when the opposite occurred, all three situations showed essentially no gain in the respective index during the following week. The observation period was 1996–2003, which contained extreme bull and bear markets.

■ An Integrated Probability Model

If there is a noticeable relationship between price, volume, and open interest (or market breadth), then a probability model can be constructed to test its importance.[13] To do this it is necessary to construct a 1-day-ahead forecast using a simple linear regression model and then backtest weighting factors for each element. Because of powerful software products, this has become a very manageable process. Using TradeStation's *EasyLanguage*, each 1-day-ahead forecast is determined using the previous n days:

Price forecast:	$Pf = Price + LinearRegSlope(close, n)$
Volume forecast:	$Vf = Volume + LinearRegSlope(volume, n)$
Open interest forecast:	$Of = Opint + LinearRegSlope(opint, n)$
On-Balance Volume forecast:	$OBVf = OBV + LinearRegSlope(OBV, n)$

The function *LinearRegSlope* returns the 1-period increase or decrease in the input value based on a straight-line fit of the past n days. That value can be added to the current price, volume, open interest, or On-Balance Volume to get the 1-day-ahead forecast. The calculation period n can be selected by subtracting the actual next-day value from the forecast and creating an error series that can be measured using a

---

[12] Larry Connors, "Fade the Breadth," *Futures* (January 2005).
[13] Based on the May 1995 "CSI Technical Journal," Commodity Systems Inc., Boca Raton, Florida.

standard deviation. The number of days, n, that generates the smallest standard deviation is the best forecast period. It is possible that the optimal forecast period will differ for each of the four items above but a robust solution would seem to be the one period that minimized the errors across all the components. These and other testing issues are thoroughly discussed in Level III, Chapter 10.

Having found the four 1-day-ahead forecasts, an index can be created that gives one weight w_1 to the price forecast and the remaining weights, $1 - w_1$, to a combination of the other three factors. This assumes that price is the most important predictor of price. Then

$$Forecast\ index = w_1 Pf + (1 - w_1) \times (w_2 Vf + w_3 Of + w_4 OBVf)$$

This formula can be backtested for values of w_1, w_2, w_3, and w_4 where $\sum w = 1$. The final index can be used instead of price for determining the trend. It will still require a moving average, or some smoothed line, to signal new uptrends and downtrends; however, the results, if successful, should be more reliable than using only price.

One advantage of testing the weighting factors is that, if one of the four elements is not helpful in predicting a trend, the weighting factor should be near zero. Another approach, that does not cluster the nonprice data together, would be to treat each item separately in the classic form:

$$Forecast\ index = w_1 Pf + w_2 Vf + w_3 Of + w_4 OBVf$$

■ Intraday Volume Patterns

Identifying increases and decreases in volume during the trading day must consider the patterns caused by the flow of orders during the day and the way traders enter orders. During the past five years, there has been a great improvement in timely reporting of intraday volume for both stocks and futures markets. Services such as Bloomberg have continually updated volume for nearly all markets. Prior to this, only tick volume was the practical alternative. Tick volume represents the number of price changes that occurred during any time interval. It turns out that the frequency of price changes is directly related to the actual volume traded. If you purchase intraday data from CQG, it will have tick volume in each price bar.

Time Stamps

One point to note is that CQG time stamps each bar at the beginning of the interval. It is because they accumulate the data as it occurs, so that 5-minute bars that are stamped 10:00, 10:05, and 10:10 have the data from 10:00:00 through 10:04:59, 10:05 through 10:09:59, and 10:10:00 through 10:14:59, respectively. For many applications, users may want to shift those times to show the end of the bar rather than the beginning. That way, if you are matching the time of the bar with the closing time of the session, those times will match. Otherwise, if the closing time is 4 p.m., or 16:00, the last 5-minute bar will be stamped 15:55. Also note that because these bars are time stamped at the beginning, the last bar of the day will have only the trading that occurred in the last 1 minute of the session. For example, the U.S. bond chart has the last interval posted at 14:00, the Chicago closing time. All trading starting at 14:00 will be captured, which is only the last minute, yet it shows very high volume. You may want to combine the last bar with the previous bar.

Intraday Patterns

Figure 13.15 shows the intraday tick volume patterns for four futures markets, crude oil, the German DAX, NASDAQ, and U.S. 30-year bonds. The charts represent the average number of price changes in each 15-minute interval for the years 1995 through 2005, for the nearest contract to delivery. Each market has a somewhat different pattern.

Before Europe became a viable, accessible market, intraday volume patterns tended to have a very symmetric U-shaped pattern, with the highest volume at the open and close. The bottom of the U always came at midday when traders took their lunch break. This can still be seen in the NASDAQ chart, Figure 13.15c. As European markets increased in volume the patterns changed so that volume was greatest while both the United States and Europe were open, then declined as European traders ended their business day. In Figure 13.15b, the DAX shows a sharp drop from 17:30, then one strong bar on the close at 18:00 (6 pm). Soon after 2005, the Eurex extended hours to match the U.S. trading sessions, so the DAX now trades until 20:00, the close of the U.S. equity index markets. We should expect the U-shaped pattern in the late session to be extended to 20:00.

Crude oil shows two U-shaped patterns, the first for the primary session, originally called the *pit session*, and the second for the evening session. Now crude trades 24 hours, although we should always expect this same volume pattern bounded by normal daily business hours in the country where the product is traded. Then the CME Nikkei contract will have very low volume and an unclear pattern because we trade it during our business hours, while Japanese business sleeps.

It should not be surprising to see the extreme clustering at both ends of the trading day. Orders enter the market early in reaction to news and events that occurred after the close of the previous day's trading. Many analysts based trading decisions on the previous day's data but perform their calculations and analyses after the close. The end of day is active due to liquidation of the positions of day traders who do not want overnight risk. Orders that allow you to specify that you want to be filled at the settlement have reduced the slippage and increased the benefit of trading on the close.

Relative Changes in Volume

Whether using actual or tick volume, decisions made using, for example, 15-minute volume patterns should compare each 15 minutes of the current day with the same 15 minutes of the prior day or with the average of that 15-minute interval over some range of days. While it may be sensible to use increasing intraday volume as a condition for entering a new trade, if the trade signal is in the second half of the day,

FIGURE 13.15 Intraday, 15-Minute Tick Volume Patterns, 1995 to 2005.

then each interval generally increases in volume; therefore, the condition is always true. If the trading signals were in the morning, the condition would always be false.

In order to use intraday volume correctly, you must consider different cases:

1. The volume of the opening bar must be compared to the volume of the same bar on the previous day, or the average volume of that bar on the past *n* days.
2. The second bar can then show volume as a percentage of the first bar. By keeping a history of this percentage value, we then will know if today's second bar is relatively stronger or weaker than the average.
3. We can track the relative strength or weakness of every bar compared to the opening bar and compared to the average bar of the same time.

Using this information, it is possible to anticipate a stronger or weaker close for the day. It is also generally true that an open on higher volume will indicate higher volume throughout the day. We could then also expect higher volatility. Days with significantly lower volume would be associated with less volatility and less directional movement.

■ Filtering Low Volume

Minutes, hours, or even days that have little market activity are likely to be associated with uncertain price direction. If the British pound moves $0.50 in the mid afternoon of the U.S. market, we know that volume is normally light because the London and European markets are closed. The intention of a volume indicator is to identify positive moves in volume that can be used as a confirmation of price direction. Eliminating those days with low volume, or with marginal price moves, may increase the dependability of the volume indicator.

Removing Low-Volume Periods

Including low-volume periods in a volume index may make the index movements unreliable. There is a similar situation in statistics, where a number of statistical values are slightly skewed to one side. Each value on its own is not noticeably important, but collectively they cause a bias. Some analysts believe that the collective weight creates significance, while others favor ignoring values that are so small they are insignificant and perhaps confusing.

The decision to remove low volume days, or intervals, means that a series of low volume days that results in a collective change will be ignored. If you have decided that removing those days makes sense, then measure the daily or intraday volume against a threshold created using the average volume minus one or two standard deviations of the volume. Using a 1 standard deviation filter will remove the lowest 16% of the days; a 2 standard deviation filter removes 32% of the days.

This type of filter is best applied to a volume index, such as On-Balance Volume. For example, we find that the average volume on the New York Stock Exchange is 1.5 billion shares, and 1 standard deviation of the volume is 0.25 billion shares. We decide that the volume filter is 2 standard deviations; therefore, any day with volume below 1.0 billion shares will be ignored. Applying this to On-Balance Volume, using TradeStation code:

```
Volumethreshold = average(volume, n) - volumefilter*stddev(volume, n)
  If volume < volumethreshold then VFOBV = VFOBV[1]
    else VFOBV = VFOBV + (close - close[1])/
        absvalue(close - close[1])) + volume;
```

we would effectively ignore all days, leaving the OBV unchanged, when the volume was below the threshold.

Removing Volume Associated with Small Price Moves

If you agree with the concept of removing days with low volume, then there is the similar case of very small price moves. Indicators such as On-Balance Volume post all volume as either a positive or negative contribution to the index, based on the direction of prices on that day. It is fair to question the validity of posting all volume to the upside when the S&P 500 closed up a minimum move of 25 basis points (+0.25) or the Dow closed up 1 point. It could just as easily have closed down that amount. In a manner similar to filtering low-volume, periods in which prices moved very little may be eliminated by using a standard deviation of the price changes as a filter. Days that are within ± 0.10 or ± 0.25 standard deviations of the average would be ignored. The *Price-Filtered On-Balance Volume*, *PFOBV*, would then be found using the code:

```
pricethreshold = average(price - price[1], n) +
    f*stddev(price - price[1], n)
if absvalue(price - price[1]) < price threshold then PFOBV = PFOBV[1]
    else PFOBV = PFOBV[1] + ((close - close[1])/
        (absvalue(close - close[1])) * volume
```

where n = the number of periods in both the average and standard deviation

       f = the number of standard deviations used to filter minimum volume

Note that, in the case of a minimum price threshold, the rules look at price change, which can be positive or negative. For a volume threshold, there is only a one-sided test using the value of volume.

◼ Market Facilitation Index

In weighing the likelihood that prices are indicating a direction, rather than a false start, the tick volume compared to the price range for the same period, called the *Market Facilitation Index*,[14] can measure the willingness of the market to move the price. This concept is interesting because it is not clear that high volume results in a large price move, although high volume appears to set up the conditions for high

---

[14] Bill Williams, *Trading Chaos* (New York: John Wiley & Sons, 1995).

volatility. If the Market Facilitation Index increases, then the market is willing to move the price; therefore trading that benefits from higher volatility should improve.

$$Market\ Facilitation\ Index_t = \frac{Trading\ range_t}{Volume_t} = \frac{H_t - L_t}{V_t}$$

The results of combining the change in tick volume and the Market Facilitation Index are interpreted as:

Tick Volume	Market Facilitation Index	Interpretation
Up	Up	Confirmation of direction
Down	Down	False direction, do not take trade
Down	Up	Poor entry timing, approach with caution
Up	Down	Potential new trend, end of old trend

CHAPTER 14

A Stock Market Model

From Ned Davis, *Being Right or Making Money*, 3rd edition (Hoboken, New Jersey: John Wiley & Sons, 2014), Chapter 3.
Loren Flath

■ A Stock Market Model

I can almost hear Ned telling his partner, Eddie Mendel, at the dawn of Ned Davis Research back in 1979, that he would need only one programmer for one year. For over a decade, Ned had been charting his favorite indicators by hand, and the work was becoming overwhelming. There were many more indicators to chart and not enough time in the day to do so. And as Ned has pointed out, he not only needed better charting, but more importantly, he needed to replace subjective trading decisions with a more objective approach. So he hired a programmer and challenged him to create software that could not only draw effective charts, but could also analyze markets in a rather unusual way. Together they developed the concept of *timing models*, and these models formed the basis of NDR's core positions in a variety of markets and economies. It turns out, however, that predicting that he'd need just one programmer for one year was Ned's worst call. Today we have an IT staff of nearly 30!

As Ned has pointed out many times, the bane of the investor is the Big Mistake. On the following pages I detail the makeup of one of our major models, the Fab Five. The goal of any NDR model is to keep us open-minded and disciplined, and to let our profits run while avoiding big mistakes. We realize models can be quite fickle, no matter what their ingredients are or how they are built. This model is no exception (there are no exceptions!). The game is to recognize potential capriciousness and pay attention to the effectiveness of each individual component and to the overall mix of indicators. One must always be vigilant when depending on models.

The Fab Five is an environmental model that uses what we call modes. Its job is to assemble the major internal and external factors that affect markets and combine them to produce a single objective verdict: bearish, neutral, or bullish. Offering only three possibilities might seem a bit too simplistic, like asking someone to rate a product on a scale of 1 to 3, instead of 1 to 10. But the goal is to keep things simple, and as you will see later, each mode can be open to subtle interpretation. To quote Ned, "The evidence is rarely black or white—rather, shades of gray."

Just what is an environmental model? In essence, it's one that can keep risk at arm's length without sacrificing too much on the long side. Such models effectively gauge how good conditions are for investing: do we have calm waters or are we about to enter the lower 40 latitudes? An environmental model takes into account what the Federal Reserve is doing, what the so-called smart money is doing, how speculators are feeling, what interest rates and inflation are doing, and, above all else, what the primary trend is. Using a weight-of-the-evidence approach gives us an educated feel for the risks in the market. The environmental model's job is not necessarily to give concrete buy and sell signals. Its job is to measure the level of risk in the market.

Before we examine the Fab Five in detail, let's briefly discuss some of the indicators we use to build models.

We look at two types of indicators: internal and external.

Internal indicators relate to the price action of a market or index and include the usual list of suspects, along with a multitude of variations: moving averages, momentum, advances and declines, and volume trends. All of these can be found in the bottomless bag of tools used by the creative technical analyst. I've seen enough momentum tricks alone to last a career. Ditto for moving averages. There seems to be no end of possibilities when it comes to manipulating an index or its components in order to come up with a so-called objective opinion on a market's direction.

We break down internal indicators into two distinct types: trend following and trend sensitive.

Trend-following indicators keep us in harmony with the market's primary trend, and with enough weight in a model they act as our stop-loss when needed. Used well, they can help investors let profits run and cut losses short. These indicators include moving-average crosses and slopes and some measures of momentum, used either alone or aggregated. Trend-following indicators are rarely neutral and can generate great returns, but sometimes give notoriously false signals. By their very nature they are late. Consequently, they require patience.

Trend-sensitive indicators, also known as overbought-oversold indicators, include mean reversion, momentum variations, and deviation from the trend. These indicators have a tendency for picking tops and bottoms and can influence models when price trends reach extremes. They are very accurate but not adept at generating significant gains. Since they spend a good part of the time in the neutral zone they tend to work well in multi-indicator models asserting themselves only at potential extremes.

Rounding out internal indicators is market breadth, an extremely useful tool in determining the technical environment. At NDR we gauge this by watching A/D data (advances, declines, unchanged), new highs and lows, the percent of stocks in a universe meeting a specified criteria (e.g., above or below a moving average), volume data (advancing and declining volume), and combinations of A/D and volume. Over the years we've developed our own stock database. We use only common shares for our calculations in order to get a pure view of the stock market that's unsullied by closed-end funds, preferred stocks, structured products, and so on. One day recently, 3,164 securities were being actively traded on the New York Stock Exchange but only 1,965 of them were common stocks. In fact, nearly 40 percent of the actively traded securities listed on the Big Board aren't common stocks.

External indicators include anything outside of price action: the monetary environment, crowd psychology, valuation, and economic conditions. At NDR we tend to lump valuation and crowd psychology in the sentiment category. We also tend to include economic indicators that can influence markets (e.g., inflation) in the monetary category and sometimes, to a lesser extent, the sentiment category. So basically we're looking at two sets of external indicators: monetary and sentiment. To analyze them, we can use the identical arsenal of measures we use for internal indicators, including moving averages, momentums, and deviations from trend.

My introduction to model building started in 1984, when Ned taught me the basics of creating what he called timing models. I was introduced to his major models with names like Big Mo, Little Mo, Lexi, Bondito, and Bondo Grande. There was also the Economic-Timing Model and the Inflation-Timing Model. He had models on 600 stocks, on gold, all the major currencies, crude, you name it. I was dizzy looking at all these models, and yet his approach to constructing them was amazingly simple: find some indicators that work, give them all equal weight by assigning +1, 0, or −1 to each, and add them up. I had cut my teeth on much more complicated systems. This was a whole new ball game. I came to believe that Ned had invented a simplified version of multiple linear regression, which makes predictions based on the relationships between dependent and independent variables. And the beauty was not only in the methodology but in the results. Here, I thought, was the ultimate KISS—keep it simple, stupid—system. But as it turns out, although the concept is quite uncomplicated the process can be complex and time-consuming. The devil is in the details. Done poorly, it's garbage in, garbage out.

I quickly learned the ropes and spent some serious time tweaking software and acquiring faster and faster computers (the difference in computing power between the machines back then and those available now is roughly a factor of 3,500—and today's computers are a whole lot cheaper!). My objective was to keep several computers busy crunching models 24/7, in the hope of building more and better models while expanding our universe of trading vehicles. All of this was fine, but no matter how much output the computers generated, the process still required a researcher to hand pick the indicators and the final model. Obviously this was a limiting factor. By the late 1980s I had written software to do the actual picking, which paved the way for a soup-to-nuts system for cranking out models. I was quite proud of myself and began building individual equity models.

However, a number of these models didn't hold up very well; some incurred pretty big losses. To remedy the problems I tweaked the programs. For example, we limited the amount of relative-strength indicators because even as a stock's price is falling, an RS (relative strength) line can rise. Another problem was insufficient diversity in the mix of indicators, which led to an overweighted indicator theme going bad and taking the model with it. In addition, too many models were accurate but lost money. And then there was the occasional so-called creative researcher who thought that making calls by pairing, say, IBM stock with COMEX (Commodity Exchange) gold was a cool idea (the old throw-it-at-the-wall-and-see-what-sticks approach).

Finally, I realized that to build a truly diverse, objective model requires finesse, diligence, a bit of artistic panache, and a strong knowledge of macroeconomic relationships, ranging from company fundamentals to macroeconomic fundamentals to Fed watching. Ironically, computing power takes a back seat in building good models.

■ Overview of the Fab Five

To create the Fab Five, we combined individual models covering our favorite areas of the market. The name comes from the famous basketball team that my alma mater, the University of Michigan, had in the early 1990s. (Ned is a huge basketball fan; we joke that if he fell and cracked open his head little basketballs would bounce out.) However, the model has only four components—sentiment, monetary readings, Combo, and the tape—but the tape is given double weight. I'll start with it because it accounts for two-fifths of the Fab Five.

Figure 14.1 shows the past 10 years of the Fab Five model. In the following pages, each component of the model is presented in the same fashion. The mode boxes at the bottom summarize the results for the full date range as well as for the past 10 years. The top clip has an additional series on it that represents an equity line based on going

FIGURE 14.1 *Top,* S&P 500 Index and Model Allocation Line; *Bottom,* Fab Five Composite Model.

long the S&P 500 when the model is above the upper bracket, going into T-bills when the model is between the brackets, and shorting the S&P 500 when the model is below the lower bracket. This equity line is only for perspective; it's there to give a close-up view of how the model has behaved in the past. The stats tell a story, but not the whole story.

■ Tape Component

There are seven individual indicators in the tape component. As with all the other Fab Five components, and in keeping with our KISS philosophy, these indicators are each assigned −1, 0, or +1, and the result is produced through simple addition.

The first indicator in the tape component is shown in Figure 14.2. This simple, trend-following indicator is what technical analysts call a golden cross (a point at which a short-term moving average breaks above a long-term average, signaling a bull market to come). It is positive when the 50-day moving average of the S&P 500 is above its 200-day average and negative otherwise.

The box on the top part of the chart summarizes the indicator's performance since 1929. At Ned Davis Research the box is called a mode bat. Ned invented this in the late 1980s, and it shows what the returns have been when buying during the bullish mode (when the 50 is above the 200) or the bearish mode (when the 50 is below the 200). It tells us that the 50-day has been above the 200-day nearly two-thirds of the time and that during those times the S&P 500 on a price-only basis has returned 9.1 percent per annum. When the 50-day has been below the 200-day the market has retreated at a 1.1 percent annual rate. Not shown in the mode bat are two other interesting statistics: a buy-and-hold approach would have generated a 5.5 percent yearly return, and reinvesting dividends while in the bullish mode would have produced a 13 percent return. Obviously an indicator like this is long-term: designed to catch the major moves.

FIGURE 14.2 *Top,* **S&P 500 Index;** *Bottom,* **50-Day versus 200-Day S&P 500 MA.**

The indicator in the chart in Figure 14.3 is a typical trend-sensitive indicator and is called a stochastic, which measures variation in momentum. The idea is to look back a set number of market days, pick the low and the high in that period, and calculate where the market's current value is relative to that range. The result is a percent; 100 percent is a new high, while 0 percent is a new low. The ambivalence of this indicator is reflected in whether you want to catch a thrust early and go long (called a bracket) or wait until the thrust is over and go short when it starts to fall (called a reverse bracket). It can be used either way, depending on the number of market days being looked at, whether a moving average is applied, and how wide the brackets are.

This chart's signals are summarized in what's known as a batting average, or bat. NDR, since its inception in 1980, has been using bats to evaluate indicators. The factors used include how accurate the long signals have been and what the overall annualized return has been. To illustrate a practical use of this indicator, Figure 14.3 assumes that on sell signals for stocks an investor will buy T-bills rather than short the market.

This 85-day stochastic is derived from NDR's All-Cap Equal-Weighted Index, based on our full Broad Market Equity Series universe. It is equally weighted and rebalanced quarterly. The result is smoothed with a five-day moving average and has brackets at 11 and 65. As the chart points out, a buy signal is generated when the smoothed result dips below then rises above 11, while a switch to T-bills is signaled when the indicator crosses above and then below 65. At NDR we call this method of signal generation a reverse bracket.

To generate a signal, the indicator either has to cross above the upper bracket and then cross below the upper bracket (sell) or cross below the lower bracket and then cross above the lower bracket (buy).

The indicator also can go neutral: if a signal is given across the upper bracket, that signal stands until either the indicator drops below the bottom bracket and then

FIGURE 14.3 *Top*, S&P 500 Index with Stochastic Indicators; *Bottom*, 85-Period Stochastic NDR Equal-Dollar-Weighted Equity Series (Five-Day Smoothing).

crosses back above the bottom bracket, or the indicator crosses back above the upper bracket before crossing the lower bracket. If the latter happens, the indicator becomes neutral. I call that an *oops* signal. The bottom bracket is treated the same way.

As it turns out, the reverse bracket indicator has been negative only 19 percent of the time (it throws out a lot of oops signals), neutral 25 percent of the time (mostly from the sell side), and positive 56 percent of the time. As of this writing, the indicator is neutral and therefore has no influence on the tape component.

Moving away from direct price action, we turn to one of our favorite broad-market tool sets: breadth. This indicator is one of Ned's favorites. It's based on another fairly simple yet effective concept: evaluating the impact of volume supply and volume demand.

If a stock advances on the day, we consider all of the volume traded on that day to be advancing volume—this is the demand side. If a stock falls on the day, the volume is tallied on the declining, or supply side. If a stock's price stays steady, all of its trading volume is considered unchanged and is discarded in our calculations. (The percentage of unchanged stocks on a typical day has fluctuated around 1.5 percent since decimalization in 2001. Prior to 1997, when stocks traded in eighths, nearly one in five stocks were unchanged on the day!)

To stabilize the volatility and gain a useful perspective, we typically sum both supply and demand over a substantial period ranging from days to months. The percent of summed supply volume plus the percent of summed demand volume always adds to 100. They meet in the middle at 50 percent. The universe we are using for these calculations is the NDR Broad Market Equity Series All-Cap Index. This index represents 99 percent of the market value of the common shares trading on the big three exchanges. Its history goes back to September 1980.

The mode box in Figure 14.4 shows that when demand has been above supply, as it has been 79.0 percent of the time, the S&P 500 has advanced at 11.8 percent a

FIGURE 14.4   S&P 500 Index versus NDR Supply and Demand.

year. But when supply is above demand, the market retreats 1.2 percent per annum. This indicator's contribution to the Fab Five tape component is +1 when demand is above supply and −1 otherwise.

There are many ways to look for excitement in the stock market: exuberance, whether rational or irrational, can be measurable. A couple of our favorite indicators look at the relationship between advancing and declining volume, or advances versus declines. Figure 14.5 evaluates the ratio of advances to declines. The ratio is actually a 10-day sum of NDR Multi-Cap advancing issues divided by a 10-day sum of declining issues. The NDR Multi-Cap universe covers the top 97 percent of tradable market cap and includes the NDR Large Cap plus the NDR Mid-Cap plus some of the NDR Small Cap (enough to get the market cap to 97 percent).

When the advance/decline ratio exceeds 1.9, we call that a *breadth thrust*. The table in Figure 14.5 shows the history of this indicator back to 1947. Now I know what you're thinking: Hold on—if the Multi-Cap started in 1980, just exactly how did you do this? Especially given that lecture about following only common stocks on the NYSE? Well, we consider ourselves market historians, and we love historical data—as much as we can get. So yes, we borrowed the NYSE advance/decline data going back to 1947 to help illustrate the point that breadth thrusts can be quite significant. It also turns out that, according to our database, stocks other than common stocks made up only 20 percent of listed NYSE issues in 1980.

Now how exactly do we get these thrusts to work for us? Typically, we try to determine how long initial momentum is likely to last based on history and then refine our prediction from there. In the case of the indicator shown in Figure 14.5, 80 market days seemed to work well. But what if a signal is repeated in that period? One could approach it in at least two ways: either by simply resetting the count every time a new signal occurs in the 80-day window or by ignoring that signal. After some quick testing we decided on the latter.

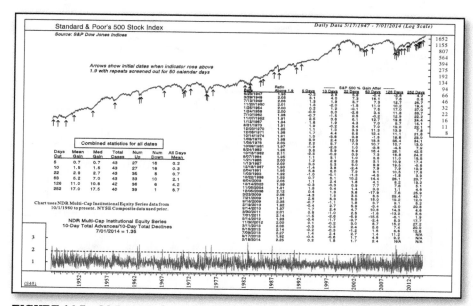

FIGURE 14.5 S&P 500 Index with Advance/Decline Breadth Thrust.

FIGURE 14.6 *Top,* S&P 500 Index; *Bottom,* NDR Combination High-Low Logic Index.

The contribution of this indicator to the Fab Five tape component is either +1 or 0. It can never go negative.

If there ever was a cool breadth gauge, the *high-low logic indicator*—developed by Norman Fosback and shown in Figure 14.6—is it. It's basically a measure of how in gear, or bullish, the market is. I'll admit I was quite baffled by this at first. How could a single indicator with opposite messages give the same signal, regardless of the message?

Well, the market is considered in gear when new 52-week highs overwhelm new 52-week lows; it is also in gear when new 52-week lows overwhelm new 52-week highs. The rest of the time, this indicator is either neutral or out-of-gear (bearish).

The high-low logic is calculated by taking the ratio of either new 52-week highs or new 52-week lows, whichever is less, to the total number of issues and then smoothing this ratio with a 10-week exponential moving average.

Fosback's original work used NYSE data back to 1941. Here we use the NYSE in combination with the NASDAQ and the AMEX for a broader look. This also helps us get past our issue with the NYSE listings by adding in higher concentrations of common stocks.

Here's Ned's view of the concept:

> Since market tops are typically slow to form, the increased risk of a peak is evident when the quality market averages are reaching higher levels without confirmation from increasing numbers of 52-week new highs. Whereas a churning, out-of-gear market is most effective as an indicator of tops after rallies, upside confirmation indicates that the market is in gear and that the current uptrend is healthy. Since market bottoms are usually formed relatively quickly, it is also bullish when the market is in

gear at selling extremes characterized by new lows on the vast majority of stocks, a sign that a selling climax has left the market oversold.

When many stocks are making new highs at the same time that many are making new lows, the index reading is high, indicating a divergent market. When very few stocks are diverging from the prevailing trend, the index reading is low, a reflection of confirmation.

In other words, high index readings reflect widespread divergence, which is bearish, whereas low index readings point to one of two bullish conditions: a selling panic with almost no new highs, the sign of an extremely oversold market; or a selling vacuum with almost no new lows, the sign of a market with strong upside momentum. The indicator is able to identify new bull markets with buy signals, while remaining on sell signals during bear market rallies or the blow-off moves that tend to occur near the end of bull markets.

Another of our favorite breadth indicators is the diffusion index. It's more or less a consensus of certain measures for a host of similar vehicles; in this case, world stock markets relative to their 50-day moving averages. Why 50 and not 83 or 27? We like to keep things simple, and virtually everyone is familiar with the 50-day moving average.

Figure 14.7 shows the relationship between global equity markets and the U.S. market. If 71 percent or more of global markets are above their 50-day moving averages, the U.S. market, as represented by the NDR All-Cap Index, appreciates at 20.2 percent per annum. Since 1980, this has occurred 41.1 percent of the time. Conversely, when the percent of markets drops below 41 percent, the NDR All-Cap retreats at 2.3 percent per annum. The contribution to the Fab Five tape component is −1, 0, or +1.

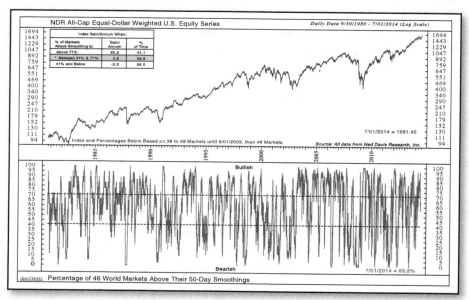

FIGURE 14.7 *Top,* **NDR All-Cap Equal-Dollar Weighted U.S. Equity Series;** *Bottom,* **Percentage of 46 World Markets above Their 50-Day Smoothings.**

The 46 world markets are MSCI (Morgan Stanley Capital International) All Country World Index members—23 developed economies and 23 emerging ones.

A long-standing tenet of NDR is to *go with Mo*. If the market's momentum is up, we're in; if it's down, we're out. We use this model as a gauge of technical health. Big Mo is a diffusion index that represents the percentage of bullish individual trend and momentum indicators taken from 96 of our own BMES subindustry indices. The trend indicators are based on the direction of a subindustry's moving average, while the momentum indicators are based on the rate of change of the subindustry's price index. The ratio of momentum to trend indicators is around two to one.

In the past we have had several versions of Big Mo. The first one I remember, from 1982, used industry groups that were defined by S&P. (We also had a daily version called Little Mo, built with individual stocks.) After developing our own geometric industry groups in the late 1980s, we rebuilt Big Mo. By the mid-1990s, having added to our stock database, developed our industry work even further, and added new analytical techniques, we took another shot at it. The current version was created in January 2013. As fate would have it, we were forced into a rebuild due to a data vendor technicality; we liked the old model but had no choice but to rebuild.

The indicator shown in Figure 14.8 introduces a modification of our standard mode bat: the directional mode bat. The two mode boxes in the upper left show results based on whether Big Mo is higher or lower than it was six weeks earlier. In the bottom section, the brackets are fixed at 56 and 79, and the results are quite different depending on Big Mo's direction. Whether the model is improving (rising) or weakening (falling) can give valuable information in addition to the model's current level: when Big Mo Tape has been high and rising, the returns have tended to be best, while a low and falling model reading has been associated with the weakest returns.

FIGURE 14.8 *Top,* **S&P 500 Index;** *Bottom,* **Big Mo Multi-Cap Tape Composite (Directional Mode Basis).**

The weight of this indicator in the tape component of the Fab Five is tricky but sensible. When Big Mo is rising and above 56 we assign a +1; when it's rising and below 56, it gets a 0; falling and above 79 is another +1; falling and between the brackets is a 0, while falling and below 56 gets the only −1 reading. If Big Mo is unchanged on a six-week basis the reading from the prior week is used.

■ The Final Tape Component

Now that we have all of our indicators, it's a simple matter to add them up to produce a result (see Figure 14.9).

Since there are seven components to the model, the range should be −7 to +7. But remember, the thrust indicator can't go negative, so the overall sum ranges from −6 to +7. The brackets for the model are set at −1.5 and 14.5 (bottom chart section). As with all of the components of the Fab Five, this model is designed to work in four separate time frames. Its contribution to the overall Fab Five is −2, 0, or +2 (remember, it gets double weight).

■ The Sentiment Component

During my initial interview with Ned back in 1984 I was a bit nervous, to say the least. I really had no idea what Ned Davis Research was, and I had never heard of Ned Davis himself. Being new to Florida, I had been scanning the want ads when I came upon a two-line blurb for a statistical researcher. When I phoned the employment agency that had placed the ad, the woman there told me that the client was looking for someone with an MBA who could program in Basic, a once-popular computer

FIGURE 14.9 *Top*, S&P 500 Index; *Bottom*, Fab Five Tape Component.

language. After I told her I had an MS, had recently worked for a research organization, and could program in Basic, she set up an interview. No information about the company was forthcoming; I went in blind. The address was a house in a semiresidential area. I thought I had the wrong place until I saw a small weather-beaten sign out front that simply said, Ned Davis Research, Investments. I noticed a gleaming maroon Jaguar out back under a carport. My initial interview was in a converted bedroom. When I met Ned, he was wearing shorts, a T-shirt, and boat shoes. I felt a little out of place in my spanking new suit. As I sat there, Ned asked me if I knew the difference between a stock and a bond. My life flashed before my eyes. I had never read a newspaper's business section in my life. I had studied biology, chemistry, and statistics, and generally viewed business majors the way I viewed psychology majors—students from another planet. When I answered with a no, I thought it was curtains for my chances of getting the job, but as it turned out Ned viewed my ignorance as a plus, because it meant I had no preconceived notions about stocks or bonds. I was a bias-free blank slate.

After several months of working for Ned, I began to perceive the relationship between investor psychology and markets. I realized I had gone from analyzing seasonal zooplankton populations to analyzing what basically amounted to fear and greed.

It's hard to find an investor or a trader, or anyone for that matter, who doesn't have an opinion on the direction of the stock market. From blogs to books to PhD dissertations to (above all else) the media, we find no end to sentiment-indicator pay dirt. The terms *irrational exuberance* and *the madness of crowds* reflect the fact that we humans have a flair for exposing our hand. And what better place to show what we're made of than in the stock market?

Fortunately, analysts and market historians have access to a smorgasbord of sentiment indicators. These include polls of investors, newsletter writers, professionals, nonprofessionals, and so on; people who put their money where their mouths are. In addition, there are other ways of determining sentiment. For example, a high price/earnings or price/dividend ratio reflects optimistic investors, while a low P/E or price/dividend ratio shows fearful investors. We can also say the same thing about market momentum in the context of optimism or pessimism. The whole idea is to look for extremes in these indicators. When investors are at their maximum bullish level (when virtually everyone is invested) that indicates a market top. When the vast majority of investors are bearish or have sold whatever they can sell, we generally find market bottoms. The trick, of course, is to detect these extremes.

The sentiment component of the Fab Five uses some of these concepts in its seven indicators. Each indicator delivers +1, 0, or −1 to the overall component, with one exception: our Daily Sentiment Composite (shown later in Figure 14.16), which gets double weight.

I wouldn't go so far as to call its name an oxymoron, but Investors Intelligence has been producing the Advisors' Sentiment Report for over 40 years. This survey is one of our favorites. The firm tracks more than 100 independent market newsletters, classifying each as bullish, bearish, or on the fence. In Figure 14.10, we're interested in bullish advisors as a percentage of those with an opinion (bullish + bearish). This presents a longer-term picture of how advisors are feeling, given that it's weekly and

FIGURE 14.10 *Top*, DJIA with Buy/Sell Signals; *Bottom*, Bulls/(Bulls + Bears) with 10-Week Smoothing.

the ratio is smoothed over 10 weeks. The presence of too many bulls indicates a market top, while too few bulls points to a market bottom. Again, the trick is discovering how many are too many or too few.

There are three brackets and two analyses on the chart, adding a bit of complexity to this fairly straightforward concept. Let's deal with the signals first. In the bottom section of the chart, excessive optimism is evident when the indicator moves above the upper bracket. Using our reverse-bracket trick, the sell signal comes on the reversal as the indicator drops back below the upper bracket. This provides confirming evidence that a bullish extreme has been reached.

There are two ways to get buy signals, and both use reverse brackets. The most obvious comes when the indicator drops below the very bottom bracket and then reverses back above it. This confirms the bearish extreme. The second way to obtain a buy signal is for the indicator to drop below the middle bracket and reverse back above that bracket (without going below the bottom bracket) while on a sell. Obviously, there is quite a difference in bearish extremes between the middle and bottom brackets, but this only works directly after a period of extreme bullishness.

The second analysis is the mode bat on the bottom right of the top clip. This mode bat shows a straightforward perspective using brackets at 53 and 69. This indicates that the market does well when the reading is below 53 and not so well when it's above 69. It also hints that the indicator is neutral nearly half of the time.

This indicator's contribution to the Fab Five sentiment component is essentially the signals just described but with neutrals thrown in. Having a sentiment indicator that's always on can be a problem, so we employ the reverse-bracket oops trick I mentioned earlier. Doing this has the indicator in a neutral mode roughly 28 percent of the time, keeping it agnostic during repeat extremes.

FIGURE 14.11 *Top*, NDR Multi-Cap Equal-Dollar Weighted Institutional Equity Series; *Bottom*, NDR Multi-Cap Institutional Equity Series Median P/E Ratio.

The P/E ratio indicator shown in the bottom clip of Figure 14.11 is equally comfortable in the valuation or sentiment camp. Even if you know absolutely nothing else about stocks, no one will realize it if you can work P/E into a conversation. The ratio is calculated by dividing the stock price by the latest earnings per share. The P/E shown here is based on the median earnings yield of the stocks in the NDR Multi-Cap Equity Series. (In our calculations, we invert the median yield.) We use the median earnings yield because it's less likely to be influenced by questionable earnings reports.

When Ned explained the concept of P/E to me for the first time, he basically said that it's what investors are willing to pay for one dollar of a company's earnings; in other words, a P/E of 20 indicates that investors are willing to pay 20 times earnings. This chart shows us that over the long term, investors have been willing to pay $19.20 for one dollar in NDR Multi-Cap profits. When the P/E ratio goes beyond a factor of 24 or one standard deviation, we're getting into optimism and as it breaches the next bracket up, we're looking at pure euphoria.

The mode bat reveals our actionable levels. The indicator shows excessive optimism or overvaluation at a P/E of 22.5. In that zone, the NDR Multi-Cap Index has fallen at a rate of 14.7 percent per annum. Dropping below 14.5 takes the indicator into too much pessimism or undervaluation. At that position, the Multi-Cap has appreciated at 18.3 percent a year.

This indicator's contribution to the Fab Five sentiment component is +1 below 14.5, 0 from 14.5 to 22.5, and −1 above 22.5. This is one of the few Fab Five indicators that is calculated monthly.

In Figure 14.12 we have a sentiment indicator that could also fit into the valuation category or even the monetary category. This one is a relative measure of earnings to

FIGURE 14.12 *Top,* **S&P 500 Index;** *Bottom,* **S&P 500 Stock Earnings Yield (GAAP) Compared to Interest Rate Composite Ratio.**

interest rates. While it's true that absolute valuation indicators can be at odds with relative valuation indicators, both can be extremely useful. In this case, very low interest rates can cause this particular indicator to be more bullish than the absolute P/E in Figure 14.11.

The interest-rate component is a composite calculated as the average yield of 91-day T-bills, 10-year Treasury notes, and Moody's Baa corporates. This gives us a more general view of the interest-rate situation.

To find extremes, we use a 60-week moving standard deviation, with plus or minus 1.3 standard deviations as the brackets. We examine earnings in two ways—relative to interest rates, and relative to time.

The contribution to the Fab Five sentiment component is −1 below the bottom bracket, 0 in between the brackets, and +1 above the upper bracket.

We first started using "moving standard-deviation brackets" in the late 1980s. This developed along with our use of reverse brackets, and indeed, they go well together (although this particular indicator uses regular brackets). An indicator that should be confined to some range but occasionally gets excited is difficult to pin down with absolute brackets. I have seen indicators that spent years in a well-defined range suddenly get trend-happy and then spend years above or below the magic range. Basically, the brackets adjust automatically to changing conditions, creating a new normal as indicators move strongly up or down. This also helps to correct for volatility. To illustrate this point, Figure 14.13 shows the Big Block Index, whose very nature has shifted dramatically over time due to changes in the size of the blocks, the move to decimals, and other factors. So moving standard-deviation brackets have kept this indicator relevant.

In Figure 14.14 we have an indicator whose basic components are more associated with breadth than sentiment. The TRIN (also known as MKDS or the Trading Index)

FIGURE 14.13 *Top*, DJIA with Buy/Sell Signals; *Bottom*, Big Block Index.

compares upside volume to downside volume and shows whether trading is concentrated in advancing or declining issues (i.e., it indicates whether the path of least resistance is upward or downward). It is calculated by dividing the ratio of advancing issues to declining issues by the ratio of advancing volume to declining volume.

TRIN's normal 10-day moving average is calculated by adding up individual daily readings and dividing the result by 10. In contrast, the Open 10 Trading Index uses the 10-day totals of each TRIN component (up stocks, down stocks, up volume, and down volume) rather than using individual daily computations. Once these component

FIGURE 14.14 S&P 500 Index versus Open 10 and Open 30 Trading Indices.

totals are determined for 10 days, they are inserted in the usual TRIN formula: (up stocks/down stocks)/(up volume/down volume). The Open 30 TRIN is derived in the same fashion, but with 30-day totals.

High levels in the Open 10 and Open 30 Trading Indices indicate an oversold market and a cash build-up by the big money. They occur just prior to significant market upswings. The mode boxes show that the market tends to post much better gains when the Open TRINs are high (above the upper dashed lines) and poor results when the Open TRINs are low (below the lower dashed lines). If an investor followed just one of these indicators, he'd be in the market 30 percent of the time. But combining the two would increase that to about 45 percent.

Contribution to the sentiment component is −1 when both TRINs are negative or one is negative and the other is neutral, 0 when they sum to 0, and +1 when both are positive or one is positive while the other is neutral.

Back in the 1980s, Ned conducted weekly research meetings. He was a huge Value Line fan; he loved that firm's approach to research and loved its indicators. One day he told us a story about Arnold Bernhard, the founder of Value Line, who had built a hugely successful investment research firm that ultimately stood on its own two feet, independent of him. When Arnold Bernhard died in 1987 his death was widely reported but had no effect on the company; it was business as usual, and Value Line is still very strong and well-respected. Ned's point was that he hoped Ned Davis Research, the firm he founded, would someday have the same foundation. (Granted, Arnold Bernhard's firm was called Value Line and not Arnold Bernhard Research, but. . . .)

The indicator shown in the bottom clip of Figure 14.15 is one of Value Line's key fundamental indicators and is based on its analysts' three- to five-year P/E projections for the stocks in their universe. The estimate of the median price appreciation

FIGURE 14.15 *Top,* **S&P 500 Index with Buy/Sell Indicators;** *Bottom,* **Value Line Median Appreciation Potential (VLMAP) with SD Brackets (Six-Week Moving Average).**

potential is found by multiplying each stock's current earnings by its future P/E projection as determined by Value Line analysts. Each stock gets a value and the median of these values is the VLMAP. As Value Line points out, though, the VLMAP tends to be a bit high (earnings estimates tend to be a little optimistic, to say the least).

We have applied the NDR moving standard-deviation reverse bracket solution to this indicator. The standard deviation is nine months and the brackets are asymmetric at −1.0 and +0.6. Although it can't be seen on the chart, we allow the signal to go neutral in typical oops fashion. The contribution to the Fab Five sentiment component is +1 when the six-week smoothing of the VLMAP drops below the upper bracket and −1 when it moves from below to above the lower bracket. That sell signal at the end of 2012 looked bad, but in Fab Five reality, it was negative for only seven weeks before it hit oops, or neutral, mode.

Although the Daily Trading Sentiment Composite shown in Figure 14.16 is just an indicator to the Fab Five, in reality this is a model composed of 27 individual indicators from six areas:

1. Advisory Service Sentiment (44.4 percent) is based on results from various polls, including those from the National Association of Active Investment Managers, Investors Intelligence, the American Association of Individual Investors, Mark Hulbert, and others.
2. Asset flows (13.3 percent) looks at the commitment of traders reports and mutual-fund flows.
3. Overbought/oversold (13.3 percent) includes various volume-related indicators as well as A/D indicators.
4. Valuation/sentiment (8.9 percent) looks at earnings relative to interest rates.
5. Volatility (8.9 percent) is based on the VIX (the Chicago Board Options Exchange's volatility index, which analysts use to help gauge how worried or

FIGURE 14.16 *Top*, S&P 500 Index; *Bottom*, NDR Daily Sentiment Composite.

confident investors are) and SKEW (an index that essentially tries to show the probability of an extreme market event, such as a crash).

6. Put/call options ratios (11.1 percent) include various ISE (International Securities Exchange) and CBOE ratios.

Each of the 27 indicators uses moving standard deviation brackets (not reverse brackets). During testing, each indicator had to work in all four predetermined time frames before being selected for inclusion. For an indicator to make the final model there had to be plenty of good results to pick from. This is true for any indicator in any Ned Davis Research model—if you have a feeling that an indicator has a strong relationship to the market and you're using the appropriate techniques, then you should get piles of output that reflect your perception of the indicator. If an analysis turns up only a small percentage of decent results then either (1) the indicator isn't any good, or (2) the analytical technique needs refinement. If there are only a handful of acceptable results after exhausting all possibilities for analysis, chalk those results up to luck, toss the indicator, and move on. In the case of the Daily Trading Sentiment Composite, virtually all of the indicators had plenty of acceptable results.

The composite itself is basically an inverted diffusion index: inverted so that high numbers are excessively optimistic and therefore bearish, and low numbers are pessimistic and therefore bullish.

The three charts that follow illustrate several components. The first is the Hulbert Newsletter Stock Sentiment Index (Figure 14.17). Mark Hulbert measures average equity exposure among a subset of advisors who focus on timing the overall stock market's short-term gyrations. This is a typical Daily Trading Sentiment Composite indicator, showing the moving standard deviation brackets in the middle clip with the bottom clip reflecting the same thing but in a form called a z-score. Doing this allows us to compare one z-score with another without the fog of periods and brackets. When most of the advisors move to the bullish side that's negative for the market, and vice versa.

FIGURE 14.17 S&P 500 Index versus the Hulbert Newsletter Stock Sentiment Index.

The classic overbought-oversold indicator shown in Figure 14.18 is based on extreme volume movements. We have taken the NDR Multi-Cap universe and presented advancing volume as a percentage of advancing and declining volume combined. When advancing volume reaches an extreme by violating the upper bracket of the standard-deviation window it's typically negative for the market. This is another one of Ned's favorite get-ready-to indicators.

Volatility is sentiment in motion; Figure 14.19 shows the VIX to be bearish during low volatility periods and bullish during high volatility periods. The reversals are when most of the gains are made.

FIGURE 14.18 **S&P 500 Index versus Multi-Cap Institutional Equity Series Advancing/(Advancing + Declining) Volume.**

FIGURE 14.19 **S&P 500 Index versus CBOE VIX (Inverted).**

The contribution to the Fab Five sentiment component is +2 when the daily sentiment composite is below the lower bracket, 0 in between the brackets, and −2 when above the upper bracket.

Sentiment Summary

The final sentiment component, shown in Figure 14.20, is a sum of the indicators discussed (plus one more P/E indicator) for a range of -8 to +8 (remember, the daily sentiment composite has double weight). The brackets are set at −1.5 and 1.5.

The Monetary Component

Our third major piece is the Fab Five monetary component. The adage "money moves markets" is probably as old as the markets themselves; without demand in some form of purchasing power, there would be no markets. The availability of money equates to liquidity, and measures of liquidity help us get a handle on risk. Of course, the source and quality of money also matter, and our view of the monetary situation comes from two major sources: (1) the price of money, meaning interest rates; and (2) the supply of money.

Rates of change in interest rates—regardless of what maturities we're looking at or whether we're examining government or corporate securities—yield consistently good results against the stock market. My first real look at this was in 1987, when Ned came up with the idea of bulls/(bulls + bears) in the context of the monetary environment. He thought that when a bull market was under way it would take a much higher percentage of bulls to send a bearish signal than it would in a

FIGURE 14.20 *Top*, S&P 500 Index and Model Allocation Line; *Bottom*, Fab Five Sentiment Component.

bear market. He hypothesized the same should be true for buying the market under favorable conditions: the percentage of bulls shouldn't have to drop as far as it would have to under bear market conditions. To test this, we used a 26-week rate of change in intermediate government bond prices as a proxy for bull and bear markets. Bond momentum above a certain level would indicate a bull market, while momentum below a lower level would indicate a bear market. I can remember Ned standing behind me, tossing out ideas while I sat at my desk doing my best to program them into a computer. Sure enough, the concept worked, and thus Ned's dynamic brackets were hatched. This led to our embracing moving standard deviation brackets the following year.

The indicator shown in Figure 14.21 presents Moody's corporate Baa yields as a 26-week percent change. It's just that simple: when interest rates are heating up, it's bad for stocks. When interest rates are coming down, it's good for stocks. The brackets are set for the NDR Multi-Cap Geometric Total Return Index, but they work just as well for the S&P 500. The contribution to the monetary component is +1 below −3 percent, 0 between −3 and 6 percent, and −1 above 6 percent.

Figure 14.22, which shows the annual rate of growth of industrial production and the commodity price component of the producer price index (PPI) subtracted from the 12-month change of the M2 money supply, illustrates the relationship between monetary and economic environments, with industrial production and PPI commodities representing the economy and what is produced with available money.

Liquidity is represented by the current-dollar M2 money supply, a measure of the money available for spending. When M2's rate of growth exceeds that of industrial production and PPI commodities, there is excess liquidity in the system, some of

FIGURE 14.21 *Top,* NDR Multi-Cap Geometric Total Return Index; *Bottom,* Moody's Baa Bond Yield (26-Week Change).

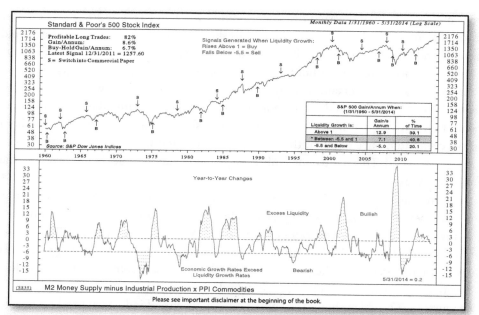

FIGURE 14.22 *Top*, S&P 500 Index with Liquidity Signals; *Bottom*, M2 Money Supply—(Industrial Production × PPI Commodities).

which flows into stocks. The periods of excess liquidity shown on this chart correspond well with stock-market uptrends.

When economic growth far exceeds the growth rate of liquidity, a rapidly expanding economy is siphoning liquidity away from financial assets and placing downward pressure on the stock market. Nearly all past bear markets have occurred when economic growth outstripped liquidity growth.

The mode box in the top clip of Figure 14.22 shows us that bullish conditions are best indicated when this indicator rises above the top bracket, while bearish conditions occur when the indicator falls below the lower bracket. The contribution to the Fab Five monetary component is −1 below the lower bracket, 0 between the two brackets, and +1 above the upper bracket.

Figure 14.23 uses a variation on a deviation-from-trend calculation to create an interest-rate indicator for the stock market using the benchmark 10-year Treasury note's yield. Instead of being represented by a longer term moving average, the trend is defined by a 70-week moving simple linear regression of the yield against time. The regression line represents the interest rate trend and the difference between the prediction and the actual result represents the deviation (see bottom clip).

To determine whether a given differential should be considered high or low, we plot moving standard deviation brackets around a three-year (156-week) moving average of the differential (+/− 0.4 standard deviation above and below). By doing this, roughly a third of the time historically is spent above the upper bracket (indicating rising interest rates), a third of the time is spent below the lower bracket (falling interest rates), and a third of the time is spent between the brackets (neutral rates). The three-year time frame gives us a longer term perspective in the level and volatility of the indicator. The mode box in the top clip summarizes the results from

FIGURE 14.23 S&P 500 Index versus 10-Year Yield Deviation-from-Trend.

1969–2014. It shows that the S&P 500 has had subpar returns, on average, when the differential has been above the upper bracket, while it has posted strong annualized gains when the differential has been below the lower bracket. Neutral readings have been associated with average returns. Only the latest 10 years of data are plotted for better visibility.

The concept behind the chart is that the rolling regression trend line could reflect a simplistic estimate of where investors might think interest rates should be, and incorporates their tendency to extrapolate an uptrend or downtrend in rates into the future, which a simple moving average doesn't do. This indicator thus gives a different perspective on where current bond yields are relative to their recent trend. This is a useful timing indicator for the stock market.

The contribution to the Fab Five monetary component is −1 above the upper bracket, 0 in between the brackets, and +1 below the lower bracket.

Early in my tenure at NDR, Ned mentioned the classic definition of inflation: too much money chasing too few goods. With the possible exception of interest rates, inflation is his favorite macro indicator; its effect on stocks has been featured in his *Hotline* many times. In the indicator shown in Figure 14.24 we use the rate of change of the Reuters Continuous Commodity Index (CCI) as a proxy for inflation. Since this is a weekly chart, updates are more timely than official consumer price data, so in a sense this gives us an early heads-up on inflation trends.

Rising commodity prices indicate inflationary pressures. When the year-to-year change in the three-week moving average of the Reuters CCI is above 8.2 percent, it has a negative effect on the stock market. When the year-to-year change drops by 4 percent or more, the market surges ahead.

The contribution to our Fab Five monetary component is +1 below 96, 0 between 96 and 108.2, and −1 above 108.2.

FIGURE 14.24 *Top*, DJIA; *Bottom*, Reuters CCI (Year-to-Year Change).

In Figure 14.25 we have the AMEX Securities Broker/Dealer Index, which tracks interest rate–sensitive financial stocks. The operative phrase is "interest rate–sensitive." These stocks do well when interest rates are falling and poorly when they're rising. They also tend to lead markets. If there are systemic risks, Financials generally will ferret them out. This is why Financials nearly always turn down on a relative basis before the overall stock market goes into a bear market. By smoothing the index over 10 days and employing moving standard deviation brackets, we can get a preview of where the market thinks interest-rate risk is headed. The standard

FIGURE 14.25 S&P 500 Index versus AMEX Securities Broker/Dealer Index.

deviation is done over 200 days, and brackets are just under plus or minus one standard deviation.

During and just after the Great Recession, we were looking for new monetary indicators that had weathered the storm. Ned thought this might work, and indeed it did and continues to do so.

The contribution to the monetary component is +1 when the smoothed price is above the upper standard deviation, 0 between the upper and lower deviations, and −1 when below the lower deviation.

As we know, liquidity or lack of liquidity helps to move markets. One way to tell whether the Fed's monetary policy is easy or tight is to follow the trend of free reserves (called *net borrowed reserves* when negative).

Most banks must keep a certain percentage of their deposits with the Federal Reserve. Since the banks can use excess reserves (total reserves less required reserves) to make investments, a free reserve position (excess reserves less borrowed reserves) usually indicates easy money. On the other hand, when money is tight banks often must borrow to meet the Fed's reserve requirements.

For the indicator shown in Figure 14.26, we take Federal Reserve Board data and normalize it by calculating the spread between the three-week moving average and the 52-week moving average. This shows us any deviations from the longer term trend. When the three-week rises faster than the 52-week, the chart indicates that Fed ease is accelerating. When the opposite occurs, this suggests that the Fed is becoming increasingly restrictive.

While the trend of free reserves is important, so is the level. As a rule, the market is in good shape when the normalized level of free reserves exceeds $200 million ($0.2 billion on the chart). When the normalized level of free reserves drops below

FIGURE 14.26 *Top*, **S&P 500 Index with Buy/Sell Signals**; *Bottom*, **Free Reserves (3-Week minus 52-Week Smoothings).**

−$180 million (−$0.18 billion on the chart), it indicates that the market is in trouble. As occurred in 1984, however, extremely low liquidity levels suggest that Fed easing is likely, a positive for stocks.

The Federal Reserve Board's actions can be inferred from the trend and level of free reserves. When free reserves are negative and falling, the Fed is putting the brakes on monetary policy. When they are positive and rising, the central bank is stepping on the accelerator.

The break we see in 2009 reflects the massive liquidity programs designed to ease strains in the banking system during the financial crisis and changes in reserve requirements. It also suggests that the Fed's policy of paying 0.25 percent interest on reserves had a longer term effect on this indicator. There is an obvious new normal here that begs the question: Is it time to reanalyze this indicator using our moving standard deviation tool? At some point, we will revisit this indicator.

The contribution to the Fab Five monetary component is +1 above the upper bracket, 0 between the two brackets, and −1 below the bottom bracket.

Figure 14.27 shows that growth in M1 can be so good, it's bad. But it also can be so bad, it's good. This is a reflection of the Fed's influence on the monetary base. Theoretically, an increasing monetary base and money supply should help depress the cost of money—interest rates. When the growth rate reaches an extreme, however, a change in Fed policy is likely. Extremely high money supply growth rates tend to be bearish for stocks, since they indicate that the Fed may tighten its monetary policy (due to inflationary pressures) and send interest rates upward. Conversely, extremely low money supply growth rates are actually bullish for stocks, since they indicate that the Fed may ease its monetary policy and allow interest rates to fall.

Extremes are determined by moving standard deviation brackets with the monetary component getting +1 below the bottom bracket, 0 in between the brackets, and −1 above the upper bracket.

FIGURE 14.27 S&P 500 Index versus M1 Annualized 13-Week Rate of Change.

Monetary Component Summary

The final monetary component in Figure 14.28 is a sum of the indicators discussed in the preceding section (plus an additional interest rate indicator, not discussed) for a range of −8 to +8. The brackets are set at −1.5 and 2.5. Because the brackets are asymmetric, it's easier to get a sell than it is to get a buy. As with all of our other Fab Five components, this model was constructed to work in all four of our preset time frames.

Fab Five Combo Component

We now come to the Fab Five's final component. We call it Combo because it's composed of six stock-market models, each with a different mix of indicators. The six range from the very simple to the very complex, but they each have the same weight. In choosing them, we simply grabbed models that Ned is comfortable with and watches every day (he watches a lot each day, and I still don't know how he does it). We've found that it helps to have a variety of models, each with its own indicator mix. Aggregating these models produces a consensus to help clarify risk and reward. Adding to our comfort level is that some of our best researchers have worked on these models over the years. And we've had some very smart, very creative analysts at what we sometimes call NDR University.

The model shown in Figure 14.29 is far and away the simplest; we call it Don't Fight the Tape or the Fed II, which says it all. It has only a tape indicator and a monetary indicator. Adding to its simplicity is that it's monthly (and thus a longer term indicator). The tape indicator is a 12-month moving average cross of the S&P 500

FIGURE 14.28 *Top*, S&P 500 Index and Model Allocation Line; *Bottom*, Fab Five Monetary Component.

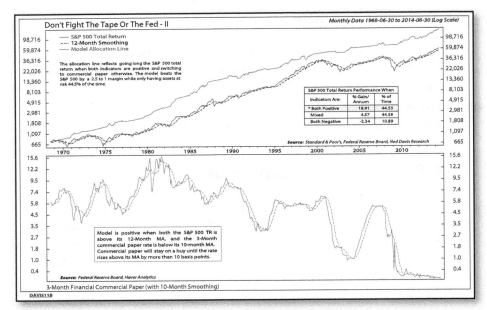

FIGURE 14.29 *Top,* S&P 500 Total Return with Model Allocation Line; *Bottom,* Three-Month Financial Commercial Paper (with 10-Month Smoothing).

Total Return Index. It's positive when the total return is above the moving average, and negative when it's below. The second indicator is also a moving-average cross. It's positive when the 90-day commercial paper rate drops below its 10-month moving average, and negative when the yield moves above its average by 10 basis points (each equal to 1 / 100th of a percentage point). When both indicators are positive (as they are 44 percent of the time), the market cranks at a nearly 19 percent rate. When they're both negative, it's best to be out of the market. The allocation line in the top clip is a good reflection of what has happened going long the S&P 500 Total Return when both indicators are positive, and holding 90-day commercial paper otherwise.

The contribution to the Fab Five Combo component is −1 when both are negative, 0 when mixed, and +1 when both indicators are positive.

Figure 14.30 is a mix of trend-sensitive, monetary, and sentiment indicators (sound familiar?). Half of the model is trend-sensitive (based on breadth, to be specific) and half is external. This model was highlighted in Tim Hayes' 2000 book *The Research Driven Investor.* Back then it was called the Nine-Indicator Model, and the only change to it has been the dropping of the NYSE Member Short Ratio. This is a case of a decent indicator no longer being published. There have been many over the years. Here's a quick list of the eight:

1. NYSE weekly new lows is a simple indicator based on new 52-week lows as a percentage of total issues. Very low values are positive, while high values are negative.

2. Net new highs is basically NYSE weekly new highs minus new lows, as a percentage of total NYSE issues. High values are positive, while low values are negative.

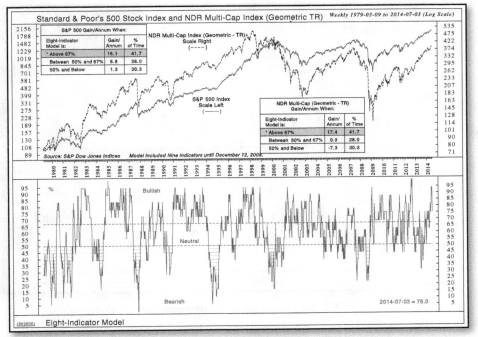

FIGURE 14.30 *Top,* **S&P 500 Index and NDR Multi-Cap Index (Geometric TR);** *Bottom,* **Eight-Indicator Model.**

3. S&P 500 reversals is a simple slope of the S&P 500. When the S&P 500 falls from a high by a certain percentage, this indicator goes negative. When it rises from a low by a certain percentage, it goes positive.

4. All Markets Open 40 Trading Index is an indicator that combines breadth data from all three U.S. markets (AMEX, NASDAQ, and NYSE) and calculates TRIN on a 40-day basis. This TRIN is then treated with a 6-month moving standard deviation with brackets. It's very similar to the TRIN indicator in the Fab Five sentiment component (which combines a 10 and a 30).

5. Bond yield/earnings yield change is a relative valuation indicator that compares bond yields to earnings yields. When the 6-month change in this ratio is high, the indicator is negative, while low is positive.

6. Composite bond yield reversals is another slope indicator; in this case the slope is applied to the long-term Treasury bond yield. A drop in the yield by a certain percentage is positive, while a rise is negative.

7. Prime rate reversals is another great Don't Fight the Fed indicator. When the prime rate falls by a certain percentage it's time to buy; when it rises by another percentage it's time to sell.

8. CCI momentum was discussed in the Fab Five monetary component.

The contribution to the Fab Five Combo component is –1 below 50 percent, 0 between 50 percent and 67 percent, and +1 above 67 percent.

The Environmental Risk Index shown in Figure 14.31 is a composite of four external components, including monetary, economic, sentiment, and valuation. There are 71 total indicators in the model. It's another Ned Davis Research original and is

FIGURE 14.31 *Top*, S&P 500 Index; *Bottom*, Environmental Risk Index.

designed to reflect the investing environment, but is not meant as a trading model. The seeds of the model go back to the 1980s, and although it has been reworked over the years it has remained essentially unchanged since 1995. However, we have had some attrition in the indicator mix: we lost a *BusinessWeek* index in 2009 and our big favorite, the Zweig sentiment indicator, in 2004.

The contribution to the Fab Five Combo component is –1 below 40 percent, 0 between 40 and 60 percent, and +1 above 60 percent.

The model shown in Figure 14.32 was built to call the MSCI Europe ex UK Index (which captures 14 developed markets in Europe excluding the United Kingdom), and it turns out, does a decent job calling the S&P 500 as well. It combines eight trend-sensitive indicators, and it's presented as a diffusion index. This adds a bit more diversity to the Combo component and cements the fact that big moves in stocks tend to be global, and that U.S. corporations have become more tied to world markets.

The contribution to the Fab Five Combo component is –1 below 40 percent, 0 between 40 percent and 75 percent, and +1 above 75 percent.

I discussed Big Mo Tape in the Fab Five tape section; now it's time to discuss this model's other half shown in Figure 14.33. As with a number of our external composites, this contains a thematic mix of indicators: economic, interest rates, sentiment, and valuation. The overlap with other external composites is pretty small. Three of these indicators are used elsewhere in the Fab Five, but that shouldn't pose a problem since they make up just 15 percent of this model. There are five indicators in each theme (for a total of 20 indicators), and they are added up to create the Big Mo External Diffusion Index. As with all of our models, each indicator is monitored periodically, and we replace any that are misbehaving.

The contribution to the Fab Five Combo component is –1 below 45 percent, 0 between 45 and 75 percent, and +1 above 75 percent.

FIGURE 14.32 *Top*, **MSCI Europe ex UK Index in Local Currency;** *Bottom*, **Europe ex U.K. Internal Composite.**

We now come to the last piece of the puzzle—the Adaptive Trading Model in Figure 14.34. It consists of three components. Component number one is designed to distinguish between a trending market and a mean-reverting market (that's the adaptive part). In a trending market, component number two, the ATM Trend Model, takes over. And in a mean-reverting market, component number three, the Mean-Reverting Model, takes the helm.

FIGURE 14.33 *Top*, **S&P 500 Index;** *Bottom*, **Big Mo External Composite.**

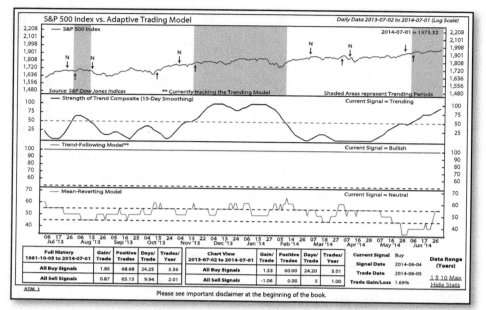

FIGURE 14.34 S&P 500 Index versus the Adaptive Trading Model.

While this all sounds complicated, it's really quite straightforward. The ATM Trend Model has only four fairly uncomplicated indicators, while the Mean-Reverting Model has five. The model controlling the switch has four. Still, this model has the same weight as the other six in the Fab Five Combo component and the contribution can be −1, 0, and +1. The Trend Model is never neutral, but the Mean-Reverting Model can be.

■ Combo Model Summary

Since there are six total indicators, the range of the model shown in Figure 14.35 is −6 to +6. The brackets are set at −1.5 and 2.5, and to be consistent with the other major Fab Five components, the model is designed to work in four preset date ranges.

■ Summing Up the Fab Five

Now that we've seen the components of the Fab Five, it's (finally!) time to add them together. Each component model is reduced to +1, 0, or −1 (with the exception of the tape component, which gets +2, 0, or −2), and the result is a simple sum. This leaves the overall model's range at −5 to +5, with the brackets set at −1.5 and 1.5 (see Figure 14.1).

FIGURE 14.35 *Top*, S&P 500 Index and Model Allocation Line; *Bottom*, Fab Five Combo Component.

■ How We Use the Fab Five

I opened this chapter explaining that the Fab Five is an environmental model that provides a unified view and ties together sometimes opposing investment themes. If the model is outright bullish then our outlook will be on the bullish side. If it's merely flirting with the upper bracket we might temper our bullishness. We might make a distinction between high neutral and low neutral, depending on whether the model is moving up or down. For example, if it shifts from bearish to neutral, we might consider that hopeful. But going from bullish to neutral could make us cautious. We would never deviate too far from the Fab Five's basic verdict. If it's bullish we won't be bearish: we might be mildly bullish, but never bearish. Even though this model isn't designed for trading, traders can still use it to make decisions about whether they should have a bullish or bearish bias. If the short side is your thing then you should be a little more careful if the Fab Five is in bullish mode, and vice versa. At any rate, we still look to other inputs when evaluating our market position, but always in the context of the Fab Five.

CHAPTER 15

A Simple Model for Bonds

From Ned Davis, *Being Right or Making Money,*
3rd edition (Hoboken, New Jersey: John Wiley &
Sons, 2014), Chapter 4.

Loren Flath

About 10 years ago Ned got wind of a TradeStation seminar at the Venetian Hotel in Las Vegas. He is always looking for new ideas on markets and trading, and he thought I might learn something about new software or new analytical techniques. It was a three-day ordeal, with workshops of various kinds hosted by some very sharp people with truly interesting—and in some cases, somewhat complicated—trading methodologies. A number of the presenters had advanced degrees and managed money with the techniques they were showing us. Originally called System Writer, TradeStation started as a computer program for developing trading systems that could use a plethora of technical analysis tools. By 2004 it had evolved into a very sophisticated platform complete with automated trading: If you built a model with specific rules for buying and selling, you could put the system on automatic pilot.

On the last day of the seminar there was an elaborate lunch. Following our meal we were introduced to the guest speaker, Nelson Freeburg. I remember quite well his discussion of real-time models, and how so few of them actually continue to work as time passes. After investigating many models he had found only four true to their back-testing promises. He discussed the details of each, and when he got to number four he emphasized that he had saved the best for last. Then he proceeded to show the real-time results for the bond model presented in Marty Zweig's book *Winning with New IRAs*. I nearly choked on my carrot cake as I listened to him go over the details of the model that I had built for Marty's book in early 1986! I had long forgotten that model and had no inkling of its real-time performance. Ned was right: I did learn something!

I'll go over the model in detail, but in reality there is not a whole lot to go over. The late, great Marty Zweig, an accomplished investment advisor and market technician, was adamant that the model be as simple as possible. He wanted his readers to be able to calculate each indicator weekly in just a few minutes themselves. No laborious calculations, no hard-to-find data, no complicated concepts. As he pointed out in his book: "We tried to keep the model as simple as possible while adhering to two of my key general principles, which apply to the stock market as well—namely, staying in gear with the tape and in gear with the Fed."

Ned and I had our guidelines, but Marty had the final say. Since the book was about individual retirement accounts, it would have been nice to have developed the model with something tradable, like a bond mutual fund. But there was a dearth of historical mutual-fund data, so we instead used the Dow Jones 20 Bond Average, for which we had the weekly history going back to 1965. That index was composed of Baa-graded corporate bonds, and we had a facsimile for its yield. That let us back-test the model and then evaluate its predictive results against the index's actual total return. The very first version of the model I sent to Marty included moving-average and momentum calculations. "No," he said, "too complicated." (Computers weren't too common in the average home in 1986.) I made it still simpler. Here are the model's original four indicators:

1. The short-term slope of the Dow Jones 20 Bond Average: buy when the index rises from a bottom by 0.6 percent and sell when the index falls from a peak by 0.6 percent.
2. The longer term slope of the Dow Jones 20 Bond Average: buy when the index rises from a bottom by 1.8 percent and sell when it falls from a peak by 1.8 percent.
3. Changes in the discount rate: buy when the discount rate—the rate at which banks borrow from the Federal Reserve Bank—drops by at least one half of a percentage point and sell when the discount rate rises by at least a half point. This series ceased to be very relevant in 1989 when the central bank began influencing short-term rates via the Fed Funds rate—the rate at which banks borrow from one another. Now the indicator looks at half-point moves in the target rate that the Fed sets for Fed Funds.
4. The yield curve, based on the difference between the yields on AAA corporate bonds and 90-day commercial paper: buy when the spread crosses above 0.6 of a percentage point and sell when the spread falls below −0.2. Go neutral between −0.2 and 0.6.

In keeping with our KISS methodology, the model is a simple sum of the indicators' values. Thus its range is −4 to +4. Marty designed this model to give concrete buy and sell signals that were to be followed implicitly—no questions asked. He gave a detailed account of the model in Chapter 12 of *Winning with New IRAs*, complete with examples of how to trade with it and instructions on how to calculate each indicator. Figure 15.1 is a modernized version of the original chart of the model equity line as it appeared in the book. This was obviously a time in which managing risk was very important; in much of the 1966–1986 period interest rates climbed and bond

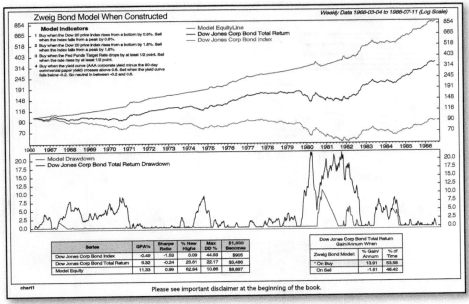

FIGURE 15.1 Zweig Bond Model When Constructed (1966–1986).

prices fell. The model was long the benchmark only 54 percent of the time. Since this is a trading model, I have added the equity drawdown history in the bottom panel. (*Drawdown* is a Wall Street euphemism for a word investors despise: loss.) This reveals a nearly 11 percent drop on September 26, 1980.

The chart in Figure 15.2 shows how the model has done since Marty's book was sent to press in July 1986. During this period bond prices have gone nearly straight up. Timing a move like that is challenging and quite often disappointing. In this case,

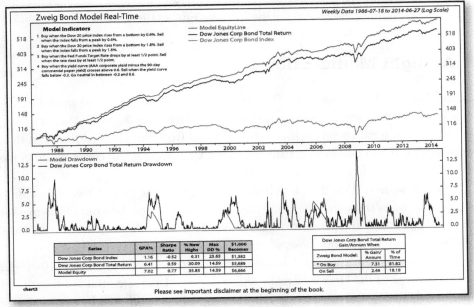

FIGURE 15.2 Zweig Bond Model Real-Time (1986–2014).

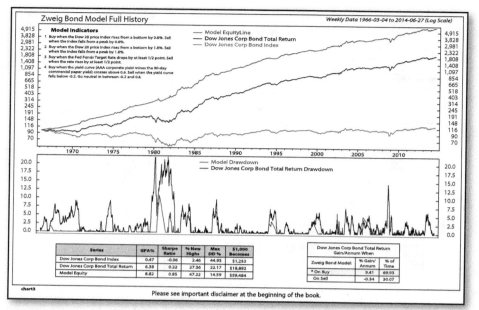

FIGURE 15.3 Zweig Bond Model Full History (1966–2014).

the model has spent only about a quarter of the time in cash. The worst period was during the 2008 debacle, when both monetary indicators were bullish while both trend indicators went bearish, causing the prior buy signal to become locked in. This caused a drawdown of 14.6 percent. The same thing happened in 2013, although the drawdown was somewhat less painful at just above 6 percent. Still, as can be seen from the Sharpe ratios the model has handily beaten a buy-and-hold strategy, with less risk. (The Sharpe ratio measures risk-adjusted performance; the higher the number, the better.)

Figure 15.3 shows the model for the full date range (1966–2014).

■ A Slight Modification

Back in 2004, following the TradeStation seminar, I put revisiting the model on the back burner. When the decision was made to update *Being Right or Making Money*, we thought we would just reprise the bond model from the 2000 edition. But then we thought it might be fun to actually highlight a model that had come to life in the mid-1980s and had been quite successful.

Now that we have done that, let's look more deeply at the model. Two things jump out: (1) the losses show that the trend component doesn't get you out of the market when the Fed is easy and prices are falling, and (2) you couldn't really trade the Dow 20 when it existed, let alone now, when it doesn't.

To minimize potential losses, I added a simple trend indicator: a 50-day (10-week) moving average of the Dow 20's price with a cross of 1 percent (this is a favorite of ours for calculating diffusion indices). If the Dow 20's price crosses below its 50-day average by at least 1 percent, this indicator goes negative. Crossing above the 50-day by at least 1 percent sends the indicator positive. With this addition the model is now a five-indicator model, and as with the original model, the sum of all the indicators needs to be a −1 or a +1 to get a signal. Figures 15.4, 15.5, and 15.6 show the modified model for the time ranges shown in Figures 15.1, 15.2, and 15.3, respectively. Note the dramatic reduction in losses and the added amount of time spent long. Also, the equity line spends more time making new highs in all three periods shown.

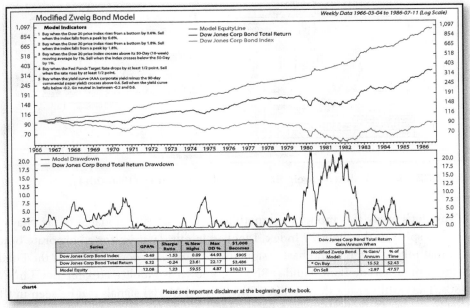

FIGURE 15.4 Modified Zweig Bond Model (1966–1986).

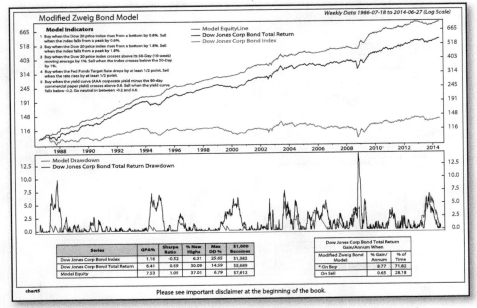

FIGURE 15.5 Modified Zweig Bond Model (1986–2014).

FIGURE 15.6 Modified Zweig Bond Model Full History (1966–2014).

Now let's apply this model to something that is actually tradable today. Staying with the spirit of the Dow 20 Index, I looked in our database for a corporate bond fund that might match it and have a significant history. A good match was the Fidelity Investment Grade Bond Fund (FBNDX), known as Fidelity Flexible Bond in the 1980s. The results using the modified Zweig Bond Model signals can be seen in the chart in Figure 15.7. At the outset they don't appear impressive. But remember that we have been dealing with a very strong bond market during the time frame covered

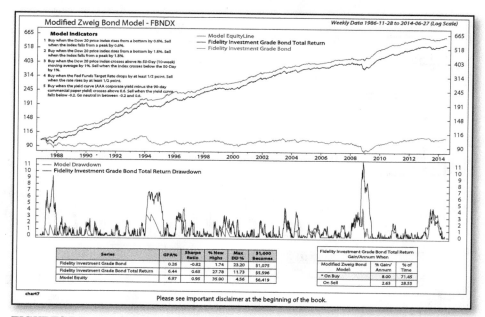

FIGURE 15.7 Modified Zweig Bond Model with FBNDX.

Modified Zweig Bond Model - JNK   Weekly Data 1998-08-07 to 2014-06-27 (Log Scale)

Model Indicators

— Model EquityLine
— SPDR Barclays Hi Yld Bond Total Return
— SPDR Barclays Hi Yld Bond

1. Buy when the JNK price index rises from a bottom by 0.6%. Sell when the index falls from a peak by 0.6%.
2. Buy when the JNK price index rises from a bottom by 1.8%. Sell when the index falls from a peak by 1.8%.
3. Buy when the JNK price index crosses above its 50-Day (10-week) moving average by 1%. Sell when the index crosses below the 50-Day by 1%.
4. Buy when the Fed Funds Target Rate drops by at least 1/2 point. Sell when the rate rises by at least 1/2 point.
5. Buy when the yield curve (AAA corporate yield minus the 90-day commercial paper yield) crosses above 0.6. Sell when the yield curve falls below -0.2. Go neutral in between -0.2 and 0.6.

— Model Drawdown
— SPDR Barclays HI Yld Bond Total Return Drawdown

Series	GPA%	Sharpe Ratio	% New Highs	Max DD %	$1,000 Becomes
SPDR Barclays Hi Yld Bond	-1.03	-0.27	2.53	51.56	$849
SPDR Barclays Hi Yld Bond Total Return	6.64	0.38	25.18	40.08	$2,779
Model Equity	9.40	0.99	30.48	11.28	$4,173

SPDR Barclays Hi Yld Bond Total Return Gain/Annum When

Modified Zweig Bond Model:	% Gain/ Annum	% of Time
* On Buy	12.17	70.05
On Sell	-5.25	29.95

chart8   Please see important disclaimer at the beginning of the book.

FIGURE 15.8 Modified Zweig Bond Model with JNK.

(1986–2014). What is significant is that the model does work, as reflected by the higher Sharpe ratio, lower drawdowns, and increased time spent long.

For those of you who really like to trade: we've found over the years that a decent model built for one index can produce surprising results when applied to another that's highly correlated but more volatile. Figure 15.8 shows the same model shown in Figure 15.7 calculated on the price of the SPDR Barclays High Yield Bond ETF (JNK) instead, with the results based on its total return. As for trade frequency, the trades averaged about 0.7 per year.

■ Summary

A note for those of you who have Marty Zweig's *Winning with New IRAs* or plan to obtain a copy: in it, Marty did a great job explaining this model. His book includes numerous details, tables, and charts to accompany the dialog. However, he writes that a buy signal comes at +3 and a sell at −3. This reflects an error in communication between the two of us. In reality, all of the results summarized in Chapter 12 of his book are based on signals at −1 and +1. Since Marty's book was published, the Dow Jones 20 Bond Index has morphed into the Dow Jones Equal Weight U.S. Issued Corporate Bond Index, and it can be found in many places, including Google and Yahoo Finance.

In sum, the Zweig Bond Model shows that keeping it simple can pay off. Marty Zweig knew this when he approached us to build it back in 1985. The basic principles were true then and still true now: don't fight the tape, and don't fight the Fed. In the words of the inimitable Stan Lee: 'nuff said!

CHAPTER 16

Perspectives on Active and Passive Money Management

From Robert A. Weigand, *Applied Equity Analysis and Portfolio Management* (Hoboken, New Jersey: John Wiley & Sons, 2014), Chapter 1.

This chapter introduces key perspectives designed to help you get the most out of the readings, exercises, and activities featured in the chapters that follow. The learning objectives for this chapter are:

1. Display an understanding of the chapter terminology and describe the top-down fundamental analysis process.
2. Explain why stocks with superior fundamentals often have higher returns and lower risk over long horizons.
3. Summarize the results of studies that investigate the performance of professional investors and what motivates investors to trade more actively.
4. Identify the three major theories of the way information gets incorporated into stock prices, and summarize the major premises of each theory.
5. Summarize the perspectives of esteemed investors and authors provided in the chapter.
6. Interpret the insights into financial markets from Chapter 23 of John Maynard Keynes's *General Theory of Employment, Interest and Money*.
7. Discuss the importance of an investment policy statement.

▪ Terminology: Investors, Investment Vehicles, Risk and Return

Equity investing can be divided into two main categories: passive and active. ***Passive investors*** buy and hold stocks for the long term. They construct portfolios or choose investment vehicles that minimize costs, including research costs, trading costs, administrative costs, performance fees, and taxes on realized gains. The most popular types of passive investment vehicles include "index" mutual funds and exchange-traded funds (ETFs), which are designed to imitate the performance of indexes like the S&P 500. ***Active investors***, however, seek to outperform the indexes by identifying individual stocks to buy and sell. Because they trade more often, active investors turn their portfolios over more frequently than passive investors and usually incur higher costs.

Relative versus Absolute Return Investing

Active investing can be further divided into two main categories. ***Relative return*** vehicles seek to outperform a benchmark index (like the Standard & Poor's [S&P] 500), where "outperformance" is measured as a combination of either earning higher returns and/or achieving lower risk exposure. Most equity portfolios, including equity mutual funds and student investment funds, are relative return vehicles, where the fund's performance is evaluated relative to a widely followed benchmark. ***Absolute return*** vehicles seek to deliver returns that are less risky but are also usually lower than the returns of most index benchmarks. Many equity hedge funds are absolute return vehicles. Examples include long-short funds that make both positive bets (by owning stocks long) and negative bets (by selling stocks short).

You may notice that the terms active and passive are, to some degree, "loaded" words. In many cultures (especially the United States), being passive is usually considered less desirable than being active. Later in this chapter, you will learn that this is rarely the case in investing, however. The results of numerous research studies show that one of the main reasons passive, buy-and-hold investing is so prevalent is that the majority of active professional investors underperform their benchmarks.

Alpha and Beta: Excess Returns and Market Risk

Alpha refers to the *excess* returns earned by relative return investors, either above or below the market index to which their performance is benchmarked. When a portfolio outperforms its benchmark index, the percentage return by which the portfolio exceeds the index return will be termed positive alpha. If a portfolio underperforms its benchmark index, we'll say it earned a negative alpha.

Beta is a measure of risk that can apply to an individual stock or to a portfolio of stocks. The average market beta = 1.0. In the case of an individual stock, beta measures how much risk, or ***volatility***, that stock is expected to contribute to the overall volatility of a diversified portfolio. High-beta stocks usually exhibit a more volatile reaction to market-wide or macroeconomic news, on both the upside and downside. Examples of high-beta stocks include ***cyclical stocks*** like Caterpillar and Ford. The stock prices of these companies are more volatile because businesses and consumers buy more tractors, cars, and trucks during strong economic times, and cut back on investments in capital assets and purchases of durable goods during weak economic times. Low-beta stocks tend to be less volatile, however, and therefore contribute less volatility to a diversified portfolio. Examples include consumer staples stocks like Nestlé and pharmaceutical stocks like Bristol-Myers. These companies produce items consumers tend to buy regardless of economic conditions.

When applied to a well-diversified equity portfolio, beta is a measure of the market risk, or volatility, of the portfolio. If a portfolio emphasizes high-beta stocks, its returns will tend to be more volatile, and vice-versa if it emphasizes low-beta stocks. Finance theory asserts that *risk and expected returns are positively related*, which implies that high-beta stock stocks should earn higher returns and low-beta stocks should earn lower returns over long holding periods. Thus, high-beta stock portfolios should outperform low-beta portfolios, as higher returns compensate investors for bearing greater risk. One of the principles of this book is that investors can construct winning portfolios by investing in *low*-beta stocks, which contradicts the basic wisdom of finance. After introducing a clearer picture of the job of the fundamental analyst in the following section, we will revisit this apparently contradictory assertion. Can investors really have it both ways—lower risk and *higher* returns?

■ The Top-Down Fundamental Analysis Process

Next we'll take an overview of the fundamental analysis process featured in this book. Our process is termed *top-down* because it begins with an analysis of the overall economy, with an emphasis on gauging the stage of the business cycle in which the economy is operating. As we'll see, this activity helps the analyst identify sectors of the stock market in which to deploy new capital, and sectors from which capital should be withdrawn and redeployed.

Analysts divide the stock market into 10 sectors. When an actively managed portfolio allocates funds by sector in a way that differs from their current market weights, we will say the portfolio manager is employing **sector overweights and underweights**. In Level III, Chapter 22 we will attribute the under- or outperformance of a portfolio relative to a benchmark to the sector weights used in the portfolio (in addition to other factors). Once an analyst determines the sectors to over- and underweight relative to the market, he will next determine the stocks with the best prospects to overweight within each sector (and the stocks to sell or sell short, if the fund allows short selling). Figure 16.1 depicts the stages of the top-down fundamental analysis process.

The decision to buy a stock and hold it in a portfolio indicates confidence, or conviction, in the security. But it is unlikely that managers will have the same degree of conviction regarding each stock they own. Figure 16.2 shows the possible "weights" (the percentage of total portfolio wealth invested in each stock) in a 12-stock portfolio, ranked by analyst conviction. Notice how the highest-conviction stocks receive the highest weight and the lowest-conviction stocks receive the lowest weight.

FIGURE 16.1 The Top-Down
Fundamental Analysis Process.

FIGURE 16.2 Analyst Conviction and Active
Portfolio Weights.

Active investors therefore allocate portfolio wealth among stocks differently than these stocks' market-determined weights in the benchmark index. The active investor's weighting scheme will be called *active portfolio weights*.

Why Stocks with Solid Fundamentals Outperform over Long Horizons

Now that you understand the overall fundamental process, let's take a closer look at exactly how portfolios emphasizing stocks with solid fundamentals outperform over long horizons. First, let's be more specific about what we mean by fundamentals. We're going to learn how to identify stocks whose prices are well supported by the basic building blocks, or fundamentals, that support intrinsic value: revenues, profits, free cash flows, and a commitment to return a large share of that free cash flow to investors, preferably in the form of cash dividends. These characteristics conform to another basic finance principle, which states that *an asset's* **intrinsic value** *equals today's value of the future free cash flows the asset is expected to generate over its lifetime*. This means that we'll learn to identify:

1. Stocks with steadily growing revenues, profits, free cash flows, and dividends.
2. Stocks that achieve this growth by making prudent capital investments.
3. Companies with strong competitive positions that allow them to defend and maintain their market presence, which supports further growth in their fundamentals.

Next, recall the idea of beta—the index of how volatile a stock is likely to be and how much volatility it will contribute to a diversified portfolio. Beginning students of finance often ask an obvious question about volatility that shows more savvy than finance theorists have been able to handle: "Don't we only want to avoid *downside* volatility?"

There is a lot of wisdom contained in that question, because it indirectly describes how stocks with superior fundamentals win. These types of stocks almost never surge ahead during the market's bull phase. But when markets correct or enter a bear phase—and they always do—stocks with superior fundamentals tend to decline in value much less than their high-beta counterparts. Moreover, after the market correction is over, these stocks usually resume following the market's next upward trend, albeit at a somewhat slower pace. We'll consider three examples to help you better understand these tendencies.

The second quarter of the year is an excellent period to study how the stock market works. Research shows that the stock market tends to earn much of its total annual return early in the calendar year (usually beginning in late December). After the first quarter, however, an old adage holds that investors can "sell in May and go away," as the market tends to trend sideways or correct after the early-year euphoria fades and investors become more discriminating about the specific stocks they want to own. Let's take a look at the returns of several stocks with solid fundamentals during the second quarter of 2012: Bristol-Myers and Johnson & Johnson.

Figure 16.3 shows how Bristol-Myers (BMY) follows the market through early April, but as investors become increasingly nervous about an impending correction, buyers gradually bid BMY's stock price up until it decouples from the market trend. This occurs because during market corrections, investors sell many of their risky, high-beta stock positions and invest the proceeds in stocks with superior fundamentals. The prices of these stocks are supported by their fundamentals, which makes them most attractive to investors during the market's darkest moods. And because these stocks have a predictable tendency to decline in value by much less than the market, investors' portfolios suffer far less damage (known as drawdowns) during corrections and bear markets. Warren Buffett best summed up this essential

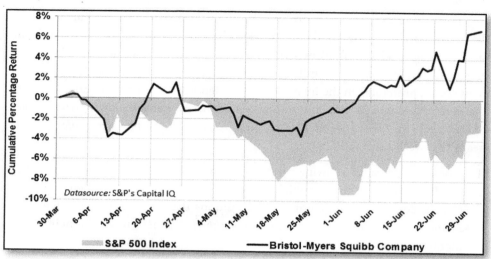

FIGURE 16.3 **Bristol-Myers Rises During the Spring 2012 Market Correction.**
Source: S&P's Capital IQ.

principle of investing when he said, "The best way to make a dollar is not to lose a dollar" (Lowe, 1997).

Figure 16.4 depicts a similar pattern for Johnson & Johnson (JNJ), which is one of the "most widely held stocks" among institutional investors. The graph reveals why so many institutions hold JNJ: because it's a great portfolio diversifier. Notice how the stock initially follows the market's downward move, but investors only allow it to fall so far before it offers compelling value in a declining market. Toward the end of the three-month market correction, JNJ has outperformed the market by almost 6 percent. And, in the world of investing, not losing 6 percent is just as good as gaining 6 percent. This is how stocks with solid fundamentals contribute to superior portfolio returns and lower volatility over long horizons.

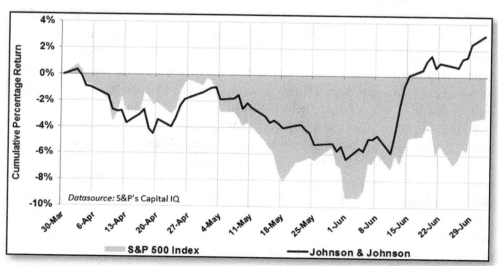

FIGURE 16.4 **J&J Reaches a 3-Month High During the Spring 2012 Market Correction.**
Source: S&P's Capital IQ.

FIGURE 16.5 Citigroup Outperforms Wal-Mart in Early 2012.

Source: S&P's Capital IQ.

Let's consider one more example to fully make the point. Figure 16.5 depicts the cumulative returns to Wal-Mart, Citigroup, and the S&P 500 during the first quarter of 2012 (we begin in mid-December, which is when large turn-of-the-year moves in the stock market often begin). The stock market gained 16 percent through late March, propelled by speculative names like Citigroup. Years of blunders by this financial services giant directly contributed to the financial crisis of 2008, and it has subsequently suffered through a series of scandals and mismanagement—none of which prevented it from accepting government assistance that enabled it to continue operating without proper financial discipline. In late 2011 through early 2012, a bet on Citigroup was a purely speculative play.

Notice how a stock like Wal-Mart, which models up well on a fundamental basis, initially gets left behind in the market's turn-of-the-year frenzy. During the first quarter of 2012, Wal-Mart's stock earns less than half of the total market return, and far less than Citigroup. At this point you might be thinking "Why *wouldn't* an investor want to own Citigroup?"

Next we'll shift our attention to Figure 16.6, which shows the cumulative returns to Wal-Mart, Citigroup, and the S&P 500 during the second quarter, when the market corrected downward by approximately 10 percent. What a difference 90 days makes. Citigroup's stock declines by more than three times as much as the market because they were weighed down by poor fundamentals. Notice how midway through the market correction, investors began the same predictable rotation into safer stocks with strong fundamentals. Wal-Mart outperforms the S&P 500 by approximately 16 percent during this period, and it beats Citigroup by almost 40 percent!

Figure 16.7 completes the story. Despite Citigroup's strong showing in the first quarter, Wal-Mart handily outperforms Citigroup through spring, summer, and most of the fall, albeit in a sort of tortoise-versus-the-hare manner. Fundamental

FIGURE 16.6   Wal-Mart Outperforms Citigroup During Spring 2012 Market Correction.
Source: S&P's Capital IQ.

investors might have felt a little nervous early in 2012 when Citigroup was bounding ahead, but in the slow and patient buy-and-hold race, the stock with the superior fundamentals eventually won out—as most often happens. Moreover, Wal-Mart outperformed with lower volatility, taking investors on less of a roller-coaster ride. Wal-Mart's beta versus the S&P 500 equals only 0.35, versus Citigroup's beta of approximately 2.0.

Now that we understand why fundamentally sound stocks outperform over long horizons, we're going to take a closer look at the long-term track record of professional money managers.

FIGURE 16.7   Citigroup Plays Catch-up for the Rest of the Year.
Source: S&P's Capital IQ.

■ The Record of Professional Money Managers

Earlier in this chapter, we reduced fundamental analysis to a multistep process that sounded as easy to implement as following a recipe. As we'll see, things are not quite that simple. In this section we'll review the record of professional money managers, and consider why they often achieve such disappointing results.

Most research into active money management concludes that the majority of managers underperform their benchmarks (they earn negative alphas). Let me assure you that this is not some abstract academic result, or a partisan misreading of the facts. It's probably one the best-kept secrets on Wall Street, however. The prevalence of negative alphas among mutual funds (net of expenses and trading costs) is well documented by studies conducted by respected researchers, including Elton et al. (1993), Carhart (1997), and John Bogle (2002), the founder of Vanguard. More recently, Standard & Poor's Indices vs. Active Funds (SPIVA) 2009 scorecard reported that over the period 2004–2008, 63 percent of large-cap mutual funds, 74 percent of mid-cap funds, and 68 percent of small-cap funds underperformed their benchmarks. Among international mutual funds, the underperformance rates ranged between 60 and 90 percent. If those results aren't bad enough, Standard & Poor's reported that 84 percent of actively managed funds underperformed in 2011. And these findings are not confined to calendar-year periods. For example, Ludwig (2012) reports that almost 90 percent of professionally managed funds underperformed from June 2011 through June 2012. These findings are not unusual. It is extremely rare for active investment vehicles to outperform passive vehicles in the aggregate, and it has never occurred consistently over any extended period of time.

The performance of investment managers in the absolute return/hedge fund space is similarly disappointing. Malkiel and Saha (2005) conclude that hedge fund returns are lower than commonly supposed, and that hedge funds are significantly riskier than more conventional investments. Fung, Xu, and Yau (2004) also report negative average alphas for hedge funds, and Pojarliev and Levich (2008) find negative risk-adjusted alphas among a sample of funds that invest in international currencies. Writing about long-short funds for *Institutional Investor* magazine, O'Hara (2009) asks, "If managers can't beat the market, what purpose do they serve?" Statman (2010) provides one possible answer to O'Hara's question. His research suggests that investors use their relationships with money management firms to express their social class and lifestyles, implying that investors are willing to accept lower returns if they can place funds with prestigious firms and/or managers.

Mark Hulbert is well known for publishing the *Hulbert Financial Digest*, a newsletter that tracks the performance and sentiment of mutual fund managers. Hulbert's survey shows that investment manager sentiment is a contrarian indicator (meaning that investment managers are too pessimistic at market bottoms and too optimistic at market tops).

Hulbert is also a columnist for the *New York Times* and *Dow Jones Marketwatch*. In 2008 he reviewed a working paper by Barras, Scaillet, and Wermers (published in 2010) that concludes that even fewer managers beat the market than previously thought. After accounting for fees, the vast majority of active mutual funds had negative returns. But these authors also conclude that the proportion of zero-alpha mutual funds is *higher* than previously thought. They find that 75 percent of funds earn zero alphas, implying that the pros earn just enough to cover their fees and other costs. Less than 1 percent of funds delivered positive alpha in a way that is consistent with manager skill, however.

Why Do Active Managers Underperform?

The research reviewed in the previous section convincingly concludes that in the aggregate, active managers underperform their benchmarks, and they do so with surprising consistency. These results were not covered with the purpose of picking on the pros—just the opposite, as the key mission of this book is to teach you to conduct your own stock research effectively and professionally. It's necessary to confront the track record of the pros to illustrate the challenging and competitive landscape of professional money management, however. We need to understand why such a group of intelligent, competitive, well-trained individuals consistently post such disappointing results so that we don't make the same mistakes. We'll start by taking a closer look at step 3 of the top-down process: conducting fundamental analysis to determine which stocks to under- and overweight relative to their weights in the overall market.

After we determine the financial health and stability of a company, we will conduct a valuation analysis to determine if the company's stock is trading above or below what we'll call its **intrinsic value**. As mentioned previously, a stock's intrinsic value equals today's value of all the free cash flows the company is expected to generate over its remaining lifetime. Estimating intrinsic value is as much a science as an art, as it involves forecasting the company's future revenues, expenses, and a variety of other income statement and balance sheet items.

This step of the fundamental analysis process involves a logical inconsistency, or paradox, that only the best analysts confront. The paradox occurs whenever an analyst concludes that a stock is under- or overvalued, because the analyst is implicitly asserting that the market is making a mistake in the way it's valuing the stock. Notice that market mistakes are a possibility that we must allow for if we're going to be active investors. If we believe the market price is correct 100 percent of the time, then only low-cost indexing makes sense. Why would anyone spend time and money researching companies and estimating the intrinsic value of stocks when all they have to do is check their market price?

So here's the paradox: if the analyst believes the market is mispricing a stock today, why shouldn't it be the case that this mispricing will continue to persist? For an analyst to rationally make the case, for example, that shares of ABC are worth $100, but are temporarily undervalued at $80, he should also be able to identify the upcoming information or change of perception that will convince other investors and traders to begin paying more for the stock. There must be an event that changes the market's mind about the value of ABC, or the analyst will simply own many shares of a stock whose price is stuck at $80.

Therefore, identifying a mispriced security (an irrational valuation by the overall market) is a necessary but insufficient step in the fundamental analysis process. The final step is to anticipate the *catalysts* that will help the rest of the market recognize the true value of the under- and overvalued securities identified by our fundamental process. There are many stocks that model up as undervalued—some based on their dividends alone. But concluding that a stock is undervalued is not the same as concluding that it's overdue for a significant price correction. Yet the investment theses of many professional analysts fail to include this important perspective.

Before an analyst can anticipate the forthcoming catalysts that will finally move a stock's price closer to his estimate of fair value, he needs a theory, or model, of how the market processes information under certain conditions. This model will inform his understanding of why the market may be mispricing a certain security, and also guide his thinking about how information regarding the company's true value will eventually become reflected in its stock price.

■ Market Efficiency, Behavioral Finance, and Adaptive Expectations

In this section we'll consider three competing explanations of the way investors process information and incorporate it into their trading decisions, and thus securities prices as well. The first explanation, the *efficient markets hypothesis* (EMH), is the oldest, known for emphasizing a high level of rationality in investor behavior and aggregate market outcomes. The second comes from the newer field of *behavioral finance*, which allows investor emotions to play a larger role in securities pricing. Behavioral finance recognizes that pricing errors can not only exist but sometimes persist for long periods. The third explanation, the *adaptive markets hypothesis* (AMH), is the newest of the three. The AMH views the interactions among investors, securities, markets, and institutions as a dynamically evolving ecosystem. Within the AMH framework, winners are determined by their ability to both compete and adapt to constantly changing circumstances.

Market Efficiency

We begin with a discussion of the concept of market efficiency, formally known as the efficient markets hypothesis, or EMH. No matter how much you may have heard this theory praised or ridiculed in previous coursework or via other exposure, it's important to understand what this theory says and its implications for active investors. Any time we're talking about "beating the market"—actively investing to earn risk-adjusted returns that are higher than the returns of a benchmark index—we're talking about market efficiency, because we're asserting that we possess tradable information that the market does not fully understand, or cannot accurately pass through to a security's price for some reason. Understanding market efficiency is a useful first step in understanding and exploiting deviations from efficiency. When information is not accurately reflected in a stock's price, there may be an opportunity to buy or sell the mispriced security and earn excess returns.

Based on the typical textbook treatment, one could get the idea that market efficiency is a theoretically abstract concept that has no application in the real world, yet nothing could be further from the truth. Securities traders and finance professionals of all types are concerned with the issue of market efficiency (as we'll see in the Morgan Stanley investment policy statement below). They just employ a perspective and use a vocabulary that's different than those of finance professors. This point is best illustrated by comparing an academic perspective on market efficiency with a practitioner perspective.

The academic perspective says: "A securities market is informationally efficient when news is rapidly and accurately reflected in the prices of financial securities." Although that's a perfectly accurate statement, representing the usual treatment of this topic in finance textbooks, thinking about market efficiency this way makes it sound dull, abstract, and uninteresting.

The practitioner perspective, however, asks the question: "Are there any trading strategies based on historical and/or publicly available information that outperform the market with reasonable consistency after adjusting for risk?" Although both definitions are concerned with whether all available information is accurately reflected in the price, approaching the topic from this perspective allows for the possibility that our understanding of market efficiency will make us better investors, which is our main goal.

Securities Prices in an Efficient Market The prices of stocks and other securities in an efficient market will react rapidly and accurately to news, where news is defined as information that is (1) relevant to the value of the security and (2) unanticipated by the market (in other words, "new"). Thus, securities prices are thought to reflect all information that is relevant regarding stocks' valuation all the time. Markets are thought to be efficient due to the research conducted by rational, wealth-maximizing analysts and investors. The large potential profits from making the right call motivate analysts to work hard to identify new information, assess its relevance for securities prices, and immediately trade on the results of their analysis. It's the diligent efforts of investors that keep prices efficient.

The Three Levels of Market Efficiency Market efficiency is often described as having three possible "levels," which define the type and amount of information assumed to be fully reflected in prices. This classification can be understood by inserting one of the three bullet-point phrases into the first and second blank spaces shown in the following sentence: "Securities markets are _____ efficient if gathering and analyzing all _____ information does *not* consistently produce excess returns."

- Weak form/historical

- Semistrong form/current and publicly available

- Strong form/private or inside

If you believe market prices fully reflect all historical information, but not necessarily current, publicly available information, then you are classifying the market as weak form efficient. In other words, all historical information is so well reflected in market prices that it's almost always impossible to trade on that information to earn excess returns. If, however, you believe market prices fully reflect both historical and current, publicly available information, then you are classifying the market as semistrong efficient. In this case, analyzing past *and* current information is not useful in consistently outperforming the market (although occasional outperformance by investors is not ruled out). There's not much point in talking about whether prices fully reflect private or inside information because it's impossible to investigate scientifically (questionnaires asking about illegal trading are never completed and returned for some strange reason). We will focus on the semistrong level of efficiency and assume that investors are proficient in both technical analysis (studying past price patterns by using charts) and fundamental analysis (studying all historical and current information, including financial statements, research conducted by other analysts, etc.).

The Behavior of Securities Prices in an Efficient Market   Let's say that news is released regarding a large, unexpected change in the profit outlook for a firm. In an efficient market we would expect to see the stock price react immediately upon release of that information. Since the market is so competitive, only the investors who receive the news first and immediately act on it will earn excess returns. Everyone else will be too late to use the news profitably, as the trades of the first investors cause the stock's price to quickly correct to fair value.

Figure 16.8 depicts an efficient market reaction to news. IBM announced its earnings for the third quarter of 2012 after the market closed on October 16. Analysts were expecting earnings of $25.4 billion, but IBM came in a little light at $24.7 billion. As shown in the graph, IBM's stock price reaction was swift. The stock declined 4.92 percent on October 17, and another 2.83 percent on October 18. Over those two days the S&P 500 rose 0.17 percent, so IBM's large price decline was clearly due to the company-specific news release and not broader information pertaining to the entire market.

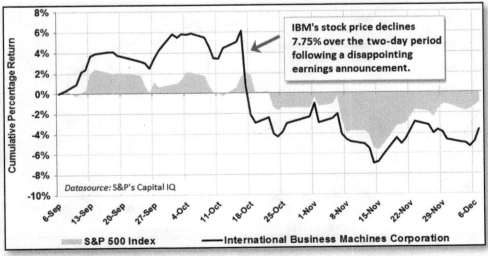

FIGURE 16.8   IBM's Earnings Miss Analysts' Expectations in October 2012.
Source: S&P's Capital IQ.

IBM's reaction is also considered efficient due to the way the stock price behaves *after* the announcement. Notice that after the two-day price adjustment, IBM's price begins following the market trend once again. There is no significant price "drift" in either a positive or negative direction. For the following two trading months, IBM loses another 1.5 percent and the market loses 2.9 percent. IBM's reaction to the earnings news therefore appears to be confined to the two-day period following the announcement, consistent with the predictions of the EMH.[1]

Now that we've considered an example of when the efficient markets theory works, let's consider a more subtle example that is representative of the type of criticism many have leveled at the EMH. This criticism concerns market participants' ability and willingness to see all the way through the numbers reported by companies. Do analysts really think critically, or are they too eager to parrot back the information that's fed to them?

Do Analysts Dig Deep Enough? Figure 16.9 shows Amazon's stock price reaction to its April 26, 2012, earnings announcement. The market was expecting Amazon to earn 7 cents a share, but the company reported 28 cents—*four times* the expected number. There was a large, positive stock price reaction of 17.97 percent over the following two trading days. Over those same days, the S&P 500 declined by 0.15 percent, so once again, the stock price reaction was almost certainly due to the release of company-specific news rather than market-wide information.

Next we'll focus on Amazon's stock returns following the announcement. Through mid-June, the stock lost 6.58 percent. Is it possible that Amazon's price overreacted to the news, and the market "took back" some of those large gains from the April earnings announcement? In this case, probably not. Even though the downward postannouncement price drift is evident in the graph, the market declined by 5.27 percent over the same period. Amazon's stock returns following the

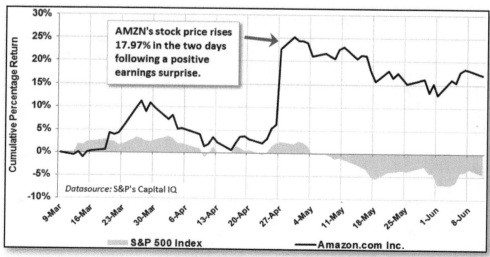

FIGURE 16.9   **Amazon's Earnings Beat Analysts' Expectations in April 2012.**
Source: S&P's Capital IQ.

announcement are therefore most likely due to the overall market trend, and not a reconsideration of Amazon's valuation based on their earnings.

Thus far, it looks like the market was efficient around Amazon's earnings announcement. There are actually several reasons to think that the market was not functioning with perfect accuracy and objectivity in this case, however. The first reason is that Amazon was on pace to report earnings per share of 7 cents in the weeks leading up to the earnings announcement, according to the "guidance" the company provided to analysts in the preannouncement period. It was only a last-minute decision to transfer profits from other entities in which Amazon has minority ownership onto their income statement that allowed Amazon to report earnings that were four times larger than analysts anticipated. Of course, there was nothing illegal about this move. It is allowed based on the "equity-method investment activity, net of tax" provision in U.S. generally accepted accounting principles (GAAP) rules. What's concerning about Amazon's decision to declare these profits is that the average value for that equity-method account was −$500,000 for the past eight quarters. Amazon's decision therefore looks a bit like opportunistic "earnings management," a practice used by many companies to make their profits look larger and more consistent than they would be without some manipulation.

The second, somewhat more disturbing criticism regarding the accuracy of the market's reaction was described by Peter Eavis, writing for the *New York Times*' Deal-Book blog on April 27, 2012. Mr. Eavis's article makes note of the following facts:

- Amazon's first-quarter earnings diverged significantly from the guidance provided by the company.

- Amazon offered no explanation for this large divergence.

- There were 17 analysts on the earnings call, yet none thought to ask why earnings were four times larger than the preannouncement number.

- Amazon's investor relations department did not respond to Mr. Eavis's subsequent e-mail inquiries and phone messages.

I find it odd that there were 17 analysts on the earnings announcement call, but none of them asked the simple question, "Why were your profits four times larger than expected?" That type of behavior is not consistent with analysts' digging deep to uncover the ultimate truth about a company. The criticism of the EMH in this case is that without access to all relevant information, including information that requires fervent due diligence by analysts, markets can't be efficient.

Taking a longer-term perspective on this issue, analysts have consistently ignored a variety of "inconvenient truths" about Amazon's profitability for quite some time. Figure 16.10 depicts Amazon's operating margin from the first quarter of 2010 through the third quarter of 2012. The graph shows that Amazon's operating margin has been in a steady downtrend for years. The company does not comment on this trend, and analysts don't ask. As shown in the graph, Amazon's operating margin turned *negative* in the third quarter of 2012. The only way to declare positive profits with negative margins is via accounting gimmicks, such as suddenly switching to the

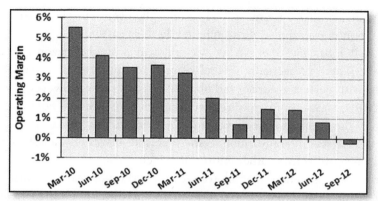

FIGURE 16.10 Amazon's Operating Margin 2010–2012.
Source: S&P's Capital IQ.

equity method for reporting subsidiary profits described above. As of early 2013, the market remained unconcerned, and Amazon's stock price continued achieving new record highs. The key question is whether Amazon's stock price objectively reflects all relevant information about the company.

Anomalies the EMH Cannot Explain   While the efficient markets hypothesis is a good starting point for understanding markets, researchers have documented numerous empirical facts about investing and markets that are inconsistent with the EMH. The existence of consistent patterns in securities prices and price volatility implies tradable opportunities based on past and current information that would not exist in a highly efficient market. A short list of these anomalies includes:

- *Correlations in security returns.* Individual security returns are negatively correlated on a daily basis, positively correlated over intermediate horizons, and negatively correlated over long horizons. Consistent correlation patterns would not exist in highly efficient markets.

- *Mean reversion or a reversal effect in securities prices.* Portfolios of stocks with the best records over the past two to three years subsequently underperform the market, and portfolios of stocks with the worst records over the past two to three years go on to outperform the market.

- *Underreaction to news.* There is significant short-term "drift" in prices following both good and bad news announcements (drift is the tendency for stock prices to keep moving in the same direction).

- *The size effect.* Small stocks outperform large stocks by more than would be expected based on their higher volatility. From 1931 to 1975, the 50 smallest stocks on the NYSE outperformed the 50 largest by 1 percent per month.

- *The price-to-earnings ratio (P/E) or value stock effect.* Studies show that the risk-adjusted returns of the lowest P/E stock portfolios are as much as 7 percent per year larger than the risk-adjusted returns of the highest P/E stock portfolios.

- *The January effect.* Stocks of small-cap companies experience unusually high returns in the first two weeks of January, then their returns revert to average for the rest of the year.

- *Patterns in volatility.* Returns are more volatile during bear markets, market volatility is greater at the open and the close than during the trading day, and overall market volatility is excessive relative to changes in the fundamentals affecting stocks' intrinsic values.

While the EMH remains the most studied theory of how information is reflected in securities prices and is a good entry point for understanding the extent to which prices accurately reflect relevant information, it is also clear that the EMH is subject to much criticism because it does not explain many outcomes observed in financial markets. Next, we'll consider an alternative explanation for investor behavior and the level of rationality reflected in securities prices, known as behavioral finance.

Behavioral Finance

The growing field of behavioral finance can trace its roots to a study by Amos Tversky and Daniel Kahneman, published in *Econometrica* in 1979. Their paper, "Prospect Theory: An Analysis of Decision Under Risk," is the most widely cited work in the history of this influential journal. Their original "prospect theory" has evolved into what we now call behavioral finance, a theory of information, securities prices, and investor behavior that competes with and frequently contradicts the highly rational premises and predictions of the efficient markets hypothesis.

Behavioral finance maintains that investors suffer from cognitive biases, or inefficiencies in the way they process information and draw conclusions. Some of the major biases include the use of **heuristics**, or mental shortcuts that make decision making easier. These mental "rules of thumb" can lead to biased reasoning and suboptimal investment decisions, however, especially when circumstances are changing (because the old mental shortcuts are no longer applicable). **Extrapolation errors**, which occur when investors assume that current and recent conditions will prevail well into the future, also cause them to ignore evidence of changing circumstances. Research by Barber and Odean (2001) shows that people tend to be **overconfident** regarding their abilities, which leads to mistakes such as too little diversification and too much trading. Barber and Odean find that men are more overconfident than women and thus trade more, despite the fact that the performance of their stock portfolios worsened as the tendency to trade increased.

Statman (2010), Nofsinger (2010), and others have identified additional cognitive biases that often derail investors' thinking. Some of the most popular biases include **hindsight error**, which tricks people into thinking they can foretell the future because they can easily observe the past. **Confirmation errors** occur when investors place too much weight on information that confirms their prior opinions (**cognitive consonance**), but underweight or completely disregard evidence that contradicts their prior opinions (**cognitive dissonance**). Whitney Tilson (2005), managing director of the T2 Partners Hedge Fund, cites additional biases that affect the behavior of value investors, including **misunderstanding randomness**, which involves seeing patterns where none exist, and **vividness bias**, which causes investors to overweight particularly memorable experiences, even though they may not be relevant given current circumstances.

A complete treatment of behavioral finance is beyond the scope of this book, but the point should be well made: recent research in this field leaves little doubt that individuals are not consistently rational and frequently make cognitive errors. Behavioral finance adds to our understanding of markets because it alerts us to the many intellectual errors that investors and traders are capable of committing, and allows that aggregate market outcomes can reflect these errors (such as systematic market mispricings, or **bubbles**). Next, we'll consider the latest theory of information and investor behavior, the adaptive markets hypothesis.

The Adaptive Markets Hypothesis

The adaptive markets hypothesis (AMH) views financial markets from a biological perspective. This theory of investor behavior asserts that the interactions among markets, institutions, securities, and investors result in an evolutionary-type process that unfolds according to the laws of "economic selection." The AMH allows for economic agents to adapt via their competitive interactions, but does not require that markets and institutions evolve toward optimal outcomes (see Farmer and Lo 1999; Farmer, 2002; and Lo, 2002, 2004, and 2005). This is the first major conflict between the AHM and the EMH, which maintains that market outcomes are always optimal.

The roots of the AMH can be found in E.O. Wilson's (1975) concept of sociobiology, which applied the principles of competition and natural selection to social interactions. Joseph Schumpeter's (1942) view of business cycles, which emphasized the need for "creative destruction" in capitalism that clears the way for "bursts of entrepreneurial activity," also provides a foundation for the adaptive markets theory.

According to Lo (2008), one of the major proponents of the adaptive markets view, the AMH is preferable as a theory of investor behavior because it allows for the cognitive biases identified by behavioral finance while also recognizing that the high level of competition prevailing in markets requires agents to continually adapt to change. The AMH can explain how market behaviors that appear anomalous under the EMH can emerge, persist for a while, and then disappear. This would include pricing bubbles that can plague markets for years, as well as shorter-term trading fads, such as the "dollar down, stocks up" trade that dominated the U.S. stock market in 2011, and the "risk-on, risk-off" trade, which seemed to be all markets were concerned with for much of 2012. These (and many other) trading opportunities often become popular overnight, dominate traders' thinking for months or years, and then vanish just as quickly as soon as traders adapt and invent new ways to stay ahead of the competition.

Researchers continue to make progress in understanding the connections between emotions, rationality and investor behavior. Some of this research appears to come full circle, such as Lo and Repin's (2002) study, which asserts that emotional responses are not always confusing or harmful, but can actually be important in helping investors understand financial risk in real time. These authors document that the ability to channel emotions in specific ways under certain market conditions can be a valuable tool for traders, which contradicts the EMH-based view that strong emotions confound the decision-making process because they interfere with rationality.

Summary of the Three Theories   In this section we considered three competing explanations of how information becomes incorporated into securities prices. The first, known as the efficient markets hypothesis, emphasizes a high degree of rationality in the market pricing mechanism. The second, behavioral finance, expressly recognizes that investors commit numerous cognitive errors and that these mistakes can affect market prices. The third, the adaptive markets hypothesis, views markets as a complex evolutionary system in which investors are constantly evolving and adapting to both rational and irrational circumstances. Under the AMH, real-world investors aren't concerned with being rational or irrational—they are just trying to figure out if what worked yesterday will still work today. If not, they quickly move on and invent new methods for remaining competitive.

   In the sections that follow, we will consider additional perspectives from well-known investors to further synthesize our understanding of these three theories into a practical investment framework. Renowned investors like John Bogle and Charles Ellis will caution us against careless attempts to beat the market; as we've already established, this can be much harder than it sounds. We'll also consider the results of recent research that examines why some investors trade excessively, and finish with a review of Chapter 23 of John Maynard Keynes's *General Theory of Employment, Interest and Money* (1936), a work that anticipated the efficient markets versus behavioral finance debate decades before academics embraced it in earnest.

■ Additional Perspectives on Investing

This section of the chapter presents a variety of perspectives that will further inform our investment philosophy and guide our efforts to construct and manage a portfolio of stocks that outperforms its benchmark. This section reviews the main points of several articles representative of the approach and analytical methods featured in the chapters that follow.

John Bogle: An Index Fund Fundamentalist (2002)

John Bogle is the founder of Vanguard Investments and is widely credited as the creator of the equity index fund. Bogle was invited to review and extend his work regarding the superiority of indexing by the *Journal of Portfolio Management*, one of the leading investment journals. Bogle shows that for almost all types of equity portfolios (various combinations of large versus small and growth versus value stocks), passively managed index funds earn higher returns with lower risk versus actively managed funds. This finding holds for every category except small-capitalization growth stocks, implying that active managers were able to add value only for stocks that require the most research to fully understand. (Small-cap stocks are less widely followed by analysts, therefore, less information is available about these stocks; growth stocks have little or no previous track records, which means that most of their success or failure is dependent on future activities that are hard to predict.)

Bogle also refutes a view regarding market efficiency by Minor (2001). (If the founder of Vanguard thinks understanding the subtleties of market efficiency is important, then we probably should as well.) Minor makes a clever argument: If investors increasingly believe in market efficiency, they will engage in more indexing and less active investing. After a while, security prices will reflect greater mispricings from this lack of research, and active investors will once again have an advantage as the market becomes less efficient. Bogle disagrees, arguing that Minor does not take the higher costs of active investing into account. Bogle argues that even if active investors earn higher gross returns, after considering the fees they charge, their clients would still have been better off indexing. As reviewed earlier, subsequent research by Barras, Scaillet, and Wermers (2010) confirms that Bogle's view is correct.

Charles Ellis: "Levels of the Game" (2000)

Charles ("Charley") Ellis is a legendary investment manager and the author of 16 books at the latest count. In addition to managing a significant portion of the Yale Endowment for years, he sits on the board of Vanguard Investments, and serves as an associate editor of the two most influential investments journals, *The Journal of Portfolio Management* and *Financial Analysts Journal*. Like John Bogle, Ellis is a valuable source of well-intentioned advice regarding investments and financial markets.

In his 2000 article "Levels of the Game," Ellis cites Bogle's earlier research, which shows that over the most recent 10-year period (at the time the article was published), 89 percent of all actively managed U.S. mutual funds had underperformed their benchmarks. Ellis attributes this underperformance to the increasing competitiveness of the active money management industry, which is dominated by highly educated, motivated professionals—consistent with the view of efficient markets developed earlier in this chapter.

Ellis points out that over the past several decades, professionals have become the market. Well over 90 percent of all trading volume is now generated by the pros, with over 50 percent generated by the top 50 firms. This means that the pros are constantly buying and selling shares to and from each other. Thus, if a firm raises its rating on a stock from hold to buy and wants more shares, they're probably buying from another professional who wants to sell (as Meir Statman (2010) humorously phrases it, "the idiot on the other side of the trade"). Ellis also classifies investing activities into one of five "levels":

- *Level 1: Asset Mix.* Determining the optimal proportion of equities, bonds, currencies, commodities, real estate and cash to hold in a portfolio or fund.

- *Level 2: Equity Mix.* Establishing a "normal" policy of growth versus value stocks, large-cap versus small-cap, and domestic versus international stocks.

- *Level 3: Active versus Passive Management.* This level involves further implementation of the normal policy established in Levels 1 and 2, specifically addressing the proportion of an investor's assets that should be in active versus passive vehicles.

- *Level 4: Specific Manager Selection.* Deciding which investment firms will manage each component of the investor's portfolio.

- *Level 5: Active Portfolio Management.* Deciding when to change portfolio strategy, the selection of specific securities or assets, and how to execute transactions.

Ellis's experience has led him to believe that keeping investors focused on Levels 1 and 2 helps them avoid major mistakes and, most important, maximizes their wealth accumulations over long horizons. Notice that Ellis's advice regarding the need to diversify and hold positions for long periods is consistent with the efficient markets hypothesis, and how his recommendation that investors avoid complex, higher-level activities that result in more errors that lower their portfolio returns follows from behavioral finance.

Charles Ellis: "The Winner's Game" (2003)

One of the most valuable perspectives Ellis provides in his 2003 article "The Winner's Game" is to partition life's activities into one of two categories: winner's games and loser's games. In loser's games, outcomes are most often determined by participant mistakes—like amateur tennis. In winner's games, however, outcomes are usually determined by decisive winning moves, as is the case in most high-level professional sports. Ellis's point is that individuals are the amateurs in the game of investments, and should focus more on minimizing mistakes instead of attempting higher-level winning moves versus professional investors. Additionally, with so many well-trained investments professionals competing against each other, individuals should not be incurring the costs of competing with the pros. Ellis stresses that individuals need to remain aware that in most cases they are disadvantaged in terms of the information they possess, the trading strategies they're capable of executing (and the skill with which they can trade), and their total cost of trading.

Perhaps the most valuable perspective Ellis brings to the active investing debate is his belief that *active investing triggers a higher error rate*, and that this is the most plausible explanation regarding why actively managed equity funds underperform their benchmarks so consistently. His recommendation: "Most investors would benefit from giving more attention to their defenses, and to not losing." Ellis is also well versed in behavioral finance, as illustrated by the following advice regarding which mistakes to avoid:

1. We are confirmation-biased—we seek out and overweight the significance of data that support our initial impressions.
2. We allow ourselves to use an initial idea or fact as a reference point for future decisions even when we know it is "just a number" (the behavioral error known as "framing" or "anchoring").
3. We distort our perceptions of our decisions, almost always in our favor, so that we believe we are better than we really are at making decisions (cognitive consonance).
4. We have a tendency to be overconfident.

Ellis closes his article by pointing out that another common error he sees investors make is switching to a new money manager with a superior record just as that manager is about to begin underperforming. This is consistent with the previously reviewed research findings on mean reversion, which describes how portfolios that outperform their benchmarks for two- to three-year periods tend to underperform over the next two to three years (and vice versa).

Dorn, Dorn, and Sengmueller: "Why Do People Trade?" (2008)

This article by Dorn, Dorn, and Sengmueller (2008) is based on a previous paper entitled "Trading as Entertainment." The bottom line of the study is that investors who indicated on surveys that they "enjoy investing" and "enjoy risky propositions" traded twice as much as peer investors. The authors provide us with an important conclusion: "Entertainment appears to be a straightforward explanation for why . . . active traders trade much more than others, and why active traders underperform their peers after transactions costs." The Dorn et al. findings complement results from the behavioral finance literature and Ellis's advice: sticking to a simple game plan and avoiding cognitive errors should be an important part of an investor's strategy. These authors remind us to ask ourselves: "Am I trading for strategic or tactical reasons, or simply to entertain myself?"

John Maynard Keynes: Chapter 23 of the *General Theory*

Keynes' *General Theory of Employment, Interest and Money* is an inarguable classic in the economics literature. In Chapter 23 Keynes dispenses practical advice for investors, along with many keen observations about human nature. His genius—and elegant writing style—are on full display. Keynes's unique perspectives can be attributed to the many roles he undertook in his lifetime. He served as chancellor of the Exchequer in England (equivalent to secretary of the Treasury in the United States) during the Great Depression. Accordingly, much of his *General Theory* is concerned with understanding how free-market economies can jolt themselves out of depressionary cycles. In addition to being recognized as one of the most brilliant economists of his day, Keynes was also a currency speculator; much of his advice therefore stems from his practical experiences as an investor. He amassed a significant fortune through his trading activities, lost it all, and earned it back again. In the analysis of Keynes's Chapter 23 that follows, notice in particular how he anticipates both the efficient markets and behavioral finance theories, which would be further developed by economists and psychologists decades later.

Long-Term Expectations Keynes begins with a thought experiment on how investors form their expectations regarding the future. Keynes writes that it would be foolish to put too much weight on matters that are highly uncertain (the future is, of course, inherently unknown). In particular, Keynes has noticed that humans have a habit of taking the current situation—whatever it is—and extrapolating it into the future, until they see definite evidence that they need to change that expectation (behavioral finance now refers to these tendencies as "extrapolation errors").

Keynes goes on to write that our long-term expectations should not depend only on the best forecast we can make, but also on the certainty with which we can make this forecast. Predictions regarding the future are usually made on an extremely precarious basis, but investors are overconfident regarding their ability to forecast (here he anticipates the overconfidence bias identified by the behaviorists).

Keynes then launches into a long meditation on the state of business and financial markets in the 1930s. He notes that, in earlier times, business ventures were started by people who focused less on precise calculations of profits and returns, and more on the adventure associated with the enterprise. These old-time entrepreneurs often earned lower returns than they had planned on—but, according to Keynes, earning high returns was not their primary focus; they were more concerned with building something.

Keynes is particularly concerned with how the stock market allows for such a profound disconnection between ownership and management—something that was relatively new in his day, but we take for granted in the twenty-first century. With this observation Keynes anticipates another field of finance and economics, known as agency theory, which has long recognized the "separation of ownership and control" as a key factor contributing to suboptimal corporate performance.

Long-Term Expectations and Stock Values   Keynes connects his ideas regarding how long-term expectations are formed and the way modern financial markets allow for investment valuation to be determined by those who are far removed from the operations of the businesses. Thus, he notes, stock values may often reflect irrelevant concerns and ideas, and not the close knowledge of the people actually running the companies. Keynes not only anticipates the efficient markets hypothesis with this statement but goes on to criticize the idea. He notes that the convention in the stock market is to assume that whatever value a stock is selling for is correct, and that the habit of continuously projecting the current state of affairs into the future is what led to both the 1920s stock market bubble and the prolonged bear market of the 1930s (extrapolation errors). Keynes asserts that in both cases prices remained on a trend determined by people who don't really know what's going on in the businesses they are valuing (a question of market efficiency). Additionally, note that Keynes is working on the problems of asset bubbles and market crashes over half a century before the dot-com, credit, and residential real estate bubbles wreaked havoc on modern markets.

Keynes Says Markets Can't Be Efficient   Keynes reinforces his point that market valuations cannot be correct most of the time because they result from a flawed expectations-forming process conducted by people who are far removed from the businesses they are valuing. Keynes says these conventions persist because people like the appearance of stability and continuity in their daily lives. This makes people feel that, at least in the short term, they are not exposed to excessive risk, because stock values must at least be close to their fair value (cognitive consonance). Of course, Keynes believes people are deluding themselves in this regard:

> Due to the gradual increase in the proportion of equity owned by persons who neither manage nor have special knowledge of the enterprise,

the element of real knowledge in the valuation of investments has declined. Day-to-day fluctuations in the profits of existing investments, which are obviously of an ephemeral nature, have an excessive—even absurd—influence on markets.

Groundless Expectations Are the Source of Excessive Volatility   One of the criticisms of the EMH is that securities prices exhibit more volatility than would be justified based on changes in companies' fundamentals alone. Keynes asserts that investors' "groundless expectations" are actually the source of this excess market volatility:

> A conventional valuation that is established as the outcome of the mass psychology of a large number of ignorant individuals is liable to change violently as the result of a sudden fluctuation of opinion due to factors that do not really make much difference to future returns, since there will be no strong roots to hold it steady.

Keynes goes on to say that during abnormal times when things are changing fast, and investors are deprived of the comfort of believing in the "indefinite continuance of the existing state of affairs," markets will be subject to waves of optimistic and pessimistic sentiment that is irrational, but also somewhat legitimate, because no solid basis exists for reasonable calculations of any sort. Even though Keynes is describing his own mid-1930s period, his observations also apply to the behavior of global financial markets from 2008 to 2013, an era characterized by alternating periods of both unusually high and low volatility.

Investment Professionals and Market Efficiency   Keynes goes on to write that there is one viewpoint in particular that deserves our attention. We might suppose that competition among expert professionals, who are supposed to have knowledge beyond that of the average private investor, would correct the pricing mistakes committed by ignorant individuals. Not exactly, Keynes says:

> The energies and skill of the professional investor are not concerned with making long-term forecasts of the probable return of an investment, but with foreseeing changes in valuation a short time ahead of the public. Professional investors are not concerned with what an investment is worth to a man who buys it "for keeps," but rather what the market will value it at, under the influence of mass psychology, three months or a year hence. Moreover, this behavior is not the result of a wrong-headed propensity . . . it is not sensible to pay $25 for an investment you believe is worth $30 if you also believe the market will value it at $20 in three months.

How the Pros Play the Game   Keynes further writes that the professional investor is therefore forced to concern himself with the anticipation of impending changes—in the news or in the atmosphere—that most influence the mass psychology of the market. This is an inevitable result of investment markets organized with the goal of so-called "liquidity" (which Keynes calls a "fetish"). Keynes's point is that there is no such thing as liquidity for the entire investment community at the same time. When everyone wants to sell, there is no liquidity without dramatic price declines (a.k.a. panic). This, of course, describes the essence of our recent global financial crisis. From 2000 to 2007 there was a boom in the origination of mortgage loans to people who could not afford to make the payments. Many of these loans were created simply because they could be bundled into complex financial instruments and sold to the next greater fool. Everything worked fine until the day that *everyone* wanted to sell their securities, which caused the market—and the balance sheets of most large banks—to collapse.

Keynes goes on to say that the game of investing might be called "beat the gun." The investors he knows are more concerned with outwitting the crowd and passing the "bad, ever-depreciating half-crown to the other fellow." Keynes further notes that this game can be played by professional investors among themselves. No uninformed individuals are required, and it is not even necessary that any of the players believe in the long-term validity of the value of any of the securities they are trading.

Keynes's Famous Beauty Contest Analogy This is probably Keynes's most memorable passage. He compares professional investing to newspaper competitions that were popular in his day in which readers voted for the prettiest faces from a hundred photographs. Depending on which face they voted for, readers' choices were placed into a jar, and a winning card was randomly selected from the jar containing the most votes. Keynes says that the stock market works just like this game. Intelligent investors don't simply pick the stocks they think are best, but the winning strategy instead involves anticipating which face will get the most votes. If your card is not in the right jar—determined by popular opinion—then you cannot win the contest:

> It is not a case of choosing those faces which, to the best of one's judgment, are really the prettiest, nor even those which average opinion genuinely thinks the prettiest. We have reached the third degree where we devote our intelligences to anticipating what average opinion expects the average opinion to be.

The Reduced Role of Fundamental Investors Next, Keynes anticipates—and refutes—the type of objections that believers in market efficiency still raise today:

> If the reader is motivated to interject that there must surely be large profits to be gained in the long run by a skilled individual who remains undistracted by the prevailing pastime and continues to purchase investments on the best genuine long-term expectations he can frame, he must be answered, first of all, that there are such serious-minded individuals, and that it makes a vast difference to an investment market whether or not they predominate in their influence over the game-players.

But Keynes adds that there are several factors that jeopardize the predominance of such individuals in modern investment markets:

> Investment based on genuine long-term expectation is so difficult today that it is basically impractical. He who attempts it must surely lead more laborious days and run greater risks than he who tries to guess better than the crowd how the crowd will behave; and, given equal intelligence, he may make more disastrous mistakes.

This statement echoes Ellis's advice about the importance of avoiding mistakes.

Keynes's Warning for Long-Term Investors

> Notice that it is the long-term investor—he who most promotes the public interest—who will in practice come under the greatest criticism whenever investment funds are managed by committees or boards or banks. For it is the essence of his behavior that he should appear eccentric, unconventional and rash in the eyes of average opinion. If he is successful, that will only confirm his rashness; and if in the short run he is unsuccessful, which is very likely, he not receive much mercy.

Keynes has a little career advice for us as well: "Worldly wisdom teaches that it is better for one's reputation to fail conventionally than to succeed unconventionally." (I have found this to be an ironic truth in my own professional career path from time to time.)

Keynes on Bubbles

> Speculators may do little or no harm when they are only bubbles on a steady stream of long-term investors; but they can be seriously harmful when long-term investors become the bubble on a whirlpool of speculators. When the capital development of a country becomes a by-product of the activities of a casino, the job is likely to be ill-done.

And Keynes coins a term—bubble—that has remained in the investor's lexicon ever since.

Animal Spirits

> A large proportion of our positive activities depend on spontaneous optimism rather than on a mathematical expectation. Our decisions to do something positive are usually taken as a result of animal spirits—a spontaneous urge to action rather than inaction—and not as the outcome of a weighted average of quantitative benefits multiplied by quantitative probabilities. If the animal spirits are dimmed and the spontaneous optimism falters, leaving us to depend on nothing but a mathematical expectation, enterprise will fade and die.

Animal spirits is another Keynes term that investors and traders still use every day.

■ Professional Investment Policy Statements

We will wrap up this chapter by examining a professional investment policy statement (IPS) and synthesizing the viewpoints from this chapter into a sample IPS that summarizes the type of stocks we'll be looking for and the type of portfolio we'll construct using these stocks. An IPS makes clear statements about an investor's or fund's objectives, return expectations, risk tolerance, time horizon, and portfolio allocations. Highlights from the IPS from Morgan Stanley's Focus Growth Strategy team are presented below. You will notice similarities with items mentioned in this chapter (including market efficiency), as well as considerations that we'll emphasize in our stock selection process in upcoming chapters (such as favorable trends in return on invested capital, focusing on free cash flow instead of accounting earnings, taking a long-term perspective, and analyzing whether a company has a genuine competitive advantage that is sustainable).

Morgan Stanley Focus Growth Strategy Profile (2013, Edited)

Investment Philosophy[2]

- Permitted market capitalization: within the market capitalization of the benchmark index

- Sector concentrations result from security selection; no specified minimum or maximum exposure

- Security weight: 1 to 5 percent of the portfolio

- Typical number of holdings: 20–30 securities

- Invest in high-quality established and emerging companies

- The investment team seeks companies with:

  - Inherent sustainable competitive advantages

  - Favorable return on invested capital trends

  - Long-term capital appreciation rather than short-term events

- Stock selection is informed by rigorous fundamental analysis

- Guiding principles combined with intellectual and process flexibility are critical to strong decision-making in pursuit of attractive investments

When assessing businesses, the team seeks to capitalize on market inefficiencies by investing in companies that it believes are underappreciated due to one or more of the following reasons:

- *Relative lack of coverage.* Companies transitioning from one market capitalization category to another—as well as recapitalizations or spin-offs—tend to be underfollowed, creating potential investment opportunities for the team.

- *Conventional valuation bias:* There is a tendency to view companies with low price-to-earnings (P/E) ratios as more attractive than those with higher ratios. However, the team believes that earnings-related measures can be limiting, as they do not incorporate the return on invested capital (ROIC) or free-cash-flow generation profile of a company. In addition, corporate earnings can often make comparisons both within industries and across sectors less meaningful.

- *Coverage bias.* Experts typically use traditional valuation rules of thumb to assess companies in their coverage areas—rules that the team believes may be less appropriate in analyzing companies with new or unique business models that are generating substantially different economic value.

- *Short-term bias.* The team believes that it can exploit inefficiencies stemming from the fact that market participants increasingly focus on short-term considerations (such as quarterly earnings) in their analysis rather than on long-term value creation.

Investment Process   The team follows a disciplined investment process that entails the following steps:

- *Idea generation.* The team generates investment ideas through an ongoing set of activities conducted individually and collaboratively, including: (1) involvement in contact networks across industries and in the investment management business; (2) its reading network; (3) its focus on ROIC and free-cash-flow yield; (4) team discussions; (5) the identification of patterns; (6) conventional-valuation and coverage biases, among others; and (7) continual research on current company holdings.

- *Bottom-up analysis and valuation.* The team narrows its idea generation by seeking stocks that reside in the intersection between its views of a company's business quality, growth quality, and risk/reward characteristics (see diagram, Figure 16.11). Valuation focuses on free-cash-flow yield three to five years in the future.

- *Disruptive change research.* To complement its in-depth, bottom-up research, the team's disruptive change researcher investigates big ideas and emerging themes that typically may have far-reaching consequences, such as nanotech, infrastructure and the global water shortage.

- *Portfolio construction and implementation.* The team's portfolios are actively managed and built to maximize expected value. Company weightings are primarily determined by the quality of the idea and the team's conviction. Each member of the investment team helps drive stock-picking, with at least two of the three most senior members typically involved in final construction decisions. The team reviews factor analysis on a monthly basis in order to ensure that the portfolio's risk is more idiosyncratic than systematic. The team anticipates holding between 20 and 30 securities.

- *Culture.* The team's culture is shaped by four core values that are cultivated and reinforced in many ways: intellectual curiosity and flexibility, perspective, self-awareness, and partnership.

FIGURE 16.11   The Investment Thesis: Business Quality, Growth Quality, and Risk/Reward Trade-off.

Source: Morgan Stanley Investment Management (2013).

A Sample Investment Policy

After reading through the highlights of the Morgan Stanley IPS, you should be ready to draft one for your portfolio or student investment fund. Following is a draft of a basic IPS (adapted from Krinsky and Hall (2012) and Putnam Investments (2013)):

Description of the Client. The University Foundation (or other entity).

Purpose of the IPS. To establish a clear understanding between the investor and the adviser regarding the Student Investment Fund's (SIF) objectives for return, risk management, security suitability, and portfolio review.

Duties of the Parties. The adviser shall design and implement an appropriate portfolio, monitor the performance of the portfolio, periodically review the investment strategy and investment policy statement, and prepare and make available all related reports. The University Foundation will promptly notify the adviser of changes in risk tolerance or other issues pertaining to security suitability.

Objectives: Return. The SIF aims to outperform the S&P 500 on a risk-adjusted basis over the long term. We favor large-capitalization stocks with sustainable competitive advantages that earn a high return on invested capital and pay above-average dividends.

Objectives: Risk. The SIF targets a level of risk (defined as portfolio beta) equal to or less than the S&P 500.

Constraints: Sector Weightings. None. Sector concentrations result from a combination of macroeconomic analysis and favorable investment opportunities identified by stock-specific fundamental analysis; no specified minimum or maximum exposure to any particular sector.

Constraints: Liquidity. None. The SIF's goal is to be fully invested in equities at all times.

Constraints: Time Horizon. The SIF assumes an infinite time horizon. The investment thesis for all securities must specify if the security is a short-term (1–2 years) or long-term (3–5 years) component of the SIF portfolio. Short-term positions are limited to 50 percent of the portfolio's holdings.

Constraints: Taxes. The University Foundation is a tax-free not-for-profit.

Constraints: Legal and Regulatory. The SIF strives to maintain compliance with the Uniform Prudent Investor Act (UPIA) to the best of its ability, subject to the constraints it faces in terms of enrollment and the current class's ability to perform a comprehensive portfolio review.

Unique Circumstances. No leverage, short selling, derivative securities or non-equity securities. The SIF invests in equities and cash. Equities may be U.S. or international, provided the security trades on a major U.S. exchange (American depositary receipts, or ADRs, are acceptable securities for the SIF).

Asset Allocation Targets and Ranges. U.S./global equities approaching 100 percent, with a small cash balance until proceeds from security sales or dividends can be prudently reinvested.

Guidelines for Portfolio Adjustments and Rebalancing. The SIF's goal is to review the entire portfolio annually. A full allocation to a new position is approximately 5 percent of the total value of the portfolio. Positions approaching 10 percent of the total value of the portfolio must be reviewed for possible rebalancing in the current or next semester.

Sell Discipline. We will reduce or sell a position if valuation levels significantly exceed industry or sector averages, a previous investment thesis is invalidated by subsequent events, our confidence in management's integrity and ability to execute is compromised, or new ideas offer better risk/reward profiles than an existing holding. If a stock experiences a sudden decline and our research signals a deterioration of our original investment thesis, we will sell the position.

Schedule for Portfolio and IPS Review. Annually, or as permitted by course enrollment and the capacity of the current class to perform a complete portfolio review.

■ Summary

- Active equity investors seek to outperform a market index benchmark by identifying individual stocks to buy and sell.

- Passive investors buy and hold stock portfolios for the long term or choose other investment vehicles that minimize costs, including research costs, trading costs, administrative costs, performance fees, and taxes on realized gains.

- The fundamental analysis process featured in this book is termed *top-down* because it begins with an analysis of the overall economy. Gauging the stage of the business cycle in which the economy is operating helps an analyst identify sectors of the stock market to over- and underweight in pursuit of market-beating returns.

- Passive investors outperform active investors in the aggregate.

- Research suggests that two main factors contribute to the outperformance of passive investors: lower costs of trading and committing fewer cognitive errors.

- Active investors need a theory, or model, of how rapidly and accurately new information affects stock prices.

- The three main theories of information and prices are the efficient markets hypothesis, behavioral finance, and the adaptive markets hypothesis.

- An investment policy statement makes clear statements about an investor's or fund's objectives, return expectations, risk tolerance, time horizon, and portfolio allocations that inform the decisions of stock analysts and portfolio managers.

NOTES

1. If we were conducting a formal academic study, we would have also adjusted IBM's stock returns around the announcement for risk by taking IBM's risk (measured as beta) into account.
2. Excerpted with permission of Morgan Stanley Investment Management, © 2013.

■ References

Barber, Brad, and Terry Odean. 2001. "Boys Will Be Boys: Gender, Overconfidence, and Common Stock Investment." *Quarterly Journal of Economics* 116: 261–92.

Barras, Laurent, Olivier Scaillet, and Russ Wermers. 2010. "False Discoveries in Mutual Fund Performance: Measuring Luck in Estimated Alphas." *Journal of Finance* 65, February 179–216.

Bogle, John. 2002. "An Index Fund Fundamentalist Goes Back to the Drawing Board." *Journal of Portfolio Management*, Spring 31–38.

Carhart, M. 1997. "On Persistence in Mutual Fund Performance." *Journal of Finance* 52: 57–82.

Dorn, Anne, Daniel Dorn, and Paul Sengmueller. 2008. "Why Do People Trade?" *Journal of Applied Finance,* Fall/Winter: 37–50.

Eavis, Peter. April 27, 2012. "Analyzing the Unusual Items in Amazon's Earnings." Dealbook, *New York Times Online*, http://dealbook.nytimes.com/2012/04/27/analyzing-the-unusual-items-in-amazons-earnings/. Accessed January 28, 2013.

Ellis, Charles D. "Levels of the Game." *Journal of Portfolio Management,* Winter: 12–15.

Ellis, Charles D. "The Winner's Game." *Journal of Portfolio Management,* Spring: 27–24.

Elton, Edwin, Martin Gruber, Sanjiv Das, and Matthew Hlavka. 1993. "Efficiency with Costly Information: A Reinterpretation of Evidence from Managed Portfolios." *Review of Financial Studies* 6(1): 1–22.

Farmer, D. 2002. "Market Force, Ecology and Evolution." *Industrial and Corporate Change* 11: 895–953.

Farmer, Doyne, and Andrew Lo. 1999. "Frontiers of Finance: Evolution and Efficient Markets." *Proceedings of the National Academy of Sciences* 96: 9991–92.

Fung, H., X. Xu, and J. Yau. 2004. "Do Hedge Fund Managers Display Skill?" *Journal of Investing* 6 (4): 22–31.

Hulbert, Mark. 2008. "The Prescient Are Few." *New York Times*, July 13, www.nytimes.com/2008/07/13/business/13stra.html. Accessed March 2013.

Keynes, John Maynard. 2010. *The General Theory of Employment, Interest and Money.* Whitefish, MT: Kessinger Publishing, LLC (originally published in 1936).

Krinsky, Simon, and Kathryn Hall. 2012, March. "A Roadmap for the Roadmap: Creating an Investment Policy Statement for Endowments and Foundations." San Francisco, CA: Hall Capital Partners, LLC.

Lo, A. 2008. "Where Do Alphas Come From?" Working paper, MIT Sloan School of Management and AlphaSimplex Group (October).

Lo, A., and D. Repin. 2002. "The Psychophysiology of Real-Time Financial Risk Processing." *Journal of Cognitive Neuroscience* 14: 323–39.

Lo, Andrew. 2002. "Bubble, Rubble, Finance in Trouble?" *Journal of Psychology and Financial Markets* 3: 76–86.

Lo, Andrew. 2004. "The Adaptive Markets Hypothesis: Market Efficiency from an Evolutionary Perspective." *Journal of Portfolio Management* 30: 15–29.

Lo, Andrew. 2005. "Reconciling Efficient Markets with Behavioral Finance: The Adaptive Markets Hypothesis." *Journal of Investment Consulting* 7: 21–44.

Lowe, Janet. 1997. *Warren Buffett Speaks: Wit and Wisdom from the World's Greatest Investor.* New York: John Wiley & Sons.

Ludwig, Olly. 2012. "Passive Reigns as of First Half of 2012." Index Universe. Available online at www.indexuniverse.com/sections/features/14686-spiva-passive-reigns-as-of-first-half-2012.html. Accessed January 28, 2013.

Malkiel, Burton, and Atanu Saha. 2005. "Hedge Funds: Risk and Return." *Financial Analysts Journal* 61(6): 80–88.

Minor, Dylan. 2001. "Beware of Index Fund Fundamentalists." *Journal of Portfolio Management,* Summer: 45–50.

Morgan Stanley. 2013. *Focus Growth Strategy Profile.* New York: Morgan Stanley Investment Management.

Nofsinger, John. 2010. *The Psychology of Investing.* Upper Saddle River, NJ: Prentice Hall.

O'Hara, N. 2009. "They're Supposed to Be Better Than This." *Institutional Investor,* February 19. Available online at www.institutionalinvestor.com/Article/2113414/Theyre-Supposed-to-Be-Better-Than-This.html. Accessed January 28, 2013.

Pojarliev, M., and R. M. Levich. 2008. "Do Professional Currency Managers Beat the Benchmark?" *Financial Analysts Journal* 64(5): 18–32.

Putnam Investments. 2013. "Investment Policy Statement and Sample Checklist." Putnam Investments, available online at https://content.putnam.com/literature/pdf/ID093.pdf. Accessed January 28, 2013.

Schumpeter, J. 1975. *Capitalism, Socialism and Democracy.* New York: Harper (originally published in 1942).

Standard & Poor's. 2008. Standard & Poor's Indices Versus Active Funds (SPIVA) Scorecard, Mid-Year 2008, November 12, www.standardandpoors.com. Accessed March 2013.

Statman, Meir. 2010. *What Investors Really Want.* New York: McGraw-Hill.

Tilson, W. 2005, November. "Applying Behavioral Finance to Value Investing." Monograph. Denver, CO: T2 Partners LLC.

Wilson, E. 1975. *Sociobiology: The New Synthesis.* Cambridge, MA: Belknap Press of Harvard University Press.

CHAPTER 17

Understanding Chart Patterns

From Thomas N. Bulkowski, *Visual Guide to Chart Patterns* (Hoboken, New Jersey: John Wiley & Sons, 2002), Chapters 1–3.

■ The Basics

This section of the book reviews the basics: minor highs and lows, trendlines, gaps, throwbacks, pullbacks, support, and resistance. I provide many exhibits so that we agree on terms and techniques. The basics will become important when we move to identifying chart patterns and then using them to signal trades.

■ Pattern Recognition Made Easy

While working at Tandy Corporation, I hung on my office wall a price chart of the company's stock. I did not know if the head-and-shoulders top I found was one or not, but it looked like a person's head in the middle of a pair of shoulders. To the left and right of that pattern, price dropped back to earth, making it seem like the pattern was a ghost rising from a moat.

That was my first attempt at finding a chart pattern. Since that time, I taught myself to recognize chart patterns—a skill almost anyone can learn. Let us begin looking at a few charts to see how to recognize patterns.

The Empty Chart

The empty chart is not empty at all, is it? Price bars form a mountain range that climbs higher until July after which a hiker walking on those bars would probably fall to their death. (See Figure 17.1.)

In that brief description, we have learned two things: Price rises until July and then dies. If you owned this stock, you would be looking for chart patterns that predict the coming decline. Why? Because you might want to sell before the tumble or act to protect your position.

FIGURE 17.1 MMM US Equity (3M Co).

In October, in addition to searching for the remains of our dead hiker, you would be looking for signs that the downward price trend had reversed. If it had, then you might want to buy the stock or buy more to capture the recovery.

How do you find patterns that predict a decline? Begin with peaks.

Finding Peak Patterns

When I look at a price chart, my eyes find peaks that stop at or near the same price. At line A, for example, several peaks approach or touch the upper red line. That line represents **overhead resistance**. When price finally breaks through that ceiling, it signals a change in trend from moving sideways to up. (See Figure 17.2.)

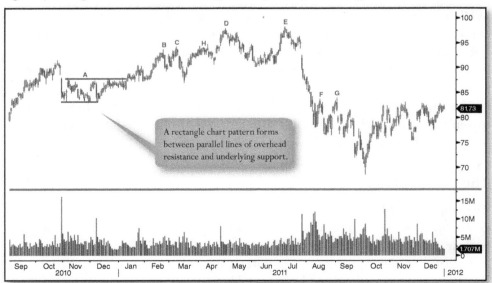

A rectangle chart pattern forms between parallel lines of overhead resistance and underlying support.

FIGURE 17.2 MMM US Equity (3M Co).

After finding the top horizontal red line, look for a corresponding line parallel to the top one, but drawn along the valleys. I show that as the lower red line. The two lines form a rectangle chart pattern. The name of the chart pattern is not as important as how I found it. Just imagine a horizontal line that touches several peaks and another line that touches several valleys.

Peaks B and C also exhibit overhead resistance. How do I know that? Because they top out near the same price. An imaginary ceiling exists above those peaks, holding the stock down—for a time. Peak H slams its head against that ceiling, too.

Compare the BCH trio with peaks D and E. The DE pair form twin tops, but further apart—larger. Larger patterns tend to be more important than smaller ones. Price will tend to drop further after a large pattern than after a small one. In this case, the stock declines more after DE than after BC.

Peaks F and G are another pair showing overhead resistance. In this case, a downward price trend leads to this pair whereas BC and DE appeared in an upward price trend.

Peak pairs BC, DE, and FG show the major ingredient of double top chart patterns, that of two peaks finding overhead resistance near the same price.

Finding Valley Patterns

Figure 17.3 highlights price valleys. In a manner similar to peaks, look for two or more valleys that bottom near the same price. Those valleys may rest upon a floor where support is strong enough to launch another move up. One example is CD.

I highlight this pair because it forms **underlying support**. Price finds a floor at C and bounces off it at D. Eventually, though, the stock tunnels its way through support at E, and plummets like a stone through water.

Valley patterns are useful for determining when a downward price trend changes to horizontal or upward.

FIGURE 17.3   MMM US Equity (3M Co).

Notice the peaks that bump up against line G, shown in red. The first two poke through the line, but that is fine since rarely will peaks or valleys stop at exactly the same price. The line represents a temporary barrier to an upward move.

For the moment, ignore the V-bottom at I. Search below line G for valleys that bottom near the same price. I found them and drew line F. It represents a support area connecting bottoms J and H, and extending to the right with additional touches along the way.

Does the GF trading range mean price is changing trend from down to up? Perhaps. It is too early to tell for sure.

What about the emergency dive to I? That submarine plunge may have been panic selling, forcing the stock down to a level low enough that it represented a steal to value investors. The needle shape of the V bottom supports this theory (that is, price remained at I for just one day before dumping its ballast and rising).

Notice pattern HIJ. It is an inverted (upside down) **head-and-shoulders pattern**. H and J represent shoulders and I is the head. K could be a cancerous growth on the neck, but lab results have not come back yet. It is not important to the survival of the pattern.

> **DEFINITION:**
> Head-and-shoulders pattern
> A head-and-shoulders bottom and inverted head-and-shoulders are synonyms.

Another head-and-shoulders bottom (a synonym for an inverted head-and-shoulders) occurs at ABC. This one is unusual—and rarer—because price trends upward into the pattern, not downward.

For now, though, the inbound price trend is not important. What is important is to train your eyes to find peaks that top out near the same level and find valleys that

THEORY AND ANALYSIS

bottom near the same price. When you can do that, you can find chart patterns. It is that simple.

> **Smart Investor Tip**
>
> In a rising price trend, try forming curved patterns beneath price bars. In a falling price trend, curves often appear smoother along the tops. Either method works.

> **Smart Investor Tip**
>
> Train your eyes to find peaks that top out near the same price and valleys that bottom near similar prices.

Curved Patterns

After finding peaks and valleys that align, try imagining price tracing curves. I show two examples in Figure 17.4.

Notice that the price bars at A begin rising, following a straight line of trend, but then curve at the top. Connecting the underside of price bars in a rising price trend often shows the curve better than connecting the tops. Either way is fine.

Pattern A is called an inverted and ascending scallop. The chart pattern appears often on the charts, but it is not popular or well known. The fishy sounding name refers to the bowl shape and not the mollusk. If you find one, never eat it.

The rounding turn at B forms another curved pattern. The B turn would be a rounding bottom, but price needs to enter the pattern trending down and not up. B is an example of a failed cup with handle pattern. The handle is at C. Cups have many qualifications, so strictly speaking, this is not one. However, the pattern does show the important parts: a rising price trend followed by a rounded turn and a short handle.

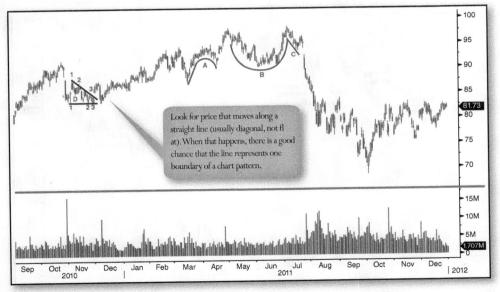

Look for price that moves along a straight line (usually diagonal, not flat). When that happens, there is a good chance that the line represents one boundary of a chart pattern.

FIGURE 17.4   MMM US Equity (3M Co).

Diagonal Patterns

Staying with the same chart, look at pattern D on the left. What happened to the rectangle bottom identified in an earlier chart? It is still there, of course, but the new lines form a different chart pattern. Chart patterns can nest (one inside the other) and the same pattern can appear as two different types. Think of it as explaining the words "there," "their," and "they're" to someone learning English. They sound the same, but are different.

Look on the chart where price forms diagonals. I show one as a slanting blue trendline above D. The line touches price three times as marked. Another trendline touches the pattern's bottom, also three times. The blue pattern is an example of a descending triangle.

> **Smart Investor Tip**
> Chart patterns can nest—one inside the other. The same price pattern can also appear as two (or more) differently named patterns.

Constructing Patterns

When you look at a price chart, train your eyes to search for peaks that top out near the same price. They may form chart patterns (double tops) that warn of a coming trend change from up to down.

Train your eyes to find valleys that bottom near the same price (double bottoms). Bottoming patterns can alert you to a stock ready to fly like the model rockets I launched as a kid (not the homemade gasoline one that ignited a water puddle—sorry about that, Mom).

Patterns that form diagonals (descending triangle, for example) or curves (scallops, rounding bottoms, or cup with handles) also foretell the direction that price may take.

Visually connect peaks, valleys, curves, and diagonals to form chart patterns.

Figure 17.5 highlights the valid patterns identified so far.

FIGURE 17.5   MMM US Equity (3M Co).

THEORY AND ANALYSIS

LS means left shoulder and RS means right shoulder. A complex head-and-shoulders bottom (lower right) takes the place of the rectangle bottom. A complex head-and-shoulders bottom has multiple shoulders and multiple heads, but rarely both.

Think of pattern recognition as like trying to find the Big Dipper or Cassiopeia in the heavens at night.

In the next section, I begin to develop a common language, starting with minor highs and lows. Do not be alarmed. This is not as hard as learning French. However, I could be lying because I never learned French.

Test Yourself

Decide which of the following statements are true or false.

1. Overhead resistance occurs when price stalls or reverses, and is always below price.
2. Underlying support happens when price stalls at the same level as it has in the past. Support is never above price.
3. A rectangle forms between underlying resistance and overhead support.
4. On the same price scale (daily scale or weekly scale, but not mixed), tall chart patterns tend to outperform smaller ones.
5. The same price pattern can have multiple names.
6. Like an expectant mother, one price pattern can be inside another.

Answers: 1. False 2. True 3. False 4. True 5. True 6. True.

■ Minor Highs and Lows

Minor highs and lows are synonyms for peaks and valleys except that they have strict definitions that can help with pattern recognition. I will use these terms throughout this book, so we might as well go through the pain of learning what they mean and how to recognize them.

A minor high does not refer to an overdose, and a minor low is not lingo for a bad trip. Rather, they represent the building blocks of pattern recognition. If you can program a computer to find them, then you can automate pattern recognition. For example, a triple top has three minor highs near the same price.

Since you are a human computer, I have created definitions for minor highs and lows to help you find them until your eyes become trained to spot them. String them together in your mind and patterns will emerge, patterns that repeat, patterns that can make you money.

Peaks: Minor Highs

A minor high is a significant peak on the price chart. What does *significant* mean? I had to answer that question when I wrote Patternz—free software that automatically finds chart patterns. I discovered that peaks between three and five days apart led to the best pattern recognition (the exact number is pattern specific).

Use five days between peaks for **minor highs,** but be flexible.

DEFINITION:

Minor highs

A minor high is a peak separated by about five days from a higher high. It should represent a significant peak.

Figure 17.6 shows each peak highlighted with an asterisk that is at least five days away from a higher peak. For example, point A is the highest high from at least five days before to five days after the peak.

Notice that peak B does not have an asterisk. According to my computer, it is not a minor high. Why? Because C has a high that is above peak B, and C is five days away from B.

The same situation occurs at D with a higher high occurring three days later. Nevertheless, I consider peaks B and D to be minor highs. Grasp the concept that a minor high is a significant peak in a price trend and worry less about counting days between peaks. Once you train your eyes to see minor highs, you will not need to count. It also helps if you are sober.

Valleys: Minor Lows

In a manner similar to minor highs, **minor lows** are valleys separated by at least five days from a lower low. That means five days before to five days after the minor low.

Figure 17.7 shows an example, with asterisks highlighting minor lows.

FIGURE 17.6   GE US Equity (General Electric Co).

FIGURE 17.7   GE US Equity (General Electric Co).

For example, valley A is below the adjacent price bars such that none are lower than it is for at least five days on either side.

Look at B. Notice the absence of an asterisk. If you count five candles to the right of B, you will see that a price bar is slightly lower than B (it may be hard to tell, so just take my word for it). Candle B is not strictly a minor low, but I consider it one anyway.

Candle C is another example of a bottom that is not strictly a minor low because it is too close to lower candles. However, if this were the left shoulder of a head-and-shoulders bottom, then I would probably consider it a valid minor low.

In other words, be flexible when searching for minor lows. If it looks like price is making a turn, then it is a minor low. If you need to count the price bars to be sure it is a minor low, then do so.

The inset shows bottoms with two days of separation instead of five, highlighted with asterisks. Notice that point E qualifies, but does it look like a minor low? No. It appears as part of the upward price trend and not a significant turning point. It is not a minor low.

In the next section, I discuss trendlines, and there are three types. Can you name them?

Need a hint? One is curved, but the others are not straight and diagonal. Wait until you read my exercises. You may find it easier to eat a bowling ball than to get them right!

For Further Reading

You may find my free website useful, including the link to Patternz:

Over 500 articles on chart patterns: www.thepatternsite.com

Free pattern recognition software that finds 66 chart patterns and 105 candlesticks: www.thepatternsite.com/patternz.html

---

Test Yourself

Answer the following.

1. True or false: As used in this book, a minor high can represent a *major* turning point.
2. True or false: A minor low represents a *minor* turning point.
3. A minor high is the highest peak from five days before to five days after the peak. If peak A is the highest price four days from a higher peak, is peak A still a minor high?

   A. Always.
   B. Never.
   C. Sometimes.

Answers 1. True; 2. True; 3. C

■ Trendlines

Trendlines are to technical analysis as hammers are to carpentry. Knowing how to use trendlines properly can save you money and allow you to enter a new trade with confidence.

Earlier in this chapter, I asked if you could name the three types of trendlines. They are internal, external, and curved. Before I get to that, let us discuss scaling (this is not a fish joke).

Figure 17.8 shows a chart on the logarithmic price scale. Notice that the price divisions at A (lower right) are spaced further apart than they are at B (upper right). On charts that show price making large moves (such as charts using weekly or monthly data), the log scale will make chart patterns taller at the lower end of the scale so you can see them better.

I drew a line connecting the peaks. The line slopes downward and touches each peak using a straight line.

The same exhibit on the linear scale looks warped, but it could be your eyeglasses. Check for scratches. (See Figure 17.9.)

A curved line touches the same peaks. Why? Each vertical division is the same height whereas in the prior exhibit, price was on the log scale.

Which scale should you use to view chart patterns? Hint: I prefer the log scale. Most of the charts in this book are on the linear scale.

For an example of why scaling is important, look at Intel during the technology bubble of 2000 (monthly, linear scale). Figure 17.10 shows a price mountain that would make Tenzing Norgay pause.

FIGURE 17.8   ABGX US Equity (Abgenix Inc).

FIGURE 17.9   ABGX US Equity (Abgenix Inc).

A descending triangle appears in 1998. Notice that at the lower price ranges, you cannot see any other chart patterns. The price looks smooth as if a giant stomped on the foothills (until 1995, anyway).

Compare the same chart using a log scale. (See Figure 17.11.)

The rugged terrain becomes apparent. Other chart patterns appear, too, such as a rising wedge and a second descending triangle. Which scale would you rather use?

KEY POINT:
The logarithmic price scale gives a clearer view of historical price data when the stock makes a large vertical move. Chart patterns are easier to see on the log scale.

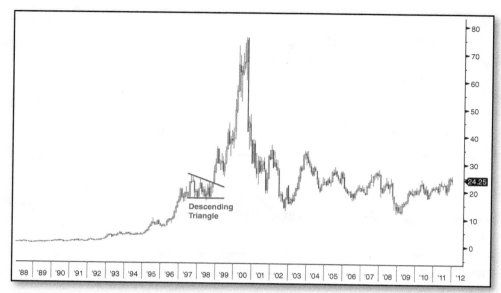

FIGURE 17.10   INTC US Equity (Intel Corp).

However, whenever you need to physically measure the height of a chart pattern (like using a ruler held up to a computer screen), use the linear scale. For example, measuring one inch on the linear scale may mean a $10 rise, but on the log scale, that same one inch could measure $50. Height becomes important for the measure rule, which I will discuss later in the book.

Whichever scale you decide to use, do not go flipping from log to linear to log. It will only confuse you. Pick one scale and stay with it when searching for chart patterns. Only switch when needed.

Uptrend Connections

Price forms trends. Sometimes, you can connect those trends with lines, called **trendlines**. Most often those lines will be diagonal and straight, but not always.

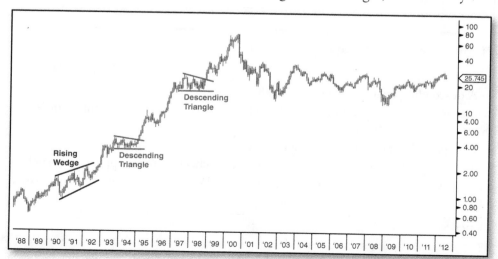

FIGURE 17.11   INTC US Equity (Intel Corp).

When you look at a price chart, look for places where price trends. In your mind, connect the valleys with a straight line, highlighting an up-sloping trend.

For example, Figure 17.12 shows price trending at blue line A (far left). The line works well, meaning it follows the minor lows until F, G, and H. Those candles poke through the line. In fact, H begins a new trend downward.

Line B shows a horizontal price trend, also drawn along the minor lows. Trendlines C and D are about the same length as A and at nearly the same slope.

As you experiment with drawing trendlines, you may discover that steep, up-sloping trendlines do not last long. Why? Because traders take profits if the stock rises too fast. That selling pressure will force the stock to move sideways or down, piercing the trendline—at least temporarily.

Shallower trendlines tend to be powerhouses. From them, strong moves are born. In between the shallow and vertical trendlines are the also-rans. They show breaks in the prevailing short- to intermediate-term trend only to see a new trend emerge, perhaps at a shallower angle.

Look at trendline E, drawn in red. It is the longest on the chart, and it is also the most important. Why? Because price plunges through it in July, signaling the end of the uptrend.

Notice that I have drawn each up-sloping trendline along the valleys and not the tops. Why? To signal a trend change. Up-sloping trendlines drawn along peaks will not do that.

Trendline Types: Internal, External, and Curved

Trendline A is (Figure 17.12) called an **internal trendline** because it slices through price at F and G (H does not count because it ends the trend).

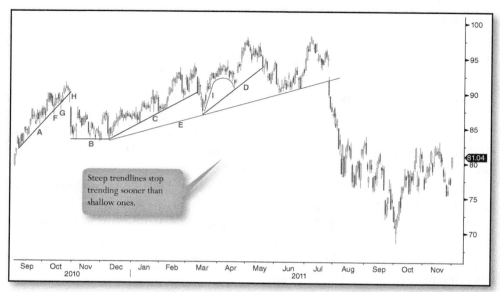

FIGURE 17.12   MMM US Equity (3M Co).

The thinking behind drawing internal trendlines is that the line best represents the majority of traders. Few will receive a fill at the day's exact high or low, so why draw a trendline connecting those outliers?

I have a different view. If I were to place a stop below the trendline, I do not want to be stopped out because my trendline sliced through price and an outlier hit my stop. I prefer to draw my trendlines like line C. This line follows the price bottoms as it trends. Line C is an example of an **external trendline**. An external trendline connects only the price ends; it does not slice through price.

Line I represents the third type of trendline: a **curved trendline**. It begins straight, but curves over at the top of the inverted and ascending scallop chart pattern. Curved trendlines become important for some chart patterns and for parabolic moves (curved moves that resemble a biplane flying level then going vertical).

DEFINITION:

External trendline

An external trendline hugs the end of price.

DEFINITION:

Curved trendline

A curved trendline also hugs price, but it is curved (although a curved trendline can be external or internal, too).

Draw trendlines for the best fit. If a trendline happens to slice through price, do not get your knickers in a twist. If a curved line better represents a trend, then use it.

KEY POINT:

Draw trendlines for the best fit, whether they look curved or slice through price.

FIGURE 17.13   ACET US Equity (Aceto Corp).

Downtrend Connections

Down trendlines are the same as up trendlines except you draw them along peaks. Why? To detect a trend change.

Figure 17.13 shows an example of several trendlines highlighting a falling stock. Line A is short and steep. It is an external trendline that touches the candle tops three times.

I originally drew line B from the start in May until point B, but then extended it. It touched another candle at the line's end, forming a chart pattern called a bump and run reversal bottom. The pattern predicts an upward breakout, which is what happened. I used to call them bump and run formations but changed it because of the acronym (BARF).

Line C, drawn in red, is a major trendline not only for its length, but also because it signals a trend change. Price not only slices through the line at E, but closes above it. A new up trend may be underway.

Minor low D finds support near the trendline, too, although price pierced the trendline for a day before reversing. The E to D move is a throwback, a pattern I will discuss in a later chapter.

Notice the two chart patterns outlined in blue on the far left of the chart. Those are broadening tops. A top trendline connects the peaks and a bottom trendline connects the valleys, creating a megaphone appearance.

If you know how to draw trendlines, you probably could have found these two patterns. Not only do trendlines signal a trend change, but they also outline pattern boundaries.

On a price chart, look for peaks that align. Draw trendlines connecting them to see what they reveal. Draw trendlines along valleys and see what they show, too. This is especially significant along the hard right edge (the right side of the chart) because trends there suggest where price is going in the future.

Trendline Guidelines

Now that we have experimented with drawing trendlines, what are the guidelines and tips for their use? Here is a nine-item list.

1. Trendlines should connect at least two peaks(minor highs) or two valleys (minor lows), preferably three or more.
2. Like horseshoes and hand grenades, closeness counts. Price need not touch the trendline, but it should come close.
3. To detect a trend change, draw trendlines along the valleys when price is trending up. Draw trendlines along the peaks in a declining stock.
4. Trendlines with widely spaced touches are more significant than are those with narrow ones (I proved this).
5. In 2006, I wrote in my book *Getting Started in Chart Patterns*, "Trendlines are like diving boards. You get a bigger bounce from a longer diving board than a shorter one."
6. Steep trendlines underperform shallow ones. That means larger moves occur after a trendline pierce from a shallow trendline than a steep one.
7. Rising volume along an up-sloping trendline *powers* (a larger decline) price downward after a trendline break more than does a receding volume trend leading to the breakout.
8. For downward sloping trendlines, receding volume leads to better performance after price pierces the trendline, moving up.
9. Just because price closes above a down-sloping trendline or below an up-sloping one is no reason to believe that the trend has changed. It is only a hint of a trend change, not a guarantee.

The next chapter discusses one of the most important topics: support and resistance. If you can determine when price is going to reverse, you can make a bundle. If you save wisely and invest carefully, you can retire at 36 just as I did. Learning about support and resistance is a good first step to achieving that goal.

This just in: All you have to do is turn the page!

DEFINITION:
Trendlines
Trendlines not only follow trends, but also outline chart patterns.

For Further Reading

Bulkowski, Thomas N. *Getting Started in Chart Patterns*. Hoboken, NJ: John Wiley & Sons, 2006.

Bulkowski, Thomas N. *Trading Classic Chart Patterns*. Hoboken, NJ: John Wiley & Sons, 2002.

THEORY AND ANALYSIS

CHAPTER 18

Understanding Chart Pattern Breaks

From Thomas N. Bulkowski, *Visual Guide to Chart Patterns* (Hoboken, New Jersey: John Wiley & Sons, 2002), Chapters 4–6.

■ Support and Resistance

If trendlines are like hammers, then support and resistance (SAR) are like boards. Price stalls or even reverses at SAR areas and that makes predicting future price trends easier. Fortunately, there are many techniques that show SAR, and this chapter discusses them.

In the fall of 1987, a friend of mine said that she had purchased shares in a mutual fund. This was her first time investing in the stock market, and she was excited!

On black Monday, October 19, 1987, the Dow Jones industrials lost over 22 percent of their value in *one* session.

She was not excited! In fact, she vowed to sell as soon as she got her money back, which she did.

Her behavior is typical of novices. Imagine that others acted the same way. Their emotional selling would force price down. People buying the stock just before the drop or as the selling begins also get upset as the stock tumbles. They vow to sell when they get their money back, too.

If you were to plot this behavior on a chart, you would see the stock peak and then peak again near the same price. That concerted selling forms a barrier to upward movement called **overhead resistance**. Price will eat through that resistance, so it is not made of concrete.

> **DEFINITION:**
> **Overhead resistance**
> Overhead resistance occurs when selling pressure overcomes buying demand, sending price lower—at least for a time.

A similar behavior pattern exists for valleys. People want to buy a stock at $10, but price gaps higher and zooms away from them, rising to $15. They missed the move and vow to buy the stock if it ever gets back to $10.

When the stock drops to $10, they buy, joining others doing the same thing. That buying demand builds a floor underneath the stock, which we call **support**. The floor is not made of concrete either, so price can act as termites do and eat its way through.

> **DEFINITION:**
>
> Support
>
> Underlying support occurs when buying demand overcomes selling pressure, putting a temporary floor beneath the stock.

Support and resistance is human nature at work—a pictorial representation of emotion.

Support and resistance represent *areas* or *bands* where price is likely (but not guaranteed) to stall or reverse. Price can motor through a support zone and a week later, it will stop there as if taking a snooze at a roadside rest stop.

> **KEY POINT:**
>
> Support areas can act as resistance and resistance areas can act as support.

Trendline SAR

Trendlines highlight and act as SAR areas. For example, Figure 18.1 shows a trendline connecting the valleys beginning at A, touching B, C, D, and E. At F, however, price pierces the trendline, heading down.

Notice that at G, H, and I, price bumps up against a ceiling formed by the same trendline. The trendline that once acted as support now acts as resistance.

The blue trendline shows the same principle, but not as clearly. The trendline acts as support from J to M and as overhead resistance at N and O.

FIGURE 18.1   ANF US Equity (Abercrombie & Fitch Co).

After drawing a trendline, imagine what price might do in the future. By extending trendline AF, a trader can guess where price might reverse when it hits the trendline.

Trendlines can be powerful prediction tools, but they do not always work.

Down-sloping trendlines show the same behavior by acting as support or resistance at any time. An example of this is trendline PQR. Down-sloping trendline PQ acts as overhead resistance at the two peaks, and at R it acts as underlying support.

SAR at Gaps

Price gaps when the day's low remains above the prior day's high, leaving a bullish gap on the daily chart. A bearish gap forms when the day's high remains below the prior day's low.

> **DEFINITION:**
>
> **Price gaps**
>
> A price gap is a blank area on the chart that shows the high price below the prior day's low, or the low price above the prior day's high. Gaps do not work well as support or resistance areas.

Figure 18.2 shows examples of several gaps that act as support and resistance. I measured how often gaps show SAR (support: 20 percent, resistance: 25 percent) and found them to be as reliable as a coworker who promised to pick me up at the airport and then forgot.

Gap A has difficulty supporting price at valley B. At peak C, it does provide overhead resistance to block the upward move.

Gap D shows support at valley E (notice that price pierces the gap but soon reverses) and resistance at peak F before the effect wears off.

FIGURE 18.2 **APD US Equity (Air Products & Chemicals Inc).**

In February, gap G supports price, but the support melts like snow in spring during the strong downtrend in March.

Now look at gaps H, I, J, and K. Those gaps do not impede price at all.

In candlestick land, gaps are called windows probably because traders that depend on gaps climb out windows and jump.

Horizontal Consolidation Regions

Unless you have read my other books, you probably have never heard of **horizontal consolidation regions (HCRs),** and yet they are some of the most powerful SAR areas (they work 41 percent to 55 percent of the time). Figure 18.3 shows examples.

> **DEFINITION:**
>
> Horizontal consolidation regions (HCRs)
>
> A horizontal consolidation region is an area of horizontal price movement that has lots of price overlap with a flat bottom, flat top, or both. When price bumps against it, the stock often reverses direction or stalls. Long and tight HCRs (lots of price overlap) work better than do short or loose ones (meandering price).

An HCR is an *area* on the price chart where the stock crawls horizontally. The best HCRs have flat tops, flat bottoms, or both. When an HCR appears in the path leading to a chart pattern, any breakout that takes price back into the path of the HCR will often run into support or resistance.

To explain this, the inset shows the ideal case. A horizontal consolidation region appears as the grey box. Price drops out of this area and heads down, eventually forming a symmetrical triangle chart pattern. After an upward breakout from the triangle, price climbs to the HCR region (the area between the red lines) and then reverses.

FIGURE 18.3   AYI US Equity (Acuity Brands Inc).

The rest of Figure 18.3 shows how HCRs can act. For example, at A, price forms an HCR about a month long, and I show it bounded by two red lines extended into the future. At D, the HCR is a ceiling that acts as overhead resistance. At B and C, price stops at a new level of overhead resistance.

The area between D and G is a weak HCR because price tends to meander. Area E finds support in the DG region.

I drew the blue trendline, starting at F, toward G, just to see where it was in relation to the DG horizontal consolidation region. Notice that F finds support at the bottom of the DG area.

Round Number SAR

Support and resistance is a product of fear and greed, and round number SAR fits into that definition as snugly as a bug in a rug.

When novice traders buy a stock, they ask their brokers to buy at $10 and not at $9.91. Those round numbers—numbers that end in a zero—tend to show support and resistance. When traders set price targets, they choose round numbers at which to sell—$50 and not $49.87. When investors pick the same round number at which to trade, their buying and selling creates overhead resistance or underlying support. Figure 18.4 shows examples of this behavior.

Circled in red are areas that either touch or come close to the blue lines. The blue lines are round numbers like 20, 30, 40, and so on.

A good example of round number SAR is at A in the upper middle of the chart. Price bumps up against 80 from May to December before throwing in the towel and giving up.

Since people will be selling at round numbers, get in ahead of them. Instead of selling at 80, sell at 79.93.

FIGURE 18.4   ADS US Equity (Alliance Data Systems Corp).

Apply the same logic to stop placement. Avoid round numbers because that is where many novice traders will position their stops. If those stops trigger, it can start an avalanche where price drops, triggering more stops, and so on. The selling pressure forces price to tumble in what is called running or gunning the stop. If this happens to your stock, do not shoot yourself. Aim for something less valuable.

You can use round numbers to guess where price is going to stall, even if it has never reached that high before (no apparent overhead resistance).

For example, if a stock is breaking out to new highs at 17, you can guess that it will run into overhead resistance at 20. Traders and investors will use 20 as a sell point, and if enough actually sell, price will reverse there. Beat the crowds and sell at 19.95.

Day traders can use round numbers, too, as targets. When price reaches a round number, consider selling.

SAR at Peaks, Valleys, and Chart Patterns

Support and resistance forms at peaks, valleys, and chart patterns. Figure 18.5 shows examples of all three.

FIGURE 18.5   AWI US Equity (Armstrong World Industries Inc).

Starting on the left, an ascending triangle appears at G. The horizontal consolidation region has a flat top, but it looks loose with price wandering up and down between the two red trendlines. That region should show support or resistance in the future, and it does. The symmetrical triangle forms in the middle of the HCR and point I on the far right also peaks near the top of G.

H is an **exhaustion gap**. Notice that price later finds support at the bottom of the gap.

DEFINITION:

Exhaustion gap

An exhaustion gap appears at the end of a trend. Price usually closes the gap within a week or two.

The symmetrical triangle is a delight because it is a perfect example of the chart pattern. Price bounces from trendline to trendline, filling the pattern with movement. The tops and bottoms of the pattern touch each trendline without leaving whiskers behind for your shaver.

Notice that price turns at A, directly above the triangle apex.

The apex is also a place of future support and resistance (as is the entire triangle, for that matter). Although valley B slides below the apex, it does reverse within the triangle.

The horizontal red line joining peaks C and D show peak SAR. Price bumps up against a ceiling there. During an advance, expect price to reverse at the level of a prior peak (it may not, so keep that in mind, too).

Smart Investor Tip

Objects that show support will often show resistance in the future and vice versa.

This idea also applies to valleys. Circled in blue is a loose horizontal congestion region at E. When price attempts to exceed this level at F, it hits the HCR and finds overhead resistance.

Finally, price drops to find support at K setup by peak J (and the loose congestion area to its left).

When looking at price trends, imagine where price may stall or reverse. Those reversals can happen at the price level of prior peaks, prior valleys, horizontal congestion regions, gaps, trendlines, chart patterns, and round numbers.

It sounds like I am covering every possible number on the price chart, right? Have faith that price will reverse at support or resistance and when it fails, squeal like a stuck pig.

The next section discusses four types of gaps. Traders love gaps. Why? I have no idea. I prefer women.

■ Gaps

There are several types of gaps, but we will cover only four of them. Others, like the ex-dividend gap and the opening gap, are inconsequential or too advanced.

Gaps are exciting! Those that appear at a chart pattern breakout can push a stock like a booster stage does to a rocket. For example, breakout day gaps in symmetrical triangles (bull markets, up breakouts) show gains averaging 36 percent compared to 28 percent for those without gaps.

Sometimes the booster stage fails to ignite as it does in ascending triangles. There, gaps hurt performance: 29 percent versus 35 percent gain for those with and without gaps, respectively.

Being able to tell the gap type can help traders decipher what will happen with the stock. Will a stock begin a new price trend as it does after a breakaway gap, or will an exhaustion gap signal the party is over faster than champagne left uncorked?

Four Types

I show a bar chart to find examples of the four major gap types: area, breakaway, continuation, and exhaustion. The bar chart makes finding gaps easier. (See Figure 18.6)

FIGURE 18.6   JNY US Equity (Jones Group Inc/The).

Look at gap B1, located to the right of the circled congestion region. A breakaway gap always leaves a congestion area. A congestion area is where price moves sideways for a time. It can be just a few days wide—or more—like that circled. The breakaway gap breaks away from the area, hence its name.

Slaloming downhill, we find gap E1. This is an example of an exhaustion gap. The gap exhausts the trend, thus its name. After an exhaustion gap, expect to see a quick reversal, sometimes a powerful one, but also one that does not last long.

Gap A1, on the far left of the chart, is an area gap. These little stinkers carry a load in their pants. They look like breakaway gaps, but a trend does not develop. The **gap closes** quickly by curling around and filling the gap.

> **DEFINITION:**
>
> **Gap closes**
>
> A gap is said to close when future price action covers the same price level as the gap. Price fills the gap, closing it.

The inset shows an ideal example of the last type of gap, a continuation gap. A trend develops with a breakaway gap (B) that appears after a congestion region. Then a continuation gap appears (Co) during the trend. An exhaustion gap (E) ends the trend.

A continuation gap is also known as a **measuring gap** because it sometimes forms midway in a price trend. Continuation gaps are rare, and I found only one on the far right of the chart.

> **DEFINITION:**
>
> **Measuring gap**
>
> A continuation, measuring, or runaway gap is one that appears midway in a price trend. Measure from the start of the trend to the gap and project from the gap onward to determine how far price might move.

Gap Type	Discussion
Area, Common, or Pattern:	Occurs in areas of congestion (trendless markets) and close rapidly. Volume on the day of the gap can be high, but returns to normal in a day or two. No significant highs (in uptrends) or lows (in downtrends) occur immediately after the gap. A distinctive curl as the gap closes is a key indication of this gap type.
Breakaway:	Identifies the start of a new trend and occurs on breakout from a consolidation region. Is accompanied by high volume on the day of the gap and continuing for several days. The trend continues long enough for several new highs (for uptrends) or new lows (downtrends) to occur after the gap.
Continuation, Measuring, or Runaway:	Happens in the midst of a straight-line advance or decline. Price continues making new highs or lows without filling the gap. Volume is usually high, propelling price in the direction of the trend.
Exhaustion:	Occurs at the end of a trend on high volume. The gap is not followed by new minor highs or minor lows and the gap itself may be unusually tall. After the gap, price consolidates. Commonly occurs after a continuation gap. The gap closes quickly, usually within a week.

Identification Guidelines

What differentiates gaps? The following table describes what to look for.

I studied each gap type and found that area gaps close in an average of 3 days.

Breakaway gaps take an average of 136 days to close in a bull market, upward trend, and 168 days in a downward trend.

Continuation gaps close in an average of 98 days (uptrends) and 77 days (downtrends).

Exhaustion gaps close in 9 days (uptrends) and 14 days (downtrends).

Exercise

When I visit my dentist every year, I pull out the *Highlights* magazine and search the drawing for a comb, rake, toothbrush, and other utensils hidden on the page. These exercises are just like that search except that here you are looking for chart patterns.

The next chart tests your knowledge of gaps, based on the earlier table and discussion. Try to identify each gap. The numbers point to the gaps and the associated volume. All four gap types appear in Figure 18.7.

Figure 18.8 shows the answers.

Breakaway gaps exit a congestion area as if it were on fire, so they are easy to spot. Sometimes, however, they become area gaps. Continuation gaps are rare and will appear only in strong price trends. It took a while to find a chart that had them. Exhaustion gaps end a trend, so look for a strong trend, and find a gap that leads to a consolidation region.

Trading Gaps

If you are a day trader, the only gaps important to you are opening gaps. Other intraday gaps that may appear happen because of low volume. Ignore them.

FIGURE 18.7 OLN US Equity (Olin Corp).

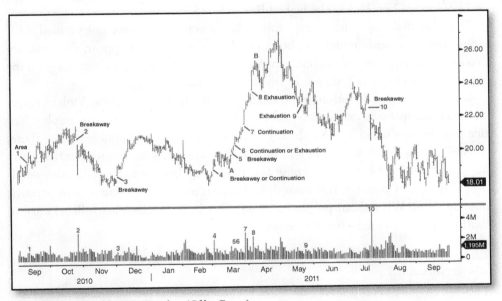

FIGURE 18.8 OLN US Equity (Olin Corp).

If you are a swing trader, then gaps are important. When a gap forms out of a consolidation region on high volume, you know that a trend is underway. It is a buy signal (but not one you should necessarily take).

If a trend fails to appear, then the gap becomes an area gap. That situation should become clear if the gap closes in two or three price bars. If the gap closes, exit the trade immediately.

Area gaps show a hook as price curls back to the gap. That hook should happen within a handful of price bars of the gap. If it does not, then it is a breakaway gap.

When a gap appears in a strong price trend that is already underway, it is probably an exhaustion gap. It could be a continuation gap, so waiting another price bar or two should provide confirmation, and perhaps a better exit price. If you see lots of overlap between one gap bar and the next, then it is an exhaustion gap and time to sell. If the trend continues with little overlap, then it is a continuation gap.

Since continuation gaps are rare, a gap in a trend already underway is most likely an exhaustion gap.

Gap Measure Rule   For continuation gaps, measure from the start of the trend to the middle of the gap and project upward from the middle of the gap to get a price target.

For example, in Figure 18.8, continuation gap 7 shows a trend start at A that ends at B. The gap is about midway in the trend. To put numbers to this, the low at A is at 18.95 and the middle of the gap is at 21.57 for a height of 2.62. That gives a target of 21.57 + 2.62 or 24.19. The high at B is at 25.45

Some say that continuation gaps follow breakaway gaps (I have not verified this). If the trend is already underway, but a breakaway gap did not appear, then you are probably looking at an exhaustion gap. Also, exhaustion gaps can be very large. If the gap you are seeing is tall, then it is probably an exhaustion gap.

If you do see an exhaustion gap, consider trading the new direction. Violent reversals can accompany an exhaustion gap. Gaps 8 and 9 in Figure 18.8 are examples. Notice that the new trend lasts for about a week, so you have to be nimble trading these.

Now that we have filled the *gaps* in your knowledge, what comes next? Throwbacks and pullbacks. Do you know the difference between them, besides spelling? Hint: Chart patterns that have throwbacks often perform worse than patterns missing them. What about pullbacks? Are pullbacks to stocks what fullbacks are to football? I have no idea what that means.

Test Yourself

Answer the following questions to test for gaps in your knowledge.

1. What does closing the gap mean?
   A. The window of opportunity to trade a gap is dwindling.
   B. Price covers the gap within a month.
   C. Price in the future retraces far enough to fill the gap.
   D. None of the above.

2. A breakaway gap has the following characteristics:
   A. Is accompanied by high volume.
   B. Is accompanied by low volume.
   C. Usually closes quickly.
   D. Often remains open a long time.
   E. Leaves a congestion region.
3. True or false: Exhaustion gaps close quickly.
4. True or false: The appearance of an exhaustion gap means the stock is tired, hence the name exhaustion gap.
5. True or false: A continuation gap always appears midway in a price trend.
6. The differences between a breakaway gap and an area gap are:
   A. Only one occurs on high volume.
   B. The breakaway gap is unusually tall.
   C. The breakaway gap closes quickly.
   D. The area gap closes quickly.
   E. The breakaway gap remains open longer.

Answers : 1. C; 2. A, D, E; 3. True; 4. False; 5. False; 6. D and E

■ Throwbacks and Pullbacks

Throwbacks and pullbacks are important patterns. Why? Because they happen about half the time after the breakout from a chart pattern. Not knowing about them invites disaster when the stock returns to the breakout price and continues lower. You sell for a loss only to watch the stock recover.

Figure 18.9 provides a typical example of what a **throwback** looks like.

> **DEFINITION:**
>
> **Throwback**
>
> A throwback occurs after an upward breakout when price returns to the breakout price or chart pattern boundary within 30 days.

FIGURE 18.9 AMTD US Equity (TD Ameritrade Holding Corp).

Imagine that you have a buy stop placed a penny above the top of this ascending triangle. The order triggers at A. Since you are a seasoned pro, you always use a stop and decide to place it below the prior minor low, at D.

Price rises for a few days and then the company announces earnings before the market opens, at C. The stock opens below the bottom trendline and then plummets far enough to catch your stop and take you out of the trade. By day's end, the stock has closed *higher!*

The injury to your ego continues when the stock performs like a killer bee chasing a bird, soaring 38 percent to B.

Congratulations! You have just been stung by a throwback.

Pullbacks

You learn from your mistake and decide that you placed the stop too close. In your next trade, you are looking to boost income so you select the dividend pay-ing utility stock shown in Figure 18.10, and buy at A.

Since ascending triangles break out upward 67 percent of the time in a bull mar-ket, you feel confident that this stock will do well. You place a stop loss order further away this time, a penny below the bottom of the triangle, at B.

The day after you buy the stock, it breaks out downward and a day later, it stops you out (C). Then price recovers almost as quickly and begins the move up that you expected. In fact, at D, the stock has climbed 32 percent above your buy price. Not only did you take a loss, but you missed out on all of those dividend checks.

The drop to C and the recovery is called a **pullback**.

> **DEFINITION:**
>
> Pullback
>
> A pullback occurs after a downward breakout from a chart pattern when price returns to the breakout price or chart pattern boundary within 30 days.

FIGURE 18.10   UIL US Equity (UIL Holdings Corp).

Identification Guidelines

What should you look for when trying to identify throwbacks and pullbacks? The following table provides the answer.

Characteristic	Discussion
Chart pattern breakout	From a chart pattern, price breaks out upward in a throwback and downward in a pullback.
Loop	Price continues in the direction of the breakout for a few days, but then loops back to the breakout price.
White space	After the stock returns to the breakout price, it leaves white space on the chart between the breakout and return.
Time	The stock must return to the breakout price or trendline boundary within 30 days.

Look at Figure 18.11, which helps explain the *average* behavior of throwbacks and pullbacks.

The left panel shows a throwback. Buying enthusiasm pushes price upward until it explodes out the top of any chart pattern. However, that buying demand slowly fades in the face of mounting selling pressure. In an average of six days, the stock has peaked after climbing 8 percent. Then it begins the return trip to the chart pattern.

The return takes only four days to either touch or come near the trendline boundary or breakout price, for a total of 10 days to make the round trip.

From there, price may continue lower or it may rebound immediately. In 65 percent of the cases, price resumes the upward breakout direction and rises. The other 35 percent close below the bottom of the chart pattern.

Pullbacks show a similar pattern except they apply to downward breakouts from any chart pattern. Price shoots lower at the breakout when excessive selling overpowers weak buying demand.

FIGURE 18.11 The Typical Behavior of Throwbacks and Pullbacks.

In an average of six days, the stock has bottomed and buying demand reverses the downtrend. The return journey takes five days for a total of eleven for the round trip from breakout to pullback.

Price may continue rising from there, and in 53 percent of the cases it does by closing above the top of the chart pattern. The remaining 47 percent of the time, the stock drops.

Figure 18.11 shows averages of thousands of chart patterns, so each individual case may vary.

Not all chart patterns will throwback or pullback, either. The accompanying table shows the throwback and pullback rates for popular chart patterns.

The highest throwback rate is for rectangle tops, and triple tops have the highest pullback rate. Descending triangles have the lowest throwback rate and rectangle tops have the lowest pullback rate.

This chapter ends the boot camp. The next chapter begins playing with live ammo by discussing individual chart patterns. It is an exciting time, so gather the children, and you may want to make popcorn.

Chart Pattern	Throwback Rate	Pullback Rate
Ascending triangles	60%	56%
Descending triangles	50%	55%
Double bottoms	56%	N/A
Double tops	N/A	57%
Head-and-shoulders bottoms	57%	N/A
Head-and-shoulders tops	N/A	59%
Rectangle bottoms	59%	59%
Rectangle tops	64%	54%
Symmetrical triangles	58%	58%
Triple bottoms	58%	N/A
Triple tops	N/A	63%

N/A: Not applicable

Test Yourself

Answer the following questions.

1. True or false: A pullback occurs when price pulls back to the chart pattern from above.

2. True or false: A throwback never happens after a downward breakout.

3. If price breaks out downward from a descending triangle at $10 and 31 days later it is at $10, what has happened?

    A. A throwback has occurred.
    B. A pullback has occurred.
    C. Nothing.

4. Price completes a pullback after a breakout. What is the probability that price will continue higher?

    A. Over 50 percent.
    B. Under 50 percent.
    C. 50 percent.
    D. Unknown.

Answers: 1. False; 2. True; 3. C; 4. A

CHAPTER 19

Triangles, Pennants, and Flags

From Thomas N. Bulkowski, *Visual Guide to Chart Patterns* (Hoboken, New Jersey: John Wiley & Sons, 2002), Chapters 7–11.

■ Pattern Identification

This chapter focuses on identifying individual chart patterns. How do you find them? What should you look for, and why do they form? I answer these questions and others, as well as ask you to find patterns in the exercises in each chapter.

■ Rectangles

Now that we are experts at identifying minor highs and lows, drawing trendlines, and knowing what support and resistance look like, let us begin by finding our first chart pattern: a rectangle.

Think of a rectangle as a sewer pipe snaking through a construction site. It has a flat top and flat bottom, and price is a rattlesnake winding its way through the pipe. Figure 19.1 shows an example of a rectangle bottom.

After trending downward, the stock bumped up against an invisible ceiling of overhead resistance and stood on a floor of underlying support from October to December, forming a rectangle bottom.

That ceiling and floor I show as two horizontal trendlines in red. Notice that price touches each trendline three times on the top (1–3) and three on the bottom (4–6). Also notice that price enters the pattern from the top, trending down.

The exit from the chart pattern, called a **breakout**, is downward in this example, but can be in any direction for rectangles. I highlight the breakout location in the figure. Price must *close* below the bottom of the rectangle to stage a downward breakout.

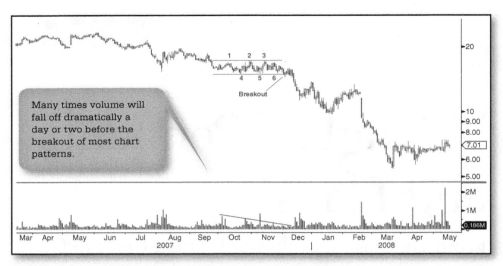

Many times volume will fall off dramatically a day or two before the breakout of most chart patterns.

FIGURE 19.1   ACMR US Equity (AC Moore Arts & Crafts Inc).

Notice the volume trend. Just before the breakout, volume recedes to a low level. Many times volume will fall off dramatically a day or two before the breakout of most chart patterns (not just rectangles).

KEY POINT:
In a rectangle, price moves horizontally between overhead resistance and underlying support.

DEFINITION:
Breakout
A breakout occurs when price closes outside the boundary of a chart pattern.

Identification Guidelines

Rectangles are rare, so finding them is about as common as seeing a hummingbird in the middle of a housing subdivision. The following table lists the identification guidelines.

Characteristic	Discussion
Price Trend	The short-term price trend leading to the rectangle is downward for bottoms and upward for tops.
Horizontal Trendlines	Two horizontal, or nearly so, trendlines bound price along the top and bottom of the rectangle.

Characteristic	Discussion
Touches	There should be at least two touches of each trendline.
Volume	For rectangle bottoms: Volume tends to follow the breakout direction: upward for upward breakouts, and downward for downward breakouts. For rectangle tops: Volume usually recedes until the breakout.

When searching a chart for rectangles, begin looking for a congestion region where price moves horizontally, often for weeks. In fact, the average length of 1,228 rectangles in a study I did using daily price data from 1991 to 2011 was 71 days (about 2 1/2 months).

Price should bounce between a support zone at the bottom and resistance at the top.

Connect the minor highs with a horizontal or nearly horizontal trendline. A similar line drawn below the minor lows forms a parallel trendline. Occasionally, one of the trendlines will not be horizontal. That is fine providing the slope is not too steep to disturb the overall picture. Consider the varying **trend lengths**.

> **DEFINITION:**
>
> **Trend lengths**
>
> A short-term trend lasts up to three months. An intermediate-term or secondary trend lasts between three and six months. A long-term trend or primary trend lasts longer than six months.

At least two touches (but three is better) of each trendline are required for a valid rectangle. The touches need not alternate from top to bottom, but should have at least two clearly defined minor highs and two minor lows coming close to or touching each trendline.

In the ideal case, the trendline touches should be spaced evenly along the pattern, not bunched together on one end only. In other words, the trendline should not appear like a diving board, with one end unsupported.

To determine whether the rectangle is a top or bottom, look at the price trend leading to the start of the rectangle. Rectangle bottoms have price trending downward into them, but tops have price trending upward. Ignore any overshoot or undershoot in the price bars within a week or so before the start of the rectangle.

For rectangle bottoms, the volume pattern tends to track the breakout direction. For tops, volume often recedes over the length of the rectangle. Do not discard a rectangle because the volume pattern is wrong.

For example, Figure 19.2 shows a rectangle top on the weekly scale. Price bounces between two horizontal trendlines B and C, touching each plenty of times, spread along its length. No diving board here!

Price begins the uptrend at A and although price bobbles up and down in early 2004 (before the start of the rectangle), it is clear that this rectangle is at the top of the trend and not at the bottom.

Volume trends upward during the first half of the rectangle and recedes thereafter.

The top trendline cuts through price (an internal trendline) to best show the horizontal nature of this rectangle.

FIGURE 19.2   BSET US Equity (Bassett Furniture Industries Inc).

A smaller rectangle appears at E. The price trend off the chart to the left shows that this is a rectangle bottom because price trends downward into it.

Figure 19.3 shows a rectangle bottom on the weekly scale. Price trends higher at B, peaks at A, and drops into the rectangle bottom. There, price slides between two horizontal trendlines before breaking out upward.

Notice that the exit trend, C, nearly matches the slope of trendline B. In fact, the exit velocity of price leading out of a chart pattern nearly matches the velocity going into a pattern. That behavior applies not only to rectangles, but to all chart pattern

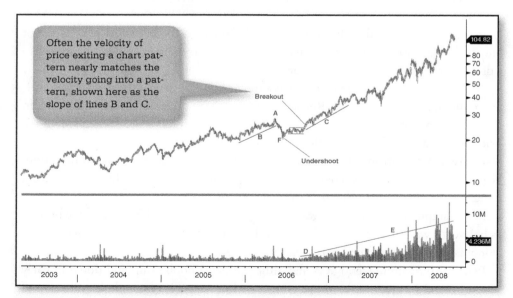

Often the velocity of price exiting a chart pattern nearly matches the velocity going into a pattern, shown here as the slope of lines B and C.

Breakout

Undershoot

FIGURE 19.3   AGU US Equity (Agrium Inc).

varieties. If you have limited dollars to spend and find two stocks showing chart patterns, choose the one with a higher velocity (cents per day).

> **SMART INVESTOR TIP**
> Tops have price trending into a chart pattern from the bottom, and bottoms have price trending into a chart pattern from the top.

> **SMART INVESTOR TIP**
> The price velocity leading to and exiting from a chart pattern are often similar even if the direction is reversed.

Notice that volume, D, slopes upward. This upward slope grows dramatically as price climbs, forming a long hill at E that would scare bicyclists like me trying to climb it.

I also show price undershoot (F) a few weeks before the rectangle begins. Ignore it. **Undershoot or overshoot** is a short dip or rise, respectively, before the start of a chart pattern. The only influence they have is to confuse novices and give authors like me something to write about.

> **DEFINITION:**
> **Undershoot or overshoot**
> Both undershoot and overshoot occur before a chart pattern begins. Undershoot happens when price briefly dips below the entrance of a chart pattern. Overshoot happens when price briefly soars above it.

The inbound price trend is downward leading to this rectangle bottom (starting from A), not upward starting from the undershoot (F).

Rectangle Psychology

Why do rectangles form? Imagine that you run a small mutual fund and your fundamental and technical analysis says that Friedman Industries is a steal at 5.50. You order the trading department to buy the stock at that price. (See Figure 19.4.)

Since you want to own several hundred thousand shares and the stock averages only 16,000 shares traded daily, it could take weeks to buy all that you want. Why? Because if you hit the market with an order for 450,000 shares, it will likely send price soaring. That would boost the average cost of ownership.

One tip I learned is that your buying or selling should not be for more than 1 percent of the average daily volume. In this example, that would amount to 1,600 shares. Recently, I had to use a limit order to exit a stock for fear that my selling would punish price—it was that thinly traded.

FIGURE 19.4   FRD US Equity (Friedman Industries Inc).

Beginning in early January, point A in the Figure, the trading department starts buying the stock. That buying demand causes price to rise, and your traders stop buying because the stock is too expensive. Price floats up to almost 6.

Another fund wants to dump the stock since they believe that the company will suffer in the coming economic slowdown. But they want to sell at a price no less than 5.75. Other institutional investors and retail traders join both sides. The result is that price hits a ceiling near 6 and a floor at 5.45.

When price bubbles up to the sell price, the mutual fund jumps in and sells as many shares as they can before forcing the price back down. When it drops to the buy price, the other mutual fund begins buying, sending the price higher.

Eventually, one side fulfills their mission to either establish a position or liquidate one. The price will either drop out of the bottom or rise through the top.

In this example, an upward breakout happens like a cork flying off a champagne bottle. C is the breakout day and 40,700 shares trade that day. The prior day saw only 12,200 shares traded.

Variations

This section looks at variations that you may come across in your quest to find rectangles. For example, Figure 19.5 shows an unusual chart pattern, but is it a rectangle?

Starting from A, the stock plunges like a bungee jumper whose cord breaks, splashing into the water, and slowly sinking into the top of the chart pattern. That means this rectangle is a bottom and not a top.

Our jumper surfaces three times near B, touching the top trendline. The guidelines say that at least two touches are necessary, preferably widely spaced. Does this qualify, or is it a diving board?

Since the chart pattern is so long, the three clustered touches are a problem. However, it helps that C is there to hold up the far end of the trendline.

Consider redrawing the top trendline parallel at F. It will slice through price as an internal trendline, but that is fine. Draw the line where it best shows overhead resistance.

> **SMART INVESTOR TIP**
> Volume is not an important *identification* feature of most chart patterns, including rectangles. Volume plays a bigger role in performance.

Now look at the bottom trendline. How many trendline touches do you see? The chart shows one at D, but the line is drawn incorrectly. Ignore that touch and move the line higher until it hugs the price valleys, connecting E. If you do that, the support area becomes clearer.

FIGURE 19.5 ARWR US Equity (Arrowhead Research Corp).

FIGURE 19.6 GLBL US Equity (Global Industries Ltd).

This is a rectangle bottom, but not a pretty one. If it helps, keep in mind what you are looking for—price moving sideways in a horizontal congestion region.

The next chart is one that reminds me of an e-mail that read as if the sender had overdosed on his medication. "Is this a flat base? Is this a rectangle? What kind of chart pattern is it? Price gaps up and then goes horizontal!" (See Figure 19.6.)

One glance at the chart told me all I needed to know, but I checked the news anyway. At A, the company received an offer to merge their operations with another company. These types of buyout offers make the stock soar and then flatline like a dead animal until the merger completes.

I do not consider the pattern to the right of A to be a rectangle. Why? Because of the news surrounding the stock. This is an example of an event pattern—how a stock behaves after it receives a buyout offer.

Exercise

This section presents two exercises. Find the rectangles on each chart. It will help if you look for minor highs that peak near the same price. In your mind, connect those peaks with a horizontal trendline. Then look below that line for minor lows that bottom near the same price. If you find that combination, then you have a rectangle.

Is it a rectangle top or bottom? Look at the short-term price *trend* leading to the rectangle. Tops have price trending upward into the chart pattern and bottoms have price trending downward.

Figure 19.7 has at least two rectangles. Find them.

Figure 19.8 shows the answer. The pattern highlighted in red is a rectangle bottom. Price begins sliding after A, trending down into the chart pattern, just as it is supposed to do for a rectangle bottom. Then it begins moving horizontally, forming minor highs (1 through 5) and minor lows (6 through 11).

FIGURE 19.7 DPL US Equity (DPL Inc).

FIGURE 19.8 DPL US Equity (DPL Inc).

The peak at 1 slices through the top trendline, but does it matter? No. Why not? Because by the time you recognize the price pattern as a rectangle bottom, that peak ceases to have any significance. Drawing the top trendline above peak 1 would make the other top touches seem too far away.

The same argument applies to valley 8. Price pokes below the red trendline but is not important to the overall picture.

The volume trend (F) rises and price breaks out upward.

Pattern CED is a rectangle top because price trends upward into the chart pattern. Price touches the bottom trendline three times and several times along the top. I drew the top trendline through E to show how price touches the top trendline better. Also, the first bottom touch, B, is part of a straight-line run. It is a minor low, but one that is not easy to see without a trendline connecting it. This is not a perfect example of a rectangle top, but be flexible.

The volume trend (G) is upward even though this rectangle breaks out downward. Rectangle tops often have a receding volume trend, but do not let that throw you off.

Look at pattern J. Did you find this one? The bottom trendline touches only one point. I show it redrawn in the inset as a V-shaped price trend. This V-shape more accurately represents the trend, not a horizontal line.

The top trendline rests on one peak, H. Point I is not a minor high. It is just a price bar on the side of a hill, not an individual peak (minor high). Avoid counting a trendline touch that is not a minor high or minor low. Pattern J is just squiggles on a chart and not a rectangle.

Figure 19.9 also shows at least one rectangle. Find as many as you can, and have tissues ready in case you get it wrong.

Figure 19.10 shows the answers. Let us begin with the red one (C) on the far right, since that is the only rectangle bottom on this chart.

Price trends downward into the chart pattern and then bounces up and down between two horizontal trendlines, touching each at least twice.

Look at peak B. This is an example of overshoot that I mentioned earlier. Price trends upward into the chart pattern, but overshoots the entry for a week or so before sliding into the rectangle. This is a rectangle top.

For rectangle top E, the price trend is horizontal leading to this pattern but upward before that (sharing the same inbound trend as rectangle D). Notice that point

FIGURE 19.9 OLN US Equity (Olin Corp).

FIGURE 19.10   OLN US Equity (Olin Corp).

A is NOT a minor high so it does not qualify as a top trendline touch. Be careful about touch counts and include only minor highs or minor lows.

Pattern E is a rectangle top. However, I prefer to call pattern DE one long rectangle top instead of thinking of it as two separate ones.

The next section discusses ascending triangles. I used to love trading them until I discovered that they did not perform well. In other words, I lost my shirt. Have you seen it?

Test Yourself

Answer the following statements or questions.

1. True or false: A rectangle bottom *always* has price trending down into the chart pattern.
2. True or false: It is fine if *one* of the trendlines bounding the rectangle bottom is almost horizontal.
3. True or false: It is fine if *both* trendlines are not horizontal, providing they are not too far from level.
4. True or false: A down-sloping volume trend is a key factor in determining whether the chart pattern is a rectangle bottom.
5. True or false: A breakout occurs when price pierces one of the horizontal trendlines.
6. How is a rectangle bottom different from a top (pick all that apply)?
   A. Rectangle bottoms are shorter in duration.
   B. Rectangle bottoms have price entering the chart pattern from the bottom, and tops have it entering from the top, hence the bottom and top names.
   C. They have different names because the volume pattern is different.
   D. A rectangle bottom is a horizontal consolidation region but a top is not.
   E. By definition, price enters tops from the bottom and enters bottoms from the top.
7. True or false: A rectangle top is a horizontal congestion region.

Answers: 1. True; 2. True; 3. True; 4. False; 5. False; 6. E; 7. True

■ Ascending Triangles

This section begins looking at chart patterns not bounded by twin horizontal lines. Triangles use a more complicated shape: diagonal trendlines. Training your eye to recognize them is still easy, though, because the technique builds on what we have learned.

Figure 19.11 shows an example of an ascending triangle, highlighted by red trendlines.

Price overshoots (A) the entry to this chart pattern, but who cares? There are no ascending triangle top and bottom variations to worry about (where the inbound price trend is important); there are only ascending triangles.

The stock breaks out upward at B, which happens the majority of the time, but this one sees price quickly turn down, closing below the bottom of the chart pattern at C. When that happens, it **busts the ascending triangle**.

KEY POINT:
Ascending triangles are wedge-shaped patterns that break out most often upward. The triangle can act as a reversal or continuation of the existing price trend.

DEFINITION:

Busts the ascending triangle

A busted ascending triangle occurs when price breaks out in one direction, moves less than 10 percent before reversing, and continues in the new direction to close above the top or below the bottom of the triangle.

The popularity of ascending triangles stems from the belief that price will start a robust uptrend. However, I stopped trading most of them because too many looked like this chart. Price climbed a few percent and then died, killing my trade as well.

FIGURE 19.11   LXU US Equity (LSB Industries Inc).

Some volume disciples will look at the chart and say, "Look at volume! It should be well above average, but it isn't!" Point D shows the breakout day's volume, and they are right. Volume was well below average, but I have seen profitable trends start on mediocre volume, too. In fact, I do not even show volume on my charts. It is as useful to me as asking if fish like seafood. I am a vegetarian: I eat weeds.

Identification Guidelines

When searching for ascending triangles, look for minor highs close together (weeks apart, but usually not months between tops) that peak near the same price. Then look directly below those peaks to see if the valleys trend upward following a straight line.

Sometimes I will see an up-sloping line of valleys following a trend. Then I look above them and see a horizontal line of peaks. That combination spells triangle.

The accompanying table lists the important characteristics of ascending triangles.

Characteristic	Discussion
Horizontal top line	Price along the top follows a horizontal trend.
Up-sloping bottom line	Price makes a series of higher valleys, following a trendline. The two trendlines converge.
Price crossing	Price must cross the pattern from side to side, filling the triangle with movement. Avoid patterns with excessive white space in the center of the triangle.
Volume	Volume in the pattern recedes and can be especially low the day before the breakout.
Breakout	Can be in any direction, but is upward the majority of the time.

Price along the top of the ascending triangle follows a horizontal or nearly horizontal trendline. Along the bottom, the minor lows bounce off an up-sloping trendline drawn connecting them.

Look at Figure 19.12.

Minor highs A through D stop near the same price. Minor lows E through G touch the bottom trendline. Together they form an ascending triangle, only this one has a downward breakout.

Make sure that price crosses the chart pattern plenty of times. What you do not want to see is white space in the middle of the pattern. I show an example of that later in this chapter.

Volume tends to recede over the life of the triangle, but that varies from triangle to triangle. The chart shows volume trending higher in the first half of the pattern and then downward leading to the breakout. Do not discard an ascending triangle simply because of an abnormal volume trend.

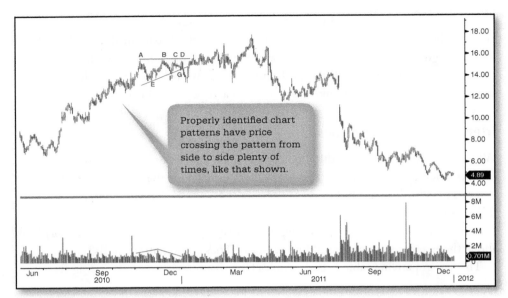

Properly identified chart patterns have price crossing the pattern from side to side plenty of times, like that shown.

FIGURE 19.12   **FOE US Equity (Ferro Corp).**

The breakout from an ascending triangle can be in any direction, but is usually upward.

This is another example of a busted ascending triangle. Price breaks out downward and does not drop far (less than 10 percent) before reversing and closing above the top of the triangle. When that happens, it busts the downward breakout.

Unfortunately, this bust did not result in a tasty move upward. That might be because of the extended rise leading to the triangle. In fact, the downward breakout was a clue to weakness to begin with.

Ascending Triangle Psychology

In ascending triangles, price peaks for the same reason it does in rectangles: Traders sell when the stock reaches their target price.

Suppose that Molly runs a mutual fund and wants to sell several hundred thousand shares of ABC Chewing Gum. Every time the stock reaches $35, she sells some. Her selling creates a ceiling on the stock.

KEY POINT:

When searching for ascending triangles, make sure price crosses the chart pattern from side to side several times. Price should not be bunched up near the start nor near the end with an empty white hole in the middle.

KEY POINT:

An ascending triangle forms because of increasing demand at lower prices matched with selling at a constant price.

Harry runs the trading department of a hedge fund, and he loves ABC Chewing. When the stock drops to 30, he buys as many shares as he can, but the stock runs away from him and becomes too expensive to chase.

Johnny is a rich swing trader. He watches Mutual Fund Molly create overhead resistance at 35 and sees Hedge Fund Harry put a floor in the stock at 30. When the stock drops to 30.25, he starts buying, knowing that he can probably sell when it approaches 35. "Easy money," he says and smiles.

Harry sees volume tick up and believes that others are buying ahead of him. He raises his buy price to 30.50 and starts eating as many shares as he can before they disappear from his plate.

On the next cycle, Harry has to raise his buy price to 31 to stay ahead of the other cannibals. The hunt continues until Molly sells all of her shares or Harry bags his quota and quits. When one side gives up, the other side yells, "Tag! You're it!" and snatches the stock; then a breakout ensues, ending the pattern.

Variations

Figure 19.13 shows an example of an ascending triangle on the weekly scale.

Price touches the top trendline (A) three times at three minor highs and the bottom trendline (B) also three times, although the individual spikes may be hard to see.

Notice the white space at C. I would prefer that A slide to the left a bit, filling some of that white space, but I also think this pattern works as an ascending triangle. It is not perfect, but few chart patterns are.

You will notice that if I changed the time scale to days or intraday, the pattern shape would not change. An ascending triangle on the 1-minute scale would still have a flat top and an up-sloping bottom.

FIGURE 19.13   GD US Equity (General Dynamics Corp).

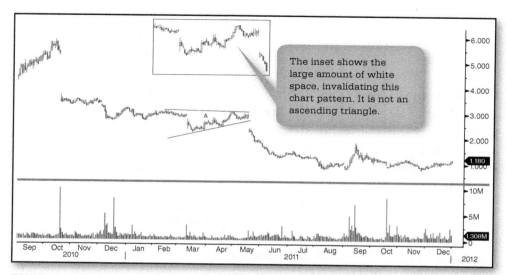

FIGURE 19.14   CWTR US Equity (Coldwater Creek Inc).

Before we move on to the next figure, notice the head-and-shoulders bottom that appears. The pattern is a wonderful example of a reversal that signaled the turn from bear market to bull.

The left (LS) and right (RS) shoulders look fine. The stretched head and neck, however, warn us to never play tag with black holes.

Figure 19.14 shows an invalid ascending triangle.

Price touches the top trendline twice and the bottom line multiple times, just as the guidelines require. The top trendline is horizontal and the bottom one slopes upward. But the gaping hole of white space at A seems large enough to fly a 747 through. Price does not cross the triangle often enough to qualify this as a valid ascending triangle.

Exercise

Look for ascending triangles in Figure 19.15. You should find two of them, maybe three if you are creative, along with a broadening top, head-and-shoulders top, and double top. If you do not know what the non-triangle patterns are, that is fine. I just want your eyes to get used to seeing a variety of patterns.

Figure 19.16 shows the answers, including examples of how the triangle's apex aligns with price.

FIGURE 19.15   TREX US Equity (Trex Co Inc).

FIGURE 19.16   TREX US Equity (Trex Co Inc).

Compare apex A with turn B, apex E with F, and G with H. Above or below each apex is a corresponding price turn. The turn may not last long or it could start a new trend. The duration of the turn is unknown, but this technique does highlight short-term turns.

Look at pattern C. Price along the bottom of the pattern (D) touches the trend-line three times (the end point does not count since price plunges through the pattern there). Along the top, it also touches the trendline multiple times, but there is a problem. The top line is not horizontal.

Does it have to be level? No. Now look at the blue inset directly above the triangle. This depiction makes the top line appear horizontal. Is it an ascending triangle or not?

FAST FACTS
The apex of a triangle is where price tends to form a short-term peak or valley.

Depending on how you draw the top trendline, the blue outline appears to have an upward breakout whereas the red depiction shows a downward breakout (a small red circle in each case).

I believe that the red image better represents a rising wedge and not an ascending triangle.

Before moving on to the next figure, look at the other chart patterns so that you can become accustomed to finding them, too.

Search Figure 19.17 for two ascending triangles, a double bottom, and a head-and-shoulders top and bottom. We have not covered many of those patterns, but do your best anyway.

Figure 19.18 reveals the locations of these chart patterns.

Hopefully, you were able to pick out the ascending triangles in February and April.

FIGURE 19.17 CX US Equity (Cemex SAB de CV).

FIGURE 19.18 CX US Equity (Cemex SAB de CV).

The next section discusses descending triangles. Think of them as ascending triangles who forgot to refill their anti-depressant medication.

■ Descending Triangles

Descending triangles share characteristics of their ascending brothers including one horizontal trendline and another sloping.

Figure 19.19 shows two examples in red.

Starting in May, the stock drops like a Texas hailstone and slams into support at A, bounces several times and forms a descending triangle.

Points A, B, and C highlight valleys that align along a horizontal bottom trendline. Along the top, peaks D, E, and F touch another line, but this one slopes downward. The two trendlines merge at the triangle's apex.

Volume trends downward (G) until spiking on the breakout day, and that behavior is typical of many chart patterns.

Be still my heart: This is an example of a trading setup that I love. Price breaks out downward but reverses, pushes upward, and closes above the top of the triangle. When it does that, it busts the pattern. Busted patterns can lead to good performance, as this example shows.

FIGURE 19.19 NWY US Equity (New York & Co Inc).

I was hesitant to show triangle H because the bottom trendline, although shown flat, is probably better drawn sloping upward. If you redraw it, the pattern becomes a symmetrical triangle, the subject of the next section. However, the bottoms are close enough to the trendline that the pattern qualifies as a descending triangle, too.

> **KEY POINT:**
> A descending triangle is a wedge-shaped chart pattern that breaks out downward most often. It can act as a reversal or continuation of the price trend.

Identification Guidelines

The following table lists the important characteristics that help identify descending triangles.

Characteristic	Discussion
Horizontal bottom line	Price along the bottom follows a horizontal trend.
Down-sloping top line	Price along the top slopes downward, following a trendline.
Price crossing	Price must cross the pattern from side to side, filling the triangle with movement. Avoid patterns with excessive white space in the center of the triangle.
Volume	Volume in the pattern recedes and can be especially low the day before the breakout.
Breakout	Can be in any direction, but is downward the majority of the time.

> **SMART INVESTOR TIP**
> If price touches the bottom trendline only twice, it should touch the down-sloping trendline at least three times. This is not a requirement, but five touches for many chart patterns works well to help avoid selecting boneheaded ones.

To help explain the guidelines, look at Figure 19.20.

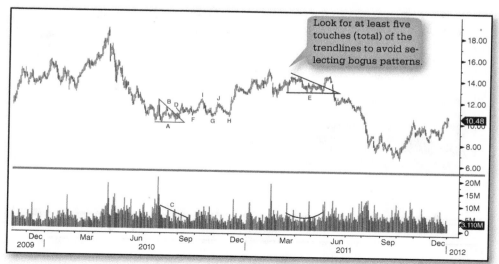

FIGURE 19.20   MAS US Equity (Masco Corp).

The bottom of triangle A shows three touches of a horizontal trendline. The valleys do not bottom at exactly the same price, but they come close. They *look* as if they belong on the same trendline.

Along the top, B, another trendline connects peaks that form at successively lower levels and yet still touch the trendline. I look for three touches along the diagonal if only two touch the bottom. That is a safety measure to prevent selecting triangles that are just random squiggles on the price chart.

Price crosses the triangle from side to side, leaving no room for white space. This is another important safety tip to avoid selecting bogus patterns.

SMART INVESTOR TIP

Avoid excessive white space between the two trendlines when selecting descending triangles. Price should cross the triangle plenty of times to fill the area.

Volume typically recedes in the chart pattern, but do not discard a descending triangle just because the volume pattern shows increasing volume. Triangle E has U-shaped volume and yet it is a valid descending triangle.

Price can break out of a descending triangle in any direction, but most often, it will be downward.

Look at points F through J. Is this a descending triangle? Yes. I dislike only two touches on the top, and the bottom trendline could be straighter, but the combination works.

There is another descending triangle on the chart that is not marked. Where is it? Go look for it before I tell you where it is.

Hint: Look on the far left of the chart.

In mid-November 2009, the stock began forming a descending triangle that extended to early January, breaking out upward. It has three touches on the top and three on the bottom.

Descending Triangle Psychology

Suppose you are a large institutional investor that wants to own Cemex, pictured in Figure 19.21, at $5 a share.

When the stock drops to $5, you buy (A). Notice the associated rise in volume.

I watch the ticker tape and see large blocks roll across my screen at $5 and below, so I conduct research and discover that the stock represents a compelling value. I buy too. Together, along with other buyers, we send the price moving up.

When the stock hits $6, I dump the turkey, pass Go, and collect my $200. Other sellers that view it as overvalued decide to cash in as well (D).

This selling pressure causes price to ease lower and eventually trigger more buying at a lower price (B). When the stock rises, those that missed selling as the stock approached $6 sell now.

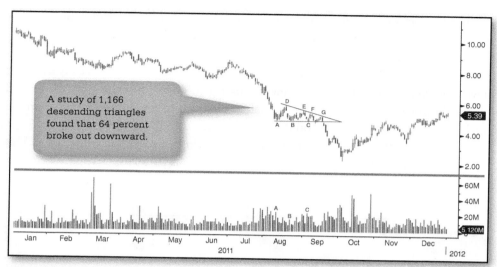

FIGURE 19.21   CX US Equity (Cemex SAB de CV).

The cycle of buying and selling continues at E, C, F, and G. At G, well into the traditional worst performing month of the year (September), selling pressure increases, overwhelming buying demand, forcing the stock to push through support. The stock tumbles.

The footprint that remains on the chart outlines a descending triangle.

Variations

Look at Figure 19.22 because it reveals a flaw in pattern identification.

Price anchors the bottom of the chart pattern at A and B with minor low trendline touches at the same price. Along the top, price touches the trendline multiple times on the way to C. The peak at C pokes up through the top of the triangle, staging a breakout.

FIGURE 19.22   EXPD US Equity (Expeditors International of Washington Inc).

What is wrong with this triangle? It contains too much white space in the middle of the pattern. Price does not cross the triangle from side to side, filling the chart pattern with price movement.

> **KEY POINT:**
> A descending triangle forms when buyers acquire the stock at a fixed price, forming a line of support. Others sell when the stock becomes overpriced.

If you look at the blue inset, with the triangle boundaries removed, you can see that this is nothing more than the stock climbing to a peak and withdrawing. It is not a triangle.

> **SMART INVESTOR TIP**
> It is helpful to look at a price chart without any trendlines connecting the pattern boundaries to make sure that what you are seeing is really a chart pattern. Can you draw each trendline a different way, by connecting other nearby peaks or valleys? Will others see the same pattern as you? If there are doubts, then skip the pattern and look for another one.

Compare pattern ABC with the one in the red inset at D. The D triangle shows plenty of price crossings as well as trendline touches spaced throughout the triangle. Image D is how a descending triangle should look.

Exercise

You will likely have difficulty finding a descending triangle in Figure 19.23. Here is a hint: Look for the down-sloping trendline first. You should also find a double bottom. Another hint? Both are large patterns.

FIGURE 19.23   NOC US Equity (Northrop Grumman Corp).

FIGURE 19.24 **NOC US Equity (Northrop Grumman Corp).**

The next chart (see Figure 19.24) reveals the descending triangle. It has three touches on the top and two on the bottom. Price crosses the pattern and fills the white space, but because the triangle is so large, it may look like too much white space. It takes time for price to cross the pattern, so it is fine.

Notice that the double bottom shares the triangle's space. Both are valid chart patterns.

I think that the next exercise is easy, but then I know where to look. You will find a descending triangle, two double tops, one double bottom, and a symmetrical triangle. Try to find as many of those as you can. (See Figure 19.25.)

The descending triangle is at A, in red. Price touches each trendline, forming a beautiful wedge shape. It reminds me of the rubber doorstop I use to keep the wind from slamming the door shut in summer. (See Figure 19.26.)

FIGURE 19.25 **CACH US Equity (Cache Inc).**

FIGURE 19.26 CACH US Equity (Cache Inc).

You probably did not select triangle B, and that is good because it is not a descending triangle. There is too much white space between the trendlines to qualify this as a valid triangle.

On the right of the chart is a symmetrical triangle. It is a more complicated shape, with two converging trendlines. Unlike ascending and descending triangles, the shape of the pattern does not hint at the breakout direction. Symmetrical triangles are as plentiful as fleas on a dog, and can be just as annoying. They are the subject of the next section.

Test Yourself

Answer these statements with true or false.

1. An ascending triangle has a horizontal top trendline.
2. A descending triangle has a down-sloping top trendline.
3. At least four touches, total, of the two trendlines is required, but five or more is better.

Answers: 1. True; 2. True; 3. True

■ Symmetrical Triangles

Symmetrical triangles take pattern recognition to a new level. We ditch horizontal trendlines and use diagonal ones to outline the pattern.

Figure 19.27 shows a pair of symmetrical triangles swimming in a price sea. They remind me of angelfish I had in my 55-gallon aquarium when I lived near Boston.

I like the red triangle at C. Price touches two sloping trendlines that merge at the triangle apex. Directly above the apex, in this example, is a price peak. I have

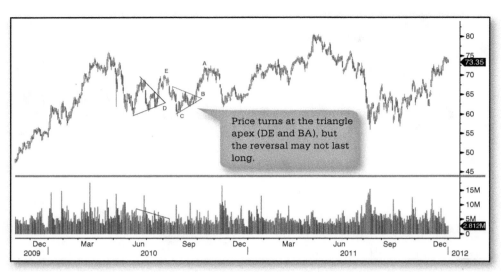

FIGURE 19.27   BA US Equity (Boeing Co/The).

mentioned this apex and turning behavior before because it works well and gives traders a clue where the trend might shift.

Notice that the blue triangle apex (D) sits beneath peak E. It is not as timely (it comes late as price is about to slide) as the other triangle's prediction, but it is valuable, too.

Triangle D cuts through price on both trendlines, so it is not ideal. Volume trends lower as it does in many symmetrical triangles.

Identification Guidelines

The following table lists important characteristics that help identify symmetrical triangles.

Characteristic	Discussion
Two sloping and converging trendlines	Price follows two sloping trendlines that join at the triangle apex.
Price crossing	Price must cross the pattern from side to side, filling the triangle with movement. Avoid patterns with excessive white space in the center of the triangle.
Volume	Volume in the pattern recedes and can be especially low the day before the breakout.
Breakout	Can be in any direction.
Duration	Should be longer than three weeks; otherwise they could be pennants.

KEY POINT:

A symmetrical triangle appears like an angelfish bounded by two converging trendlines. The breakout can be in any direction.

THEORY AND ANALYSIS

FIGURE 19.28   ALK US Equity (Alaska Air Group Inc).

To help explain the guidelines, look at Figure 19.28.

This is an example of a large symmetrical triangle at C, bounded by red trendlines. Price touches each trendline three times (twice is a minimum, but I like to see three) in distinct minor highs and minor lows. As price crosses the chart pattern from side to side, it fills the white space. Since this is a large example, do not expect price to fill the entire area. White space will be present, but should not look like a cavity too large for a dentist to fill.

Volume recedes, but is often irregular looking. Do not discard a symmetrical triangle because the volume pattern is wrong.

The breakout can be in any direction, including horizontal where price oozes out the front of the triangle.

Most symmetrical triangles should be longer than three weeks to help distinguish them from pennants. The exception is when a pennant is missing a flagpole. In that case, the pennant is really a small symmetrical triangle.

Symmetrical Triangle Psychology

Symmetrical triangles are the epitome of confusion. Price does not know which way to trend. Figure 19.29 shows another example of a symmetrical triangle.

FIGURE 19.29 GFF US Equity (Griffon Corp).

At the start of the pattern, bulls push price up in the hopes that the double bottom will **confirm** as a valid chart pattern. That means price must close above the highest peak between the two bottoms, which it does.

> **DEFINITION:**
> Confirm
> Price confirms many patterns when the stock closes outside the pattern boundaries. For example, in a double bottom, price must close above the highest peak between the two bottoms; otherwise, it is not a double bottom.

The straight-line run continues until meeting overhead resistance set up by bears wanting to dump the stock at a price they believe is too rich.

Their selling forces price back down. When it approaches the price level of the prior minor low, eager bulls who missed their opportunity to buy do so now. Others may add to existing positions. That buying demand pushes price up until meeting bears wanting to take profits.

The oscillations continue, with bears taking profits earlier and bulls buying sooner, tightening the coil. Eventually, buying demand outpaces selling pressure and the coil releases, springing upward in this example.

Almost as soon as that happens, the bears regroup and force price back down, and they keep selling until the stock bottoms in August. What remains on the chart is a long symmetrical triangle.

Variations

Figure 19.30 shows several chart patterns, including some that hint of being symmetrical triangles, but are not.

Look at triangle A. What attracts me are the three touches of the bottom trendline. However, the top shows only two touches. That is not optimum.

The widest part of a symmetrical triangle should be at or near the start, not in the middle of the chart pattern.

FIGURE 19.30 ASNA US Equity (Ascena Retail Group Inc.).

Triangle B is flawed because erasing the first touch on the bottom makes the line horizontal (but it may be difficult to see).

The top of triangle C is near the middle of the chart pattern instead of the start, making it difficult to approve as a valid triangle, too. Nevertheless, all three qualify as symmetrical triangles even though none is perfect.

Now look at pattern D. Along the bottom is an up-sloping trendline with three touches. Peak D is in the middle of the pattern. Using D as the start of the triangle would make it look too lopsided, too unbalanced. It is not a symmetrical triangle.

Confused? If any chart pattern looks questionable, look for another one. They are as plentiful as ants at a picnic.

Pattern E has many touches along the peaks, but too much white space on the bottom. It is not a symmetrical triangle.

Figure 19.31 gives a warning of how not to draw a symmetrical triangle.

Price along the bottom touches points A and B, widely separated. Along the top are two minor high touches.

Look at C. The white space is obvious. This is not a symmetrical triangle. It is just a peak with red lines drawn to resemble one. The inset shows the peak without the lines.

Exercise

In Figure 19.32, I found three symmetrical triangles, two double tops, and a head-and-shoulders top, but no partridge in a pear tree. See if you can find the chart patterns as well.

Figure 19.33 shows the answers. The symmetrical triangle at A is the easiest to find, probably because it is large with so many trendline touches.

FIGURE 19.31   HW US Equity (Headwaters Inc).

FIGURE 19.32   MEA US Equity (Metalico Inc).

FIGURE 19.33   MEA US Equity (Metalico Inc).

Triangle B is harder to spot because the top spike upward at the start might not register as a minor high touch. Without it, the pattern would resemble an ascending triangle.

Triangle C is the hardest to find. It seems buried in an area where price is directionless. There are three touches along the top trendline, but only two along the bottom. Notice that D does not qualify as a touch since it is not a minor low. D is part of a straight-line run downward that just happens to gap where the trendline touches.

SMART INVESTOR TIP

To avoid selecting bogus symmetrical triangles, look for at least three touches of each trendline.

Figure 19.34 has three symmetrical triangles. Also look for a descending triangle, head-and-shoulders bottom, and Big W, which is a type of double bottom with tall sides.

Figure 19.35 shows the answers. If you picked A as a symmetrical triangle, be careful because candle A is not a minor low and should not be used to anchor the start of the pattern. However, the pattern does appear wedge shaped. It is a symmetrical triangle.

Triangle B is large with plenty of trendline touches and should have been easy to spot.

Point C is the same height as D. That means the down-sloping trendline does not quite touch C. Even so, I think it is fine as a symmetrical triangle.

I hope you found the descending triangle. The Big W, even if you did not know what to look for, has an evocative name that just speaks to me. Perhaps it did to you as well. If you left your hearing aid turned off, then you could be talking to yourself.

FIGURE 19.34   VMC US Equity (Vulcan Materials Co).

FIGURE 19.35   VMC US Equity (Vulcan Materials Co).

The next section discusses flags and pennants, so we will have a better understanding of those patterns and what a flagpole is. Why is there no such thing as a pennantpole?

Test Yourself

Answer these statements with true or false.

1. Ascending and descending triangles have only one slanted trendline, but symmetrical triangles have two.
2. Symmetrical triangles longer than three weeks are called pennants when they rest upon a flagpole.
3. If price does not confirm a chart pattern, you are looking at squiggles on a price chart and not a chart pattern.
4. Price confirms a symmetrical triangle when it first pierces the trendline border.

Answers : 1. True; 2. False; 3. True; 4. False

■ Flags and Pennants

Pennants remind me of those pointed streamers that line roped-off areas at festivals. They are the same as flags except that the trendlines bounding the pattern converge. In flags, they are parallel.

Figure 19.36 shows a sprinkling of flags and pennants.

Let us start with pennant B. This is the kind of pennant that traders dream about. The trend begins at A in a straight-line run up to the pennant (B). Price consolidates, forming a triangle shape (the pennant). After that, price resumes a strong move up to C. The AB move is about the same as BC. Thus, the pennant can act as a half-staff pattern; it can appear midway in a price trend. The same is true of flags and other chart patterns, too.

C is another pennant. Unlike B, where price moved sideways in the pennant, this one has a more traditional slope—downward against the trend.

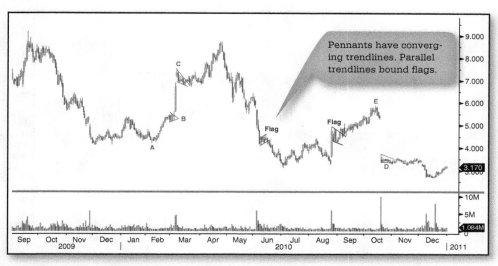

Pennants have converging trendlines. Parallel trendlines bound flags.

FIGURE 19.36   CWTR US Equity (Coldwater Creek Inc).

Pennant D, on the far right of the chart, looks like a small version of a descending triangle, a pattern that has a flat bottom and down-sloping top.

Flags have parallel trendlines whereas pennants converge. The flags appear in blue, but not because they have been holding their breath like a child throwing a tantrum.

KEY POINT:

Flags and Pennants

Flags are short chart patterns that appear as small rectangles in a strong price run. They can act as reversals, but are usually continuation patterns.

A pennant is a short triangular-shaped chart pattern. It can act as a trend reversal or continuation pattern.

Identification Guidelines

The following table lists important characteristics to help identify flags and pennants. For such simple patterns, why does it seem so complicated?

Characteristic	Discussion
Price trends	Flags and pennants always rest upon a flagpole, so look for a strong price run leading to them.
Two converging trendlines	For flags, price follows two parallel or nearly parallel trendlines. For pennants, price follows two converging trendlines.
Volume	Volume in the pattern recedes.
Breakout	Can be in any direction.
Duration	Flags and pennants are shorter than three weeks.

The easiest way to find a flag or pennant is to begin with the flagpole. Look for a straight-line price run. Price will consolidate along that run. When it does, it can take the shape of a flag or pennant.

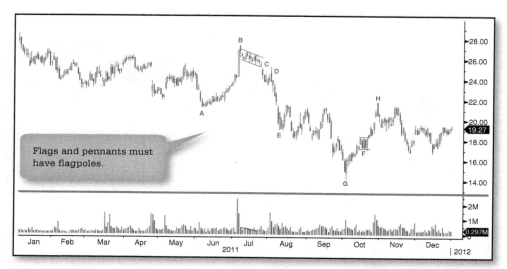

FIGURE 19.37 ABFS US Equity (Arkansas Best Corp).

To help explain the guidelines, look at Figure 19.37.

The flag pattern begins with the flagpole, AB. If a strong trend (a straight-line price run) does not exist, then look elsewhere. Atop the pole, price consolidates and forms flag BC. After that, price breaks out downward (C) and drops, pulling back briefly at D, but then powering down to the launch price and digging a crater (E).

Flags should form between two parallel or nearly parallel trendlines. The two lines do not have to be exactly parallel. Pennants should form between two converging trendlines. For both flags and pennants, trendline touch count is not important.

Price in the flag or pennant can slope in any direction, including sideways, but is usually against the prevailing trend. In this case, the trend is up from A to B and the flag slopes down from B to C.

Volume typically recedes in a flag or pennant just as it does in many other chart patterns. The breakout can be in any direction, too, but usually follows the trend leading to the flag or pennant.

Flags and pennants are short, no longer than three weeks. This is an arbitrary value. What you are looking for is a small knot of congestion in a strong price run. Once the knot unties (breaks out), price should continue on its way.

Flag F is notable because it rests in the middle of the GH move.

Flag and Pennant Psychology

Figure 19.38 highlights one pennant and one flag.

At A, the smart money began buying, believing or knowing that a good earnings report was coming.

Two days later, the company announced earnings and raised their outlook to the top end of the target range while increasing the dividend.

Buying demand propelled the stock higher like an overly excited kid gobbling Halloween candy. Then the bears returned to the trading table and started a food fight with the bulls. The fight between evenly matched opponents pushed price sideways, forming the pennant. This one had a flat base and down-sloping top, suggesting a group of investors wanted to buy the stock at a set price (49.50) but stopped buying when price climbed too high. Their buying put a floor underneath the stock.

After the bears digested the news and ran for the exits, the bulls took over and sent the stock moving higher again, rising from C to D. Notice how one good earnings report can launch a stock toward the heavens. Or maybe it was the candy.

SMART INVESTOR TIP

If the chart pattern does not have a flagpole, then it is not a flag or a pennant.

FIGURE 19.38 HSY US Equity (Hershey Co/The).

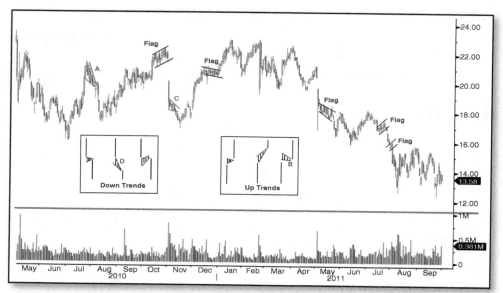

FIGURE 19.39 CKP US Equity (Checkpoint Systems Inc).

Variations

Figure 19.39 shows five flags (blue) and two pennants (red) with four additional variations in the inset. Although the insets show pennants, use your creative mind to redraw the pennant trendlines as parallel lines for flag variations.

Pennant A forms after a mediocre uptrend. I would call it powerful if price broke out of the pennant upward, but it does not. Rather, the pennant slopes downward, which is typical, but then price continues down, oozing out the end of the pennant like caulking. That configuration follows pattern B (except for a downward breakout, of course).

Pennant C forms after price gaps lower. The pennant boundary is irregular in shape, but highlights a small congestion region where price gathers its strength for the coming drop. That drop occurs, completing the configuration like that shown at D.

In the two insets, I show various pennant shapes in up and down trends. Be aware that pennants can break out in any direction, so expect that. I show only the patterns acting as continuations of the prevailing price trend and not reversals.

Exercise

Figure 19.40 has a multitude of flags. Try to find as many as you can that obey the identification guidelines discussed earlier. I found eight and stopped there. One is large and may not qualify. That is a hint, of course.

Figure 19.41 shows the answers. I numbered the flags, making them easier to see. Flag 5 is the likely offender to the three-week rule. It is about a month long. That would still be fine if the flagpole were long, too. Strong and long trends tend to precede extended sideways movement. This flag has the extended sideways movement, but the flagpole height is unexciting.

FIGURE 19.40   NST US Equity (NSTAR).

> Flags and pennants should be no longer than three weeks and look proportional to the flagpole.

FIGURE 19.41   NST US Equity (NSTAR).

In other words, the flag or pennant should be proportional to the height of the flagpole. This pole begins at A and ends at B, which looks too short for the flag.

Are you rested enough to try again? Figure 19.42 shows pennants. Find as many as you can.

Hint: I found five.

Figure 19.43 shows the answers. Starting from the left at A, price begins trending to pennant B, breaking out upward and ending at C. The trend start (A) is important when the pennant acts as a half-staff pattern, as in this case.

SMART INVESTOR TIP

When looking for flags and pennants, try using a bar chart instead of a candlestick chart.

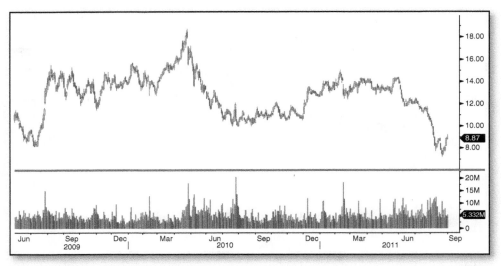

FIGURE 19.42   MAS US Equity (Masco Corp).

The rise from D to E matches the decline from E to F, only EF takes more time.

Pennant G is perhaps the prettiest on the chart. The trend begins at F and goes to H. The stock, from the bottom of G to H, only climbs about half the FG move.

You may argue that J is a flag and not a pennant, so I show the price action in the inset. The pattern resembles a small ascending triangle, but due to its size, becomes a pennant.

Pennant K is large and loose looking. Price meanders up and down within its boundaries. The straight-line run down from J looks proportional to the pennant size.

The next chapter shifts the focus from drawing trendlines to finding potholes that bottom near the same price. We call them double bottoms.

FIGURE 19.43   MAS US Equity (Masco Corp).

CHAPTER 20

Tops and Bottoms

From Thomas N. Bulkowski, *Visual Guide to Chart Patterns* (Hoboken, New Jersey: John Wiley & Sons, 2002), Chapters 12–15.

■ Double Bottoms

This chapter begins discussing chart patterns not bounded by trendlines. How can you find them if not looking for straight or diagonal trendlines? You find them by looking for two potholes that bottom near the same price.

If I were to ask my brother to find a double bottom on a price chart, he might pick AB shown in Figure 20.1. Price from peak C forms a hill filled with moguls that my brother would love skiing down. At the bottom of that hill, the double bottom at AB acts as a reversal.

Is there more to correctly identifying a double bottom than finding two valleys? Yes.

Identification Guidelines

The following table shows the identification guidelines.

Characteristic	Discussion
Downward price trend	The short-term price trend leading to a double bottom is down.
Two valleys	Look for two valleys that bottom near the same price. Near means within about 5 percent. The bottoms should look as if they are at the same price.
Valley separation	The time between bottoms varies, but two to seven weeks results in the best performance.
Peak	The peak between the two bottoms should measure at least 10 percent, but exceptions are numerous, making this guideline almost useless.
Volume	Volume is higher on the left bottom than the right, but this is an observation, not a requirement.
Confirmation	Price must close above the highest peak between the two bottoms. If price closes below the lowest bottom before confirmation, it invalidates the double bottom.

FIGURE 20.1   HON US Equity (Honeywell International Inc).

Look at Figure 20.2 while we discuss identification guidelines.

FIGURE 20.2   LIZ US Equity (Liz Claiborne Inc).

After trending down from the April peak, the stock bottoms at A, bounces up to E and down to B. The two valleys do not bottom at the same price, but they are just 17 cents apart (4 percent). On this scale, though, it looks as if an earthquake shifted the pavement.

The time between bottoms is about two weeks, but after studying thousands of double bottoms, the separation is not a concern.

The peak between the two bottoms, E, is supposed to be at least 10 percent above the lowest bottom. I do not even measure this nor do I care. What I am looking for is a reversal of the downward price trend.

SMART INVESTOR TIP

The time between bottoms and the price variation is less important than confirmation. An unconfirmed double bottom is just squiggles on a price chart.

Volume is often higher on the left bottom than the right, as in this case.

Confirmation is the key to double bottoms. Price must confirm the chart pattern. By that, I mean price must *close* above the highest peak (E) between the two bottoms (AB). If price closes below the lowest bottom first, it is not a double bottom. AB is a valid double bottom.

The exhibit also shows additional double bottoms at GH, IJ, and KL. If you consider AB as one bottom (C), then CD is also a double bottom. In all cases, the horizontal red line starting from the peak between the two bottoms marks confirmation. They point to where the stock closes above the peak.

SMART INVESTOR TIP

Reversal chart patterns, such as double bottoms, must have something to reverse. If the price trend leading down to the double bottom is shallow, do not expect a large rise after confirmation.

Double Bottom Psychology

Why do double bottoms form? Look at Figure 20.3 while I discuss one possible answer.

The exhibit shows a stock that I love to own. Why? Because it pays a tasty dividend while it bounces between the 30s and 50s. I buy below 40 and sell above 50 while collecting 5.5 percent in between. Yum!

Imagine that you are a big game hunter searching for income, and decide that when double bottom CD confirms, you will buy.

Unfortunately, price hides by tunneling down to A, invalidating the double bottom. The decline comes as a shock, so you sit paralyzed and just watch it weekly, wondering if the slide is over.

FIGURE 20.3   CHG US Equity (CH Energy Group Inc).

Eventually it bottoms at A, but you wait because you are not sure the decline has ended. When you look again, the stock has climbed too far to chase, despite the power of your hunting rifle.

At E, you vow that if the stock ever returns to the price level of A, you will bag it. The stock cooperates, reaching B. You shoot and score some shares!

Others do the same, putting a floor on the stock. Price rises, eventually confirming the twin valley pattern as a valid double bottom.

Who actually hunts like that? I do. I bought at 39.72 on June 3 (B) and sold it at 54 a year later, pocketing a 5.4 percent dividend along the way.

Variations

Double bottoms have several variations and Figure 20.4 shows three of them.

Pattern A is called an Eve & Eve double bottom. B is an **Eve & Adam**, and C is an Adam & Adam double bottom.

> **DEFINITION:**
>
> **Eve & Adam**
>
> Adam bottoms are narrow, often single-day price spikes. Eve is wider, more rounded looking. If Eve has price spikes, they are shorter and more numerous. Adam tends to remain narrow vertically whereas Eve broadens out.

The difference between Adam and Eve is the shape of the bottom. Adam bottoms are thin, narrow price spikes, often composed of a single day or two. Eve is wider and more rounded looking. If Eve has price spikes, they are more numerous and stubby.

FIGURE 20.4 EXC US Equity (Exelon Corp).

Eve bottoms tend to be wide and widen out as price climbs. Adam bottoms tend to remain narrow.

For example, look at the width of Eve at B. The two vertical red lines at D show how it widens out. Compare that to the Adam bottom at E. The lines remain narrow.

I often use the width of the bottom in this manner to determine whether I am looking at an Eve or Adam bottom.

Another way to determine the type is to ask if the two bottoms look alike. If so, then you have Adam & Adam or Eve & Eve. Otherwise, it is a mix of the two: Eve & Adam or Adam & Eve.

> **SMART INVESTOR TIP**
>
> To differentiate between Adam and Eve bottoms, ask if the two bottoms look the same or different. If they look the same, then they are either Adam & Adam or Eve & Eve. If they look different, then they are either Adam & Eve or Eve & Adam.

Why the emphasis on Adam and Eve? Because the various types perform differently. Figure 20.5 shows the last two variations.

An Adam & Eve double bottom appears in February and it has a narrow bottom (three days wide) followed by a wide one. The chart pattern confirms as a valid double bottom when price closes above the peak between the two valleys.

The other double bottom variation is probably one you have never heard of. I call it an ugly double bottom. Price bottoms at A and then bounces to form a higher

FIGURE 20.5 CRH US Equity (CRH PLC).

bottom, B (at least 5 percent higher, by the way). When price confirms the chart pattern by closing above the peak between the two bottoms, it indicates that the trend has changed from down to up.

Exercise

Find as many valid double bottoms as you can in Figure 20.6. Do not concern yourself with any of the identification guideline numbers, such as two to seven weeks

FIGURE 20.6 EXP US Equity (Eagle Materials Inc).

FIGURE 20.7   EXP US Equity (Eagle Materials Inc).

between bottoms, or 5 percent apart, and so on. Just look for two valleys that bottom at or near the same price and confirm as valid patterns. Do not look for ugly double bottoms, and do not worry about the Adam and Eve variations. Also pretend that the long green downward spike in May does not exist.

Figure 20.7 shows what I found. First, in the lower right of the chart is the only valid double bottom, AB. Price confirms it when the stock closes above the top of the pattern, at C.

If you marked DE, that would be wrong because it does not confirm.

Bottom FG confirms, but it is not a bottom. Price must trend downward into the chart pattern, not rise up from the grave. The rule I use is that in-bound price must be higher than the peak in the middle of the double bottom to guarantee that it is indeed trending down into the chart pattern. That does not occur on the FG bottom.

Confused? I explain it again in the next section.

All of the other potential double bottoms on the chart have one or both of those flaws. They do not confirm or are located in an uptrend.

Figure 20.8 has multiple double bottoms in it. Find as many as you can, but do not look for those narrower than about two weeks and forget about ugly double bottoms, too.

Figure 20.9 shows the answers. I drew a line connecting the bottoms for your viewing pleasure. Bottom A confirms as a valid pattern in a downward price trend. If you excluded it because the two valleys did not bottom at the same price (they are 72 cents apart or 1.7 percent), then, good. I still consider it one.

G is one of those double bottoms I told you not to worry about because the valleys are too narrow. If you found it anyway, wonderful! It is a double bottom. Price makes a third bottom, but that happens after the double bottom confirms.

FIGURE 20.8   VMC US Equity (Vulcan Materials Co).

FIGURE 20.9   VMC US Equity (Vulcan Materials Co).

B, D, and E should have been easy (maybe C, too). E is especially delicious since the Eve bottom is so much wider than Adam.

What about bottom F? That is not a double bottom. Why? Look at bottoms 1 and 2. They do not confirm until *after* bottom 3 forms. This is an example of a triple bottom, the subject of our next section.

If you found bottoms 2 and 3, you should have looked to the left and found bottom 1, again, forming a triple bottom.

By now, you probably hate me. Are you going to remove me from your will? Do that after you die, and after you read the next section on triple bottoms.

■ Triple Bottoms

Now that we have trained ourselves to find two bottoms that line up at the same price, let us look for triplets: three bottoms in a row. It is as easy as it sounds, except that triple bottoms are sometimes confused with head-and-shoulders bottoms. Maybe it is not so easy . . .

Triple bottoms are considerably rarer than double bottoms, but the technique used to find them is the same. Find a double bottom and then look to the left and right to see if a third bottom exists at the same price.

> **KEY POINT:**
> Triple bottoms are three valleys that bottom near the same price. The chart pattern acts as a bullish reversal of the downward price trend.

Figure 20.10 shows an example.

Based on what you have learned in this book, which of the three patterns are triple bottoms (guess)?

Look at bottom ABC. Price trends downward into the chart pattern. If you do not see a downward price trend, then it is not a bottom reversal. The pattern has three price spikes, with A slightly above the other two. Price confirms the pattern by *closing* above the highest peak between the three bottoms.

It is a triple bottom.

> **KEY POINT:**
> Price must *trend* downward into a bottom and upward into a top. That trend is what qualifies the chart pattern as a bottom or top, respectively. Without the trend, then you do not have a reversal pattern.

A reversal chart pattern must have something to reverse. The ABC pattern is a good example with a strong downward move leading to it.

FIGURE 20.10   CHS US Equity (Chico's FAS Inc).

DEF is similar to ABC in that two of three bottoms are near the same price. However, F is much higher than DE so this would work better as double bottom DE with throwback F.

HIJ has a center valley (I) below the other two. That is a dead giveaway. It is a head-and-shoulders bottom, a chart pattern I will be discussing later in the book.

Identification Guidelines

What is involved in identifying triple bottoms? You can probably guess most of them, but the following table provides a list.

Characteristic	Discussion
Downward price trend	The short-term price trend leading to the triple bottom is down.
Three bottoms	Three minor lows are involved in a triple bottom. Sometimes they can be one-day price spikes or wider, more rounded turns. Each valley tends to look similar to the others.
Same price	Each minor low should bottom *near* the same price. Rarely will all three bottom at exactly the same price, so be flexible.
Volume	Volume recedes, meaning it is higher on the left than the right, but each bottom can show significant volume. Do not exclude a pattern because it has an unusual volume shape.
Confirmation	Price must confirm the triple bottom by closing above the highest peak between the three bottoms.

SMART INVESTOR TIP

If the middle peak of an alleged triple bottom is *significantly* below the other two, then it is probably a head-and-shoulders bottom.

FIGURE 20.11 KWR US Equity (Quaker Chemical Corp).

Figure 20.11 shows an example of a triple bottom.

Price climbs a cliff to D and then turns into a waterfall, tumbling to the stream below and forming triple bottom ABC. The D peak is too far away to be an example of overshoot.

Three valleys appear similar in shape, all of them narrow and bottoming near the same price. Volume trends upward, which is odd for triple bottoms.

The pattern confirms as a valid triple bottom when price closes above the highest peak (E) between the three bottoms. Confirmation happens at F.

Figure 20.12 occurs on the weekly scale.

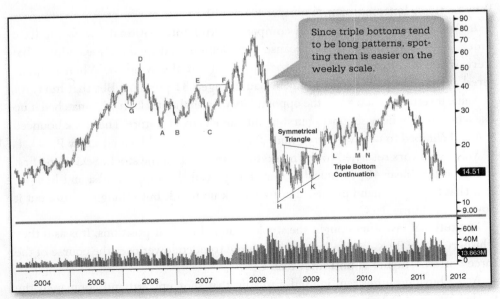

FIGURE 20.12 ACI US Equity (Arch Coal Inc).

I chose this chart because of its similarity to the prior exhibit. Price climbs to D and then tumbles to the triple bottom reversal at ABC.

This time, though, the valleys are wider and more rounded looking. If you were to flip to the daily scale, you would see them expand as if they overdosed on potato chips.

Price confirms the triple bottom at F when it closes above peak E. Price must *close* above the highest peak in the pattern, or else it is not a triple bottom.

Look at G, the three brief spikes down in early 2006. This is also a triple bottom, but due to the weekly scale, it is harder to spot.

Valleys H, I, and J form three bottoms—and you can throw in K for another triple (IJK)—but the valleys do not bottom at or near the same price. They are better classified as a symmetrical triangle, shown outlined in blue.

Triple L, M, and N form three bottoms near the same price, but it is not a reversal. Price climbs into the start of the chart pattern from the bottom, not trends lower as required. However, some may call this a triple bottom continuation pattern. Price rises going into this chart pattern and continues rising on exit.

Triple Bottom Psychology

Why do triple bottoms form? Consider Figure 20.13.

In April 2010, pharmaceutical company Baxter International was facing hard times. How do I know this? Because they announced quarterly earnings that were worse than expected. The stock jumped out the window. When it splattered against the pavement in May, it had plunged 31 percent. Bet that hurt.

Value investors, when given the opportunity to grab the stock on sale, snatched it up like a horde of holiday shoppers bursting into an electronics store. The stock bounced at A and climbed to nearly 43 from mid 40 then retreated and formed valley B.

Value investors returned to the market and scooped up the stock. Seeing the first valley bottom near 40, technical players recognized the support area and bought, too. That buying demand pushed the stock back up to 43, but selling pressure cut it down a third time, to C.

Institutional investors bought the stock or added to their positions. It is as if they whispered "Buy BAX, but do it quietly." Volume trended lower over the course of the three bottoms, higher at bottom A than C.

At C, buying enthusiasm ignited a missile that shot upward and confirmed the triple bottom at D, but within a week was parachuting back down in a throwback.

FIGURE 20.13   BAX US Equity (Baxter International Inc).

Months later, market enthusiasts could look back and see the triple bottom for what it was: a reversal that marked a significant bottom for the stock.

Variations

Variations in triple bottoms center around the price level of the three valleys. Look at Figure 20.14, starting with A on the far left.

This triple bottom has a middle valley (red dot) that is well above the other two. The triple bottom appears in a downward price trend and acts as a reversal. Price

FIGURE 20.14   PMTI US Equity (Palomar Medical Technologies Inc).

confirms the chart pattern as a valid one when it closes above the peak between the three valleys. I consider it a valid triple bottom.

FAST FACTS

Tall triple bottoms tend to outperform short ones (gains averaging 39 percent versus 27 percent, respectively), according to a study of bull market patterns from mid-1991 to 2011 using 609 samples.

B shows three spikes near the same price level. Everything looks good except for one thing. Price closes below the bottom of the pattern first, so it is not a triple bottom.

Pattern C looks like a head-and-shoulders bottom because the middle red dot is much lower than the other two. When pattern A showed a higher middle, that was fine, but a lower middle often qualifies the chart pattern as a head-and-shoulders. C is not a triple bottom.

D is also not a triple bottom reversal because price rises into the chart pattern (starting at C) instead of trending downward. The rule I use is that the price mountain to the left of the chart pattern must be above the highest peak in the triple bottom.

I show what I mean using the two variations in the blue inset. The blue lines represent price. G has price trending downward (H) into the triple bottom from above the red line. The triple bottom acts as a reversal of the downward trend.

I has price rising (from J) into the three bottoms. The inbound price trend remains below the middle peak. This triple bottom acts as a continuation pattern, not a reversal. Pattern D resembles scenario I, so it is not a triple bottom reversal.

E is a triple bottom even though the right valley is lower than the other two. When looking at this on a historical basis, which we are, the triple bottom is a reversal with price rising above the three valleys on either side. It *looks* like a reversal. It *acts* like a reversal. It even quacks like a reversal.

Pattern F also has a lower middle valley but if this were a person, he would have the nickname "No neck." It is a valid triple bottom and not a head-and-shoulders bottom.

Exercise

To test what you have learned in this chapter, the first exercise (see Figure 20.15) is easy. There are only four patterns on the chart that I want to highlight. Two are triple bottoms and two are head-and-shoulders bottoms. See if you can find all of them even though we have not yet covered the head-and-shoulders.

Figure 20.16 shows the answers.

A and B are the triple bottoms. They exist in a downward price trend, form three bottoms near the same price, and confirm when price closes above the highest peak between the three valleys in each pattern.

The two head-and-shoulders bottoms would be difficult to confuse as triple bottoms since the heads are much lower than the surrounding valleys.

FIGURE 20.15 TIE US Equity (Titanium Metals Corp).

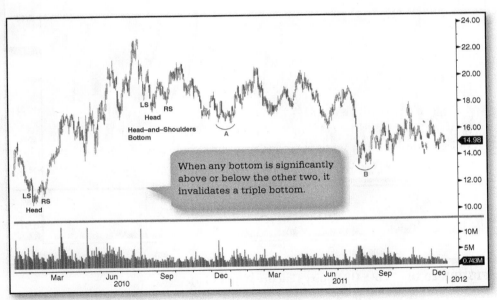

FIGURE 20.16 TIE US Equity (Titanium Metals Corp).

This next exercise (see Figure 20.17) is trickier than the last one. Look for three triple bottoms and one head-and-shoulders bottom.

Figure 20.18 shows the answers. Triple bottom A has a right bottom below the other two, but it still acts as a reversal of the downward price run. Price on the right valley does not sink too far below (just 20 cents) the other two to invalidate the triple bottom.

FIGURE 20.17   WIRE US Equity (Encore Wire Corp).

FIGURE 20.18   WIRE US Equity (Encore Wire Corp).

You might quibble with pattern B, and this is certainly a hard triple bottom to find. Cover up the additional valleys after the right one and it looks like a triple bottom. Price confirms this, too, by closing above the highest peak between the three valleys. Once the pattern confirms as a triple bottom, it does not matter if the stock nosedives into the ground or flies to the stars. The pattern remains a valid triple bottom.

Triple bottom C is a small one that you may have overlooked. It is valid, too.

The head-and-shoulders is a three valley pattern, but the head is well below the surrounding shoulders. It is not a triple bottom.

In the next section, we abandon bottoms and switch to tops: double tops. I like my double tops shaken, not stirred.

■ Double Tops

Double tops are dual price mountains that peak near the same price. They are the same as double bottoms except flipped upside down. In this section, we will discuss what to look for when searching for double tops.

Figure 20.19 shows two examples of double tops on the daily scale. At F, price begins the steep march up the sides of the double top. It peaks at A, withdraws to G, and then forms another peak, B, at a price similar to A.

When price closes below G, it confirms the twin peaks as a valid double top.

I chose this chart because the long climb up reminds me of a trek up K2. The double top acts like storm clouds, warning of the coming decline.

Look at CDE. This is a triple top, but is CD also a double top? Yes. CD confirms as a double top before peak E forms. When E appears, the double top also becomes a triple top, but only when the trio confirms.

What do I mean by confirmation, and what should you look for in double tops? That question brings us to identification.

KEY POINT:
Double tops are bearish reversals of an uptrend formed by twin peaks near the same price.

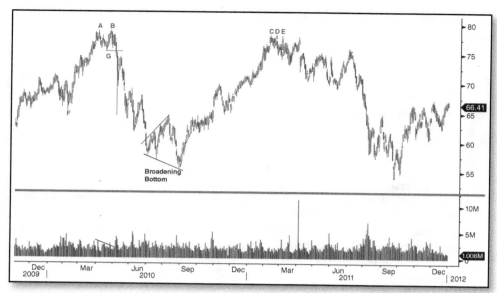

FIGURE 20.19   GD US Equity (General Dynamics Corp).

Identification Guidelines

The following table lists the criteria that double tops share.

Characteristic	Discussion
Upward price trend	The short-term price trend leading to the double top is up.
Two peaks	Look for two peaks that top out near the same price. Near means within about 3 percent. The tops should *look* as if they are at the same price.
Peak separation	The time between peaks varies, but two to six weeks is typical.
Valley	The valley drop between the two peaks should measure at least 10 percent, but allow exceptions. The drop should look proportional to the width of the double top.
Volume	Volume is usually higher on the left top than the right, but this is an observation, not a requirement.
Confirmation	Price must close below the lowest valley between the two peaks. If price closes above the highest peak before confirmation, it invalidates the double top.

Consider the double top shown in Figure 20.20.

Price begins the upward trend at F, leading to the double top. Twin peaks appear as an Adam & Eve double top at the cleverly chosen letters A and E. The double top begins to reverse the FA climb.

SMART INVESTOR TIP

A reversal chart pattern must have something to reverse. If the rise leading to a double top is small, then do not expect a big drop. The stock might try digging to the earth's core, but do not count on it.

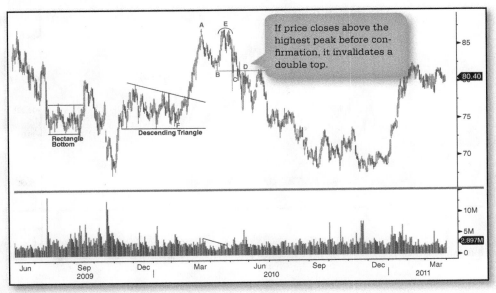

FIGURE 20.20   LMT US Equity (Lockheed Martin Corp).

The time between the two peaks is usually less than two months, frequently rang-ing between two and six weeks. They can be further apart, especially when using the weekly or monthly scales, or narrower for day traders.

The valley between the two peaks sees price drop, but the depth should be propor-tional to the width of the peaks. Peaks separated by two weeks probably will not see a massive plunge between the two tops. Usually the drop measures in the 10 to 20 percent range, but allow exceptions, especially when using other time scales (like intraday).

Volume tends to be higher on formation of the left peak than the right, which this example shows.

The twin peaks become a valid double top when price closes below the valley between the two peaks. The valley bottom is at B and it confirms at C when the red candle closes below the price of B. A pullback to the breakout price at D gives trad-ers another opportunity to exit before the decline resumes.

FAST FACTS

A study of 2,333 double tops shows that a pullback occurs 58 percent of the time.

Double Top Psychology

Why do double tops form? The answer is the same as it is for other chart patterns: fear and greed, sometimes powered by fundamentals.

Figure 20.21 shows an example of a double top standing like a castle overlooking a sea of prices.

At C, the company released first quarter earnings and announced the completion of a merger with Amrep Inc., a chemical supplier. The stock went nowhere that day.

FIGURE 20.21   ZEP US Equity (Zep Inc).

Two days later, the institutions finished digesting the news and decided the stock represented a good value. Their buying pushed the stock up the price mountain to A where traders encountered a group of angry bears. The bears pushed them off the cliff, forcing the stock back down.

Since the bears remained at the top of the cliff, the bulls bought the stock at the bottom and their buying demand made it climb back up a new slope to B, forming a second peak.

FAST FACTS

Double tops show their best performance in bear markets, not bull. Adam & Adam performs best in a bull market, but worst in a bear market.

A day later, a brokerage firm downgraded the stock.

The bulls and bears fought again, tearing into each other, but not making or losing much ground. Even so, the smart money started selling ahead of the second quarter's earnings announcement.

At E, the company reported earnings and had a conference call to discuss them the next day. The news herded some of the bulls into the slaughterhouse and bears pushed the rest over the edge. The stock did a cliff diver plunge back to the sea at D.

Variations

I show variations of the basic double top, beginning with Figure 20.22.

I have already discussed Adam and Eve double bottoms, and the top variety is similar to the bottoms. Adam peaks are narrow, often one-day price spikes. Eve peaks look more rounded. If she has price spikes, they are numerous and short.

FIGURE 20.22   POL US Equity (PolyOne Corp).

The exhibit shows an Adam & Adam double top at AA. Following that, an Eve & Adam top appears. Notice how wide Eve appears compared to Adam. Another Eve & Adam double top appears about a year later.

Figure 20.23 shows the two missing varieties of Adam and Eve.

FIGURE 20.23   ANF US Equity (Abercrombie & Fitch Co).

An Adam & Eve double top appears in February, and you may be scratching your head because the two peaks look similar. That is the problem with labeling the various peaks. Recall that Adam tends to remain narrow whereas Eve widens out, which appears to be the case here.

The Eve & Eve tops look more rounded, especially when you consider the entire top on the left (blue arc) as part of the turn.

FAST FACTS

The failure rate can almost double from one type of double top to another, depending on the Adam and Eve combinations compared.

Exercise

The Adam and Eve combinations of double tops can confuse even the experts, so I am not going to test you on them. Look at Figure 20.24 to find three double tops, four flags, and a symmetrical triangle. Here is a hint for the flags. Look for the flagpole first (a straight-line price run), and then see if a flag is attached to it.

Figure 20.25 shows the locations of the chart patterns. A is an Eve & Eve double top. B is an Adam & Eve and C is an Eve & Adam. These should have been easy to locate, and I hope you found the flags and triangle as well.

This next exercise is more difficult because I chose a chart in which you may select some bogus patterns. Look for three valid double tops. (See Figure 20.26.)

FIGURE 20.24   COH US Equity (Coach Inc).

FIGURE 20.25 COH US Equity (Coach Inc).

Figure 20.27 shows the answers. Twin peak A is not a double top because it does not confirm (price does not close below line B).

C, D, and E are the correct choices for double tops. F, however, is an unconfirmed double top (at least so far).

The next section extends the twin peak pattern to three to create a triple top.

FIGURE 20.26 XLB US Equity (Materials Select Sector SPDR Fund).

FIGURE 20.27 XLB US Equity (Materials Select Sector SPDR Fund).

■ Triple Tops

A double top can become a triple after growing another peak near the same price. Let us take a closer look at this medical miracle to see how traders recognize it.

Figure 20.28 shows two examples of real triple tops and one implant.

The triple top at A has three peaks near the same price after the stock trends upward into the chart pattern. The stock becomes a base jumper and confirms the chart pattern on the way down through the horizontal red line.

The middle triple top, at B, is also a triple top with the same features as A. The skydiver pops his chute, and the drop ends soon after.

C is not a triple top because it does not confirm. You can guess what that means, but the next section makes the various components of a triple top clear.

KEY POINT:

A triple top is a three-peak pattern with the three minor highs topping out near the same price. The pattern acts as a reversal of the upward price trend.

FIGURE 20.28   ALK US Equity (Alaska Air Group Inc).

Identification Guidelines

The following table lists guidelines for finding triple tops.

Characteristic	Discussion
Upward price trend	The short-term price trend leading to the triple top is up.
Three peaks	Look for three minor highs. Sometimes the peaks can be oneday price spikes or wider, more rounded turns. Each peak tends to look similar to the others, but allow variations.
Same price	Each minor high should peak near the same price. Rarely will all three top out at exactly the same price, so be fl exible. In fact, the middle peak is sometimes lower than the other two.
Volume	Volume recedes, meaning it is higher on the left than the right, but each peak can show signifi cant volume. Do not exclude a pattern because it has an unusual volume shape.
Confirmation	Price must confi rm the triple top by closing below the lowest valley between the three peaks.

Figure 20.29 shows another example of a triple top.

I chose this one because the middle peak is depressed and needed cheering up. Do not trash a valid triple top because the middle peak is slightly lower than its neighbors.

Price trends upward from below the chart pattern at E. Peaks A and C have more rounded looking turns than does needle B, but that is fine.

To confirm a triple top, price has to close below the lowest valley in the chart pattern. That happens at D.

FIGURE 20.29 SXI US Equity (Standex International Corp).

Volume trends downward as the blue line shows. Receding volume is typical of triple tops, but do not discard a potential triple top because of unusual volume.

> **FAST FACTS**
> When the middle peak has higher volume than the last peak in the triple top, performance tends to be better.

Triple Top Psychology

Figure 20.30 shows selling near a fixed price that halts the upward movement in the stock, forming triple top ABC. It might play out something like this.

Imagine that you run a hedge fund that bought the stock at 18 in 2009 just after the bear market ended (not shown). At A, the stock reached 38 and change, more than double what you paid. Based on your analysis, it is time to sell.

> **FAST FACTS**
> The average length of a triple top on the daily chart is about three months in a bull market.

However, since you own a large position, you cannot just dump your shares on the market all at once. That would force the stock down into the Hudson faster than an airliner striking a flock of birds.

FIGURE 20.30 HAYN US Equity (Haynes International Inc).

At A, you let loose your first volley, but since the stock is thinly traded (less than 40,000 shares), you have difficulty selling 10,000 share blocks. You have to break it up into smaller chunks each day.

At B, you are having a bad day. You feel frustrated because other trades are going badly and you need to raise cash to cover redemptions. Your selling punishes the stock. Others see the panic selling and join in, sending the stock tumbling below 30.

At C, the stock is once again at your sell price, but you still have plenty of this lame turkey left in your portfolio. You sell as quietly as you can, as quickly as you can, but others sense the weakness and sell, too. Together, that sends the stock plunging quicker than a submarine during a crash dive. Momentum grows, keeping the stock trending down.

The stock reaches a long-term trendline (shown in blue) and bobbles up and down along that line for months. When the stock recovers to D, you sell more shares and finish dumping them when the stock powers higher at E.

Now that you have sold your position, the stock doubles, which really pisses you off.

Variations

Only one variation needs to concern you: a head-and-shoulders top. In the next two chapters, we discuss head-and-shoulders patterns but until then, just avoid picking triple tops in which the center peak rises too far above the other two. It should not look like a person's bust.

For example, consider Figure 20.31.

FIGURE 20.31 FOE US Equity (Ferro Corp).

The head-and-shoulders has a head above the shoulders (LS and RS) far enough to make it look like a person's bust.

> **SMART INVESTOR TIP**
> Select three peak patterns in which the middle peak is not too far above the other two. If the pattern resembles a human bust, then the pattern is better described as a head-and-shoulders top.

Compare that to the triple top ABC. B is slightly above A and C, but hardly enough to notice. It *looks* like a triple top and not a head-and-shoulders top.

Exercise

The first exercise is easy (see Figure 20.32). Find at least one triple top, a head-and-shoulders top (guess), and a double top. Except for the head-and-shoulders top, you should be able to identify the other patterns.

When searching for a triple top, imagine the outline of a mountain range. Three of the mountains line up at the same height to form a triple top.

Figure 20.33 shows the answers.

The head-and-shoulders top has a head sticking above the other two peaks, helping to differentiate it from a triple top.

The triple top at ABC forms three peaks near the same price. It confirms when price closes below the lowest valley in the chart pattern.

The double top may have given you some trouble because the two peaks are not at the same price (45 cents difference, or less than 1 percent).

FIGURE 20.32   GPN US Equity (Global Payments Inc).

FIGURE 20.33   GPN US Equity (Global Payments Inc).

Peak D is not a triple top. I shy away from peaks that align like this one does, forming a diagonal trend downward. Often that is a clue to a symmetrical triangle.

Figure 20.34 shows a target-rich environment. In it you should find at least two triple tops, two flags, a pennant, a double bottom, and a head-and-shoulders top.

Figure 20.35 shows where the chart patterns are located. Starting on the left, a small head-and-shoulders top appears in April. Since the price difference between the first two peaks is just 15 cents, if you want to call this a triple top, fine.

FIGURE 20.34 TFX US Equity (Teleflex Inc).

FIGURE 20.35 TFX US Equity (Teleflex Inc).

Next is the large pattern ABC. Although these three peaks line up near the same price, the chart pattern does not confirm, so it is not a triple top.

The flag in July is difficult to spot because it acts as a reversal of the uptrend.

The December flag and February pennant follow price higher surrounding the holidays.

D is the first triple top. The upward spike that occurs after the third peak also occurs after confirmation. The chart pattern reversal leads to a huge drop that sees a double bottom form as another reversal.

Following that is the second triple top, at E.

In the next chapter, I discuss head-and-shoulders bottoms. Just two days ago, I received an e-mail asking why I have not discussed the inverted head-and-shoulders pattern. I do not call them by that name. It has something to do with the federal eyewitness protection program.

Test Yourself

Answer the following.

1. If a fourth peak appears at the same price as the other three, what does it mean?
   A. If price closes below the lowest valley in the triple top before the fourth peak appears, you have a valid triple top.
   B. If the triple top is unconfirmed, it becomes a quad or multiple top pattern.
   C. If the four-peak pattern confirms, it suggests price is going down.
   D. Overhead resistance is strong.
   E. All of the above.
2. True or false: If price trends lower into a three-peak pattern, you have a triple top.
3. How close do the peaks have to be from each other to qualify as a triple top?
   A. It depends on scaling.
   B. No more than 25 cents.
   C. Within 4 percent.
   D. It does not matter providing they appear near the same price.
   E. All of the above.
4. True or false: Triple tops tend to be wide patterns with many lasting from two to three months.

Answers: 1. E; 2. False; 3. A or D; 4. True

CHAPTER 21

Head-and-Shoulders Patterns

From Thomas N. Bulkowski, *Visual Guide to Chart Patterns* (Hoboken, New Jersey: John Wiley & Sons, 2002), Chapters 16–17.

■ Head-and-Shoulders Bottoms

The head-and-shoulders is perhaps the best-known chart pattern. It has an evocative name, but recognizing a valid one takes an understanding of the rules. Let us begin by looking at a few samples. (See Figure 21.1.)

In this figure, I show three head-and-shoulders patterns. Pattern A is a head-and-shoulders bottom. The right shoulder (RS) bottoms at a price above the left (LS), but not too far. If this were the bust of a real person, yes, they might be in need of medical attention.

Notice that the head is below the adjacent shoulders. That is a key feature of a head-and-shoulders bottom.

Pattern B is similar to A. The two shoulders bottom close to the same price and they are almost symmetrical about the head in terms of time. Symmetry is important to head-and-shoulders patterns.

> **KEY POINT:**
> A head-and-shoulders bottom is a three-valley chart pattern that resembles a person's bust, inverted. The head is below the adjacent shoulders, and it acts as a reversal of the downward price trend.

C is a good example of a head-and-shoulders top. That chart pattern is the subject of the next section.

Besides a miracle, what does it take to find a valid head-and-shoulders bottom?

Identification Guidelines

The following table lists the identification guidelines.

FIGURE 21.1   SMRT US Equity (Stein Mart Inc).

Characteristic	Discussion
Downward price trend	Look for a short-term price trend leading down to the head-and-shoulders bottom.
Three valleys	The head-and-shoulders is a three valley pattern with the middle valley bottoming below the other two. The three valleys and two armpits (peaks between the valleys) should be well-defined minor highs and lows.
Symmetry	The entire pattern has a symmetrical feel to it. The left and right shoulders should have similar distances to the head; both should bottom at or near the same price, and be positioned on either side of the head.
Volume	Weakest on the right shoulder and often highest on the left shoulder, but head volume can be high, too. Do not exclude a head-and-shoulders bottom because of an unusual volume pattern.
Neckline, confirmation	The neckline is a line drawn across the two armpits. A close above this line confirms the head-and-shoulders as a valid chart pattern. For up-sloping necklines, use a close above the right armpit as the confirmation price.

Figure 21.2 shows one valid head-and-shoulders bottom and a wannabe. Let us determine the differences.

FAST FACTS

The average length of a head-and-shoulders bottom is over two months.

Pattern AB is a valid head-and-shoulders bottom. From the peak in February, price tumbles down a waterfall into the chart pattern and forms the left shoulder as a minor low. Following that, a lower valley appears as the head. After recovering from the head, price makes a higher low that becomes the right shoulder.

Pattern DEF has price trending upward into the pattern. There is nothing to reverse.

FIGURE 21.2   CF US Equity (CF Industries Holdings Inc).

Points A and B are the armpits. Connecting those is the neckline, shown in red.

The two shoulders are almost the same distance from the head, but hardly bottom at the same price. It is hard to tell which of the three valleys have higher volume.

In other words, the guidelines are just that, guidelines, not firm rules. Be flexible when prospecting for head-and-shoulders bottoms since wide variations are common.

Pattern DEF would seem to be a better example of a head-and-shoulders bottom. The two shoulders are more symmetrical looking both in price level and head distance. The pattern confirms when price closes above the neckline.

What is the flaw? Answer: The left shoulder is not a valid minor low. Recall that a minor low should be the lowest price from five days before to five days after. The left shoulder appears to be just a small blip in a rising price trend and not a minor low.

Head-and-Shoulders Bottom Psychology

Why do head-and-shoulders bottoms form? The chart pattern represents the struggle to find the lowest price at the best value. (See Figure 21.3.)

FIGURE 21.3 PFE US Equity (Pfizer Inc).

For example, the chart shows volume spiking even as the stock descends, going into the left shoulder. That higher turnover is a sign of a bottom, but one the stock has seen plenty of times as it rolled down the hill from the January high. What is different this time?

Buying demand puts a crimp on the downward slide and price moves up, but only for about a week. Then, the downtrend resumes, going into the head. Volume on formation of the head is less than on the left shoulder, but that configuration is typical for head-and-shoulders bottoms.

The smart money is accumulating the stock in anticipation of a change in the fundamentals and a rising price. The stock finds support and bottoms at the head low. Then the stock begins recovering, taking volume with it, signaling the change from bear to bull.

Price rounds over at the right armpit and drops to form the right shoulder. Volume is subdued here as if the smart money knows a good value when they see it, but are keeping it quiet. Their buying sends the stock moving higher again, above the neckline, confirming the turn from bear to bull.

Now firmly entrenched in their positions, the smart money can sip margaritas while others do the hard work of pushing the stock higher.

Variations

I show Figure 21.4 because of the right head-and-shoulders bottom (the one with measles). What is so special about this one compared to the others? It has multiple shoulders.

The right shoulder has two small valleys and the left has three. I show four of them as red dots. Strictly speaking, only two of these five are minor lows because of the five-day count on either side of the low to qualify it as a minor low.

FIGURE 21.4   LLY US Equity (Eli Lilly & Co).

This variation is called a complex head-and-shoulders bottom. Those are chart patterns with multiple shoulders, multiple heads, or both (rarely). As you scan for head-and-shoulders bottoms, look to the left and right and check for additional shoulders or another head. Treat the more complex pattern as a simple head-and-shoulders bottom.

As for the other two head-and-shoulders bottoms, notice the higher left shoulder bottom in each case. Irregularities such as these will cause doubt until you become accustomed to identifying flawed patterns.

Figure 21.5 shows a chart pattern that you may think is a head-and-shoulders bottom, and you would be wrong. This one has two twists. What are they?

FIGURE 21.5   TXI US Equity (Texas Industries Inc).

First, price does not trend downward into the chart pattern as the blue channel lines show. Price rises instead. This head-and-shoulders acts as a continuation of the upward price trend and not a reversal.

One might argue that point, saying that price drops from the peak in July 2009 and bottoms a year later with the middle section being a retrace of that downtrend. Fine.

The second "flaw" is that it never confirms as a valid head-and-shoulders bottom. That means price did not *close* above the neckline (A) or right armpit high (B) before closing below the bottom of the pattern. The armpit measure is the correct one to use when the neckline slopes upward, as in this case.

SMART INVESTOR TIP

If the neckline slopes upward from a head-and-shoulders bottom, use a close above the right armpit as confirmation instead of a close above the neckline.

Exercise

The first exercise shows three head-and-shoulders bottoms, but one you may disagree with. See if you can find all three. (See Figure 21.6.)

Figure 21.7 shows the answers. The questionable head-and-shoulders bottom is at A. Why? Because price trends upward into the chart pattern. It does not act as a "bottom" reversal but as a continuation pattern.

The other two chart patterns are valid head-and-shoulders bottoms. They reverse the short-term downtrend.

Note the horizontal red confirmation line in patterns A and B where the neckline slopes upward.

FIGURE 21.6 ANF US Equity (Abercrombie & Fitch Co).

FIGURE 21.7   ANF US Equity (Abercrombie & Fitch Co).

The next exercise is easier, but just as tricky. There is at least one head-and-shoulders bottom in Figure 21.8. See how many you can find.

Figure 21.9 shows the answers. Pattern A is not a head-and-shoulders bottom. Why? Because it is not symmetrical. The right shoulder is just too far away from the head compared to the left shoulder–head distance.

Pattern B is a valid head-and-shoulders bottom chart pattern.

The next section discusses another variation of the head-and-shoulders pattern: a top! If you had trouble finding the bottom variety, then spotting tops may be easier.

FIGURE 21.8   COH US Equity (Coach Inc).

FIGURE 21.9   COH US Equity (Coach Inc).

■ Head-and-Shoulders Tops

Spotting tops is easier for me. Perhaps it is the idea that preservation of capital is more important than profit. Whatever the reason, let us look at the last chart pattern in this section of the book.

The head-and-shoulders top appears on the chart just as it sounds and Figure 21.10 shows examples. In both chart patterns, a head towers above the shoulders, making it look like a person's bust.

KEY POINT:

A head-and-shoulders top is a three-peak reversal pattern with a centrally located head priced above two adjacent (shoulder) peaks. The pattern confirms as a valid chart pattern when price closes below the neckline or right armpit.

FIGURE 21.10   TREX US Equity (Trex Co Inc).

Price trends upward into the head-and-shoulders reversal. Then a left shoulder forms (LS), followed by a head and right shoulder. When price closes below the neckline, it confirms the chart pattern as valid. Price drops like a falling climber whose pitons have released.

Identification Guidelines

The following table lists guidelines for identifying head-and-shoulders tops.

Characteristic	Discussion
Upward price trend	Look for an upward price trend leading to a head-and-shoulders top.
Three peaks	The head-and-shoulders top is a three-peak pattern with the middle peak above the other two. The three peaks and two armpits (valleys between the peaks) should be well-defined minor highs and lows.
Symmetry	The entire pattern has a symmetrical feel to it. The left and right shoulders should have similar distances from the head; both shoulders should top out near the same price, and be positioned on either side of the head.
Volume	Weakest on the right shoulder and often highest on the left shoulder, but head volume can be high, too. Do not exclude a head-and-shoulders top because of an unusual volume pattern.
Neckline, confirmation	The neckline is a line drawn across the two armpits. A close below this line confirms the head-and-shoulders as a valid chart pattern. For down-sloping necklines, use a close below the right armpit as the confirmation price.

Figure 21.11 shows a head-and-shoulders top on the weekly scale. It appears as a three-bump pattern sitting atop a hill as if it were playing King of the Mountain.

FIGURE 21.11 HOV US Equity (Hovnanian Enterprises Inc).

Notice that the chart pattern on the weekly scale appears similar to ones on the daily chart or any other scale.

FAST FACTS

The head-and-shoulders top, in a bull market after a breakout, has the best average decline of 21 chart patterns tested.

Two shoulders appear at similar distances from the head, but not quite at the same price, with a head that towers above the shoulders.

This head-and-shoulders top has a down-sloping neckline in red (A). The blue line (B) shows how much sooner price validates the pattern when using a close below the right armpit instead of the neckline.

Volume is higher on the left shoulder than the right.

Head-and-Shoulders Top Psychology

Why do head-and-shoulders tops form? Pretend that you represent the smart money—high wealth individuals, financial institutions, hedge or mutual funds. You are searching for a stock to buy and believe that Hovnanian, shown in Figure 21.12, represents an intriguing situation.

You start buying at A, and that buying pressure sends the stock exploding out of a loose consolidation region that ended in March.

FAST FACTS

When volume is highest on the right shoulder in a bull market, the average head-and-shoulders top underperforms.

FIGURE 21.12   HOV US Equity (Hovnanian Enterprises Inc).

Others join in and buy the stock, sending the price into orbit like a shuttle launching.

As stars appear out the shuttle's window and the stock rises above 7, you have made 40 percent in about two weeks. Time to sell.

Your selling causes the stock to halt its upward move and begin a retrace, forming the left shoulder.

Sensing weakness, you stop selling but monitor the situation. Buy-the-dip players, believing that this is a chance to get in on a mission to deep space, buy the stock on the retrace. The decline halts, and the stock begins rising again.

As the stock moves up, momentum players join the trend. Once the stock rises above 8, you resume selling, not heavily at first because you have a large number of shares to dump. Still, the market players notice your selling and the stock heads back down.

You dump your remaining shares as the stock begins tumbling. Volume rises as other players sell their shares to unsuspecting buyers. The stock continues moving down and slides back below 6. Believing the stock oversold, demand picks up and sends the price moving up again for the last time.

You watch from the sidelines. The stock climbs to form the right shoulder. Lacking support for a continued rise, the stock turns down.

Investors versed in technical analysis see the head-and-shoulders top for what it is: a reversal. They quietly take profits. Others initiate short sales by selling high and hoping price hits zero.

The stock moves lower and forms a pennant before breaking out downward, leading to a head-and-shoulders bottom reversal.

Variations

Figure 21.13 shows a variety of head-and-shoulders tops. Let us begin on the left.

The head-and-shoulders at A is a traditional-looking pattern because it has wide, rounded shoulders and deep recessions that form the armpits. The pattern confirms when price closes below the horizontal line.

Pattern B is an outlier. The left and right shoulders do not qualify as minor highs because they are not wide enough, and yet the head-and-shoulders acts as a reversal of the uptrend. It confirms when price closes below the up-sloping neckline.

Pattern C has a spike for its head with unevenly priced shoulders, but they are close to symmetrical about the head. The pattern also confirms when price closes below the up-sloping neckline.

Pattern D is the only invalid head-and-shoulders top. The left shoulder is much wider than the right one, and the two shoulders are not symmetrical about the head.

Notice that the stock closes above the top of the head (E) before price closes below the red confirmation line, invalidating the chart pattern.

FIGURE 21.13   CHD US Equity (Church & Dwight Co Inc).

When searching for head-and-shoulders tops, I have found it beneficial to ask if the pattern *looks* like a person's bust. If the neck is unusually long or if the two shoulders are crooked, then look for another head-and-shoulders top.

Exercise

In this exercise, find as many head-and-shoulders tops as you can. Also, look for double and triple tops and bottoms, ascending and descending triangles. (See Figure 21.14.)

The answers appear in Figure 21.15. I show the patterns spread out like peanut butter across bread, but there are other patterns that may qualify (like additional double bottoms or double tops).

Head-and-shoulders tops A, B, and C are all valid. Pattern D confirms as a head-and-shoulders top, but the trend is downward leading to the chart pattern. It is not a reversal, but a continuation head-and-shoulders top.

Notice that since the head-and-shoulders pattern appeared at the end of the trend, the downward breakout did not amount to much. That is a trading tip you might want to remember.

FIGURE 21.14   RYL US Equity (Ryland Group Inc/The).

FIGURE 21.15   RYL US Equity (Ryland Group Inc/The).

As for the other chart patterns, the double bottom in November 2010 has uneven bottoms (3 percent apart), making the pattern difficult to identify.

Figure 21.16 has many patterns that look like head-and-shoulders tops, but are not. Find two valid ones.

Figure 21.17 shows the answers. The valid head-and-shoulders tops are marked A and B, flavored with red necklines. The other chart patterns do not confirm before price rises above the top of the chart pattern.

FIGURE 21.16   TOL US Equity (Toll Brothers Inc).

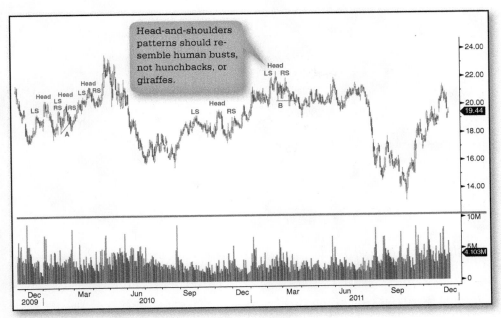

FIGURE 21.17   TOL US Equity (Toll Brothers Inc).

It's a Wrap

This chapter completes the introduction to chart pattern identification. We learned to use horizontal trendlines to highlight rectangles. Then we sloped one of the lines to find ascending and descending triangles. Two converging trendlines outlined a symmetrical triangle.

After that, we switched to peaks and valleys to find double and triple tops and bottoms. Completing the group were the head-and-shoulders, a complex pattern that is not much different from a triple top or bottom.

Now that we know what to look for, we can use the patterns as buy signals. The next section describes how.

Test Yourself

Answer the following.

1. How close must the two shoulders of a head-and-shoulders top be in price?
   A. Within 25 cents
   B. Within 50 cents
   C. It does not matter.
   D. It does not matter providing the entire pattern looks like a human bust.
   E. All of the above.

2. True or false: In a head-and-shoulders top, the chart pattern confirms when price closes below the left armpit.

3. True or false: To qualify as a top, price must trend upward into the bottom of a chart pattern.

4. True or false: In a triple top, the middle peak can be slightly below the other two.

Answers: 1. D; 2. False; 3. True; 4. True

CHAPTER 22

Computers in Trading

From Dr. Alexander Elder, *The New Trading for a Living* (Hoboken, New Jersey: John Wiley & Sons, 2014), Part 4, Chapter 21.

Computerized technical analysis is more objective than classical charting. You can argue whether support or resistance is present—but there can be no argument about an indicator's direction. Of course, you still need to decide what to do after you identify an indicator's message.

■ Toolboxes

When working with wood or metal, you can go to a hardware store and buy a set of tools that can help you work smartly and efficiently. A technical analysis toolbox provides a set of electronic tools for processing market data.

When you decide to get into computerized technical analysis, begin by drawing a list of tasks you want your computer to perform. This will take some serious thinking, but it's much better than getting a package first and scratching your head later, trying to figure out what it might do for you. Decide what markets you want to track, what types of charts to view and what indicators to use.

A toolbox draws weekly, daily, and intraday charts; it splits the screen into several windowpanes for plotting prices and indicators. A good toolbox includes many popular indicators, such as moving averages, channels, MACD, Stochastic, Relative Strength Index, along with dozens if not hundreds of others. It allows you to modify all indicators and even construct your own.

A good toolbox allows you to compare any two markets and analyze their spreads. If you trade options, your toolbox must include an options valuation model. Advanced packages allow you to backtest trading systems.

Another feature of a good toolbox is its ability to scan stocks. For example, you may want to find all stocks among the Nasdaq 100 whose exponential moving aver-ages are rising, but whose prices are no more than 1% above their EMAs. Can your software scan for that? Can it add fundamental parameters to your search, such as rising earnings? Think what you want to find and then ask software vendors whether their products can do it for you.

There are good toolboxes at all price levels. A beginner making his first steps may sign up with an online service that offers a basic set of computerized tools for free; you can upgrade to a paid level later. Most charts in this book are drawn using just such a service, StockCharts.com, because I want you to see how much you can do while spending very little. Some traders find that sufficient, while many of us buy programs that reside on our computers, allowing greater customization. With prices of software in a steady decline, you don't have to worry too much. Buy something simple and inexpensive and upgrade later—it's a date, not a marriage.

Once you've decided what package to use, you may want to hire somebody who already uses it to help you set it up on your machine. This can save a great deal of time and energy for inexperienced users.

A growing number of brokerage firms offer free analytic software to their clients; the price is right, but they tend to have two serious limitations. First, for legal reasons, they make their software very hard to modify and second, it only works online. Traders often ask how to add my indicators to their brokerage software, and the usual answer is—you can't.

Most brokerage house programs enable you to place and change your orders using the same analytic software. This can be quite handy and useful for day traders, but less important for longer-term traders. Be sure to disable a common feature that shows your equity gains or losses in real time. Watching dollars jump up or down at every tick is stressful and distracting. As the song goes, "…never count your money while you're sitting at the table—there'll be time enough for counting when the dealing's done." Focus on prices and indicators instead of watching dollars and thinking what you can buy with them.

Technical analysis software is constantly changing and evolving; a book is not the right place for software recommendations. My firm Elder.com maintains a brief Software Guide, which we periodically update and e-mail to any trader who asks for it, as a public service.

As mentioned earlier in this book, most programs for technical analysis fall into one of three groups: toolboxes, black boxes, and gray boxes. Toolboxes are for serious traders, black boxes are for people who believe in Santa Claus, and gray boxes are in between. When considering a new software package, be sure to know which group it belongs to.

■ Black Boxes and Gray Boxes

Black Box

Software is pure magic: it tells you what and when to buy and sell without telling you why. You download the data and push a button. Lights blink, gears click, and a message lights up, telling you what to do. Magic!

Black boxes always come with impressive track records that show profitable past performance. Every black box eventually self-destructs because markets keep changing. Even systems with built-in optimization don't survive because we don't know what kind of optimization will be needed in the future. There is no substitute for human judgment. The only way to make money from a black box is to sell one. Most black boxes are sold by hustlers to gullible or insecure traders.

Each black box is guaranteed to fail, even if sold by an honest developer. Complex human activities, such as trading, cannot be automated. Machines can help but not replace humans.

Trading with a black box means using a slice of someone else's intelligence, as it existed at some point in the past. Markets change, and experts change their minds, but a black box keeps churning out its buy and sell signals. It would have been funny if it wasn't so expensive for losers.

A Gray Box

Generates trading signals based on proprietary formulas. Unlike a black box, it discloses its general principles and allows you to adjust its parameters to some degree. The closer a gray box is to a toolbox, the better it is.

■ Computers

While online programs can run on any computer, most stand-alone programs are written for the Windows environment. Some traders run them on Macs, using emulation software. There are even programs for tablets, such as iPads.

Technical analysis software tends to be not very demanding of processing power, but still, it makes sense to get the most modern machine so that it remains useful for years.

Many day traders like to use multiple screens for a multidimensional view of the markets and the ability to watch several trading vehicles at once. Since I like to travel, I carry a small external screen that helps me monitor markets and trade from the road. It's the size of my laptop but much thinner and attaches to it with a USB cable, without a power cord.

■ Market Data

Swing and position traders enter and exit trades within days or weeks, while day traders enter and exit within a few hours if not minutes. End-of-day data is sufficient for position traders, but day traders need real-time data.

When you download the daily data for research, it pays to cover two bull-and-bear-market cycles, or about 10 years. Whenever I approach a stock, I like to look back at 12 years of trading history to see whether it is cheap or expensive relative to its 12-year range.

Whenever you approach a trade, you must know your edge—what will help you make money. The ability to recognize patterns is a part of my edge, but if a stock's history is too short, there are no reliable patterns to identify. That's why I avoid trading very young stocks, those with less than a year's history.

When collecting and analyzing data, don't chase too many markets at once. Focus on quality and depth rather than quantity. Begin by following the key market indexes, such as the Dow, the NASDAQ, and the S&P. Many professional traders focus on a relatively small number of stocks. They get to know them well and become familiar with their behavior patterns.

You could start out by focusing on a dozen stocks. Many professionals limit them-selves to fewer than 100 stocks, which they review every weekend and mark their opinions in a fresh column of their spreadsheet. They may select fewer than 10 stocks from that pool that look promising for the week ahead and focus on them. Build your watch list gradually from the popular stocks of the year; add a few stocks from the most promising industries and some stocks you've traded before. Building a watch list is like gardening: you can't get a beautiful garden in a single season, but you can get there over several seasons.

Try to stick to the data in your own time zone. When I teach overseas, traders often ask whether I trade in their country. I remind them that whenever you put on a trade, you're trying to take money out of some other trader's pocket, while others are trying to pick yours. This game is hard enough when you're awake, but it is risky to trade in a different time zone, allowing locals to pick your pockets while you sleep. This is why I largely limit my trading to the U.S. markets. Many overseas traders complain that they find their domestic markets too thin and ask whether it would make sense for them to trade in the huge and liquid U.S. market. The answer depends on how different their time zone is from the U.S. market's time zone. For example, the U.S. markets are easy to trade from Europe where they open at 3:30 p.m. local time and close at 10 p.m. It is much harder to do from Asia or Australia, but it can work if you take a longer view and aim to catch longer-term trends.

Beginning traders should steer clear of day-trading. It demands instant decision making, and if you stop to think, you're dead. Learn to trade in a slower environment. Become a competent position or swing trader before you consider day-trading. If you compare swing trading and day-trading, it is like playing the same video game at level one or level nine. You run the same mazes and dodge the same monsters, but the pace of the game is so fast at level nine that your reactions must be automatic. Learn to analyze markets at level one—become a swing trader before attempting to day-trade. We'll return to this topic in Chapter 34, "Trading Timeframes."

A good place to get started is swing trading, i.e., holding positions for several days. Select popular stocks that have good swings on a good volume. Start out by following just a handful. Some swing traders who hold positions for only a few days use real-time data for timing entries and exits, while others manage quite well with end-of-day data.

■ Three Major Groups of Indicators

Indicators help identify trends and reversals. They are more objective than chart patterns and provide insight into the balance of power between bulls and bears.

A great challenge is that various indicators may contradict one another. Some of them work best in trending markets, others in flat markets. Some are good at catching turning points, while others are better at riding trends. That's why it pays to select a small number of indicators from various groups and learn to combine them.

Many beginners look for a "silver bullet"—a single magic indicator, but markets are too complex to be handled with a single tool. Others try to poll a multitude of indicators and average their signals. The results of such a "poll" will be heavily skewed by the indicators you select.

Most indicators are based on the same five pieces of data: open, high, low, close, and volume. Prices are primary; indicators are derived from them. Using ten, twenty, or fifty indicators will not deepen your analysis because they share the same base.

We can divide indicators into three groups: trend-following indicators, oscillators, and miscellaneous. Trend-following indicators work best when markets are moving, but the quality of their signals sharply deteriorates when the markets go flat. Oscillators catch turning points in flat markets but give premature and dangerous signals when the markets begin to trend. Miscellaneous indicators provide insights into mass psychology. Before using any indicator, be sure to understand what it measures and how it works. Only then can you have confidence in its signals.

Trend-Following Indicators

Include moving averages, MACD Lines (moving av-erage convergence-divergence), the Directional System, On-Balance Volume, Accumulation/Distribution, and others. Trend-following indicators are coincident or lagging indicators—they turn after trends reverse.

Oscillators

Help identify turning points. They include MACD-Histogram, Force Index, Stochastic, Rate of Change, Momentum, the Relative Strength Index, Elder-ray, Williams %R, and others. Oscillators are leading or coincident indicators that often turn ahead of prices.

Miscellaneous Indicators

Provide insights into the intensity of bullish or bearish camps. They include the New High–New Low Index, the Put-Call Ratio, Bullish Consensus, Commitments of Traders, and others. They can be leading or coincident indicators.

It pays to combine several indicators from different groups so that their negative features cancel each other out, while their positive features remain undisturbed. This is the aim of the Triple Screen trading system.

As we begin to explore indicators, a few words of caution. Sometimes their signals are very clear, while at other times they are quite vague. I've learned long ago to enter trades only when indicator signals "grab me by the face." If I find myself squinting at a chart while trying to understand its signals, I flip the page and move to the next stock.

If you look at a familiar indicator but can't understand its message, it is most likely because the stock you're trying to analyze is in a chaotic stage. If indicator signals aren't clear, don't start massaging them or piling on more indicators, but simply leave that stock alone for the time being and look for another one. One of the great luxuries of private traders is that no one pushes us to trade—we can wait for the best and clearest signals.

As you read about the signals of different indicators, remember that you cannot base trading decisions on a single indicator. We need to select several indicators we understand and trust and combine them into a trading system. In the following chapters, we'll be exploring indicators, while later in the book we'll see how to build your own system from them.

For more information regarding Dr. Alexander Elder's work, please visit www.elder.com.

CHAPTER 23

Moving Averages

From Dr. Alexander Elder, *The New Trading for a Living* (Hoboken, New Jersey: John Wiley & Sons, 2014), Part 4, Chapter 22.

Wall Street old-timers say that moving averages were brought to the financial markets after World War II. Antiaircraft gunners used moving averages to site guns on enemy planes and after the war, applied this method to moving prices. The two early experts on moving averages were Richard Donchian and J. M. Hurst—neither apparently a gunner. Donchian was a Merrill Lynch employee who developed trading methods based on moving average crossovers. Hurst was an engineer who applied moving averages to stocks in his classic book, *The Profit Magic of Stock Transaction Timing.*

A moving average (MA) reflects the average value of data in its time window. A 5-day MA shows the average price for the past 5 days, a 20-day MA for the past 20 days, and so on. Connecting each day's MA value gives you a moving average line.

$$\text{Simple MA} = \frac{P_1 + P_2 + \ldots + P_N}{N}$$

where P is the price being averaged

         N is the number of days in the moving average (selected by the trader)

The level of a moving average reflects values that are being averaged and depends on the width of the MA window. Suppose you want to calculate a 3-day simple moving average of a stock. If it closes at 19, 21, and 20 on three consecutive days, then a 3-day simple MA of closing prices is 20 (19 + 21 + 20, divided by 3). Suppose that on the fourth day the stock closes at 22. It makes its 3-day MA rise to 21—the average of the last three days (21 + 20 + 22), divided by 3.

There are three main types of moving averages: simple, exponential, and weighted. Simple MAs used to be popular because they were easy to calculate in precomputer days, and both Donchian and Hurst used them. Simple MAs, however, have a fatal flaw—they change twice in response to each price.

Twice as Much Bark

First, a simple MA changes when a new piece of data comes in. That's good—we want our MA to reflect the latest prices. The bad thing is that MA changes again when an old price is dropped off at the end of its window. When a high price is dropped, a simple MA ticks down. When a low price is dropped, a simple MA rises. Those changes have nothing to do with the current reality of the market.

Imagine that a stock hovers between 80 and 90, and its 10-day simple MA stands at 85 but includes one day when the stock reached 105. When that high number is dropped at the end of the 10-day window, the MA will dive, as if in a downtrend. That meaningless dive has nothing to do with the current trend.

When an old piece of data gets dropped off, a simple moving average jumps. This problem is worse with short MAs but not so bad with long MAs. If you use a 10-day MA, those drop-offs can really shake it because each day constitutes 10% of the total value. On the other hand, if you use a 200-day MA, where each day is responsible for only 0.5%, dropping off a day isn't going to influence it a lot.

Still, a simple MA is like a guard dog that barks twice—once when someone approaches the house, and once again when someone walks away from it. After a while, you don't know when to believe that dog. This is why a modern computerized trader is better off using exponential moving averages, which we'll discuss later in this chapter.

Market Psychology

Each price is a snapshot of the current consensus of value among all market participants. Still, a single price doesn't tell you whether the crowd is becoming more bullish or bearish, just as you can't tell from a single photo whether a person is an optimist or a pessimist. If, on the other hand, you take a daily photo of a person for ten days, bring them to a lab, and order a composite picture, it'll reveal that person's typical features. You can monitor trends in that person's mood by updating that composite photo each day.

A moving average is a composite photograph of the market—it combines prices for several days. The market consists of huge crowds, and the MA slope identifies the direction of mass inertia. **A moving average represents an average consensus of value for the period of time in its window.**

The most important message of a moving average is the direction of its slope. When it rises, it shows that the crowd is becoming more optimistic—bullish. When it falls, it shows that the crowd is becoming more pessimistic—bearish. When prices rise above a moving average, the crowd is more bullish than before. When prices fall below a moving average, the crowd is more bearish than before.

Exponential Moving Averages

An exponential moving average (EMA) is a better trend-following tool because it gives greater weight to the latest data and responds to changes faster than a simple MA. At the same time, an EMA doesn't jump in response to dropping old data. This guard dog has better ears, and it barks only when someone approaches the house.

$$EMA = P_{tod} \bullet K + EMA_{yest} \bullet (1 - K)$$

where $\quad K = \dfrac{2}{N + 1}$

N = the number of days in the EMA (chosen by the trader).

P_{tod} = today's price.

EMA_{yest} = the EMA of yesterday.

Technical analysis software allows you to select EMA length. An EMA has two major advantages over a simple MA. First, it assigns greater weight to the last trading day. The latest mood of the crowd is more important. In a 10-day EMA, the last closing price is responsible for 18 percent of EMA value, while in a simple MA all days are equal. Second, EMA does not drop old data the way a simple MA does. Old data slowly fades away, like a mood of the past lingering in a composite photo.

■ Choosing the Length of a Moving Average

It pays to monitor your EMA slope because a rising line reflects bullishness and a declining one bearishness. A relatively narrow window makes an EMA more sensitive to price changes. It catches new trends sooner, but leads to more whipsaws. A whipsaw is a rapid reversal of a trading signal. An EMA with a wider time window produces fewer whipsaws but misses turning points by a wider margin.

You can take several approaches to deciding how long to make your moving average or any other indicator. It would be nice to tie EMA length to a price cycle if you can find it. A moving average should be half the length of the dominant market cycle. If you find a 22-day cycle, use an 11-day moving average. If the cycle is 34 days long, then use a 17-day moving average. Trouble is, cycles keep changing and disappearing.

There is no single magic "best" number for the EMA window. Good indicators are robust—not too sensitive to small changes in their parameters. When trying to catch longer trends, use a longer moving average. You need a bigger fishing rod to catch a bigger fish. A 200-day moving average works for long-term stock investors who want to ride major trends.

Most traders can use an EMA between 10 and 30 days. A moving average should not be shorter than 8 days to avoid defeating its purpose as a trend-following tool. Among the numbers I like are 22 because there are approximately 22 trading days in a month and 26—half of the number of trading weeks in a year.

Creating individualized parameters for every trading vehicle is practical only if you track a tiny handful of stocks or futures. Once their number reaches double digits, individualized parameters create confusion. It is better to have a yardstick that's one yard long and use the same parameters for all your moving averages in the same timeframe.

Don't change indicator parameters while looking for trades. Fiddling with parameters to obtain signals you'd like to see robs your indicators of their most valuable feature—their objectivity. It is better to set your parameters and live with them.

■ Trading Rules

Beginning traders try to forecast the future. Professionals don't forecast; they measure the relative power of bulls and bears, monitor the trend, and manage their positions.

Moving averages help us trade in the direction of the trend. The single most important message of a moving average comes from the direction of its slope (Figure 23.1). It reflects the market's inertia. When an EMA rises, it is best to trade the market from the long side, and when it falls, it pays to trade from the short side.

1. When an EMA rises, trade that market from the long side. Buy when prices dip near the moving average. Once you are long, place a protective stop below the latest minor low, and move it to the break-even point as soon as prices close higher.

2. When the EMA falls, trade that market from the short side. Sell short when prices rally toward the EMA and place a protective stop above the latest minor high. Lower your stop to break even as prices drop.

3. When the EMA goes flat and only wiggles a little, it identifies an aimless, trendless market. Do not trade using a trend-following method.

Old traders used to follow fast and slow MA crossovers. The favorite approach of Donchian, one of the originators of trading with moving averages, was to use crossovers of 4-, 9-, and 18-day MAs. Trading signals were given when all three MAs turned in the same direction. His method, like other mechanical trading methods, only worked during strongly trending markets.

Trying to filter out whipsaws with mechanical rules is self-defeating—filters reduce profits as much as losses. An example of a filter is a rule that requires prices to close on the other side of MA not once, but twice, or to penetrate MA by a certain margin. Mechanical filters reduce losses, but they also diminish the best feature of a moving average—its ability to lock onto a trend at an early stage.

FIGURE 23.1 DIS Daily 22-Day EMA. *(Chart by StockCharts.com)*

An Exponential Moving Average (EMA)
The direction of the slope of a moving average helps identify trends of trading vehicles, such as the Walt Disney Company (DIS).

A trader must accept that an EMA, like any other trading tool, has good and bad sides. Moving averages help you identify and follow trends, but they lead to whipsaws in trading ranges.

■ More on Moving Averages

Moving averages often serve as **support and resistance**. A rising MA tends to serve as a floor below prices, and a falling MA serves as a ceiling above them. That's why it pays to buy near a rising MA, and sell short near a falling MA.

Moving averages can be applied to **indicators** as well as prices. For example, some traders use a 5-day moving average of volume. When volume falls below its 5-day MA, it shows reduced public interest in the minor trend and indicates that it is likely to reverse. When volume overshoots its MA, it shows strong public interest and confirms the price trend. We'll be using moving averages of an indicator when we work with Force Index.

The proper way to plot a simple moving average is to **lag** it behind prices by half its length. For example, a 10-day simple MA properly belongs in the middle of a 10-day period and it should be plotted underneath the 5th or 6th day. An exponential moving average is more heavily weighted toward the latest data, and a 10-day EMA should be lagged by two or three days. Most software packages allow you to lag a moving average. .

Moving averages can be based not only on closing prices but also on the **mean between the high and the low**, which can be useful for day traders.

An exponential moving average assigns greater weight to the latest day of trading, but a **weighted moving average** (WMA) allows you to assign any weight to any day, depending on what you deem important. WMAs are so complicated that traders are better off using EMAs.

■ Dual EMAs

Whenever I analyze charts, I like to use not one but two exponential moving averages. The longer EMA shows a longer-term consensus of value. The shorter-term EMA shows a shorter-term consensus of value.

I keep the ratio between them at approximately two to one. For example, I may use a 26-week and a 13-week EMA on a weekly chart, or a 22-day and an 11-day EMA on a daily chart. Please understand there is no magic set of numbers. You should feel free to play with these values, selecting a set that will be unique to you. Just keep in mind to keep the difference between the two EMAs near 2:1. It might be simpler and more efficient to use the same set of values (for example 26/13 or 22/11) in all timeframes: weekly, daily, and even intraday.

Since the shorter EMA represents the short-term consensus of value and the longer-term EMA the long-term consensus, I believe that value "lives" between these two lines. **I call the space between the two EMAs the value zone.**

Moving Averages and Channels

A channel consists of two lines drawn parallel to a moving average. Oddly enough, the distance between the upper and the lower channel lines is sometimes described as "height" and at other times as "width" of the channel, even though both refer to the same measurement.

A well-drawn channel should contain approximately 95% of all prices that occurred during the past 100 bars. Longer-term markets have wider channels because prices can cover greater distances in 100 weeks than in 100 days. Volatile markets have wider (or taller) channels than quiet, sleepy markets.

Channels are very useful for trading and performance tracking.

Prices, Values, and the Value Zone

One of the key concepts in market analysis—the concept that all of us intuitively understand but almost never spell out—is that prices are different from values. We buy stocks when we feel that their current prices are below their true value and expect

FIGURE 23.2   DIS Daily, 26- and 13-Day EMAs. *(Chart by Stockcharts.com)*

EMAs and the Value Zone

A short-term MA identifies a short-term consensus of value, while a long-term MA reflects a long-term consensus of value. Value "lives" in the zone between the two moving averages. Select the parameters for this pair so that the long-term average is approximately twice the length of the short-term EMA. Looking at a chart, you can immediately tell which EMA is longer or shorter—the fast one hugs prices more closely, while the slow one moves more slowly. The slow EMA helps identify the trend, while the fast MA sets the boundary of the value zone.

When looking to buy a stock, it pays to do it in the value zone, rather than overpay and buy above value. Similarly, when shorting, it pays to wait for a rally into the value zone to establish a short position rather than sell short when prices collapse.

During the uptrend shown on this chart, you can see pullbacks to value, offering attractive buying opportunities in areas marked 1, 2, 3, and 4. The downward reversal of the slow EMA marks the end of the uptrend. At the right edge of the chart, the trend is down, while a pullback to value in area 5 offers a shorting opportunity.

prices to rise. We sell and sell short when we think that stocks are priced above their real value and are likely to come down.

We buy undervalued stocks and sell overvalued shares—but how to define value?

Fundamental analysts do it by studying balance sheets and annual reports, but those sources aren't nearly as objective as they seem. Companies often massage their financial data. Fundamental analysts don't have a monopoly on the concept of value. Technical analysts can define values by tracking the spread between a fast and a slow EMA. One of these EMAs reflects a short-term and the other a long-term consensus of value. *Value lives in the zone between the two moving averages* (Figure 23.2).

Very important: it's impossible to trade successfully with just a single indicator or even a pair of moving averages. Markets are too complex to extract money from them with a single tool. We need to build a trading system using several indicators as well as analyze markets in more than one timeframe. Keep this in mind as we review various indicators—they are the building blocks of trading systems, which we'll review later in the book.

Keeping this in mind will help you become a more rational trader. Once you know how to define value, you can aim to buy at or below value and sell above value.

For more information regarding Dr. Alexander Elder's work, please visit www.elder.com.

CHAPTER 24

Moving Average Convergence-Divergence: MACD Lines and MACD-Histogram

From Dr. Alexander Elder, *The New Trading for a Living* (Hoboken, New Jersey: John Wiley & Sons, 2014), Part 4, Chapter 23.

Moving averages help identify trends and their reversals. A more advanced indicator was constructed by Gerald Appel, an analyst and money manager in New York. Moving Average Convergence-Divergence, or MACD for short, consists of not one, but three exponential moving averages. It appears on the charts as two lines whose crossovers give trading signals.

◼ How to Create MACD

The original MACD indicator consists of two lines: a solid line (called the MACD line) and a dashed line (called the Signal line). The MACD line is made up of two exponential moving averages (EMAs). It responds to changes in prices relatively quickly. The Signal line smooths the MACD line with another EMA. It responds to changes in prices more slowly. In Appel's original system, buy and sell signals were given when the fast MACD line crossed above or below the slow Signal line.

The MACD indicator is included in most programs for technical analysis. To create MACD by hand:

1. Calculate a 12-day EMA of closing prices.
2. Calculate a 26-day EMA of closing prices.
3. Subtract the 26-day EMA from the 12-day EMA, and plot their difference as a solid line. This is the fast MACD line.
4. Calculate a 9-day EMA of the fast line, and plot the result as a dashed line. This is the slow Signal line.

Market Psychology

Each price reflects the consensus of value among the mass of market participants at the moment of the trade. A moving average represents an average consensus of value for a selected period of time—it is a composite photo of mass consensus. A longer moving average tracks longer-term consensus, and a shorter moving average tracks shorter-term consensus.

Crossovers of the MACD and Signal lines identify shifts in the balance of power of bulls and bears. The fast MACD line reflects mass consensus over a shorter time period. The slow Signal line reflects mass consensus over a longer period. When the fast MACD line rises above the slow Signal line, it shows that bulls dominate the market, and it is better to trade from the long side. When the fast line falls below the slow line, it shows that bears dominate the market and it pays to trade from the short side.

Trading Rules for MACD Lines

Crossovers of the MACD and Signal lines identify changes of market tides. Trading in the direction of a crossover means going with the flow of the market. This system generates fewer trades and whipsaws than mechanical systems based on a single moving average.

1. When the fast MACD line crosses above the slow Signal line, it gives a buy signal. Go long, and place a protective stop below the latest minor low.
2. When the fast line crosses below the slow line, it gives a sell signal. Go short, and place a protective stop above the latest minor high (Figure 24.1).

Bottoms A, B, and C of ABX could be seen as an inverted head-and-shoulders bottom. Still, our technical indicators deliver much more objective messages than classical chart patterns.

More on MACD Lines

Sophisticated traders tend to personalize their MACD Lines by using other moving averages than the standard 12-, 26-, and 9-bar EMAs. Beware of optimizing MACD too often. If you fiddle with MACD long enough, you can make it give you any signal you'd like.

A **"quick-and-dirty"** way to plot MACD can be used by traders whose software doesn't include this indicator. Some packages allow you to draw only two

FIGURE 24.1 ABX Weekly, 26- and 13-Week EMAs, 12-26-9 MACD Lines. *(Chart by StockCharts.com)*

MACD Lines

Barrick Gold Corporation (ABX), which has the largest market capitalization of all U.S. listed gold companies, was dragged down in 2012 and 2013 by the bear market in gold. Notice the sell signal, marked by a red vertical arrow, when the fast line crossed below the slow line. That signal reversed more than a year later, when the fast line crossed above the slow line, marked with a green vertical arrow.

Notice several additional patterns on this chart. When ABX fell to a record low, marked B, MACD Lines refused to confirm: they didn't fall to a new low but traced out a double bottom. That new low B turned out to be a false downside breakout, a bullish sign. Bears' last attempt to drive ABX lower, in area C, wasn't confirmed by MACD Lines, which maintained a steady uptrend. At the right edge of the chart, MACD Lines have reached a new high for the upmove, indicating strength. Both EMAs are rising, confirming the bullish trend.

EMAs. In that case, you can use crossovers between two EMAs, such as 12-day and 26-day EMAs as a proxy for MACD and Signal lines.

■ MACD-Histogram

MACD-Histogram offers a deeper insight into the balance of power between bulls and bears than the original MACD Lines. It shows not only whether bulls or bears are in control but also whether they are growing stronger or weaker. It is one of the best tools available to market technicians.

$$\text{MACD-Histogram} = \text{MACD line} - \text{Signal line}$$

MACD-Histogram measures the difference between the MACD line and the Signal line. It plots that difference as a histogram—a series of vertical bars. That distance may appear puny, but a computer rescales it to fill the screen (Figure 24.2). If the fast line is above the slow line, MACD-Histogram is positive and plotted above the zero line. If the fast line is below the slow line, MACD-Histogram is

FIGURE 24.2 DJIA Daily, 26- and 13-Day EMAs, 12-26-9 MACD Lines. *(Chart by StockCharts.com)*

MACD-Histogram

When MACD Lines cross over, MACD-Histogram, which is derived from them, crosses above or below its zero line. You can see buy and sell signals of MACD lines, marked by green and red arrows. These signals are often delayed, but MACD-Histogram gives its own fine signals. We'll return to them later in this chapter, but at this point let's look at just one.

Compare the Dow bottoms D and F. The second bottom was slightly lower (it turned out to be a false downside breakout), but the corresponding bottom of MACD-Histogram was more shallow than the first, warning that bears were weaker than before and an upside reversal was likely to occur.

negative and plotted below the zero line. When the two lines touch, MACD-Histogram equals zero.

When the spread between the MACD and Signal lines increases, MACD-Histogram becomes taller or deeper, depending on its direction. When the two lines draw closer, MACD-Histogram becomes shorter.

The slope of MACD-Histogram is defined by the relationship between any two neighboring bars. If the last bar is higher (like the height of letters m–M), the slope of MACD-Histogram is up. If the last bar is lower (like the depth of letters P–p), then the slope of MACD-Histogram is down.

Market Psychology

MACD-Histogram reveals the difference between long-term and short-term consensus of value. The fast MACD line reflects market consensus over a shorter period. The slow Signal line reflects market consensus over a longer period. MACD-Histogram tracks the difference between them.

The slope of MACD-Histogram identifies the dominant market group. A rising MACD-Histogram shows that bulls are becoming stronger. A falling MACD-Histogram shows that bears are becoming stronger.

When the fast MACD line rallies ahead of the slow Signal line, MACD-Histogram rises. It shows that bulls are becoming stronger than they have been—it is a good time to trade from the long side. When the fast MACD line drops faster than the slow line, MACD-Histogram falls. It shows that bears are becoming stronger—it's a good time to trade from the short side.

When the slope of MACD-Histogram moves in the same direction as prices, the trend is safe. When the slope of MACD-Histogram moves in a direction opposite to that of prices, the health of the trend is in question.

The slope of MACD-Histogram is more important than its position above or below the centerline. It is best to trade in the direction of the slope of MACD-Histogram because it shows whether bulls or bears dominate the market. The best buy signals occur when MACD-Histogram is below its centerline but its slope turns up, showing that bears have become exhausted. The best sell signals are given when MACD-Histogram is above its centerline but its slope turns down, showing that bulls have become exhausted.

Trading Rules

MACD-Histogram gives two types of trading signals. One is common, occurring at every price bar. The other is rare but extremely strong. It may occur only a few times a year on the daily chart of a stock. It's even more rare on the weekly charts, but more frequent on the intraday charts.

The common signal is given by the slope of MACD-Histogram. When the current bar is higher than the preceding bar, the slope is up. It shows that bulls are in control and it's time to buy. When the current bar is lower than the preceding bar, the slope is down. It shows that bears are in control and it's time to be short. When prices go one way but MACD-Histogram moves the other way, it shows that the dominant crowd is losing its enthusiasm and the trend is weaker than it appears.

1. Buy when MACD-Histogram stops falling and ticks up. Place a protective stop below the latest minor low.
2. Sell short when MACD-Histogram stops rising and ticks down. Place a protective stop above the latest minor high.

MACD-Histogram ticks up and down on the daily charts so often that it's not practical to buy and sell every time it turns. The changes of slope of MACD-Histograms are much more meaningful on the weekly charts, which is why it is included in the Triple Screen trading system.

When to Expect a New Peak or Valley

A record peak for the past three months of daily MACD-Histogram shows that bulls are very strong and prices are likely to rise even higher. A record new low for MACD-Histogram for the past three months shows that bears are very strong and lower prices are likely ahead.

When MACD-Histogram reaches a new high during a rally, the uptrend is healthy and you can expect the next rally to retest or exceed its previous peak. If

MACD-Histogram falls to a new low during a downtrend, it shows that bears are strong and prices are likely to retest or exceed their latest low.

MACD-Histogram works like headlights on a car—it gives you a glimpse of the road ahead. Not all the way home, mind you, but enough to drive safely at a reasonable speed.

More on MACD-Histogram

MACD-Histogram works in all timeframes: weekly, daily, and intraday. Signals in longer timeframes lead to greater price moves. For example, the signals of weekly MACD-Histogram lead to greater price changes than the daily or intraday MACD. This principle applies to all technical indicators.

When you use MACD Lines and MACD-Histogram on the weekly charts, you don't have to wait until Friday to find your signals. A trend can turn in the middle of the week—the market does not watch the calendar. It makes sense to perform weekly studies each day. I set my software to plot weekly charts in the traditional manner, from Monday through Friday, but with a twist: the latest weekly bar reflects trading for the current week, starting on Monday. After the market closes on Monday, my latest "weekly bar" is identical to Monday's daily bar. The weekly bar on Tuesday reflects two trading days, and so on. Because of this, on Monday I take the new weekly bar at a heavy discount, but by Thursday I start trusting it a great deal more.

■ Divergences

Divergences are among the most powerful signals in technical analysis. In this subchapter, we'll focus on MACD-Histogram, but this concept applies to most indicators.

Divergences between MACD-Histogram and prices are infrequent, but they give some of the most powerful signals. They often mark major turning points. They don't occur at every important top or bottom, but when you see one, you know that a big reversal is probably at hand.

Bullish Divergences

Occur towards the ends of downtrends—they identify market bottoms. A classical bullish divergence occurs when prices and the oscillator both fall to a new low, rally, with the oscillator rising above its zero line, then both fall again. This time, prices drop to a lower low, but an oscillator traces a higher bottom than during its previous decline. Such bullish divergences often precede sharp rallies (Figure 24.3).

I'm showing you this weekly chart of DJIA and its MACD-Histogram as a perfect example of a divergence. It deserves to be pinned to a wall near your trading desk. You won't always get such a perfect picture, but the closer you get to it, the more reliable it'll be.

Notice that the **breaking of the centerline** between two indicator bottoms is an absolute must for a true divergence. MACD-Histogram has to cross above that line before skidding to its second bottom. If there is no crossover, there is no divergence.

Another key point: MACD-H gives a **buy signal when it ticks up from the second bottom**. It does not have to cross above the centerline for the second time.

FIGURE 24.3 DJIA Weekly, 26- and 13-Day EMAs, 12-26-9 MACD Lines and MACD-Histogram. *(Chart by TC2000 from the book Two Roads Diverged:Trading Divergences)*

A Bullish Divergence

Here you see a divergence that signaled the 2007–2009 bear market bottom, giving a strong buy signal right near the lows. In **area A**, the Dow appeared in a free fall, as Lehman Brothers went bust and waves of selling hit the market. The record low A of MACD-H indicated that bears were extremely strong and that the price bottom A was likely to be retested or exceeded. In **area B**, MACD-H rallied above its centerline, "breaking the back of the bear." Notice that the brief rally reached the "value zone" between the two moving averages. This is a fairly common target for bear market rallies. In **area C**, the Dow slid to a new bear market low, but MACD-H traced a much more shallow low. Its uptick completed a bullish divergence, giving a strong buy signal.

The buy signal occurs when MACD-H, still below zero, simply stops declining and traces out a bar that is less negative than its preceding bar.

This divergence of MACD-Histogram in Figure 24.3 was reinforced when MACD Lines traced a bullish pattern between the bottoms A and C, with the second bottom more shallow than the first. Such patterns of MACD Lines are quite rare. They indicate that the coming uptrend is likely to be especially strong, even though we cannot call them divergences because this indicator has no zero line. The rally that began in 2009 lasted almost a year before its first meaningful correction.

Also, we can't call the pattern of lower indicator tops after the bottom C a divergence. The lower tops reflect a gradual weakening of the uptrend with the passage of time. In order to count as a divergence, MACD-Histogram has to cross and recross its zero line.

Bearish Divergences

Occur in uptrends—they identify market tops. A classical bearish divergence occurs when prices reach a new high and then pull back, with an oscillator dropping below its zero line. Prices stabilize and rally to a higher high, but an oscillator reaches a lower peak than it did on a previous rally. Such bearish divergences usually lead to sharp breaks.

A bearish divergence shows that bulls are running out of steam, prices are rising out of inertia, and bears are ready to take control. Valid divergences are clearly visible—they seem to jump at you from the charts. If you need a ruler to tell whether there is a divergence, assume there is none (Figure 24.4).

The previous chart featured a striking bullish divergence at the 2009 stock market bottom. Now, for a similarly striking illustration of a massive bearish divergence, let's roll back the clock and examine the 2007 bull market top.

Notice that the **breaking of the centerline** between the two indicator tops is an absolute must for a true divergence. MACD-Histogram has to drop below its zero line before rising to the second top.

Another key point: MACD-H gives a **sell signal when it ticks down from the second top**. We don't need to wait for it to cross below the centerline again. The sell signal occurs when MACD-H, still above zero, simply stops rising and traces out a bar shorter than the preceding bar.

FIGURE 24.4   DJIA Weekly, 26- and 13-Day EMAs, 12-26-9 MACD Lines and MACD-Histogram. *(Chart by TC2000 from the book Two Roads Diverged: Trading Divergences)*

A Bearish Divergence

In **area X**, the Dow rallied to a new bull market high and MACD-Histogram rallied with it, rising above its previous peak and showing that bulls were extremely strong. This indicated that the price peak X was likely to be retested or exceeded. Note that the top X of MACD-H, despite its complex form, was not a divergence because the valley in its middle never sank below zero.

In **area Y**, MACD-H fell below its centerline, "breaking the back of the bull." Notice that prices punched below the value zone between the two moving averages. This is a fairly common target for bull market breaks. Notice also a kangaroo tail at the bottom Y. In **area Z**, the Dow rallied to a new bull market high, but the rally of MACD-H was feeble, reflecting the bulls' weakness. Its downtick from peak Z completed a bearish divergence, giving a strong sell signal and auguring in the nastiest bear market in a generation.

The message of a bearish divergence in Figure 24.4 was reinforced by MACD Lines, which traced a bearish pattern between the tops X and Z. The second top of MACD Lines was more shallow than the first, confirming the bearish divergence of MACD-H. Such patterns of MACD Lines tell us that the coming downtrend is likely to be especially severe.

"Missing right shoulder" divergences in which the second peak fails to cross the zero line are quite rare, but produce very strong trading signals. An experienced trader can look for them, but they are definitely not for beginners. They are described and illustrated in the e-book *Two Roads Diverged: Trading Divergences*.

Kerry Lovvorn performed extensive research to find that the most tradable divergences occur when the distance between the two peaks or the two bottoms of MACD-H is between 20 and 40 bars—and the closer to 20, the better. In other words, the two tops or two bottoms cannot be too far apart. 20 bars translate into 20 weeks on a weekly chart, 20 days on a daily chart, and so on. Kerry also found that the best signals come from divergences in which the second top or bottom is no more than half the height or the depth of the first.

Triple Bullish or Bearish Divergences

Consist of three price bottoms and three oscillator bottoms or three price tops and three oscillator tops. They are even stronger than regular divergences. In order for a triple divergence to occur, a regular bullish or bearish divergence first has to abort. That's another good reason to practice tight money management! If you lose only a little on a whipsaw, you will preserve both the money and psychological strength to re-enter a trade. The third top or bottom has to be more shallow than the first but not necessarily the second.

■ The Hound of the Baskervilles

This signal occurs when a reliable chart or indicator pattern doesn't lead to the action you expected and prices move in the opposite direction. A divergence may indicate that an uptrend is over, but if prices continue to rise, they give the Hound of the Baskervilles signal.

This signal is named after the story by Sir Arthur Conan Doyle in which Sherlock Holmes was called to investigate a murder at a country estate. He found the essential clue when he realized that the family dog didn't bark while the murder was being committed. That meant the dog knew the criminal and the murder was an inside job. The signal was given by the lack of expected action—by the lack of barking!

When the market refuses to bark in response to a perfectly good signal, it gives you the Hound of the Baskervilles signal. This shows that something is fundamentally changing below the surface. Then it is time to get in gear with the new powerful trend.

I am not a fan of "stop-and-reverse" orders, but make an exception for the Hound of the Baskervilles. On those rare occasions when a bearish divergence aborts, I may go long. In the rare instances when a bullish divergence aborts, I look to go short.

CHAPTER 25

The Directional System

From Dr. Alexander Elder, *The New Trading for a Living* (Hoboken, New Jersey: John Wiley & Sons, 2014), Part 4, Chapter 24.

T he Directional system is a trend-following method developed by J. Welles Wilder, Jr., in the mid-1970s and modified by several analysts. It identifies trends and shows when a trend is moving fast enough to make it worth following. It helps traders to profit by taking chunks out of the middle of important trends.

■ How to Construct the Directional System

Directional Movement is defined as the portion of today's range that is outside of the previous day's range. The Directional system checks whether today's range extends above or below the previous day's range and averages that data over a period of time. These complex calculations are best performed on a computer. The Directional system is included in most programs for technical analysis.

1. Identify **"Directional Movement"** (DM) by comparing today's high-low range with yesterday's high-low range. Directional Movement is the largest part of today's range outside of yesterday's range. There are four types of DM (Figure 25.1). DM is always a positive number (+DM and −DM refer simply to movement above or below yesterday's range).

2. Identify the **"True Range"** (TR) of the market you analyze. TR is always a positive number, the largest of the following three:
   a. The distance from today's high to today's low
   b. The distance from today's high to yesterday's close
   c. The distance from today's low to yesterday's close

3. Calculate daily **Directional Indicators** (+DI and −DI). They allow you to compare different markets by expressing their directional movement as a percentage of each market's true range. Each DI is a positive number: +DI equals

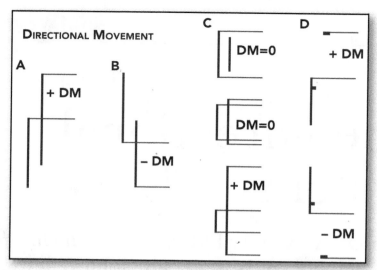

FIGURE 25.1 Directional Movement.

Directional movement is the largest part of today's range that is outside of yesterday's range.

1. If today's range extends above yesterday's range, Directional Movement is positive (+DM).
2. If today's range extends below yesterday's range, Directional Movement is negative (−DM).
3. If today's range is inside of yesterday's range or extends above and below it by equal amounts, there is no Directional Movement (DM = 0). If today's range extends both above and below yesterday's range, DM is positive or negative, pending on which part of the "outside range" is larger.
4. On a limit-up day, +DM equals the distance from today's close to yesterday's high. On a limit-down day, −DM equals the distance from today's close to yesterday's low.

zero on a day with no directional movement up; −DI equals zero on a day with no directional movement down.

$$+DI = \frac{+DM}{TR} \qquad -DI = \frac{-DM}{TR}$$

4. Calculate **smoothed Directional Lines** ($+DI_{13}$ and $-DI_{13}$). Smooth +DI and −DI are created with moving averages. Most software packages allow you to pick any period for smoothing, such as a 13-day moving average. You get two indicator lines: smoothed Positive and Negative Directional lines, $+DI_{13}$ and $-DI_{13}$. Both numbers are positive. They are usually plotted in different colors.

The relationship between Positive and Negative lines identifies trends. When $+DI_{13}$ is on top, it shows that the trend is up, and when $-DI_{13}$ is on top, it shows that the trend is down. The crossovers of $+DI_{13}$ and $-DI_{13}$ give buy and sell signals.

5. Calculate the **Average Directional Indicator** (ADX). This unique component of the Directional system shows when a trend is worth following. ADX measures the spread between Directional Lines $+DI_{13}$ and $-DI_{13}$. It is calculated in two steps:

a. Calculate the daily **Directional Indicator** DX:

$$DX = \frac{+DI_{13} - -DI_{13}}{-DI_{13} + -DI_{13}} \times 100$$

For example, if $+DI_{13} = 34$ and $-DI_{13} = 18$, then,

$$D = \frac{34 - 18}{34 + 18} \times 100 = 30.77, \text{ rounded off to } 31$$

b. Calculate the Average Directional Indicator ADX by smoothing DX with a moving average, such as a 13-day EMA.

During a persistent trend, the spread between two smoothed Directional lines increases, and ADX rises. ADX declines when a trend reverses or when a market enters a trading range. It pays to use trend-following methods only when ADX is rising.

■ Crowd Behavior

The Directional system tracks changes in mass bullishness and bearishness by measuring the capacity of bulls and bears to move prices outside of the previous day's range. If today's high is above yesterday's high, it shows that the market crowd is more bullish. If today's low is below yesterday's low, it shows that the market crowd is more bearish.

The relative positions of Directional lines identify trends. When the Positive Directional line is above the Negative Directional line, it shows that bullish traders dominate the market. When the Negative Directional line rises above the Positive Directional line, it shows that bearish traders are stronger. It pays to trade with the upper Directional line.

The Average Directional Indicator (ADX) rises when the spread between Directional lines increases. This shows that market leaders, for example bulls in a rising market, are becoming stronger, the losers weaker, and the trend is likely to continue.

ADX declines when the spread between Directional lines narrows down. This shows that the dominant market group is losing its strength, while the underdogs are gaining. It suggests that the market is in turmoil, and it's better not to use trend-following methods.

■ Trading Rules

1. Trade only from the long side when the positive Directional line is above the negative one. Trade only from the short side when the negative Directional line is above the positive one. The best time to trade is when the ADX is rising, showing that the dominant group is getting stronger.
2. When ADX declines, it shows that the market is becoming less directional. There are likely to be many whipsaws. When ADX points down, it is better not to use a trend-following method.
3. When ADX falls below both Directional lines, it identifies a flat, sleepy market. Do not use a trend-following system but get ready to trade, because major trends emerge from such lulls.

4. The single best signal of the Directional system comes after ADX falls below both Directional lines. The longer it stays there, the stronger the base for the next move. When ADX rallies from below both Directional lines, it shows that the market is waking up from a lull. When ADX rises by four steps (i.e., from 9 to 13) from its lowest point below both Directional lines, it "rings a bell" on a new trend (Figure 25.2). It shows that a new bull market or bear market is being born, depending on what Directional line is on top.

5. When ADX rallies above both Directional lines, it identifies an overheated market. When ADX turns down from above both Directional lines, it shows that the major trend has stumbled. It is a good time to take profits on a directional trade. If you trade large positions, you definitely want to take partial profits.

Market indicators give hard signals and soft signals. For example, when a moving average changes direction, it is a hard signal. A downturn of ADX is a soft signal.

FIGURE 25.2 ANV Daily, 22-Day EMA, Directional System (13). *(Chart by StockCharts.com)*

Directional System

Swings between strength and weakness are a typical market feature. Strong stock groups grow weak while the weak ones become strong, and then they swap roles again. Gold and silver stocks were the two weakest stock industry groups in 2013, but they began bottoming out in December. Allied Nevada Gold Corp. (ANV) was one of several stocks I began buying at that time.

The low at point A was $3.07, at point B the stock dipped to $3.01 and recoiled, leaving behind a false downside breakout, and at point C it retested support by declining to $3.08—and from there it was off to the races, with its EMA turning up. The Directional system gave its buy signal during the bar marked with a vertical green arrow: the green bullish Directional line was above the red bearish line, while the ADX penetrated above the red line.

You may find a similar shorting signal in the lettered area, but a discretionary trader doesn't trade every signal he sees: shorting a stock near $3 that has already declined from $45 would mean chasing a very old trend. Near the right edge you see a pullback to value, offering a good opportunity to add to the long position.

Once you see ADX turn down, you ought to be very, very careful about adding to positions. You should start taking profits, reducing positions, and looking to get out.

■ Average True Range—Help from Volatility

Average True Range (ATR) is an indicator that averages True Ranges (described in "How to Construct the Directional System" above) over a selected period of time, such as 13 days. Since volatility is a key factor in trading, you can track it by plotting a set of ATR lines above and below a moving average. They will help you visualize current volatility and you can use that for decision making.

Kerry Lovvorn likes to plot three sets of lines around a moving average: at one, two, and three ATRs above and below an EMA. These can be used for setting up entry points and stops, as well as profit targets (Figure 25.3).

FIGURE 25.3   LULU Daily, 21 EMA, Volume with 8 EMA, ATR Channels. *(Chart by TradeStation)*

ATR Channels

This diary of a trade, Lululemon Athletica Inc. (LULU), was posted by Kerry in SpikeTrade .com, where we post diaries of our trades. It shows using ATR channels for profit-taking.

LULU gapped down on a wide range bar on September 18 after an earnings announcement. There was no downside follow-through, and as the stock rallied, Kerry drew a horizontal line at the midpoint of its tall bar A, which tends to serve as short-term support.

As LULU pulled back, its daily ranges narrowed, and volume dried up in area B. Kerry bought LULU at $72.02 on Monday, September 30, during bar C, as it recovered from a false downside breakout. He took profits on 1/3 of his position at $73.70 later that day, as LULU came within a few cents of plus 1 ATR. On Thursday, during bar D, LULU hit its plus 2 ATR at $76.63, and Kerry exited another 1/3 of his position. He took the remaining 1/3 near the mid-range of bar D.

Entries We saw that it was a good idea to buy below value—below the EMA. But how far below? Normal pullbacks tend to bottom out near the minus one ATR.

Stops You want your stop to be at least one ATR away from your entry. Anything less than that would place your stop within the zone of normal market noise, making it likely to be hit by a random short-term move. Placing your stop further away makes it more likely that only a real reversal can hit your stop.

Targets After you buy a stock, depending on how bullish it appears to you, you can place an order to take profits at +1, +2, or even +3 ATRs. Kerry likes to get out of his winning positions in several steps, placing orders for taking profits for one third at 1 ATR, another third at 2 ATR, and the rest at 3 ATR.

It is highly unusual for any market to trade outside of three ATRs—three times average true range—for a long time. Those tend to be the extreme moves. Whenever you see a market trade outside of its three ATRs, either up or down, it is reasonable to expect a pullback.

ATR channels work not only with prices. We can also use them to bracket technical indicators to help identify the extreme levels where trends are likely to reverse. I use ATR channels on the weekly charts of Force Index.

THEORY AND ANALYSIS

For more information regarding Dr. Alexander Elder's work, please visit www.elder.com.

CHAPTER 26

Oscillators

From Dr. Alexander Elder, *The New Trading for a Living* (Hoboken, New Jersey: John Wiley & Sons, 2014), Part 4, Chapter 25.

While trend-following indicators, such as MACD Lines or Directional system, help identify trends, oscillators help catch turning points. Whenever masses of traders become gripped by greed or fear, they surge but after a while their intensity fizzles out. Oscillators measure the speed of any surge and show when its momentum is starting to break.

Oscillators identify emotional extremes of market crowds. They allow you to find unsustainable levels of optimism and pessimism. Professionals tend to fade those extremes. They bet against deviations and for a return to normalcy. When the market rises and the crowd gets up on its hind legs and roars from greed, professionals get ready to sell short. They get ready to buy when the market falls and the crowd howls in fear. Oscillators help us time those trades.

■ Overbought and Oversold

Overbought means a market is too high and ready to turn down. An oscillator becomes **overbought** when it reaches a high level associated with tops in the past. Oversold means a market is too low and ready to turn up. An oscillator becomes **oversold** when it reaches a low level associated with bottoms in the past.

Be sure to remember that those aren't absolute levels. An oscillator can stay overbought for weeks when a new strong uptrend begins, giving premature sell signals. It can stay oversold for weeks in a steep downtrend, giving premature buy signals. Knowing when to use oscillators and when to rely on trend-following indicators is a hallmark of a mature analyst.

We can mark overbought and oversold oscillator levels by horizontal reference lines. Place those lines so that they cut across only the highest peaks and the lowest valleys of that oscillator for the past six months. The proper way to draw those lines is to place them so that an oscillator spends only about 5 percent of its time beyond each line. Readjust these lines once every three months.

When an oscillator rises or falls beyond its reference line, it helps identify an unsustainable extreme, likely to precede a top or a bottom. Oscillators work spectacularly well in trading ranges, but they give premature and dangerous signals when a new trend erupts from a range.

We've already reviewed one important oscillator—MACD-Histogram. We looked at it "ahead of schedule" because it's derived from a trend-following indicator, MACD Lines. We'll now explore very popular oscillators: Stochastic and Relative Strength Index (RSI) in Chapters 27 and 28.

For more information regarding Dr. Alexander Elder's work, please visit www.elder.com.

CHAPTER 27

Stochastic

From Dr. Alexander Elder, *The New Trading for a Living* (Hoboken, New Jersey: John Wiley & Sons, 2014), Part 4, Chapter 26

Stochastic is an oscillator popularized by the late George Lane. It's now included in many software programs and widely used by computerized traders. Stochastic tracks the relationship of each closing price to the recent high-low range. It consists of two lines: a fast line called %K and a slow line called %D.

1. The first step in calculating Stochastic is to obtain "raw Stochastic" or %K:

$$\%K = \frac{C_{tod} - L_n}{H_n - L_n} \bullet 100$$

where C_{tod} = today's close.

L_n = the lowest point for the selected number of days.

H_n = the highest point for the selected number of days.

n = the number of days for Stochastic, selected by the trader.

The standard width of Stochastic's time window is 5 days, although some traders use higher values. A narrow window helps catch more turning points, but a wider window helps identify more important turning points.

2. The second step is to obtain %D. It is done by smoothing %K—usually over a three-day period. It can be done in several ways, such as:

$$\%D = \frac{\text{3-day sum of } (C_{tod} - L_n)}{\text{3-day sum of } (H_{tod} - L_n)} \bullet 100$$

There are two ways to plot Stochastic—Fast and Slow. **Fast Stochastic** consists of two lines—%K and %D—plotted on the same chart. It's very sensitive but leads to many whipsaws. Many traders prefer to use **Slow Stochastic**, adding an extra layer of smoothing. The %D of Fast Stochastic becomes the %K of Slow Stochastic

FIGURE 27.1 CVX Daily, 26-Day EMA. 5-Day Slow Stochastic. *(Chart by Stockcharts.com)*

Stochastic

This chart of Chevron Corporation (CVX) illustrates both helpful and dangerous aspects of Stochastic. As long as the stock stays in a sideways trading range, which is where it was for most of the time covered by this chart, Stochastic keeps nailing down short-term tops and bottoms. Stochastic gives buy signals, marked here with vertical green arrows, when it rises above its lower reference line. It gives sell signals, marked by vertical red arrows, by sinking below its upper reference line. Those signals are reinforced by broad, down-sloping Stochastic tops, marked by diagonal black arrows.

A careful reader will find several instances of false breakouts in Figure 27.1 that reinforce Stochastic signals. Using Stochastic signals during a trading range is like going to a cash machine. That machine stops working and eats your card after a trend erupts from the trading range. A sharp downtrend near the right edge overrides the Stochastic buy signal.

A trader may rely on Stochastic in a trading range, but should use protective stops because the last trade in a range always creates a loss when a trend begins.

and is smoothed by repeating step 2 to obtain %D of Slow Stochastic. Slow Stochastic does a better job of filtering out market noise and leads to fewer whipsaws (Figure 27.1).

Stochastic is designed to fluctuate between 0 and 100. Reference lines are usually drawn at 20 percent and 80 percent levels to mark overbought and oversold areas.

■ Crowd Psychology

Each price is the consensus of value of all market participants at the moment of transaction. Daily closing prices are important because the settlement of trading accounts depends on them. The high of any period marks the maximum power of bulls during that time. The low of that period shows the maximum power of bears during that time.

Stochastic measures the capacity of bulls or bears to close the market near the upper or lower edge of the recent range. When prices rally, markets tend to close near the high. If bulls can lift prices during the day but can't close them near the top, Stochastic turns down. It shows that bulls are weaker than they appear and gives a sell signal.

Daily closes tend to occur near the lows in downtrends. When a bar closes near its high, it shows that bears can only push prices down during the day but cannot hold them down. An upturn of Stochastic shows that bears are weaker than they appear and flashes a buy signal.

■ Trading Rules

Stochastic shows when bulls or bears become stronger or weaker. This information helps decide whether bulls or bears are likely to win the current fight. It pays to trade with winners and against losers.

Stochastic gives three types of trading signals, listed here in the order of importance: divergences, the level of Stochastic lines, and their direction.

Divergences

The most powerful buy and sell signals of Stochastic are given by divergences between this indicator and prices.

1. A bullish divergence occurs when prices fall to a new low, but Stochastic traces a higher bottom than during its previous decline. It shows that bears are losing strength and prices are falling out of inertia. As soon as Stochastic turns up from its second bottom, it gives a strong buy signal: go long and place a protective stop below the latest low in the market. The best buy signals occur when the first bottom is below the lower reference line and the second above it.

2. A bearish divergence occurs when prices rally to a new high, but Stochastic traces a lower top than during its previous rally. It shows that bulls are becoming weaker and prices are rising out of inertia. As soon as Stochastic turns down from the second top, it gives a sell signal: go short and place a protective stop above the latest price peak. The best sell signals occur when the first top is above the upper reference line and the second below.

Overbought and Oversold

When Stochastic rallies above its upper reference line, it shows that the market is overbought. It means that a stock or even the entire market is unusually high and ready to turn down. When Stochastic falls below its lower reference line, it shows that a stock or even the entire market is oversold: too low and ready to turn up.

These signals work fine during trading ranges but not when a market develops a trend. In uptrends, Stochastic quickly becomes overbought and keeps giving sell signals while the market rallies. In downtrends, it quickly becomes oversold and keeps giving premature buy signals. It pays to combine Stochastic with a long-term trend-following indicator. The Triple Screen trading system allows traders to take buy signals from daily Stochastic only when the weekly trend is up. When the weekly trend is down, it allows traders to take only sell signals from daily Stochastic.

1. When you identify an uptrend on a weekly chart, wait for daily Stochastic lines to decline below their lower reference line. Then, without waiting for their crossover or an upturn, place a buy order above the high of the latest price bar. Once you are long, place a protective stop below the low of the trade day or the previous day, whichever is lower.

   The shape of Stochastic's bottom often indicates whether a rally is likely to be strong or weak. If the bottom is narrow and shallow, it shows that bears are weak and the rally is likely to be strong. If it is deep and wide, it shows that bears are strong and the rally is likely to be weak. It is better to take only strong buy signals.

2. When you identify a downtrend on a weekly chart, wait for daily Stochastic lines to rally above their upper reference line. Then, without waiting for their crossover or a downturn, place an order to sell short below the low of the latest price bar. By the time Stochastic lines cross over, the market is often in a free fall. Once you are short, place a protective stop above the high of the trade day or the previous day, whichever is higher.

   The shape of Stochastic's top often indicates whether a decline is likely to be steep or sluggish. A narrow top of Stochastic shows that bulls are weak and a severe decline is likely. A Stochastic top that is high and wide shows that bulls are strong—it is safer to pass up that sell signal.

3. Do not buy when Stochastic is overbought, and don't sell short when it is oversold. This rule filters out most bad trades.

Line Direction

When both Stochastic lines are headed in the same direction, they confirm the short-term trend. When prices rise and both Stochastic lines rise, the uptrend is likely to continue. When prices slide and both Stochastic lines fall, the short-term downtrend is likely to continue.

■ More on Stochastic

You can use Stochastic in any timeframe, including weekly, daily, or intraday. **Weekly** Stochastic usually changes its direction one week prior to weekly MACD-Histogram. If weekly Stochastic turns, it warns you that MACD-Histogram is likely to turn the next week—time to tighten stops on existing positions or start taking profits.

Choosing the **width of the Stochastic window** is important. Shorter-term oscillators are more sensitive. Longer-term oscillators turn only at important tops and bottoms. If you use Stochastic as a stand-alone oscillator, a longer Stochastic is preferable. If you use Stochastic as part of a trading system, combined with trend-following indicators, then a shorter Stochastic is preferable.

For more information regarding Dr. Alexander Elder's work, please visit www.elder.com.

CHAPTER 28

Relative Strength Index

From Dr. Alexander Elder, *The New Trading for a Living* (Hoboken, New Jersey: John Wiley & Sons, 2014), Part 4, Chapter 27.

Relative Strength Index (RSI) is an oscillator developed by J. Welles Wilder, Jr. It measures any trading vehicle's strength by monitoring changes in its closing prices. It's a leading or a coincident indicator—never a laggard.

$$RSI = 100 - \frac{100}{1 + RS}$$

$$RS = \frac{\text{Average of net UP closing changes for selected period of days}}{\text{Average of net DOWN closing changes for the same number of days}}$$

RSI fluctuates between 0 and 100. When it reaches a peak and turns down, it identifies a top. When it falls and then turns up, it identifies a bottom. The pattern of RSI peaks and valleys doesn't change in response to the width of its time window. Trading signals become more visible with shorter RSI, such as 7 or 9 days. (Figure 28.1)

Overbought and oversold RSI levels vary from market to market and even from year to year in the same market. There are no magical levels for all tops and bottoms. Oversold and overbought signals are like hot and cold readings on a window thermometer. The same temperature levels mean different things in summer or winter.

Horizontal reference lines must cut across the highest peaks and the lowest valleys of RSI. They are often drawn at 30% and 70%. Some traders use 40% and 80% levels in bull markets or 20% and 60% in bear markets. Use the 5 percent rule: draw each line at a level beyond which RSI has spent less than 5 percent of its time in the past 4 to 6 months. Adjust reference lines once every three months.

FIGURE 28.1 CVX Daily, 13-Day RSI. *(Chart by Stockcharts.com)*

Relative Strength Index (RSI)

Here we apply a 13-day RSI to the chart of Chevron Corporation (CVX) that we already examined in Figure 16.1, in the chapter on Stochastic. Both RSI and Stochastic work well in trading ranges, but give premature and dangerous signals when prices begin to trend.

RSI, based exclusively on closing prices, is less noisy than Stochastic. It calls for rallies when it rises above its lower reference line, marked here by vertical green arrows. It signals declines by sinking below its upper reference line, marked here by vertical red arrows. Comparing both charts, you see that the RSI signals emerge earlier.

A very powerful sell signal is given by a bearish divergence of RSI, marked here by a diagonal solid arrow and a dashed red arrow. The stock rallied to a new high, while RSI couldn't reach its upper reference line, pointing to that rally's hidden weakness.

The sharp break near the right edge pushes prices lower despite the RSI buy signal. To avoid getting hurt, we must use protective stops because the last trade in a range can easily create a loss when a new trend begins.

■ Mass Psychology

Each price represents the consensus of value of all market participants at the moment of transaction. The closing price reflects the most important consensus of the day because the settlement of traders' accounts depends on it. When the market closes higher, bulls make money and bears lose. When the market closes lower, bears make money and bulls lose.

Traders pay more attention to closing prices than to any other prices of the day. In the futures markets, money is transferred from losers' to winners' accounts at the end of each trading day. RSI shows whether bulls or bears are stronger at closing time—the crucial money-counting time in the market.

■ Trading Rules

RSI gives three types of trading signals. They are, in order of importance, divergences, chart patterns, and the level of RSI.

Bullish and Bearish Divergences

Divergences between RSI and prices tend to occur at important tops and bottoms. They show when the trend is weak and ready to reverse.

1. Bullish divergences give buy signals. They occur when prices fall to a new low but RSI makes a higher bottom than during its previous decline. Buy as soon as RSI turns up from its second bottom, and place a protective stop below the latest minor price low. Buy signals are especially strong if the first RSI bottom is below its lower reference line and the second bottom is above that line.
2. Bearish divergences give sell signals. They occur when prices rally to a new peak but RSI makes a lower top than during its previous rally. Sell short as soon as RSI turns down from its second top, and place a protective stop above the latest minor high. Sell signals are especially strong if the first RSI top is above its upper reference line and the second top is below it.

Charting Patterns

RSI often breaks through support or resistance a few days ahead of prices, providing hints of likely trend changes. RSI trendlines are usually broken one or two days before price trend changes.

1. When RSI breaks above its downtrend line, place an order to buy above the latest price peak to catch an upside breakout.
2. When RSI breaks below its uptrend line, place an order to sell short below the latest price low to catch a downside breakout.

RSI Levels

When RSI rises above its upper reference line, it shows that bulls are strong but the market is overbought and entering its sell zone. When RSI declines below its lower reference line, it shows that bears are strong but the market is oversold and entering its buy zone.

It pays to buy using overbought signals of daily RSI only when the weekly trend is up. It pays to sell short using sell signals of daily RSI only when the weekly trend is down.

1. Buy when RSI declines below its lower reference line and then rallies above it.
2. Sell short when RSI rises above its upper reference line and then crosses below it.

When we analyze markets, we deal with only a few numbers—the opening, high, low, and closing prices for each bar, plus volume, and also open interest for derivatives, such as futures and options. A typical beginner error is "shopping for indicators." A trader may feel bullish about the stock market, but then he notices that the moving averages of the Dow and the S&P are still declining. Their bearish message doesn't sit well with him; he starts scrolling through his software menu and finds several oscillators, such as Stochastic or RSI. Sure enough, they look oversold, which is normal in a downtrend. The eager beginner takes those oversold readings as a signal to buy. The downtrend continues, he loses money—and then complains that technical analysis didn't work.

It is much better to use only a small number of indicators with a strict hierarchy for their analysis, including multiple timeframes.

For more information regarding Dr. Alexander Elder's work, please visit www.elder.com.

CHAPTER 29

Volume

From Dr. Alexander Elder, *The New Trading for a Living* (Hoboken, New Jersey: John Wiley & Sons, 2014), Part 5, Chapter 28.

Volume reflects the activity of traders and investors. Each unit of volume represents actions of two individuals: one sells a share or a contract and another buys that share or a contract. Daily volume is the number of shares or contracts traded in one day (Figure 29.1).

Traders usually plot volume as a histogram—vertical bars whose height reflects each day's volume. They usually draw it underneath prices. Changes in volume show how bulls and bears react to price swings and provide clues to whether trends are likely to continue or to reverse.

Some traders ignore volume. They think that prices already reflect all information known to the market. They say, "You get paid on price and not on volume." Professionals, on the other hand, know that analyzing volume can help them understand markets deeper and trade better.

Volume depends on the size of the trading crowd and the activity levels of buyers and sellers. If you compare volumes of two markets, you'll see which is more active or liquid. You are likely to receive better fills and suffer less slippage in liquid markets than in thin, low-volume markets.

There are three ways to measure volume:

1. The actual number of shares or contracts traded. For example, the New York Stock Exchange reports volume this way. This is the most objective way of measuring volume.
2. The number of trades that took place. Some international exchanges report volume this way. This method is less objective because it doesn't distinguish between a 100-share trade and a 5000-share trade.
3. Tick volume is the number of price changes during a selected period of time, such as 10 minutes or an hour. It is called tick volume because most changes equal 1 tick. Some exchanges don't report intraday volume, forcing day traders to use tick volume as a proxy for real volume.

FIGURE 29.1   BID Daily, 22-Day EMA, Volume. *(Chart by StockCharts.com)*

Volume

Sotheby's Holdings Inc. (BID) is the world's biggest publicly traded auction house. It provides a window into what the world's big money is doing in terms of their conspicuous consumption. This company's business was buoyed in 2013 by the influx of new money from Asia, but the stock hit its head on the ceiling during that year's last quarter.

In areas A and B, volume increased during the rally, confirming the uptrend and calling for higher prices ahead. In areas C and D, volume flashed warning signs for the bulls—it shrank during each rally attempt. Notice false upside breakouts in those areas and an atypical form of a kangaroo tail in area C. Rising volume near the right edge confirms the power of bears.

A note to forex traders: since that market is decentralized and reports no volume, you can use the volume of currency futures as its proxy. Futures of all major currencies, measured against the U.S. dollar, are traded in Chicago and on the electronic exchanges. We can assume that their volume trends are reasonably similar to those in the forex markets, since both respond to the same market forces.

■ Crowd Psychology

Volume reflects the degree of financial and emotional involvement, as well as pain, among market participants. A trade begins with a financial commitment by two persons. The decision to buy or sell may be rational, but the act of buying or selling creates an emotional commitment in most people. Buyers and sellers crave to be right. They scream at the market, pray, or use lucky talismans. The level of volume reflects the degree of emotional involvement among traders.

Each tick takes money away from losers and gives it to winners. When prices rise, longs make money and shorts lose. When prices fall, shorts gain and longs lose. Winners feel happy and elated, while losers feel depressed and angry. Whenever prices move, about half of the traders are hurting. When prices rise, bears are in pain, and when prices fall, bulls suffer. The greater the volume, the more pain in the market.

Traders react to losses like frogs to hot water. If you throw a frog into a hot pail, it'll jump in response to sudden pain, but if you put a frog into cool water and heat it slowly, you can boil it alive. If a sudden price change hits traders, they jump from pain and liquidate losing positions. On the other hand, losers can be very patient if their losses increase gradually.

You can lose a great deal of money in a sleepy stock or a future, such as corn, where a one-cent move costs only $50 per contract. If corn goes against you just a few cents a day, that pain is easy to tolerate. If you hang on, those pennies can add up to thousands of dollars in losses. Sharp moves, on the other hand, make losing traders cut their losses in a panic. Once weak hands get shaken out, leaving behind a volume spike, the market is ready to reverse. Trends can persist for a long time on moderate volume but can expire after a burst of volume.

Who buys from a trader who is selling his losing long position? It may be a short seller who wants to cover and take profits. It may be a bargain hunter who steps in because prices are "too low." A bottom-picker takes over the position of a loser who washed out—he either catches the bottom or becomes the next loser.

Who sells to a trader who buys to cover his losing short position? It may be a savvy investor who takes profits on his long position. It also may be a top-picker who sells short because he thinks that prices are "too high." He assumes the position of a loser who covered his shorts, and only the future will tell whether he is right or wrong.

When shorts give up during a rally, they buy to cover and push the market higher. Prices rise, flush out even more shorts, and the rally feeds on itself. When longs give up during a decline, they sell, pushing the market lower. Falling prices flush out even more longs, and the decline feeds on itself. Losers who give up on their trades propel trends. A trend that moves on steady volume is likely to persist. It shows that new losers are replacing those who washed out.

When volume falls, it shows that the supply of losers is running low and a trend is ready to reverse. It happens after enough losers catch on to how wrong they are. Old losers keep bailing out, but fewer new ones come in. Falling volume is a sign that the trend is about to reverse.

A burst of extremely high volume also gives a signal that a trend is nearing its end. It shows that masses of losers are bailing out. You can probably recall holding a losing trade longer than you should have. Once the pain became intolerable and you got out, the trend reversed and the market went the way you expected, only without you. This happens time and again because most humans react to stress similarly and bail out at roughly the same time. Professionals don't hang on while the market beats them up. They quickly close out losing trades and reverse or wait on the sidelines, ready to re-enter.

Volume spikes are more likely to signal an imminent reversal of a downtrend than an uptrend. Volume spikes in downtrends reflect explosions of fear. Fear is a powerful but short-term emotion—people run fast, dump shares, and then the trend is likely to reverse. Volume spikes in uptrends are driven by greed, which is a slower-moving, happy emotion. There may be a slight pause in an uptrend after a volume spike, but then the trend is quite likely to resume.

Volume usually stays relatively low in trading ranges because there is relatively little pain. People feel comfortable with small price changes, and flat markets can drag on a long time. A breakout is often marked by a dramatic increase in volume because losers run for the exits. A breakout on low volume shows little emotional commitment to a new trend. It indicates that prices are likely to return into their trading range.

Rising volume during a rally shows that more buyers and short sellers are pouring in. Buyers are eager to buy even if they have to pay up, and shorts are eager to sell to them. Rising volume shows that losers who leave are being replaced by a new crop of losers.

When volume shrinks during a rally, it shows that bulls are becoming less eager, while bears are no longer running for cover. The intelligent bears have left long ago, followed by weak bears who could not take the pain. Falling volume shows that fuel is being removed from the uptrend and it's ready to reverse.

When volume dries up during a decline, it shows that bears are less eager to sell short, while bulls are no longer running for the exits. The intelligent bulls have sold long ago, and the weak bulls have been shaken out. Falling volume shows that the remaining bulls have greater pain tolerance. Perhaps they have deeper pockets or bought later in the decline, or both. Falling volume identifies an area in which a downtrend is likely to reverse.

This reasoning applies to all timeframes. As a rule of thumb, if today's volume is higher than yesterday's, then today's trend is likely to continue.

■ Trading Pointers

The terms "high volume" and "low volume" are relative. What's low for Amazon may be very high for a less popular stock, while what's low for gold is high for platinum, and so on. We compare volumes of different stocks, futures, or options only when selecting higher-volume trading vehicles. Most of the time, we compare current trading volume of a stock to its average volume. As a rule of thumb, "high volume" for any given market is at least 25 percent above its average for the past two weeks, while "low volume" is at least 25 percent below average.

1. High volume confirms trends. If prices rise to a new peak and volume reaches a new high, then prices are likely to retest or exceed that peak.
2. If the market falls to a new low and the volume reaches a new high, that bottom is likely to be retested or exceeded. A very high volume "climax bottom" is almost always retested on low volume, offering an excellent buying opportunity.
3. If volume shrinks while a trend continues, that trend is ripe for a reversal. When a market rises to a new peak on lower volume than its previous peak, look to take profits on a long position and/or for a shorting opportunity. This technique does not work as well in downtrends because a decline can persist on low volume. There is a saying on Wall Street: "It takes buying to put prices up, but they can fall of their own weight."

4. Watch volume during reactions against the trend. When an uptrend is punctuated by a decline, volume often picks up in a flurry of profit taking. When that dip continues but volume shrinks, it shows that bulls are no longer running or that selling pressure is spent. When volume dries up, it shows that the reaction is nearing its end and the uptrend is ready to resume. This identifies a good buying opportunity. Major downtrends are often punctuated by rallies that begin on heavy volume. Once weak bears have been flushed out, volume shrinks and gives a signal to sell short.

For more information regarding Dr. Alexander Elder's work, please visit www.elder.com.

CHAPTER 30

Volume-Based Indicators

From Dr. Alexander Elder, *The New Trading for a Living* (Hoboken, New Jersey: John Wiley & Sons, 2014), Part 5, Chapter 29.

Several indicators help clarify volume's trading signals. For example, a 5-day EMA of volume can identify volume's trends. A rising EMA of volume affirms the current price trend, while a declining one points to the price trend's weakness.

This and other volume-based indicators provide more precise timing signals than volume bars. They include On-Balance Volume and Accumulation/Distribution, described below. Force Index combines price and volume data to help identify areas where prices are likely to reverse.

■ On-Balance Volume

On-Balance Volume (OBV) is an indicator designed by Joseph Granville and described in his book, *New Strategy of Daily Stock Market Timing*. Granville used OBV as a leading indicator of the stock market, but other analysts applied it to futures.

OBV is a running total of volume. Each day's volume is added or subtracted, depending on whether prices close higher or lower than on the previous day. When a stock closes higher, it shows that bulls won the day's battle; that day's volume is added to OBV. When a stock closes lower, it shows that bears won the day, and that day's volume is subtracted from OBV. If prices close unchanged, OBV stays unchanged. On-Balance Volume often rises or falls before prices, acting as a leading indicator.

■ Crowd Psychology

Prices represent the consensus of value, but volume represents the emotions of market participants. It reflects the intensity of traders' financial and emotional commitments, as well as pain among losers, which is what OBV helps to track.

A new high of OBV shows that bulls are powerful, bears are hurting, and prices are likely to rise. A new low of OBV shows that bears are powerful, bulls are hurting, and prices are likely to fall. When the pattern of OBV deviates from the pattern of prices, it shows that mass emotions aren't in gear with mass consensus. A crowd is more likely to follow its gut than its mind, and that's why changes in volume often precede price changes.

■ Trading Signals

The patterns of OBV tops and bottoms are much more important than the absolute levels, which depend on the starting date of your calculations. It is safer to trade in the direction of a trend that is confirmed by OBV (Figure 30.1).

1. When OBV reaches a new high, it confirms the power of bulls, indicates that prices are likely to continue to rise, and gives a buy signal. When OBV falls below its previous low, it confirms the power of bears, calls for lower prices ahead, and gives a signal to sell short.
2. OBV gives its strongest buy and sell signals when it diverges from prices. If prices rally, sell off, and then rise to a new high, but OBV rallies to a lower high,

FIGURE 30.1 MCD Daily, 22-Day EMA, On-Balance Volume (OBV). *(Chart by StockCharts.com)*

On-Balance Volume

McDonald's Corp. (MCD) is a stable, slow-moving stock. You can see a fairly tight trading range, marked with dashed lines (two lines at the lows, one tight and the other loose). Notice the tendency of MCD towards false breakouts (bottoms A and C and tops B and D). Notice a kangaroo tail in area A.

At the right edge of the chart, the stock market is in a free-fall, but while MCD trades near its recent lows, its OBV indicator is trading near the highs. It points to strength and suggests buying rather than selling.

it creates a bearish divergence and gives a sell signal. If prices decline, rebound, and then fall to a new low, but OBV falls to a more shallow bottom, it traces a bullish divergence and gives a buy signal. Long-term divergences are more important than the short-term ones. Divergences that develop over the course of several weeks give stronger signals than those created over a few days.

3. When prices are in a trading range and OBV breaks out to a new high, it gives a buy signal. When prices are in a trading range and OBV breaks down and falls to a new low, it gives a signal to sell short.

■ More on OBV

One of the reasons for Granville's success in stock market timing was that he combined OBV with two other indicators—the **Net Field Trend indicator** and the **Climax indicator**. Granville calculated OBV for each stock in the Dow Jones Industrial Average and rated its OBV pattern as rising, falling, or neutral. He called that a Net Field Trend of a stock: It could be $+1$, -1, or 0. Climax indicator was a sum of the Net Field Trends of all 30 Dow stocks.

When the stock market rallied and the Climax indicator reached a new high, it confirmed strength and gave a buy signal. If the stock market rallied but the Climax indicator made a lower top, it gave a sell signal.

You can look at the Dow Jones Industrial Average as a team of 30 horses pulling the market wagon. The Climax indicator shows how many horses are pulling uphill, downhill, or standing still. If 24 out of 30 horses pull up, 1 down and 5 are resting, then the market wagon is likely to move up. If 9 horses pull up, 7 pull down, and 14 are resting, that wagon may soon roll downhill.

Remarkably, Granville did his calculations by hand.[1] Now, of course, OBV, the Net Field Trend indicator, and the Climax indicator can be easily programmed. It would be worthwhile to apply them to a database that includes all stocks of the S&P 500 index. This method may produce good signals for trading the S&P 500 futures and options.

■ Accumulation/Distribution

This indicator was developed by Larry Williams and described in his 1973 book, *How I Made One Million Dollars*. It was designed as a leading indicator for stocks, but several analysts applied it to futures. The unique feature of Accumulation/Distribution (A/D) is that it tracks the relationship between opening and closing prices, in addition to volume. Its concept is similar to that of Japanese candlesticks, which at the time Williams wrote his book weren't known to Western traders.

---

[1] I visited Granville in 2005 in Kansas City. Not only did he do all his calculations by hand, he avoided going online, as he was suspicious of pervasive snooping—and that was years before the disclosures of government spying. He disconnected his computer from the Internet until it was time to send out his newsletter. Granville monitored intraday prices by tuning his TV into CNBC with the sound turned off and a towel draped over the upper portion of the screen, so that all he could see was the tape, running along the bottom of his screen.

Accumulation/Distribution is more finely calibrated than OBV because it credits bulls or bears with only a fraction of each day's volume, proportionate to the degree of their win for the day.

$$A/D = \frac{Close - Open}{High - Low} \times Volume$$

If prices close higher than they opened, then bulls won the day, and A/D is positive. If prices close lower than they opened, then the bears won, and A/D is negative. If prices close where they opened, then nobody won, and A/D is zero. A running total of each day's A/D creates a cumulative A/D indicator.

For example, if today's high-low spread was five points but the distance from the open to the close was two points, then only 2/5 of today's volume is credited to the winning camp. Just as with OBV, the pattern of A/D highs and lows is important, while its absolute level simply depends on the starting date.

When the market rises, most people focus on new highs, but if prices open higher and close lower, then A/D, which tracks their relationship, turns down. It warns that the uptrend is weaker than it appears. If, on the other hand, A/D ticks up while prices are down, it shows that bulls are gaining strength.

◼ Crowd Behavior

Opening prices reflect pressures that have built up while the market was closed. Openings tend to be dominated by amateurs who read their news in the evening and trade in the morning.

Professional traders are active throughout the day. They often trade against the amateurs. As the day goes on, waves of buying and selling by amateurs as well as slow-moving institutions gradually subside. Professionals tend to dominate the markets at closing time. Closing prices are especially important because the settlement of trading accounts depends on them.

A/D tracks the outcomes of daily battles between amateurs and professionals. It ticks up when prices close higher than they opened—when professionals are more bullish than amateurs. It ticks down when prices close lower than they opened—when professionals are more bearish than amateurs. It pays to bet with the professionals and against the amateurs.

◼ Trading Rules

When the market opens low and closes high, it moves from weakness to strength. That's when A/D rises and signals that market professionals are more bullish than amateurs, and the upmove is likely to continue. When A/D falls, it shows that market professionals are more bearish than amateurs. When the market weakens during the day, it's likely to reach a lower low in the days to come.

FIGURE 30.2   GOOG Daily, Accumulation/Distribution Index. *(Chart by Stockcharts.com)*

Accumulation / Distribution

"Coming events cast their shadows before" is an old proverb with a lot of meaning for technical analysts. Google Inc. (GOOG) was trending lower for months, but the uptrend of the Accumulation/Distribution Index (A/D) showed that big money was buying. The stock has fallen lower at point B than at A, but the A/D Index traced out a much higher bottom. Just as important, it broke out to a new high (marked with a vertical green arrow) before prices gapped up following a surprisingly good earnings announcement. Somebody knew what was coming, and their massive buying was identified by the A/D accumulation pattern and its upside breakout. Technical analysis helps even out the imbalance of knowledge between outsiders and insiders.

The best trading signals are given by divergences between A/D and prices.

1. If prices rally to a new high but A/D reaches a lower peak, it gives a signal to sell short. This bearish divergence shows that market professionals are selling into the rally.
2. A bullish divergence occurs when prices fall to a new low but A/D bottoms out at a higher low than during its previous decline. It shows that market professionals are using the decline for buying, and a rally is coming (Figure 30.2).

■ More on Accumulation/Distribution

When you go long or short, following a divergence between A/D and price, remember that even market professionals can go wrong. Use stops and protect yourself by following the **Hound of the Baskervilles** rule (see Chapter 24).

There are important parallels between A/D and Japanese candlestick charts, since both focus on the differences between opening and closing prices. A/D goes further than candlesticks by taking volume into account.

For more information regarding Dr. Alexander Elder's work, please visit www.elder.com.

CHAPTER 31

Force Index

From Dr. Alexander Elder, *The New Trading for a Living* (Hoboken, New Jersey: John Wiley & Sons, 2014), Part 5, Chapter 30.

Force Index is an oscillator developed by this author. It combines volume with prices to discover the force of bulls or bears behind every rally or decline. Force Index can be applied to any price bar for which we have volume data: weekly, daily, or intraday. It brings together three essential pieces of information—the direction of price change, its extent, and the volume during that change. It provides a practical way of using volume for making trading decisions.[1]

Force Index can be used in its raw form, but its signals stand out much more clearly if we smooth it with a moving average. Using a short EMA of Force Index helps pinpoint entry and exit points. Using a longer EMA helps confirm trends and recognize important reversals.

How to Construct Force Index

The force of every move is defined by three factors: direction, distance, and volume.

1. If prices close higher than the close of the previous bar, the force is positive. If prices close lower than the close of the previous bar, the force is negative.
2. The greater the change in price, the greater the force.
3. The bigger the volume, the greater the force.

$$\text{Force Index} = \text{Volume}_{today} \bullet (\text{Close}_{today} - \text{Close}_{yesterday})$$

A raw Force Index can be plotted as a histogram, with a horizontal centerline at a zero level. If the market closes higher, Force Index is positive and rises above the centerline. If the market closes lower, Force Index is negative and extends below the centerline. If the market closes unchanged, Force Index is zero.

---

[1] Remember, we're talking about the force of market crowds, not the formula in physics.

The histogram of a raw Force Index is very jagged. This indicator gives much better trading signals after being smoothed with a moving average (see Level II, Chapter 23). A 2-day EMA of Force Index provides a minimal degree of smoothing. It is useful for finding entry points into the markets. It pays to buy when the 2-day EMA is negative and sell when it's positive, as long as you trade in the direction of the trend.

A 13-day EMA of Force Index tracks longer-term changes in the force of bulls and bears. When the 13-day EMA crosses above the centerline, it shows that bulls are in control and suggests trading from the long side. When the 13-day EMA turns negative, it shows that bears are in control and suggests trading from the short side. Divergences between a 13-day EMA of Force Index and prices identify important turning points.

■ Trading Psychology

When the market closes higher, it shows that bulls won the day's battle, and when it closes lower, it shows that bears carried the day. The distance between today's and yesterday's closing prices reflects the margin of victory by bulls or bears. The greater this distance, the larger the victory achieved.

Volume reflects the degree of emotional commitment by market participants (see Chapter 29). High-volume rallies and declines have more inertia and are more likely to continue. Prices moving at high volume are like an avalanche that gathers speed as it rolls. Low volume, on the other hand, shows that the supply of losers is thin, and a trend is probably nearing an end.

Prices reflect what market participants think, while volume reflects the strength of their feelings. Force Index combines price and volume—it shows whether the head and the heart of the market are in gear with each other.

When Force Index rallies to a new high, it shows that the force of bulls is high and the uptrend is likely to continue. When Force Index falls to a new low, it shows that the force of bears is intense and the downtrend is likely to persist. If the change in prices is not confirmed by volume, Force Index flattens and warns that a trend is about to reverse. It also flattens and warns of a nearing reversal if high volume generates only a small price move.

■ Trading Rules

Short-Term Force Index

A 2-day EMA of Force Index is a highly sensitive indicator of the short-term force of bulls and bears. When it swings above its centerline, it shows that bulls are stronger, and when it falls below the centerline, it shows that bears are stronger.

Since the 2-day EMA of Force Index is a sensitive tool, we can use it to fine-tune signals of other indicators. When a trend-following indicator identifies an uptrend, the declines of the 2-day EMA of Force Index below zero pinpoint the best buying points: buying pullbacks during a long-term rally (Figure 31.1). When a trend-following tool identifies a downtrend, rallies of a 2-day EMA of Force Index mark the best shorting areas.

FIGURE 31.1 ADBE daily, 26-day EMA, 2-day Force Index. *(Chart by StockCharts.com)*
Short-Term Force Index.

Later in this book we'll return to the all-important topic of using multiple timeframes to make trading decisions. For example, you may make your strategic decision—to be a bull or a bear—on a weekly chart and then make your tactical decisions on where to buy or sell short using a daily chart.

In the case of Adobe Systems, Inc. (ADBE), there is a steady uptrend on the weekly chart, confirmed by its rising EMA (not shown). When the weekly trend is up, a 2-day Force Index on the daily chart provides an ongoing series of signals that identify buy points. Instead of chasing strength and buying high, it's better to buy during short-term pullbacks, when a wave goes against the tide. Those waves are marked by the 2-day Force Index dropping below zero. Once the 2-day Force Index goes negative, it makes sense to start placing buy orders above the latest bar's high. This will ensure you'll be stopped into a long trade as soon as the downwave loses its power.

1. Buy when a 2-day EMA of Force Index turns negative during uptrends.
   Even a fast and furious uptrend has occasional pullbacks. If you delay buying until the 2-day EMA of Force Index turns negative, you'll buy closer to a short-term bottom. Most people chase rallies and then get hit by drawdowns they find hard to tolerate. Force Index helps find buying opportunities with lower risks.

   When a 2-day EMA of Force Index turns negative during an uptrend, place a buy order above the high price of that day. When the uptrend resumes and prices rally, you'll be stopped in on the long side. If prices continue to decline, your order will not be executed. Keep lowering your buy order to near the high of the latest bar. Once your buy stop is triggered, place a protective stop below the latest minor low. This tight stop is seldom touched in a strong uptrend, but it'll get you out early if the trend is weak.

2. Sell short when a 2-day EMA of Force Index turns positive in a downtrend.
   When trend-following indicators identify a downtrend, wait until the 2-day EMA of Force Index turns positive. It reflects a quick splash of bullishness—a shorting opportunity. Place an order to sell short below the low of the latest price bar.

If the 2-day EMA of Force Index continues to rally after you place your sell order, raise your order the next day to near the previous bar's low. Once prices slide and you enter a short trade, place a protective stop above the latest minor peak. Move your stop down to a break-even level as early as possible.

Additionally, a 2-day EMA of Force Index helps decide when to pyramid positions. You can add to longs in uptrends each time Force Index turns negative; you can add to shorts in downtrends whenever Force Index turns positive.

Force Index even provides a glimpse into the future. When a 2-day EMA of Force Index falls to its lowest low in a month, it shows that bears are strong and prices are likely to fall even lower. When a 2-day EMA of Force Index rallies to its highest level in a month, it shows that bulls are strong and prices are likely to rise even higher.

A 2-day EMA of Force Index helps decide when to close out a position. It does it by identifying short-term splashes of mass bullishness or bearishness. A short-term trader who bought when this indicator was negative can sell when it turns positive. A short-term trader who went short when this indicator was positive can cover when it turns negative. A longer-term trader should get out of his position only if a trend changes (as identified by the slope of a 13-day EMA of price) or if there is a divergence between the 2-day EMA of Force Index and the trend.

3. Bullish divergences between the 2-day EMA of Force Index and price give strong buy signals. A bullish divergence occurs when prices fall to a new low while Force Index makes a more shallow low.

4. Bearish divergences between the 2-day EMA of Force Index and price give strong sell signals. A bearish divergence occurs when prices rally to a new high while Force Index traces a lower second top.

5. Whenever the 2-day EMA of Force Index spikes down to five times or more its usual depth and then recoils from that low, expect prices to rally in the coming days.

   Markets fluctuate between overbought and oversold, and when they recoil from a down spike, we can expect a rally. Note that this signal doesn't work well in uptrends—markets recoil from down spikes but not from up spikes. Spikes that point down reflect intense fear, which doesn't persist for very long. Spikes that point up reflect excessive enthusiasm and greed, which can persist for quite a long time.

   A 2-day EMA of Force Index fits well into the Triple Screen trading system (see Level III, Chapter 1). Its ability to find short-term buying and selling points is especially useful when you combine Force Index with a longer-term trend-following indicator.

Intermediate-Term Force Index

A 13-day EMA of Force Index identifies longer-term changes in the balance of power between bulls and bears. When it rises above zero, the bulls are stronger, and when it falls below zero, the bears are in charge. Its divergences from prices identify intermediate and even major turning points (Figure 31.2). It spikes, especially near the bottoms, mark approaching trend reversals.

The raw Force Index identifies the winning team in the battle between bulls and bears in any price bar, be it weekly, daily, or intraday. We get much clearer signals by smoothing the raw Force Index with a moving average.

1. When a 13-day EMA of Force Index is above the centerline, bulls are in control of the market. When it is below the centerline, bears are in charge.

   When a rally begins, prices often jump on heavy volume. When a 13-day EMA of Force Index reaches a new high, it confirms the uptrend. As an uptrend grows older, prices tend to rise more slowly, and volume becomes thinner. That's when a 13-day EMA of Force Index starts tracing lower tops. When it drops below its zero line, it signals that the back of the bull has been broken.

2. A new peak of the 13-day EMA of Force Index shows that bulls are very strong and a rally is likely to continue. A bearish divergence between a 13-day EMA of

FIGURE 31.2 SSYS daily, 26-day EMA, 13-day Force Index. *(Chart by StockCharts.com)*
Long-Term Force Index.

Stratasys, Inc. (SSYS) is one of the two leading companies in the rapidly emerging additive manufacturing (AM) market. In the two years since I wrote the world's first popular e-book on investing in this technology, AM stocks have become investors' favorites. A technical pattern has emerged, with rallies driven by amateurs piling in and sharp declines as they panic and bail out. The 13-day Force Index does a good job of catching those waves.

When the 13-day Force Index crosses above its zero line (marked by vertical green arrows), it shows that buying volume is coming in. That's where a longer-term trader buys and holds. When the 13-day Force declines below its zero line and stays there, it shows that bears predominate.

Near the right edge of the screen, we see a record low of Force Index, but then bears begin to weaken, as Force Index starts inching towards zero. Keep your powder dry as you wait for an accumulation pattern to emerge and be confirmed by Force Index crossing above zero. This see-saw movement of stocks passing from strong hands into weak ones near the tops and back again near the lows goes on forever. Force Index can help you position yourself with the right group.

Force Index and price gives a strong signal to sell short. If prices reach a new high but this indicator traces a lower peak, it warns that bulls are losing power and bears are ready to take control.

Note that for a divergence to be legitimate, this indicator must make a new peak, then fall below its zero line, and then rise above that line again, but tracing a lower peak, which creates a divergence. If there is no crossover, then there is no legitimate divergence.

3. A new low in the 13-day EMA of Force Index shows that a downtrend is likely to continue. If prices fall to a new low but this indicator rallies above zero and then falls again, but to a more shallow low, it completes a bullish divergence. It reveals that bears are losing power and gives a buy signal.

When a downtrend begins, prices usually drop on heavy volume. When a 13-day EMA of Force Index falls to a new low, it confirms the decline. As the downtrend grows old, prices fall more slowly or volume dries up—that's when a reversal is in the cards.

Adding an envelope to the chart of Force Index can help you detect its extreme deviations from the norm, which tend to lead to price trend reversals. This method for catching deviations and potential reversals works well with weekly charts, but not with the daily and intraday charts. This is truly a longer-term tool.

For more information regarding Dr. Alexander Elder's work, please visit www.elder.com.

CHAPTER 32

Open Interest

From Dr. Alexander Elder, *The New Trading for a Living* (Hoboken, New Jersey: John Wiley & Sons, 2014), Part 5, Chapter 31.

Open interest is the number of contracts held by buyers or owed by short sellers in any derivative market, such as futures or options.

Stock market shares are traded for as long as the company that listed them stays in business as an independent unit. Most shares are held as long positions, with only a small percentage of shorts. In futures and options, on the other hand, the total size of long and short positions is always identical, due to the fact that they are contracts for future delivery. When someone wants to buy a contract, someone else has to sell it to them, i.e., go short. If you want to buy a call option for 100 shares of Google, another trader has to sell you that option; in order for you to be long, someone else has to be short. **Open interest equals the total long or the total short positions**.

Futures and options contracts are designed to last for only a set period of time. A futures or options buyer who wants to accept delivery and a seller who wants to deliver have to wait until the first delivery day. This waiting period ensures that the numbers of contracts held long and short are always equal. In any case, very few futures and options traders plan to deliver or accept delivery. Most traders close out their positions early, settling in cash long before the first notice day.

Open interest rises when new positions are being created and falls when positions are being closed. For example, if open interest in April COMEX gold futures is 20,000 contracts, it means that bulls are long and bears short 20,000 contracts. If open interest rises to 20,200, it means that the net of 200 new contracts have been created: both bought and sold short.

Open interest falls when a bull who is long sells to a bear who is short but wants to cover his short position. As both of them get out, open interest falls by the size of their trade, since one or more contracts disappear from that market.

TABLE 32.1

Buyer	Seller	Open Interest
New buyer	New seller	Increases
New buyer	Former buyer sells	Unchanged
Former seller buys to cover	New seller	Unchanged
Former seller buys to cover	Former buyer sells	Decreases

If a new bull buys from an old bull that is getting out of his long position, open interest remains unchanged. Nor does the open interest change when a new bear sells to an old bear who wants to buy to cover his short position. In summary, open interest rises when "fresh blood" enters that market and falls as current bulls and bears start leaving that market, as illustrated in Table 32.1.

Technicians usually plot open interest as a line below price bars (Figure 32.1). Open interest in any market varies from season to season because of massive hedging by industrial users and producers at different stages of the annual production cycle. Open interest gives important messages when it deviates from its seasonal norm.

FIGURE 32.1 TYH14 Daily, 13-Day EMA, Open Interest. *(Chart by TradeStation)*

Open Interest

Open interest (OI) reflects the number of all short or long positions in any futures or options market. Since the two are equal in the derivatives markets, OI reflects the degree of conviction among bulls and bears.

Rising OI shows that the conflict between bulls and bears is becoming more intense and confirms the exiting trend. Falling OI, on the other hand, shows that losers are leaving the market, while the winners are cashing in—it signals that the trend is nearing its end.

Near the left edge of this chart of March 2014 Treasury Notes futures (TYH14), the trend is down, but the declining OI warns bears not to overstay the downtrend. OI bottomed out in area A, T-Notes in area B, and in area C, both were in clear uptrends, with rising OI calling for higher prices ahead. OI topped out in area D, and while prices continue to rise in area E, the new downtrend of OI serves up a warning to the bulls near the right edge of the chart.

Not all charts of open interest look as smooth and clear as this one. Serious traders don't expect to find a magic tool of a single indicator—they use several indicators and act only when their messages confirm one another.

◼ Crowd Psychology

It takes one bull and one bear to create a futures or options contract. A bull who believes that prices will rise buys a contract. A bear who thinks that prices are going to drop goes short by selling a contract for future delivery. With a trade between a new bull and a new bear, open interest rises by the number of contracts they traded. A single trade is unlikely to move any market, but when thousands of traders make similar trades, they propel or reverse market trends.

Open interest reflects the intensity of conflict between bulls and bears. It depends on their willingness to maintain long and short positions. When bulls and bears don't expect the market to move in their favor, they close out their positions, reducing open interest.

There are two people on the opposite sides of every trade, and one of them will be hurt when prices change. In a rally, bears will get hurt, and in a decline, bulls will suffer. As long as the losers hold on, hoping and hanging on to their positions, open interest doesn't change.

A rise in open interest shows that a crowd of confident bulls is facing down a crowd of equally confident bears. It points to a growing disagreement between the two camps. One group is sure to lose, but as long as potential losers keep pouring in, the trend will continue. These ideas have been clearly put forth in L. Dee Belveal's classic book, *Charting Commodity Market Price Behavior*.

It takes conviction among both bulls and bears to maintain a trend. Rising open interest shows that both camps keep adding to their positions. If they strongly disagree about the future course of prices, then the supply of losers is growing, and the current trend is likely to persist. An increase in open interest gives a green light to the existing trend.

If open interest rises during an uptrend, it shows that longs are buying while bears are shorting because they believe that the market is overvalued. They are likely to run for cover when the uptrend squeezes them harder—and their buying will propel prices higher.

If open interest rises during a downtrend, it shows that shorts are aggressively selling, while bottom pickers are buying. Those bargain hunters are likely to bail out when falling prices hurt them, and their selling will push prices even lower.

When a bull is convinced that prices are going higher and decides to buy, but a bear is afraid to sell short, that bull can buy only from another bull who bought earlier and now wants to cash out. Their trade creates no new contract, and open interest stays unchanged. When open interest goes flat during a rally, it shows that the supply of losers has stopped growing.

When a bear is convinced that prices are going lower and wants to sell short, but a bull is afraid to buy from him, that bear can sell only to another bear who shorted earlier and now wants to cover, take profits and leave. Their trade creates no new contract, and open interest does not change. When open interest stays flat during a decline, it shows that the supply of bottom pickers isn't growing. Whenever open interest flattens out, it flashes a yellow light—a warning that the trend is aging and the best gains are probably behind.

When a bull decides to get out of his long position, a bear decides to cover his short position, and the two trade with one another, a contract disappears, and open interest shrinks. Falling open interest shows that losers are bailing out, while winners are taking profits. When the disagreement between bulls and bears decreases, the trend is ripe for a reversal. Falling open interest shows that winners are cashing in and losers are giving up hope. It signals that the trend is approaching its end.

■ Trading Rules

1. When open interest rises during a rally, it confirms the uptrend and gives a green light to add to long positions. It shows that more short sellers are coming into the market. When they bail out, their short covering is likely to push the rally higher.

    When open interest rises as prices fall, it shows that bottom pickers are active in the market. It gives a green light to shorting because those bargain hunters are likely to push prices lower when they throw in the towel.

    If open interest rises when prices are in a trading range, it's a bearish sign. Commercial hedgers are much more likely to sell short than speculators. A sharp increase in open interest while prices are flat shows that savvy hedgers are probably shorting the market. You want to avoid trading against those who likely have better information than you.

2. If open interest falls while prices are in a trading range, it identifies short covering by major commercial interests and gives a buy signal. When commercials start covering shorts, they show that they expect the market to rise.

    When open interest falls during a rally, it shows that winners and losers alike are becoming cautious. Longs are taking profits, and shorts are covering. Markets discount the future, and a trend that is accepted by the majority is ready to reverse. If open interest falls during a rally, consider selling and getting out.

    When open interest falls during a decline, it shows that shorts are covering and buyers are taking losses and bailing out. If open interest falls while prices slide, take profits on short positions.

3. When open interest goes flat during a rally, it shows that the uptrend is getting old and the best gains have already been made. This gives you a signal to tighten stops on long positions and avoid new buying. When open interest goes flat during a decline, it warns you that the downtrend is mature and it is best to tighten stops on short positions. Flat open interest in a trading range does not contribute any new information.

■ More on Open Interest

The higher the open interest, the more active the market, and the less **slippage** you risk when getting in and out of positions. Short-term traders should focus on the contracts with the highest open interest. In the futures markets, the highest open interest tends to be in the front months. As the first notice day approaches and open interest of the front month begins to drop, while open interest in the next month begins to rise, it signals to roll over your position into the next month.

CHAPTER 33

Time

From Dr. Alexander Elder, *The New Trading for a Living* (Hoboken, New Jersey: John Wiley & Sons, 2014), Part 5, Chapter 32.

Most people conduct their lives as if they will live forever — repeating the same mistakes, not learning from the past, and hardly ever planning for the future. Freud showed that the unconscious mind doesn't have the notion of time. Our deep-seated wishes remain largely unchanged throughout our lives.

When people join crowds, their behavior becomes even more primitive and impulsive. Individuals may be ruled by the calendar and the clock, but crowds pay no attention to time. They act out their emotions as if they had all the time in the world.

Most traders focus only on changing prices but pay little attention to time. That's just another sign of being caught up in mass mentality.

The awareness of time is a sign of civilization. A thinking person is aware of time, while someone who is acting impulsively is not. A market analyst who pays attention to time becomes aware of a dimension hidden from the market crowd.

■ Cycles

Long-term price cycles are a fact of economic life. For example, the U.S. stock market tends to run in approximately four-year cycles. They exist because the ruling party inflates the economy going into the presidential election every four years. The party that wins the election deflates the economy when voters can't take revenge at the polls. Flooding the economy with liquidity lifts the stock market, while draining liquidity pushes it down.[1]

Major cycles in agricultural commodities are due to weather and fundamental production factors, coupled with the mass psychology of producers. For example, when livestock prices rise, farmers breed more animals. When those animals reach the market, prices fall and producers cut back. When the supply is absorbed, scarcity pushes prices up, breeders go to work again, and the bull/bear cycle repeats. This cycle is shorter in hogs than in cattle because pigs breed faster than cows.

---

[1] This cycle was grossly distorted by the Fed's "quantitative easing" following the 2008 debacle, but it's likely to return, once we crawl out of the Great Recession.

Long-term cycles can help traders identify market tides. Instead, many traders get themselves in trouble by trying to use short-term cycles to predict minor turning points.

Price peaks and valleys often seem to flow in an orderly manner. Traders measure distances between neighboring peaks, and project them into the future to forecast the next top. Then they measure distances between bottoms and extend them into the future to forecast the next low. Cycles put bread and butter on the tables of analysts who sell forecasts. Few of them realize that what appears like a cycle on the charts is often a figment of the imagination. If you analyze price data using a mathematically rigorous program, such as John Ehlers's MESA (Maximum Entropy Spectral Analysis), you'll find that approximately 80 percent of what looks like cycles is simply market noise. A human mind looks for order—and even an illusion of order is good enough for many people.

If you look at any river from the air, it appears to have cycles, swinging right and left. Every river meanders in its valley because water flows faster in its middle than near the shores, creating turbulences that force the river to turn. Looking for short-term market cycles with a ruler and a pencil is like searching for water with a divining rod. Profits from an occasional success are erased by many losses due to unsound methods.

■ Indicator Seasons

A farmer sows in spring, harvests in late summer, and in the fall, lays in supplies for the winter. There is a time to sow and a time to reap, a time to bet on a warm trend and a time to get ready for a frost. We can apply the concept of seasons to financial markets. Taking a farmer's approach, a trader should look to buy in spring, sell in summer, go short in the fall, and cover in winter.

Martin Pring developed the model of seasons for prices, but this concept works even better with technical indicators. Their seasons help recognize the current stage of the market cycle. This simple but effective model helps you buy when prices are low and sell short when they are high, setting you apart from the market crowd.

We can define the seasons of many indicators by two factors: their slope as well as their position above or below the centerline. For example, let's apply the concept of indicator seasons to MACD-Histogram (see Chapter 24). We define the slope of MACD-Histogram as the relationship between two neighboring bars. When MACD-Histogram rises below its centerline, it is spring; when it rises above its centerline, it is summer; when it falls above its centerline, it is autumn; and when it falls below its centerline, it is winter. Spring is the best season for going long, and autumn is the best season for selling short (Figure 33.1).

Indicator Slope	Position Relative to Centerline	Season	Preferred Action
Rising	Below	Spring	Go long
Rising	Above	Summer	Start selling
Falling	Above	Fall	Go short
Falling	Below	Winter	Start covering

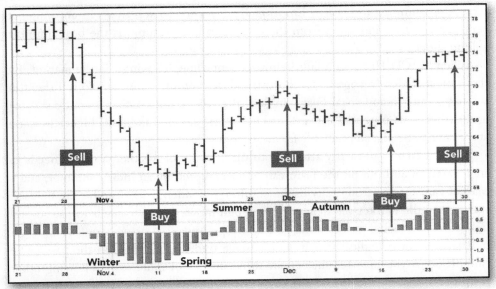

FIGURE 33.1 VRTX Daily, MACD-Histogram 12-26-9. *(Chart by StockCharts.com)*

Indicator Seasons

We can apply the concept of seasons to most indicators and timeframes, including intraday. This can be done with a multitude of trading vehicles, even though this example focuses on the daily MACD-Histogram of Vertex Pharmaceuticals, Inc. (VRTX), a stock in the Nasdaq 100.

> Autumn—The indicator is above the centerline but falling. This is the best season for establishing shorts.
>
> Winter—The indicator drops below its centerline. Use weakness to take profits on short positions.
>
> Spring—The indicator turns up from below its centerline. It is the best time to establish longs.
>
> Summer—The indicator rises above its centerline. As the weather gets hot, use strength to take profits on long positions.

MACD-Histogram looks very smooth in this example, but be prepared for brief fluctuations, both above and below the centerline. Spring can be interrupted by a frost, there can be a warm spell in winter, etc.

When MACD-Histogram is below its centerline but its slope is rising, it is spring in the market. The weather is cool but turning warmer. Most traders expect the winter to return and are afraid to buy. Emotionally, it is hard to buy because the memories of a downtrend are still fresh. In fact, spring is the best time for buying, with the highest profit potential, while risks are relatively small because we can place a protective stop slightly below the market.

When MACD-Histogram rises above its centerline, it's summer in the market—and by now most traders recognize the uptrend. It's emotionally easy to buy in summer because bulls have plenty of company. In fact, profit potential in summer is lower than in spring, while the risks are higher because stops have to be farther away from the market due to heightened volatility.

When MACD-Histogram is above its centerline but its slope turns down, it's autumn in the market. Few traders recognize that change and keep buying, expecting summer to return. Emotionally, it's hard to sell short in autumn—it requires you to stand apart from the crowd. In fact, autumn is the best time for selling short.

When MACD-Histogram falls below its centerline, it's winter in the market. By then, most traders recognize the downtrend. It is emotionally easy to sell short in winter, joining many vocal bears. In fact, the risk/reward ratio is rapidly shifting against bears, as potential rewards are becoming smaller and risks higher because stops have to be placed relatively far away from prices.

Just as a farmer must pay attention to the vagaries of weather, a trader needs to stay alert. An autumn on the farm can be interrupted by an Indian summer, and a market can stage a strong rally in the autumn. A sudden freeze can hit the fields in spring, and the market can drop early in a bull move. A trader needs to use several indicators and techniques to avoid getting whipsawed.

The concept of indicator seasons focuses a trader's attention on the passage of time. It helps you plan for the season ahead instead of mindlessly following other people.

■ Market Time

We measure time using calendars and watches, but seldom stop to think that our own perceptions of time are far from universal. We keep track of time in human terms, while huge areas of life move on vastly different timelines.

For example, we think that the ground under our feet is stable, while in fact continents move constantly. They traverse only a few inches per year, but this is enough to radically change the face of the globe over millions of years. Within shorter timeframes, weather patterns change over centuries. Ice ages and warming periods alternate with one another.

At the other end of the scale, there are physical particles that survive only a tiny fraction of a second. There are insects that are born, mature, procreate, and die within a single day.

Turning to trading, let's keep in mind that time flows at a different speed in the market than it does for us as individuals. The market, composed of huge masses of human beings, moves at a much slower speed. The patterns you recognize on your charts may have predictive value—but the turns they anticipate are likely to occur much later than you expect.

The relative slowness of crowds can bedevil even experienced traders. Time and again we find ourselves entering trades too early. Beginners are typically late. By the time they recognize a trend or a reversal, that move had been underway for so long that they miss most, if not all of it. Newbies tend to chase old trends, but the more experienced analysts and traders tend to run into an opposite problem. We recognize approaching reversals and emerging new trends from far away—and jump in too soon. We often buy before the market finishes tracing a bottom or sell short well before it completes a top. By getting in too early we can end up losing money in trends that are too slow to turn.

What should we do? First of all, you need to become aware that the market time is much slower than your own. Second, consider not putting on a trade when you notice an early reversal signal. A better signal may well emerge later, especially at market tops, which take longer to form than bottoms.

It pays not to be greedy and trade a smaller size. A smaller position is easier to hold while a reversal is taking its sweet time. Be sure to use multiple timeframes for market analysis: this is the essence of Triple Screen.

■ The Factor of Five

Most beginners casually pick a timeframe that looks good to them—it can be a daily or a 10-minute chart, or any other—and ignore others. Few are aware of the fact that the market lives in multiple timeframes. It moves simultaneously on monthly, weekly, daily, and intraday charts—often in opposite directions.

The trend may be up on the daily charts but down on the weeklies, and vice versa. Which of them will you follow? And what will you do about the intraday charts, which may well contradict either the weeklies or the dailies? Most traders ignore all timeframes except for their own—until a sudden move from outside of their timeframe hits their account.

Keep in mind that neighboring timeframes are linked by the factor of approximately 5. If you start with a monthly chart and proceed to the weekly, you'll notice that there are 4.5 weeks to a month. As you switch from a weekly to a daily chart, you know that there are 5 trading days to a week. Turning to intraday analysis, you may look at an hourly chart—and there are approximately 5–6 hours to a trading day. Day traders can proceed even further and look at 10-minute charts, followed by 2-minute charts. Each is related to its neighboring timeframes by approximately the factor of five.

The proper way to analyze any market is to review at least two neighboring timeframes. You must always start with the longer timeframe for a strategic view and then switch to the shorter timeframe for tactical timing. If you like using daily charts, you must first examine weekly charts, and if you want to day-trade using 10-minute charts, you first need to analyze hourly charts. This is one of the key principles of the Triple Screen trading system.

CHAPTER 34

Trading Timeframes

From Dr. Alexander Elder, *The New Trading for a Living* (Hoboken, New Jersey: John Wiley & Sons, 2014), Part 5, Chapter 33.

How long do you plan to hold your next trade? Do you think it'll be a year, a week, or an hour? A serious trader plans the expected duration of every trade. Various timeframes offer different opportunities and carry different risks. We can roughly divide all trades into three groups:

1. **Long-term trading or investing**—The expected duration of a position is measured in months, sometimes years.
   Advantages: requires little day-to-day attention and may lead to spectacular gains.
   Disadvantage: drawdowns can be intolerably severe.
2. **Swing trading**—The expected duration of a trade is measured in days, sometimes weeks.
   Advantages: a wealth of trading opportunities, fairly tight risk control.
   Disadvantage: will miss major trends.
3. **Day-trading**—The expected duration of a trade is measured in minutes, rarely hours.
   Advantages: great many opportunities, no overnight risk.
   Disadvantages: demands instant reflexes; transaction costs become a factor.

If you decide to operate in more than one timeframe, consider making those trades in different accounts. This will allow you to evaluate your performance in each timeframe rather than lump together apples and oranges.

■ Investing

The decision to invest or trade for the long term is almost always based on some fundamental idea. You may recognize a new technological trend or an exciting product that can greatly increase the value of a company. Investing demands a firm conviction and a great supply of patience if you are to hold that position through the inevitable pullbacks and periods of flat prices. These tough challenges make successful investing extremely hard.

Major trends that are easily seen on long-term charts appear uncertain and foggy in real time, especially when a stock enters a drawdown. When your investment drops 50% or more, wiping out the bulk of paper profits—a common development for long-term positions—few of us have enough conviction and fortitude to continue to hold. Let me illustrate this using an example of Apple Inc. (AAPL), a darling of several bull markets (Figure 34.1).

AAPL survived its near-death experience in 2003, when its battered stock was rumored to be a takeover candidate, and grew to become the highest-capitalized, publicly traded company in the world, before collapsing from that top in 2012. Its uptrend looks grand in retrospect, but ask yourself, honestly, would you have been able to hold through multiple drawdowns, some of them exceeding 50%. Remember that such drawdowns often mark the ends of uptrends.

A sensible way to deal with the challenge of investing is to implement your fundamental idea with the help of technical trading tools. When you decide to buy, check out technical signals to ensure you're getting a relative bargain rather than paying full price. If your investment soars, use technical tools to identify overvalued zones; take your profits there and be ready to repurchase during the inevitable pullbacks. This plan demands a high degree of attention, focus, and perseverance. Figure 34.2 is an example that was taken from my trading diary.

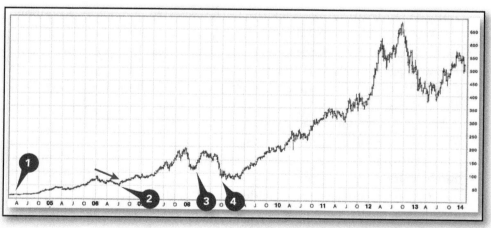

FIGURE 34.1   AAPL Weekly. *(Chart by StockCharts.com)*

Investing

The tremendous challenges of holding an investment, even a market leader like Apple Inc. (AAPL), can be seen on this 10-year chart:

1. 2003—AAPL collapses below $10. Company's survival in question. Would you buy?
2. 2006—AAPL rallies to $86, then sinks to $51. If you had a thousand shares, would you hold? Would you sell when it got back above $80 and appeared to stall?
3. 2008—AAPL rallies to $202, drops to $115. If you had a thousand shares, showing an $87,000 drawdown, would you hold or sell?
4. 2009—AAPL recovers to $192, sinks to $78, below its previous low. Your drawdown is over 50%. Are you holding or cashing out?

FIGURE 34.2 F Monthly, 26- and 13-Months EMA with the Impulse System, Auto-envelope, MACD Lines and MACD-Histogram (12-26-9), and Force Index 13-Months EMA with ATR Channels. *(Chart by Tradestation)*

Technical Analysis with Fundamentals

1. 2007—Ford was on the ropes when the new CEO arrived—the man who earlier spearheaded saving Boeing. In the heady atmosphere of a bull market, Ford seemed to have a shot at recapturing its $30 high. I saw a false downside breakout coupled with a bullish divergence and bought. I then grimly held through the bear market.
2. 2011—Ford spiked above its monthly channel, which was narrower at that time, tracing a kangaroo tail, while monthly MACD weakened. I took profits.
3. 2011—As monthly prices stabilized in their value zone, I repurchased my position.

Fundamental analysis can help you find a stock that may be worth buying. Use technical analysis to time your entries and exits. Be prepared to buy and sell more than once during a major uptrend.

■ Swing Trading

While major trends and trading ranges can last for years, all are punctuated by short-term upswings and downswings. Those moves create multiple trading opportunities, which we can exploit. Many charting examples in this book feature swing trades.

I especially recommend swing trading for beginning and intermediate traders. The more trades you make, the more you learn, provided you manage risk and keep good records. Swing trading teaches you faster than long-term investing, whose lessons take years to complete. Swing trading gives you time to think, unlike day-trading, which demands instant reactions. Day-trading is too fast for beginners.

Short-term swings can be substantial enough to generate meaningful profits, without the gut-wrenching drawdowns of position trades. Swing trades don't require watching the screen all day. In SpikeTrade.com, where hundreds of traders compete, most trades last a few days. Some members carry their trades for weeks and even months, while others hop in and out within hours—but the holding period for most members is measured in days. Swing trading hits the sweet spot among time horizons.

I piggyback one or more of the Spiketrade group's picks almost every week. The chart of HES in Figure 34.3 comes from my diary of one of those trades.

My profit in the HES trade was $1.92 per share. You can calibrate the amount of risk you accept and the size of potential profit by deciding how many shares to trade.

One of the best learning techniques involves returning to your closed-out trades two months later and replotting their charts. Trading signals that looked foggy when you saw them at the right edge of the screen become clear when you see them in the middle of your chart. Now, with the passage of time, you can easily see what worked and what mistakes you may have made. Creating these follow-up charts teaches you what to repeat and what to avoid in the future. Updating the charts of closed trades turns you into your own instructor.

FIGURE 34.3 HES Daily, 26- and 13-Day EMA with 4% Envelope, MACD Lines and MACD-Histogram (12-26-9), the Impulse System, and 2-Day Force Index. *(Chart by StockCharts.com)*

A Swing Trade

Professional traders are just as comfortable selling short as buying. The signals are similar but the action quicker—stocks fall twice as fast as they rise.

This chart shows where I shorted the stock of Hess Corporation (HES) as it was tracing a short-term double top, with bearish divergences in all indicators. I covered and took profits, as prices appeared to stall just below the value zone between the two EMAs, while the indicators became oversold.

The chart and text in Figure 34.4 come from SpikeTrade.com. Each week the Spiker who won that week's competition posts a diary of his trade. Different people use different indicators and parameters.

Peter's trade gained almost 11% in three days. Of course, we can't allow ourselves to get intoxicated by such numbers. A beginner looks at them, multiplies them by the number of weeks in a year, and goes crazy throwing his money at the markets. Such spectacular gains are inevitably interspersed with losses. A professional trader carefully manages his money, quickly cuts losing trades and protects his capital to allow his equity to grow.

If investing is like hunting the big game, swing trading is like rabbit hunting. If your livelihood depends on hunting, shooting rabbits is a much more reliable way of

FIGURE 34.4 TRQ Daily, 22- and 12-Day EMA with 11% Envelope, MACD Lines and MACD-Histogram (12-26-9), and 20-Day RSI. *(Chart by StockCharts.com)*

A Swing Trade near the Bottom

This trade was submitted by Peter D., a long-term Spiker from the Netherlands. His post was headlined "Fishing near the Lows."

"Weekly conditions: Indicators don't show much movement. MACD very shallow but positive and RSI slowly improving. Daily: MACD was about to confirm a positive divergence, and so was RSI. Prices dove last week but stopped near support.

"I set the initial entry at $3.02, in line with recent lows. It was hit on Monday morning, which turned out to be one cent above the low for the day and the week. Price closed near the high of the day and continued surging on Tuesday and Wednesday. My target was hit on Wednesday, on the way up. The rest of the day saw some pulling back, but price kept in range to close the week on a relatively high note."

putting meals on the table. Carefully entering and exiting swing trades, while cautiously managing money, is a realistic way of surviving and prospering in the markets.

■ Day-Trading

Day-trading means entering and exiting trades within a single market session. Rapid buying and selling in front of a flashing screen demands the highest levels of concentration and discipline. Paradoxically, it attracts the most impulsive and gambling-prone people.

Day-trading appears deceptively easy. Brokerage firms hide customer statistics from the public, but in 2000, state regulators in Massachusetts subpoenaed brokerage house records, which showed that after six months only 16% of day-traders made money.

Whatever gaps you may have in your knowledge or discipline, day-trading will find them fast and hit you hard in your weak spots. In swing trading, you have the luxury of being able to stop and think, but not in day-trading.

The person who is learning to trade is much better off using end-of-day charts. After you grow into a consistently profitable swing trader, you may wish to explore day-trading. You'll use your already developed skills and will only need to adjust to a faster game. A market newbie who stumbles into day-trading is a gift to the pros.

Make sure to write down your action plan for day-trading: what will prompt you to enter or exit, to hold or cut. Be prepared to invest plenty of time: day-trading chews up long hours in front of multiple screens.

Another difficulty of day-trading is that you shoot at much smaller targets. This is reflected in the height of price channels. Elsewhere in this book, you'll read that a good measure of a trader's performance is the percentage of the channel or an envelope he captures in a trade. Taking 30% or more of a channel's height earns you an A grade, while capturing 10% of that channel earns you a C. Let's apply these ratings to several stocks that are popular with day traders. The exact figures will change by the time you read this book, but today I get the following numbers for channel heights on the daily and 5-minute charts (Table 34.1).

A swing trader who uses daily charts can do very well in these active stocks. He can really clean up if he is an A level trader, but even if he is a C trader, taking only 10% out of a channel, he can stay comfortably ahead of the game while learning to trade. On the other hand, a person who day-trades the very same stocks must be a straight A trader in order to survive. Anything less and his account will be ground up by slippage, commissions, and expenses.

TABLE 34.1

	Daily Channel	"A" Trader	"C" Trader	5-Min Channel	"A" Trader	"C" Trader
AAPL	55	16.5	5.5	2.5	0.75	0.25
AMZN	27	8.1	2.7	2.2	0.66	0.22
MON	7	2.1	0.7	0.6	0.18	0.06

If, after developing a successful track record as a swing trader, you decide to day-trade, you'll be able to use most of the tools and techniques you've already learned.

When a friend who is an Olympic rowing coach taught me to row, he focused on developing the correct stroke. A competent rower always moves his oars exactly the same way, whether it's a leisurely weekend row or the final stretch of a race. What changes are power and speed. The same with day-trading: the technique is the same, but the speed is different. If you learn to swing trade, you can apply your technique to day-trading. And then you can go in reverse, and apply day-trading techniques to swing-trade entries and exits.

Day-trading can be a profitable pursuit, but keep in mind that it's a highly demanding professional game and most definitely not a casual activity for beginners.

For more information regarding Dr. Alexander Elder's work, please visit www.elder.com.

CHAPTER 35

The New High–New Low Index

From Dr. Alexander Elder, *The New Trading for a Living* (Hoboken, New Jersey: John Wiley & Sons, 2014), Part 6, Chapter 34.

Stocks that reach their highest level in a year on any given day are the leaders in strength. Stocks that fall to their lowest point for that year on the same day are the leaders in weakness. The New High–New Low Index (NH-NL) tracks the behavior of market leaders by subtracting the number of New Lows from the New Highs. In my experience, NH-NL is the best leading indicator of the stock market.[1]

■ How to Construct NH-NL

The New High–New Low Index is easy to calculate, using information that appears in many online sources and in major newspapers.

$$NH\text{-}NL = \text{New Highs} - \text{New Lows}$$

Most data services in the United States report the daily numbers of New Highs and New Lows, but it is shocking how loosely they define their data. Some are too narrow and track only the NYSE stocks, ignoring other exchanges. Others are too broad and track everything, including interest rate ETFs. My favorite source of reliable data is www.barchart.com. I take their data, subtract New Lows from New Highs, and plot the result underneath the daily chart of the S&P 500.

The task of constructing NH-NL is harder for traders outside the United States, in countries where such data isn't reported. There you'll need to do a bit of programming. First, run a daily scan of the database of all stocks in your country to find those that have reached the highest high and the lowest low for the year during the day. Once you have those two lists, take the above formula and apply it to the numbers you found.

---

[1] In 2012, I wrote an e-book with Kerry Lovvorn on the New High–New Low Index. We publish nightly updates on its signals on SpikeTrade.com.

On the days when there are more new highs than new lows, NH-NL is positive and plotted above the centerline. On the days when there are more new lows than new highs, NH-NL is negative and plotted below the centerline. If the numbers of new highs and new lows are equal, NH-NL is zero. We normally plot the New High–New Low Index as a line, with a horizontal reference line at a zero level.

While I plot NH-NL underneath the S&P 500, keep in mind that it has a much broader reach than the S&P—NH-NL includes data from the NYSE, AMEX, and NASDAQ, excluding only ETFs, unit investment trusts, closed-end funds, warrant stocks, and preferred securities. The chart of the S&P 500 is there simply for a comparison.

■ Crowd Psychology

A stock appears on the list of new highs when it's the strongest it's been in a year. It means that a herd of eager bulls is chasing its shares. A stock appears on the list of new lows when it's the weakest it's been in a year, showing that a crowd of aggressive bears is selling its shares.

The New High–New Low Index compares the numbers of the strongest and the weakest stocks on the exchange. It reveals the balance of power between the leaders in strength and the leaders in weakness.

You can visualize all stocks on the New York Stock Exchange, the NASDAQ, or any other exchange as soldiers in a regiment. The new highs and new lows are their officers. The new highs are the officers who lead an attack uphill. The new lows are the officers who are deserting and running downhill.

The quality of leadership is a key factor in any conflict. When I was in officer training, they kept telling us that there are no bad soldiers, only bad officers. The New High–New Low Index shows whether more officers are leading an attack uphill or deserting downhill. Where the officers lead, soldiers follow. The broad indexes, such as the S&P 500, tend to follow the trend of NH-NL (Figure 35.1).

When NH-NL rises above its centerline, it shows that the bullish leadership is dominant. When NH-NL falls below its centerline, it shows that bearish leadership is in charge. If the market rallies to a new high and NH-NL climbs to a new peak, it shows that bullish leadership is growing and the uptrend is likely to continue. If the market rallies but NH-NL shrinks, it shows that the leadership is becoming weak and the uptrend is in danger. A regiment whose officers are starting to desert is likely to retreat.

A new low in NH-NL shows that the downtrend is well led and likely to persist. If officers are running faster than the men, the regiment is likely to be routed. If stocks fall but NH-NL turns up, it shows that officers are no longer running. When officers regain their morale, the whole regiment is likely to rally.

■ Trading Rules for NH-NL

Traders need to pay attention to three aspects of NH-NL: the level of NH-NL above or below its centerline, the trend of NH-NL, and divergences between the patterns of NH-NL and prices.

FIGURE 35.1   S&P 500 Daily, 26- and 13-Day EMAs, Autoenvelope, NH-NL Daily.
(Chart by TradeStation)

NH-NL—Daily Chart, Yearly Look-Back

This chart tracks daily NH-NL during a mostly bullish year in the stock market. Still, every bullish trend gets interrupted by pullbacks. Bearish deterioration patterns of NH-NL, marked here by diagonal red arrows, warn you of coming declines. These signals emerge because officers start shifting towards the rear before the soldiers retreat.

Declines end and rallies begin when NH-NL rallies from negative into positive territory, marked here by purple circles. Those signals work especially well when the S&P is oversold, i.e., near its lower channel line. As always, trading messages are especially strong when independent signals confirm each other.

NH-NL Zero Line

The position of NH-NL in relation to its centerline shows whether bulls or bears are in control. When NH-NL is above its centerline, it shows that more market leaders are bullish than bearish and it is better to trade from the long side. When NH-NL is below its centerline, it shows that bearish leadership is stronger, and it's better to trade from the short side. NH-NL can stay above its centerline for months at a time in bull markets and below its centerline for months in bear markets.

If NH-NL stays negative for several months but then rallies above its centerline, it signals that a bull move is likely to begin. It is time to look for buying opportunities, using oscillators for precise timing. If NH-NL stays positive for several months but then falls below its centerline, it shows that a bear move is likely to begin. It is time to look for shorting opportunities using oscillators for precise timing.

NH-NL Trends

When the market rallies and NH-NL rises, it confirms uptrends. When NH-NL declines together with the market, it confirms downtrends.

1. A rise in NH-NL shows that it's safe to hold long positions and add to them. If NH-NL declines while the broad market stays flat or rallies, it is time to take profits on long trades. When NH-NL falls below zero, it shows that bearish

leadership is strong and it's safe to hold short positions and even add to them. If the market continues to fall but NH-NL rises, it shows that the downtrend is not well led—it's time to cover shorts.

2. If NH-NL rises on a flat day, it flashes a bullish message and gives a buy signal. It shows that officers are going over the top while the soldiers are still crouching in their foxholes. When NH-NL falls on a flat day, it gives a signal to sell short. It shows that officers are deserting while the troops are still holding their positions. Soldiers aren't stupid—if their officers start running away, they will not stay and fight.

NH-NL Divergences

If the latest market peak is confirmed by a new high of NH-NL, that rally is likely to continue, even if punctuated by a decline. When a new market low is accompanied by a new low in NH-NL, it shows that bears are well led and the downtrend is likely to persist. On the other hand, divergences between the patterns of NH-NL and broad market indexes show that leaders are deserting and the trends are likely to reverse.

1. If NH-NL traces a lower peak while the market rallies to a new high, it creates a bearish divergence. It shows that bullish leadership is weakening even though the broad market is higher. Bearish divergences often mark the ends of uptrends, but pay attention to the height of the second peak. If it is only slightly above zero, in the low hundreds, then a big reversal is probably at hand and it's time to go short. If, on other hand, the latest peak is in the high hundreds, it shows that the upside leadership is strong enough to prevent the market from collapsing.

2. If the market declines to a new low, but NH-NL traces a shallower bottom than its previous decline, it creates a bullish divergence. It shows that bearish leadership is shrinking. If the latest low of NH-NL is shallow, in the low hundreds, it shows that the bearish leadership is exhausted and a major upside reversal is near. If the latest low sinks deep, then bears still have some strength, and the downtrend may pause but not reverse. Keep in mind that bullish divergences at stock market bottoms tend to develop faster than bearish divergences at market tops: buy fast and sell slowly.

▣ NH-NL in Multiple Timeframes and Look-Back Periods

Markets move simultaneously in different timeframes. My original work on the NH-NL focused on the daily charts with a one-year look-back period—counting stocks that have reached a new high or a new low for their latest 52-week range. I have since added several dimensions for a deeper understanding of this key indicator.

Weekly NH-NL

The weekly NH-NL helps confirm major stock market trends and identify major reversals. I build it from the daily data of barchart.com, mentioned above, by running a five-day moving total. I plot the result underneath a weekly chart of the S&P 500.

The weekly NH-NL gives its most important signals when it reaches extreme levels and also by divergences. To understand its logic, keep in mind how the weekly NH-NL is constructed. For example, if the weekly NH-NL rises to a +1,500 level, it means that in each of the past five trading days there were on average 300 more New Highs than New Lows. It takes a period of sustainable bullishness or bearishness to push the weekly NH-NL to an extreme.

These are the most important signals of weekly NH-NL:

■ When it drops below minus 4,000 and then rallies above that level, it delivers major buy signals.

■ When the weekly NH-NL rises above plus 2,500, it confirms bull markets.

■ When the tops or bottoms of weekly NH-NL diverge from price patterns, they signal important reversals.

A drop below −4,000 reflects an unsustainable market panic. To fall that low, the market has to deliver an average of 800 more daily New Lows than New Highs for five days in a row. Such massive panic is not going to last. When the weekly NH-NL rises above −4,000, it flashes a buy signal I call a Spike. It's so powerful and effective in both bull and bear markets that I named our SpikeTrade group after it. This signal misfired only once in several decades, as you'll see on the chart in Figure 35.2.

FIGURE 35.2 S&P 500 Weekly, 26-Week EMA, NH-NL Weekly. Green Line at +2,500, Purple Line at −4,000. *(Chart by TradeStation)*

NH-NL—Weekly Chart

When the weekly NH-NL falls below −4,000 and then rises above that level, it nails important bottoms, marked here with vertical green arrows. This chart covers 11 years—the signal works in bull and bear markets. There was only one exception—in October and November 2008, during the worst bear market of a century (marked by a purple oval). Let this serve as a reminder that no market signal works 100% of the time, making risk management essential for survival and success.

Red diagonal arrows mark major bearish divergences. Weekly NH-NL touching the +2,500 level confirms bull markets and calls for higher prices ahead, even if interrupted by a correction.

When the weekly NH-NL rises to the +2,500 level, it confirms bull markets. This indicator never rises this high during bear market rallies. When you see it above that level, you know you're in a bull market, with higher prices likely ahead.

The 65-Day and 20-Day NH-NL

One of the great innovations in the New High–New Low analysis in recent years was the addition of two new look-back windows: a 20-day and a 65-day. While the regular daily NH-NL compares each day's high and low to the high-low range for the preceding year, a 20-day NH-NL compares it only to the preceding month and a 65-day NH-NL to the preceding quarter. These shorter-term views of the NH-NL are useful for short-term timing.

These two new time windows deliver more sensitive signals than the standard year-long NH-NL. The logic is simple: before a stock reaches a new high for the year, it must first make a new high for the month and then for the quarter. If a stock has been in a downtrend, it may take a long time to recover and reach a new yearly high, but it can reach monthly and quarterly highs much sooner.

In addition to the usual signals, such as trends and divergences, a very sharp short-term buy signal occurs when the 20-day NH-NL drops below minus 500 and then rallies above that level. It shows that the market has touched and rejected a short-term bearish extreme, and afterwards it usually launches a short-term rally. We call this a "Spike bounce" signal.

Tracking market leaders with the help of NH-NL helps improve timing. There are two ways to utilize the New High–New Low signals. First, since individual stocks largely depend on broad market trends, we can use NH-NL signals to decide when to buy or sell our stocks. Furthermore, we can use NH-NL signals to trade vehicles that track the broad market, such as the S&P e-mini futures.

CHAPTER 36

Stocks above 50-Day MA

From Dr. Alexander Elder, *The New Trading for a Living* (Hoboken, New Jersey: John Wiley & Sons, 2014), Part 6, Chapter 35.

This broad stock market indicator is based on the key concepts regarding prices and moving averages (Figure 36.1). Each price represents a momentary consensus of value among market participants, while a moving average represents an average consensus of value during its time window. This means that when a stock trades above its MA, the current consensus of value is above average—bullish. When a stock trades below its MA, the current consensus of value is below average—bearish.

When the market is trending higher, the percentage of stocks above their moving averages keeps growing. In a broad downtrend, the number of stocks above their MAs keeps shrinking.

This indicator tracks all stocks traded on the New York Stock Exchange, American Exchange, and NASDAQ and calculates how many of them trade above their moving averages. It plots that percentage as a line that fluctuates between 0% and 100%. We can use the pattern of this line to confirm market trends and anticipate reversals.

The indicator for tracking the number of stocks above their 50-day MAs is included in many software packages. I like to view it on a weekly chart, where it helps catch intermediate reversals—market turns that augur in trends that last anywhere from several weeks to several months. You don't need to look at this indicator daily, but it can be an important part of weekend homework.

In theory, the highest possible reading of this indicator would be 100%, if all stocks rallied above their MAs. Its lowest possible reading of 0% would occur if all stocks were to fall below their MAs. In practice, only exceptional market moves swing it near the 90% or 10% extremes. Normally, this indicator tends to top out near 75% and bottom out near 25%. I draw two reference lines on its chart at 75% and 25% and start looking for the market turn as this indicator approaches those levels.

FIGURE 36.1   S&P 500 Weekly and 26-Week MA; Stocks above 50 MA with Reference Lines at 75% and 25%. *(Chart by TradeStation)*

Stocks above 50-Day MA

When the "stocks above their 50-day MA" indicator reaches an extreme—above 75% or below 25% and then moves away from that level, it shows that the intermediate-term trend has reached a likely turning point. A reversal of this indicator flashes a signal for the entire market: buy when it turns up and sell when it turns down. In the latter part of 2013, as the market started going up with almost no pullbacks, buy signals from upside reversals began to occur at levels higher than 25%. These signals don't mark every reversal—no indicator does—but when it flashes its signal, we had better pay attention.

The percentage of stocks above their 50-day MA gives its trading signals not by reaching any certain levels but rather by reversing near those levels. It signals the completion of a top by rising to or above the upper reference line and then sinking below that line. It signals that a bottom has been formed when it falls below or even near the lower reference line and then turns up.

Notice that the tops of this indicator tend to be broad, while its bottoms are sharper. Tops are formed by greed, which is a happier, longer-lasting emotion. Bottoms are formed by fear—a more intense and shorter-lived emotion.

While some of this indicator's signals are right on time in catching reversals, others mark only temporary pauses in major trends. Let this serve as a reminder never to rely on a single indicator for trading decisions. Use multiple tools: when they confirm each other's signals, they reinforce one another.

CHAPTER 37

Other Stock Market Indicators

From Dr. Alexander Elder, *The New Trading for a Living* (Hoboken, New Jersey: John Wiley & Sons, 2014), Part 6, Chapter 36.

Only a handful of general market indicators have stood the harsh test of time. Many that used to be popular in previous decades have been swept away by the flood of new trading vehicles. The New High–New Low Index and Stocks Above 50-day MA, reviewed above, continue to work because of their clear logic. Several other indicators are listed below. Whatever tools you choose, be sure to understand how they work and what exactly they measure. Select a few and track them on a regular basis, until you come to trust their signals.

609

■ Advance/Decline

The Advance/Decline line (the A/D line) tracks the degree of mass participation in rallies and declines. Each day it adds up the number of stocks that closed higher and subtracts the number of stocks that closed lower.

While the Dow Jones Industrials track the behavior of the generals and the New High–New Low Index focuses on the officers, the A/D line shows whether soldiers are following their leaders. A rally is more likely to persist when the A/D line rises to a new high, while a decline is likely to deepen if A/D falls to a new low in step with the Dow.

The A/D line is based on the day's closing prices for each stock at any exchange: take the number of advancing stocks, subtract the number of declining stocks, and ignore unchanged stocks. The result will be positive or negative, depending on whether more stocks advanced or declined during the day. For example, if 4,000 stocks were traded, 2,600 advanced, 900 declined, and 500 were unchanged, then Advance/Decline equals +1,700 (2,600–900). Add each day's Advance/Decline figures to the previous day's total to create a cumulative A/D line (Figure 37.1).

FIGURE 37.1   S&P 500 Daily and the Advance/Decline Line. (Chart by StockCharts.com)

Advance/Decline Line

The turns of this indicator usually coincide with price turns, but occasionally precede them. This ability to give early warnings makes A/D line worth following. In area A, prices are scratching the bottom and make a new low, while the uptrend of the A/D line calls for a rally. In area B, the opposite occurs—prices press higher, while a downturn of the A/D line calls for a decline. In area C, prices continue to decline, while the A/D line turns up and calls for a rally. Those warnings don't occur at every turning point.

Traders should watch for new peaks and valleys in the A/D line rather than its absolute levels, which depend on its starting date. If a new high in the stock market is accompanied by a new high of the A/D line, it shows that the rally has broad support and is likely to continue. Broadly based rallies and declines have greater staying power. If the stock market reaches a new peak, but the A/D line reaches a lower peak than during the previous rally, it shows that fewer stocks are participating, and the rally may be near its end. When the market falls to a new low but the A/D line traces a shallower bottom than during the previous decline, it shows that the decline is narrowing down and the bear move is nearing an end. These signals tend to precede reversals by weeks if not months.

The **Most Active Stocks indicator** (MAS) is an Advance/Decline line of the 15 most active stocks on the New York Stock Exchange. It used to be listed daily in many newspapers. Stocks appeared on this list when they caught the public's eye. MAS was a big money indicator—it showed whether big money was bullish or bearish. When the trend of MAS diverged from the price trends, the market was especially likely to reverse.

Hardly anyone today uses an indicator called **TRIN**, which was important enough to have its own chapter in the original *Trading for a Living*. Very few people track another formerly popular indicator called **TICK**. Old stock market books are full of fascinating indicators, but you have to be very careful using them today. Changes in the market over the years have killed many indicators.

Indicators based on the volume of **low-priced stocks** lost their usefulness when the average volume of the U.S. stock market soared and the Dow rose tenfold. The **Member Short Sale Ratio** and the **Specialist Short Sale Ratio** stopped working after options became popular. Member and specialist short sales are now tied up in the intermarket arbitrage. **Odd-lot** statistics lost value when conservative odd-lotters bought mutual funds. The **Odd-lot Short Sale Ratio** stopped working when gamblers discovered puts.

CHAPTER 38

Consensus and Commitment Indicators

From Dr. Alexander Elder, *The New Trading for a Living* (Hoboken, New Jersey: John Wiley & Sons, 2014), Part 6, Chapter 37.

Most private traders keep their opinions to themselves, but financial journalists, letter writers, and bloggers spew them forth like open hydrants. Some writers may be very bright, but the financial press as a whole has a poor record of market timing.

Financial journalists and letter writers tend to overstay trends and miss turning points. When these groups become intensely bullish or bearish, it pays to trade against them.

It's "monkey see, monkey do" in the publishing business, where a journalist's or an advisor's job may be endangered by expressing an opinion that differs too sharply from his group. Standing alone feels scary, and most of us like to huddle. When financial journalists and letter writers reach a high degree of bullish or bearish consensus, it's a sign that the trend has been going on for so long that a reversal is near.

Consensus indicators, also called contrary opinion indicators, are not suitable for precision timing, but they draw attention to the fact that a trend is near its exhaustion level. When you see that message, switch to technical indicators for more precise timing of a trend reversal.

A trend can continue as long as bulls and bears remain in conflict. A high degree of consensus precedes reversals. When the crowd becomes highly bullish, get ready to sell, and when it becomes strongly bearish, get ready to buy. This is the contrary opinion theory, whose foundations were laid by Charles Mackay, a Scottish barrister. His classic book, *Extraordinary Popular Delusions and the Madness of Crowds* (1841) describes the infamous Dutch Tulip Mania and the South Seas Bubble in England. Humphrey B. Neill in the United States applied the theory of contrary opinion to stocks and other financial markets. In his book, *The Art of Contrary Thinking*, he made it clear why the majority must be wrong at the market's turning points: prices are established by crowds, and by the time the majority turns bullish, there aren't enough new buyers to support a bull market.

Abraham W. Cohen, an old New York lawyer whom I met in the early 1980s, came up with the idea of polling market advisors and using their responses as a proxy for the entire body of traders. Cohen was a skeptic who spent many years on Wall Street and saw that advisors as a group performed no better than the market crowd. In 1963, he established a service called *Investors Intelligence* for tracking letter writers. When the majority of them became bearish, Cohen identified a buying opportunity. Selling opportunities were marked by strong bullishness among letter writers. Another writer, James H. Sibbet, applied this theory to commodities, setting up an advisory service called Market Vane.

■ Tracking Advisory Opinion

Letter writers follow trends out of fear of losing subscribers by missing major moves. In addition, bullishness helps sell subscriptions, while bearish comments turn off subscribers. Even in a bear market, we rarely see more bears than bulls among advisors for more than a few weeks at a time.

The longer a trend continues, the louder the letter writers proclaim it. They are most bullish at market tops and most bearish at market bottoms. When the mass of letter writers turns strongly bullish or bearish, it's a good idea to look for trades in the opposite direction.

Some advisors are very skilled at doubletalk. The man who speaks from both sides of his mouth can claim that he was right regardless of what the market did, but editors of tracking services have plenty of experience pinning down such lizards.

When the original *Trading for a Living* came out, only two services tracked advisory opinions: *Investors Intelligence* and *Market Vane*. In recent years, there has been an explosion of interest in behavioral economics, and today many services track advisors. My favorite resource is SentimenTrader.com, whose slogan is "Make emotion work for you instead of against you." Jason Goepfert, its publisher, does a solid job of tracking mass market sentiment.

■ Signals from the Press

To understand any group of people, you must know what its members crave and what they fear. Financial journalists want to appear serious, intelligent, and informed; they are afraid of appearing ignorant or flaky. That's why it's normal for them to straddle the fence and present several sides of every issue. A journalist is safe as long as he writes something like "monetary policy is about to push the market up, unless unforeseen factors push it down."

Internal contradiction is the normal state of affairs in financial journalism.[1] Most financial editors are even more cowardly than their writers. They print contradictory articles and call this "presenting a balanced picture."

For example, an issue of a major business magazine had an article headlined "The Winds of Inflation Are Blowing a Little Harder" on page 19. Another article on page 32 of the same issue was headlined "Why the Inflation Scare Is Just That." It takes a powerful and lasting trend to lure journalists and editors down from their fences. This happens only when a tide of optimism or pessimism sweeps up the market near the end of a major trend. When journalists start expressing strongly bullish or bearish views, the trend is ripe for a reversal.

This is why the front covers of major business magazines serve as contrarian indicators. When a leading business magazine puts a bull on its cover, it's usually a good time to take profits on long positions, and when a bear graces the front cover, a bottom cannot be too far away.

■ Signals from Advertisers

A group of three or more ads touting the same "opportunity" in a major newspaper or magazine warns of an imminent top. This is because only a well-established up-trend can break through the inertia of several brokerage firms. By the time all of them recognize a trend, come up with trading recommendations, produce ads, and place them in a newspaper, that trend is very old indeed.

The ads on the commodities page of *The Wall Street Journal* appeal to the bullish appetites of the least-informed traders. Those ads almost never recommend selling; it is hard to get amateurs excited about going short. You'll never see an ad for an investment when its price is low. When three or more ads on the same day tout gold or silver, it is time to look at technical indicators for shorting signals.

A more malignant breed of promoters appeared on the scene in the past decade: thanks to the Internet, "pump and dump" operators have migrated online. The scammers touting penny stocks know that they need to wait for an uptrend to hook their victims. Whenever a higher than usual number of promo pitches starts showing up in my spam filter, the top can't be too far away (Figure 38.1).

■ Commitments of Futures Traders

Government agencies and exchanges collect data on buying and selling by various groups of traders and publish summary reports of their positions. It pays to trade with the groups that have a track record of success and against those with track records of persistent failure.

For example, the Commodity Futures Trading Commission (CFTC) reports long and short positions of hedgers and big speculators. Hedgers—the commercial producers

---

[1] And not only journalism: in 2013 three academicians shared a Nobel Prize in economics. The work of one of them showed that the market was efficient and couldn't be timed; the work of another showed that the market was irrational and could be timed. Take your pick and wait for next year's prize.

FIGURE 38.1   Monthly Total Dollar Value of OTC Stocks. *(Courtesy SentimenTrader.com)*

Money pours into penny stocks when the market is up and dries up when it is down. This is reflected in the monthly reports of penny stock volume at the NASDAQ. After markets have hit new highs and the news is good, volume often spikes up for these "lottery ticket" stocks. When the stock market hits the skids, their volume dries up.

and consumers of commodities—are the most successful market participants. The Securities and Exchange Commission (SEC) reports purchases and sales by corporate insiders. Officers of publicly traded companies know when to buy or sell their shares.

Positions of large futures traders, including hedge funds, are reported to the CFTC when their sizes reach the so-called **reporting levels**. At the time of this writing, if you are long or short 250 contracts of corn or 200 contracts of gold, the CFTC classifies you as a big speculator. Brokers report those positions to the CFTC, which compiles the data and releases summaries on Fridays.

The CFTC also sets up the maximum number of contracts a speculator is allowed to hold in any given market— these are called **position limits**. Those limits are set to prevent very large speculators from accumulating positions that are big enough to bully the markets.

The CFTC divides all market participants into three groups: commercials, large speculators, and small speculators. **Commercials**, also known as **hedgers**, are firms or individuals who deal in actual commodities in the normal course of their business. In theory, they trade futures to hedge business risks. For example, a bank trades interest rate futures to hedge its loan portfolio, while a food processing

THEORY AND ANALYSIS

company trades wheat futures to offset the risks of buying grain. Hedgers post smaller margins and are exempt from speculative position limits.

Large speculators are those whose positions have reached reporting levels. The CFTC reports buying and selling by commercials and large speculators. To find the positions of **small traders**, you need to take the open interest and subtract from it the holdings of the first two groups.

The divisions between hedgers, big speculators, and small speculators are somewhat artificial. Smart small traders grow into big traders, dumb big traders become small traders, and many hedgers speculate. Some market participants play games that distort the CFTC reports. For example, an acquaintance who owns a brokerage firm sometimes registers his wealthy speculator clients as hedgers, claiming they trade stock index and bond futures to hedge their stock and bond portfolios.

The commercials can legally speculate in the futures markets using inside information. Some of them are big enough to play futures markets against cash markets. For example, an oil firm may buy crude oil futures, divert several tankers, and hold them offshore in order to tighten supplies and push up futures prices. They can take profits on long positions, go short, and then deliver several tankers at once to refiners in order to push crude futures down a bit and cover shorts. Such manipulation is illegal, and most firms hotly deny that it takes place.

As a group, commercials have the best track record in the futures markets. They have inside information and are well-capitalized. It pays to follow them because they are successful in the long run. Big speculators used to be successful wealthy individuals who took careful risks with their own money. That has changed, and today most big traders are commodity funds. These trend-following behemoths do poorly as a group. The masses of small traders are the proverbial "wrong-way Corrigans" of the markets.

It is not enough to know whether a certain group is short or long. Commercials often short futures because many of them own physical commodities. Small traders are usually long, reflecting their perennial optimism. To draw valid conclusions from the CFTC reports, you need to compare current positions to their historical norms.

■ Legal Insider Trading

Officers and investors who hold more than 5 percent of the shares in a publicly traded company must report their buying and selling to the Securities and Exchange Commission. The SEC tabulates insider purchases and sales, and releases this data to the public.

Corporate insiders have a long record of buying stocks when they're cheap and selling them high. Insider buying emerges after severe market drops, and insider selling accelerates when the market rallies and becomes overpriced.

Buying or selling by a single insider matters little: an executive may sell shares to meet major personal expenses or he may buy them to exercise stock options. Analysts who researched legal insider trading found that insider buying or selling was meaningful only if more than three executives or large stockholders bought or

Apple Incorporated	$ 534.97	Green Mountain Coffee Roasters	$ 119.74
AAPL	-1.00	GMCR	0.34
Daily Short Sale Volume	view	Daily Short Sale Volume	view
Short Interest (Shares Short)	16,538,900	Short Interest (Shares Short)	32,931,300
Days To Cover (Short Interest Ratio)	0.9	Days To Cover (Short Interest Ratio)	15.1
Short Percent of Float	1.86 %	Short Percent of Float	25.76 %

FIGURE 38.2 AAPL and GMCR Shorting Data. *(Source: Shortsqueeze.com)*

Short Interest and Days to Cover

Compare short interest data for two popular stocks on the day I'm editing this chapter. "Short Percent of Float" is 1.86% for Apple, Inc. (AAPL), but nearly 26% for Green Mountain Coffee Roasters, Inc. (GMCR). "Days to Cover" are 0.9 for AAPL but over 15 for GMCR. These numbers reflect much more aggressive shorting of GMCR. Not to forget, each and every one of those shorts at some point will need to buy in order to cover his short position.

Perhaps savvy shorts know something very bad about GMCR, but what if its stock rallies even a little? Many bears will run for cover, and as they scramble to cover shorts, the stock may soar. Whatever its long-term prospects, it could be sent flying in the near term.

sold within a month. These actions reveal that something very positive or negative is about to happen. A stock is likely to rise if three insiders buy in one month and to fall if three insiders sell within a month.

Clusters of insider buying tend to have a better predictive value than clusters of selling. That's because insiders are willing to sell a stock for many reasons (diversification, buying a second home, sending a kid to college) but they are willing to buy for one main reason—they expect their company's stock to go up.

■ Short Interest

While the numbers of futures and options contracts held long and short is equal by definition, in the stock market there is always a huge disparity between the two camps. Most people, including professional fund managers, buy stocks, but very few sell them short.

Among the data reported by exchanges is the number of shares being held short for any stock. Since the absolute numbers vary a great deal, it pays to put them into a perspective by comparing the number of shares held short to that stock's float (the total number of publicly owned shares available for trading). This number, **"Short Percent of Float,"** tends to run about one or two percent. Another useful way to look at short interest is by comparing it to the average daily volume. By doing this, we ask a hypothetical question: if all shorts decided to cover, while all other buyers stood aside and daily volume remained unchanged, how many days would it take for them to cover and bring short interest down to zero? This **"Days to Cover"** number normally oscillates between one and two days.

When planning to buy or short a stock, it pays to check its Short Percent of Float and Days to Cover. If those are high, they show that the bearish side is overcrowded. A rally may scare those bears into panicky covering, and send the stock sharply higher. That would be good for bulls but bad for bears.

Fear is a stronger emotion than greed. Bulls may look for bargains but try not to overpay, while squeezed bears, facing unlimited losses, will pay any price to cover. That's why short-covering rallies tend to be especially sharp.

Whenever you look for a stock to buy, check its Short Percent of Float and Days to Cover. The usual, normal readings don't provide any great information, but the deviations from the norm often deliver useful insights (Figure 38.2).

High shorting numbers mark any stock as a dangerous short. By extension, if your indicators suggest buying a stock, its high short interest becomes an additional positive factor—there is more fuel for a rally. It makes sense for swing traders to include the data on shorting when selecting which of several stocks to buy or sell short. I always review these numbers when working up a potential trade.

CHAPTER 39

The Scientific Method and Technical Analysis

From David Aronson, *Evidence-Based Technical Analysis: Applying the Scientific Method and Statistical Inference to Trading Signals* (Hoboken, New Jersey: John Wiley & Sons, 2006), Chapter 3.

621

TA's central problem is erroneous knowledge. As it is traditionally practiced, much of TA is a body of dogma and myth, founded on faith and anecdote. This is a consequence of the informal, intuitive methods used by its practitioners to discover patterns with predictive power. As a discipline, TA suffers because it is practiced without discipline.

Adopting a rigorous scientific approach would solve this problem. The scientific method is not a cookbook procedure that automates knowledge discovery. Rather it is "a set of methods designed to describe and interpret observed or inferred phenomena, past or present aimed at building a testable body of knowledge open to rejection or confirmation. In other words, (it) is a specific way of analyzing information with the goal of testing claims."[1] This chapter summarizes its logical and philosophical foundations and discusses the implications of its adoption by TA practitioners.

■ The Most Important Knowledge of All: A Method to Get More

"Of all the kinds of knowledge that the West has given to the world, the most valuable is the scientific method, a set of procedures for acquiring new knowledge. It was invented by a series of European thinkers from about 1550 to 1700."[2] Compared to informal approaches it is unsurpassed in its ability to separate fact from falsehood. The dramatic increase in our understanding of and control over the natural world over the last 400 years attests to the power of the scientific method.

The method's rigor protects us from the frailties of mind, which often impair what we learn from experience using less formal methods. Although informal knowledge acquisition works well for many of the obvious truths of daily living, sometimes what seems obvious is not true. It was obvious to the ancients that the sun revolved around the earth. It took science to show this was false. Informal observation and intuitive inference are especially prone to failure when phenomena are complex or highly random. Financial market behavior displays both.

Historically, TA has not been practiced in a scientific manner, but this is now changing. In academia and the business world, a new breed of practitioners, known as quants, have been adopting a scientific approach. Indeed, some of the most successful hedge funds are using strategies that could be called scientific TA.

Unsurprisingly, many traditional TA practitioners have resisted this change. Vested interests and habitual ways of thinking are hard to abandon. No doubt there was opposition when folk medicine evolved into modern medicine, when alchemy progressed into chemistry, and when astrology advanced into the science of astronomy. Rancor between traditional and scientific practitioners is to be expected. However, if history is any guide, traditional TA will, in the end, be marginalized. Astrologers, alchemists, and witch doctors still practice, but they are no longer taken seriously.

■ The Legacy of Greek Science: A Mixed Blessing

The Greeks were the first to make an effort at being scientific, though their legacy proved to be a mixed blessing. On the positive side of the ledger was the invention of logic by Aristotle. The formal reasoning procedures he developed remain a pillar of today's scientific method.

On the negative side were his faulty theories of matter and motion. Instead of being generalized from prior observations and tested against freshly observed facts, as is the practice in modern science, his theories were deduced from metaphysical principles. When observations conflicted with theory, Aristotle and his disciples were prone to bending the facts rather than altering or abandoning the theory. Modern science does the opposite.

Aristotle ultimately realized that deductive logic was insufficient for learning about the world. He saw the need for an empirical approach based on inductive logic—observation followed by generalization. Its invention was his most significant contribution to science. However, he failed in the application of his own invention. At his institution of higher learning, the famed Lyceum in Athens, Aristotle and his students made meticulous observations on a wide range of natural phenomena. Unfortunately, the inferences they drew from these facts were biased by Aristotelian dogma and often based on inadequate evidence.[3] There was too much theorizing from too little evidence. When facts contradicted favored first principles, Aristotle would contort the facts to conserve the principle.

Ultimately the Aristotelian legacy would prove to be an obstruction to scientific progress. Because his authority was so great, his flawed theories were transmitted as unquestioned dogma through the next 2,000 years. This hindered the growth of scientific knowledge, or at least the sort of knowledge that we now characterize as scientific.[4] In a like manner, the teachings of TA's pioneers like Dow, Schabacker, Elliott, and Gann have been passed along unquestioned and untested. Just as there is no room for dogma in science, neither should there be in TA.

■ The Birth of the Scientific Revolution

"Science was the major discovery, or invention, of the seventeenth century. Men of that time learned—and it was a very revolutionary discovery—how to measure, explain, and manipulate natural phenomena in a way that we call scientific. Since the seventeenth century, science has progressed a great deal and has discovered many truths, and it has conferred many benefits that the seventeenth century did not know, but it has not found a new way to discover natural truths. For this reason, the seventeenth century is possibly the most important century in human history."[5]

The revolution began in Western Europe around 1500 in an atmosphere of intellectual stagnation. At that time, all knowledge was based on authoritarian pronouncements rather than observed facts. The doctrines of the Roman Church and the dogma of Greek science were taken as literal truths. On Earth, objects were assumed to be governed by Aristotelian physics. In the heavens, the laws invented by the Greek astronomer Ptolemy and later endorsed by the Church were thought to rule. The Ptolemaic system held that the earth was the center of the universe and that the sun, stars, and planets orbited about it. To the casual observer, the facts seemed to agree with the Church's orthodox theory.

Everyone was happy until people began to notice facts that conflicted with these accepted truths. Artillerymen observed that projectiles hurled by catapults and shot from cannons did not fly in conformity with Aristotle's theory of motion (Figure 39.1). The objects were repeatedly observed to follow arced paths—a distinct departure from the

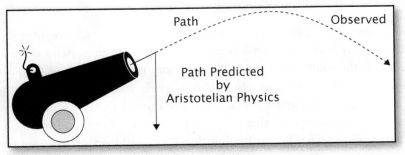

FIGURE 39.1 Prediction versus Observation.

trajectory predicted by Greek theory, which would have had them fall directly to earth as soon as they left the apparatus. Either the theory was wrong or the solders were deceived by their senses. The notion of testing the validity of a theory by comparing its predictions with subsequent observations is fundamental to the modern scientific method. This was an early step in that direction.

Also, at that time, observations of the heavens began to collide with the Church's theory of an Earth-centered universe. Increasingly accurate astronomical measurements revealed that planets did not move as the theory said they should. For a time, bewildered astronomers were able to patch up the Church's theory to make it agree with observed planetary paths. As discordant observations occurred, new assumptions were added to the theory, in the form of smaller orbits revolving about a planet's principal orbit. These ad hoc fixes, called epicycles, permitted the theory to account for the troublesome observations. For example, epicycles were able to explain why planets were sometimes seen to move backwards (retrograde motion) rather than follow a continuous path across the sky. Over time, a succession of epicycle fixes transformed the fundamentally incorrect theory of an Earth-centered universe into an unwieldy monstrosity of complexity with epicycles upon smaller epicycles upon even smaller epicycles.

A landmark in scientific history took place when the telescope of Galileo Galilei (1564–1642) showed that four moons circled the planet Jupiter. This observation contradicted Church orthodoxy that all celestial objects must revolve around the Earth. Galileo's findings would have called for the rejection of deeply held beliefs and the destruction of the Church's view of reality. Religious authorities were not about to face these facts. Though Galileo had originally been given permission by the Church to publish his findings, it subsequently withdrew the permission and found him guilty ex post facto. As punishment, he was forced to give up astronomy and live out his days under house arrest.[6]

Eventually, the Church's theory of the heavens was replaced by the far simpler and more correct Copernican model. It placed the sun at the center of the universe and managed to explain astronomical observations with far fewer assumptions. Today we know that the sun is not the center of the universe, but at the time the Copernican model represented a true increase in man's knowledge of the heavens.

■ Faith in Objective Reality and Objective Observations

Science makes a fundamental assumption about the nature of reality; there is an objective reality that exists outside and independent of those who observe it, and this reality is the source of the observer's sensory impressions. This faith is the basis of science's emphasis on observation. It is properly characterized as a faith because there is no experiment or logic that can prove the existence of an objective reality. For example, I cannot prove that my perception of a red traffic signal is caused by a light that exists outside of myself rather than by something that arose entirely within my own mind.

One might ask why we should make a big deal about a fact that seems so obvious to common sense. Everyone can see there is a world out there. However, in the eyes of science this issue is a mountain and not a molehill, and it points to an important difference between knowing scientifically and knowing intuitively. Science does not accept something as true simply because it seems to be so. The history of science has shown repeatedly that the obvious is not necessarily true. Science assumes the truth of an independent objective reality, not because it is self-evident, but because it is consistent with a principle that shapes much of the scientific enterprise—*the principle of simplicity*.

The principle says simpler is better. Thus, when judging which of several theories is most likely to be true, when all theories are equally good at fitting a set of observed facts, the principle of simplicity urges us to accept the simplest theory. This is the theory that invokes the fewest and least complicated assumptions. The principle of simplicity, also known as Ockham's Razor, tells us to cut away a theory's excess complexity. The Copernican model of the universe was preferable to the Church's model because it replaced a complex arrangement of epicycles with one orbit for each planet. In a like manner, if a segment of market history can be explained either as a random walk, which assumes very little, or as an Elliott wave pattern that assumes waves embedded within waves, golden ratios, Fibonacci sequences, and a host of other complexities, the random walk is the preferred explanation. That is, unless the Elliott Wave Principle is able to make more accurate predictions than the random-walk theory.

Assuming the existence of an external reality simplifies matters greatly. To do otherwise would require a far more complex set of assumptions to explain why two people, observing the same phenomenon, will come away with generally the same impression. Explaining why I see other cars stopping when I see the traffic signal turning red is simple if I assume that there really is a traffic light out there. However, without that assumption, many more complicated assumptions would be required to explain why other motorists stop when I do.

As a consequence of its faith in an objective reality, science holds that objective and subjective perceptions are essentially different. My objective observation of a red traffic signal and my subjective experience of being annoyed because it will make me late for work are not the same. Objective observations can be shared with and confirmed by other observers. For this reason, objective observations lend themselves to the establishment of knowledge that can be shared with and confirmed by others. Subjective thoughts, interpretations, and feelings cannot, and this flaw alone is sufficient to disqualify subjective TA as legitimate knowledge.

■ The Nature of Scientific Knowledge

Albert Einstein once said; "One thing I have learned in a long life: that all our science, measured against reality is primitive and childlike—and yet it is the most precious thing we have."[7] Scientific knowledge is different than wisdom gained by other modes of inquiry such as common sense, faith, authority, and intuition. These differences, which account for science's higher reliability, are considered in this section.

Scientific Knowledge Is Objective

Science strives for maximum objectivity by confining itself exclusively to facts about the world out there, although it is understood that perfectly objective knowledge is never attainable. This eliminates from consideration subjective assessments that are inherently private and accessible by only one person. Inner thoughts and emotive states cannot be shared accurately with others, even when that is the intent of an artist, poet, writer, or composer. In *Naked Lunch*, William Burroughs attempts to convey his personal experience of heroin. However, I will never know his experience and may take away from those passages something quite different than Burroughs's experience or that of someone else reading it. Scientific knowledge is, therefore, public in the sense that it can be shared with and verified by as many people as possible. This promotes maximum possible agreement among independent observers.

Scientific knowledge is empirical or observation based. In this way it differs from mathematical and logical propositions that are derived from and consistent with a set of axioms but need not refer to the external world or be confirmed by observation. For example, the Pythagorean Theorem tells us that the squared length of the hypotenuse of a right triangle, c, is equal to the sum of the squares of the other two sides a and b or

$$c^2 = a^2 + b^2$$

However, this truth was not derived by studying thousands of examples of right triangles and generalizing from those many observations. Rather, it is derived from a set of accepted mathematical postulates.

Scientific Knowledge Is Quantitative

The notion that the world is best understood when described in quantitative terms originated with the Greek mathematician Pythagoras [569 B.C.–approx. 475 B.C.]. It was his contention that both the world and the mind are essentially mathematical. The importance science places on quantification cannot be overemphasized. "Wherever mankind has been able to measure things, which means transform or reduce them to numbers, it has indeed made great progress in understanding them and controlling them. Where human beings have failed to find a way to measure, they have been much less successful, which partly explains the failure of psychology, economics, and literary criticism to acquire the status of science."[8]

Observations must be reduced to numbers if they are to be analyzed in a rational and rigorous fashion. Quantification makes it possible to apply the powerful tool of statistical analysis. "Most scientists would say that if you cannot describe what you are doing in mathematical terms, you are not doing science."[9] Quantification is the best way to ensure the objectivity of knowledge and to maximize its ability to be shared with and tested by all qualified practitioners.

The Purpose of Science: Explanation and Prediction

The goal of science is the discovery of rules that predict new observations and theories that explain previous observations. Predictive rules, often referred to as scientific laws, are statements about recurring process, such as 'event A tends to predict event B,' but laws don't try to explain why this happens.

Explanatory theories go further than predictive rules by telling us why it is that B tends to follow A, rather than simply telling us that it does.

Scientific laws and theories differ with respect to their generality. The most prized are the most general—that is, they predict and/or explain the widest range of phenomena. A TA rule that is effective on all markets and all time scales would have higher scientific stature than one that works only on copper futures on hourly data.

Laws also differ with respect to their predictive power. Those that depict the most consistent relationships are the most valuable. All other things being equal, a TA rule that is successful 52 percent of the time is less valuable than one that works 70 percent of the time.

The most important type of scientific law is the functional relationship. It summarizes a set of observations in the form of an equation. The equation describes how a variable that we wish to predict (dependent variable) typically denoted by the letter Y, is a function of (i.e., dependent on) one or more other variables called predictors, usually designated by the letter X. This is illustrated as

$$Y = f(X_i)$$

Typically the values of the predictors are known, but the value of the dependent variable is not. In many applications, this is because the dependent variable Y refers to a future outcome, whereas the X variables refer to values that are currently known. Once a functional relationship has been derived, it is possible to predict values for the dependent variable by plugging in known values of the predictor variables.

Functional relationships can be derived in two ways. They can be deduced from explanatory theories or they can be estimated (induced) from historical data by function fitting (e.g., regression analysis). Currently, TA is primarily constrained to the latter because theories of TA are just now being formulated

■ The Role of Logic in Science

Scientific knowledge commands respect, in part because its conclusions are based on logic. By relying on logic and empirical evidence to justify its conclusions, science avoids two of the common fallacies that contaminate informal reasoning: *appeals to authority* and *appeals to tradition*. An appeal to authority offers as proof the statement of a purportedly knowledgeable person. An appeal to tradition offers a long-standing way of doing things as proof.

To its detriment, much of popular TA is justified on grounds of tradition or authority rather than formal logic and objective evidence. In many instances, current authorities merely quote prior authorities who, in turn, quote yet earlier experts and so on back to an original source whose knowledge was primarily intuitive. Thus the fallacies of authority and tradition are mutually reinforcing.

The First Rule of Logic: Consistency

Aristotle (384–322 B.C.) is credited with the invention of formal logic, which evolved from geometry. The Egyptians had been making accurate measurements of lines and angles and calculating areas for over two thousand years, but it was the "Greeks who extended these basic notions and transformed them into a compelling system of irrefutable conclusions derived from mathematical definitions (axioms)."[10]

Formal logic is the branch of mathematics concerned with the laws of correct reasoning that are used to formulate and evaluate the validity of arguments. In contrast to informal inference, if the rules of formal logic are followed, a true conclusion is guaranteed.

The most fundamental principle of formal logic is the rule of consistency. It is expressed in two laws: the *Law of the Excluded Middle* and the *Law of Noncontradiction*. "The law of the excluded middle requires that a thing must either possess or lack a given attribute. There is no middle alternative. Or said differently, the middle ground is excluded."[11] A statement is either true or false. It cannot be both. However, the law is only properly applied to situations that are binary and is easily misapplied to situations that are not truly two-state.

"Closely related to the law of the excluded middle is the law of noncontradiction. It tells us that a thing cannot both be and not be at the same time."[12] A statement cannot be true and not true at the same time. An argument that allows for its conclusion to be true and not true at the same time is said to be a self-contradictory.

As will be shown in subsequent sections, these laws of logic are used to great effect in science. Although observed evidence, such as the profitable back test of a TA rule, cannot logically prove that the rule has predictive power, that same evidence can be used to logically disprove (contradict) the assertion that the rule is devoid of predictive power. By the Law of Noncontradiction, this indirectly proves that the rule does possess predictive power. This method of proving empirical laws, called the method of indirect proof or proof by contradiction, is the logical basis of the scientific method.

Propositions and Arguments

Logical inference takes two distinct forms: deduction and induction. We will consider each separately and then see how they are used together in the logical framework of modern science, the hypothetico-deductive method. However, before considering these forms of inference some definitions are in order.

- *Proposition:* a declarative statement that is either true or false sometimes referred to as a claim. For example, the statement *The head-and-shoulder pattern has more predictive power than a random signal* is a proposition. A proposition differs from other kinds of statements that do not possess the attribute of truth of falsity such as exclamations, commands, and questions. Therefore, only propositions may be affirmed or denied.

- *Argument:* a group of propositions, one of which is referred to as the *conclusion*, which is claimed to follow logically from the other propositions, called *premises*. Thus, an argument asserts that its premises provide the evidence to establish the truth of its conclusion.

Deductive Logic

As mentioned earlier, the there are two forms of logic, deductive and inductive. This section considers deductive logic; the next considers inductive.

Categorical Syllogisms   A deductive argument is one whose premises are claimed to provide conclusive, irrefutable evidence for the truth of its conclusion. A common form of deductive argument is the categorical syllogism. It is comprised of two premises and a conclusion. It is so named because it deals with logical relations between categories. It begins with a premise that states a general truth about a category, for example *All humans are mortal*, and ends with a conclusion that states a truth about a specific instance, for example *Socrates is mortal*.

Premise 1: *All humans are mortal.*

Premise 2: *Socrates is a human.*

Therefore: *Socrates is mortal.*

Notice that the argument's first premise establishes a relationship between two categories, humans and mortals: *All humans are mortal.* The second premise makes a statement about a particular individual member of the first category: *Socrates is a human.* This forces the conclusions that this individual must also be a member of the second category: *Socrates is mortal.*

The general form of a categorical syllogism is as follows:

Premise 1: *All members of category A are members of category B.*

Premise 2: *X is a member of category A.*

Therefore: *X is a member of category B.*

Deductive logic has one especially attractive attribute—certainty. A conclusion arrived at by deduction is true with complete certainty, but this is so if and only if two conditions are met: the premises of the argument are *true* and the argument has *valid* form. If either condition is lacking, the conclusion is false with complete certainty. Therefore, a valid argument is defined as one whose conclusion must be true if its premises are true. Or, said differently, it is impossible for a valid argument to have true premises and a false conclusion.

In summary, conclusions arrived at by deduction are either true or false. If either valid form or true premises are lacking, then the conclusion is false. If both are present, the conclusion is true. There is no middle ground.

It is important to note that *truth* and *validity* are two distinct properties. Truth, and its opposite, falsity, are properties that pertain to an individual proposition. A proposition is true if it conforms to fact. Because premises and conclusions are both propositions, they are aptly characterized as either true or false. The premise *All pigs can fly* is false. The premise *Socrates is a man* is true as is the conclusion *Socrates is mortal*.

Validity is a property that pertains to the form of an argument. In other words validity refers to the logical relationships between the propositions comprising the argument. Validity or lack thereof describes the correctness of the logical inference linking the premises to the conclusion, but validity makes no reference to the factual truth of the argument's premises or conclusion. An argument is said to be valid if, when its premises are true, its conclusion must also be true.

However, an argument can be valid even if is composed of false propositions so long as the logical connections between the propositions are sound. The categorical syllogism that follows has valid form because its conclusion is logically compelled by its premises, yet its premises and conclusion are clearly untrue.

All humans are immortal.

Socrates is a human.

Therefore, Socrates is immortal.

Because validity has nothing to do with matters of fact, validity can best be demonstrated with arguments or diagrams of arguments, called Euler circles, which make no factual references whatsoever. In a Euler diagram, the set of elements comprising a category is represented by a circle. To show that one category, such as sports cars, is a subset of the more general category—cars in general—the circle representing sports cars resides within the larger circle representing cars. See Figure 39.2.

Figure 39.3 makes clear why argument 1 is valid but argument 2 is not. Argument 1 is valid because its conclusion, *X is a B*, follows necessarily from (i.e., is compelled by) its premises. However, Argument 2 is not valid because it conclusion, *X is an A*, is not logically compelled by its premises. X may belong to category A but not necessarily. The Euler diagrams portray validity more forcefully than the argument itself because the argument alone requires some thinking.

FIGURE 39.2 Euler Circles.

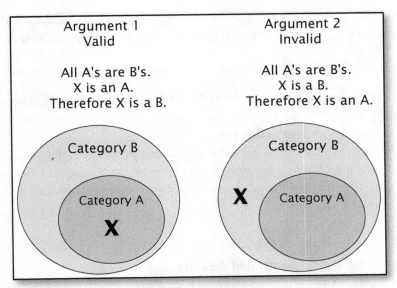

FIGURE 39.3 Valid and Invalid Categorical Syllogisms.

Argument 1

All A's are B's.

X is an A.

Therefore, X is a B.

Argument 2

All A's are B's.

X is a B.

Therefore, X is an A.

Conditional Syllogisms: The Logic of Scientific Arguments Another form of deductive argument, and the one that is central to scientific reasoning, is the *conditional* syllogism. It is the logical basis for establishing the discovery of new knowledge.

Like the categorical syllogism, the conditional syllogism is also composed of three propositions: two premises and a conclusion. It is so named because its first premise is a conditional proposition.

A conditional proposition is a compound statement that combines two simple propositions using the words *If–then*. The proposition following *if* is referred to as the *antecedent* clause and the proposition following *then* is referred to as the *consequent* clause. The general form of a conditional proposition is

If (antecedent clause), then (consequent clause)

For example:

If it is a dog, then it has four legs.

In the example, *it is a dog* is the antecedent clause and *it has four legs* is the consequent clause. A second example that is closer to the purpose at hand would be

If the TA rule has predictive power, then its back tested rate of return will exceed zero.

Our ultimate goal will be to establish the truth of the antecedent clause of these conditional propositions like the preceding example. As will become clear, the route to establishing its truth is an indirect one!

The second premise of a conditional syllogism is a proposition that either affirms or denies the truth of either the antecedent clause or the consequent clause of the first premise. Referring to the prior example, the second premise could be one of the following four statements:

It is a dog: Affirms the truth of the antecedent.

It is not a dog: Denies the truth of the antecedent.

It has four legs: Affirms the truth of the consequent.

It does not have four legs: Denies the truth of the consequent.

The conclusion of the conditional syllogism affirms or denies the truth of the remaining clause of the first premise. In other words, the conclusion references the clause that is not mentioned in the second premise. For example, if the second premise refers to the antecedent clause of the first premise, *It's a dog*, then the conclusion would refer to the consequent clause, *It has four legs*.

An example of a conditional syllogism is as follows:

If it is a dog, *then it has four legs.*

It is a dog (affirms the truth of the antecedent).

Therefore, it has four legs (affirms the truth of the consequent).

When a conditional syllogism possesses valid form, its conclusion is logically compelled by the two premises. Moreover, if it has valid form and its premises are factually true, then the conclusion of the conditional syllogisms must also be true.

Valid Forms of the Conditional Syllogism   There are two valid forms of the conditional syllogism; *affirming the antecedent* and *denying the consequent*. In an argument that affirms the antecedent, the second premise affirms the truth of the antecedent clause of the first premise. In an argument that *denies the consequent*, the second premise asserts that the consequent clause of the first premise is not true. These two valid forms of argument are shown here. They assume all dogs possess four legs.

Affirming the antecedent:

Premise 1: *If it is a dog, then it has four legs.*

Premise 2: *It is a dog.*

Valid Conclusion: *Therefore, it has four legs.*

In this valid form, the second premise *affirms the antecedent* clause by stating *It is a dog*. These two premises deductively compel the conclusion *It has four legs*. The general form of a conditional syllogism in which the antecedent is affirmed is

Premise 1: *If A is true, then B is true.*

Premise 2: *A is true.*

Valid Conclusion: *Therefore, B is true.*

The other valid form of the conditional syllogism is *denial of the consequent*. In this form, the second premise asserts that the consequent clause of premise 1 is a falsehood. From this, one may conclude that the antecedent clause of premise 1 is also false. This is illustrated by the following example:

Premise 1: *If it is a dog, then it has four legs.*

Premise 2: *It does NOT have four legs.*

Valid Conclusion: *Therefore, it is not a dog.*

Denial of the consequent follows the general form:

Premise 1: *If A is true, then B is true.*

Premise 2: *B is not true.*

Valid Conclusion: *Therefore, A is not true.*

This is sometimes shortened to

If A, then B.

Not B.

Therefore, not A.

Notice that this form of argument uses evidence (creature does not have four legs) to prove that antecedent (*It is a dog*) is false. It is this form of reasoning that is used in science to prove that a hypothesis is false. The hypothesis plays the role of the antecedent. We hypothesize that the creature is a dog. The consequent clause predicts what will be observed if the hypothesis is true. That is, if the creature is truly a dog, then, when it is observed, it will be seen to possess four legs. In other words, the conditional proposition, *If A, then B*, predicts that B would be observed in an experiment if the hypothesis (A) were in fact true. The second premise states that when the observation was made, the observation contradicted the prediction, that is, B was not observed. Given this, we can validly deduce that the hypothesis A is false.

As will be shown in due course, if we can prove that hypothesis A is false, we can indirectly prove that some other hypothesis is true. That other hypothesis is the new knowledge that we wish to establish as true, for example that a new vaccine is more effective than a placebo or that some TA rule predicts more effectively than a randomly generated signal.

Invalid Form of the Conditional Syllogism   An important reason for using formal logic is the difficulty people often have when reasoning informally about conditional syllogisms. Psychological studies[13] have shown that people tend to commit two fallacies when reasoning about conditional propositions: the fallacy of *affirming the consequent*, and the fallacy of *denying the antecedent*. An example of the fallacy of affirming the consequent is

> Premise 1: *If it is a dog, then it has four legs.*
>
> Premise 2: *It has four legs.*
>
> Invalid Conclusion: *Therefore, it is a dog.*

The fact that a creature has four legs certainly does not compel the conclusion that the creature is a dog. It may be a dog. The evidence is consistent with the fact that it is a dog. However, the evidence is also consistent with other conclusions. It could just as easily be a cow, a horse, or any other four-legged creature. The fallacy of affirming the consequent has the general form:

> Premise 1: *If A is true, then B is true.*
>
> Premise 2: *B is true.*
>
> Invalid Conclusion: *Therefore, A is true.*

This fallacy is a very common error in poor scientific reasoning and one committed in many articles on TA. Consider the following syllogism, which commits the fallacy of affirming the consequent.

> Premise 1: *If TA rule X has predictive power, then it should produce profits in a back test.*
>
> Premise 2: *The back test was profitable.*
>
> Invalid Conclusions: *Therefore, the TA rule has predictive power.*

Both of these premises may be true, but the conclusion is not necessarily true. With respect to the first premise, it is true that if the TA rule X does possess predictive power it should back test profitably. In other words, a profitable back test would be consistent with the supposition that the rule has predictive power. However, a profitable back test could also be consistent with the supposition that the rule was merely lucky. Similarly, just as evidence of four legs is consistent with a dog, it is also consistent with all other four-legged creatures.[14] The fallacy of affirming the consequent is the reason that empirical evidence cannot be used to prove that a hypothesis is true. As we shall see, one philosopher of science, Karl Popper, contended that the scientific method must, therefore, rest on denial (falsification) of the consequent, which, as pointed out earlier, is a valid form of inference.

The other fallacy associated with conditional syllogisms is the fallacy of denying the antecedent. It is illustrated here:

Premise 1: *If it is a dog, then it has four legs.*

Premise 2: *It is not a dog.*

Invalid Conclusion: *Therefore, it does not have four legs.*

The fact that a creature is not a dog does not preclude its having four legs. The general form of this fallacy is

Premise 1: *If A is true, then B is true.*

Premise 2: *A is not true.*

Invalid Conclusion: *Therefore, B is not true.*

In logical shorthand

If A, then B.

Not A.

Therefore, not B.

Invalid arguments can be hard to notice when they concern complex subjects. The best way to reveal them is to plug in commonplace items for A and B and see if the conclusion follows from the premises.

Figures 39.4 and 39.5 summarize the preceding discussion of the conditional syllogism.

As mentioned, the great strength of deductive reasoning is its ability to deliver conclusions that are true with certainty. However, deductive logic has a great weakness; it is unable to reveal new knowledge about the world. All that a deductive argument can do is to reveal truths that were already implicit in its premises. In other words, deductive reasoning can only tease out truths that were already present in the premises though they may not have been evident.

Valid	Invalid
Affirming the Antecedent If A, then B. A. Therefore, B.	**Denying the Antecedent** If A, then B. Not A. Therefore, Not B.
Denying the Consequent If A, then B. Not B. Therefore, Not A.	**Affirming the Consequent** If A, then B. B. Therefore, A.

FIGURE 39.4 Conditional Syllogisms: General Form.

	Valid	Invalid
	Affirming The Antecedent If a dog, then has 4 legs. It is a dog. Therefore, has 4 legs.	**Fallacy: Denying Antecedent** If a dog, then has 4 legs. It is not a dog. Therefore, not 4 legs.
	Denying The Consequent If a dog, then has 4 legs. Legs not equal to 4. Therefore not a dog.	**Fallacy: Affirming Consequent** If a dog, then has 4 legs. Has 4 legs. Therefore dog.

FIGURE 39.5   Conditional Syllogisms: Example.

This is not meant to minimize or trivialize deduction but to clarify its role. It may well be that a conclusion implied by the premises is far from obvious. Great mathematical discoveries are exactly that—the revealing of truths that had been implicit in the axioms of a mathematical system but that had not been understood prior to being proven. Such was the case with the much-publicized proof of Fermat's last theorem. It was first hinted at in the margin of a book in 1665 but not proven until 1994, by Andrew Wiles and Richard Taylor.

Inductive Logic

Induction is the logic of discovery. It aims to reveal new knowledge about the world by reaching beyond the knowledge contained in the premises of an inductive argument. However, this new knowledge comes with a price—uncertainty. Conclusions reached by induction are inherently uncertain. That is, they can only be true with some degree of probability. Thus, the notion of probability is intimately connected with induction.

Induction proceeds in a manner opposite to deduction. We saw that deduction progresses from a premise expressing a general truth that is held to apply to an unlimited number of instances, *All men are mortal* to a conclusion about a specific instance *Socrates is mortal*. In contrast, inductive reasoning moves or, better said, leaps from a premise based on a limited number of observed instances to a general conclusion about an unlimited number of similar but not-yet-observed instances. Thus, this form of inference is often referred to as inductive generalization. It is in leaping beyond what has been directly experienced by observation that induction incurs uncertainty—the possibility that its conclusion may be wrong.

Inductive generalization is illustrated by the following:

Premise: *Each of one thousand healthy dogs had four legs.*

General conclusions: *All healthy dogs will have four legs.*

The conclusion, in this example, is called a universal generalization, because it asserts that *all* members of the class dog have the attribute four legs. Universal generalizations have the form

All X's are Y's.

or

100 percent of X's have the attribute Y.

Generalizations need not be universal. Nonuniversal generalizations have the form

P percent of X's are Y's.

or

P percent of X's have attribute Y.

or

X's have attribute Y with probability P.

Again, we see that probability is inextricably tied to the concept of generalization. In fact, nonuniversal generalizations are also known as probabilistic generalizations. An example would be: *A higher percentage of bulldogs are prone to violence than poodles.* This statistically sound nonuniversal generalization[15] does not claim all bulldogs are prone to violent behavior, nor does it claim that even a majority are so inclined. However, it does say that, as a group, statistics show that bulldogs have a higher probability of being dangerous than poodles.

Aristotle's defeat as scientist was in part attributable to his failure to appreciate that nonuniversal generalizations convey useful knowledge. His fascination with the certainty of deductive proofs led him to restrict his search to universal generalizations. He was unable to see that many important regularities of the natural world are inherently probabilistic.

Induction by Enumeration

The most common form of inductive argument is based on enumeration. It proceeds from a premise that enumerates the evidence contained in a set of observations, and then draws a general conclusion that pertains to all similar observations outside the enumerated set.

Premise: *Over the past 20 years there have been 1,000 instances in which TA rule X gave a buy signal and in 700 of those instances the market moved higher over the next 10 days.*

Conclusion: In the future, when rule X gives a buy signal, there is a 0.7 probability that the market will be higher at the end of 10 days.

This conclusion or any conclusion reached by induction is inherently uncertain because it extends to observations that have not yet been made. However, some inductive arguments are stronger than others, and hence, arrive at conclusions that are more certain. The strength of an inductive argument and the certainty of its conclusion depend upon the quantity and quality of the evidence enumerated in its premise. The more numerous the instances cited and the higher their quality, the more likely the conclusion will generalize accurately to future observations.

Suppose that the conclusion about TA rule X had been based on only 10 instances with a 70 percent success rate instead of 1,000. In such a case, the conclusion would have been at least 10 times more uncertain.[16] This means we should be less surprised if the signal's future accuracy differs greatly from its historic success rate. In science, the evidence offered in support of a conclusion is typically evaluated with statistical methods. This allows one to make quantitative statements about the conclusion's uncertainty. This topic is discussed in Level III, Chapters 23 and 24.

The strength of an inductive argument also depends upon the quality of the evidence. Evidence quality is an entire subject unto itself, but suffice it to say that some observational methods produce higher quality evidence than others. The gold standard in science is the controlled experiment, where all factors but the one under study are held constant. TA does not permit controlled experiments, but there are better and worse ways to make observations. One issue that is relevant to TA is the matter of systematic error or bias. As will be discussed in Level III, Chapter 24, objective TA research is prone to a particular type of systematic error called *data mining bias* if careful steps are not taken.

Also relevant to the strength of an inductive argument is the degree to which the evidence cited is representative of the kinds of observations that are likely to be encountered in the future. An inference about a rule that generates long/neutral $(+1,0)$ signals that was back-tested only during rising markets is unlikely to be accurate about the rule's performance in a declining market environment. Even if the rule had no predictive power, its restriction to long or neutral positions makes it likely that it would have generated a profit because it was tested during a rising market period.

The most common fallacy of induction is the hasty generalization—an induction based on too little evidence or evidence of poor quality. Rule studies that cite a small number of successful signals as a basis for concluding that the rule has predictive power are likely to be hasty generalizations.

■ The Philosophy of Science

The philosophy of science seeks to understand how and why science works. It explains such things as: the nature of scientific propositions and how they differ from nonscientific and pseudoscientific propositions; the way scientific knowledge is produced; how science explains, predicts, and, through technology, harnesses nature; the means for determining the validity of scientific knowledge; the formulation and use of the scientific method; and the types of reasoning used to arrive at conclusions.[17]

That the scientific method is one of man's greatest inventions and is by far the most effective method for acquiring objective knowledge about the natural world is beyond question. "The part of the world known as the Industrial West could, in its entirety, be seen as a monument to the Scientific Revolution. . . ."[18] Humankind's ability to predict and control the natural world has improved more in the last 400 years, since the scientific revolution began, than it had in the prior 150,000 years that modern humans, *homo sapiens*, walked the face of the Earth.

Strange as it may seem, the invention of the scientific method and its first fruits came before it was understood why the method worked as well as it did. That insight came gradually, over the course of several centuries, as practicing scientists and their erstwhile critics, the philosophers of science, wrestled with perfecting the method and, in parallel, developed an understanding of how and why it worked.

The mere fact that the scientific method did work was not enough. It was seen as necessary to understand why. What philosophers found so vexing was the following apparent contradiction. On the one hand were the great victories of science, such as Newton's laws of motion and gravity and humanity's expanding technological control over nature. On the other was the fact that scientific knowledge was inherently uncertain, because conclusions arrived at by logical induction were inherently uncertain. How could so much useful knowledge result from such a flawed method of inference?

This section discusses the keys steps in the method's development and the milestones in our deepening understanding of how and why it works. The reader may wish to skip this historical development and go directly to the summary of the key aspects of the scientific method.

Bacon's Enthusiasm

Without invitation, philosophers poke their noses into all sorts of matters. It's their nature. They tell us how to act (ethics), how governments should rule (political philosophy), what is beautiful (aesthetics), and of greatest concern to us, what constitutes valid knowledge (epistemology) and how we should go about getting it (philosophy of science).

The scientific revolution was, in part, a revolt against Aristotelian science. The Greeks regarded the physical world as an unreliable source of truth. According to Plato, mentor of Aristotle, the world was merely a flawed copy of the truth and perfection that existed in the world of *Forms*, a metaphysical nonmaterial realm, where archetypes of the perfect dog, the perfect tree, and every other imaginable thing could be found.

When the revolt against this view of reality finally arrived, it was harsh and unremitting.[19] The new school of thought, empiricism, resoundingly rejected the Greek paradigm. It contended that, not only was the natural world worthy of study, but that careful observation could lay bare its truths. A pioneer of empiricism and perhaps the first philosopher of science was Francis Bacon (1561–1626). "Nature, for Bacon was an open book that could not possibly be misread by an unprejudiced mind."[20] In his famous work the *Novem Organum* (the new tool) Bacon extolled the power of observation and induction. He held science to be a completely objective rational practice that could conclusively confirm or falsify knowledge simply by observing without bias or prejudice and then generalizing from those observations. In many situations, this approach seemed to work.

However, empiricism was not the perfect tool Bacon and his disciples claimed, and philosophers made it their business to say why. First, they pointed out that empiricism, an observation-based enterprise, rested on a crucial assumption that could not be confirmed by observation, the assumption that nature was uniform over all time and space. That assumption was critical in justifying the empiricists' position that if a scientific law was observed to hold true here and now it would also hold true everywhere and forever. Because the uniformity of nature assumption could not be confirmed by observation, it had to be taken on faith. Second, science often deals with phenomena and concepts that defy direct observation: atomic structure, the force of gravity, and electric fields. Though their effects are observable, these constructs could not be arrived at exclusively by observation and induction. They are better understood as human inventions that explain and predict rather than observable physical realities.

Nevertheless, Bacon's contributions to the development of the scientific method were important. He promoted the idea of experiment and made room for doubt by taking special note of discordant observations. Both ideas eluded the Greeks.

Descartes's Doubt

If philosophers are good for anything it's raising doubt, and no one was better than Rene Descartes (1596–1650). Regarded as the father of modern philosophy and a key figure in the birth of science, Descartes shared Bacon's skepticism for the authoritarian knowledge of the Greeks and the dogma of the Roman Church. However, Descartes was just as skeptical of the claims made by the empiricists about the power of observation and inductive generalization. His famous expression, "I think, therefore I am," expressed the position that science must start by doubting everything except the existence of the person who experiences doubt. From that point of solidity, knowledge must be built purely by deductive reasoning without being contaminated by error-prone observations made with the imperfect five senses.

As a consequence of Descartes' anti-empirical stance and penchant for theorizing in a factual vacuum, his scientific findings were almost meaningless.[21] However, his contributions to science were lasting. Skepticism is central to the scientific attitude. In addition, Descartes' invention of analytic geometry paved the way for Newton's invention of the calculus which, in turn, allowed him to specify his famous equations of motion and gravity.

Hume's Critique of Induction

Another dose of doubt was administered by Scottish empiricist and philosopher David Hume (1711–1776). His seminal work, the *Treatise on Human Nature*, published in 1739, grappled with a central problem of epistemology: how to distinguish knowledge from lesser forms of knowing, such as opinions that happen to be true. Prior to Hume's publication, philosophers generally agreed that the distinction was related to the quality of the method used to acquire the knowledge. What justified calling one bit of wisdom knowledge but not another was the pedigree of the method of inquiry.[22]

Philosophers could not, however, agree on the best method of knowledge acquisition. Empiricists argued that objective observation followed by inductive generalization was the route to wisdom. Rationalists, on the other hand, contended that pure deductive reasoning from self-evident truths was the correct method.

Hume took issue with both schools of thought and ultimately even with himself. As an empiricist, Hume disparaged the rationalists' purely deductive approach because it was disconnected from observed facts. Also, in the spirit of empiricism, Hume said that it was wise to adjust the strength of one's beliefs in proportion to the evidence and that theories should be evaluated by the degree to which they matched observation. But then Hume went on to contradict himself by attacking the logical basis of empiricism. He denied the validity of inductive generalization and disparaged the ability of science to establish causal laws. His searing critique of induction has come to be known as Hume's problem.

Hume's attack on induction was on both psychological and logical grounds. First, he said the belief that induction could establish correlative or causal connections between events was a nothing more than a by-product of human psychology. Hume asserted that the perception of cause and effect was merely an artifact of the mind. The belief that A causes B or is even correlated to B, simply because A has always been followed by B was nothing more than a habit of mind, and a bad habit at that.

From a logical perspective, Hume claimed that induction was flawed because no amount of observed evidence, no matter how objectively collected, can compel a conclusion with the force of a valid deduction. Moreover, he said that there was no rule of induction that tells us when we have evidence of sufficient quantity or quality to justify the leap from a finite set of observations to a conclusion about an infinite number of similar but not yet observed instances. A rule of induction would, itself, have had to be the result of a prior valid induction made on the basis of an even earlier rule of induction, and so forth and so on, ad infinitum. In other words, an attempt to justify induction inevitably rests on an infinite regress—a logically impossible absurdity.

In light of Hume's attack, supporters of induction retreated to a narrower claim saying inductive generalizations were merely correct in a probabilistic sense. So as evidence accumulates in favor of a relationship between A and B, the probability that the relationship is authentic also increases. However, philosophers were quick to point out that a probabilistic justification of induction was also flawed. The probability that A predicts B is equal to the number of times that A was followed by B divided by the total number of instances of A regardless of whether it was followed by B.[23] Because the future holds an infinite number of instances, the probability will always be zero, no matter how numerous the past observations (any number divided by an infinitely large number is still zero).

Thus, Hume and his allies created a paradox. On one hand were their seemingly valid concerns about the flaws of induction. On the other hand was the accumulation of stunning scientific discoveries. If science was based on such a flawed logic, how could it have managed to be so successful?

William Whewell: The Role of Hypothesis

It took philosophers and scientists two hundred years of watching the scientific method succeed to understand how it worked and why it had been so triumphant. By the middle of the nineteenth century, it was becoming clear that science employs a synergistic combination of inductive and deductive logic. In 1840, William Whewell (1794–1866) published *The History and Philosophy of Inductive Sciences*.

Whewell was the first to understand the crucial role of induction in the formulation of a hypothesis. Whewell called it a happy guess, He said that scientific discovery starts with a bold inductive leap to a new hypothesis, but it is followed by deduction. That is to say, after a hypothesis has been induced, a prediction is deduced from said hypothesis. This prediction takes the form of a conditional statement:

If the hypothesis is true, then specific future observations are predicted to occur.

When the observations are made, they will either be consistent with the prediction, thus confirming the hypothesis, or conflict with the prediction, thus contradicting the hypothesis.

What is a scientific hypothesis? It is a conjecture of a suspected pattern, for example:

X predicts Y.

or

X brings about Y.

This conjecture is spawned by a scientist's prior experience—noticing repeated pairings of X and Y. Once the XY hypothesis has been put forward, a testable prediction is deduced from it. This takes the form of a conditional proposition, which is composed of two clauses: an antecedent and a consequent. The hypothesis serves as the antecedent clause, and the prediction serves as the consequent clause. In situations where it is merely asserted that X is correlated (predicts) with Y the following conditional proposition would apply:

IF X predicts Y, then future instances of X will be followed by instances of Y.

In cases where the hypothesis asserts that X causes Y, the following conditional proposition would apply:

IF X causes Y, then if X is removed, Y should not occur.

The predictions embodied in the consequent clause of the conditional proposition are then compared with new observations. These must be observations whose outcome is not yet known. This is crucial! This does not necessarily mean that the observations concern some future event. It simply means that when the prediction is made, the outcome of the observations is not yet known. In historical sciences like geology, archeology, and so forth, the observations are about events that have already taken place. However, the outcomes have not yet been observed.

If it turns out that future observations of X are not followed by Y or if removal of X does prevent the occurrence of Y, then the hypothesis (antecedent) is proven to be false by the valid deductive form falsification of the consequent.

> If X, then Y.
>
> Not Y.
>
> Valid Deduction: *Therefore, not X.*

If, however, future instances of X are indeed followed by Y, or if the removal of X does cause the disappearance of Y, the hypothesis is not proven! Recall that affirming the consequent is not a valid deductive form.

> If X, then Y.
>
> Y.
>
> Invalid: *Therefore, X.*

That the prediction has been confirmed merely offers tentative confirmation of the hypothesis. The hypothesis survives for the moment, but more stringent tests of it are sure to follow.

Whewell agreed with Hume that inductive conjecture was a habit of human thought, but the habit that Hume so disparaged Whewell regarded as fruitful though mysterious. He was unable to explain the mental processes that gave rise to such creative thoughts though he believed inductive generalization was part of it. He called the ability to conjure a hypothesis an unteachable inventive talent but a crucial one, because, without a hypothesis, a set of observations remain nothing more than a disconnected collection of facts that could neither predict nor explain. However, with one came the breakthroughs of science.

Whewell's description of this crucial creative aspect of science reminds me of a conversation I had many years ago with Charles Strauss, a prolific composer of some of Broadway's most successful musicals. In my early twenties at the time, short on tact and long on audacity, I asked him to explain how he managed to be so productive. With more forbearance than I deserved, Charles described a daily discipline of religiously sitting at the piano from 8 until 11 each morning and from 2 until 5 each afternoon, whether he felt inspired or not. He told me he treated composing music like a job. During this time he would test tentative melodies—musical hypotheses. He modestly attributed his high productivity to 99 percent discipline and 1 percent creative talent. However, as I thought about this conversation years later, it seemed otherwise. With an almost infinite number of note combinations, his success at creating infectious tunes had to be a creative talent—some special ability to see which of those musical conjectures had the potential to be melodies and which did not. This was what Whewell called the happy guess—that unteachable talent of seeing a theme that meaningfully relates a disparate set of observations or notes that eludes the average person. A few folks have it. The vast majority do not.

Whewell's realization that proposing a hypothesis was an act of invention no less than the creation of the steam engine or the light bulb represented a profoundly important advance in thinking about science.[24] Induction could not produce truths on its own, but it was a necessary first step. This was a profound departure from the prior notion of science as a systematic objective investigation followed by inductive generalization. Whewell saw the scientist as a creator as much as an investigator.

Karl Popper: Falsification and Bringing Deduction Back into Science

In two landmark works, *The Logic of Scientific Discovery*[25] and *Conjectures and Refutations*,[26] Karl Popper (1902–1994) extended the insight of Whewell and redefined the logic of scientific discovery by clarifying the role of deduction. Popper's central contention was that a scientific inquiry was unable to prove hypotheses to be true. Rather, science was limited to identifying which hypotheses were false. This was accomplished by using observed evidence in combination with the valid deductive form of falsification of the consequent.

> **If** hypothesis H is true, **then** evidence E is predicted to occur under specified conditions (e.g., back test of a TA rule).
>
> *Evidence E did not occur under the specified conditions.*
>
> *Therefore, hypothesis H is false.*

In taking this stance, Popper challenged the prevailing view advocated by a school of philosophy called logical positivism. Just as Francis Bacon had revolted against the strictures of the Greek tradition, Popper was in revolt against the Vienna Circle, the home of logical positivism. Logical positivists believed that observations could be used to prove hypotheses to be true. Popper demurred, saying that observed evidence could only be used to prove a hypothesis false. Science was a baloney detector, not a truth detector.

Popper justified his method, called falsificationism, as follows. A given set of observations can be explained by or is consistent with numerous hypotheses. Therefore, the observed data, by itself, cannot help us decide which of these hypotheses is most likely correct.[27] Suppose the data is that one of my shoes is missing. One hypothesis that might explain this observation is that I'm a disorganized housekeeper who is always misplacing things. Another hypothesis, which is equally consistent with the observation of a missing shoe, would be that my house was burglarized by a one-legged thief who only had use for one shoe. In fact, an infinite number of hypotheses could be proposed that are consistent with (explain) the missing shoe.

We have already seen that data cannot be used logically to deduce the truth of a hypothesis. Attempts to do so commit the fallacy of affirming the consequent.[28] However, and this is the key to Popper's method of falsificationism, data can be used to validly deduce the falsehood of a hypothesis by denial of the consequent. In other words, disconfirming evidence can be used to reveal a false explanation. For example, finding the other shoe would be evidence that would falsify the one-legged thief hypothesis. The logical argument is as follows:

Premise 1: *If a one-legged thief is responsible for my missing shoe, then I will not find the shoe in my home.*

Premise 2: *Missing shoe is found (consequent denied).*

Conclusion: *Therefore, the one-legged thief hypothesis is false.*

Popper's method of falsification runs against the grain of common sense, which is biased in favor of confirmatory evidence. Intuition often tells us to test the truth of a hypothesis by seeing if confirmatory evidence can be found. We do so under the mistaken impression that confirmatory evidence is sufficient to establish truth. However, using evidence in this way commits the fallacy of affirming the consequent. We are not wrong to suspect that confirmatory evidence should be found if the hypothesis is true, but we are wrong to think that confirmatory evidence is sufficient to establish its truth. Said differently, confirmatory evidence is a necessary condition of a proposition's truth but not a sufficient condition.[29] Popper's point was that the absence of necessary evidence is sufficient to establish the falsity of a hypothesis, but the presence of necessary evidence is not enough to establish its truth. Having four legs is a necessary condition of a creature being a dog, but the presence of four legs is not sufficient to establish that a creature is a dog. However, the observation that the creature does not have four legs is sufficient to falsify the contention it is a dog. Popper's logic of falsification can be seen as a protection against the confirmation bias that infects informal inference.

One final example may help clarify the power of falsifying evidence and the weakness of confirmatory evidence. It is the famous problem of the black swan posed by philosopher John Stuart Mill (1806–1873). Suppose we wish to ascertain the truth of the proposition: 'All swans are white.' Mill said, and Popper concurred, that no matter how many white swans have been observed—that is, no matter how voluminous the confirmatory evidence—the proposition's truth is never proven. A black swan may lurk just around the next corner. This is the limitation of induction that so upset Hume. However, by merely observing a single non-white swan, one may declare with certitude that the proposition is false. The conditional syllogism below shows that the falsity of the proposition *All swans are white* is based on the valid deductive form falsification of the consequent.

Premise 1: *If it is true that all swans are white, then all future observations of swans will be white.*

Premise 2: *A nonwhite swan is observed.*

Valid Conclusion: *The proposition that all swans are white is false.*

The general form of argument used to test a hypothesis under Popper's method of falsification is:

Premise 1: *If the hypothesis is true, then future observations are predicted to have property X.*

Premise 2: *An observation occurs that lacks property X.*

Valid Conclusion: *Therefore, hypothesis is false.*

As will be seen in Level III, Chapter 23, this is the logic used to test statistical hypotheses.

The Provisional and Cumulative Nature of Scientific Knowledge One implication of Popper's method of falsification is that all existing scientific knowledge is provisional. Whatever theory is currently accepted as correct is always a target for empirical challenge and the possibility of its being replaced by a more correct theory always exits. Today Einstein's Theory of Relativity is taken as correct. Though its predictions have withstood countless tests, tomorrow a new test may show it to be false or incomplete. Thus, science is a never-ending cycle of conjecture, prediction, testing, falsification, and new conjecture. It is in this way that the body of scientific knowledge continually evolves toward an ever more accurate representation of objective reality.

In most instances when older theories are replaced, it is not because they are proven false so much as they are shown to be incomplete. When Newton's laws of motion were replaced by Einstein's theories, Newtonian physics was still mostly correct. Within the limited domain of everyday experience, where bodies travel at normal speeds (approximately less than 90 percent of the speed of light), Newton's laws still held true. However, Einstein's theory was correct in a wider domain, which not only included the motions of everyday objects, but also objects traveling up to and including the speed of light. In other words, Einstein's theory, which built upon Newton's, was more general and thus subsumed it.

The net result of building upon prior successful ideas (those whose predictions have been confirmed) and pruning away wrong ideas (those whose predictions have been falsified) is a body of knowledge that continually improves. This cannot be said of any other intellectual discipline, where new styles are introduced but where newer is not necessarily better. The fact that a scientist in any field of science knows more today than even the best one living just a generation ago is beyond debate. However, whether gangsta rap is better or worse than Mozart could be argued endlessly.

The Restriction of Science to Testable Statements Another implication of Popper's method is that science must restrict itself to testable hypotheses—propositions that generate predictions about observations not yet made. To say that a hypothesis has been tested and has survived or has been tested and falsified means that predictions deduced from it have either been confirmed or contradicted by new observations. The comparison of predictions with new observations is the crucial mechanism that fosters the continual improvement of scientific knowledge. For this reason, propositions that do not generate testable predictions must be excluded from the domain of scientific discourse.

The term *prediction*, in the context of hypothesis testing, warrants some clarification, because TA is essentially an enterprise dedicated to prediction. When we speak of prediction as it pertains to testing a hypothesis, it does not necessarily mean foretelling the future though the predicted observations may indeed lie in the future. Rather, the term *prediction* refers to the fact that the observations' outcomes are not yet known.

Predictions made in historical sciences, such as geology, refer to events that have already taken place perhaps eons ago. For example, geology's dominant theory, plate tectonics, may predict that specific geologic formations that were created millions of years ago would be observed if an investigation of some specific location were to be carried out tomorrow. In finance, the efficient market's hypothesis predicts that if a TA rule were to be back tested, its profits, after adjustment for risk, would not exceed the risk adjusted return of the market index.

Once the prediction has been deduced from the hypothesis, the operations necessary to produce the new observations are carried out. They may involve a visit to the location of the predicted geologic formation or the back test of the TA rule. Then it becomes a matter of comparing prediction with observation. Measuring the degree of agreement between observation and prediction and making the decision about whether the hypothesis is left intact or falsified is what statistical analysis is all about.

What is important from the standpoint of science is that the hypothesis is able to make predictions about observations whose outcomes are not yet known. This is what allows a hypothesis to be tested. Observations whose outcomes are known cannot serve this purpose because it is always possible to fashion an explanation, after-the-fact that is consistent with said observations. Therefore, activities that are unable or unwilling to make testable predictions, thus opening them to the possibility of falsification, do not qualify as scientific.

The Demarcation Problem: Distinguishing Science from Pseudoscience An important consequence of Popper's method was that it solved a key problem in the philosophy of science—defining the boundary between science and nonscience. The domain of science is confined to propositions (conjectures, hypotheses, claims, theories, and so forth) that make predictions that are open to refutation with empirical evidence. Popper referred to such propositions as falsifiable and meaningful. Propositions that cannot be challenged in this manner are unfalsifiable or meaningless. In other words they do not say anything of substance, something that sets up a testable expectation.

Unfalsifiable propositions may appear to assert something, but, in fact, they do not. They cannot be challenged because they do not say, with any degree of specificity, what can be expected to happen. In effect, they are not informative. Hence, the falsifiability of a proposition is related to its information content. Falsifiable propositions are informative because they make specific predictions. They may prove to be wrong, but at least they say something of substance. A proposition that cannot generate falsifiable predictions essentially says any outcome can happen. For example, a weather forecast that says, *It will be cloudy or sunny, wet or dry, windy or calm, and cold or hot*, allows for all possible outcomes. It cannot be falsified. The only thing good that can be said about it is that its lack of information is completely obvious.

The problem is that pseudoscientists and pseudoforecasters are clever about the way they word their predictions so as to obscure their lack of information and non-falsifiability. Consider the astrologer's forecast "You will meet a tall dark stranger, and your life will be changed." This statement is impossible to refute no matter what the outcome. Should you ever go back for a refund, you will be given one of two answers: (1) be patient—you will meet the stranger soon, or (2) you already did meet a dark stranger and you life is indeed different, but you are oblivious to the change. These answers cannot be challenged because the prediction was vague. It neither stated when your life would change or in what measurable (verifiable) manner. This is a far cry from the prediction, "Before 7:00 p.m. next Wednesday you will see a man wearing one red shoe, walking east on 42nd Street whistling 'Satin Doll.'" By 7 p.m. next Wednesday, the evidence will be in and you will have had the opportunity to evaluate the prediction as true or false. Even if the prediction turns out to be false, it was at least falsifiable allowing you to decide if future visits to the astrologer are worthwhile.

The infomercial pitchmen that inhabit late-night television are masters of the meaningless claim. "Wearing our copper bracelet will improve your golf game." What does *improve* mean? How is it to be measured and when? As with the astrologer's forecast, the claim's vagueness makes it impossible to deduce a testable (falsifiable) prediction. However, it is quite easy to imagine after-the-fact anecdotal evidence that is seemingly confirmatory. "Holy cow, I feel so much more relaxed wearing my copper bracelet. I used get all tensed up before teeing off. Now my drives seem straighter. Last week I almost had a hole in one, and I don't curse nearly as much as I used to. My wife even says I look more handsome in my golf outfit, and I think my hair has stopped falling out." Although meaningless claims invite confirmatory anecdotes, they are protected from objective falsifying evidence. The claimant never gets nailed and the claim gains support from seemingly confirmational anecdotal reports.

In contrast, the statement, "Wearing a copper bracelet will increase the length of your drives by 25 yards," is informative and meaningful because it generates a testable prediction. You hit 100 golf balls not wearing the copper bracelet and determine their average distance. The next day, do the same thing while wearing a copper bracelet and get their average distance. Repeat this alternating series of experiments for 10 days. If the drives on copper-bracelet days are less than 25 yards better, evidence refuting the claim would be in hand.

Limitations of Popper's Method As important as Popper's method of falsification is to modern science, it has been criticized on a number of grounds. Critics assert that Popper's contention that hypotheses can be definitively falsified overstates matters. Although the observation of a black swan can neatly and logically falsify the universal generalization that all swans are white, the hypotheses of real science are far more complex[30] and probabilistic (nonuniversal). They are complex in the sense that a newly proposed hypothesis rests on numerous auxiliary hypotheses that are assumed to be true. Thus, if a prediction deduced from the new hypothesis is later falsified, it is not clear whether the new hypothesis was in error or one of the many auxiliary hypotheses was incorrect. This proved to be the case when the solar system's eighth planet, Neptune, was discovered. The aberrant path of Uranus was not due to flaws in Newton's laws but in the auxiliary hypothesis that the solar system contained only seven planets. However, when the theory did fail early in the twentieth century, it was indeed because of imperfections in Newton's laws. Doing real science is tricky business. TA is a long way from facing these problems because we are still at the at the point of scratching the data for reliable predictive rules.

Moreover, because many of the hypotheses of science are probabilistic, as would be the case in TA, an observation that contradicts the hypothesis can never be taken as certain evidence of falsity. The aberrant observation may be a chance occurrence. It is here that statistical analysis enters the picture. As will be pointed out in Level III, Chapter 23, the decision to reject a hypothesis on the basis of observed evidence runs a certain probability of being wrong. Statistics helps us quantify this probability.

Despite these and other limitations that go beyond our concerns here, Popper's contributions to the development of the scientific method have been enormous.

The Information Content of Scientific Hypotheses

To recap, a hypothesis is informative if it can make testable predictions. This opens it to the possibility of being found false. Thus, the falsifiability of a hypothesis and its information content are related.

Within the domain of scientifically meaningful hypotheses, there are degrees of information content and falsifiability. Some hypotheses are more information rich and hence more falsifiable than others.

When Popper referred to a *bold conjecture* he was speaking of a highly informative hypothesis from which many falsifiable predictions could be deduced. The scientist's job, therefore, is to continually attempt to refute an existing hypothesis and to replace it with an even more informative one. This spurs the improvement of scientific knowledge.

An information-rich hypothesis makes many precise (narrow ranged) predictions about a broad range of phenomena. Each prediction presents an opportunity to show the hypothesis is false. In other words, the more informative a hypothesis the more opportunities it presents for falsification. In contrast, low information, timid hypotheses make fewer or less-precise predictions. Consequently they are more difficult to falsify. For example, a TA rule that claims high profitability on any instrument in any time frame makes a bold and information-rich claim that that could be falsified by showing that it is unprofitable on one market in one time frame. In contrast, a method that only claims to be marginally profitable on S&P futures on the one-week bar time scale is timid, has low information content, and is hard to falsify. The only opportunity to refute it would be limited to back test of the S&P 500 on a weekly showing that was not at all profitable.

Some TA methods that are seemingly informative are not. Elliott Wave Principle is a case in point. On the surface, it bravely proclaims that all price movement in all markets over all time scales can be described by a single unifying principle. This proposition is seemingly confirmed by the ability of EWP practitioners to produce a wave count for any prior segment of price data. In fact, EWP is timid to the point of being meaningless because it makes no falsifiable predictions of future price motion.[31]

A second case in point, one more pleasing to the TA community, is the Efficient Markets Hypothesis (EMH). In this context, the term *efficiency* refers to the speed with which prices reflect all known and knowable information that is relevant to the future returns of an asset. In an efficient market, relevant information is presumed to be reflected in price almost instantaneously. EMH comes in three flavors. In descending order of boldness, information content, and falsifiability they are: EMH strong, EMH semistrong, and EMH weak.

EMH strong asserts that financial markets are efficient with respect to all information, even private inside information. This version predicts that all investment strategies, be they based on an inside tip from the president about an impending takeover, or based on public information of a fundamental or technical nature, will be useless in earning market-beating (excess) returns. This most audacious version of EMH is also seemingly the most informative and falsifiable because any evidence of abnormal profits from any investment strategy whatsoever, irrespective of the type of information or form of analysis used, would be sufficient to refute EMH strong. However, because information that is known privately can never be confirmed, this version is not testable in a practical sense.

The semistrong version of EMH makes a less informative and narrower claim, saying that the market is only efficient with respect to public information. This version of EMH can be falsified with any evidence of market-beating returns produced by an investing strategy based on either public fundamental data (P/E ratios, book values, and so forth) or technical data (relative strength rank, volume turnover ratios, and so forth). In effect, EMH semistrong denies the utility of fundamental and technical analysis.

Finally we have EMH weak, which makes the least bold and least informative claim. It asserts that the market is only efficient with respect to past price, volume, and other technical data. Because EMH weak only denies the utility of technical analysis, it presents the smallest and hardest-to-hit target by would-be falsifiers. Their only hope would be to present evidence that shows excess returns generated by an investment strategy based on TA.

Because EMH weak is the hardest version to falsify and is thus the least likely to be proven false, its falsification would also generate the most surprise. In other words, of all versions of EMH, falsification of EMH weak would generate the biggest increase in knowledge. This points out a general principle of science: the largest gains in knowledge occur when the most timid and hardest to falsify hypotheses are falsified. A test showing that inside information, like the tip from a corporate president, was able to generate excess returns (i.e., falsification of EMH strong) would not be surprising nor would we learn very much from it. Big deal, so inside information generates profits. What else is new? In contrast, the falsification of EMH weak would be a highly informative event for both TA practitioners and EMH supporters. Not only would it mean the final destruction of the EMH, an important principle of finance for over 40 years, but it would be an important confirmation of TA's validity. Both would represent large changes in the current state of knowledge.

Thus, it can be said that the gain in knowledge that occurs upon falsification of a hypothesis is inversely related to its information content. Likewise, it can be said that the knowledge gained by confirmation of a hypothesis (observations consistent with its predictions) is directly related to the information content of the hypothesis. The most informative hypotheses make the most audacious claims of new knowledge. They attempt to bring within the realm of understanding the broadest range of phenomena with the greatest degree of precision while at the same time involving the fewest assumptions. When such a hypothesis is falsified, we are not very surprised nor do we learn very much. Few would have expected the hypothesis to be confirmed, except perhaps for the bold scientist proposing it. For example, suppose a bold new theory of physics is put forward, one of whose predictions is that it is possible to build an antigravity device. If true, such a theory would represent a major increase in knowledge. However, if the device fails to work, no one would be surprised by the prediction's failure. However, it is exactly the opposite when a timid hypothesis is falsified. For example a timid hypothesis would be one that merely asserts that the currently accepted theories of physics are true and predicts that the antigravity device should fail. The falsification of this weak hypothesis via observations of the antigravity device working would result in a very significant gain in knowledge—the verification of new physics.

The most timid hypothesis that can be put forward is one that asserts that there have been no new discoveries. In other words, it says that all that is currently known is all that there is to know. This hypothesis denies the truth of any other hypothesis that asserts that something new has been discovered. The timid hypothesis that asserts that nothing new had been discovered has a special name in science. It is called the *null hypothesis* and it is the starting assumption in the investigation of any claim that a new discovery has been made. Whether that claim asserts that a new vaccine will cure a dreaded disease, that a new principle of physics tells us how to nullify gravity, or that a TA rule has predictive power, we always start by assuming that the null hypothesis is true. Then, if evidence can be produced that falsifies the null hypothesis, a most timid claim, it generates a big gain in knowledge.

Thus, science proceeds as follows. Every time a bold new hypothesis is put forward, it spawns an opposing claim, the null hypothesis. The null is as timid as the new hypothesis is bold. Jonas Salk's bold hypothesis that his vaccine would prevent polio better than a placebo spawned a competing claim, the null hypothesis. It made the timid prediction that the vaccine's ability to prevent infection would be no better than a placebo. This was a timid prediction because every prior attempt to develop a vaccine against polio had failed. These two competing claims left no middle ground. If one hypothesis could be falsified, by logic's Law of the Excluded Middle, we know that the other must be true. Salk's experimental evidence made it clear that the rate of infection among those receiving the real vaccine was significantly less than those receiving the placebo. In other words it was sufficient to falsify the null's prediction. This was a surprising result that represented a huge increase in medical knowledge!

How Scientists Should Respond to Falsification

How should a scientist respond when a hypothesis or theory that has survived many prior tests is ultimately falsified because recent observations conflict with predictions? The proper response is whatever leads to the biggest increase in knowledge. Because scientists are human beings, they sometimes fail to do what is scientifically correct.

There are two possible responses that increase knowledge. The first is to preserve the existing hypothesis by using it to predict new, previously unknown facts. If these new facts are confirmed and can explain why the observations that had been in conflict with the hypothesis are no longer in conflict, then the hypothesis deserves to be retained. The new facts represent an increase in what we know about the world. A second proper response is to throw out the old hypothesis and propose a new one that not only accounts for all observations that had been explained by the prior hypothesis but also explains the new discordant observations. This also represents an increase in knowledge in the form of a new hypothesis with greater explanatory or predictive power. However, in either case the correct response is to do whatever advances the frontier of knowledge the most.

Unfortunately the interests of science sometimes take a back seat to personal agendas. Human nature gets in the way of good science. Emotional, economic and professional ties to a prior hypothesis can motivate attempts to explain away the discordant evidence in a way that reduces the information content and falsifiability of their cherished hypothesis. This moves the frontier of knowledge backward. Fortunately science is a collective self-correcting enterprise. The community of scientists happily takes their fallen brothers to task when they stray from the path of righteousness in this way.

Some examples will clarify these abstract concepts. First, I present an example of a proper response to predictions being contradicted by new observations. In this case, new facts were predicted to rescue an established theory from falsification. This high road was taken by two astronomers during the nineteenth century, and it led to new knowledge in the form of a new planet being discovered. At that time, Newton's laws of motion and gravity were the accepted physics of planetary motion. They had been confirmed and reconfirmed by countless observations, but then, to the surprise of astronomers of that day, new and more powerful telescopes showed the planet Uranus was deviating from the orbit predicted by Newton's laws. A rigid and improper application of falsificationism would have called for an immediate rejection of Newtonian mechanics. However, all theories rest on a bed of auxiliary assumptions. A key assumption in this case was that the solar system contained only seven planets with Uranus being the seventh and furthest from the sun. This led astronomers Adams and Leverrier to boldly predict the existence of a yet undiscovered eighth planet (the new fact), lying beyond Uranus. If this were true, that new planet's gravitational effects could explain the aberrant motion of Uranus, which seemed to be in conflict with Newton's laws. In addition, if an eighth planet did exist, one of Newton's laws would predict the exact spot in the sky where the new planet would be observable. This was a bold, informative, and highly falsifiable prediction that put Newton's laws to a most stringent test. The astounding prediction made by Adams and Leverrier about where the new planet would appear in the sky was indeed confirmed in 1846 with the discovery of Neptune. They saved Newton's laws from falsification by demonstrating that the theory was not only able to explain the deviant behavior of Uranus but was also able to make a highly accurate prediction. This is the kosher way to retain a theory when it is confronted with dissonant observations.

In the end, however, Newton's laws proved to be provisionally true, as is ultimately the case for all laws and theories. Although Newton's laws had worked perfectly for more than 200 years, early in the twentieth century more precise astronomical observations were found to be truly inconsistent with the theory's predictions. The old theory had finally been falsified and it was time for a new one. In 1921, Albert Einstein responded properly by putting forward his new and more informative Theory of General Relativity. Today, almost one hundred years later, Einstein's theory has survived all attempts to falsify it.

Newton's theory qualified as scientific because it was open to empirical refutation. In fact, Newton's theory was not wrong so much as it was incomplete. Einstein's General Theory of Relativity not only accounted for all of the phenomena covered by the Newtonian model, but it accommodated the new observations that conflicted with Newton's more limited theory. This is how science progresses. Longevity and seniority mean nothing. Predictive accuracy and explanatory power are everything.

The case of Adams and Leverier make clear why claims must be open to empirical refutation. Falsifiability alone gives scientific knowledge a large advantage over conventional wisdom. The ability to jettison false or incomplete ideas and replace them with ever more informative ones produces a body of knowledge that is self-correcting and in a continual state of improvement. This in turn provides a stable base upon which new ideas can be erected that reach ever higher levels of understanding. Intellectual activities that have no procedure for eliminating erroneous knowledge inevitably get bogged down in nonsense. This is precisely the problem with the popular version of TA.

Now we will consider an example of an improper response to falsification. It occurs in the field of finance. The injection of science into finance is relatively recent. Perhaps this explains the defensive, unscientific response of those who support the efficient markets hypothesis. When observations collided with their favorite theory, they tried to save it from falsification by reducing its information content. As mentioned earlier, its least informative version, EMH weak, predicts that investment strategies based on TA[32] will not be able to earn risk adjusted returns that beat the market index. When EMH supporters were faced with studies showing that TA-based strategies were able to earn excess returns,[33] they responded by trying to immunize their theory from falsification. They did so by inventing new risk factors and claimed that the excess returns earned by TA were merely compensation for risks inherent in pursuing such a strategy. In other words, EMH defenders claimed that investors who followed the TA strategy were exposing themselves to a risk that was specific to that strategy. This allowed the EMH supporter to characterize the TA strategy's returns as non-market-beating. Recall EMH does not claim that earning returns higher than the market is impossible. It only says that higher returns entail the assumption of additional risk. If the returns earned by the TA strategy were indeed compensation for bearing higher risk, then EMH would remain intact despite the studies that show TA strategy earning a return higher than the market index.

There was one problem with the way EMH supporters did this. They cooked up the risk factor after the TA studies had been performed.[34] This is not kosher science. It would have been scientifically correct if EMH had defined the risk factor in advance of the study and predicted that a test of the TA method would generate what appeared to be market-beating returns. Had they done this, the status of EMH would have been enhanced with a successful prediction. Instead, EMH supporters took the low road to save their favored hypothesis by giving themselves the license to invent a new risk factor any time they needed to explain away findings that conflicted with their favored theory. In so doing, EMH supporters rendered their hypothesis unfalsifiable, thereby draining it of any information content.

The precedent for this knowledge-regressive method of immunizing the EMH hypothesis against falsification had already been established by earlier flawed defenses of EMH. These earlier, and similarly misguided, efforts to save EMH were in response to studies that had shown that public fundamental information, such as the price-to-book ratio and PE ratio, could be used to generate excess returns.[35] In response to this inconvenient evidence, EMH defenders claimed that low price-to-book ratios and low PE ratios were merely signals of stocks with abnormally high risk. In other words, the fact that a stock's price is low relative to its book value is an indication that the company is facing difficulties. Of course, this reasoning is circular. What is key here is the fact that EMH advocates had not defined low price-to-book or low PE as risk factors in advance of the studies showing that stocks with these traits were able to earn excess returns. Had EMH theorists done so, it they would have bolstered the information content of EMH with an additional dimension of risk. Instead, EMH theorists invented these risk factors after the fact, for the specific purpose of explaining away discordant observations that had already been made. Such explanations are termed ad-hoc hypotheses— explanations invented after the fact for the specific purpose of saving a theory or hypothesis from being falsified. Popper referred to this knowledge regressive, save-the-theory-at-any-cost behavior as falsification immunization.

Had Popper known of it, he would have chastised the die-hard supporters of EMH, but he would have probably applauded the efforts of those advocating behavioral finance. This relatively new field has proposed testable hypotheses that explain the profitability of strategies based on public technical and fundamental data as arising from the cognitive biases and illusions of investors. It is ironic that erroneous beliefs in the validity of subjective TA and the valid profitability of some forms of objective TA may both be the result of cognitive foibles.

The Scientific Attitude: Open yet Skeptical

Falsificationism makes a clear distinction between two phases of scientific discovery: proposal and refutation. These phases demand different mindsets—openness and skepticism. The coexistence of these opposite mindsets defines the scientific attitude.

An attitude of openness to new ideas is vital when hypotheses are being formulated. The willingness[36] to see things in a new way, to advance new explanations and take bold inductive leaps characterizes the proposal phase. Most practitioners of TA function well in this mode. New indicators, new systems, and new patterns get proposed all the time.

However, once a bold conjecture has been made, receptivity must morph into skepticism. Doubt about the new idea motivates a relentless search for its flaws. Thus, there is an ongoing tension in the scientist's mind between speculative curiosity and hard-nosed disbelief. However, the doubt is not an unremitting skepticism but one that yields to persuasive new evidence. This is the quasi-schizoid state that defines the scientific attitude.

Beyond the distrust of the new hypothesis, another form of skep-ticism thrives in the mind of a scientist: doubt about the mind itself. This springs from a profound awareness of the all-too-human tendency to generalize hastily and leap to unfounded conclusions. The procedures of science can be seen as safeguards against these tendencies.

■ The End Result: The Hypothetico-Deductive Method

Some would say there is no such thing as the scientific method.[37] "The scientific method, as far as it is a method is nothing more than doing one's damnedest with one's mind no holds barred."[38] At its essence it is intelligent problem solving.

The problem-solving method used in science today has come to be known as the hypothetico-deductive method. It is commonly described as having five stages: observation, hypothesis, prediction, verification, and conclusion. "In actual scientific work these stages are so intertwined that it would be hard to fit the history of any scientific investigation into this rigid scheme. Sometimes the different stages are merged or blurred, and frequently they do not occur in the sequence listed."[39] Rather, it is a useful way to think about the process.

The hypothetico-deductive method was initiated by Newton in the seventeenth century, but was not formally named until after Popper's contributions were introduced. It is the outgrowth of several hundred years of tussling between scientists and philosophers. The method integrates both inductive and deductive logic, paying heed to their individual limits while leveraging their respective powers.

The Five Stages

1. **Observation:** A possible pattern or relationship is noticed in a set of prior observations.

2. **Hypothesis:** Based on a mysterious mixture of insight, prior knowledge, and inductive generalization, it is hypothesized that the pattern is not an artifact of the particular set of observations but one that should be found in any similar set of observations. The hypothesis may merely assert that the pattern is real (scientific law) or it may go further and offer an explanation about why the pattern exists (scientific theory).

3. **Prediction:** A prediction is deduced from the hypothesis and embodied in a conditional proposition. The proposition's antecedent clause is the hypothesis and its consequent clause is the prediction. The prediction tells us what should be observed in a new set of observations if the hypothesis is indeed true. For example: **If** the hypothesis is true, **then** X should be observed if operation O is performed. The set of outcomes defined by X makes clear which future observations would confirm the prediction and, more importantly, which future observations would be in conflict with it.

4. **Verification:** New observations are made in accordance with the operations specified and compared to the predictions. In some sciences the operation is a controlled experiment. In other sciences it is an observational study.

5. **Conclusion:** An inference about the truth or falsity of the hypothesis is made based on the degree to which the observations conform to the prediction. This stage involves statistical inference methods such as confidence intervals and hypothesis tests, which are described in Level III, Chapter 23.

An Example from TA

The following is an example of the hypothetico-deductive method as it would be applied to testing a new idea about technical analysis.

1. **Observation:** It is noticed that when a stock market index, such as the Dow Jones average or the S&P 500, rises above its 200-day moving average, it generally continues to appreciate over the next several months (probabilistic generalization).

2. **Hypothesis:** On the basis of this observation, inductive generalization, and prior findings of technical analysis, we propose the following hypothesis: Upward penetrations of the 200-day moving average by the DJIA will, on average, produce profitable long positions over the next three months. I'll refer to this hypothesis as 200-H.

3. **Prediction:** On the basis of the hypothesis, we predict that an observational investigation, or back test, will be profitable. The hypothesis and the prediction are turned into the following conditional statement: **If** 200-H is true, **then** the back test *will be profitable*. However this prediction creates a logical problem. Even if the back test is profitable it will not be helpful in proving the truth of 200-H because, as previously pointed out, while a profitable back test would be consistent with the truth of 200-H, it cannot prove that 200-H is true. An attempt to do so would commit the fallacy of affirming the consequent (see argument 1 below).

If, on the other hand, the back test turns out to be unprofitable, it would be valid to conclude 200-H is false by the valid logical form falsification of the consequent. See Argument 2 below.

Argument 1

Premise 1: *If 200-H is true, then a back test will be profitable.*

Premise 2: *The back test was profitable.*

Invalid Conclusion: Therefore, 200-H is true. (fallacy of affirming the consequent)

Argument 2

Premise 1: *If 200-H is true, then a back test will be profitable.*

Premise 2: *The back test was NOT profitable.*

Valid Conclusion: *Therefore, 200-H is false.*

However, our objective is to prove the truth of 200-H. To get around this logical problem, suppose we had formulated a null hypothesis at stage 2, specifically, *Upward penetrations of a 200-day moving average do not generate profits over the following three months.* Let's refer to this as Null-200. From this we can formulate the following conditional proposition: **If *Null-200 is true,* then** *a back-test will NOT be profitable.* If the back test does turn out to be profitable, we can validly argue that the null hypothesis has been falsified (falsifying the consequent). By the Law of the Excluded Middle, either 200-H is true or Null-200 is true. There is no middle ground; there is no other hypothesis possible. Thus by disproving the null we will have indirectly proven that 200-H is true. Thus we have the following conditional syllogism:

Premise 1: *If Null-200 is true, then the back test will be unprofitable.*

Premise 2: *The back test was NOT unprofitable (i.e., it was profitable).*

Valid Conclusion: Null-200 is false, therefore 200-H is true.

4. **Verification:** The proposed rule is back tested and its profitability is observed.
5. **Conclusion:** Determining the meaning of the results is a matter of statistical inference.

■ Rigorous and Critical Analysis of Observed Results

The fifth phase of the hypothetico-deductive method points to another important difference between science and nonscience. In science, observed evidence is not taken at face value. In other words, the obvious implication of the evidence may not be its true implication. The evidence must be subjected to rigorous analysis before a conclusion can be drawn from it. The evidence of choice in science is quantitative data, and the tool of choice for drawing conclusions is statistical inference.

An important scientific principle is the preference for simpler explanations (Ockham's Razor). As such, astounding hypotheses are given serious consideration only after more commonplace hypotheses have been rejected. Sightings of a UFO are not immediately interpreted as evidence of an alien visit. More mundane accounts such as ball lightning, weather balloons, or a new aircraft must first be discredited before an invasion from outer space is taken seriously.

Thus a scientific attitude toward an extraordinarily profitable rule back test would first consider and reject other explanations before entertaining the possibility that a significant TA rule has been discovered. The possible explanations of good performance unrelated to a rule's predictive power are good luck due to sampling error (see Level III, Chapter 23) and systematic error due to data-mining bias (see Level III, Chapter 24).

■ Summary of Key Aspects of the Scientific Method

The following is a summary of the key points of the scientific method:

- No matter how voluminous the evidence, the scientific method can never conclusively prove a hypothesis to be true.

- Observed evidence used in combination with the deductive form falsification of the consequent can be used to disprove a hypothesis with a specified degree of probability.

- Science is restricted to testable hypotheses. Propositions that are not testable are not within the domain of scientific discourse and are considered to be meaningless.

- A hypothesis is testable if and only if predictions about yet-to-be-made observations can be deduced from the hypothesis.

- A hypothesis that can only explain past observations but that cannot make predictions about new observations is not scientific.

- A hypothesis is tested by comparing its predictions with new observations. If predictions and observations agree, the hypothesis is not proven, but merely receives tentative confirmation. If they don't agree, the hypothesis is taken to be false or incomplete.

- All currently accepted scientific knowledge is only provisionally true. Its truth is temporary until a test shows it to be false, at which point it is replaced or subsumed by a more complete theory.

- Scientific knowledge is cumulative and progressive. As older hypotheses are shown to be false, they are replaced by newer ones that more accurately portray objective reality. Science is the only method of inquiry or intellectual discipline which can claim that newer is better. Though knowledge, styles, and methods in other disciplines, such as music, art, philosophy, or literary criticism, may change over time, it cannot be claimed that new is necessarily better.

- Any set of past observations (data) can be explained by an infinite number of hypotheses. For example, Elliott Wave Theory, Gann Lines, classical chart patterns, and a roster of other interpretive methods can all explain past market behavior according to their own paradigm of analysis. Therefore, all these explanations are said to be empirically equal. The only way to decide which ones are better is by seeing how well they can predict observations whose outcomes are not yet known. Those methods that cannot generate testable (falsifiable) predictions about new observations can be eliminated immediately on the grounds that they are scientifically meaningless. Those methods that can generate predictions that are found to conflict with future observations can be eliminated on grounds that they have been falsified. Thus, only methods that can make testable predictions that display genuine predictive power deserve to be retained in the body of TA knowledge.

■ If TA Were to Adopt the Scientific Method

This section examines consequences of TA adopting the scientific method.

The Elimination of Subjective TA

The most important consequence of TA adopting the scientific method would be the elimination of subjective approaches. Because they are not testable, subjective methods are shielded from empirical challenge. This makes them worse than wrong. They are meaningless propositions devoid of information. Their elimination would make TA an entirely objective practice.

Subjective TA would be eliminated in one of two ways: by transformation into objective methods or abandonment. Perhaps Gann Lines, subjective divergences, trend channels, and a host of subjective patterns and concepts embody valid aspects of market behavior. In their present subjective form, however, we are denied this knowledge.

Transforming a subjective method into an objective version is not trivial. To illustrate a case where this has been done, I discuss an algorithm for the automated diction of head and shoulder patterns and test results in the section "Objectification of Subjective TA: An Example."

Elimination of Meaningless Forecasts

It is not practical to assume that all subjective practitioners will follow my call to objectify or close up shop. For those who continue to use subjective approaches, there is an important step that can be taken to make their output, if not their methodology, objective. Henceforth, they would issue only falsifiable forecasts. This would at least make the information they provide meaningful and informative. In this context, informative does not necessarily mean correct but rather that the forecasts have cognitive content that passes the discernable difference test discussed in the Introduction. In other words, the forecast would convey something of substance, the truth of which can be clearly determined by subsequent market action. In other words, the forecast will make explicit or clearly imply which outcomes would show it to be wrong. As stated previously, a forecast that does not make clear what future events constitute prediction errors in essence says that any outcome can happen.

At the present time, most subjective forecasts, often referred to as market calls, are meaningless. In all likelihood, this is not obvious to either consumers or the analysts issuing the forecasts. First, consider a forecast that is clearly meaningless: "My indicators are now predicting the market will either go up an infinite percentage, down 100 percent, or something in between." On its face, the statement is unfalsifiable because there is no outcome that could possibly conflict with the prediction. The only good thing about the forecast is that its lack of meaning and lack of falsifiability are transparent. A more typical market call goes something like this: "On the basis of my indicators [fill in one or more TA methods], I am bullish." This unfalsifiable statement is just as meaningless, but its lack of substance is not obvious. Though there is a prediction of a rise, the prediction leaves unclear when it might occur or under what circumstances the prediction would be wrong.

This bullish stance could have been made meaningful by clearly excluding certain outcomes. For example, *I expect the market to rise more than 10 percent from current levels before it declines by more than 5 percent from current levels.* Any instance of a decline of greater than 5 percent before a rise of 10 percent would be sufficient to classify the forecast as an error.

If you ever suspect that you are being fed a meaningless prediction, here are some good antidotes. Ask the following question: "How much adverse movement (opposite to the direction predicted) would have to occur for you to admit this forecast is mistaken?" Or "What outcomes are precluded by your prediction?" Or "When, and under what conditions, can the forecast be evaluated, such as the passage of time, change in price (adverse or favorable), or a specific indicator development?" Reader, I warn you not to do this if you are squeamish about watching people squirm.

Making subjective forecasts meaningful with an up-front statement of when and how the forecast will be evaluated would eliminate the market guru's after-the-fact wiggle room. Some ways of adding meaning to a subjective forecast include (1) defining a future point in time when the forecast will be evaluated, (2) defining the maximum degree of adverse movement that would be allowed without declaring the prediction wrong, and (3) predicting a specified magnitude of favorable movement prior to a specified magnitude of unfavorable movement (X percent favorable before Y percent unfavorable). Steps like these would allow a subjective practitioner to develop a track record of meaningful market calls. Meaningful track records can also result from specific transaction recommendations made in real time.

One limitation of this recommendation is that it would still leave unclear what the profitable track record represents. This is because subjective forecasts are derived in an undefined way, so even if a profitable track record of meaningful predictions is built up over time, it cannot be known that they were the result of a consistent analysis procedure that can be repeated in the future. In fact, it is likely that the method of analysis is not stable over time. Studies of expert subjective judgment indicate that experts do not combine information in a consistent manner from one judgment to the next. "Intuitive judgments suffer from serious random inconsistencies due to fatigue, boredom, and all the factors that make us human."[40] In other words, given the exact same pattern of market data at different times, it is quite possible that a subjective analyst would not give the same forecast.[41]

Paradigm Shift

Refashioning TA into an objective practice would be what Thomas Kuhn calls a paradigm shift. In his highly influential book, *The Structure of Scientific Revolutions*, Kuhn rejected Popper's notion that science evolves strictly by falsification and conjecture. Instead, Kuhn saw the evolution of a science as a sequence of paradigms, or world views. While a given paradigm is in place, practitioners indoctrinated in that point of view confine their activities to posing questions and hypotheses that are consistent with and answerable within that view.

A large number of TA analysts have been indoctrinated with the nonscientific, intuitive analysis paradigm developed by TA pioneers like Dow, Gann, Shabacker, Elliott, Edwards and Magee, and so forth. They established the subjective research tradition and postulated the background wisdom that is accepted as true and taught to aspiring practitioners. The certification exam given by the Market Technicians Association to aspiring Chartered Market Technicians (CMT) exemplifies this tradition.

The shift to an evidence-based objective approach would challenge much of this material as either meaningless or not sufficiently supported by statistical evidence. Many of the teachings will go the way of early Greek physics and astronomy. Some methods will survive objectification and statistical testing and will warrant a position in a legitimate body of TA knowledge.

Lest the reader think my position too harsh, I am not advocating that the falsifiability criterion be used to cut off all research in budding TA methods just as they are being formulated. Many of the brilliant theories of science began as half-backed prescientific ideas on the wrong side of the falsifiability criterion. These ideas needed time to develop, and one day some turned into meaningful science. One example in TA is the new field of socionomics, an outgrowth of Elliott Wave Theory. At the current time, I regard this newly developing discipline as prescientific, though it may have the potential to become a science. According to a conversation I had with Professor John Nofsinger, who is working within the field of socionomics, at this time the discipline is not yet able to make testable predictions. This will require the quantification of social mood, the key determinant of market movement according to socionomics.

Nascent areas of research such as this and others should not be short-circuited simply because they are not at this time able to generate testable predictions. One day they may be able to do so.

■ Objectification of Subjective TA: An Example

One of the challenging aspects of moving TA to a science will be transforming subjective chart patterns into objectively defined testable patterns. This section presents an example of how two academic technicians, Keving Chang and Carol Osler (C&O) objectified the head-and-shoulders pattern).[42] Not all elements of their pattern are included here. Rather, I have included enough of their rules and the problems they faced and solved to illustrate the challenges of transforming a subjective method into an objective one. For further details please refer to their original articles.

Descriptions of the head-and-shoulders pattern can be found in many TA texts[43] and are typically accompanied by a diagram similar to the one in Figure 39.8. It represents the pattern as a sequence of noise-free price swings. When the pattern manifests in perfect textbook form, even a beginning student of TA can spot it.

The problem occurs when an actual chart pattern departs from this ideal. Even seasoned chartists can debate whether a given pattern qualifies as a legitimate head and shoulders, an unavoidable consequence of the lack of an objective pattern definition. Subjective pattern definitions generally describe how the head-and-shoulders pattern should look, but they do not provide clear rules for discriminating patterns that do qualify as head and shoulders from patterns that possess some head-and-shoulders-like features but do not qualify. In other words, the definitions lack clear rules for which patterns to exclude. This problem is conceptualized in Figure 39.6.

Without objective rules for deciding what does and what does not qualify as a legitimate head-and-shoulders pattern it is impossible to evaluate the pattern's profitability or predictive power. The solution to the problem is to define objective rules that discriminate valid head-and-shoulders patterns from those that are not.[44] This notion is illustrated in Figure 39.7. The challenge of turning a subjective pattern into an objective one can be thought of as the problem of defining the pattern as a clear subset in the super-set of all possible TA price patterns.

C&O defined the head-and-shoulders top pattern as composed of five pivot or price reversal points that, in turn, define the pattern's three peaks and two troughs.

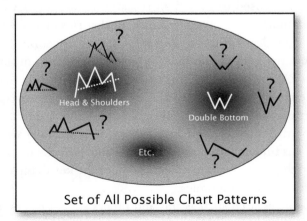

FIGURE 39.6   Subjective Patterns—No Definitive Exclusion Rules.

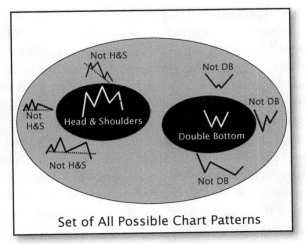

FIGURE 39.7 Objective Patterns—Definitive Exclusion Rules.

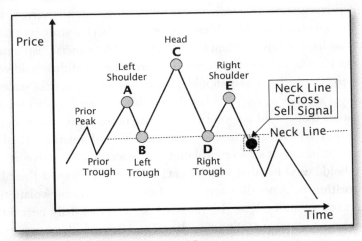

FIGURE 39.8 Head and Shoulders.

These pivots are denoted by letters A through E on Figure 39.8. All eight texts consulted by C&O were clear that the head, denoted by letter C, must be higher than the two surrounding peaks (shoulders) denoted by letters A and E. There has been some debate among chartists about several auxiliary features including the Adam's apple, the double chin, and the cowlick. However, the TA manuals consulted by C&O were inconsistent on these aspects and they were not included.

One challenge that faces the real-world chartist is the fact that actual price oscillations do not trace out clearly identifiable peaks and troughs. Rather, peaks and troughs occur at numerous oscillation scales from tiny waves lasting minutes to very large ones lasting years or decades. This property, called fractal scaling, imposes a burden on the subjective analyst trying to identify a head-and-shoulders pattern. The analyst must visually filter the price behavior to isolate peaks and troughs at one particular scale of interest. This is relatively easy in retrospect, but it is quite difficult as the pattern is actually unfolding in real time.

C&O addressed this problem by using a percentage filter, also known as an Alexander filter[45] or a zigzag indicator, which is discussed by Merrill in *Filtered Waves*.[46] It is an objective method for identifying peaks and troughs as prices evolve. Troughs are identified after prices have moved up from a recent price low by an amount greater than a specified threshold percentage and peaks are identified after prices have moved down from a recent price high by the threshold percentage. The problem is that the identification occurs with a time lag, the time it takes for prices to move the threshold amount. For example, if the threshold is set at 5 percent, then a peak is not detected until prices have fallen at least 5 percent from the most recent price maximum, and troughs are not detected until prices have risen at least 5 percent from the recent price minimum. The minimum required price movement causes a lag between the time the peak or trough actually occurred and the time at which it is detected by the zigzag filter.

Next, C&O addressed how to determine the correct threshold percentage to define the zigzag filter. Different filter thresholds would reveal head-and-shoulders patterns of different size (scale). For example, a 3 percent filter might reveal a head-and-shoulders pattern that a 10 percent filter would completely ignore. This makes it possible for multiple head-and-shoulders patterns of differing scale to exist simultaneously. C&O addressed this problem by subjecting each financial instrument (stock or currency) to 10 different zigzag filters employing a range of threshold values. This allowed them to identify head-and-shoulders patterns on a variety of scales.

This raised yet another problem. What should the 10 filter thresholds be? Clearly, a set of thresholds that would be good for one instrument may not be good for another because they are characterized by different levels of volatility. Realizing this, C&O take each instrument's recent volatility into account to arrive at the set of 10 filter thresholds used for that instrument. This insight allowed their head-and-shoulders algorithm to generalize across markets with different volatilities. C&O defined a market's volatility, V, as the standard deviation of daily percentage price changes over the most recent 100 trading days. The 10 thresholds were arrived at by multiplying V by 10 different coefficients; 1.5, 2.0, 2.5, 3.0, 3.5, 4.0, 4.5, 5.0, 5.5, 6.0. This resulted in 10 zigzag filters with varying sensitivity. The validity of the set of coefficients chosen by C&O were confirmed by visual inspection of price charts by TA practitioners who agreed that the 10 zigzag filters did a reasonable job of identifying head-and-shoulders patterns.

Next C&O addressed the problem of defining rules that qualify a candidate pattern as a valid head-and-shoulders. These rules were applied to the instrument once its price had been zigzag filtered and the peaks and troughs at a given scale had been identified.

First, the head and shoulders identified by C&O's algorithm had to satisfy the following basic rules:

1. The head of the pattern must be higher than both the left and right shoulders.
2. The instrument must be in an uptrend prior to the formation of the head-and-shoulders pattern. Thus, the pattern's left shoulder has to be above the prior peak (PP) and the pattern's left trough has to be above the prior trough (PT).

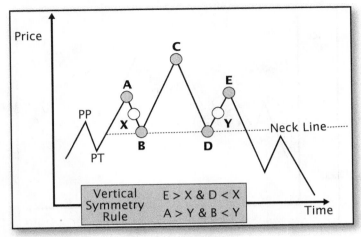

FIGURE 39.9 Good Vertical Symmetry.

Next C&O grappled with more subtle and complex issues to qualify a candidate pattern as a valid head-and-shoulders. They accomplished this with a set of innovative measurements that qualified the pattern in terms of its vertical and horizontal symmetry and the time it took for the pattern to complete. These rules allowed them to definitively label a candidate pattern as either head-and-shoulders or a non–head-and-shoulders.

Vertical Symmetry Rules

The vertical symmetry rules exclude patterns with necklines that are too steeply sloped. The pattern in Figure 39.9 has acceptable vertical symmetry.

The rules compare the price levels of the right and left shoulders (A and E) and the price levels of the right and left troughs (B and D) with a price level defined by the midpoint of segment AB, designated as point X, and the midpoint of segment DE designated as point Y. To qualify as a vertically symmetrical head-and-shoulders, the pattern must satisfy the following rules.

1. The price level of the left shoulder peak, point A, must exceed the price level of point Y.
2. The price level of the right shoulder peak, point E, must exceed the price level of point X.
3. The price level of the left trough, point B, must be less than the price level of point Y.
4. The price level of the right trough, point D, must be less than the price level of point X.

Figures 39.10 and 39.11 show two head-and-shoulders patterns that would be excluded because the vertical symmetry criteria have not been satisfied.

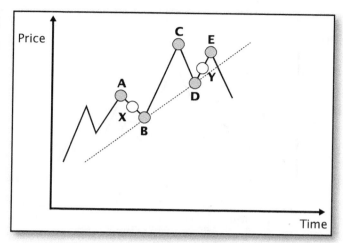

FIGURE 39.10 Poor Vertical Symmetry—Neckline Slope Too Steep.

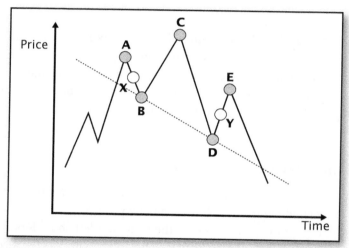

FIGURE 39.11 Poor Vertical Symmetry—Neckline Slope Too Steep.

Horizontal Symmetry Rule

Another feature used by C&O to distinguish head-and-shoulders patterns from non-head-and-shoulders patterns was horizontal symmetry. A pattern with good horizontal symmetry is one for which the head, at point C, is roughly equidistant from the peaks representing the pattern's two shoulders (points A and E). C&O's rule was that the distance from the head to one shoulder should not be greater than 2.5 times the distance of the head to the other shoulder. There is nothing magical about the value 2.5 other than it seemed reasonable. See Figure 39.12.

Figure 39.13 is an example of a pattern that fails the test for horizontal symmetry. Note the right shoulder is stretched too far to the right. A pattern with excessive leftward stretch would also be disqualified.

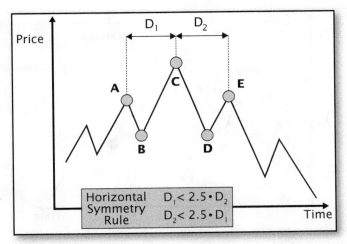

FIGURE 39.12 Good Horizontal Symmetry.

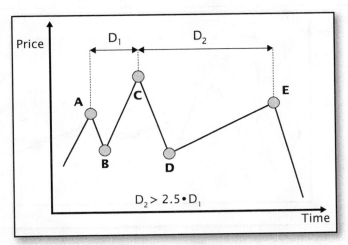

FIGURE 39.13 Poor Horizontal Symmetry.

Pattern Completion Rule: Maximum Time to Neckline Penetration

C&O also specified a rule that excludes patterns that take too long to penetrate the neckline once the right shoulder, point E, has been formed. As with other features, this criterion is defined in terms of the pattern's internal proportions rather than some fixed number of time units. This allows the rule to be applied to all patterns irrespective of their time frame or scale.

The maximum time allowed for the movement from the right shoulder, point E, until the penetration of the neckline is the temporal distance separating the two shoulders, points A and E. The pattern in Figure 39.14 meets the time to completion criterion because the temporal distance from the right shoulder until neckline penetration (D4) is less than the temporal separation of the shoulders (D3). The pattern in Figure 39.15 does not qualify because D4 exceeds D3.

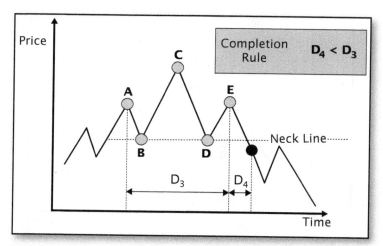

FIGURE 39.14 Pattern Completion Rule Satisfied.

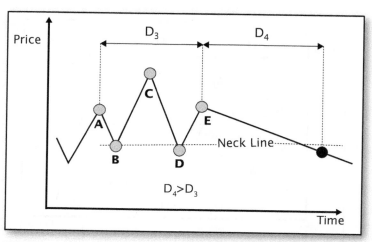

FIGURE 39.15 Pattern Completion Rule Not Satisfied.

Future Information Leakage: Look-Ahead Bias

In their simulation of head-and-shoulders patterns, C&O took precautions against the future information leakage or look-ahead bias problem. This problem afflicts back tests that assume the possession of knowledge that was not truly available when a trading decision was made. In the context of back testing, this can make results appear more profitable than would be possible in actual trading. An extreme example would be assuming access to the *Wall Street Journal* the day before its publication.

In the context of back testing the head-and-shoulders pattern, future information leakage can occur if the zigzag threshold percentage is larger than the percentage distance between the right shoulder peak and the neckline. It would not be legitimate to assume a short-sale signal due to a neckline penetration until the right shoulder (point E) has been detected. However, it is possible for prices to cross the neckline before the right shoulder is identified by the zigzag filter. To clarify, suppose the right shoulder, point E, lies only 4 percent above the neckline, but the threshold for the zigzag filter is 10 percent. It would not be legitimate to assume that a trader knew about the neckline penetration because a 10 percent decline from the right shoulder would have been required to identify the right shoulder of the head-and-shoulders pattern. In this example, assuming an entry price only 4 percent below the right shoulder would be more favorable than waiting for a price 10 percent below the right shoulder, the price movement required to have a fully formed head-and-shoulders pattern. To avoid this problem, C&O assumed an entry after the right shoulder had been objectively identified by the zigzag filter. Though this was a less favorable entry price in some instances, the back test was unencumbered by look-ahead bias. I mention this because it shows C&O's attention to detail.

C&O's pattern definition also deals with numerous other issues regarding entry and exit of positions, stop-loss levels, and so forth, but the point has been made that it is possible to transform subjective chart patterns into objective testable patterns. Readers may take exception to arbitrary aspects of C&O's pattern. All well and good if the reader has a better objective definition to offer.

As a final sanity check, C&O showed patterns that had been identified by their automated head-and-shoulders algorithm to a number of chartists. C&O claim that the chartists agreed that the patterns identified by the objective head-and-shoulders algorithm did indeed conform to subjective head-and-shoulders criteria.

Head-and-Shoulders Back Test Results

Does the head-and-shoulders pattern carry predictive information with respect to stocks or currencies? In a word, the pattern hailed as a cornerstone of charting is a bust. Tests by C&O show that it is worthless on stocks and only modestly profitable on currencies. The pattern was profitable in two out of six currencies tested, but the relatively complicated head-and-shoulders algorithm was far outperformed by a much simpler objective signal based on zigzag filters. Moreover, when C&O tested the occurrence of a head-and-shoulders in conjunction with the zigzag rule either as a confirming or disconfirming signal, the head-and-shoulders pattern added no value. In other words, zigzag signals did no better when the head-and-shoulders signal was in the same direction as the zigzag signal and the zigzag did no worse when the head-and-shoulders signal was in the opposite direction. The bottom line for currency traders: the value of head-and-shoulders is doubtful.[47]

The head-and-shoulders performed worse on stocks. C&O evaluated the head-and-shoulders on 100 randomly selected equities[48] over the period from July 1962 until December 1993. On average, each stock gave one head-and-shoulders signal per year, counting both long and short signals, giving a sample of over 3,100 signals. To test the pattern's profitability on actual stock prices, C&O established a benchmark based on the pattern's performance on pseudo-price histories. These simulated price histories were generated from actual historical price changes strung together in a random fashion. By using actual price changes, the pseudo-price histories had the same statistical characteristics as real stocks, but any predictability due to authentic temporal structure—the structure TA patterns are intended to exploit—was

eliminated Despite the fact that the pseudo-price histories were randomly generated, head-and-shoulders patterns that fit C&O's definition still emerged. This confirms the results of Harry Roberts referred to earlier.

If the head-and-shoulders patterns appearing in real stock data are useful, they
should generate profits superior to those achieved by trading the patterns appearing
in the fake stock price histories. C&O found that head-and-shoulders patterns in
actual stock prices lost slightly more money than the signals on pseudo-price histories. According to the study "the results uniformly suggest that head-and-shoulders
trading are not profitable." The signals lose on average about 0.25 percent over a
10-day holding period. This compares with an average loss of 0.03 percent for head-
and-shoulders patterns in the pseudo-stock data. C&O referred to traders using the
pattern as "noise traders," speculators who mistake a random signal for an informative one.

Confirming C&O's findings is the work of Lo et al.[49] Lo used an alternative method of objectifying the H&S pattern based on kernel regression, a sophisticated local[50]
smoothing technique. Their study was unable to unseat the null hypothesis that the
head-and-shoulders pattern is useless.[51]

Bulkowski[52] found the head-and-shoulders was profitable, but his research falls
short. He does not provide an objective pattern definition that back-testable pattern
or entry and exit rules. In other words, his study is subjective TA. In addition, his
results fail to adjust for the trend of the general stock market over the time period
in which he tested the patterns.

■ Subsets of TA

Given the preceding discussion, TA can be seen as comprised of four subsets: (1) subjective TA, (2) objective TA with unknown statistical significance, (3) objective TA
that is not statistically significant, and (4) objective TA that is statistically significant.

The first subset, subjective TA, has already been defined as methods that cannot be
reduced to a back-testable algorithm. Subsets two, three, and four refer to objective
methods.

The second subset is comprised of objective methods of unknown value. Though
these methods are objective and may have been back tested, their results have not
been evaluated for statistical significance. Here, it is simply a matter of applying the
methods discussed in Level III, Chapters 23 and 24. This is not meant to suggest that
applying statistical methods to back test results is simple, but rather that the decision
to do so is.

The third subset, which I refer to as useless TA, consists of objective TA rules for
which results have been comprehensively back tested and evaluated with statistical
methods, but have been reveled to add no value either on a stand-alone basis or when
used in combination with other methods. In all likelihood, the majority of objective
TA methods will fall into this subset. This is to be expected because financial markets
are extremely difficult to predict due to their inherent complexity and randomness. In fact, in all fields of science, most proposed ideas do not work. Important

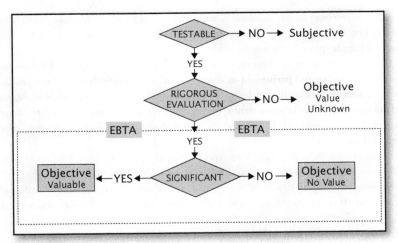

FIGURE 39.16 Subsets of Technical Analysis.

discoveries are rare. This is not obvious because the numerous failures are typically not reported in the lay press or even in scientific journals. What is most important is having a procedure in place for getting rid of methods that do not work.

The fourth subset, useful TA, consists of objective methods that produce statistically significant or, better yet, economically significant results. Though some rules will be useful on a stand-alone basis, the complexity and randomness of financial markets make it likely that most rules will add value when used in combination with other rules to form complex rules.

Evidence-based technical analysis (EBTA) refers to subsets (3) and (4)—objective TA that has been back tested and subjected to statistical analysis. Given the preceding discussion, the categorization of TA is illustrated in Figure 39.16.

■ Notes

1. M. Shermer, *Why People Believe Weird Things: Pseudoscience, Superstition, and Other Confusions of Our Time* (New York: W.H. Freeman, 1997).
2. C. Van Doren, *A History of Knowledge: Past, Present, and Future* (New York: Ballantine Books, 1991).
3. S. Richards, *Philosophy & Sociology of Science: An Introduction* (Oxford, UK: Basil Blackwell, 1983), 45.
4. Ibid.
5. Ibid., 189.
6. Ibid., 201.
7. As quoted by Shermer, *Why People Believe*.
8. Van Doren, *History of Knowledge*, 189.
9. Ibid.
10. Richards, *Philosophy & Sociology of Science*, 14.
11. D.J. Bennett, *Logic Made Easy: How to Know When Language Deceives You* (New York: W.W. Norton, 2004), 30.
12. Ibid., 31.
13. Ibid., 99 and 108; referring to P.C. Wason, "Self-Contradictions," in *Thinking: Readings in Cognitive Science* (Cambridge, UK: Cambridge University Press, 1977), 114–128; S.S. Epp, "A Cognitive

Approach to Teaching Logic," *DIMACS Symposium, Teaching Logic and Reasoning in an Illogical World*, Rutgers, The State University of New Jersey, July 25–26, 1996, available at www.cs.cornell. edu/Info/People/gries/symposium/symp.htm.

14. The fact that a given set of observations can be consistent with (explained by) more than one theory or hypothesis and perhaps an infinite number of alternative theories is a problem known in philosophical and scientific circles as the *underdetermination of theories problem*. Because a multitude of hypotheses can be consistent with the same set of observations, the hypotheses are said to be empirically identical. The implication is that observational data, on its own, cannot tell us which of them is correct.

15. F. Schauer, *Profiles, Probabilities and Stereotypes* (Cambridge, MA: Belknap Press of Harvard, 2003), 59. References to studies on dog breed behavior are found in footnote 7.

16. In a subsequent chapter it will be shown that in this case the uncertainty would be 10 times greater with 10 observations than with 1,000 if price changes conform to the normal distribution, but may be far more uncertain if they do not.

17. http://en.wikipedia.org/wiki/Philosophy_of_science.

18. Shermer, *Why People Believe*, 24.

19. Richards, *Philosophy & Sociology of Science*, 45.

20. B.L. Silver, *The Ascent of Science* (New York: Oxford University Press, 1998), 15.

21. Ibid., 14.

22. R.S. Percival, *About Karl Popper*, adapted from his PhD thesis, available at www.eeng.dcu.ie/~tkpw/intro_popper/intro_popper.html.

23. This is the frequency definition of probability. There are others.

24. Richards, *Philosophy & Sociology of Science*, 52.

25. K.R. Popper, *The Logic of Scientific Discovery* (London: Hutchinson, 1977).

26. K.R. Popper, *Conjectures and Refutations* (London: Routledge & Kegan 1972).

27. This is known as the underdetermination of theories problem.

28. *If hypothesis is true, then X should be observed. X is observed* (affirms the consequent). Invalid conclusion: *The hypothesis is true* (fallacy of affirming the consequent).

29. A *necessary* condition is one that is required to produce an effect, but it alone is not enough to produce the effect. For example if X is a necessary condition of Y, it means that, if X is lacking, Y will not occur but the fact that X is present is not enough to insure Y. In shorthand: *If not X, then not Y*. A *sufficient* condition is more comprehensive in that its presence is enough (is sufficient) to produce the effect. Thus it means: *If W, then Y*.

30. Richards, *Philosophy & Sociology of Science*, 59.

31. My contention may be challenged in the near future by an objective version of EWT called EWAVES developed by Robert Prechter's firm, Elliott Wave International. Prechter claims it generates definitive signals for which financial performance can be measured.

32. Descriptions of EMH-weak vary. Some say only historical price data cannot be used to generated excess returns. Other versions say any stale market data, price, volume, or any other data series that TA practitioners study cannot be used to generated excess returns.

33. N. Jegadeesh and S. Titman, "Returns to Buying Winners and Selling Losers: Implications for Stock Market Efficiency," *Journal of Finance* 56 (1993), 699–720.

34. R.A. Haugen, *The Inefficient Stock Market: What Pays Off and Why* (Upper Saddle River, NJ: Prentice-Hall, 1999), 63.

35. F. Nicholson, "Price-Earnings Ratios in Relation to Investment Results," *Financial Analysts Journal* (January/February 1968), 105–109; J.D. McWilliams, "Prices and Price-Earnings Ratios," *Financial Analysts Journal* 22 (May/June, 1966), 136–142.

36. Because there are not infinite time and resources to test all ideas, receptivity is tempered with prior knowledge, experience, and intuition. Some new ideas merit more attention than others. However, being overly restrictive at this phase could have a big cost—missing a breakthrough. In this phase, if one is to err, it is better to err on the side of openness.

37. W.A. Wallis and H.V. Roberts, *Statistics: A New Approach* (New York: The Free Press of Glencoe, 1964), 5.

38. P.W. Bridgman, "The Prospect for Intelligence," *Yale Review* 34 (1945), 444–461, quoted in J.B. Conant, *On Understanding Science* (New Haven: Yale University Press, 1947), 115.

39. Wallis and Roberts, *Statistics*, 6.

40. J.E. Russo and P.J.H. Schoemaker, *Decision Traps: The Ten Barriers to Brilliant Decision-Making and How to Overcome Them* (New York: Doubleday, 1989), 135.

41. L.R. Goldberg, "Man versus Model of Man: A Rationale, Plus Some Evidence for a Method of Improving Clinical Inference," *Psychological Bulletin* 73 (1970), 422–432.

42. P.H.K. Chang and C.L. Osler, "Methodical Madness: Technical Analysis and the Irrationality of Exchange-Rate Forecasts," *Economic Journal*, 109, no. 458 (1999), 636–661; C.L. Osler, "Identifying Noise Traders: The Head-and-Shoulders Pattern in U.S. Equities," Publication of Federal Reserve Bank of New York, 1998.

43. R.D. Edwards, J. Magee, and W.H.C. Bassetti (Eds.), *Technical Analysis of Stock Trends*, 8th ed., (Boca Raton, FL: CRC Press, 2001); M.J. Pring, *Technical Analysis Explained*, 4th ed. (New York: McGraw-Hill, 2002); J.J. Murphy, *Technical Analysis of the Financial Markets: A Comprehensive Guide to Trading Methods and Applications* (New York: New York Institute of Finance, 1999).

44. It may be possible to define chart patterns using fuzzy logic where class membership is given a class membership function (0 to 1.0) rather than a yes or no. However, evaluating pattern effectiveness will still require a threshold on the class membership function to decide which patterns belong in a given class and which do not.

45. S.S. Alexander, "Price Movements in Speculative Markets: Trends or Random Walks," *Industrial Management Review* 2 (1961), 7–26; S.S. Alexander, "Price Movements in Speculative Markets: Trends or Random Walks No. 2," *Industrial Management Review* 5 (1964), 25–46.

46. A.A. Merrill, *Filtered Waves: Basic Theory* (Chappaqua, NY: Analysis Press, 1977).

47. P.H.K. Chang, and C.L. Osler, "Methodical Madness: Technical Analysis and the Irrationality of Exchange-Rate Forecasts," *Economic Journal* 109, no. 458 (1999), 636–661.

48. C.L. Osler, "Identifying Noise Traders: The Head-and-Shoulders Pattern in U.S. Equities," Publication of Federal Reserve Bank of New York, 1998.

49. A.W. Lo, H. Mamaysky, and W. Jiang, "Foundations of Technical Analysis: Computational Algorithms, Statistical Inference, and Empirical Implementation," *Journal of Finance* 55, 4 (August 2000), 1705–1765.

50. Kernel regression estimates the value of a smoothed curve by averaging nearby or local observations, where the weight of each observation is inversely related to its distance from the location for which a smoothed value is desired. Thus, nearby observations are given the greatest weight. The term *kernel* refers to the shape of the weighting function used. One common weight function is based on the shape of the normal probability distribution (Gaussian kernel).

51. The authors of the paper do not come out directly and say the patterns are not useful for forecasting trends, but the data they present indicates this as does the commentary on the paper provided by Narasimhan Jegadeesh (pp. 1765–1770). In Table 1 he shows that the post pattern returns (trends) are not significantly different than when the patterns are not present.

52. T.N. Bulkowski, *Encyclopedia of Chart Patterns* (New York: John Wiley & Sons, 2000), 262–304.

CHAPTER 40

Theories of Nonrandom Price Motion

From David Aronson, *Evidence-Based Technical Analysis: Applying the Scientific Method and Statistical Inference to Trading Signals* (Hoboken, New Jersey: John Wiley & Sons, 2006), Chapter 7.

At the risk of stating the obvious, if market fluctuations were completely random, TA would be pointless. TA is a justifiable endeavor if and only if price movements are nonrandom to some degree some portion of the time. This chapter offers several theories explaining why episodes of nonrandom price movements ought to occur in financial market prices.

Although the occurrence of nonrandom price motion is necessary to justify TA, this alone is not sufficient to justify any specific TA method. Each method must demonstrate, by objective evidence, its ability to capture some part of the nonrandom price motion. Part Two will evaluate a large number of TA rules with respect to their ability to do just that.

■ The Importance of Theory

Several new theories from the field of behavioral finance explain why price movements are nonrandom to some degree and therefore potentially predictable. Thus, these novel theories take a position that is contrary to the efficient markets hypothesis (EMH), a cornerstone of finance theory for over 40 years. EMH contends that price changes in financial markets are random and, therefore, unpredictable. Therefore, these new theories hold out hope for TA.

The reader may wonder why theoretical support for nonrandomness is even necessary. If a TA method has a profitable back test, isn't that all that should be needed? It could be asserted that a significantly profitable back test not only establishes that markets are nonrandom, it also establishes that the method is able to exploit some portion of the market's nonrandomness.

This view misses the importance of theoretical support. Even when all statistical precautions have been taken, a profitable back test that is not supported by sound theory is an isolated result and possibly still a lucky one. A successful back test always provokes the question: Will the rule continue to work in the future? Theory can be helpful here because a back test that is consistent with sound theory is less likely to be a statistical fluke. When a back test has theoretical foundation, it is no longer an isolated fact, but part of a larger cohesive picture in which theory explains fact and fact confirms theory.

For example, the profitability of technical trend-following systems in commodity futures can be explained as compensation (i.e., a risk premium) for providing a valuable service to commercial hedgers, that of risk transference. In other words, economic theory predicts that futures markets should manifest enough profitable trends to motivate trend followers to accept the price risks hedgers wish to shed.[1] This is discussed later in this chapter.

■ Scientific Theories

In everyday speech, a theory is a speculative conjecture about why something is the way it is. As explained in Chapter 39, a scientific theory is something different. First, it offers a succinct explanation for a broad range of prior observations. Second, and most importantly, it makes specific predictions that are later confirmed by new observations.

Kepler's laws of planetary motion[2] concisely explained a large number of prior astronomical observations and made specific predictions that were subsequently confirmed by additional observations. However, as good as Kepler's laws were, Newton's theory of gravitation was better because it was broader in scope. It not only explained why Kepler's laws worked but explained a far wider variety of phenomena. Theories of nonrandom price motion need not predict with the accuracy of physical theories. However, to be useful, they must not only succinctly describe a wide variety of previously observed market behavior, but must also make testable predictions confirmed by subsequent observations.

■ What Is Wrong with Popular TA Theory?

Many TA texts offer no explanation about why their proposed methods work. The statement of John Magee, author of one of TA's seminal works[3] is typical. He said, "We can never hope to know why the market behaves as it does, we can only aspire to understand how. History obviously has repetitive tendencies and that's good enough."

Some TA texts do offer explanations, but these are typically ad-hoc rationales that generate no testable predictions. According to author John Murphy, the cornerstone premise of TA is "anything that can possibly affect the price—fundamentally, politically, psychologically, or otherwise—is actually reflected in the price of that market."[4] One would be hard pressed to extract testable predictions from such a vague statement.

Actually, this statement, which purports to explain why TA works, contains a logical contradiction. For, if it were true that price did reflect (i.e., discount) all possible information, it would imply that price was devoid of any predictive information. To understand why, assume a hypothetical price pattern has just occurred in stock XYZ, which is currently at $50, and based on the pattern a move to $60 is implied. Then, by definition, when the pattern occurs its predictive implication has yet to be reflected in prices. However, if the premise that price reflects all information were true, the price would already be at the level predicted by the pattern, thus negating the pattern's forecasting ability.

This logical contradiction is even more apparent when it is pointed out that EMH, a school of thought that rejects the efficacy of TA, rests on the very same premise; "prices fully reflect all available information."[5] Technical analysis cannot be based on the same premise as its mortal enemy. This contradiction is an example of cloudy uncritical thinking that is all too common in the popular version of TA.

Fortunately for TA, its cornerstone premise that price reflects all information appears to be contradicted by fact. One example is the so-called underreaction effect, which has been postulated by behavioral finance. It says that, because prices sometimes fail to respond to new information as rapidly as EMH theorists contend, a systematic price movement, or trend, toward a price level that does reflect the new information occurs. The failure of prices to respond rapidly is caused by a several cognitive errors that afflict investors, such as the conservatism bias and the anchoring effect. These are discussed later in this chapter.

Another popular justification of TA is based on pop psychology. By pop psychology, I mean principles of human behavior that seem plausible but lack scientific support. According to noted economist and authority in the field of behavioral finance, Robert Shiller, "In considering lessons from psychology, it must be noted that the many popular accounts of the psychology of investing are simply not credible. Investors are said to be euphoric or frenzied during booms or panic-stricken during market crashes. In both booms and crashes, investors are descried as blindly following the herd like so many sheep, with no minds of their own."[6] The fact is, people are more rational than these pop-psychology theories suggest. "During the most significant financial events, most people are preoccupied with other personal matters, not with the financial markets at all. So it is hard to imagine that the market as a whole reflects the emotions described by these psychological theories."[7] We will need to look beyond the platitudes of popular texts for TA's justification. Fortunately, theories developed in the field of behavioral finance and elsewhere are beginning to offer the theoretical support TA needs.

■ The Enemy's Position: Efficient Markets and Random Walks

Before discussing theories that explain why nonrandom price movements should exist, we need to consider the enemy's position, the EMH. Recently, some have argued that EMH does not necessarily imply that prices follow unpredictable random walks,[8] and that efficient markets and price predictability can coexist. However, the pioneers of EMH asserted that random walks were a necessary consequence of efficient markets. This section states their case and examines its weaknesses.

What Is an Efficient Market?

An efficient market is a market that cannot be beaten. In such a market, no fundamental or technical analysis strategy, formula, or system can earn a risk-adjusted rate of return that beats the market defined by a benchmark index. If the market is indeed efficient, the risk-adjusted return earned by buying and holding the market index is the best one can hope for. This is so because prices in an efficient market properly reflect all known and knowable information. Therefore, the current price provides the best estimate of each security's value.

According to EMH, markets achieve a state of efficient pricing because of the vigorous efforts of numerous rational investors attempting to maximize their wealth. In their pursuit of true value, these investors are constantly updating their beliefs with the latest information in a probabilistically correct manner[9] so as to project each security's future cash flows. Although no single investor is all knowing, collectively they know as much as can possibly be known. This knowledge motivates investors to buy and sell in such a way that prices settle at the *equilibrium* or rational price level.

In such a world, prices change only when new information arrives. When it does, prices change almost instantly to a new rational price that properly reflects the news. Thus, prices do not gradually trend from one rational price level to the next, giving the trend analyst a chance to get on board. Not at all. In the world posited by EMH, prices trace a step function as they move almost instantly from one rational level to the next. If the news is favorable, prices rise, and if it's unfavorable, prices fall. Because it is not predictable whether the news will be favorable or unfavorable (it wouldn't be news if it was), price changes will be unpredictable as well. This is illustrated in Figure 40.1.

The Consequences of Market Efficiency: Good and Bad

Market efficiency has good and bad implications. They are good for the economy as a whole but bad—very bad—for TA. They are good for the economy because rational prices send vital signals of asset values that, in turn, encourage the efficient allocation of scarce resources, such as capital and labor. This fosters economic growth.[10]

However, prices in an efficient market are unpredictable rendering all forms of TA useless. According to Paul Samuelson, financial market prices follow a random walk because of the actions of many intelligent/rational investors. In seeking to maximize wealth, they buy undervalued assets pushing their prices higher and sell overvalued assets pushing prices lower.[11] "Taken to its logical extreme, it means that a blindfolded

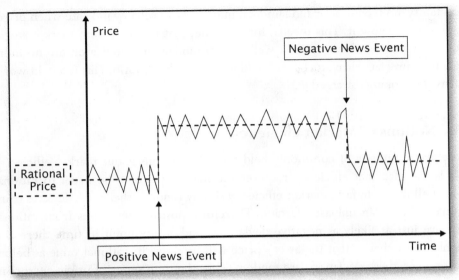

FIGURE 40.1 Efficient Market's Response to Positive and Negative News.

monkey selecting stocks by throwing darts at a newspaper's financial pages could do just as well as one carefully selected by the experts."[12]

"EMH rules out the possibility of trading systems, based on available information, that have expected profits or returns in excess of equilibrium expected profit or return."[13] "In plain English, an average investor—whether an individual, pension fund, or a mutual fund—cannot hope to consistently beat the market, and the vast resources that such investors dedicate to analyzing, picking and trading securities are wasted."[14] Although, under EMH, it is still possible to generate positive returns from an investment strategy, when those returns are adjusted for risk, they will not be superior to the return of buying and holding the market index portfolio.

The efficient markets hypothesis also declares that when there is no news entering the market, prices tend to oscillate in a random and unbiased fashion above and below the rational price level. See Figure 40.2. Because this level is itself subject to

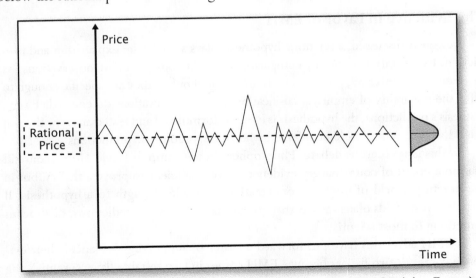

FIGURE 40.2 Efficient Market Hypothesis (Random and Unbiased Pricing Errors).

uncertainty, no technical or fundamental indicator can reliably indicate when prices are above or below it. This means, for example, that in an efficient market stocks with a low price to book ratio, a well known fundamental indicator, are no more likely to appreciate than stocks with a high price to book ratio. This is a cold world for anyone looking for an edge.

False Notions of Market Efficiency

There are a number of commonly held but false notions about market efficiency. First is the idea that efficiency requires the market price to be equal to rational value at all times. In fact, market efficiency simply requires that price deviates from rational value in an unbiased fashion. Therefore, positive deviations from rational value are just as likely as negative deviations, and at any point in time there is a roughly equal chance that the asset's price will be above its rational value as below it. Moreover, these deviations are random. Thus the time series of pricing errors in an efficient market is a random variable whose probability distribution is centered at the rational price and is approximately symmetrical about it.

A second false notion about market efficiency is that it implies that no one can beat the market. Actually, in any given time period, about 50 percent of all investors will outperform the benchmark index, while the remaining 50 percent underperform. The notion that no single investor or money manager can beat the market over the long term is equally false. Given enough players, a small number are likely to have lengthy streaks of market beating returns even if their strategies are totally without merit. Nassim Taleb[15] shows that even if we assume money managers are no better than a blind monkey throwing darts[16] (probability of beating the market = 0.5) and the universe of managers is large enough, say 10,000, after five years there is likely to be about 312 firms who have beaten the market five years in a row. These lucky folks are the ones who will send salesmen calling. The other 9,682 are less likely to knock on your door.

The Evidence in Favor of EMH

As previously discussed, a scientific hypothesis plays a dual role: explanation and prediction. Its veracity is tested by comparing its predictions with new observations. As discussed in Chapter 39, predictions are meaningful only if they are specific enough to offer the possibility of empirical falsification. If new observations do contradict a hypothesis's predictions, the hypothesis is either reformulated and tested anew or thrown out. However, what should be inferred when observations and predictions agree?

On this issue there is debate. Philosophers in the camp of David Hume contend that no amount of confirmatory evidence is ever sufficient to prove a theory, but in the practical world of science, confirmation does add strength to a hypothesis. If test after test yields observations that are consistent with its predictions, that means something to most scientists.

So EMH advocates have put forward a roster of supporting evidence. Their evidence comes in two flavors because EMH comes in two testable flavors: semistrong

FIGURE 40.3 Efficient Market Response to Bullish News.

and weak.[17] The semistrong form asserts it is impossible to beat the market with public information. Because this includes all fundamental and technical data, the semistrong form predicts that neither fundamental nor technical analysis can beat the market. This informal prediction is not sufficiently specific to be testable, but it is in agreement with the observation that people have great difficulty profiting consistently from market fluctuations—and a lot try.

The semistrong form also makes several specific predictions that are testable. One is that a security's price will react quickly and accurately to any news that bears on its value. The proper response of an efficient market to news is illustrated in Figure 40.3.

This prediction implies prices should neither overreact nor underreact to news. This is testable in the following way. Imagine for a moment that prices did not behave efficiently and did systematically over- or underreact to new information. If this were the case, it would imply that price movements would be predictable. To see why, consider what would happen if a stock overreacted to news either by going up too much in response to good news or down too much in response to bad. Because EMH says prices must stay close to rational values, overshooting rational value would necessarily lead to a corrective movement back toward rational value. This correction would not be random meandering but rather a purposeful movement, as if the price were being magnetically drawn to the rational level. Such a movement would be, to some degree, predictable. Because EMH denies predictability, it must also deny the possibility of overreactions to news. A hypothetical overreaction to bullish news and a subsequent systematic movement back to rational levels is illustrated in Figure 40.4.

By the same logic, EMH must also deny the possibility of underreaction to news, where prices move less than the news justifies. In this case, a systematic price movement would also develop as prices continued to trend (drift) toward

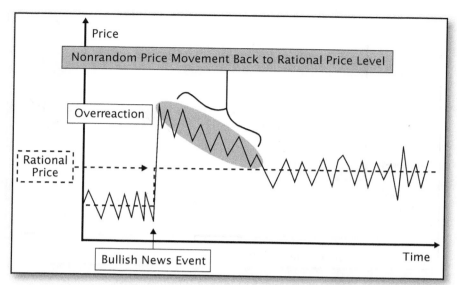

FIGURE 40.4 **Overreaction to Bullish News (Implies Nonrandom Price Movements).**

the new rational level implied by the news. Underreaction to bullish and bearish news events and the resultant nonrandom movement toward rational value are illustrated in Figure 40.5.

Evidence supporting EMH's prediction that overreactions and underreactions do not occur is presented in the event studies of Eugene Fama.[18] He examined all types of corporate news events such as earnings and dividend announcements, takeovers, mergers, and so forth and found that after an initial, almost instantaneous, nonexploitable price movement triggered by the news, there was no additional movement.

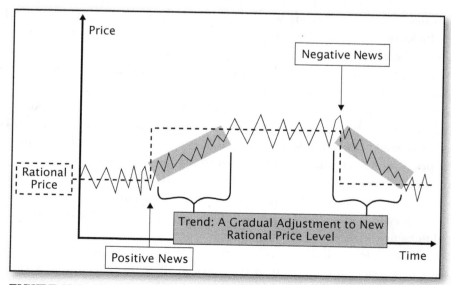

FIGURE 40.5 **Underreaction to News Can Explain Nonrandom Trends.**

These observations are consistent with EMH's prediction that the markets quickly and accurately discount news events.[19]

A second prediction of EMH is that prices should change only when news arrives. It follows then, that prices should not change dramatically in the absence of news or in response to noninformative events.[20] These two predictions suggest yet a third that is most crucial to TA. EMH implies that stale information, information already in the public domain, should have no predictive power and be of no value in making investment profits. Clearly, all information used by TA qualifies as stale. Thus, EMH predicts that all TA methods should fail. If this were to be confirmed, it's lights out for TA.

The prediction that all stale information strategies should have no predictive power seems cut and dried until one tries to test it. Recall, EMH says an investment strategy based on stale information should not be able to generate excess profits after risk adjustment. So the mere fact that a strategy based on stale information makes gains is not sufficient to rebut EMH. To contradict EMH, it must be demonstrated that the gains are excessive after adjusting for the strategy's risk.

The notion of judging investment strategies on the basis of risk-adjusted returns is entirely reasonable. For example, if a strategy makes 20 percent per year and the benchmark makes 10 percent, but the strategy exposes the investor to three times the risk, the strategy has not beaten the index after risk adjustment. The question is: How does one define and quantify risk?

Quantifying risk requires a risk model. The most well known is the capital asset pricing model[21] (CAPM), which explains systematic differences in the returns of securities in terms of a single risk factor, the security's relative volatility. This is to say, the risk of a stock is quantified by its volatility relative to the volatility of the market as a whole. Thus, if a stock is twice as volatile as the market index, its returns should be twice that of the market. Such a stock is said to earn excess returns when it earns more than twice the market return. This approach works well when measuring the risk of a single stock or a portfolio of long stock positions. However, CAPM cannot quantify the risk exposures of more complex strategies. In response to this limitation, capital market theorists have proposed other risk models. One of the best known is APT (arbitrage pricing theory), which attributes risk to several independent risk factors.[22]

However, EMH advocates have tacitly given themselves the liberty of cooking up new risk factors whenever they wish. This makes it nearly impossible to refute their claim that stale information strategies cannot beat the market. For, it is always possible to propose a new risk model that explains away a strategy's excess returns as compensation for risk. This is not a scientific sin if the risk factor(s) were identified before the stale information strategy earning excess returns was discovered. However, proposing a new risk factor(s) after a market-beating strategy has been discovered is nothing more than an ad hoc hypothesis. This is an explanation cooked up after the fact for the specific purpose of immunizing a theory, in this case EMH, from falsification. This practice is frowned upon in science for good reason. Also, the information content of a scientific theory is roughly equivalent to the opportunities it presents for falsification. The unbridled ability to explain away any and all dissonant evidence effectively drains the theory of its information content. Thus, the freedom to concoct new risk factors to explain each and every investment strategy that beats the market with stale information effectively reduces EMH to a meaningless theory.

The evidence confirming the weak form of EMH, which states that stale prices and indicators derived from them—such as price momentum—are without value, is based on auto-correlation studies. They measure the degree to which price changes are linearly correlated with prior changes, at various lag intervals.[23] These studies have confirmed that price changes (i.e., returns) are indeed linearly independent. This means that a linear function of current and past returns cannot be used to predict future returns.[24] Based on these findings, it was concluded by EMH advocates, that security returns are an unpredictable random walk.

However, autocorrelation studies are relatively weak tests in the sense that they can only detect linear dependencies. Searching for linear structure is merely one way to determine if a time series is behaving in a nonrandom fashion. Edgar Peters[25] and Andrew Lo and A. Craig MacKinlay[26] have shown that alternative data analysis methods indicate that financial market time series do not behave like random walks. For example, the test statistic used by Lo and McKinlay, called the variance ratio, can detect more complex (nonlinear) nonrandom behaviors that would be invisible autocorrelation studies.

■ Challenging EMH

A good theory is consistent in two ways. Its logic is internally consistent and it is consistent with observed evidence. Thus a theory can be challenged either by showing that it contradicts itself or that it is contradicted by evidence.

A theory is self-contradicting if it implies or predicts something that would contradict the theory. An example was given earlier in this chapter: I showed that a cornerstone premise of popular TA, which asserts that price perfectly reflects all information, contradicts another of its central premises, that price contains predictive information.

The Smart versus Dumb Paradox

One implication of market efficiency is that knowledgeable investors should not be able to earn higher returns than investors who are less knowledgeable. This follows from the premise that market efficiency means that whatever information is known or knowable has already been reflected in security prices. In an efficient market, there is no competitive advantage to being smart or disadvantage to being dumb.

However, this implication conflicts with another of EMH's assumptions—that the arbitrage activities of rational investors are able to drive prices toward rational levels. (See the heading titled "The Assumptions of EMH" later in this chapter.) Arbitrage can only act as an enforcer of rational prices if arbitrageurs have more trading capital and, thus, greater price-moving power than irrational, dumb investors. Having more trading capital implies that smart arbitrageurs must have earned higher returns in the past than less well informed (dumb) investors. Either market prices are set by the smartest, richest participants or they are not. EMH implies both. Paradoxical, isn't it!

The Cost of Information Paradox

Another logical inconsistency of EMH has to do with the cost of information. It is reasonable to assume that it costs time, money, and intelligence to gather information and process it into useful investing strategies. At the same time EMH contends that such information cannot earn incremental returns for investors who incur these costs. Remember, EMH contends that information is instantly reflected in prices. This implies that no matter how wide or deep the research effort, whatever is discovered will be of no value.

However, if EMH is correct that there is no payoff for information gathering and processing, then investors would lack the motivation to incur the costs of doing so. With no one to dig out the information and act on it, it would not get reflected in price. In other words, if it is costly to make markets informationally efficient, investors would be motivated to do it only if they were compensated with excess risk-adjusted returns. Thus the contradiction—EMH requires that information seekers be compensated for their efforts and simultaneously denies that they will be.

This paradox is argued persuasively by Grossman and Stiglitz in their article "On the Impossibility of Informationally Efficient Markets."[27] They contend that inefficiencies are necessary to motivate rational investors to engage in information gathering and processing. The returns they earn from the market's pricing errors are compensation for their efforts, which, in turn, have the effect of moving prices toward rational levels. The gains of these rational investors are financed by the losses of noise traders and liquidity traders. Noise traders are investors who buy and sell based on signals that they think are informative but that are not. Rational investors also earn profits from the losses of investors who trade to increase their cash reserves (liquidity traders). One way for the rational investor to gain would be if there were a delay between the time information is discovered and the time it is reflected in prices, but EMH denies the possibility of gradual price adjustments. This is yet another logical inconsistency of EMH.

A similar logic applies to the costs of acting on information (e.g., commissions, slippage, bid-asked spreads). Unless investors were compensated for incurring trading costs there would be no point to their trading activities, which are required by EMH to move the price to its rational level. The bottom line is that any factor that limits trading—costs to trade, costs to generate information, the rule that impairs short-selling, and so forth—limits the ability of the market to attain efficiency. It simply does not hold logically that there would be no compensation to those engaged in trading.

The Assumptions of EMH

To appreciate the arguments made by EMH's critics, it is necessary to understand that EMH rests on three progressively weaker assumptions: (1) investors are rational, (2) investors' pricing errors are random, and (3) there are always rational arbitrage investors to catch any pricing errors. Let's examine each of these in a bit more detail.

First is EMH's contention that investors are, by and large, rational. To recap, rational investors, in aggregate, are purported to value securities correctly. This means prices will reflect, as accurately as possible, the present discounted value of a security's future cash flows and risk characteristics. As rational investors learn new information, they respond quickly, bidding up prices when news is good and letting the price fall when news is bad. As a consequence, security prices adjust, almost instantly, to new information.[28]

Even if this assumption were incorrect, EMH advocates still insist that prices adjust quickly to rational levels anyway because of their second assumption: The valuation mistakes of individual investors are uncorrelated. This means that if one investor erroneously values a security too high, that error will be offset by another investor's error of valuing it too low. Taken in aggregate, these valuation errors are self-canceling and have an average value of zero. That is to say pricing errors are unbiased. This is presumed to be true because the error-prone investors are likely to be using different, though useless, investment strategies. Therefore, their actions should be uncorrelated. To put it bluntly, as one foolish investor gets an uninformative signal to buy, another investment fool is equally likely to get an uninformative signal to sell. In effect they wind up trading with each other, leaving prices very close to rational levels.

Moreover, even if this second assumption fails to keep prices at rational levels, EMH invokes yet a third assumption. That is, if the valuation mistakes of irrational investors turn out to be biased (i.e., have an average value that is greater than or less than zero), arbitrage investors will come to the rescue. They will notice that prices have systematically diverged from rational values. The arbitrageurs will buy when prices are too low or sell when they are too high, thus forcing prices back to where they should be.

In the EMH world, arbitrage is as close as it gets to a free lunch. An arbitrage transaction incurs no risk, requires no capital, and earns a guaranteed return. As envisioned by efficient market advocates, an arbitrage trade goes something like this: Consider two financial assets, stocks X and Y, which sell at equal prices and which are equally risky. However, they have different expected future returns. Obviously, one of the two assets is improperly priced. If asset X has a higher future return, then to take advantage of the mispricing, arbitrageurs would buy asset X while short-selling Y. With the activities of like-minded arbitrageurs, the price of each stock will converge to its proper fundamental value.[29] Market efficiency attained in this manner assumes there are always arbitrageurs ready, willing, and able to jump on these opportunities. The better ones become very wealthy, thereby enhancing their ability to drive prices to proper levels, while the irrational investors eventually go broke losing their ability to push prices away from equilibrium levels. The uninformed, irrational investors are driven out of the market the way a weak species is driven from an ecosystem, while the rational, well-informed arbitrageurs thrive.

Flaws in EMH Assumptions

This section considers each of the assumptions of EMH and how they miss the mark.

Investors Are Rational Investors do not appear to be as rational as EMH assumes. Many investors react to irrelevant information, what noted economist Fischer Black calls "noise signals."[30] Though they think they are acting intelligently, these investors can expect to earn the same return as an investor who buys and sells based on a coin flip. Investors who follow the advice of financial gurus who base their advice on noise signals are noise traders by proxy.

In fact, investors are guilty of numerous departures from rationality. For example, they fail to diversify, they trade too actively, they increase their tax liabilities by selling appreciated stocks but hold onto losing positions, and they trade mutual funds with high fees. Moreover, their failures are recurring. "Investors' deviations from the maxims of economic rationality turn out to be highly pervasive and systematic."[31] These departures from rationality can be classified into three areas: inaccurate risk assessments, poor probability judgments, and irrational decision framing. I discuss each of these in turn.

Investors typically do not assess risks in conformity with the normative ideal put forward by Neumann and Morgenstern, known as "expected utility theory." In a perfectly rational world, an individual faced with choosing among several options selects the one with the highest expected value. The expected value of a particular choice is equal to a sum of products, where each product is the probability of each possible outcome multiplied by the value or utility of that outcome to the decision maker. The problem is people do not actually behave this way. Research has shown that investors make numerous systematic errors when assessing risks and making choices.

These mistakes have been incorporated into a framework called Prospect Theory, which was proposed by Kahneman and Tversky (1979).[32] It explains how people actually make decisions under conditions of uncertainty. For example, it explains that investors hold onto losing stocks but sell profitable positions to avoid the psychic pain of realizing a loss. It also explains why investors overvalue low-probability long-shot speculations.

The second way investors depart from the rational ideal of EMH is in their judgments of probability. EMH assumes that, as investors receive new information, they update their probability assessments in accordance with Bayes' theorem, a formula for combining probabilities in a theoretically correct way. However, to their detriment, investors do not behave this way. One common error is the crime of small numbers—drawing grand conclusions from small samples of data. This explains why investors will rashly conclude that a corporation with a short string of successful quarterly earnings reports is likely to continue to grow rapidly. Their overreaction to this small sample of positive earnings changes causes the stock to become overpriced.

Lastly, investors' decisions can be strongly impacted by how choices are described (framed). By incorrectly framing a decision situation, investors tend to misperceive the true expected value of a choice. For example, when choices are framed in terms of potential gains, investors tend to choose the option most likely to earn a gain, even if it is insignificant in size. However, when the same choices are framed in terms of potential losses, investors will assume the risk of a very significant loss just to avoid the certainty of a small loss. This error, called the "disposition effect," is thought to explain why investors sell winners quickly, so as to be sure to earn a gain, even if it's small, but hold on to losers even if it means there is a chance the loss will turn into a much larger one.

Investor Errors Are Uncorrelated The assumption that investors' errors are uncorrelated is contradicted by psychological research which shows people do not deviate from rationality randomly in situations characterized by uncertainty. In reality, most people tend to make similar mistakes in such situations and hence their deviations from rationality are correlated. Many investors will be tempted to buy the same stock because the stock appeals to a common heuristic rule of judgment that makes it look like a candidate for further appreciation. For example, a company that has three positive earning quarters can be perceived by many investors to be a growth stock that warrants a high price-to-earnings ratio or P/E. This problem is made worse by social interactions, or herding, between investors. "They follow each other's mistakes listening to rumors and imitating the actions of their fellow traders."[33]

Money managers, who should know better, make these mistakes as well. They are guilty of creating portfolios that are excessively close to the benchmarks against which they are measured, all in an effort to reduce the chance they will underperform. Professional money managers also engage in imitative behavior and move herd-like into the same stocks, for fear of falling behind the pack. They dress up their portfolios by adding stocks that have done well and eliminate those that have not, so year-end portfolio reports show the fund invested in the highest performing stocks.

Arbitrage Forces Prices to Rational Levels This assumption fails because the power of arbitrage activities to push prices toward rational levels is limited. First, no one rings a bell when securities become mispriced. The rational price is the discounted value of a stream of future cash flows, which is, by definition, uncertain. Investors try to estimate future earnings, but their forecasts are prone to significant error.

Second, arbitrageurs do not have unlimited tolerance for adverse price movement—for example, when an underpriced stock that has been purchased continues to go lower, or an overpriced security that has been sold short continues to soar. The actions of noise traders can easily push prices further away from rational levels before they return to them. Therefore, even if an arbitrageur spots a truly mispriced security, the pricing error may grow larger before it is finally eradicated. Should this adverse price movement become too large, the arbitrageur may have to close the position with a loss. If this happens often enough, the noise traders can drive rational investors out of business. This is referred to as noise trader risk[34] and it limits the motivation and commitments of arbitrage traders. Behavioral finance expert Andre Shleifer says even an arbitrage trade that looks nearly perfect from the outside is in reality quite risky so the number of investors who go after it will be limited. The bottom line is arbitrage activities cannot always enforce rational pricing.

Noise trader risk was a factor in the blow-up of the Long Term Capital Management (LTCM) hedge fund in the fall of 1998. The fund's crash nearly took the entire financial market with it. Ultimately, the mispricings that LTCM had identified were corrected, but because they had overleveraged their positions, the fund lacked the staying power to hold its positions through a short-term period of even greater mispricing.

Improper use of leverage is yet another factor that can impair the role arbitrage plays in driving markets to efficiency. Thus, even if arbitrageurs can accurately identify over- and under-priced securities, if they use too much leverage they can get wiped out. There is an optimal leverage for favorable bets (i.e., speculations with a positive expectancy).[35] If this level is exceeded, the probability of ruin rises despite the positive expectation.

I show this to my students during a class I call Casino Night. We play a game in which everyone starts off with an imaginary $100. I have a friend come in to act as coin flipper. Before each flip, the students determine what fraction of their capital to bet on the next coin toss. If a head results, the payoff is twice the amount of the bet. If a tail results, only the amount of the bet is lost. We play the game for 75 flips. This game has a very favorable expectation.[36] However, even in a game with such a favorable expectancy, many students wind up losing money because they bet too aggressively (i.e., the fraction of capital wagered on a bet is too large). A formula worked out by Kelly, an electrical engineer at Bell Labs in the 1950s, now known as the Kelly Criterion, specifies the optimal fraction to bet on each coin flip so as to maximize the growth rate of the bettor's capital. The optimal fraction depends on the probability of a win and the ratio of the average win to average loss. In this particular game, the optimal fraction to wager on each bet is 0.25. If this level is exceeded, the bettor faces greater risk without the benefit of a faster growth of capital. If one were to employ a bet fraction of 0.58 it is likely all funds would be lost, despite the favorable expectation. This is what happens to an arbitrageur with good information who uses too much leverage.

Another constraint on an arbitrage's ability to enforce efficient pricing is the lack of perfect substitute securities. An ideal (riskless) arbitrage transaction involves the simultaneous purchase and sale of a pair of securities with identical future cash flows and identical risk characteristics. An arbitrage transaction based on securities that do not conform to this ideal necessarily involves risk. And it is risk that limits the degree to which arbitrage activity can force prices to efficient levels. When a broad class of assets, such as all stocks, become overpriced, as they did in the spring of 2000, there is no substitute security to use as the long-side hedge to a short sale of the entire stock market. Even in the case where the securities in an arbitrage transaction are close substitutes, there can be substantial risks. Each stock has its own specific or idiosyncratic risks, and this makes arbitrageurs wary. For example, if GM were undervalued and it were purchased against an offsetting short sale in Ford, there would be the risk that some bullish event unique to Ford or a bearish event unique to GM would create a loss for the arbitrage trader.

There are still other constraints that prevent arbitrage from playing the price-policing role envisioned by EMH. Arbitrageurs do not have unlimited funds to correct pricing errors nor do they have total freedom to pursue any and all opportunities. Most arbitrage investors manage money for other investors in the form of hedge funds. The management contracts under which the fund managers operate typically constrain their actions to some degree. Without a completely free hand and unlimited funds, some mispricings will remain unarbitraged.

As a result of these limits, the EMH assumption that all arbitrage opportunities will be eradicated appears to be an oversimplification.

Empirical Challenges to EMH

The EMH is not only riddled with logical inconsistencies, its predictions are contradicted by a growing body of empirical evidence. This section summarizes these findings.

Excessive Price Volatility   If security prices were as tightly connected to fundamental values as EMH asserts, then the magnitude of price changes should be similar to the magnitude of changes in the underlying fundamentals. However, studies show prices are far more volatile than fundamentals. For example, when fundamental value is defined as the net present value of future dividends,[37] changes in fundamental value are unable to explain the high volatility of prices. The technology stock bubble that ruptured in the spring of 2000 and the bubble in Japanese stock prices in the late 1980s are examples of price movements that cannot be explained by changes in fundamental value.

EMH also predicts that large price changes should occur only when significant new information enters the market. The evidence does not agree. For example, the stock market crash of October 1987 was not accompanied by news that would have justified a price drop that exceeded 20 percent. A 1991 study by Cutler cited by Shleifer[38] examined the 50 largest one-day price movements since the end of World War II. Many of these price events were not associated with significant news announcements. In a similar study, Roll[39] showed that fluctuations in the price of frozen orange juice futures often occurred without any developments in the weather, the major fundamental influence on that market. Roll also showed that individual stock movements are often not associated with corporate news events.

Evidence of Price Predictability with Stale Information   The evidence most damning to EMH are studies showing that price movements can be predicted to a meaningful degree with publicly known (stale) information. In other words, strategies based on stale information can generate risk-adjusted returns that beat the market. If it were true that prices quickly incorporate all known information, as EMH asserts, this should not be possible.

How Cross-Sectional Predictability Studies Are Performed   The April 2001 issue of *Journal of Finance* notes that many predictability studies show that publicly available information is not fully reflected in stock prices and that numerous strategies based on this information are profitable.[40] These studies measure the degree to which indicators based on public information are able to forecast the relative performance of stocks.[41] Indicators tested included a stock's price-to-earnings ratio, its price-to-book-value ratio, its recent relative price performance, and so forth.

Predictability studies employ a cross-sectional design. That is to say, they examine a large cross section of stocks at a given point in time, for example, all stocks in the S&P 500 Index as of December 31, 1999. For that date, the stocks are ranked on the basis of an indicator[42] that is being examined for its predictive power, such as a stock's rate of return over the past six months (price momentum). With this done, the stocks are arranged into a number of portfolios on the basis of rank, with each portfolio containing an equal number of stocks. Ten portfolios is a common number. Thus portfolio 1 would contain the top 10 percent of all stocks ranked by their prior six-month rate of return. That is to say, the portfolio is composed of those stocks whose prior six-month rate of return was in greater than the ninetieth percentile. A second portfolio is formed containing stocks ranked from the eightieth percentile to the eighty-ninth percentile, and so on until a final portfolio is formed from the 10 percent of stocks with the worst prior six-month performance.

To determine if six-month momentum has predictive power, the future performance of the top decile portfolio (1) is compared to the future performance of the bottom decile portfolio (10). The forward prediction horizon is typically one time period. Therefore, using monthly data, it would be one month.[43] Typically these studies quantify the indicator's predictive power as the return earned by a long portfolio versus a short portfolio. In other words, a long position is assumed to be taken in all portfolio 1 stocks and a short position in all portfolio 10 stocks. For example, if in a given time period, the long portfolio earned 7 percent while the short portfolio lost 4 percent (e.g., the stocks sold short went up 4 percent), the long-versus-short strategy would have earned 3 percent. Although in this example the indicator used to rank stocks was the six-month price momentum, any item of information that was known at the time the portfolios are constructed could be used. I illustrate this concept in Figure 40.6, where the indicator used is each stock's P/E ratio.

FIGURE 40.6 **Cross-Sectional Study to Determine the Predictive Power of P/E Ratio.**

PE | P/B | Cap. | Mom. | Etc.
Stock 1
Stock 2
Stock 3

Stock n

Month 1 · Month 2 · Month 3 · Month 4 · Month 5 · etc.

Time

Predictor
Variables

FIGURE 40.7 Cross-Sectional Time Series Study.

I just described how a cross-sectional study is carried out for a single month (December 1999). However, cross-sectional studies are carried out over many months (cross-sectional time series). Thus, the predictive power of an indicator is measured as the average return on portfolio 1 minus the average return on portfolio 10 over an extended period of time. Such studies often examine a number of candidate predictor variables. This idea is illustrated in Figure 40.7.

Predictability Studies Contradicting Semistrong EMH The semistrong form of EMH is the boldest testable version of EMH.[44] It asserts that no information in the public domain, fundamental or technical, can be used to generate risk-adjusted returns in excess of the market index. The bottom line of numerous well-conducted cross-sectional time series studies is this: Price movements are predictable to some degree with stale public information, and excess risk-adjusted returns are possible. Here, I summarize some of these key findings:

- **Small capitalization effect:** A stock's total market capitalization, defined as the number of shares outstanding multiplied by its price per share, is predictive of future returns.[45] Stocks in a portfolio composed of the lowest decile portfolio of market capitalization earned about 9 percent per year more than stocks in the highest decile portfolio.[46] This effect is most pronounced in the month of January. Recent studies show this indicator's predictive power has disappeared since the mid to late 1980s.

- **Price-to-earnings ratio effect:** Stocks with low P/E ratios outperform stocks with high P/E ratios.[47]

- **Price-to-book-value effect:** Stocks with low price to book value ratios outperform stocks with high price to book value ratios.[48] The cheapest stocks, in terms of price to book, outperformed the most expensive stocks by almost 20 percent per year.

- **Earnings surprise with technical confirmation:** Stocks reporting unexpected earnings or giving earnings guidance that is confirmed by strong price and volume action on the day after the news is announced earn an annualized return spread (longs − shorts) over the next month of over 30 percent.[49] This strategy is a marriage of fundamental and technical information.

Predictability Studies Contradicting the Weak Form of EMH The weak form of EMH is the least bold version of the theory. It claims that only a subset of public information, past prices, and price returns[50] is unhelpful in earning excess returns. The following studies show that stale prices and other data used in technical indicators are indeed useful. This is very good news for TA and very bad news for EMH. The narrowest, most timid, and most difficult to falsify version of EMH has been contradicted with evidence.

- **Momentum persistence:** Jegadeesh and Titman (1993)[51] showed that price momentum measured over the past six to twelve months persists. In other words, the stocks that have been strongest over the past 6 months, 7 months, 8 months, and so on, up to 12 months, tend to outperform over the following 6 to 12 months. Their study simulated a strategy of holding long positions in stocks with the highest returns over the prior 6 months (top decile) and holding short positions in stocks with the worst performance (lowest decile). The portfolio of long and short positions was then held for 6 months. This strategy earned an annualized return of 10 percent. In light of this evidence, even one of the high priests of EMH, Eugene Fama, had to admit that past stock returns can predict future stock returns.[52] Score a big one for TA!

- **Momentum reversal:** Although stocks with strong trends over the past 6 to 12 months tend to maintain those trends over the following 6 to 12 months, something different is observed when momentum is measured over longer time spans. Strong trends measured over the prior three to five years display a tendency to reverse. De Bondt and Thaler tested a strategy of buying stocks with the most negative five-year trends (losers) and selling short stocks with the most positive five-year trends (winners). The long-versus-short portfolio averaged an 8 percent annualized return over the next three years,[53] and most importantly, this return difference was not attributable to risk. The prior losers (future winners) were not more risky than the prior winners (future losers).[54] This contradicts a central proposition of EMH that higher returns can only be earned by assuming higher risks. Additionally, it bolsters the notion that a very simplistic form of TA is useful.

- **Nonreversing momentum:** When a stock's momentum is measured by its proximity to its 52-week high, rather than its prior rate of return, profits are greater and momentum does not reverse.[55] The author of this study speculates that investors become mentally anchored to prior 52-week price highs. Anchoring is known to prevent people from making appropriate adjustments to new information. The author of this study, Michael Cooper, conjectured that this prevents stocks near their 52-week highs from responding to new fundamental developments as rapidly as they should. Retarded news response engenders systemic price trends (momentum) that correct the mispricing.

- **Momentum confirmed by trading volume:** Further support for the validity of TA comes from studies showing that, when trading volume is used conjointly with price momentum, even higher returns can be earned. That is to say, a synergism can be attained by combining price and volume indicators. The return of the combination is 2 to 7 percent higher than the return can be earned using price momentum alone.[56] Stocks with high volume and positive price momentum do better going forward than stocks with positive price momentum alone. Moreover, stocks with high volume and negative price momentum do worse going forward than stocks that merely have negative price momentum. Said differently, the discrimination power of price momentum is greater for high-volume stocks.

EMH Digs for a Defense

When an established theory is contradicted with empirical evidence, its supporters do not simply roll over and say never mind. The cognitive mechanisms of belief persistence don't work that way for trained scientists any more than they do for common folk. Cynical observers of science say adherents to a theory that has been falsified never really change their minds. They have far too much invested in its survival to do that. With time, they just fade away.

With EMH having served, and served well, for 40+ years, as the foundation of finance, its backers were just not about to go away with heads hanging low. Two of its standard bearers (read pall bearers), Eugene Fama and Kenneth French, said gains earned by stale-information strategies such as price-to-book value and market capitalization were nothing more than fair compensation for risk. Recall that EMH does not deny the possibility that stale public information can earn profits. It merely says that when those gains are adjusted for risk, they will not be better than investing in an index fund.

So long as the term *risk* is left undefined, EMH defenders are free to conjure up new forms of risk after the fact. As Elliott wavers have proven, after-the-fact fiddling allows any prior observations to be explained or explained away. And that, it seems to me, is what Fama and French did.[57] They invented a new, ad hoc risk model using three risk factors to replace the old standby, the capital asset pricing model,[58] which uses only one risk factor, a stock's volatility relative to the market index. Quite conveniently, the two new risk factors that Fama and French decided to add were the price-to-book ratio and market capitalization. By citing these as proxies for risk, Fama and French neatly explained away their predictive power. "According to the new risk model, stocks of smaller firms (low-market cap) or firms with low market-to-book ratios are fundamentally riskier companies and thus must offer higher average returns to compensate the investors willing to own them. Conversely, large capitalization stocks because they are safer, and high price-to-book ratio stocks, which are in effect growth stocks with more certain future prospects, earn lower average returns because they expose their owners to lower risk."[59]

This was nothing more than an ad hoc after-the-fact explanation conjured up to save a dying theory. Had Fama and French predicted that price-to-book and market capitalization were valid risk factors before these variables were discovered to earn excess returns, that would have been a much different story. It would have shown that EMH was a powerful theory whose deductive consequences were confirmed by subsequent observations. However, Fama and French did not do this. They invented the new risk factors after price-to-book and market cap had been shown to produce excess returns.

As pointed out earlier, Fama and French justified their new risk model by suggesting that low market-cap and low price relative to book are signals of corporations at higher risk of failure. If this were true, it would imply (predict) that value strategies (buying low price-to-book stocks) and small cap strategies would earn subpar returns in bad economic times, when distressed companies are most likely to suffer.

Empirical evidence contradicts this prediction. A 1994 study found no evidence that value strategies do worse when the economy suffers.[60] Also, the disappearance of the excess return to small-cap stocks in the last 15 years presents a problem. If cap size were indeed a legitimate risk factor, the returns to strategies based on it should continue to earn a risk premium. Finally, neither the Fama-French risk model, nor any other EMH model, is able to explain the predictive power of price momentum indicators or the conjoint effect of price momentum and trading volume.

■ Behavioral Finance: A Theory of Nonrandom Price Motion

New theory is needed when existing theory confronts dissonant evidence. EMH has now been bombarded with a lot of evidence that contradicts its predictions. It is time for a new theory.

The relatively new field of behavioral finance has come forward with several variations of a new theory of financial market behavior that explains phenomena that EMH cannot. These theories are scientifically meaningful in that they do not simply explain (fit) what has occurred, but they make testable predictions that have been confirmed by subsequent observational studies.

Behavioral finance incorporates elements of cognitive psychology, economics, and sociology to explain why investors depart from full rationality and therefore why markets depart from full efficiency. By considering the impact of emotions, cognitive errors, irrational preferences, and the dynamics of group behavior, behavioral finance offers succinct explanations of excess market volatility as well as the excess returns earned by stale information strategies.

Behavioral finance does not assume that all investors are irrational. Rather, it views the market as a mixture of decision makers who vary in their degree of rationality. When irrational investors (noise traders) trade with rational investors (arbitrageurs), markets can depart from efficient pricing. In fact, market efficiency is a rather special condition that is less probable than other more plausible market conditions, where prices are likely to diverge from rational levels and thus likely to experience systematic predictable movements toward those levels.[61] This explains why systematic strategies based on stale information can profit.

This is all quite ironic with respect to TA. Cognitive errors can explain how people form erroneous beliefs in the validity of subjective TA in the absences of sound supportive evidence or even in the face of contradictory evidence. At the same time, however, cognitive errors may also explain the existence of market inefficiencies that spawn the systematic price movements that allow objective TA methods to work. That which explains the foolishness of subjective TA practitioners also explains the reasonableness of some objective TA methods.

Foundations of Behavioral Finance

Behavioral finance rests on two foundational pillars: The limited ability of arbitrage to correct pricing errors, and the limits of human rationality.[62] When both notions are combined, behavioral finance is able to predict specific departures from market efficiency that produce systematic price movements. For example, under certain circumstances, trends are predicted to persist, whereas, under other circumstances, trends are predicted to reverse. We will consider each of these pillars.

Limits of Arbitrage   To recap briefly, arbitrage is not the perfect enforcer of efficient pricing that EMH assumes. The lack of perfect security substitutes turns arbitrage from a risk-free, no-investment-required transaction into one that requires capital and incurs risk. Even where there are very good substitute securities, there is a risk that prices will diverge further from rational values before returning to them. Moreover, the investors who supply trading capital to arbitrageurs don't have unlimited patience, or unlimited capital. Consequently, they do not grant unlimited latitude to arbitrageurs in terms of the types of opportunities that can be considered for exploitation.

These constraints explain why security prices do not always react properly to new information. Sometimes, prices underreact, and sometimes, they overreact. Add to this the impact of noise traders, who act on uninformative signals,[63] and it becomes clear how security prices can systematically depart from rational levels for extended periods of time.

Limits of Human Rationality   The constraints on arbitrage predict that inefficiencies will occur, but they alone do not predict under what conditions the inefficiencies will manifest. For example, arbitrage constraints do not tell us under which circumstances markets are more likely to underreact to new information than overreact. That is where the second pillar of behavioral finance, the limits of human rationality, comes in.

Cognitive psychology has revealed that, under conditions of uncertainty, human judgment tends to err in predictable (systematic) ways. By taking into account the systematic errors of human judgment, behavioral finance can predict the type of departure from market efficiencies that are most likely to occur in a given set of circumstances.

THEORY AND ANALYSIS

Of the two pillars of behavioral finance, more is understood about the limits of arbitrage than about investor irrationality. This is because arbitrageurs are expected to be rational, and economic theory has a firmer grasp on the behavior of rational actors than irrational ones. For example, it is not yet clear which specific cognitive biases and systematic judgment errors are most important in finance, but a picture is gradually emerging. This section describes the current state of behavioral finance's understanding of irrational investor behavior and the systematic price movements that arise as a result of them.

In contrast to traditional finance theory, behavioral finance asserts investors make biased judgments and choices. In effect, market prices systematically deviate from rational values because investors systematically deviate from full rationality. However, these mistakes are not a sign of ignorance, but rather a consequence of the generally effective ways human intelligence has developed to cope with complexity and uncertainty.

Behavioral finance and EMH are similar in that they both contend that the market eventually does get it right—that is, prices ultimately converge toward rational valuations. They merely differ about the character of these departures and their duration. EMH says prices depart from rational levels randomly and briefly. Behavioral finance says some departures are systematic and last long enough to be exploited by certain investment strategies.

Psychological Factors

Cognitive errors impact subjective technicians and result in erroneous beliefs. In the context of behavioral finance, we will consider how cognitive errors impact investors and result in systematic price movements. The cognitive errors discussed in the sections that follow are not completely distinct, nor do they operate independently. However, they are presented separately for the purpose of clarity.

Conservatism Bias, Confirmation Bias, and Belief Inertia   The conservatism bias[64] is the tendency to give too little weight to new information. Consequently, people fail to modify their prior beliefs as much as the new information would warrant. Prior beliefs tend to be conserved. Because of this, investors tend to underreact to new information that is relevant to security values and so security prices fail to respond adequately. Over time, however, prices do systematically catch up with value. This gradual, purposeful adjustment appears on a chart as a price trend. This is illustrated in Figure 40.5.

This conservatism bias is encouraged by the confirmation bias, which causes people to accept evidence that is consistent with a prior belief and reject or give too little credence to evidence that contradicts it. Thus, when investors hold an existing view about a security and new information arrives that confirms that belief, they will tend to give it more weight than it deserves and overreact to it. Conversely, when new information arrives that contradicts the prior belief, they tend to treat it skeptically and underreact.

The confirmation bias also causes investors' beliefs, whatever they may be, to become more extreme over time. The reason is as follows: Over time, news items arrive as a random mixture of confirmatory and contradictory information. However, the confirmation bias causes them to be treated differently. Confirmatory information is given credence, thus strengthening the prior belief, while contradictory information will tend not to be believed and thus have a negligible impact on the investors' prior belief. Consequently, over time it is likely that prior beliefs strengthen.

However, prior beliefs can be subject to a radical and irrational weakening if several bits of contradictory information arrive in a streak. Even though streaks are common in a random sequence, investors may commit the crime of small numbers and attribute too much significance when several pieces of information that contradict the prior beliefs arrive sequentially. In other words, the random streak may be erroneously interpreted as an authentic trend. These ideas are illustrated in Figure 40.8.

Too Much Anchoring and Too Little Adjustment   In uncertain situations, people rely on heuristics to simplify and speed complex cognitive tasks like estimating probabilities. One heuristic, not discussed thus far, is called anchoring. It is relied upon to estimate quantities. The rule is applied as follows: An initial estimate of the quantity is made, based on preliminary information called the anchor. Then upward or downward adjustments are made to the initial estimate based on additional information. The anchoring rule seems to make sense.

However, in practice, people commonly make two mistakes when applying this heuristic. First, initial estimates can be strongly influenced by a completely irrelevant anchor. This occurs even when the anchor's irrelevance is completely obvious. Second, even in cases where the initial estimate is based on relevant anchoring information, there is a tendency for subsequent adjustments up or down to be too small (the conservatism bias). In other words, the additional information is given too little weight relative to the initial estimate.

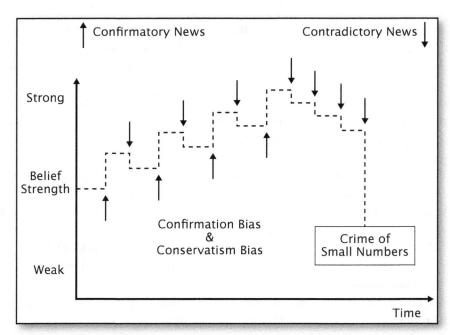

FIGURE 40.8   Revising Beliefs.

The tendency to seize on an irrelevant anchor was demonstrated in a study in which people were asked to estimate the length of the Mississippi River (actual length = 2,348 miles). Subjects were first asked if the length was greater than or less than some arbitrary length. This number assumed the role of anchor in the subject's minds. When the question posed was: Is the length greater or less than 800 miles? Most people correctly said the Mississippi was longer than 800 miles. Subjects were then asked to give an estimate of its actual length. Other subjects were given the number 5,000 miles in the greater than or less than part of the question. Again, most people correctly said the river's length was less than 5,000 miles, but their estimates of the river's actual length were, on average, greater than the estimates given by subjects who were asked to make a comparison with 800 miles. This revealed that the subjects seized on the number of miles given in the question as an anchor, and then made inadequate adjustments from there. If the figure 800 or 5,000 were not truly influencing the estimate, the estimates of length would have been about the same, irrespective of whether the question involved a comparison with 800 miles or 5,000 miles.[65] The anchor had a strong influence.

Another experiment showed that people will anchor on a number even when it is obviously irrelevant.[66] Subjects were asked about facts that are typically not part of common knowledge—for example, "What is the percentage of African nations in the United Nations?" The answers to each question involved a percentage (0 to 100). Before each question, a wheel of fortune with 100 numbered slots was spun in front of the subjects. The study showed that the subjects' answers were strongly affected by the wheel's obviously random result. For example, if the wheel landed on the number 10, the median estimate was 25 percent, but when the wheel stopped on 65 the median estimate was 45 percent.

The anchoring heuristic is thought to be related to investor underreaction. Underreactions to bullish news cause asset prices to remain too cheap, whereas underreactions to bearish news leave prices too dear. Over time, the market's temporary state of inefficiency is resolved as prices drift (trend) to the rational level. Thus, anchoring can help explain the occurrence of price trends.

Anchoring may explain the profitability of a momentum strategy alluded to earlier.[67] It is based on a simple technical indicator, a stock's proximity to its 52-week high. Because this information is available in newspapers and on various web sites, investors may fixate (anchor) on it. In other words, investors may fixate or anchor on the 52-week high price if a stock is currently trading near that level. In effect, the stock gets stuck near its 52-week high. Thus the price fails to respond properly to new bullish information, and it becomes temporarily underpriced. Ultimately the pricing error is corrected as the stock responds with a systematic movement higher.

Anchoring to Stories   Investors not only become anchored to numbers; they can get stuck on intuitively compelling[68] stories, too. The effect is the same; prices do not respond efficiently to new information and thus depart from rational valuations.

Stories are compelling because "much of human thinking that results in action is not quantitative, but instead takes the form of storytelling and justification."[69] Investors rely more on causal narratives than on weighing and combining evidence to estimate probabilities and make decisions. People seem to need simple rationales to justify their actions.[70] The most compelling rationales are plausible, easily understood, easily retold, cause and effect chains filled with concrete and colorful details. These are the tales that captivate investors and incite buying and selling. These are the stories that get stuck in investors' minds.

Optimism and Overconfidence   To recap, people are generally too confident about the quality and precision of their knowledge. Thus, investors tend to be overconfident about their private interpretations of public information and overly optimistic about the profits they will achieve. The combined effect of overconfidence and overoptimism leads investors to overreact to their private information, and in turn pushes security prices too far. Overextended price movements lead to price reversals and systematic movements back toward rational levels.

The Crime of Small Numbers (Sample Size Neglect)   The crime of small numbers is the failure to consider the number of observations comprising a sample being used to form a conclusion. Thus, it is fallacious to judge whether a datum was produced by a random or nonrandom process or to estimate a population parameter on the basis of a small sample. For example, if a sequence of 10 coin flips produces 7 heads, it would be invalid to conclude the coin has a 0.7 probability of producing heads. The true head rate for a coin can be reliably inferred from only a large number of flips.

Investors who neglect sample size are easily deceived when trying to decide if a time series is random or not. For example, by generalizing too hastily from too little evidence, investors may incorrectly conclude that a few quarters of positive earnings growth indicate that the company has established a valid growth trend. We have already seen that a small cluster of positive quarters can easily occur in a random-earnings stream. Thus, the crime of small numbers helps explain why investors may overreact to a short sequence of good earnings reports.

The crime of small numbers can cause two different judgment errors: the gambler's fallacy and the clustering illusion. Which of these two errors results depends on the observer's prior belief about the process being watched. Suppose an investor is watching a sequence of price changes that are truly independent of each other (a random walk).

If the investor holds a prior belief that the process is random, the error will most likely be the gambler's fallacy. Recall that on the basis of common sense we expect random processes to display more flip-flops and fewer streaks (trends) than actually do occur. As a result, a streak of positive price changes will lead naive observers to falsely conclude that a trend reversal (a negative price change) is due. Thus, after five heads, the observer erroneously concludes a tail is more likely than 50/50, its true likelihood. In reality, a random-walk sequence has no memory. Thus, the occurrence of a positive streak does not alter the probability of the next outcome in any way. The false expectation of a reversal is called the "gambler's fallacy" because the statistically naive tend to make this mistake when watching a roulette wheel; a sequence of black outcomes is thought to increase the chance of a red. Wrong!

The other fallacy stemming from sample-size neglect is the clustering illusion. It occurs when an observer has no prior belief about whether the process generating the data is random or nonrandom The clustering illusion is the misperception of order (nonrandomness) in data that is actually a random walk. Again, imagine someone observing the outcomes of a process that is truly a random walk trying to determine if the process is random or nonrandom (orderly, systematic).[71] Recall that small samples of random walks often appear more trended (clustered) than common sense would lead us to expect (the hot hand in basketball). As a result of the clustering illusion, a sequence of positive price or earnings changes is wrongly interpreted as a legitimate trend, when it is nothing more than an ordinary streak in a random walk.

Social Factors: Imitative Behavior, Herding, and Information Cascades[72]

We have just seen how investor behavior viewed at the level of the individual investor can explain several types of systematic price movement. This section examines investor behavior at the group level to explain systematic price movements. In contrast to conventional TA theories of investor psychology, we will see that some group behaviors are quite rational.

When faced with uncertain choices, people often to look to the behavior of others for cues and imitate their actions. This is what is meant by herd behavior. I should clarify that herd behavior is not defined by similarity of action. Similar actions by many individuals can also occur when individuals have made similar choices but those choices have been arrived at independently. Herd behavior refers specifically to similarity of action arising from imitation. As I will point out, the choice to imitate can be entirely rational.

There is a major difference between similar behaviors arising from herding and similar behaviors arising from many individual decision makers making the same choice independently. Herd behavior stops the diffusion of information throughout a group, but independent decision making does not. When information diffusion is impeded, it becomes more likely that investors will make the same mistakes and prices will systematically diverge from rational levels.

To see why herd behavior impedes the spread of information, consider the opposite case, where individuals evaluate information independently and make autonomous choices. Suppose a large number of investors are independently evaluating a stock. Some may mistakenly value it too high, while others mistakenly value it too low. Because the mistakes are made independently, they will tend to be offsetting, making the average valuation error close to zero. Here, each investor has made an individual appraisal and in effect acted on a unique signal. This makes it far more likely that all the available information about the stock will have been considered and built into the price of the stock. Even if no single investor was in full possession of all the facts, the group, taken as a whole, is likely to be nearly fully informed.

In contrast, when investors elect to imitate the behavior of others rather than deciding independently, all the relevant information about the stock is less likely to be fully diffused throughout the entire group, making it more likely that the stock's price will not reflect all relevant information. However, an individual investor electing to imitate may be making a perfectly rational choice. Not everyone has the time or expertise to evaluate a stock, so it can make sense to copy an investor with a good track record, such as Warren Buffett. Once Buffett does his analysis and makes his buy or sell decision known, investors may cease their own efforts to gather information and evaluate the stock. This makes it more likely that, if some factor has escaped Buffett's notice, it will remain unnoticed by the community of investors. So here is a case where individuals take actions that are fully rational on an individual basis but harmful to them as a group.

Why Do We Imitate? At one time it was thought that imitative behavior was a consequence of social pressure to conform. Early experimental evidence seemed to confirm this.[73] In one study, an authentic subject was asked to estimate the length of line segments in the presence of fake subjects who also gave estimates. The fakes, who were actually part of the experiment, intentionally gave wrong answers. Even though the correct answer was obvious, the authentic subjects often went along with the group rather than give the obviously correct answer. However, a later experiment,[74] in which the authentic subject was isolated from the group of confederates, showed the subject still imitated the group's obviously wrong answer. This finding implied that social pressure does not explain imitative behavior. A better explanation emerged. The subjects seemed to be relying on a social heuristic: When one's own judgment is contradicted by the majority, follow the majority. In other words, people operate with an implicit rule: The majority is unlikely to be wrong.

"This behavior is a matter of rational calculation: in everyday living we have learned that when a large group of people is unanimous in its judgment on a question of simple fact, the members of the group are almost certainly right."[75] Similarly, most of us operate with the principle that, when an expert tells us something that contradicts our common sense, we tend to heed the expert. So it is entirely rational under conditions of uncertainty to look to the advice of experts or the actions of the majority.

Information Cascades and Herd Behavior The uncertainties of investing make it likely that investors would rely on an imitation heuristic rather than independent decision making. This has important implications for the emergence of systematic price behavior because imitation gives rise to "information cascades."[76] An information cascade is a chain of imitative behavior that was initiated by the action of one or just a few individuals. In some instances that initiating action may have been a random choice.

The emergence of an information cascade can be illustrated with a hypothetical example. Suppose two new restaurants open for business on the same day, right next door to each other. The first hungry customer to arrive must choose one, and has little information on which to base a decision. That customer's choice is, therefore, a random decision. However, when the second customer arrives, there is an additional piece of information: one of the restaurants has a patron. This may trigger the second customer to go into the same place. Because the first customer's selection was a guess, we know that the second customer's choice was based on an uninformative signal.

When the third customer arrives and sees one restaurant empty and the other with two customers, the chance is increased that the third customer will also make an imitative choice. In the end, a cascade of dependent choices, triggered by the first customer's random choice, may ultimately cause one establishment to thrive and the other to fail, and it is entirely possible that the failing establishment offered better food.

Thus, an initial random event sets the course of history down one particular path (restaurant 1 succeeds) rather than another path (restaurant 2 succeeds). As time goes on, the likelihood that one restaurant will thrive increases while the likelihood that the second establishment will fail increases. In the same way, an initial random price movement can trigger successive rounds of imitative investor behavior, resulting in a long-duration large amplitude price swing.

Now consider what would have happened if many customers had made independent restaurant choices, allowing both establishments to be sampled by many customers. By combining their findings, they would have discovered which was the better of the two restaurants. However, in an information cascade, imitative behavior prevents the accumulation and sharing of many independent appraisals. Thus, information cascades block the diffusion of information and rational choice.

The information cascade model reveals the flaw in the common sense notion that financial market prices are determined by a process like voting, in which many individuals make their own assessment.[77] In an information cascade, investors make the rational choice of copying the actions of others, rather than expending the considerable effort required to arrive at an independent choice. Voters do one thing, and investors sometimes do something entirely different.

The Diffusion of Information Among Investors   We have seen that information cascades can explain why the rational behavior of individual investors can impede the diffusion of information. This is important for TA because the rate at which information spreads among investors can explain the occurrence of systematic price movements. EMH assumes almost instantaneous information diffusion and, consequently, almost instantaneous price adjustments. Such price adjustments are too quick to be exploited by TA methods. However, information that diffuses slowly allows for gradual, systematic price movements that can be exploited by TA methods.

Despite the prevalence of advanced communications technology, the preferred method of exchanging investment information is still a good story told person to person. This predilection, a result of several million years of evolution, has been confirmed by the studies of behavioral-economist Robert Shiller. He has shown that the word-of-mouth effect is strong even among people who read a lot. A story about a hot new issue has greater impact in conversation than a statistic about the high failure rate of new companies.

The way stories spread among investors has been studied with mathematical models similar to those used by epidemiologists to study the spread of disease within a population. Unfortunately, these models have not been as accurate in the investor domain as they have been in the realm of biology. This is explained by the fact that the mutation rate of circulating ideas is far higher than the mutation rate of organisms. However, the models have been enlightening in another way; they explain how stories spread so rapidly.

One reason a "new" story can spread so rapidly is that it is not really new. Investors' minds are already infested with many familiar story scripts, and it does not matter that the panoply of stories residing in investors' minds contradict each other. For example, investors can be comfortable with the notion that the stock market cannot be predicted and at the same time hold the opposing notion that it can. No doubt, most investors have been exposed to experts who have espoused both points of view. Our minds are able to accommodate a wide variety of contradictory ideas because the scripts lie there inert with no demand that we choose one side or the other.

Nevertheless, this state of affairs can change rapidly. Even a slight random perturbation in the news or the market's behavior can cause an idea that had been hibernating in investors' minds to spring to life and consume their attention.

Shifts in Investor Attention   Where investors are focusing their attention at any given moment can shift dramatically due to minor changes in the news. "The human brain is structured to have essentially a single focus of attention at a time and to move rapidly from one focus to another."[78] The brain had to evolve a capacity to selectively attend to only a tiny trickle of the torrent of information that pours in from the world. This filtering process is both a mark of human intelligence and a source of judgment error. Numerous instances of expert error are attributable to missing important details. However, before outcomes are known, we never know which details deserve our attention.

Among the automatic unconscious rules used by the brain to filter relevant from irrelevant information is the rule to look to other people for cues. In other words, we presume that what grabs the attention of others must be worthy of our attention as well. According to economist Robert Shiller, "the phenomenon of social attention is one of the great creations of behavioral evolution and is critical for the functioning of human society."[79] Although communal attention has great social value, because it promotes collaborative action, it has a downside. It can lead an entire group to hold an incorrect view and take similar mistaken actions.

In the opposite situation, where individuals form their own views independently, errors of attention would be random and self-canceling. Although this mode of thought makes it harder to organize joint efforts around common views and goals, it is less likely to overlook important details. Dramatic market movements can easily grab the attention of the community of investors and encourage them to act in ways that amplify the movement, even if there is no fundamental reason for it.

Robert Shiller has studied the way dramatic price movements capture investor attention and trigger herd behavior. Even institutional investors, who would be expected to select stocks in systematic ways based on statistically valid characteristics, are prone to buying a stock simply because it has experienced a rapid price increase.[80] This mechanism can explain how a market boom can be triggered just by a vivid initial price movement that calls attention to the stock market. Moreover, Shiller's studies show that investors are often not even aware that it was a dramatic price movement that motivated them to act.

The Role of Feedback in Systematic Price Movements Social interaction among investors creates feedback. Feedback refers to the channeling of a system's output back into the system as input. See Figure 40.9, where two systems are compared—one with no feedback and one with feedback.

There are two types of feedback, positive and negative. One way to think of the difference is as follows. In the case of negative feedback, the system output is multiplied by a negative number and the result is feedback in. In the case of positive feedback the multiplier is a positive number. This is illustrated in Figure 40.10.

FIGURE 40.9 Feedback: Output Becomes Input.

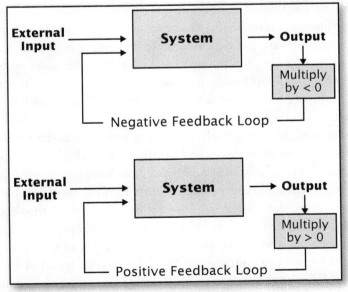

FIGURE 40.10 Positive and Negative Feedback Loops.

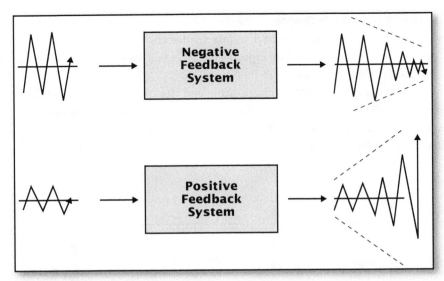

FIGURE 40.11 Positive and Negative Feedback Loops: Dampening versus Amplifying.

Negative feedback has the effect of dampening system behavior, driving the output back toward a level of equilibrium. Positive feedback has the opposite effect, amplifying a system's behavior, thus driving its output further from equilibrium. This is illustrated in Figure 40.11.

An example of a negative feedback system is a household heating & air conditioning system. When the temperature falls below a desired or equilibrium level, the thermostat turns on the furnace, returning the system's output, the household temperature, back to the desired level. Temperature above the desired level turns on the A/C, bringing the temperature back down. This is all accomplished by feeding the system's output back into the system as an input. This allows the system to self-regulate its way toward equilibrium.

Positive feedback is illustrated by the growing screech in a public-address system when the speakers are placed too close to the microphone. The normal hum coming out of the speakers (output) gets fed back into the audio system via the microphone, where it is amplified by the system. With each cycle, the sound comes out louder, developing into a loud screech. Positive feedback is also known as the snowball effect or vicious cycle.

Financial markets, like other self-organizing self-regulated systems, rely on a healthy balance between negative and positive feedback.[81] Arbitrage provides negative feedback. Prices that are too high or too low trigger arbitrage trading that pushes prices back toward rational levels. Positive feedback occurs when investor decisions are dominated by imitative behavior rather than independent choice. In this regime, investors will hop aboard an initial price movement, buying after first signs of strength or selling after first signs of weakness, thus amplifying an initial small price movement into a large-scale trend. A TA approach, known as trend following, depends on large-scale price moves for its profitability and thus is most effective during times when positive feedback dominates.

Positive feedback can cause a vicious cycle of price increases or decreases, which take prices far beyond rational levels even if the initial price move that triggered the whole affair was justified. In other words, price trends can go far above or below rational levels simply due to the amplifying effect of positive feedback.

Positive feedback can also result from the way people adapt their expectations to recent changes. Although it generally makes sense to alter expectations when conditions change, people do it imperfectly. At times, they adjust insufficiently (the conservatism bias), whereas at other times they are overly sensitive to change and alter their expectations more than is justified. Investors are especially likely to overreact to new information that is prominent. Either a single large price change or a sequence of similar changes can induce investors to alter their expectations too much. These price changes can feed on themselves, thus generating price momentum that may lead to a bubble or crash.

A judgment error that sometimes contributes to positive feedback is mental accounting. This is the irrational tendency to think about money as if it belonged in separate accounts, which should be treated differently. Gains from prior speculative ventures may be assigned to the hot-action account, whereas money accumulating in the home-equity account is treated with greater conservatism. Rationally, all of an investor's money, regardless of how it was made or in which asset it is invested, should be treated in the same way. A dollar is a dollar. However, speculative gains from a recent market rise are often, irrationally, earmarked for further speculation, thus adding fuel to a rising market.

At some point, the increasing expectations that fuel a bubble run out. Common sense would suggest, and some analysts insist, that a price bubble necessarily ends in market crashes (i.e., a negative bubble). At times they do, but other bubble termination patterns are possible. Computer simulations of systems that incorporate feedback loops show that bubbles not only develop in a jagged fashion with many intervening pauses, but they can also deflate in a similar manner. If the late 1990s was a price bubble, it seems to be ending with many intervening pauses.

Self-Organizing Ponzi Schemes

The feedback theory of price bubbles is appealing because of its plausibility and the numerous historical examples that seem to confirm its validity. However, it is hard to prove that a simple feedback mechanism involving heightened investor focus, imitative behavior, and exaggerated investor confidence is truly operational in financial markets.

Nevertheless, Yale economist Robert Shiller believes actual cases of pyramid frauds known as Ponzi schemes offer evidence that confirms the feedback theory. The scheme, named after the infamous Charles Ponzi, who invented the idea in the 1920s, involves promising investors a high rate of return from some sort of business venture or investment. However, the investors' money is never put to work in the way promised. Instead, the commitments of new investors are used to pay off earlier investors. This serves two purposes: it makes the venture look legitimate and it encourages the first investors to spread the story of their success. As the tale gains popularity, new investors are motivated to make investments. Their funds are, in turn, used to pay off a prior round of investors, who now go out and tell their story. This cycle of using Peter's investment to pay off Paul to prove the success of the enterprise continues and grows. The number of people influenced by the scam follows a curve similar to the diffusion of an infection throughout a population. Ultimately, a saturation level is reached. The supply of noninfected speculators gets exhausted, and so there are no new investments with which to pay off the last round of investors. At this point, the scheme crashes.

Recently a housewife from a small town in Alaska collected an estimated $10 to $15 million over a six-year period by promising a 50 percent return. Her business was purportedly based on unused frequent flyer miles accumulated by large companies. In fact, this was very similar to Ponzi's original scheme, which was based on international postage coupons.

Ponzi scams evolve in a typical pattern. Initially, investors are skeptical and invest only small amounts, but once early investors reap profits and tell their success story, later-stage investors gain confidence and the flow of capital into the scheme gains momentum. Frequently there are rational skeptics issuing warnings, but the greedy pay no heed. Well-founded cynical arguments cannot compete with vivid accounts of fat profits. The moths dive into the flame.

Shiller contends that speculative bubbles are naturally occurring Ponzi schemes that emerge spontaneously in financial markets, without requiring the machinations of a fraudulent promoter.[82] Such self-organizing phenomena are common in complex systems. There is no need for false stories because there is always some buzz about the stock market anyway. A trend of rising prices acts as a call to action much like the gains of early investors in a Ponzi scheme. The message is then amplified by Wall Street's salesmen, and they need not tell lies. They simply pitch the upside potential while downplaying the risk side of the story. The parallels between Ponzi schemes and speculative bubbles are so clear in Shiller's opinion that the burden of proof is on those who deny the similarity.

Competing Hypotheses of Behavioral Finance

A mathematical model quantifies a scientific hypothesis about some aspect of the world, This allows quantitative predictions to be made that can be tested against future observations. Of course, those proposing the model hope its predictions will coincide with said observations. Nevertheless, if they should clash, a true scientist stands ready to formulate a new model that both explains the discordant observations and makes additional predictions that can be tested against further observations. This cycle of refinement never ceases because knowledge is never complete.

Pseudoscientific stories resemble legitimate scientific hypotheses, but only superficially. A scientific hypothesis is compact, yet it accounts for a wide range of observations. Pseudoscientific stories tend to be complicated. Scientific hypotheses make precise predictions that can be checked against future observation. Pseudoscientific accounts make vague predictions that are consistent with prior observations but never make predictions specific enough to permit clear refutation. Thus, pseudoscientific accounts survive in the minds of the gullible, no matter how far off the mark they may be.

On this basis, behavioral finance qualifies as science, albeit a young one. Although as yet, there is no agreement on a single theory, there has been substantial progress. Within the last decade behavioral-finance practitioners have proposed several hypotheses to explain investor behavior and key features of market dynamics. These are important to TA because they provide a rationale for the occurrence of systematic price movements, the "without-which-not" of TA.

The behavioral-finance hypotheses have been formulated as mathematical models, thus allowing them to generate testable predictions of how markets would behave if the hypothesis were correct. This opens the hypotheses to refutation if markets do not manifest the predicted behaviors. For example, if a model predicts the occurrence of trend reversals similar to those actually observed in market data, the hypothesis gains some confirmation. However, if the model's predicted scenarios are contradicted by actual market behavior, then the hypothesis would be refuted. This makes the hypotheses of behavioral finance scientifically meaningful.

Recall that the random-walk model of EMH predicts that systematic price motion should not be observed in market behavior. In contrast, the behavioral-finance hypotheses described later predict the occurrence of systematic price motion and offer an explanation about why they should occur. Even though none of the hypotheses provides a comprehensive theory of market behavior, they have a common a message of importance to TA: There is good reason to believe financial markets are not entirely random walks.

Biased Interpretation of Public Information: The Barberis, Shleifer, and Vishny (BSV) Hypothesis Empirical studies show that investors display two distinct errors in response to news releases. Sometimes they underreact, and consequently prices change less than the new fundamentals say they should. At other times, investors overreact, causing prices to change more than is justified by the news. Ultimately, however, these pricing errors are rectified by systematic price movements toward price levels that accurately reflect the new information.

The puzzle is: Why do investors sometimes overreact while at other times they underreact? A hypothesis proposed by Barberis, Shleifer, and Vishny[83] (BSV) offers an explanation. First, BSV asserts that two distinct cognitive errors are involved: conservatism bias and sample-size neglect. Second, they assert that the particular error that is operative at a given point in time depends on circumstances.

To briefly recap: The conservatism bias describes the tendency to alter a prior belief less than new information would warrant. Existing opinions are sticky. Sample-size neglect, also known as the crime of small numbers, is the tendency to draw too grand a conclusion from a small sample of observations. Thus, the conservatism bias is the opposite of the crime of small numbers. In the former, new evidence is given too little weight; in the latter, it is given too much.

The conservatism bias is at work when investors underreact to news, leaving prices too low after good news or too high after bad news. However, as investors gradually realize the new information's true significance, prices make a gradual systematic march to a level that properly reflects the news. Thus, some price trends can be explained by investor underreaction.

The crime of small numbers explains investor overreaction. For example, if investors observe a small number of positive earnings changes, they may conclude, too hastily, that a valid growth pattern has been established. This stimulates overly aggressive buying that pushes prices higher than warranted. Investors can overreact in the same way to a few negative observations and push the price too low.

The mathematical model put forward by BSV makes the following simplifying assumptions: (1) the market has a single stock, (2) its earnings stream follows a random walk, but (3) investors do not realize this,[84] so (4) investors labor under the false impression that the stock's earnings stream shifts back and forth between two distinct regimes, a growth trend phase and a mean-reverting (oscillating) phase, but they do not consider the possibility that the earning may follow a random walk, (6) therefore, investors believe their job is to figure out which of these two regimes is operative at any given point in time.

Let's see how BSV's mythical investor might react to the releases of new earnings information. At any given time, the investors hold a belief that the earnings are in either one of two nonrandom regimes: a growth trend or mean reverting process. The possibility of a random walk is not considered. Recall that a random walk displays less mean reversion than a true mean-reverting process and also displays streaks that are shorter in duration than those found in a truly trending process. As we pick up the story, an investor holds some prior belief about the earnings regime and hears news about earnings. Suppose the news announcement contradicts the investor's belief. For example, if the investor had believed the stock's earnings had been in a growth trend, and a negative earnings report came out, the investor would be surprised. Similarly, if the investor had been under the belief that earnings were in a mean-reverting regime, a streak of similar changes would also be surprising. According to the BSV hypothesis, both kinds of surprises would trigger an underreaction by the investor due to the conservatism bias. In other words, regardless of whether the investor's prior belief was in a mean-reverting regime or in a growth regime, news contradicting the belief would be given too little weight causing prices to underreact to the new information. However, if news that is at odds with a prior belief continues to occur, the investor will become convinced that the regime has switched, either from mean reverting to growth or from growth to mean reverting. In this case, the BSV hypothesis predicts that investors will switch from the mistake of being too stuck with their prior beliefs and underreacting (the conservatism bias) to the mistake of committing the crime of small numbers and overreacting. Thus, the BSV model accounts for both kinds of investor error as well as the systematic price movement that corrects both forms of errors.

I illustrate the type of behavior predicted by BSV in Figure 40.12. Here I posit the case where investors initially believe that earnings are in a mean-reverting regime. Thus, they expect positive earnings reports to be followed by a negative report. For this reason, they underreact to the first two positive earnings reports. However, after the third positive report, not at all unusual in a random process

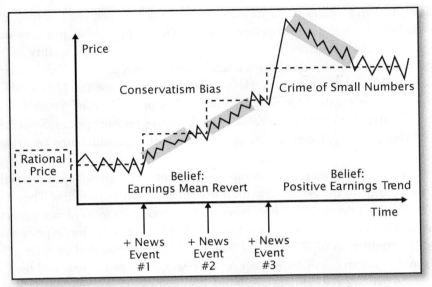

FIGURE 40.12 BSV: Underreaction Followed by Overreaction.

(three heads in a row), they abandon their earlier belief and adopt the idea that earnings have entered a growth regime and have established an uptrend. Consequently they now expect that future reports will also be positive. This causes investors to overreact, pushing the stock above a rational level. The systematic price movements resulting from both types of investor error are highlighted in grey.

Thus BSV's model also shows how a feedback loop emerges from the crime of small numbers. When investors see earnings move in the same direction several times in succession, they switch from doubting the trend to assuming it is real.[85] However, the conservatism bias initially impedes the adoption of the new belief. The interaction between the crime of small numbers and the conservatism bias determines the speed at which speculative feedback develops.[86] Simulations of the BSV model show several kinds of actual market behavior such as price trends following surprising earnings, price momentum, long-term reversals, and the forecasting power of fundamental ratios such as price-to-book. Thus, the BSV model explains how investors' biased interpretations of public information can predict the occurrence of phenomena that are observed in actual market data. This suggests that the model does capture some of the dynamics of real financial markets.

Biased Interpretation of Private Information: The Daniel, Hirshleifer, and Subrahmanyam (DHS) Hypothesis An alternative hypothesis proposed by Daniel, Hirshleifer, and Subrahmanyam (1998, 2001)[87] (DHS) suggests a different explanation for systematic price movements such as trend reversals and trend persistence (momentum). In contrast to BSV, the DHS hypothesis is founded upon investors' biased interpretations of private research. In addition, DHS emphasizes somewhat different cognitive errors: the endowment bias, the confirmation bias, and the self-attribution bias.

Private research refers to an investor's independently derived interpretations of public information (i.e., proprietary research). The hypothesis put forward by DHS predicts that investors will be overly confident about the quality of their private research and hence will have a tendency to overreact to it. This prediction is based on the endowment bias—the predisposition to place too high a value on what we own or create. This overreaction pushes prices beyond rational levels, which ultimately leads to a price reversal back toward rational prices. So in DHS's view of the world, price reversals are an effect of overconfidence in privately derived signals.

DHS also explains price momentum (nonrandom price trends) as the result of two other cognitive biases: confirmation bias and self-attribution bias. They assert price momentum develops because news releases and price movements impact investors in a biased manner. Because of the confirmation bias, news or price movements that confirm an investor's prior beliefs, (i.e., those founded on their private signals and research), will be given excessive weight. News events and/or price movements that are confirmatory have the effect of increasing the investors' confidence that their private research was indeed accurate. This induces them to take additional action (buying or selling), which amplifies the momentum of the current price trend. The self-attribution bias also causes investors to view confirmatory news or price movement as a sign that their private research is good. Recall that self-attribution causes people to take credit for outcomes, even if they occur because of good luck, but to deny responsibility for bad outcomes by attributing them to bad luck. Thus, both the confirmation bias and self-attribution bias induce investors to overreact to confirmatory evidence, thereby amplifying the market's positive feedback.

Conversely, if public information or price behavior contradicts the investor's private research, it will be given too little weight (confirmation bias) and investors will attribute it to bad luck rather than to poor private research (self-attribution bias). Therefore, regardless of whether the news or the price movement confirms or contradicts the investor's private information, the DHS model predicts that investors' confidence in their private research will increase. "This unequal treatment of new information means initial overconfidence is on average followed by even greater overconfidence, thus generating price momentum."[88] However, after a sequence of contradictory public news signals, the investors' confidence in their private information will be shattered (crime of small numbers), and price trends will reverse.

Both DHS and BSV predict that investors are sometimes excessively optimistic and sometimes excessively pessimistic. In addition, these beliefs are predicted to be subject to reversal when a streak of disconfirming information arrives. If DHS and BSV are valid, then the profits earned by strategies that exploit trend reversals should be concentrated at the times of information releases. This predicted consequence, which opens both hypotheses to refutation, has been confirmed.[89] Indeed, a large fraction of the excess returns earned by buying value stocks (low price to book, low P/E, and so forth) and buying the weakest stocks of the past three to five years do occur near the times of earnings information releases.

News Traders and Momentum Traders: The HS Hypothesis As just described, certain instances of price momentum can be explained by prices catching up with fundamentals due to an initial underreaction to news. Other trends can be explained by positive feedback, in which a price increase stimulates additional buying and price weakness stimulates additional selling.[90] Thus, some investors look for signals in recent price changes rather than news.

From the perspective of TA, trends spawned by positive feedback can be viewed as a cascade of progressively less sensitive trend-following signals being triggered. An initial price movement (news inspired or random) triggers the most sensitive trend signals (e.g., a very short-term moving average crossover signal). Transactions triggered by that signal push prices enough to trigger a somewhat less sensitive trend signal (e.g., medium-term moving average), which in turn triggers even less sensitive signals and so on. Whatever the mechanism, investor actions become correlated, forming a herd effect.

The hypothesis proposed by Hong and Stein[91] (HS) explains three market phenomena: momentum, underreaction, and overreaction. To do so, they postulate two classes of investors, news watchers (fundamentalists) and momentum traders (technicians). The HS hypothesis asserts that an interaction between these two classes of investors creates positive feedback and, therefore, price momentum. The HS assumption that there is more than one class of investors is grounded in the notion that investors, by dint of their intellectual limits, must confine their attention to a restricted portion of the available information. News watchers confine their attention to fundamental developments. On the basis of this information, they derive private estimates of future returns. In contrast, momentum traders confine their attention to past price changes and derive their private forecast of future trends.

Hong and Stein posit that news watchers pay little or no attention to price changes. As a result, their private assessments of the news fail to spread quickly throughout the community of news watchers. To understand how an exclusive focus on the fundamental news impedes the diffusion of information, consider what would happen if the news watchers also paid attention to price action. Watching price movements would allow them to infer, to some degree, the private information of other news watchers. For example, rising prices might imply that other news watchers were interpreting the news as favorable, whereas falling prices might imply the opposite. As we have seen, any investor behavior that slows the process by which prices incorporate new information can cause price trends. That is, instead of prices instantaneously adjusting to new information, they move gradually to a higher or lower level justified by new information. For momentum (trend-following) strategies to work, prices must change in a gradual enough fashion to allow signals based on an initial price change to predict additional price change. Thus, the failure of news traders to extract information from price action slows the rate at which prices adjust to new information, thus resulting in price trends.

Now consider the effect on market dynamics caused by momentum traders (trend-followers). The HS hypothesis claims that momentum traders only pay attention to signals from price behavior. Trend following assumes that newly emerging price trends are an indication that important new fundamental information is starting to diffuse throughout the market. Momentum traders make the bet that the diffusion is incomplete and that the price trend will continue after the initial momentum signal. Actions taken by subsequent waves of trend followers keep prices moving, thus generating positive price feedback. Ultimately, as more trend followers join the party, prices may carry further than fundamentals justify. The overshooting occurs because momentum traders are unable to judge the extent to which the news has been diffused and understood by all investors. When the news is fully diffused and all investors have acted on it, no further price movement is fundamentally justified. Thus, HS assert that the overshooting of rational price levels, resulting from the positive feedback of momentum traders, sets up the conditions for a trend reversal back toward rational levels based on fundamentals.

The Bottom Line   Behavioral finance has offered a number of testable hypotheses that attempt to explain systematic price motion. It is not yet clear which, if any, of these are correct. No doubt new hypotheses will be offered. So long as they generate testable (falsifiable) predictions, they should be entertained. What is of importance to TA is that these theories suggest that systematic price movements should occur in financial market prices.

■ Nonrandom Price Motion in the Context of Efficient Markets

The preceding section explained how systematic price movement can arise in markets that are not fully efficient. However, even if markets are fully efficient, the case for TA is not lost. A case can be made for the existence of systematic price motion in markets that are fully efficient. This section presents this case.

How Systematic Price Motion and Market Efficiency Can Coexist

Some economists contend that systematic price movements are possible even if markets are fully efficient.[92] In other words, the existence of nonrandom price behavior and the possibility of price prediction does not necessarily imply that financial markets are inefficient.[93]

Other economists state the case more strongly, asserting that some degree of predictability is not only possible but necessary for markets to function properly. In their book *A Non-Random Walk Down Wall Street*, Andrew Lo and Craig MacKinlay say, "predictability is the oil that lubricates the gears of capitalism."[94] A similar position is taken by Grossman and Stiglitz.[95] They contend that efficient markets must offer profit opportunities to motivate investors to engage in the costly activities of information processing and trading. For it is these very activities that drive prices toward rational valuations.

In fact, there is only one special condition under which market efficiency necessarily implies that price movement must be random and, therefore, unpredictable.

This occurs when all investors have the same attitude toward risk, a condition that is simply not plausible. Is there any type of risk about which all people have the same attitude? To see how far-fetched this assumption is, imagine for a moment a world in which all people have the same attitude toward risk. There would be either too many test pilots and high steel workers or not enough of them. Either everyone would be into skydiving and alligator wrestling, or no one would.

It is far more realistic to assume a world of investors with highly diverse attitudes toward risk. In such a world, some investors would be more adverse to risk than others, and they would be willing to pay other investors to accept the burden of additional risk. Also, there would likely be risk-tolerant investors looking to profit from the opportunity to assume additional risk. All that would be needed in such a world is a mechanism by which risk can be transferred from the risk adverse to the risk tolerant and for compensation to be paid to those willing to accept said risk.

Let's step away from markets for a moment to consider one mechanism by which the risk adverse can compensate the risk inclined—the insurance premium. Home-owners dread the possibility of a fire, so they enter into a transaction with a fire insurance company. The homeowner transfers the financial risk of a fire to the insurance company and, in exchange, the insurance company earns a premium. This is a profitable business if the insurance company can predict the likelihood of a house burning down (over a large number of homes—Law of Large Numbers) and charge a premium that compensates it for that risk plus a bit more for profit. The bottom line: The insurance company provides a risk acceptance service and is compensated for doing so.

Participants in financial markets have exposures to various risks and vary in their tolerance for them. These ingredients motivate transactions that transfer risk from one party to another. In this situation, the investors willing to bear greater risks can reasonably demand compensation in the form of a higher return than that offered by riskless investments, just as test pilots and high steel workers can demand a premium salary for the additional risks they bear. In financial market terms, compensation for accepting increased risk is called a risk premium or economic rent.

Financial markets offer several kinds of risk premiums:

- **The equity market risk premium:** Investors provide working capital for new business formation and are compensated by receiving a return that is above the risk-free rate for incurring the risk of business failure, economic downturns, and such.

- **Commodity and currency hedge risk transfer premium:** Speculators assume long and short positions in futures to give commercial hedgers (users and producers of the commodity) the ability to shed the risk of price change. Compensation is in the form of profitable trends that can be captured with relatively simple trend-following strategies.

- **Liquidity premium:** Investors assume positions in less liquid securities and in securities being aggressively sold by investors with acute short-term needs for cash. Compensation is in the form of higher returns for holding illiquid securities or in the form of short-term gains for buying stocks that have recently been very weak (i.e., engaging in countertrend strategies).

- **Information or price discovery premium for promoting market efficiency:** This premium compensates investors for making buy-and-sell decisions that move prices toward rational levels. Because these decisions are often based on complex models developed by sophisticated research, this premium might also be called a complexity premium.[96] For example, a strategy that sells overvalued stocks and buys undervalued stocks helps move prices back to rational values (price discovery).

The good news about returns that come in the form of a risk premium is that they are more likely to endure into the future. Of course, it is every analyst's dream to discover true market inefficiencies because the returns earned from them do not entail additional risk.[97] However, inefficiencies are ephemeral. Sooner or later they tend to be discovered and wiped out by other diligent researchers. However, returns that are justified as a risk premium are more likely to endure as they represent payment for service.

How do risk premiums explain the existence of systematic price movements? Such price movements can provide a mechanism for risk-accepting investors to be compensated. The investor who is willing to provide liquidity to a stockholder with a strong desire to sell winds up buying stocks that have a systematic tendency to rise over the near term. These stocks can be identified with countertrend strategies.[98]

Therefore, in the context of efficient markets, the profits-earned by TA strategies may be understood as risk premiums; compensation for the beneficial effect the strategy confers on other investors or the market as a whole. In other words, TA signals may generate profits because they identify opportunities to assume risks that other investors wish to shed.

I should point out that the mere fact that an investor is willing to bear a risk does not guarantee that a return will be earned. The risk taker must be clever about it. Just as a careless high steel worker or test pilot may not live long enough to collect a wage that includes the hazardous-duty premium, a careless seeker of risk premiums may not stay in the game long enough to collect, either.

Hedge Risk Premium and the Gains to Trend-Following Commodity Futures

This section describes how the profits to trend followers in the commodities markets may be explained as a risk transfer premium. The commodities futures markets perform an economic function that is fundamentally different from the stock and bond markets. The stock and bond markets provide companies with a mechanism to obtain equity and debt financing[99] and provide investors with a way to invest their capital. Because stocks and corporate bond investments expose investors to risks that exceed the risk-free rate (government treasury bills), investors are compensated with a risk premium—the equity risk premium and the corporate-bond risk premium.

The economic function of the futures markets has nothing to do with raising capital and everything to do with price risk. Price changes, especially large ones, are a source of risk and uncertainty to businesses that produce or use commodities. The futures markets provide a means by which these businesses, called commercial hedgers, can transfer price risk to investors (speculators).

At first blush, it may seem puzzling that commercial hedgers would even need investors to assume their price risk. Because some hedgers need to sell, like the farmer who grows wheat, and some need to buy, like the bread company that uses wheat, why don't hedgers simply contract with each other? They do, but often there is an imbalance in their hedging needs. Sometimes wheat farmers have more wheat to sell than bakery companies and other commercial users of wheat need to buy. At other times, the situation is the opposite. Thus there is often a gap between the farmers' supply and the bakers' demand. This creates the need for a third group of market participants who are willing to buy or sell. That is, they are willing to fill the supply-demand gap that develops between commercial producers and commercial users.

The existence of a supply-demand gap is a predicable consequence of the law of supply and demand; as the price of wheat rises, supply goes up while demand goes down. As the price falls, supply goes down while demand goes up. Data from the Commodity Futures Trading Commission (CFTC), which tracks the buying and selling of commercial hedgers, confirms this is exactly what occurs in the futures markets. During rising price trends, commercial hedge selling exceeds hedge buying (i.e., hedgers are net sellers). During falling trends, commercial hedge buying exceeds commercial hedge selling (hedgers are net buyers).

In the futures markets, the amount sold and the amount bought must be equal just as in real estate transactions the number of homes sold must equal the number of homes bought. It cannot be otherwise. Given that a rising trend motivates more commercial hedge selling than hedge buying, there is a need for additional buyers during rising markets to accommodate the excess hedge selling. During falling trends, excessive commercial hedge buying creates the need for additional sellers.

Enter the price trend speculator who is willing to buy during uptrends to meet the unfilled needs of commercial hedge sellers and willing to sell short during falling price trends, to meet the unmet needs of the commercial hedge buyers. In other words the futures markets need speculators to be trend followers. And it is the invisible hand of the marketplace that creates the trends to compensate them for filling this need.

However, trend followers are exposed to significant risks. For example, most trend-following systems generate unprofitable signals 50 to 65 percent of the time. These occur when markets are trendless, which is the case a majority of the time. During these times, the trend followers experience the dreaded equity drawdown. During drawdowns it is not unusual for successful trend followers to lose up to 30 percent of their trading capital. Thus they need a strong motive to tolerate drawdown risk. That motive is the opportunity, though not the guarantee, to profit from price trends when they do occur. In other words, large-scale trends provide a profit opportunity to trend followers who are adequately capitalized and who manage leverage correctly.

The Mt. Lucas Management Index of Trend Following Returns

The risk premium earned by commodity trend followers has been quantified with the creation of a benchmark index called the Mt. Lucas Management Index (MLM). It is a historical record of the returns that can be earned by an extremely simplistic trend-following formula. In other words, it assumes no specialized knowledge of a complex forecasting model. If it did it could not legitimately be called a benchmark index, whose function is to estimate the returns that can be earned by investing in an asset class with no special skill.

The risk-adjusted returns earned by the MLM index suggest that commodity futures markets contain systematic price movements that can be exploited with relatively simple TA methods. The MLM index monthly returns, which have been computed back to the 1960s, are derived by applying a 12-month moving-average crossover strategy to 25 commodities markets.[100] At the end of each month, the price of the nearby futures contract for each of the markets is compared to its 12-month moving average. If the price is greater than the moving average, a long position is held in that market for the next month. If the price is below the average, a short position is held.

The annualized return[101] and risk, as measured by the standard deviation in annual returns, of the MLM index is compared with returns and risks of several other asset-class benchmarks in Figure 40.13.

The risk-adjusted excess return or Sharpe ratio for the MLM index, and the other asset classes are shown Figure 40.14. The trend follower earns a risk premium that is somewhat better than the other asset-class benchmarks.[102] The MLM index provides some evidence that the futures markets offer compensation in the form of systematic price movements.

If a risk-transfer premium is a valid explanation of trend-follower returns, then trend following in stocks should not be as rewarding as it is in the commodity futures markets. A trend follower in stocks is not providing a risk-transfer service. There are data suggesting that trend following in stocks is indeed a less rewarding enterprise.[103] Lars Kestner compared the performance of trend-following systems for a portfolio of futures and a portfolio of stocks. The futures considered were 29

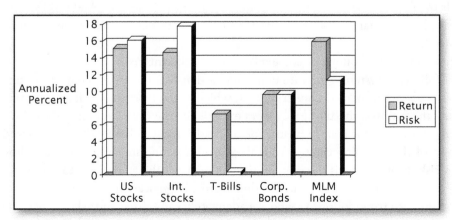

FIGURE 40.13 Returns and Standard Deviations for Five Benchmarks.

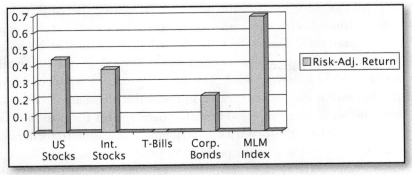

FIGURE 40.14 Risk–Adjusted Excess Returns.

commodities in 8 different sectors.[104] The stocks were represented by 31 large-cap stocks in 9 different industry sectors,[105] and 3 stock indices. Risk-adjusted performance (Sharpe ratio) was computed for 5 different trend-following systems,[106] over the period January 1, 1990 through December 31, 2001. The Sharpe ratio averaged over the five trend-following systems in futures was .604 versus .046 in stocks. These results support the notion that futures trend followers are earning a risk premium that is not available to trend followers in stocks. See Figure 40.15.

Liquidity Premium and the Gains to Counter Trend Trading in Stocks

The stock market offers risk-taking stock traders a different form of compensation. They can earn a premium for providing liquidity to highly motivated sellers. In other words, there are systematic price movements in stocks that can be exploited with countertrend strategies that buy stocks that have been very weak over the recent past.

Owners of stock with an urgent need to liquidate their holdings need buyers. This suggests that the market should offer compensation to traders who are willing to meet unmet needs for liquidity. Evidence presented by Michael Cooper shows that buyers of oversold stocks can earn above-average short-term returns.[107] His study shows that stocks that have displayed negative price momentum on declin-

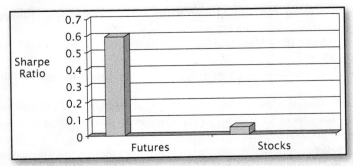

FIGURE 40.15 Risk–Adjusted Returns to Trend-Following Futures Versus Stocks.

ing trading volume earn excess returns. In other words, the pattern identifies stocks with distressed sellers in search of buyers. The excess returns appear to be a liquidity premium. Cooper's study showed that stocks that have declined sharply over the prior two weeks on declining volume display a systematic tendency to rise over the following week. The declining volume aspect of this pattern is plausible because it can be interpreted to mean that there are insufficient buyers to meet the acute needs of the sellers. To guard against the possibility of data mining, Cooper used a walk-forward out-of-sample simulation to form portfolios of long and short positions over the period 1978 to 1993. The long/short portfolios, created from 300 large capitalization stocks, earned an annualized return of 44.95 percent versus a benchmark buy-and-hold return of 17.91 percent. Again, we see evidence of systematic price movements that can be explained as a risk premium, in this case a liquidity premium, which can be exploited with TA.

In the context of efficient equity and futures markets, signals given by TA methods can be viewed as identifying opportunities to fill a market need. In effect, they are want ads, "risk adopter for hire by hedgers," or "desperately seeking liquidity provider— will pay." TA traders profiting from these signals are not getting a free lunch. They are simply reading the market's Help Wanted advertisements.

Conclusion

In this chapter, I have made a case for the existence of nonrandom price movements in financial markets. Without them, there can be no justification for technical analysis. With them, TA has an opportunity to capture some portion of that nonrandom behavior. Ultimately, it is up to each method of TA to prove that it can.

Notes

1. C.R. Lightner, "A Rationale for Managed Futures," *Technical Analysis of Stocks & Commodities* (March 1999).
2. Kepler actually proposed three distinct laws.
3. R.D. Edwards and J. Magee, *Technical Analysis of Stock Trends*, 4th ed. (Springfield, MA: John Magee, 1958).
4. J.J. Murphy, *Technical Analysis of the Futures Markets: A Comprehensive Guide to Trading Methods and Applications* (New York: New York Institute of Finance, 1999), 2.
5. E. Fama, "Efficient Capital Markets: A Review of Theory and Empirical Work" *Journal of Finance* 25 (1970), 383–417.
6. R.J. Shiller, *Irrational Exuberance* (Princeton, NJ: Princeton University Press, 2000), 135.
7. Ibid.
8. In this chapter in section "Nonrandom Price Motion in the Context of Efficient Markets," I state the case of those who say EMH allows for price predictability, namely, that random walks are not a necessary implication of EMH.
9. Updating a belief in a probabilistically correct way implies that new information impacts a prior belief in accord with Bayes' theorem, whereby the prior belief is altered in accord with the predictive value of the new information.

10. Correct prices induce the proper allocation of resources among different possible uses. For example, if the price of corn is too high, more of it than necessary will be produced, flooding the economy with more corn than is needed at the expense of something else such as wheat. Net result: too many boxes of Corn Flakes and too few boxes of Wheaties to meet consumer demand.

11. P. Samuelson, "Proof That Properly Anticipated Prices Fluctuate Randomly," *Industrial Management Review* 6 (1965), 41–49.

12. B.G. Malkiel, *A Random Walk Down Wall Street* (New York: W.W. Norton & Company, 2003).

13. E. Fama, "Efficient Capital Markets: A Review of Theory and Empirical Work," *Journal of Finance* 25 (1970), 383–417, as cited by A. Shleifer in *Inefficient Markets: An Introduction to Behavioral Finance* (Oxford, UK: Oxford University Press, 2000), 1.

14. A. Shleifer, *Inefficient Markets: An Introduction to Behavioral Finance* (Oxford, UK: Oxford University Press, 2000), 1.

15. N.N. Taleb, *Fooled by Randomness: The Hidden Role of Chance in the Markets and in Life* (New York: Texere, 2001).

16. A money manager with no skill whatsoever has a 0.5 probability of beating the market in any given time period (e.g., 1 year). In this experiment, Taleb assumed a universe of money managers with a 0.50 probability of beating the market in a given year.

17. Actually there are three forms of EMH—strong, semistrong, and weak. The strong form contends that no information, including inside information, can be used to beat the market on a risk-adjusted basis. This form is impossible to test because it cannot be reliably ascertained who knew what and when they knew it. The testimony of those who trade on inside information is notoriously untrustworthy.

18. E. Fama, L. Fisher, M. Jensen, and R. Roll, "The Adjustment of Stock Prices to New Information," *International Economic Review* 10 (1969), 1–21.

19. These results conflict with later studies in behavioral finance that found markets did not properly discount surprising earnings announcements. My interpretation is that Fama's studies did not consider the degree to which earnings announcements differed from prior Street expectations. Later studies done by V. Bernard showed that stock prices do experience trends after earnings announcements, if the degree of surprise in the announcement is large. V. Bernard, "Stock Price Reactions to Earnings Announcements," *Advances in Behavioral Finance*, R. Thaler (Ed.) (New York: Russell Sage Foundation, 1992; V. Bernard and J.K. Thomas, "Post-Earnings Announcement Drift: Delayed Price Response or Risk Premium?," *Journal of Accounting Research, Supplement* 27 (1989), 1–36; V. Bernard and J.K. Thomas, "Evidence That Stock Prices Do Not Fully Reflect the Implications of Current Earnings for Future Earnings," *Journal of Accounting and Economics* 13 (1990), 305–341.

20. A noninformative event is one that carries no implications for the future cash flows of the asset or the future returns of the security.

21. The capital asset pricing model was proposed by William F. Sharpe in "Capital Asset Prices: A Theory of Market Equilibrium under Conditions of Risk," *Journal of Finance* 19 (1964), 425–442.

22. APT was first proposed by S. Ross, "The Arbitrage Theory of Capital Asset Pricing," *Journal of Economic Theory* (December 1976). APT says a linear model relates a stock's returns to a number of factors, and this relationship is the result of arbitrageurs hunting for riskless, zero-investment opportunities. APT specifies factors, including the rate of inflation, the spread between low and high quality bonds, the slope of the yield curve, and so on.

23. In other words, the current price change is correlated with the prior change (i.e., a lag interval of 1), then with the change prior to that (lag interval = 2), and so forth. A correlation coefficient is computed for each of these lags. Typically, in a random data series, the correlations drop off very quickly as a function of the lag interval. However, if the time series of price changes is nonrandom in a linear fashion, some of the autocorrelation coefficients will differ significantly from the pattern of autocorrelations of a random sequence.

24. E. Fama, "The Behavior of Stock Market Prices," *Journal of Business* 38 (1965), 34–106.

25. E.E. Peters, *Chaos and Order in the Capital Markets: A New View of Cycles, Prices and Market Volatility* (New York: John Wiley & Sons, 1991); E.E. Peters, *Fractal Market Analysis: Applying Chaos Theory to Investment and Economics* (New York: John Wiley & Sons, 1994).

26. A.W. Lo and A.C. MacKinlay, *A Non-Random Walk Down Wall Street* (Princeton, NJ: Princeton University Press, 1999).

27. S.J. Grossman and J.E. Stiglitz, "On the Impossibility of Informationally Efficient Markets," *American Economic Review* 70, no 3 (1980), 393–408.

28. Shleifer, *Inefficient Markets*, 2.

29. V. Singal, *Beyond the Random Walk: A Guide to Stock Market Anomalies and Low Risk Investing* (New York: Oxford University Press, 2004), 5.

30. F. Black, "Noise," *Journal of Finance* 41 (1986), 529–543.

31. Shleifer, *Inefficient Markets*, 10.

32. D. Kahneman and A. Tversky, "Prospect Theory: An Analysis of Decision Making under Risk," *Econometrica* 47 (1979), 263–291.

33. R. Shiller, "Stock Prices and Social Dynamics," *Brookings Papers on Economic Activity* 2, (1984), 457–498.

34. Cited by Shleifer, *Inefficient Markets*; J.B. De Long, A. Shleifer, L. Summers, and R. Waldmann, "Noise Trader Risk in Financial Markets," *Journal of Political Economy* 98 (1990), 703–738.

35. R. Merton and P. Samuelson, "Fallacy of the Log-Normal Approximation to Optimal Portfolio Decision-Making over Many Periods," *Journal of Financial Economics* 1 (1974), 67–94.

36. The expectation of a game is (probability of a win × amount won) − (probability of a loss × amount lost). Thus, per dollar bet, the expectation is +50 cents. In investment-strategy terms, this would be called a profit factor of 2.0. Very few investment strategies have such a favorable edge.

37. R. Shiller, "Do Stock Prices Move Too Much to Be Justified by Subsequent Changes in Dividends?," *American Economic Review* 71 (1981), 421–436.

38. Cited by Shleifer, *Inefficient Markets*, 20; D. Cutler, J. Poterba, and L. Summers, "Speculative Dynamics," *Review of Economic Studies* 58 (1991), 529–546.

39. Cited by Shleifer, *Inefficient Markets*; R. Roll, "Orange Juice and Weather," *American Economic Review* 74 (1984), 861–880; R. Roll, "R-squared," *Journal of Finance* 43, (1988), 541–566.

40. Singal, *Beyond the Random Walk*, ix.

41. *Relative performance* refers to the stock's performance relative to the performance of the average stock, or a benchmark. Relative performance is also known as excess return.

42. Stocks can also be ranked on the basis of a prediction model that employs a multitude of indicators, typically referred to as factors.

43. When multiperiod horizons are used, the number of independent observations are also reduced, so a one-month horizon, based on monthly data, is often used.

44. The strong form of EMH is broader yet in claiming that not even inside information is useful in generating superior returns, but this version is not testable.

45. R. Banz, "The Relation between Market Return and Market Value for Common Stocks," *Journal of Financial Economics* 9 (1981), 3–18.

46. E. Fama and K. French, "The Cross-Section of Expected Stock Returns," *Journal of Finance* 47 (1992), 427–465.

47. Cited by Shiller, *Irrational Exuberance*; S. Basu, "The Investment Performance of Common Stocks Relative to Their Price-Earnings Ratios: A Test of the Efficient Markets," *Journal of Finance* 32, no. 3 (1977), 663–682.

48. Cited by Shiller, *Irrational Exuberance*; E. Fama and K. French, "The Cross Section of Expected Stock Returns," *Journal of Finance* 47 (1992), 427–466.

49. Singal, *Beyond the Random Walk*.

50. Although the weak form of EMH typically only talks about past prices and past price changes, I believe advocates of this position would also claim that any other data relied upon by TA would be useless for predicting future returns.

51. N. Jegadeesh, and S. Titman, "Returns to Buying Winners and Selling Losers: Implications for Market Efficiency," *Journal of Finance* 48, (1993), 65–91.

52. E. Fama, "Efficient Capital Markets: II," *Journal of Finance* 46 (1991), 1575–1617.

53. W. De Bondt and R. H. Thaler, "Does the Stock Market Overreact?," Journal of Finance 40, no. 3 (1985), 793–805.

54. In this case, risk is as defined by CAPM, volatility relative to the market.

55. T.J. George and C.-Y. Hwang, "The 52-Week High and Momentum Investing," *Journal of Finance* 59, no. 5 (October 2004), 2145.

56. C.M.C. Lee and B. Swaminathan, "Price Momentum and Trading Volume," *Journal of Finance* 55, no. 5 (October 2000), 2017–2067; S. E. Stickel and R.E. Verecchia, "Evidence That Trading Volume Sustains Stock Price Changes," *Financial Analysts Journal* 50, no. 6 (November–December 1994), 57–67. It should be noted that when the forward-looking horizon is 3 to 12 months, high volume increases the price momentum's effect. However, when the return is looked at 3 years out, high-momentum stocks with low volume are more persistent on the upside, whereas negative-momentum stocks with high volume persist on the downside.

57. E. Fama and K. French, "1996 Common Risk Factors in the Returns on Bonds and Stocks," *Journal of Financial Economics* 33 (1993), 3–56; E. Fama and K. French, "Multifactor Explanations of Asset Pricing Anomalies," *Journal of Finance* 51 (1996), 55–84.

58. W. Sharpe, "Capital Asset Prices: A Theory of Market Equilibrium under Conditions of Risk," *Journal of Finance* 19 (1964), 435–442; also see J. Lintner, "The Valuation of Risk Assets and the Selection of Risky Investments in Stock Portfolios and Capital Budgets," *Review of Economics and Statistics* 47 (1965), 13–37.

59. Shleifer, *Inefficient Markets*, 19.

60. J. Lakonishok, A. Shleifer, and R. Vishny, "Contrarian Investment, Extrapolation, and Risk," *Journal of Finance* 49 (1994), 1541–1578.

61. Shleifer, *Inefficient Markets*, 24.

62. Ibid.

63. Ibid.

64. W. Edwards, "Conservatism in Human Information Processing," in *Formal Representation of Human Judgment*, B. Kleinmutz (Ed.) (New York: John Wiley & Sons, 1968) 17–52.

65. D.G. Myers, *Intuition, Its Powers and Perils* (New Haven: Yale University Press, 2004), 157.

66. A. Tversky and D. Kahneman, *Judgment under Uncertainty Heuristics and Biases, in Judgment under Uncertainty: Heuristics and Biases*, D. Kahneman, P. Slovic, and A. Tversky (Eds.) (New York: Cambridge University Press, 1982), 14.

67. George and Hwang, "52-Week High."

68. Shiller, *Irrational Exuberance*, 138.

69. Ibid., 139.

70. E. Shafir, I. Simonson, and A. Tversky, "Reason–Based Choice," *Cognition* 49 (1993), 11–36.

71. Systematic process can exhibit real trends, which are streaks that are longer in duration than those found in random walks, or they can exhibit true meanreversion behavior, which means that streaks will be shorter in duration (i.e., more frequent flip-flops between positive and negative outcomes) than is true for random walks. In both truly trended processes and true mean-reverting process, prior observations contain useful predictive information. In true random- walk processes, prior observations contain no predictive information.

72. Shiller, *Irrational Exuberance*, 148–169.

73. A. Asch, *Social Psychology* (Englewood Cliffs, NJ: Prentice-Hall, 1952), 450–501.

74. M. Deutsch and H.B. Gerard, "A Study of Normative and Informational Social Influence upon Individual Judgment," *Journal of Abnormal and Social Psychology* 51 (1955), 629–636.

75. Shiller, *Irrational Exuberance*, 148–169.

76. R.J. Shiller cites D.D. Bikhchandani, D. Hirshleifer, and I. Welch, "A Theory of Fashion, Social Custom and Cultural Change," *Journal of Political Economy* 81 (1992), 637–654; A.V. Nanerjee, "A Simple Model of Herd Behavior," *Quarterly Journal of Economics* 107, no. 3 (1993), 797–817.

77. Shiller, *Irrational Exuberance*, 152.

78. Ibid., 164.

79. Ibid., 165.

80. Ibid., 166.

81. See Carl Anderson, "Notes on Feedback and Self-Organization," at www.duke.edu/~carl/pattern/characteristic_student_notes.htm.

82. Shiller, Irrational *Exuberance*, 67.

83. N. Barberis, A. Shleifer, and R. Vishny, "A Model of Investor Sentiment," *Journal of Financial Economics* 49 (1998), 307–343.

84. This assumption is consistent with studies showing that people have difficulty distinguishing random series from series that display systematic behavior such as mean-reversion or trending behavior. This failure accounts for sports fans' misperception of the hot hand and chartists' inability to distinguish real from random charts cited in chapter 2.

85. Shiller, *Irrational Exuberance*, 144.

86. R.J. Shiller cites Barberis, Shleifer, and Vishny, "Model of Investor Sentiment," and N. Barberis, M. Huang, and T. Santos, "Prospect Theory and Asset Prices," *Quarterly Journal of Economics* 116, no. 1 (February 2001), 1–53; K. Daniel, D. Hirshleifer, and A. Subrahmanyam, "Investor Psychology and Security Market Over and Underreaction," *Journal of Finance* 53, no. 6 (1998), 1839–1886; H. Hong and J. Stein, "A Unified Theory of Underreaction, Momentum Trading, and Overreaction in Asset Markets," *Journal of Finance* 54, no. 6 (December 1999), 2143–2184.

87. Daniel, Hirshleifer, and Subrahmanyam, "Investor Psychology"; and K. Daniel, D. Hirshleifer, and A. Subrahmanyam, "Overconfidence, Arbitrage and Equilibrium Asset Pricing," *Journal of Finance* 56 (2001), 921–965.

88. N. Barberis, "A Survey of Behavioral Finance," in *Handbook of the Economics of Finance*, Volume 1B, G.M. Constantinides, M. Harris, and R. Stulz (Eds.) (New York: Elsevier Science, B.V., 2003).

89. N. Chopra and R. Lakonishok, "Measuring Abnormal Performance: Do Stocks Overreact?," *Journal of Financial Economics* 31 (1992), 235–268; R. La Porta, R. Lakonishok, A. Shleifer, and R. Vishny, "Good News for Value Stocks: Further Evidence on Market Efficiency," *Journal of Finance* 49 (1997), 1541–1578.

90. J.B. De Long, A. Shleifer, L. Summers, and R. Waldmann, "Positive Feedback Investment Strategies and Destabilizing Rational Speculation," *Journal of Finance* 45, no. 2 (1990), 379–395; N. Barberis and A. Shleifer, "Style Investing," *Journal of Financial Economics* 68 (2003), 161–199.

91. Hong and Stein, "Unified Theory."

92. S.F. LeRoy, "Risk Aversion and the Martingale Property of Stock Returns," *International Economic Review* 14 (1973), 436–446; R.E. Lucas, "Asset Prices in an Exchange Economy," *Econometrica* 46 (1978), 1429–1446.

93. A.W. Lo and A.C. MacKinlay, *A Non-Random Walk Down Wall Street* (Princeton, NJ: Princeton University Press, 1999), 5.

94. Ibid.

95. S. Grossman, "On the Efficiency of Competitive Stock Markets Where Traders Have Diverse Information," *Journal of Finance* 31 (1976), 573–585; S. Grossman and J. Stiglitz, "On the Impossibility of Informationally Efficient Markets," *American Economic Review* 70 (1980), 393–408.

96. L. Jaeger, *Managing Risk in Alternative Investment Strategies: Successful Investing in Hedge Funds and Managed Futures* (London: Financial Times–Prentice Hall, 2002), 27.

97. Gains from a true inefficiency are not a free lunch, because it is costly to identify them, but they need not entail the risk of additional volatility in returns. Thus true inefficiencies can generate investment performance with a high relative Sharpe ratio.

98. H.D. Platt, *Counterintuitive Investing: Profiting from Bad News on Wall Street* (Mason, OH: Thomson Higher Education, 2005).

99. Equity and bond markets provide a quick way for owners of equities to sell their position to other investors. The liquidity of stocks and bonds thus makes them attractive to the initial investors, thereby making it easier for companies to raise debt and equity financing.

100. Grains (corn, soybeans, soybean meal, soybean oil, and wheat); financials (5-year T-notes, 10-year T-notes, long-term treasury bonds); currencies (Australian, British, Canadian, German, Swiss, and Japanese); energy (heating oil, natural gas, crude oil, and unleaded gas); cattle; metals (gold, copper, and silver); and soft/tropical (coffee, cotton, and sugar).

101. G.R. Jensen, R.R. Johnson, and J.M. Mercer, "Tactical Asset Allocation and Commodity Futures," *Journal of Portfolio Management* 28, no. 4 (Summer 2002).

102. An asset-class benchmark measures the returns earned and risks incurred by investing in a specific asset class, with no management skill.

103. Lars Kestner, *Quantitative Trading Strategies: Harnessing the Power of Quantitative Techniques to Create a Winning Trading Program* (New York: McGraw-Hill, 2003), 129–180.

104. The eight market sectors tested were foreign exchange, interest rates, stock index, metals, energy, grains, meats, and softs.

105. The nine industry sectors were energy, basic materials, consumer discretionary, consumer staples, health care, financials and information technology, telecom. The three stock indexes were S&P 500, NASDAQ 100, and Russell 2000.

106. The five trend-following systems were channel breakout, dual moving-average crossover, two version of momentum, and MACD versus its signal line. For more description see Kestner's *Quantitative Trading Strategies.*

107. M. Cooper, "Filter Rules Based on Price and Volume in Individual Security Overreaction," *Review of Financial Studies* 12, no. 4 (Special 1999), 901–935.

CHAPTER 41

Case Study of Rule Data Mining for the S&P 500

From David Aronson, *Evidence-Based Technical Analysis: Applying the Scientific Method and Statistical Inference to Trading Signals* (Hoboken, New Jersey: John Wiley & Sons, 2006), Chapter 8.

This chapter describes a case study in rule data mining. The study evaluates the statistical significance of 6,402 individual TA rules back tested on the S&P 500 Index over the period from November 1, 1980 through July 1, 2005.

■ Data Mining Bias and Rule Evaluation

The primary purpose of the case study is to illustrate the application of statistical methods that take into account the effects of data-mining bias. To recap, data mining is a process in which the profitability of many rules is compared so that one or more superior rules can be selected. As pointed out in Level III, Chapter 24, this selection process causes an upward bias in the performance of the selected rule(s). In other words, the observed performance of the best rule(s) in the back test overstates its (their) expected performance in the future. This bias complicates the evaluation of statistical significance and may lead a data miner to select a rule with no predictive power (i.e., its past performance was pure luck). This is the fool's gold of the objective technician.

This problem can be minimized by using specialized statistical-inference tests. The case study illustrates the application of two such methods: an enhanced version of White's reality check and Masters's Monte-Carlo permutation method. Both take advantage of a recent improvement,[1] which reduces the probability that a good rule will be overlooked (Type II error). That is to say, the improvement increases the power of the tests.

A secondary purpose of the case study was the possible discovery of one or more rules that generate statistically significant profits. However, when the case study's rules were proposed, it was unknown if any would be found to be statistically significant.

■ Avoidance of Data Snooping Bias

In addition to data mining bias, rule studies can also suffer from an even more serious problem, the *data-snooping bias*. *Data snooping* refers to using the results of prior rule studies reported by other researchers. Because these studies typically do not disclose the amount of data mining that led to the discovery of whatever it was that was discovered, there is no way to take its effects into account and hence no way to properly evaluate the statistical significance of the results. As pointed out in Level III, Chapter 24, depending on which method is being used—White's Reality Check or the Monte Carlo permutation method—information about each rule tested must be available to construct the appropriate sampling distribution.

For example, suppose the case study in this book had included a rule developed by Dr. Martin Zweig known as the *double 9:1 upside/downside volume* rule. This rule signals long positions when the daily ratio of upside to downside volume on the NYSE exceeds a threshold value of 9 on two instances within a three-month time window. Note, this rule has three free parameters: the threshold value on the ratio (9), the number of instances on which the ratio exceeds the threshold (2), and the maximum time separation between the threshold violations (3 months). According to tests of this rule conducted by students in my technical analysis class, the signal does have predictive power over the following 3, 6, 9, and 12 months. In other words, the rule is statistically significant, but only under the assumption that Zweig did not engage in data mining to discover the parameter values he recommends: 9, 2, and 3. Zweig has not reported if he tested other versions of the rule using different parameter combinations or, if he did, how many combinations were tried to find the specific set that defines his rule. If Zweig's rule were to be included in the case study and it was selected as the best rule, it would be impossible to take into account the true amount of data mining that led to its discovery.

In an effort to avoid data-snooping bias, the case study did not explicitly include any rules discussed by other researchers. Even though it is possible, perhaps even likely, that some of the study's rules were similar to those tested in prior rule studies, these similarities were by accident, not by design. This precaution mitigated the data-snooping bias but could not eliminate it entirely because, in proposing the 6,402 rules tested, I could not help but be affected by rule studies I have previously read.

■ Analyzed Data Series

Although all rules were tested for their profitability on the S&P 500 Index, the vast majority of rules utilized data series other than the S&P 500 to generate buy-and-sell signals. These other data series included: other market indices (e.g., transportation stocks), market breadth (e.g., upside and downside volume), indicators that combine price and volume (e.g., on-balance volume), prices of debt instruments (e.g., BAA bonds), and interest-rate spreads (duration spread between 10-year treasury notes and 90-day treasury bills). This approach is in the spirit of intermarket analysis as discussed by Murphy.[2] All series and rules are detailed below.

■ Technical Analysis Themes

The 6,402 rules tested were derived from three broad themes of TA: (1) trends, (2) extremes and transitions, and (3) divergences. Trend rules generate long and short market positions based on the current trend of the data series analyzed by the rule. Extreme and transition rules generate long and short positions when the analyzed series reaches an extreme high or low value or as it makes a transition between extreme values. Divergence rules generate signals when the S&P 500 Index trends in one direction while a companion data series trends in the other. The specific data transformations and signal logic for each rule are described later in this chapter.

The rules employ several common analysis methods including moving averages, channel breakouts, and stochastics, which I refer to as channel normalization.

■ Performance Statistic: Average Return

The performance statistic used to evaluate each rule was its average return over the period (1980 to 2005) when back tested on detrended S&P 500 data. Detrending involves subtracting the S&P 500's average daily price change over the back-test period from each day's actual price change. This results in a new data series for which the average daily change is equal to zero.

Detrending eliminates any benefit or detriment that would accrue to a rule's performance as a result of either a long or short position bias. A binary rule can be position biased if one of its conditions (long or short) is restrictive relative to the other condition (long or short). For example, if the long-position condition is more difficult to satisfy than the short-position condition, the rule will have a short-position bias and tend to spend a majority of its time in short positions. If such a rule were to be applied to market data with a positive trend (average daily price change > 0), its average return would be penalized. This reduction in the rule's performance would have nothing to do with its predictive power and thus cloud its evaluation.

■ No Complex Rules Were Evaluated

To keep the scope of the case study manageable, it was restricted to tests of individual rules. Complex rules, which are derived by combining two or more individual rules with mathematical and/or logical operators, were not considered. The combining method can be as simple an unweighted average or as complex as an arbitrarily nonlinear function derived with sophisticated data-modeling software.

Limiting the case study to individual rules was detrimental for two reasons. First, few practitioners rely on a single rule to make decisions. Second, complex rules exploit informational synergies between individual rules. It is not surprising, therefore, that complex rules have demonstrated higher levels of performance. At least one study[3] has shown that complex rules can produce good performance, even when the simple rules combined to form the complex rule are individually unprofitable. Combining rules intuitively is extremely difficult, but there are now effective automated methods[4] for synthesizing complex rules.

■ The Case Study Defined in Statistical Terms

The following section defines the case study in terms of the key elements of a statistical study: the population at issue, the parameter of interest, sample data used, the statistic of interest, the null and alternative hypotheses considered, and the designated significance level.

The Population

The population at issue is the set of daily returns that would be earned by a rule if its signals were to be applied to the S&P 500 over all possible realizations of the *immediate practical future*.[5] This is an abstract population, in the sense that its observations have not yet occurred and it is infinite in size.

Population Parameter

The population parameter is the rule's expected average annualized return in the immediate practical future.

The Sample

The sample consists of the daily returns earned by a rule applied to detrended S&P 500 Index prices over the back-test period from November 1, 1980 until July 1, 2005.

Sample Statistic (Test Statistic)

The sample statistic is the average annualized return earned by a rule when applied to the detrended S&P 500 price data from November 1, 1980 until July 1, 2005.

The Null Hypothesis (H_0)

The null hypothesis states that all 6,402 rules tested are without predictive power. This implies that any observed profits in a back test were due to chance (sampling variability).

In reality, there are two version of the null hypothesis in the case study. This stems from the fact that two different methods were used to assess statistical significance: White's reality check and Masters's Monte Carlo permutation method. Although both methods assert that all rules considered were devoid of predictive power, they implement this assumption differently. The null hypothesis tested by White's reality check is that all rules tested have expected returns equal to zero (or less). The null tested by Masters's Monte Carlo permutation is that all rules generated their long and short positions in a random fashion. In other words, long and short were randomly permuted with the market's one-day-forward price change.

The Alternative Hypothesis

This study's alternative hypothesis asserts that a rule's back-tested profitability stems from genuine predictive power. Again, the two methods assert this in slightly different ways. In the case of White's reality check, the alternative hypothesis says that there is at least one rule within the tested universe that has an expected return greater than zero. It should be noted that White's reality check does not assert that the rule with the highest observed performance is necessarily that best rule (i.e., the rule with the highest expected return). However, under fairly reasonable conditions, they are one and the same.[6] The alternative hypothesis declared by Masters's method is that a rule's back-tested profitability is the result of an informative pairing of its long and short positions with the market's one-day-forward price change. In other words, the rule has predictive power.

The Statistical Significance Level

A 5 percent level of significance was chosen as a threshold for rejection of the null hypothesis. This means there was a 0.05 probability of rejecting the H_0 hypothesis when the H_0 was, in fact, true.

Practical Significance

The practical significance of a result is different from its statistical significance. The latter is the probability that a rule that has no predictive power (i.e., H_0 is true) would earn a return as high as or higher than the return produced by the rule in a back test by luck. In contrast, practical significance relates to the economic value of the observed rule return. When sample sizes are large, as they are in the case study (i.e., over 6,000 days), the H_0 can be rejected even if a rule's return is positive by a very minor amount. In other words, a rule can be statistically significant even though its practical value is negligible. Practical significance depends upon a trader's objectives. One trader may be satisfied with a rule for which expected return is 5 percent whereas another may reject any rule for which expected return is less than 20 percent.

■ Rules: Transforming Data Series into Market Positions

A rule is an input/output process. That is to say, it transforms input(s), consisting of one or more time series, into an output, a new time series consisting of +1's and −1's that indicate long and short positions in the market being traded (i.e., S&P 500). This transformation is defined by the one or more mathematical,[7] logical,[8] or time series[9] operators that are applied to the input time series. In other words, a rule is defined by a set of operations. See Figure 41.1.

Some rules utilize inputs that are raw time series. That is to say, the one or more time series used as inputs to the rule are not transformed in any way prior to the rule's position logic being applied, for example the S&P 500 closing price. This is illustrated in Figure 41.2.

Other rules utilize input series that have been derived from one or more raw market series by applying various transformations to the market data. These prepro-cessed inputs are referred to as constructed data series or *indicators*. An example of an indicator is the *negative volume index*. It is derived from transformations of two raw data series; S&P 500 closing price and total NYSE daily volume. This is illustrated in Figure 41.3. The transformations used in the creation of the negative volume index and other indicators used in the case study are described in the following section.

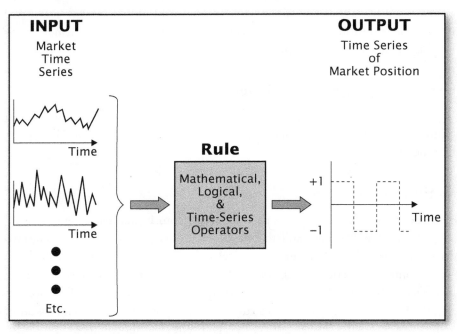

FIGURE 41.1   TA Rule Transforms Input into Output.

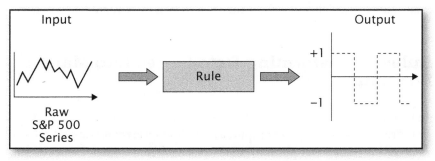

FIGURE 41.2   Raw Market Time Series as Rule Input.

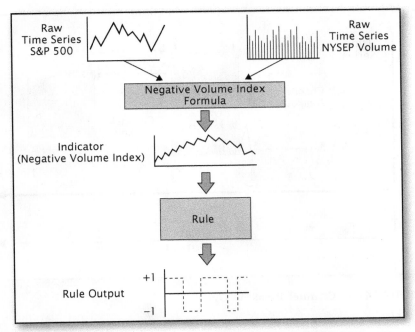

FIGURE 41.3 Transformed Market Time Series as Rule Input.

■ Time-Series Operators

This section describes the time-series operators used in the case study to transform raw data series into indicators. Time-series operators are mathematical functions that transform a time series into a new time series. The case study utilized several common time-series operators: channel breakout, moving average, and channel normalization. The channel breakout operator is used to identify trends in a time series for rules that are based on trends. The moving-average operator, which can also identify trends, is used in the case study for smoothing. The channel-normalization operator, or stochastics, is used to eliminate the trend of a time series (i.e., detrending).

Channel Breakout Operator (CBO)

"The purpose of all trend identification methods is to see past the underlying noise in a time series, those erratic moves that seem to be meaningless, and find the current direction of the series."[10] One such method is the n-period channel-breakout operator.[11] Here, n refers to the number of time periods (days, weeks, and such) into the past that are examined to define the upper and lower channel boundaries that enclose the time series. The lower boundary is defined by the minimum value of the time series over the past n-periods, not including the current period. The upper boundary is defined by the time series' maximum value over the past n-periods, not including the current period. Despite its extreme simplicity, the channel-breakout operator has proven to be as effective as more complex trend-following methods.[12]

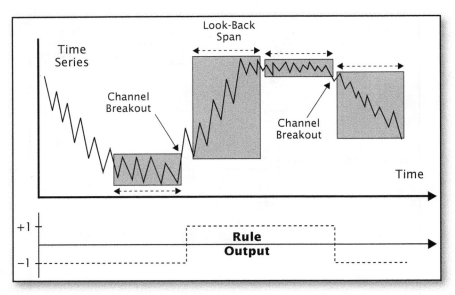

FIGURE 41.4   Channel-Breakout Operator.

As conventionally interpreted, the channel breakout operator signals long positions if the analyzed series exceeds its maximum value established over the past n-periods. Conversely, short positions are signaled when the time series falls below its *n*-period minimum. This is illustrated in Figure 41.4. In practice, the channel is redrawn as each new data point becomes available, but in Figure 41.4 only several channels are shown to illustrate its function. Although the channel has a constant look-back span with respect to the time axis, its vertical width with respect to the axis that represents the value of the time series adjusts dynamically to the range of the series over the past *n*-periods. This feature may explain the effectiveness of the method. This is to say, the channel breakout's dynamic range may reduce the likelihood of false signals caused by an increase in the series' volatility rather than an actual change in its trend.

The *n*-period breakout operator has a single free parameter, its look-back span, the number of time periods into the past used to establish the channel's boundaries. In general, the larger the look-back span, the wider the channel, and hence, the less sensitive the indicator. Thus, larger values of *n* are used to identify larger trends. The case study tested 11 different look-back spans for which lengths were separated by a factor of approximately 1.5. The specific spans used were: 3, 5, 8, 12, 18, 27, 41, 61, 91, 137, and 205 days.

Moving-Average Operator (MA)

The moving average is one of the most widely used times-series operators in TA. It clarifies trends by filtering out high frequency (short-period) fluctuations while passing through low frequency (long-period) components. Thus, the moving-average operator is said to function as a low-pass filter. This is illustrated

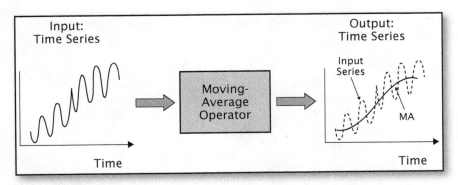

FIGURE 41.5 Moving-Average Operator: Low-Pass Filter.

in Figure 41.5, where the moving average has been centered[13] (lagged by $0.5 \times$ period -1). Note that the output of the moving-average operator is essentially the trend of the original time series with the high frequency oscillations about the trend removed.

The smoothing effect is accomplished by averaging the values of the time series within a moving data window called the *look-back span*. This eliminates or reduces the magnitude of fluctuations with durations that are equal to or less than the duration of the look-back span. Thus, a 10-day moving average will reduce the amplitude of fluctuations for which peak-to-peak or trough-to-trough duration is less than 10 days, and it will completely eliminate a fluctuation with a duration that is exactly equal to 10 days.

The benefit of smoothing comes at a cost—lag. In other words, fluctuations in the raw price that manifest in the smoothed version experience some delay. Thus, a trough in the raw price does not produce a trough in the moving average until some later date. The amount of lag depends upon the length of the look-back span. A longer look-back span produces more smoothing while producing more lag.

The lag induced by a *simple moving average*, which gives equal weight to all elements in the window, is equal to one-half of the look-back span minus one. Thus, the output of an 11-day simple moving average has a lag of $(11 - 1)/2$ or 5 days. This means that trend reversals in the input time series, which are of sufficient duration to manifest in the moving average, will not show up until 5 days later.

There are many types of moving averages, from the simple moving average that gives equal weight to each element in the data window, to sophisticated smoothing methods that use complex data-weighting functions. The benefit conferred by a complex weighting is improved filter performance—less lag for a given degree of smoothing. The field of digital signal processing is concerned with, among other things, the design of weighting functions that maximize filter performance. Digital filters that are relevant to TA are discussed in two books by Ehlers.[14]

The calculation for a simple moving average is given by the following formula.[15]

Moving Average Operator

$$MA_t = \frac{P_t + P_{t-1} + P_{t-2} \ldots + P_{t-n+1}}{n}$$

$$= \frac{\displaystyle\sum_{i=1}^{n} P_{t-i+1}}{n}$$

Where:
P_t = Price at time t
MA_t = Moving average at time t
n = Number of days used to compute moving average

The lag of a simple moving average can be reduced while maintaining the same degree of smoothing by using a linearly weighted moving average. As pointed out by Ehlers[16] the lag of a linearly weighted moving average with a look-back span of n days is $(n-1)/3$ compared with $(n-1)/2$ for a simple moving average. Thus, a linearly weighted moving average with a span of 10 days will have a lag of 3 days whereas a simple moving average with the same span will have a lag of 4.5 days. The linear-weighting scheme applies a weight of n to the most recent data point, where n is the number of days in the moving average look-back span, and then the weight is decreased by one for each prior day. The sum of the weights becomes the divisor. This is illustrated in the following equation:

Linear Weighted Moving Average

Weights

$$WMA_t = \frac{(n) \times P_t + (n-1) \times P_{t-1} + \ldots + (n-(t-n+1)) \times P_{t-n+1}}{\underbrace{n + n-1 + \ldots + n-(t-n-1)}_{\text{Sum of Weights}}}$$

Where:
P_t = Price at time t
WMA_t = Weighted moving average at time t
n = Number of days used to compute moving average

The case study used a four-day linearly weighted moving average to smooth indicators used in rules that signal when the indicator crosses above or below a critical threshold. Smoothing mitigates the problem of excessive signals that an unsmoothed version of the indicator wiggling back and forth across the threshold would produce. The calculation of a four-day linearly weighted moving average is illustrated in the following equation:

Four Day Linear Weighted Moving Average

$$WMA_t = \frac{\overbrace{(4)\times P_{t0} + (3)\times P_{t-1} + (2)\times P_{t-2} + (1)\times P_{t-3}}^{\text{Weights}}}{\underbrace{10}_{\text{Sum of Weights}}}$$

Where:
P_t = Price at time t
WMA_t = Weighted moving average at time t
n = Number of days used to compute moving average

Channel-Normalization Operator (Stochastics): CN

The channel-normalization operator (CN) removes the trend in a time series, thus clarifying short-term fluctuations around the trend. Channel normalization detrends the time series by measuring its current position within a moving channel. The channel is defined by the maximum and minimum values of the time series over a specified look-back span. In this way it is similar to the channel breakout operator discussed earlier.

The channel normalized version of a time series is scaled to the range 0 to 100. When the raw time series is at its maximum value within the look-back span, CN assumes the value of 100. When the series is at the minimum value within the look-back span the CN is equal to zero. A value of 50 indicates the series is currently midway between its maximum and minimum values.

The calculation of CN is illustrated in the following equation:

Channel Normalization Operator

$$CN_t = \left(\frac{S_t - S_{min-n}}{S_{max-n} - S_{min-n}} \right) 100$$

Where:
$CN_t = n$ day channel normalized value on day t
$S_t =$ Value of time series at time t
$S_{min-n} =$ Minimum value of time series, last n days
$S_{max-n} =$ Maximum value of time series, last n days
$n =$ Channel look-back span in days

An example of the calculation is illustrated in Figure 41.6.

In terms of its filtering properties, the CN operator functions as a high-pass filter. In contrast to the moving average, a low-pass filter, CN expresses the short-period (high-frequency) oscillations in its output while filtering out the long-period fluctuations or trend. This is illustrated in Figure 41.7. Note that the input series has a distinct upward trend, but the output series has no trend.

The CN operator has been known in TA at least as far back as 1965 when Heiby[17] used it to formulate divergence rules. He measured divergences by comparing the channel normalized value of the S&P 500 with the channel normalized value of a market breadth indicator. According to Heiby, a divergence occurred when one series was in the upper quartile of its 50-day range (CN > 74) while the other series was in the lower quartile of its range (CN <26). Sometime in the

FIGURE 41.6 Channel Normalization.

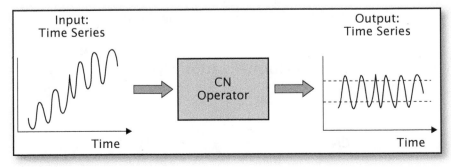

FIGURE 41.7 Channel Normalization Operator: A High-Pass Filter.

early 1970s, a virtually identical operator was described by George Lane,[18] who dubbed it *stochastic*. Unfortunately, the name is a misnomer. In reality, *stochastic* is a mathematical term that refers to the evolution of a random variable through time. There is nothing random about the CN operator, which is a completely deterministic data transformation. This text uses the term channel normalization (CN) rather than Lane's term, because it accurately describes what the operator does. Most TA writings continue use the term *stochastics*. The case study utilizes the CN operator for two types of rules: (1) extremes and transitions and (2) divergences. They are discussed in following sections.

Indicator Scripting

As discussed earlier, the time series that are used as inputs to the rules may either be in raw form, just as they comes from the market, or in the form of indicators—times series that have been created by applying one or more mathematical, logical, or time-series operators to one or more raw time series. The specification of an indicator may require the application of several operators. For example, the raw time series might first be smoothed with a moving average and then channel normalization is applied to the smoothed version. When the creation of an indicator involves multiple steps, it is convenient to express it in terms of an *indicator scripting language* (ISL). An ISL expression succinctly depicts the set of transformations used to create the indicator from raw time series.

My first exposure to an ISL was *Gener*, which was developed in 1983 for Raden Research Group by friend and colleague Professor John Wolberg. Today, ISLs are common. All rule back-testing platforms,[19] such as TradeStation, Wealth-Lab, Neuro-Shell, Financial Data Calculator, and so forth have an ISL. Though each ISL has features unique to it, they share similar syntaxes. The most basic ISL statement is a time-series operator followed by a set of parentheses that contain the arguments of the operator. The arguments are the items that must be defined for the operator to do its thing. Operators differ in terms of the number of arguments required. For example, the moving-average operator requires two arguments: a data series to which the operator will be applied and the number of periods in the look-back span. Thus a moving-average indicator would be specified by a statement such as this:

$$\text{Moving Average Indicator} = \text{MA (input series, N)}$$

Where:
MA is the moving average operator
N is the number of days in the moving average.

The general form of an indicator expression in scripting language is:

$$\text{Indicator} = \text{Operator (Argument}_1, \text{Argument}_2, \ldots, \text{Argument}_i)$$

Where:
i is the number of arguments required by the operator.

> **Channel-Breakout Operator (CBO)**
>
> Number of Arguments = 2:
>
> Indicator = CBO (Time Series, n)
>
> ---
>
> **Moving-Average Operator (MA) or Linear Weighted MA (LMA)**
>
> Number of Arguments = 2:
>
> Indicator = MA or LMA (Time Series, n)
>
> ---
>
> **Channel-Normalization Operator (CN)**
>
> Number of Arguments = 2:
>
> Indicator = CN (Time Series, n)

FIGURE 41.8   Indicator Scripting Language for Three TA Operators.

Figure 41.8 shows the ISL syntax for the operators defined thus far: channel breakout, moving average, and channel normalization.

A key benefit of ISL is the ability to define complex indicators by nesting operators. In nesting, the output of one operator becomes an argument for a second operator and so on. For example, if one wanted to define an indicator that is the 60-day channel normalization of another time series that is a 10-day moving average of the Dow Jones Transportation Index, the expression for the indicator in ISL would look something like this:

$$\text{Indicator} = CN\,[MA(DJTA, 10), 60]$$

■ Input Series to Rules: Raw Time Series and Indicators

This section describes the 24 raw time series used in the case study as well as the 39 time series that were ultimately used as rule inputs. Ten of the 39 inputs were in the form of raw unprocessed time series: S&P 500 closing price, Dow Jones Transportations Index closing price, NASDAQ Composite Index closing price, and so forth. The additional rule 29 inputs were indicators derived from one or more raw time series.

Raw Time Series

The 24 raw time series used in the case study came from two sources: Ultra Financial Systems[20] and Market Timing Reports.[21] They are shown in Table 41.1.

TABLE 41.1   Raw Time Series

Number	Raw Data Series	Abbreviation	Source
1	S&P 500 Daily Close	SPX	Ultra 8
2	S&P 500 Open	SPO	Ultra 8
3	DJIA High	DJH	Ultra 8
4	DJIA Low	DJL	Ultra 8
5	DJIA Close	DJC	Ultra 8
6	S&P Industrials	SPIA	Market Timing Reports
7	Dow Jones Transports	DJTA	Market Timing Reports
8	Dow Jones Utilities	DJUA	Market Timing Reports
9	NYSE Financial Index	NYFA	Market Timing Reports
10	Dow Jones 20 Bonds	DJB	Ultra 8
11	NASDAQ Composite Close	OTC	Ultra 8
12	Value Line Geometric Close	VL	Ultra 8
13	NYSE Advancing Issues	ADV	Ultra 8
14	NYSE Declining Issues	DEC	Ultra 8
15	NYSE Unchanged Issues	UNC	Ultra 8
16	NYSE New 52-Week Highs	NH	Ultra 8
17	NYSE New 52-Week Lows	NL	Ultra 8
18	NYSE Total Volume	TVOL	Ultra 8
19	NYSE Upside Volume	UVOL	Ultra 8
20	NYSE Downside Volume	DVOL	Ultra 8
21	3-Month T-Bill Yields	T3M	Market Timing Reports
22	10-Year T-Bond Yields	T10Y	Market Timing Reports
23	AAA Bond Yields	AAA	Market Timing Reports
24	BAA Bond Yields	BAA	Market Timing Reports

Indicators

Twenty-nine of the 39 rule inputs were indicators derived by transforming one or more raw time series with various mathematical, logical, and time-series operators. This section describes the transformations used to produce these indicators.

The indicators are presented in four categories: (1) price and volume functions, (2) market-breadth indicators, (3) prices-of-debt instruments, and (4) interest-rate-spread indicators.

Price and Volume Functions   Fifteen (15) indicators were functions that combine price and volume information. A number of studies have shown that trading volume contains useful information both on its own and when used in conjunction with price.[22] Technical analysis practitioners have suggested a number of price and volume functions: on-balance volume, accumulation distribution volume, money flow, negative volume, and positive volume. Each of these functions is described below.

The price-volume functions were used to create two types of indicators: (1) cumulative sums and (2) moving averages. An indicator defined as a cumulative sum is the algebraic sum of all prior daily values of the price-volume function. The daily value of a price-volume function can either be a positive or negative quantity. Thus, an indicator defined as the cumulative sum of the on-balance volume, at a given point in time, is equal to the sum of all prior values of the daily on-balance-volume quantity. An indicator defined as a cumulative sum will display long-term trends similar to those observed in the levels of asset prices and interest rates. In other words, these indicators are nonstationary time series.

In contrast, a moving average of a price-volume function will be a stationary time series. In other words, it will not display trends. This is explained by the fact that a moving average only considers the observations within the look-back span. Since price and volume functions can assume both positive or negative values, a moving average will tend to remain within a relatively confined range near zero. See Figure 41.9.

Cumulative On-Balance Volume   Perhaps the first invented price & volume function was the cumulative on-balance-volume indicator, which is attributed to Joseph Granville and Woods and Vignolia.[23] It is a cumulative sum of signed (+ or −) total market volume. The algebraic sign of the volume for any given day is determined by the sign of the change in a market index for the current day, week, or whatever time interval is being used. The case study used daily market changes in the

FIGURE 41.9   Cumulative Sum Versus Moving Average of Price-Volume Functions.

THEORY AND ANALYSIS

S&P 500 to determine the appropriate sign for the volume. If the price of the index rose on a given day, that day's entire NYSE volume was assigned a positive value and the number of shares traded was added to the prior cumulative sum. On days when the price declined, the NYSE volume was assigned a negative value and added to the prior cumulative sum (i.e., subtracted).

The computation for the cumulative on-balance volume is shown in the following equation:[24]

Cumulative On-Balance Volume (COBV)

$$COBV_t = COBV_{t-1} + (f_t V_t)$$

$$
\begin{array}{ll}
f_t = 1.0 & \text{if } Pc_t > Pc_{t-1} \\
f_t = -1.0 & \text{if } Pc_t < Pc_{t-1} \\
f_t = 0 & \text{if } Pc_t = Pc_{t-1}
\end{array}
$$

Where:
$OBV_t = (f_t V_t)$ = On-Balance Volume for day t
$COBV_t$ = Cumulative On-Balance Volume for day t
V_t = NYSE volume for day t
Pc_t = Closing price S&P 500 for day t

Moving Averages of On-Balance Volume In addition to the cumulative on-balance volume, two moving averages of daily on-balance volume were considered: for 10 and 30 days (OBV10, OBV30). In ISL they would be:

OBV10=MA(OBV,10)
OBV30=MA(OBV,30)

where OBV represents the on-balance volume for a given day.

Cumulative Accumulation-Distribution Volume (CADV) Another price-volume function, *accumulation distribution volume*, is attributed to Marc Chaiken.[25] However, there are several similar functions including: *Intra-day Intensity* developed by David Bostian and *Variable Accumulation Distribution* developed by Larry Williams. These transformations attempt to overcome a perceived limitation in on-balance volume, which treats the entire day's volume as positive (negative) even if the market index had a miniscule positive (negative) price change. It was felt that minor price changes should not be treated the same as large price changes. The proposed modifications to on-balance volume sought to ameliorate on-balance volume's all-or-none approach.

Chaiken proposed that a day's price activity could be more accurately characterized by quantifying the position of the closing price within the high-low range. Specifically, his calculation takes the difference between the closing price and the midpoint of the daily range and divides the difference by the size of the range. The assumption is that, when the market closes above the midpoint of its daily range, bullish or accumulation activity dominated the day's trading activity (accumulation) and should predict higher prices. Conversely when the market closes below the midpoint of its daily range, the day is said to be dominated by bearish or distribution activity and should predict lower prices. Only if the index closed at the low of the day or the high of the day is the entire day's volume assigned a negative (distribution) or positive (accumulation) value. More typically, the close is somewhere within the day's range resulting in some fraction of the volume being assigned to accumulation (positive volume) or to distribution (negative volume). The range factor, which is defined below, quantifies the position of the closing price within the day's range. The range factor is multiplied by the daily volume, and this figure is accumulated to produce the cumulative sum. The calculation is shown in the following equation.[26]

Cumulative Accumulation/Distribution Volume

$$CADV_t = CADV_{t-1} + (V_t \times Rf_t)$$

$$\text{Range Factor } (Rf_t) = \frac{(Pc_t - Pl_t) - (Ph_t - Pc_t)}{(Ph_t - Pl_t)}$$

Where:
$ADV_t = V_t \times Rf_t$ = Accumulation/Distribution Volume for day t
$CADV_t$ = Cumulative Accumulation/Distribution Volume for day t
V_t = NYSE volume for day t
Rf_t = Range factor for day t
Pc_t = Closing price Dow Jones Industrials for day t
Pl_t = Low price Dow Jones Industrials for day t
Ph_t = High price Dow Jones Industrials for day t

The case study used data for Dow Jones Industrials for the calculation of the accumulation-distribution function rather than the S&P 500 because daily high and low prices were not available for it. I assumed that the closing position of the Dow Industrials within its range would be similar to the closing position of the S&P 500 within its range.

Moving Averages of Accumulation Distribution Volume   Moving averages of daily accumulation/distribution values were constructed for 10- and 30-day periods. In ISL they are:

$$ADV10 = MA(ADV, 10)$$
$$ADV30 = MA(ADV, 30)$$

Cumulative Money Flow (CMF)   Cumulative money flow (CMF) is similar to CADV with the exception that the product of volume and range factor is further multiplied by the price level in dollars of the S&P 500 Index. This is intended to measure the monetary value of the volume. The price level used is an average of the daily high, low, and closing prices. The computation is shown in the following equation:[27]

Cumulative Money Flow

$$CMF_t = CMF_{t-1} + (V_t \times Ap_t \times Rf_t)$$

$$\text{Range Factor } (Rf_t) = \frac{(Pc_t - Pl_t) - (Ph_t - Pc_t)}{(Ph_t - Pl_t)}$$

Where:
$MF_t = (V_t \times Ap_t \times Rf_t)$ = Money Flow for day t
CMF_t = Cumulative Money Flow for day t
Ap_t = Average price S&P 500 for day t: (Hi + Lo + Close)/3
V_t = NYSE volume for day t
Rf_t = Range Factor for day t
Pc_t = Closing price Dow Jones Industrials for day t
Pl_t = Low price Dow Jones Industrials for day t
Ph_t = High price Dow Jones Industrials for day t

Moving Averages of Money Flow   Moving averages of money flow were constructed for 10- and 30-day periods. In ISL they are:

$$MF10 = MA(MF, 10)$$
$$MF30 = MA(MF, 30)$$

Cumulative Negative Volume Index (CNV)   Cumulative negative volume is an accumulation of price changes on days of lower trading volume. In other words, it is a continuous algebraic sum of daily percentage changes in a stock market index on days when volume is less than the prior day. When volume is equal to or greater than a prior day, the CNV remains unchanged.

The inventor of CNV is unclear. Several sources attribute it to Norman Fosback[28] but several sources, including Fosback, attribute the idea to Paul Dysart.[29] However, it seems clear that it was Fosback who developed objective signal rules for CNV and evaluated their predictive power.[30]

The notion of negative volume is based on the conjecture that "trading by unsophisticated investors occurs predominately on days of exuberantly rising volume, whereas informed buying and selling (i.e., smart-money activity) usually occurs during quieter periods of declining volume. Therefore, the direction that the market assumes on days of negative volume purportedly reflects accumulation (buying) or distribution (selling) of stock by those who are in the know."[31]

The computation of the index is as shown in the following equation:

Cumulative Negative Volume Index (CNV)

$$CNV_t = CNV_{t-1} + f_t$$

$$f_t = [(Pc_t/Pc_{t-1})-1] \times 100 \quad \text{if } V_t < V_{t-1}$$

$$f_t = 0 \qquad\qquad\qquad\qquad \text{if } V_t > \text{ or} = V_{t-1}$$

Where:
$NV_t = f_t$ = Negative Volume Index for day t
CNV_t = Cumulative Negative Volume Index for day t
V_t = NYSE volume for day t
Pc_t = Closing price S&P 500 for day t

Moving Averages of Negative Volume Index   Moving averages of the daily value of negative volume index (i.e., index's percentage change on lower volume days) were constructed for 10- and 30-day periods. In ISL:

$$NV10=MA(NV,10)$$
$$NV30=MA(NV,30)$$

Cumulative Positive Volume Index (CPV)   Cumulative positive volume (CPV) is the opposite of CNV. It is an algebraic accumulation of market index changes for days when volume is greater than the prior day. Positive volume index is variously attributed to Fosback[32] and to Dysart. The calculation is presented in the equation that follows. It seems as if Dysart proposed the positive volume index and suggested ways of interpreting it in a subjective manner, whereas Fosback defined objective rules and formally tested them:

Cumulative Positive Volume Index (CPV)

$$CPV_t = CPV_{t-1} + f_t$$

$$f_t = [(Pc_t/Pc_{t-1})-1] \times 100 \quad \text{if } V_t > V_{t-1}$$

$$f_t = 0 \quad\quad\quad\quad\quad\quad \text{if } V_t < \text{ or } = V_{t-1}$$

Where:
$PV_t = f_t$ = Positive Volume Index for day t
CPV_t = Cumulative Positive Volume Index for day t
V_t = NYSE volume for day t
Pc_t = Closing price S&P 500 for day t

Moving Averages of Positive Volume   Moving averages of daily values of the positive volume index were constructed for 10- and 30-day periods (PV10 and PV30). In ISL:

PV10=MA(PV,10)
PV30=MA(PV,30)

Market Breadth Indicators   *Market breadth* refers to the spread or difference between the number of stocks advancing and the number declining on a given day, week, or other defined time interval. Breadth has been measured in a variety of ways, and they are reviewed in a scholarly study by Harlow.[33] For purposes of the case study, breadth is defined as the daily advance-decline ratio; that is, it is the difference between a day's advancing and declining issues divided by the total number of issues traded. The data is based on all issues traded on the NYSE rather than an alternative version that is restricted to NYSE common stocks. The series restricted to common stocks, which some have claimed is superior because it excludes closed-end stock and bond funds and preferred stocks, was not available in computer-readable form for the time period required.

The case study's breadth indicators are of two forms: cumulative sums of daily figures and moving averages of daily figures. For reasons previously explained, the breadth indicators that are cumulative sums display long-term trends, whereas moving-average breadth indicators tend to have reasonably stable mean values and fluctuation ranges.

Cumulative Advance-Decline Ratio (CADR)   The cumulative advance decline ratio or CADR is a cumulative sum of the daily advance-decline ratio:

$$CADR_t = CADR_{t-1} + ADR_t$$

$$ADR_t = \frac{adv_t - dec_t}{adv_t + dec_t + unch_t}$$

Where:
$CADR_t$ = Cumulative Advance/Decline Ratio for day t
ADR_t = Advance/Decline Ratio for day t
adv_t = NYSE advancing issues for day t
dec_t = NYSE declining issues for day t
$unch_t$ = NYSE unchanged issues for day t

Moving Averages of Advance-Decline Ratio   Moving averages of daily advance-decline ratio (ADR) were constructed for 10- and 30-day periods (ADR10 and ADR30). In ISL they are:

ADR10=MA(ADR,10)
ADR30=MA(ADR,30)

Cumulative Net Volume Ratio (CNVR)   Another measure of market breadth is the net volume ratio. It is based on the difference between daily upside and downside volume. Upside (downside) volume is the total number of shares traded in stocks that closed up (down) for the day. The innovation of calculating and analyzing upside and downside volume separately is attributed to Lyman M. Lowry in 1938.[34] The daily net volume ratio, a quantity that can assume either positive or negative values, is the difference between upside and downside volume divided by total trading volume. The case study used statistics released daily by the New York Stock Exchange. The cumulative net volume ratio (CNVR) is the cumulative sum of daily ratios:

Cumulative Net Volume Ratio (CNVR)

$$CNVR_t = CNVR_{t-1} + NVR_t$$

$$NVR_t = \frac{upvol_t - dnvol_t}{upvol_t + dnvol_t + unchvol_t}$$

Where:
$CNVR_t$ = Cumulative Net Volume Ratio for day t
NVR_t = Net Volume Ratio for day t
$upvol_t$ = NYSE advancing volume for day t
$dnvol_t$ = NYSE declining volume for day t
$unchvol_t$ = NYSE unchanged volume for day t

Moving Averages of Net Volume Ratio   Moving averages of the daily net volume ratio were constructed for 10- and 30-day periods (NVR10 and NVR30). In ISL:

$$NVR10 = MA(NVR, 10)$$
$$NVR30 = MA(NVR, 30)$$

Cumulative New Highs-Lows Ratio (CHLR)   A third measure of breadth, the cumulative new highs and new lows ratio (CHLR), takes a longer-term view. In contrast to CADR and CNVR, which are based on daily price changes and daily volumes, CHLR is based on a stock's current price relative to its maximum and minimum price over the preceding year. Specifically, CHLR is the cumulative sum of the daily new highs-new lows ratio (HLR), a quantity that can assume positive or negative values. The high-low ratio is defined as the difference between the number of stocks making new 52-week highs on the day and the number of stocks making new 52-week lows on the same day divided by the total number of issues traded that day. This figure is accumulated algebraically to obtain CHLR.

There is nothing particularly significant about using a look-back interval of 52 weeks. It is simply the mostly widely available statistic for new high and new low data. Prior to 1978, the number of issues making highs and lows was not based on a consistent 52-week look-back span. From the middle of March in any given year, the data were based only on the current calendar year. Prior to the middle of March, the figures were based on the current and prior years. Thus, over the course of a given year, the look-back span used to determine if a stock was making a new low or a new high varied from 2.5 months in mid-March to as long as 14.5 months just before mid-March. Most of the data used in this study was post-1978.

Despite the distortions created by the variable look-back span, rule tests based on pre-1978 high-low data suggested that the indicator's information content was robust to this distortion. For example, Fosback developed and tested an indicator called the high-low logic index over the period 1944 to 1980. His results showed that indicator demonstrated predictive power over the entire period even though the bulk of the data was infected with the variable look-back span distortion.[35] The formula for constructing the CHLR series is shown here:[36]

Cumulative New Highs New Lows (CHLR)

$$CHLR_t = CHLR_{t-1} + HLR_t$$

$$HLR_t = \frac{nuhi_t - nulo_t}{adv_t + dec_t + unch_t}$$

Where:
$CNHL_t$ = Cumulative New Highs New Lows on day t
HLR_t = New Highs New Lows on day t
$nuhi_t$ = NYSE new 52-week highs day t
$nulo_t$ = NYSE new 52-week lows day t
adv_t = NYSE advancing issues for day t
dec_t = NYSE declining issues for day t
$unch_t$ = NYSE unchanged issues for day t

Moving Averages of New Highs/New Lows Ratio (HLR1 and HLR30)

Moving averages of the daily high/low ratio were constructed for 10- and 30-day periods (HLR10 and HLR30). In ISL they are:

$$HLR10 = MA(HLR, 10)$$
$$HLR30 = MA(HLR, 30)$$

Prices-of-Debt Instruments from Interest Rates   Typically, interest rates and stock price levels move inversely. However, by taking the reciprocal (1/interest rate) interest rates can be transformed into price-like time series that are, in general, positively correlated with stock prices. This reciprocal series can be multiplied by a scaling factor such as 100. Thus, a rate of 6.05 percent would be equivalent to a price of 15.38 (1/6.05 × 100).

This transformation was used in the case study and was performed on four interest rate series: three-month treasury bills, 10-year treasury bonds, Moody's AAA corporate bonds, and Moody's BAA corporate bonds.

Interest Rate Spreads   An interest-rate spread is the difference between two comparable interest rates. Two types of interest-rate spreads were constructed for the case study; the *duration* spread and the *quality* spread. The duration spread, also known as the *slope of the yield curve*, is the difference between yields on debt instruments having the same credit quality but having different durations (i.e., time to maturity). The duration spread used in the case study was defined as the yield on the 10-year treasury note minus the yield on the three-month treasury bills (10-year yield minus 3-month yield). The spread was defined in this way rather than 3-month minus 10-year so that an upward trend in the spread would presumably have bullish implications for the stock market (S&P 500).[37]

A quality spread measures the difference in yield between instruments with similar durations but with different credit qualities (default risk). The quality spread for the case study was based on two of Moody's[38] long-term corporate bond series: AAA,[39] which are the highest rated corporate debt, and BAA,[40] a lower rated grade of corporate debt. The quality spread is defined here as AAA yield –BAA yield. When rates on lower quality debt (higher default risk such as BAA rated bonds) are falling faster than rates on higher quality debt such as AAA rated bonds, it is interpreted as indication that investors are more willing to assume additional risk to earn the higher yields on lower quality debt. In other words, a rising trend in the quality spread is a signal that investors are willing to take higher risks to earn higher returns. By this reasoning, the quality spread should trend in the same direction as stocks.

■ Table of 40 Input Series Used in Case Study

Table 41.2 lists all of the data series used as rule inputs in the case study.

TABLE 41.2 Input Series Used in the Case Study

Number	Description	Abbreviation	Form
1	S&P 500 Close	SPX	Raw
2	S&P 500 Open	SPO	Raw
3	S&P Industrials Close	SPIA	Raw
4	Dow Jones Transportation Index	DJTA	Raw
5	Dow Jones Utility Index	DJUA	Raw
6	NYSE Financial Index	NYFA	Raw
7	NASDAQ Composite	OTC	Raw
8	Value Line Geometric Close	VL	Raw
9	Cumulative On-Balance Volume	COBV	Indicator
10	On-Balance Volume 10-Day MA	OBV10	Indicator
11	On-Balance Volume 30-Day MA	OBV30	Indicator
12	Cumulative Accum. Distr. Volume	CADV	Indicator
13	Accum. Distr. Volume 10-Day MA	ADV10	Indicator
14	Accum. Distr. Volume 30-Day MA	ADV30	Indicator
15	Cumulative Money Flow	CMF	Indicator
16	Money Flow 10-Day MA	MF10	Indicator
17	Money Flow 30-Day MA	MF30	Indicator
18	Cumulative Negative Volume Index	CNV	Indicator
19	Negative Volume Index 10-Day MA	NV10	Indicator
20	Negative Volume Index 30-Day MA	NV30	Indicator
21	Cumulative Positive Volume Index	CPV	Indicator
22	Positive Volume Index 10-Day MA	PV10	Indicator
23	Positive Volume Index 30-Day MA	PV30	Indicator
24	Cum. Advance Decline Ratio	CADR	Indicator
25	Advance Decline Ratio 10-Day MA	ADR10	Indicator
26	Advance Decline Ratio 30-Day MA	ADR30	Indicator
27	Cum. Up Down Volume Ratio	CUDR	Indicator
28	Up Down Volume Ratio 10-Day MA	UDR10	Indicator
29	Up Down Volume Ratio 30-Day MA	UDR30	Indicator
30	Cum. New Highs/New Lows Ratio	CHLR	Indicator
31	New Highs/New Lows Ratio 10-Day MA	HLR10	Indicator
32	New Highs/New Lows Ratio 30-Day MA	HLR30	Indicator
33	NYSE Volume	TVOL	Raw
34	Dow Jones 20 Bond Index	DJB	Raw
35	Price 3-Month T-Bill	PT3M	Indicator
36	Price 10-Year Treasury Bond	PT10Y	Indicator
37	Price AAA Corporate Bonds	PAAA	Indicator
38	Price BAA Corporate Bonds	PBAA	Indicator
39	Duration Spread (10 Year −3 Month)	DURSPD	Indicator
40	Quality Spread (BAA–AAA)	QUALSPD	Indicator

■ The Rules

The rules tested in the case study can be grouped into three categories, each representing a different theme of technical analysis: (1) trends, (2) extremes and transitions, and (3) divergence. The following sections describe the rules in each category.

Trend Rules

The first category of rules is based on trends. A foundational principle of TA is that prices and yields move in trends that can be identified in a sufficiently timely manner to generate profits. Practitioners have developed a variety of objective indicators to define the direction of the current trend and signal trend reversals. Among the most widely used are moving averages, moving-average bands, channel breakout, and Alexander filters also known as zigzag filters. These are described in Kaufman[41] and there is no need to cover them all here.

The trend rules in the case study used the channel breakout operator or CBO to define trends in the input time series. Thus, the CBO operator transformed the input time series into a binary valued time series consisting of +1 and −1. When the trend of the input series was in an uptrend, as determined by the CBO, the rule's output was +1. Conversely, when the analyzed series was determined to be in a downtrend, the output was −1.

The identification of trend reversals in the input series by CBO is subject to lag. All trend indicators necessarily incur lag—a delay between the time the input series experiences a trend reversal and the time the operator is able to detect it. Lag can be reduced by making the indicator more sensitive. For example, in the case of CBO, lag can be reduced by decreasing the number of periods in the look-back span. However, this fix creates a different problem—an increased number of false signals. In other words, there is a tradeoff between a trend-following indicator's lag and its accuracy. Therefore, all trend indicators attempt to strike a reasonable balance between signal accuracy and signal timeliness. Finding the optimum is a challenge in the design of any signaling system, be it a household smoke detector or a TA trend rule. In the end, optimal is whatever maximizes the indicator's performance, such as average return, risk-adjusted rate of return, and so forth. Since the behavior of financial market time series changes over time, the optimal look-back span for the CBO operator would change as well. Adaptive versions of CBO were not used in the case study.

Of the 40 input series depicted in Table 41.2, 39 were used as inputs for the trend rules. The open price of the S&P 500, input series 2 in Table 41.2, was excluded on grounds of being redundant of the S&P 500 close.

Each trend rule was defined by two parameters or arguments: the CBO look-back span and a time series chosen from the set of 39 candidates shown in Table 41.2. A set of 11 values were tested as look-back spans. They were 3, 5, 8, 12, 18, 27, 41, 61, 91, 137, and 205 days. The values were chosen to be separated by a multiplier of approximately 1.5. For example, the look-back span of 205 days is approximately 1.5 times 137 days. This resulted in a total of 858 trend rules, 429 (39 × 11) based on a traditional TA interpretation, and an additional 429 inverse-trend rules.

A traditional version of a trend rule produced an output value of +1 (long position in the S&P 500) when the input time series was determined to be in an upward trend by CBO operator, and an output value of −1 (short position in the S&P 500) when the time series was in downtrend according to CBO operator. Inverse trend rules simply produced the opposite signals (e.g., short S&P 500 when the analyzed series was determined to be in an uptrend).

The following shorthand naming convention will be used for the traditional and inverse trend rules. A naming convention was necessitated by the large number of rules. The syntax of the naming convention is as follows (note this syntax is different from the syntax used for indicator scripting):

Rule (TT or TI) – Input Series Number – Look-back Span
Where TT stands for a traditional trend rule
and
TI stands for an inverse trend rule

For example, the rule named TT-15-137, is a traditional trend rule applied to input series 15 (Cumulative Money Flow) using a look-back span of 137 says. A rule named TI-40-41 is an inverse trend rule applied to input series 40 (the quality spread BAA–AAA) using a look-back span of 41 days.

Extreme Values and Transitions

The second category of rules considered in the case study is "Extreme Values and Transitions" or E rules. This category is based on the notion that a time series conveys information when it assumes an extreme high or low value or as it makes the transition between extremes. High and low extremes can be defined in terms of fixed value thresholds if the time series has a relatively stable mean and fluctuation range (i.e., is stationary). All input series used for E rules were made stationary by applying the CN operator.

Thirty-nine of the 40 input series were used for the E-type rules. The open price of the S&P 500 was excluded on grounds of redundancy. The input series used for E rules were first smoothed with a four-day linearly weighted moving average (LMA) before applying the CN operator. The smoothing was done to reduce the number of signals that would have resulted from an unsmoothed version of the input series wiggling above and below the signal threshold. Though smoothing may have been inappropriate for series that were already smoothed, for example the 30-day moving average of negative volume, all series were treated with the LMA on grounds of consistency.

In ISL, the expression for the input time series used for E rules is given by the expression:

=CN (LMA (Input Series, 4), N-days)

Where:

CN is the channel normalization operator
LMA is a linearly weighted moving-average operator

This sequence of transformations is illustrated in Figure 41.10.

E-rule signals were generated when the channel normalized smoothed series crossed a threshold. Given that there are two thresholds, an upper and lower, and

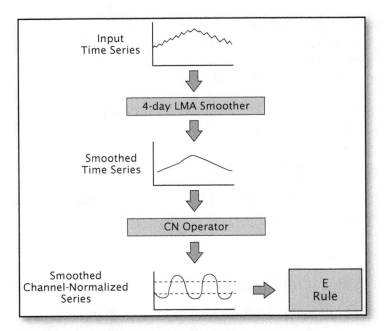

FIGURE 41.10 Smoothed Channel Normalized Series.

given that there are two directions in which a crossing can occur (up or down) there are four possible threshold-crossing events:

1. Lower threshold is crossed in the downward direction.
2. Lower threshold is crossed in the upward direction.
3. Upper threshold is crossed in the upward direction.
4. Upper threshold is crossed in the downward direction.

These events are illustrated in Figure 41.11.

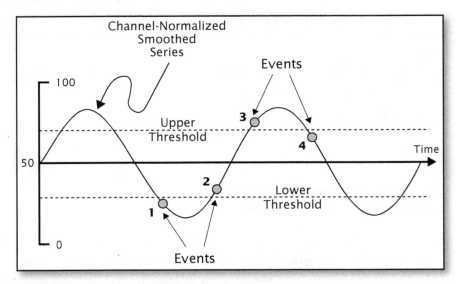

FIGURE 41.11 Threshold Crossing Events.

Each E rule was defined in terms of two threshold-crossing events: one specifying the long entry/short exit and the other specifying the short entry/long exit. This scheme yields 12 possible E-rule types. They are listed in Table 41.3. Because they cover all possibilities, there would be no point in including inverse versions. Note that type 7 is an inversion of Type 1, Type 8 is an inversion of Type 2, and so on.

The 12 E-rule types are illustrated in Figures 41.12 to 41.23.

TABLE 41.3	The 12 E-Rule Types Defined in Terms of Threshold Crossing Events	
E-Rule Types	**Long Entry/Short Exit**	**Short Entry/Long Exit**
1	Event 1	Event 2
2	Event 1	Event 3
3	Event 1	Event 4
4	Event 2	Event 3
5	Event 2	Event 4
6	Event 3	Event 4
7	Event 2	Event 1
8	Event 3	Event 1
9	Event 4	Event 1
10	Event 3	Event 2
11	Event 4	Event 2
12	Event 4	Event 3

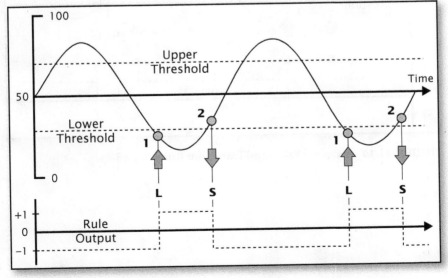

FIGURE 41.12 Extreme Value and Transition Rule: Type 1.

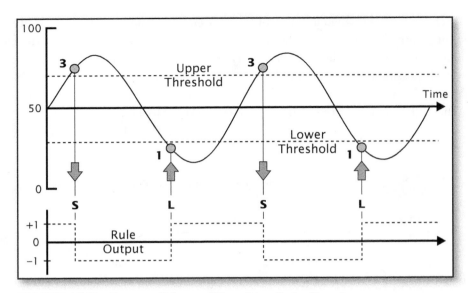

FIGURE 41.13 Extreme Value and Transition Rule: Type 2.

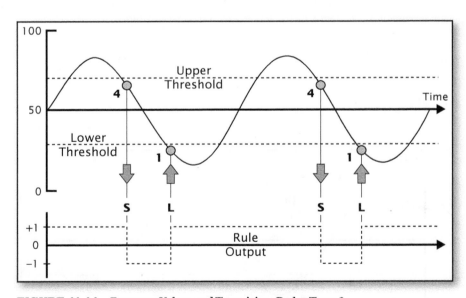

FIGURE 41.14 Extreme Value and Transition Rule: Type 3.

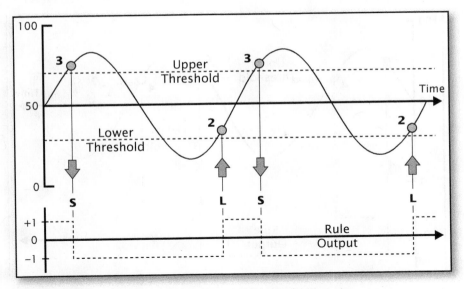

FIGURE 41.15 Extreme Value and Transition Rule: Type 4.

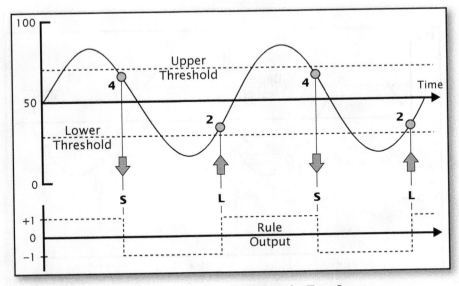

FIGURE 41.16 Extreme Value and Transition Rule: Type 5.

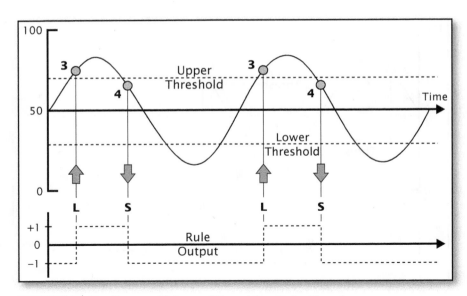

FIGURE 41.17   Extreme Value and Transition Rule: Type 6.

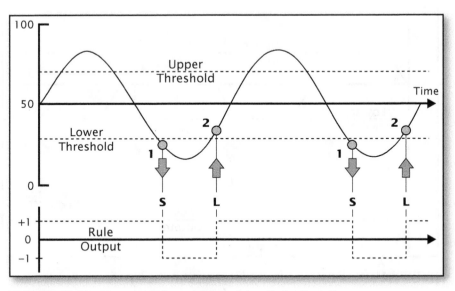

FIGURE 41.18   Extreme Value and Transition Rule: Type 7.

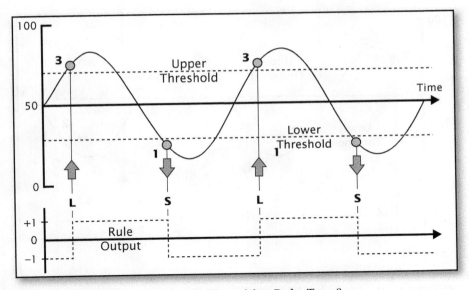

FIGURE 41.19   Extreme Value and Transition Rule: Type 8.

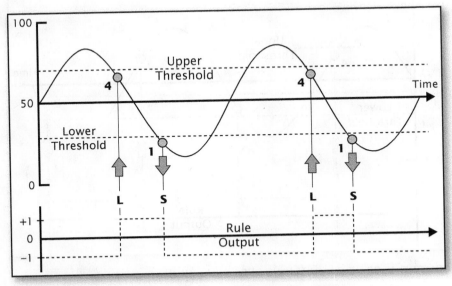

FIGURE 41.20   Extreme Value and Transition Rule: Type 9.

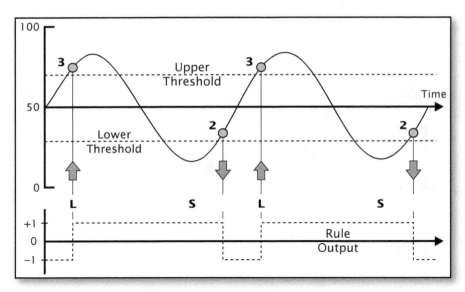

FIGURE 41.21   Extreme Value and Transition Rule: Type 10.

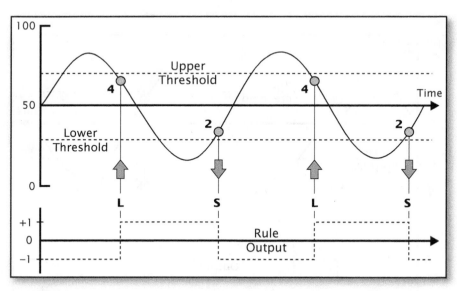

FIGURE 41.22   Extreme Value and Transition Rule: Type 11.

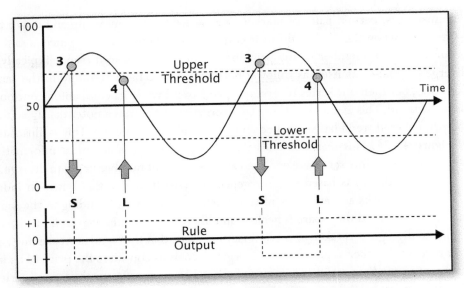

FIGURE 41.23 Extreme Value and Transition Rule: Type 12.

Parameter Sets and Total Number of E Rules An E rule is defined by four parameters: type (1 through 12), input series, displacement of the thresholds form 50,
and look-back span for the channel normalization. Because both the upper and lower
thresholds are displaced equally from the midvalue of 50, it is possible to specify
them with a single number, their displacement from 50. For example, a threshold-
displacement 10 places the upper threshold at 60 (50 + 10) and the lower threshold
at 40 (50 – 10). Two different values for the threshold displacement parameter were
tested: 10 and 20. The displacement value of 20 gave the upper threshold as 70 and
the lower threshold as 30. Three different values were considered for the channel
normalization look-back span: 15, 30, and 60. All parameter values were chosen
without optimization on the basis of intuition.

Given 12 possible rule types, 39 possible candidate input series, 2 possible threshold displacements, and 3 possible channel normalization look-back spans, there were
2,808 E-type rules (12 × 39 × 2 × 3).

Naming Convention for Extreme Value and Transition Rules The following
naming convention will be used to report results for E rules:

(E)-(type)-(Input Series)-(Threshold Displacement)-(Channel Normalization
Look-Back Span)

For example, E-4-30-20-60 would be: E rule, type 4, input series 30 (cumulative
new highs/new lows ratio), a threshold displacement of 20 (upper = 70, lower =
30), and a channel normalization look-back span of 60 days.

Divergence Rules

Divergence analysis is a foundational concept of TA that concerns the relationship between a pair of time series. It is premised on the notion that, under normal

circumstances, certain pairs of market time series tend to move up and down together, and when they fail to do so it conveys information. A divergence is said to occur when one member of the pair departs from their shared trend. Typically, a divergence manifests itself as follows: both series have been trending in the same direction, but then one series reverses its prior trend while its companion continues its prior trend. This event, according to divergence analysis, is a potential signal that the prior shared trend has weakened and may be about to reverse. This is illustrated in Figure 41.24. Hussman contends that divergence signals are most informative when numerous time series are analyzed and a significant number begin to diverge.[42]

The Dow theory is based on divergence analysis. It asserts that when an index of industrial stocks and an index of transportation stocks are trending in the same direction, the trend they share is healthy and likely to persist. However, if one series begins to diverge, it is taken as preliminary evidence that the trend is weakening and may reverse. Another application of divergence analysis considers the price of an instrument as one time series and its rate of change or momentum as the second series. Price/momentum divergence analysis is discussed by Pring.[43]

A divergence leads to one of two outcomes: either the series, for which the trend had remained undisturbed, will experience a reversal to join its diverging companion or the diverging series will end its errant ways and rejoin its companion. A completed signal of reversal is not presumed until both series have convincingly reversed and are again moving in the same direction. Thus, the fundamental idea behind divergence analysis is coherence, that is, the state of affairs when two waveforms are in phase with each other (see Figure 41.25). When two series are coherent, their common trend is considered strong and expected to continue. However, when their trends become incoherent, or out of phase, the future of the once shared trend is in question. Therefore, candidates for divergence analysis are pairs of time series that are generally coherent, but when they do diverge, one particular member of the pair

FIGURE 41.24   Divergence Analysis.

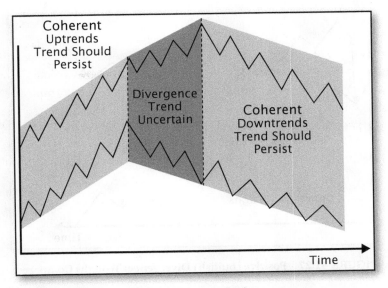

FIGURE 41.25 Trend Coherence and Divergence.

tends to have leading information about the other. In other words, there is a rather stable lead–lag relationship.

Subjective Divergence Analysis Subjective divergence analysis typically involves comparing the peaks and troughs of the two time series under consideration. A negative or bearish divergence is said to occur if one series continues to register peaks at successively higher levels while the other series begins forming peaks at lower levels. The failure by the second series to form peaks at successively higher levels is also termed a bearish nonconfirmation. This is illustrated in Figure 41.26.

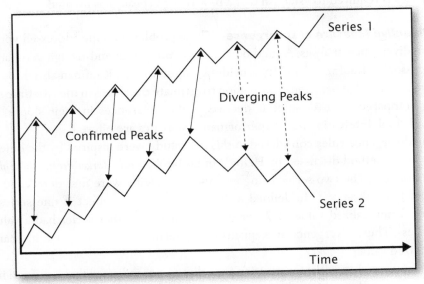

FIGURE 41.26 Negative Divergence (peaks compared).

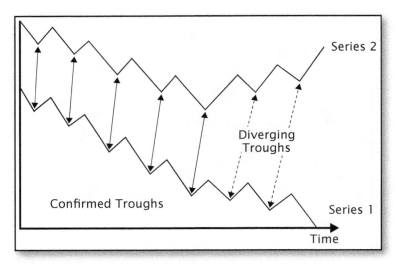

FIGURE 41.27   Positive (bullish) Divergence: Troughs Compared.

A *positive* or *bullish divergence* is said to occur when one series continues to register successively lower troughs in an established downtrend while the second series begins to form troughs at higher levels. This is also termed a *bullish nonconfirmation*. See Figure 41.27.

The problem with subjective divergence analysis, or any subjective method for that matter, is that it the procedure is neither repeatable nor testable. One issue requiring the analyst's subjective judgment is the timing of peaks and troughs. Because the two time series may not peak and trough at precisely the same time, it may be unclear which peaks and troughs should be compared. Another issue is related to duration: How long must the divergence be in existence before deciding that one has occurred? Still a third unresolved issue is how much upward (downward) movement in a series is required to establish that a new trough (peak) has formed.

An Objective Measure of Divergence   These problems can be addressed with objective divergence analysis. A method that objectifies peak and trough comparisons is discussed by Kaufman[44] and he provides computer code. Kaufman also discusses a second method that uses linear regression to estimate the slopes in the two time series being compared. A divergence is defined as the differences in their slopes. Both methods look interesting but no performance statistics are offered.

The divergence rules considered in this case study were inspired by the objective divergence method discussed by Heiby[45] in his book, *Stock Market Profits through Dynamic Synthesis*. The two series being examined by Heiby were first detrended with channel normalization. He defined a divergence to be in effect if one series had a channel-normalized value of 75 or greater while the other series had a value of 25 or less. Thus, divergence was quantified in terms of the difference in channel-normalized values.

This suggested an initial formulation for a divergence indicator that is defined in the equation that follows. Note that one series is always the S&P 500, the target market of the case study. The companion series, for example the Dow Jones Transports, is the series with which the S&P 500 is compared. The case study compared the S&P 500 to all the time series in Table 41.2, except the S&P 500 open price, which was excluded on grounds of redundancy with the S&P 500 close.

Divergence Indicator
(Initial Formulation)

$$= CN \text{ (Companion Series, } n) - CN \text{ (S\&P 500, } n)$$

Where:
CN = Channel normalization operator
n = Look-back span of the channel normalization

Because the channel normalized value of each series can vary between 0 and 100, this divergence indicator has a potential range of -100 to $+100$. For example, if the companion series is at the bottom of its channel range ($CN = 0$) and the S&P 500 is at the top of its range ($CN = 100$), the divergence indicator would have a value of -100. It should be noted that this quantification of divergence is merely one approach among several possibilities that may prove superior.

Limitations of the Proposed Divergence Indicator The proposed divergence indicator measures the degree to which two times series have similar positions within their respective channels. In general, this will give a reasonable quantification of the degree to which the series are in phase with one another. For example, when the indicator registers a value of zero, it indicates that there is no divergence; both series have the same channel normalized values and can be presumed to be trending together. However, there can be cases for which a value of zero does not indicate that the two series are in phase. For example, if two time series are negatively correlated, that is to say, they tend to move inversely with respect to each other within their channels, the divergence indicator will assume a value of zero as the series-normalized values cross paths. In this instance, a value of zero would be an erroneous indication that the two series are trending together. This is illustrated in Figure 41.28 and is clearly a limitation of the proposed divergence indicator.

This problem could have been avoided with a more complex formulation of divergence indicator based on cointegration,[46] a concept developed in the field of econometrics. Cointegration was proposed in 1987 by Engle and Granger.[47] This more sophisticated and potentially more accurate way of measuring divergences uses regression analysis to determine if a linear relationship exists between two time series. Because this method can easily accommodate the case in which the pair of series are strongly negatively correlated (180 degrees out of phase), it solves the problem discussed earlier that can occur with a divergence indicator based on channel normalization. An additional advantage of cointegration analysis is that it first applies a

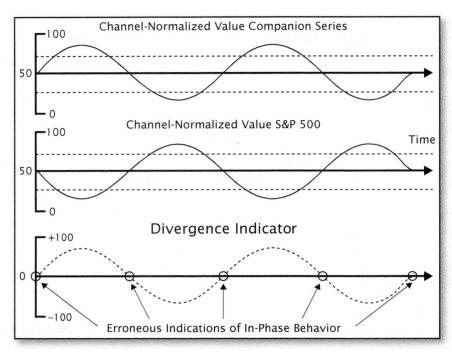

FIGURE 41.28 Erroneous Indications of In-phase Behavior.

statistical test[48] to determine if the two series have related trends (i.e., that they are cointegrated). If the test shows that they are cointegrated, a stationary divergence indicator[49] naturally falls out of the analysis. In cointegration terminology, this indicator is referred to as the *error-correction model*. It measures the degree to which one series has diverged from the typical linear relationship between the two series.

In most applications of cointegration, the error-correction model is used to predict the behavior of the spread between the cointegrated time series. In these applications, the divergence is predicted to revert back to the normal state of a shared trend when the error-correction model becomes extremely positive or negative. In other words, when the error, which is a departure from the normal linear relationship between the two series, becomes extreme, it is predicted to correct back to its normal value of zero.

A typical application of this analysis is *pairs trading*. For example, if it has been determined that Ford and GM stocks are cointegrated time series and Ford has gotten high relative to GM, a short position would be taken in Ford against a long position in GM. Thus, no matter how the divergence is corrected (Ford falls, GM rises, or some combination) the pairs trade will generate a profit.

Fosback[50] made an innovative use of cointegration analysis to develop a stock market predictor. His innovation was to use the measurement derived from the error correction model as an indicator to predict the movement of a third variable, the S&P 500, rather than predict the behavior of the spread between the cointegrated variables. The indicator, called the *Fosback Index*, exploits the fact that interest rates and mutual fund cash levels are cointegrated time series. Fosback's work is particularly noteworthy because it preceded the Engle and Granger publication on cointegration by over a decade. The Fosback Index signals when the mutual fund cash level diverges significantly from a level predicted by its linear relationship with short-term interest rates. The premise is that when mutual fund managers are excessively pessimistic about stock market prospects, they hold cash reserves that are substantially higher than the that predicted by interest rates. Excessive optimism is the opposite situation. Fosback found that both excessive pessimism and excessive optimism, measured in this fashion, correlated with future returns on the stock market. In effect, the Fosback Index removes the influence of short-term interest rates from mutual fund cash levels, thus providing a purer measure of fund manager sentiment than that provided by the raw cash level, which is contaminated by interest rates.

In the interests of simplicity, the cointegration technique was not used for the divergence indicators in the case study. It was assumed that if a companion series was not related to the S&P 500, it would be revealed by the poor financial performance of the divergence rule. However, I[51] believe that the cointegration methodology warrants further investigation in development of indicators.

Need for Double Channel Normalization   A second problem with the initially proposed version of the divergence indicator was more serious and had to be remedied. The divergence rules in the case study involved pairing the S&P 500 with 38 other time series. Given that these series had varying degrees of co-movement with the S&P 500, the fluctuation range of the divergence indicator would vary considerably from one pair to the next. This would make it impractical to use the same threshold for all pairings. This problem is illustrated in Figure 41.29. Note that the high threshold displacement that would be suitable for a companion

FIGURE 41.29   Divergence Indicator: Inconsistent Volatility.

series with a low degree of co-movement with the S&P 500 would never produce a signal for a companion series with a high degree of co-movement to the S&P 500. For this reason, the initial formulation of the divergence indicator was deemed impractical.

This problem was addressed with a modified formulation of the divergence indicator illustrated in the equation that follows. It employs the channel normalization operator twice. That is to say, the indicator is a channel-normalized version of the initial divergence indicator.

Divergence Indicator
(Double Channel Normalization)

$$= CN\{CN\,(\text{Series 1}, n) - CN\,(\text{S\&P 500}, n), 10n\}$$

Where:
CN = Channel normalization operator
Series 1 = Companion series
n = Look-back span of the first channel normalization

The second layer of channel normalization takes into account the fluctuation range of the initial formulation of the divergence indicator. This solves the problem of inconsistent fluctuation ranges across the 38 pairs of time series. As a result, the modified version of the divergence indicator will have roughly the same fluctuation range irrespective of the particular pair of time series being used, making it practical to use uniform thresholds.

The look-back span for the second level of channel normalization was set at 10 times the look-back interval used for first level. Thus, if the channel normalization used a look-back span of 60 days, the second layer of channel normalization used a look-back span of 600 days. It was assumed that a 10-fold look-back span would be sufficient to establish the fluctuation range of the basic divergence indicator. Note that a modified divergence indicator has a potential fluctuation range of 0 to 100, similar to any channel-normalized variable. See Figure 41.30.

Divergence Rule Types Upper and lower threshold were applied to the modified divergence indicator to generate signals. A positive or bullish divergence was in effect when the divergence indicator was above its upper threshold. This occurred when the companion series was moving up more or moving down less than the S&P 500. This was evidenced by the companion series having a higher relative position within its channel than the S&P 500. Conversely, a negative or bearish divergence existed when the divergence indicator was below the lower threshold. This occurred when the companion series was moving down more or moving up less than the S&P 500, resulting in its having a lower relative position within its channel than the S&P 500. This is illustrated in Figure 41.30.

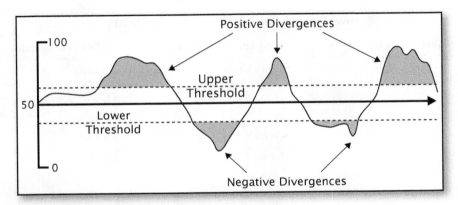

FIGURE 41.30   Modified Divergence Indicator.

The question was how to create signaling rules from the modified divergence indicator. Two rules seemed obvious: a bullish divergence rule, which would call for long positions in the S&P 500 when the divergence indicator was above the upper threshold, and a bearish divergence rule, which would call for short positions in the S&P 500 when the divergence indicator was below its lower threshold.

Both rules assumed that the companion series had leading information about the S&P 500. If the companion series was stronger than the S&P 500 (positive divergence), then a long position would be justified, whereas if the companion series was weak (negative divergence) a short position would be justified. However, this assumption may be incorrect. It may be the case that negative divergences are predictive of higher prices for the S&P 500, whereas positive divergences are predictive of lower prices. In other words, perhaps it is the S&P 500 that has the leading information. This suggests that inverse versions of each rule should be tried. In the end, it was determined that there are 12 possible divergence rule types, and all were tested.

These 12 rule types are exactly the same set used for the extreme value and transition rules. This makes sense because the modified divergence indicator is similar to the indicator used for the E rules because it has a fluctuation range of 0 to 100 and has two thresholds.

The 12 divergence rule types, presented in Table 41.4, include the basic bullish divergence (type 6), the bearish divergence (type 7) and their inversions (types 12 and 1). The 12 types are not illustrated because the illustrations would be redundant of those presented in the section on Extreme and Transition Rules.

Parameter Combinations and Naming Convention for Divergence Rules   Each divergence rule is defined by four parameters: type, companion series, threshold displacement, and channel normalization look-back span. There are 12 types of the divergence rules (see Table 41.4), 38 companion data series, 2 threshold displacement values—10 and 20, and 3 look-back spans—15, 30, and 60 days. This gives a total of 2,736 divergence rules (12 × 38 × 2 × 3).

TABLE 41.4	Divergence Rules and Associated Threshold Events	
Divergence Rule Types	**Long Entry/Short Exit**	**Short Entry/Long Exit**
1	Down Cross Lower Threshold Down Cross	Upper Cross Lower Threshold Upper Cross
2	Lower Threshold Down Cross	Upper Threshold Down Cross
3	Lower Threshold Up Cross	Upper Threshold Up Cross
4	Lower Threshold Up Cross	Upper Threshold Down Cross
5	Lower Threshold Up Cross	Upper Threshold Down Cross
6	Upper Threshold Up Cross	Upper Threshold Down Cross
7	Lower Threshold Up Cross	Lower Threshold Down Cross
8	Upper Threshold Down Cross	Lower Threshold Down Cross
9	Upper Threshold Up Cross	Lower Threshold Up Cross
10	Upper Threshold Down Cross	Lower Threshold Up Cross
11	Upper Threshold Down Cross	Lower Threshold Up Cross
12	Upper Threshold	Upper Threshold

The naming convention used for reporting results of divergence or D rules is as follows: (D)-type-companion series-threshold displacement-channel normalization look back span. Thus, a rule is named

$$D\text{-}3\text{-}23\text{-}10\text{-}30$$

Divergence rule, type 3, companion series 23 (positive volume index 30-day moving average), threshold displacement = 10 (upper threshold = 60, lower threshold = 40), 30-day channel normalization look-back span.

This completes the description of the rules tested in the case study.

■ Notes

1. J.P. Romano and M. Wolf, "Stepwise Multiple Testing as Formalized Data Snooping," *Econometrica* 73, no. 4 (July 2005), 1237–1282.

2. J.J. Murphy, *Intermarket Technical Analysis: Trading Strategies for the Global Stock, Bond, Commodity and Currency Markets* (New York: John Wiley & Sons, 1991). I was first exposed to the idea of using

relationships between markets for indicator development in 1979 by Michael Hammond and Norman Craig of Advance Market Technologies (AMTEC), Ogden, Utah. AMTEC was one of the first firms to apply artificial-intelligence methods to market prediction. AMTEC's modeling approach was based on the work of Roger Baron on adaptive learning networks, now known as polynomial networks, at Adaptronics Inc, in the 1970s. I routinely used intermarket indicators in work for clients of Raden Research Group, including Cyber-Tech Partners (1983), Tudor Investment Corporation (1987), and Manufacturer's Hanover Trust (1988).

3. P-H Hsu and C-M Kuan, "Reexamining the Profitability of Technical Analysis with Data Snooping Checks," *Journal of Financial Economics* 3, no. 4 (2005), 606–628.

4. Many of the automated methods are described in T. Hastie, R. Tibshirani, and J. Friedman, *The Elements of Statistical Learning: Data Mining, Inference and Prediction* (New York: Springer, 2001).

5. A segment of the future over which the rule's profitability persists that is long enough to compensate the effort required to discover the rule but not of unlimited duration.

6. H. White, "A Reality Check for Data Snooping," *Econometrica* 68, no. 5 (September 2000). Note that White uses the term data *snooping* to mean "datamining bias," as used in this book.

7. Mathematical operators include add, subtract, multiply, divide, powers, roots, and so forth.

8. Logical operators include *and; or; greater-than; less-than; if, then; else*, and so forth.

9. Time-series operators include moving average, moving channel normalization (stochastics), breakout channels, moving slopes, and such (described later).

10. P.K. Kaufman, 249.

11. Ibid., 200.

12. Ibid., 202. Kaufman notes that a study done in 1970 by Dunn & Hargitt Financial Services showed that a channel breakout using a four-week span, known as Donchian's four-week rule, was the best of several popular systems when tested on 16 years of data on seven commodities markets. Kaufman also compares the performance of channel breakout rules to four other trendfollowing methods (exponential smoothing, linear regression slope, swingbreakout, and point-and-figure) to Eurodollars for the 10-year period 1985 through 1994. The channel breakout method had the highest risk-adjusted performance over the 10-year period.

13. A simple moving average is centered by plotting the moving-average value in the center of the moving-data window. If N is the number of periods used to compute the moving average, the average is plotted to correspond with a value that is lagged by $(n-1)/2$ data points.

14. J.F. Ehlers, *Rocket Science for Traders: Digital Signal Processing Applications* (New York: John Wiley & Sons, 2001); J.F. Ehlers, *Cybernetic Analysis for Stocks and Futures: Cutting-Edge DSP Technology to Improve Your Trading* (New York: John Wiley & Sons, 2004).

15. Kaufman, 256.

16. Ehlers, *Rocket Science for Traders*, 27.

17. W.A. Heiby, *Stock Market Profits through Dynamic Synthesis* (Chicago: Institute of Dynamic Synthesis, 1965).

18. Although almost all sources attribute the development of this time series operator to Dr. George Lane in 1972, no source mentions the use of the same idea by Heiby at an earlier time. On this basis, I have attributed the development to Heiby. It is possible that Heiby based his work on yet an earlier author.

19. For information about various back-testing software platforms see: for TradeStation www.TradeStationWorld.com; for MetaStock www.equis.com; for AIQ Expert Design Studio www.aiqsystems.com; for Wealth-Lab www.wealth-lab.com; for eSignal www.esignal.com; for NeuroshellTrader www.neuroshell.com; for AmiBroker www.amibroker.com; for Neoticker, www.tickquest.com; for Trading$olutions www.tradingsolutions.com; for Financial Data Calculator www.mathinvestdecisions.com.

20. Ultra Financial Systems, PO Box 3938, Breckenridge, CO 90424; phone 970- 453-4956; web site www.ultrafs.com.

21. Market Timing Reports, PO Box 225, Tucson, AZ 85072; phone 520-795-9552; web site www.mktimingrpt.com.

22. Studies showing that trading volume contains useful information include the following: L. Blume and M. Easley O'Hara, "Market Statistics and Technical Analysis: The Role of Volume," *Journal of Finance* 49, issue 1 (March 1994), 153–181; M. Cooper, "Filter Rules Based on Price and Volume in Individual Security Overreaction," *Review of Financial Studies* 12 (1999), 901–935; C.M.C. Lee and B. Swaminathan, "Price Momentum and Trading Volume," *Journal of Finance* 55, no. 5 (October 2000), 2017–2069; S.E. Stickel and R.E. Verecchia, "Evidence That Trading Volume Sustains Stock Price Changes," *Financial Analysts Journal* 50 (November–December 1994), 57–67.

23. J.E. Granville, *Granville's New Strategy of Daily Stock Market Timing for Maximum Profit* (Englewood Cliffs, NJ: Prentice-Hall, 1976). The attribution to Woods and Vignolia can be found in the body of knowledge section on the web site of the Market Technicians Association.

24. This formulation of OBV is as presented in *Technical Indicators Reference* Manual for AIQ Trading Export Pro, a software product of AIQ Systems, PO Box 7530, Incline Village, NV 89452.

25. The MTA Body of Knowledge on Technical Indicators attributes the accumulation distribution indicator to Marc Chaiken, as does R.W. Colby, *The Encyclopedia of Technical Market Indicators*, 2nd ed. (New York: McGraw-Hill, 2003). No specific publication is referenced. The accumulation distribution indicator proposed by Chaiken is similar to an indicator developed by Larry Williams, *The Secrets of Selecting Stocks for Immediate and Substantial Gains* (Carmel Valley, CA: Conceptual Management, 1971), later republished by Windsor Books in 1986. Williams's indicator compares the open price to the close as the numerator of the range factor. Chaiken compares the close price to the midprice of the daily range.

26. As presented in *Technical Indicators Reference Manual for AIQ Trading Export Pro*, a software product of AIQ Systems, PO Box 7530, Incline Village, NV 89452.

27. Ibid.

28. Attribution of NVI to Norman Fosback can be found in the MTA web site Body of Knowledge and in S.B. Achelis, *Technical Analysis from A to Z* (New York: McGraw-Hill, 2001), 214.

29. Paul Dysart is credited with the creation of both positive- and negativevolume indexes by C.V. Harlow, *An Analysis of the Predictive Value of Stock Market "Breadth" Measurements* (Larchmont, NY: Investors Intelligence, 1968).

30. According to Fosback's study, the NVI identified the bullish phase of the primary trend with a probability of 0.96 over the time period 1941 to 1975. This compares to a base rate bull-trend probability of 0.70 over that time period.

31. N.G. Fosback, *Stock Market Logic: A Sophisticated Approach to Profits on Wall Street* (Dearborn, MI: Dearborn Financial Publishing, 1993), 120.

32. Ibid.

33. Harlow, *Analysis of the Predictive Value*.

34. R.W. Colby, *The Encyclopedia of Technical Market Indicators*, 2nd ed. (New York: McGraw-Hill, 2003).

35. Fosback, *Stock Market Logic*, 76–80.

36. This formulation of CNHL is as presented in *Technical Indicators Reference Manual* for AIQ Trading Export Pro, a software product of AIQ Systems.

37. C.R. Nelson, *The Investor's Guide to Economic Indicators* (New York: John Wiley & Sons, 1987), 129. The author points out that a positive spread (i.e., long-term rates higher than short-term rates) is often a bullish indicator for future changes in stock prices, especially for stock indexes that are not inflation adjusted.

38. Moody's Investors Service is a widely utilized source for credit ratings, research, and risk analysis for corporate debt instruments. Information can be found at www.moodys.com.

39. Aaa is the designated definition for the highest quality of corporate bond. Securities carrying this rating are judged to have the smallest degree of investment risk. The principal is secure and interest payments are protected by a robust margin. Although there is always a chance that various protective elements can change, these changes are easy to visualize. The Aaa rating means that it is highly unlikely for any drastic changes to occur that would erode the fundamentally strong positions on these securities. Definition provided: www.econoday.com/clientdemos/demoweekly/2004/Resource_Center/about bondmkt/morefixed.html.

40. Baa bonds are considered medium-grade obligations. They are neither highly protected nor poorly secured. Interest payments and security on the principal appear adequate for the present, but there may be certain protective elements lacking. These securities have the possibility of being unreliable over any great length of time. These bonds lack outstanding investment characteristics, making them attractive to speculators at the same time. www.econoday. com/ clientdemos/demoweekly/2004/Resource_Center/aboutbondmkt/m orefixed.html.

41. For a full discussion of alternative trend analysis methods and rules derived from them see Kaufman, Chapters 5 through 8.

42. J. Hussman, "Time-Variation in Market Efficiency: A Mixture-of-Distributions Approach," available at www.hussman.net/pdf/mixdist.pdf.

43. M.J. Pring, *Technical Analysis Explained*, 4th ed. (New York: McGraw-Hill, 2002).

44. Kaufman, 394–401.

45. Heiby, *Stock Market Profits*.

46. C. Alexander, *Market Models: A Guide to Financial Data Analysis* (New York: John Wiley & Sons, 2001), Chapter 12.

47. R.F. Engle and C.W.J. Granger, "Co-integration and Error-Correction: Representation, Estimation and Testing," *Econometrica* 55 (1987), 251–276.

48. Alexander, *Market Models*, 324–328, 353–361. One type of test used to establish the fact that a time series is stationary, called the unit-root test, is described.

49. The indicator is a time series of the errors (residuals) of the linear relationship between the two series.

50. Fosback, *Stock Market Logic*.

51. In 1983 the author, in association with Raden Research Group, developed a time series operator called *YY* that was similar in concept to cointegration analysis with the exception that *YY* values were normalized by the standard error of the regression and no explicit test was made for residual stationarity. *YY*'s development was inspired by an article by Arthur Merrill, "DFE: Deviation from Expected (Relative Strength Corrected for Beta)," *Market Technician Journal* (August 1982), 21–28. The *YY*-based indicators were used as candidate inputs for a variety of predictive modeling projects. One example was a sentiment indicator based on advisory sentiment on Tbonds. The predictive power of the raw consensus information was improved by a *YY* transformation that used past market changes as the regressor variable.

CHAPTER 42

Prospect Theory

From Edwin T. Burton and Sunit N. Shah,
Behavioral Finance (Hoboken, New Jersey:
John Wiley & Sons, 2013), Chapter 9.

E conomists assume each individual has a function that maps from every possible relevant level of wealth to a number that represents his or her happiness, and that under uncertainty each individual acts to maximize the expected level of happiness. One objection to expected utility is known as the Allais Paradox.

A second problem with expected utility maximization lies in the assumption that individuals make decisions under uncertainty based solely on the eventual levels of his or her wealth. One simple way to see that this is unlikely to be a good approximation of human behavior is to realize that most individuals are unable to report their levels of wealth in a short amount of time within a reasonable degree of accuracy. Consumers could not be acting based on anticipated levels of wealth if they are not even aware of current wealth levels.

So if wealth isn't the issue, what is?

■ The Reference Point

Consider the following set of choices, taken from Kahneman:[1]
  In addition to what you already own, you receive $1,000 for sure and either:

- Another $500 for sure, or
- A 50 percent chance of nothing and a 50 percent chance of $1,000.

  Second, consider this alternative set of choices.
  In addition to what you already own, you receive $2,000 for sure and either:

- Lose $500 for sure, or
- Face a 50 percent chance of losing nothing and a 50 percent chance of losing $1,000.

[1] Daniel Kahneman, *Thinking, Fast and Slow* (New York: Farrar, Straus and Giroux, 2011), 280.

A large majority of respondents picked the first option in the first choice set and the second option in the second choice set. Note, however, that the two choice sets represent exactly the same ending levels of wealth—what you own plus $1,500 versus what you own plus a 50 percent chance of $1,000 and a 50 percent chance of $2,000.

What is different in the two examples is the reference point. In the first example, individuals use an initial wealth of $1,000 as their beginning reference point. When considering their choices, they exhibit risk aversion, preferring the certain gain of $500 over a risky choice with an identical expected value.

In the second choice set, individuals consider $2,000 as their reference point and see a decision between a certain loss or a risky alternative with the identical expected value. In this case, the majority of individuals choose the latter option—the risky one—even though there is no risk premium to compensate them for the expected risk. In this second choice situation, individuals tend to be risk seekers, not risk averters, as in the first choice.

Economists generally would have ruled this possibility out entirely because agents would have been assumed to be risk averse in levels of wealth, and this risk aversion would apply regardless of the reference point. In contrast, what this example demonstrates is that individuals may be risk averse when considering gains but risk seeking when considering losses.

■ The S-Curve

Consider another choice between two lotteries:

- Get $900 for sure, or
- Have a 90 percent chance of getting $1,000.

Now consider this alternative set of choices:

- Lose $900 for sure, or
- Have a 90 percent chance of losing $1,000.[2]

In the first choice set, the expected value of each option is $900. Since the latter option carries more risk, a risk-averse individual would choose the first option, while a risk-loving individual would choose the second. In the latter choice set, both options have an expected value of −$900 (i.e., losing $900). The second option carries more risk, and hence would be chosen only by a risk-loving person, whereas a risk-averse individual would choose the first option.

In practice, most individuals choose the first option in the first choice set as expected. However, most choose the second option in the second choice set. In other words, when facing potential losses, individuals become risk loving rather than risk averse. This occurrence is irrespective of their initial levels of wealth—all that matters is that they take their current levels of wealth as their reference points and face losses from there.

---

[2] Kahneman, 280.

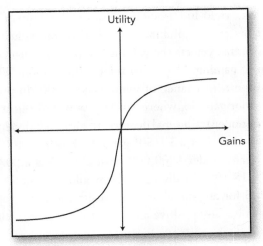

FIGURE 42.1 The S-Curve.

This behavior is not particular to this example; it is typical of the way people make choices when facing potential losses, which is fundamentally different than the way people make choices when facing potential gains. Figure 42.1 summarizes this phenomenon graphically.

For gains, an individual's utility function is concave,[3] representing his or her risk aversion. Conversely, for losses, the utility function is convex, representing risk-loving behavior.[4]

But there is more to the graph in Figure 42.1 than that observation.

■ Loss Aversion

The segment of the curve representing losses is steeper than that representing gains. This reflects the fact that for the representative individual, losses hurt much more than commensurate gains help.

As an example, consider choosing whether to take a gamble in which you have a 50 percent chance of getting $150 and a 50 percent chance of losing $100. Despite the positive expected value, most people find this lottery unappealing because the psychological cost of losing $100 is greater than the psychological gain of earning $150. This phenomenon is called *loss aversion*.[5] In the previous example, some may need a potential gain of $200 or so, or about twice as high as the loss, to accept the gamble. This loss aversion ratio has been estimated at between 1.5 and 2.5 in practice.

One might think that this loss-averse behavior could be explained by traditional wealth-based utility functions. However, in a now-famous theorem by Matthew

---

[3] Concave means the second derivative is negative, as shown in the portion of the curve above the gains axis.

[4] Convex means the second derivative is positive, as depicted in the segment of the curve below gains axis.

[5] Kahneman, 283–284.

Rabin,[6] such attempts yield ludicrous implications for human behavior in the face of other gambles. For example, Rabin shows that any individual with a concave utility function in wealth that rejects the gamble "50 percent chance of losing $100 and 50 percent chance of gaining $200" also rejects the gamble "50 percent chance of losing $200 and 50 percent chance of winning $20,000." In practice, many people might reject the former gamble, whereas very few would reject the latter.

Rabin showed that under traditional decision theory, an individual with initial wealth of $290,000 who would reject a 50/50[7] gamble of losing $100 or gaining $110 for any initial level of wealth under $300,000 must also reject a 50/50 gamble of losing $1,000 or gaining $718,190. Finally, one who would reject a 50/50 gamble of losing $100 or gaining $125 for any initial level of wealth must also reject a 50/50 gamble of losing $600 or gaining any positive amount of money, regardless of how large the potential gain is.[8]

It is not likely that these implications would hold up in practice. One could envision an individual rejecting a 50/50 gamble of winning $100 or losing $110, but it is hard to envision someone rejecting a 50/50 gamble of losing $600 or winning $10 million.

Loss aversion has an important implication for utility theory—specifically, that decisions in the face of uncertainty are *path dependent*. If an individual gains $500 and then loses $500, traditional wealth-based utility theory would predict that there was no change in the individual's happiness after both transactions took place. However, under prospect theory,[9] if there were enough time between the two transactions that the individual reset her reference point to the wealth level after the gain, she would feel an overall loss in happiness over the two transactions. Initially, she feels a benefit from the gain, but under loss aversion, the disutility she feels from the subsequent loss outweighs that benefit so that the net change is negative.

This feature of prospect theory has important consequences for utility theory. When looking at the decisions an individual makes over time, traditional wealth-based utility theory looks at the net change in wealth over the course of all decisions to assess the overall impact on utility. Under prospect theory, one must look at each of the movements in wealth in turn because the path one takes to get from initial wealth to ending wealth impacts the overall change in happiness.

This path dependence complicates the task of examining human behavior when facing various choice decisions. An econometrician who wishes to model the behavior of agents under prospect theory needs to acquire a data set complete with every decision the agent makes over time as well as the outcome of each such decision. In the case of modeling stock-trading behavior, this data set would not only need the outcome of each trade

[6] Matthew Rabin, "Risk Aversion and Expected-Utility Theory: A Calibration Theorem," *Econometrica* 68 , no. 5 (September 2000):1281–1292.

[7] 50/50 means there is a 50 percent chance of each alternative outcome occurring.

[8] Rabin, 1284–1285.

[9] Prospect theory was introduced by Daniel Kahneman and Amos Tversky in 1979. Prospect theory is an attempt to formalize a utility function approach that captures the concept of loss aversion. Daniel Kahneman and Amos Tversky, "Prospect Theory: An Analysis of Decision Under Risk," *Econometrica*, 47(1979): 263–291.

executed, but also the paper gains or losses at each time when the trader checked his or her portfolio, and the econometrician would need to approximate the trader's thoughts on the distribution of possible returns at each time the portfolio is checked as well. This is a rather onerous task, unnecessary for applications that rely on traditional utility theory, which would require data only on trades that were executed or possibly even just on the beginning and ending portfolio contents and values. Acquiring end-of-period data is a significantly easier task than acquiring much of the data within periods and part of the reason why traditional utility theory has remained a much more attractive modeling technique for finance theory.

Prospect Theory in Practice

Prospect theory has been tested in a variety of experimental settings, even in contexts outside of finance. List[10] looked at the behavior of individuals in a well-functioning marketplace and found that newcomers to the marketplace behaved in better accordance with prospect theory than with traditional utility models. Bleichrodt and colleagues[11] examine the behavior of individuals when the payoffs are in states of health rather than in monetary amounts and also finds that prospect theory explained the agents' behavior better than traditional expected utility theory did. Similar implications have been found outside of the experimental setting.

The implications of prospect theory for finance are profound. If investors consider paper gains and losses each time they check their portfolios, then not only will loss aversion tend to drive their choices, but the frequency with which they check their portfolios will greatly affect the decisions they make as well. How frequently one checks one's portfolio will lead to different levels of utility and to different investment decisions. Such behavior could account for a significant premium in markets with more active investors despite any risk factors for which such a premium should be rewarded.

Drawbacks of Prospect Theory

Despite the benefits of prospect theory in modeling how humans make decisions, the theory is not complete. There are many aspects of human behavior that are inconsistent with the implications of prospect theory. Consider the following prospects:

- A one in a thousand chance to win $1 million.
- A 90 percent chance to win $10 and a 10 percent chance to win nothing.
- A 90 percent chance to win $1 million and a 10 percent chance to win nothing.

The possibility of winning nothing exists in each choice, but it would be difficult to argue the impact of winning nothing would be the same in each case. In the first

---

[10] John A. List, "Neoclassical Theory Versus Prospect Theory: Evidence from the Marketplace," *Econometrica* 72, no. 2 (2004): 615–625.

[11] H. Bleichrodt, J. M. Abellan, J. L. Pinto, and I. Mendez, "Resolving Inconsistencies in Utility Measurement under Risk: Tests of Generalizations of Expected Utility," *Management Science* 53(2007): 469–482.

case, winning nothing is the expected outcome. In the second, it's not expected, but it would not be too harmful a result, since the individual only missed out on winning $10. However, in the last case, winning nothing would be devastating to most, since the alternative involved winning a large sum and the chances of its happening were so great the individual was probably already planning what he or she would do with the money.

In other words, prospect theory does not deal with the effect of disappointment. Winning nothing is not that disappointing when the alternative involves a modest sum, but it is extremely disappointing when one expects to win a much larger amount. Realizing you are not going to have a job on Monday is not that painful when you have been unemployed for a while, but it is much more painful when you lost your job on the previous Friday.[12]

To see a second drawback of prospect theory, consider the following gamble choice:

- A 90 percent chance to win $1 million and a 10 percent chance to win nothing, or
- Receiving $10 with certainty

versus this one:

- A 90 percent chance to win $1 million and a 10 percent chance to win nothing, or
- Receiving $100,000 with certainty,

and consider how one would feel after choosing the gamble and receiving nothing in each case. Most people would think receiving nothing would be much more painful in the latter case than in the former, but prospect theory is incapable of assigning a different value to receiving nothing in the two cases. That is, it cannot account for regret. Receiving nothing in the latter case is so painful because one is faced with the reality that he or she could have received a large sum; in the former case, the alternative was not much better than receiving nothing anyway. It is this regret that drives the increased negative value associated with receiving nothing in the second case versus the first.[13]

■ Conclusion

Traditional wealth-based utility theory falls short in a number of areas, such as the even more foundational assumption that individuals make decisions based on prospective levels of wealth. A more realistic assumption is that each person makes decisions based on gains and losses from a given starting point, and that after these gains and losses are realized, he or she resets the reference point to the current situation. That people make decisions based on the prospects available to them from a given starting point underlies the dynamics of prospect theory.

A more detailed analysis of how humans behave reveals that they also exhibit loss aversion—that is, they feel a larger pain from losses than they realize a benefit from

---

[12] Kahneman, 287.

[13] Ibid.

commensurate gains. An implication of this is that utility outcomes are path dependent. Traditional utility theory implies that a trader that starts out with a wealth of $1,000, makes five trades, and ends with a wealth of $1,500 has a particular known level of happiness at the end. However, under prospect theory, one cannot know his or her ending utility without knowing the outcomes of each trade and hence the path that the portfolio value took along the way. This model of human behavior corresponds more closely to observation, but it also complicates the business of analyzing such behavior in practice.

Prospect theory formalizes the decision process in a way that corresponds more closely to how people behave than the utility approach of traditional economics. There are limitations, however, to the use of prospect theory. The biggest single limitation is its inability to provide insight into general asset pricing theory. Prospect theory has a distinctly dynamic flavor to it because of its implicit path dependence. No one has yet constructed a satisfactory asset pricing theory based on prospect theory utility functions. Other problems with prospect theory have been emphasized by Kahneman and referenced in this chapter. The failure to deal with the emotions of disappointment and regret are major limitations of prospect theory's descriptive power.

For whatever weaknesses there may be with prospect theory, it is unquestionably a step forward in our ability to generalize actual human decision-making and provides a convenient formalization of loss aversion as well.

CHAPTER 43

Perception Biases

From Edwin T. Burton and Sunit N. Shah,
Behavioral Finance (Hoboken, New Jersey:
John Wiley & Sons, 2013), Chapter 10.

A perception bias arises when an individual has difficulty figuring out what the problem is that needs to be solved. Perception biases come in many forms. We look at several perception biases in this chapter, including saliency, framing, anchoring, and sunk-cost biases. All four of these biases have been extensively studied by Kahneman and Tversky and others and are well established. While the four perception biases that we discuss in this chapter do not exhaust the list of perception biases, these four appear to be the most important.

■ Saliency

When we have not encountered something recently, we have a tendency to ignore that thing even if it is important to an upcoming decision. No one seems interested in buying flood insurance unless there has been a recent flood. Airplane accident insurance is almost never purchased except in airports just prior to boarding a flight, though it is available to be purchased from the moment travel plans are made. When the economy has been strong and vigorous for a long time, fears of an economic slowdown recede almost to the point of being completely ignored.

Saliency works in two ways. If an event has not occurred recently, then that event tends to be perceived as having zero or negligible probability of occurring in the future. However, if the same event has occurred very recently, the perceived probability of a future occurrence becomes overstated. A dramatic example of saliency seems to take place when financial crises occur. During an economic boom, people forget that crashes can occur and underweight their likelihood of occurrence.

Gennaioli, Shleifer, and Vishny (GSV) have constructed a theory of financial intermediation[1] based upon the idea that the occurrence of "bad" economic states seems to be perceived as almost impossible when the economy is strong and the demand

---

[1] Nicola Gennaioli, Andrei Shleifer, and Robert Vishny, "Neglected Risks, Financial Innovation and Financial Fragility," *Journal of Financial Economics* 104(2012); 452–468.

for credit is high. This theory then uses an overweight of the probability of the "bad" economic state once the crisis has passed. Shleifer's theory formalizes the idea that credit standards for commercial lending seem to decline dramatically during periods of economic prosperity and then during economic recovery credit standards are tightened up to extreme levels. The opposite pattern would be more favorable to the economy, but saliency drives policy makers and market participants to incorrectly perceive the true environment in which they are operating.

The authors state their formalization of saliency in their model in the following way:

> [W]e assume that both investors and financial intermediaries do not attend to certain improbable risks when trading new securities. This assumption captures what we take to be the central feature of the historical episodes we describe: the neglect of potentially huge defaults in the housing bubble and of the sensitivity of AAA-rated securities to these defaults, the neglect of the possibility of massive prepayments in the early 1990s, or the neglect of the possibility that a money market fund can break the buck.[2]

GSV describes this as "formalization of the notion that not all contingencies are represented in the decision maker's thought process."[3]

The authors find that their model fits the financial crisis well and that attempts to account for the crisis without incorporating this element of surprise into their model significantly hinder its accuracy. They also address other research efforts that attempt to model the financial crisis. Much of this research models the crisis as an extremely low probability event that agents do rationally incorporate into their decision making. GSV finds that these models do not fit the financial crisis as well as a model incorporating saliency. They conclude that the agents involved in the crisis used incorrect investment models that assigned a zero probability to a potential financial crisis. A correct model would assign a very low, yet nonzero, probability to the chances of a prospective financial collapse.

■ Framing

The correct answer to a question should not depend on how the question is phrased. Unless the alternative way of asking a question is truly different, the answer should be independent of phrasing, or *framing*, as it has come to be known in the behavioral finance literature. The simplest setting for framing is the consideration of alternative policies that involve an unavoidable loss of life. Kahneman and Tversky pose the following example.[4]

---

[2] Ibid., 453.

[3] Ibid., 453.

[4] Daniel Kahneman and Amos Tversky, "Choices, Values, and Frames," reprinted from *American Psychologist* 39, no. 2(1984). In Daniel Kahneman and Amos Tversky, *Choices, Values and Frames* (Cambridge, UK: Cambridge University Press, 2000). The example of Problems 1 and 2 are taken, in slightly altered form, from this publication.

Problem 1

Imagine that the country is preparing for the outbreak of an unusual disease, which is expected to kill 600 people. Which of the following programs would you favor?

Program A: Has the effect of saving 200 people.

Program B: Has a 1/3 chance of saving 600 people and a 2/3 chance that no one will be saved.

Most people will choose Program A when given the choice. This is the risk-averse choice since 200 people are saved for certain as compared to the risky option in which 200 people are saved on average but it is possible that no one is saved.

Now consider the same problem phrased slightly differently.

Problem 2

Program C: 400 people will die for certain.
Program D: 1/3 chance that no one will die and 2/3 chance that 600 people will die.

In Problem 2, most respondents, when offered the choice, will opt for Program D. Program D is riskier than Program C, so risk-preferring behavior characterizes those who choose Program D over Program C.

Note that Programs A and C are identical and that Programs B and D are identical. So why are over 70 percent of respondents choosing A over B and nearly 80 percent of respondents choosing D over C? The choices are inconsistent. Kahneman and Tversky use the expression *invariance* to capture the idea that the same answer should be given to questions that vary only in phrasing but are substantively identical. Here, there seems to be a clear violation of invariance. "The failure of invariance is both pervasive and robust. It is as common among sophisticated respondents as among naïve ones, and it is not eliminated even when the same respondents answer both questions within a few minutes."[5]

What seems to drive this particular example is the reference point.[6] Problem 1 is written in the context of saving lives, while Problem 2 is written from the viewpoint of people dying. Respondents consider saving zero people the reference point in the former and zero people dying the reference point in the latter. The outcome choices are of course the same in both problems, just written from a different standpoint. But that different standpoint motivates people to make different decisions.

In Problem 1, respondents think of each person they save as a gain, and therefore make the risk-averse choice—saving 200 people for sure is more palatable than taking the chance that everyone might die. In Problem 2, respondents think of each person that dies as a loss, so they make the risk-loving choice. Sending 400 people to their deaths seems rather Draconian when the other option presents a reasonable chance that all might live.

Kahneman and Tversky[7] also provide a simple choice among lotteries that verified the failure of invariance in settings that most directly apply to finance.

---

[5] Kahneman and Tversky, 5.
[6] See Chapter 42 for a broader discussion on the effect of reference points on utility theory.
[7] Kahneman and Tversky, 6.

Problem 3

> Program E: 25 percent chance to win $240 and 75 percent chance to lose $760.
> Program F: 25 percent chance to win $250 and 75 percent chance to lose $750.

In Problem 3, virtually everyone will choose F over E since F dominates E.[8] The rational and proper choice is F. Now consider the following problem, Problem 4.

Problem 4

Imagine that you face the following pair of concurrent decisions. First, examine both decisions, then indicate the options you prefer.

Decision (i)—choose between:
A. A sure gain of $240.
B. 25 percent chance to gain $1,000 and 75 percent chance to gain nothing.

Decision (ii)—choose between:
C. A sure loss of $750.
D. 75 percent chance to lose $1,000 and 25 percent chance to lose nothing.

In Problem 4, 73 percent of respondents in Kahneman and Tversky's experiments chose A and D, while only 3 percent chose B and C. But B and C together equate to F from Problem 3, and A and D together are nothing more than E. Therefore, more than 70 percent of respondents are effectively choosing E over F. What is happening in this example is that identical options are presented to respondents and their choices will differ depending on the framing that surrounds the choices, even though the actual content of the choices presented is identical.

What framing is doing is exploiting our attitude toward bad events. In the first example, respondents do not wish to do harm. Therefore, when the choice is between saving people and rolling the dice, respondents want to save people. But when the identical choice set is presented and framed as if the respondent is choosing that 400 people will die with certainty, respondents go for the choice that presents the possibility of saving everyone, even though all 600 might die. Perception is the key.

In the monetary lotteries of Problem 3, the choice of F is obvious for almost all respondents. In Problem 4, C is where the real difficulty lies for most respondents who fail to choose the dominant B-C combination. C is a sure loss of $750 against D, which provides a way of avoiding the loss. Similarly, A is attractive because you are certain to win and avoid the possible loss entailed in choice B. Framing is taking advantage of loss aversion in Problems 3 and 4. Most respondents choose A, expressing risk aversion, and D expressing risk seeking. Such choices are routine to loss aversion. What makes Problems 3 and 4 striking is that the choice combination in 4 seems unpalatable once it is reframed as Problem 3.

---

[8] Dominance is implied since the probabilities are identical but the payoffs are better in F than in E.

■ Anchoring

Anchoring is a perception bias that arises when you are attempting to make a guess at something about which you have limited information. An *anchor* biases your guess in the direction of the anchor. A famous example of anchoring comes from attempting to guess the number of jellybeans in a jar. Staring at the jar, it would be difficult to imagine how to even begin to guess the number of jellybeans that can be stored in a jar. But imagine that just before you attempted to guess the number of jellybeans in a jar someone says: "Wow, there are a 1,000 stars in the sky!" Would that influence your guess? Would your guess be closer to 1,000 after such a comment was made? Suppose the comment were made, instead: "Wow, there are 10,000 stars in the sky!" Would your guess be significantly larger than if the anchor was 1,000?

Experiments using a single jar of jellybeans have been conducted numerous times using separated classrooms of responders. Very different estimates arise from the respondents in each room, and the average estimate for each room is biased in the direction of the anchor that applied to that room.[9]

A similar bias can occur in the context of historical guesses. Suppose one plans to ask what century Galileo lived in, but just before posing the question about Galileo, one says: "Columbus discovered America in 1492." If one compares respondent guesses when 1492 is the anchor to a different anchor such as: "The Magna Carta was signed in 1215," the group that hears 1492 will place Galileo closer to the end of the fifteenth century than the latter group, who will place Galileo's life much closer to the beginning of the thirteenth century.[10]

Anchoring can be characterized as an example of lazy thinking, but there is a possible reason for such lazy thinking. Often, limited observations can provide a reasonable basis for an estimate. One of the more famous examples of this is the Secretary Problem. Generally, this describes any situation where:

- There are *n* objects (prizes) drawn in succession.
- If all are seen together, they can be ranked from best to worst unambiguously.
- The order in which they are actually seen is random.
- Immediately after seeing each object, you must reject or accept the object most recently seen, and the decision is irreversible.
- The only information you have on the objects is the value of each object you've seen so far.
- The objective is to maximize the probability with which you select the best object.

Consider a situation where there are 10 monetary prizes available and you get to observe each prize, one by one. As you select one of the prizes and learn how much money there is, you are given a choice: You may take the money and then the game

---

[9] For similar examples, see Paul Slovic, Baruch Fischolff, and Sarah Lichtenstein, "Facts versus Fears: Understanding Perceived Risk," reprinted in Daniel Kahneman, Paul Slovic, and Amos Tversky, eds., *Judgment under Uncertainty: Heuristics and Biases* (Cambridge, UK: Cambridge University Press, 1982).
[10] Galileo was born in 1564 and died in 1642.

ends, or you can reject it, in which case that prize is discarded and you move on to the next prize. Once you get to the last prize, you must, of course, accept it as there are no other remaining prizes left to examine.

In this 10-prize situation, what is your best strategy? Remember that the only information you have are the prize values you have seen. Any arbitrary amount of money can be contained in each of the 10 prizes. Clearly, you need to gain some information—the question is how much information should you gain before making a selection. After all, each prize that you discard means that you can no longer have that prize, which may have been the largest of all the prizes.

This is a classic optimization problem and the optimal strategy is to select the first three prizes, observe the dollar amounts of each prize, and then discard each of them regardless of their values. Then consider the fourth prize. If its value is greater than what was observed in the each of the first three prizes, accept that prize and the game is over. If not, reject it and continue until you do find a prize of an amount greater than any of the first three. There is the possibility that one of the first three is the largest prize, in which case you will end up gaining the last of the 10 prizes selected, regardless of its dollar value.

Note that in some sense you are anchoring your ultimate choice by examining the first three prizes. In this process, you have constructed a "rational" anchor. It just might be that experience with rationally selecting anchors in the manner of this 10-prize example provides the backdrop for the effectiveness of seemingly irrelevant anchors in the biasing of estimates. Irrelevant anchors are latched on to in the absence of any other information. This might be harmless if the irrelevant anchor itself is unbiased noise. But if the anchor is provided intentionally such as in a purchase-and-sale situation, the perception bias triggered by anchoring can lead to biased behavior that may be in the interest of the person providing the anchor.

◼ Sunk-Cost Bias

Imagine that you paid $200 for a nonrefundable, nontransferable ticket to see a great country-and-western singer—your favorite—perform next Thursday. But when Thursday rolls around, you no longer want to go. You've decided you don't like that singer after all. You try to give away your ticket or sell it, to no avail. So do you go to the performance, even though you no longer think that you would enjoy it? Traditional economics says that a rational person will choose not to go to the performance. You might feel bad if you don't go to the performance because you will regret having wasted $200, but feelings of regret are not part of the makeup of the rational person typically assumed by economists. Utility is derived from consumption, not from wistful looks back about things you wish that you had done or not done. Feelings of regret play no role whatsoever in traditional economic analysis.

An economist normally argues that paying for something and then using it are two entirely separate decisions. The decision to pay for a ticket to attend a future event is based on expectations about the utility of that future event. Having paid for the ticket, once the future event arrives, you must make a new decision—should you attend or not? What you paid for the ticket earlier should be irrelevant, economists argue, to the decision to attend. The ticket is viewed as a *sunk cost* that is an entirely separate event from the attendance at the concert for which the ticket was purchased.

Classifying sunk costs as a perception bias is questionable. The sunk-costs bias involves something left out of the utility function, which most of us know probably does affect decisions—regret. People feel regret for things done and not done. But such things are in the past, and since they cannot be changed, they should not influence a current choice. Does having bought a ticket in the past make today's attendance at a concert more pleasurable? Not likely. But wasting the ticket one has paid for makes one regret a past decision. That regret can be avoided by going to the concert, even if you would rather not. If you had not bought a ticket and someone offered you a free one, you would likely say no. But, having paid, you wish to avoid the feeling of regret, and so you go. To an economist those two situations are identical and you should make the same decision in each.

A slight variation of the sunk-cost bias is the situation that arises if you lose your $200 ticket on the way to the concert and are faced with having to purchase or not purchase another ticket. Suppose in this case you really do want to attend the concert. If, along the way to the concert, you had lost $200, rather than the ticket that you purchased for $200, you might react differently about these two situations. Where money is lost, you might not associate the lost money with the concert and therefore you might be more likely to pay $200 for a ticket than if you had recently lost a ticket to the concert of exactly the same value. This example is usually classified as an example of mental accounting, but sunk costs are involved regardless of the classification.

Because sunk costs involve regret, the bias that results is similar to the bias an investor shows when reluctant to purchase a stock after missing the opportunity to buy the stock at a cheaper price. Investors who "go to cash" in the midst of a financial crisis are sometimes disappointed that, after they sell out, stocks rally to higher prices. Will they get back in? Often, the answer is no. The investor will wait and hope that stocks fall back to the levels at which they had made their earlier exit. What if that never happens? Then investors may wait until the regret they feel from not getting back in goes away. Once the feeling of regret is no longer present simply because of the passage of time, the investor might invest again, often at much higher prices.

■ Conclusion

Perception biases run counter to the normal utility maximization paradigm that permeates economic and finance theory. Emotions, to the extent they matter in traditional economics and finance, have their impact on the utility function, which is presumed to be a function only of expected consumption or expected net worth, where net worth is obviously a proxy for future consumption. But in real life, psychologists have found that emotions do play a role in how problems and the impact of choices are perceived. Those perceptions can be altered even when the plain substance of the problems or choices are unchanged. If a car is described as pink in color and later as rose in color, but the color has not changed, has the car changed? To the observer, it might be a different car, and that is the rub, if physically nothing has been altered.

Feelings of regret are real enough for most people and clearly affect choices that people make, but how can we take account of feelings of regret in economic or finance theory? If you choose X when Y was available, and Y turns out to be the better choice, do you feel a pang of regret? Where is that in the standard treatment of utility maximization? It is not easy to brush regret aside as of little importance when it influences investor behavior in important ways such as looking back and wishing it weren't so or worrying that if I do this, I might live to regret it. Major financial decisions seem potentially affected by feelings of regret. None of this bodes well for the efficient market hypothesis.

CHAPTER 44

Inertial Effects

From Edwin T. Burton and Sunit N. Shah,
Behavioral Finance (Hoboken, New Jersey: John
Wiley & Sons, 2013), Chapter 11.

Imagine two identical people making a choice between two options, option A and option B. The only difference between the two people is that the first starts at A and is asked whether or not he or she would like to move to B, whereas the second starts at B and is offered the ability to move to A.

It might be surprising to find that the majority of the time, individuals in these situations tend to stay where they start, regardless of the context around the decision choice or with which option they began. Experiments show that individuals tend to stick with the status quo, and that tendency persists across a variety of scenarios and in a variety of contexts. In this chapter, we explore the research that investigates such phenomena as well as the consequences of the outcomes such behavior elicits.

■ Endowment Effect

In *The Winner's Curse,* Richard Thaler tells the story of a wine-loving economist.[1] As the story goes, this particular oenophile purchased several bottles of exquisite Bordeaux wine at auction years ago at extremely low prices, $10 per bottle. The wine has since appreciated significantly in value, and now routinely sells for $200 per bottle at auction.

The economist enjoys one bottle from his collection each year. One day, the economist finds himself conversing with a student who shares his affinity for wine. The student asks why the professor does not purchase more of his beloved wine at auction, and the professor replies that the prices have grown too high for his liking. The student then asks if he could possibly buy a bottle from the professor's inventory at the auction price of $200, to which the professor replies that he cannot sell any from his stash—the bottles are simply worth too much to him.

---

[1] Richard Thaler, *The Winner's Curse: Paradoxes and Anomalies of Economic Life* (New York: Free Press, 1992), 63.

This example probably does not sound that surprising. However, the example flies directly in the face of traditional economic theory. In traditional economic theory, an individual must have a specific reservation price for a given good, such that he or she would be willing to sell some positive amount of the good for any price greater than the reservation price and buy some positive amount for any lesser price. If someone is not willing to sell a unit of a good for p_1 and is also not willing to buy one unit for p_2, with $p_2 < p_1$, according to traditional economic theory, that person would be acting irrationally.

One might argue that this is simply a question of sentimental value, but similar results have been observed in a number of experiments that eliminate such an effect. Kahneman, Knetsch, and Thaler[2] ran one experiment in which half the participants, chosen at random, were each endowed with a coffee mug (the "sellers") and the other half with nothing (the "buyers"). Each seller was asked to list his or her reservation price to sell the mug and each buyer to list his or her reservation price to buy the mug. Economic theory would predict the average selling price and buying price to be the same, but this was not the case—in fact, the average selling price was approximately twice as large as the average buying price.

In a further instantiation of the same experiment, a third group was included, called "choosers," who could receive either a mug or a sum of money. Individuals in this group were asked to list the amount of money that was as desirable as receiving the good. The reservation prices were as follows:

Buyers	$2.87
Choosers	$3.12
Sellers	$7.12

Sellers listed a reservation price approximately twice as high as both buyers and choosers. The contrast between sellers and choosers is striking, since both faced the choice of either having a mug or a commensurate amount of money—the only difference is whether they were given the mug at the outset or not. The results clearly show that the simple effect of owning the mug in the beginning nearly doubles the reservation price.

Jack Knetsch, one of the researchers from these experiments, performed a similar study[3] in which participants were chosen at random to receive either $4.50 or five ballpoint pens, and then were asked to accept or reject a series of offers that were designed to elicit their preferences for varying allotments of money and pens. From this data, Knetsch calculated indifference curves, or lines in two-dimensional space that represent allotments of the two goods (each corresponding to one of the two dimensions) such that the consumer is perfectly indifferent across those allotments.

Knetsch's results are displayed in Figure 44.1. The nearly vertical line represents the average indifference curve for those who were initially endowed with money.

[2] Daniel Kahneman, Jack L. Knetsch, and Richard H. Thaler, "Experimental Tests of the Endowment Effect and the Coase Theorem," *Journal of Political Economy* 98, no. 6 (1990): 1325–1348.
[3] Jack L. Knetsch, "Preferences and Non-Reversibility of Indifference Curves," *Journal of Economic Behavior & Organization* 17, no. 1 (1992): 131–139.

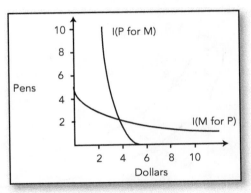

FIGURE 44.1 Crossing Indifference Curves.

These individuals needed a lot of pens to compensate for the loss of a dollar. The nearly horizontal line represents the average indifference curve for those who started with pens—they required a lot of money to give up even a single pen.

The indifference curves on this graph violate one of the basic laws of traditional economics—namely, that indifference curves can never cross. Crossing indifference curves are ruled out by the definition of the indifference curve itself. An indifference curve is the collection of all bundles that a consumer prizes equally. If two separate indifference curves cross, the consumer must be indifferent between all bundles on each curve and the crossing point between the curves—but then it must be the case that he is indifferent between any bundle on either curve and any bundle on the other curve. This is a contradiction, since each curve was supposed to represent an exhaustive collection of bundles of indifference in the first place.

At the heart of the disruption lies the underlying assumption that an individual must be indifferent across the same exhaustive set of bundles regardless of his or her starting point. Traditional economic theory assumes the value an individual places on a bundle is unaffected by what he or she is endowed with to start; behavioral finance shows that, in practice, this need not be the case.

Consider two identical individuals with the indifference curves for salary and vacation days shown in Figure 44.2.[4] Both start at position A in the graph. Each receives an offer to get either an extra $10,000 in salary per year, ending in position B, or an extra 12 vacation days per year, ending in position C. As they are both indifferent between the two outcomes, they each flip a coin, and one takes the extra money while the other takes the extra vacation.

Some time passes and then their employers allow them to reconsider their decisions. Standard economic theory states that the starting point is irrelevant, and that both individuals should still find the two options equivalent and hence still be indifferent. However, from the point of view of the first individual, the choice is between:

- Stay at Position B: Incur no gain or loss.
- Move to Position C: Receive an extra 12 vacation days but lose $10,000.

[4] Daniel Kahneman, *Thinking, Fast and Slow* (New York: Farrar, Straus and Giroux, 2011), 289–291.

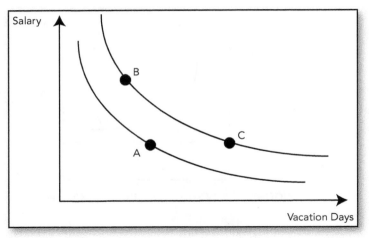

FIGURE 44.2

The second individual sees the choice as:

- Stay at Position C: Incur no gain or loss.
- Move to Position B: Receive an extra $10,000 but lose 12 vacation days.

It is not difficult to imagine that one might stay in his or her current position in both situations; in fact, it would be surprising if this were not the case. However, traditional economic theory would say that anyone in this situation should be indifferent between the choices regardless of the status quo.

Examples such as these show that indifference curves are not *reversible*—moving to another point and then back does not necessarily represent a net zero change in happiness. A movement from A to B along an indifference curve changes the indifference curve itself because the reference point changes.

Prospect theory[5] provides an explanation for this irreversibility. Regardless of the position each individual starts from, he faces a choice between a loss along one dimension plus a gain along the second and no movement at all. Since each was indifferent between the two points when starting at point A, the gain along one dimension is the same as the loss along the other. However, from prospect theory, a loss of a given size looms larger than a commensurate gain, so from a utility perspective, each individual sees the move as a net loss. Since the alternative involves no movement at all and therefore no change in happiness, neither individual will move, and both will remain at their current allocation.

The magnitude of the discrepancy in the coffee mug experiment is consistent with the results of prospect theory research—the average seller's reservation price was approximately twice as large as the average buyer's, the same two-to-one ratio that individuals exhibit when asked a question like, "How high would x have to be in order for you to accept a gamble of the following form: 50 percent chance of losing $100 and 50 percent chance of gaining x?" fMRIs[6] taken during the mug transactions

THEORY AND ANALYSIS

---

[5] For a more extensive discussion of prospect theory, see Chapter 42.
[6] fMRIs (functional magnetic resonance imaging) are brain-wave measures used in neuroeconomics.

have indicated that selling goods that have another use activated areas of the brain normally associated with disgust and pain, as did buying mugs at prices perceived to be too high, whereas buying mugs at low prices activated pleasure centers instead.[7]

The endowment effect does a better job of predicting human behavior than traditional economic theory, but it is worth noting that there are circumstances in which people do not succumb to this effect. This was shown as early as 1976, in a famous study by Vernon Smith.[8] Smith dispersed tokens, which had no alternative use outside of the experiment, as well as differing redemption values for the tokens themselves, to the various participants at random. Hence, a token may have been worth $1 to one participant and $3 to another. The participants were then allowed to publicly announce offers to buy or sell tokens which could be accepted or rejected publicly by the other participants. The results went as predicted by economic theory—the tokens ended up in the hands of those with the highest redemption values for them[9] and the market prices ended up as predicted by economic theory as well.

Similar results occur in more commonplace scenarios, such as when one changes a large bill for smaller ones or buys a product from a retail merchant in exchange for cash. Kahneman provides an explanation for such results. In such transactions, as in the token experiment by Smith, the item at hand serves as a placeholder for the other item in the exchange that will be received at a future point in time. When a lamp merchant trades a lamp for $20, the merchant feels no endowment effect from the lamp itself; mentally, the lamp served simply as a placeholder for the $20 that would be received for it in the future. Similarly, in the token experiment, the participants saw the tokens solely as a means to a monetary end; that the tokens had no alternative use outside of the experiment is key to the results. Along a similar vein, many of the results of experiments where the endowment effect does occur disappear when the participants are simply instructed to "think like traders" as they are making their decisions. Ironically, traders often do not think like traders themselves, as will be seen later in this chapter in the discussion of the disposition effect.[10]

■ Status Quo Effect

A similar result occurs when individuals are asked to choose among several options, with one option being the default, defined as the option implicitly chosen if no action is taken at all. In such situations, standard economic theory predicts that individuals should make the same choice regardless of which option is selected as the default. Experiments, however, show that individuals are influenced by which option is presented as the default one. The tendency to stick with the default option is known in the literature as the *status quo bias*.

---

[7] Kahneman, 296.

[8] Vernon Smith, "Experimental Economics: Induced Value Theory," *American Economic Review* 66, no. 2 (1976): 274–279.

[9] This is an example of the Coase Theorem, which states (in part) that, absent transaction costs and barriers to trade, resources will end up in the hands of those that place the highest value on them.

[10] Kahneman, 294.

Many experiments have demonstrated and explored this bias. Samuelson and Zeckhauser[11] asked a group of participants a series of questions phrased one of two ways, one providing a clear status quo default option and another providing no default option. For example, one question involved a decision about what to do with a significant sum of money that had been inherited. Two versions of the question appeared. Both listed investing in Company A as the first possibility. However, one version prefaced the explanation with the quote "A significant portion of this portfolio is invested in moderate-risk Company A." Samuelson and Zeckhauser found that a significantly higher percentage of individuals choose to invest in company A when it was listed as the status quo than would otherwise. Other research has consistently found the same effect.

Thaler and Sunstein have suggested that governments take advantage of such a phenomenon in the course of making policy decisions.[12] They argue for a school of thought they term *libertarian paternalism*. They define this as a central body giving several options to its constituents with the one that it deems the best for the greatest percentage of people as the default (this is the *paternalism* part), while still giving individuals the right to opt out of the default and into another choice if they deem it appropriate for themselves (the *libertarian* part). At the heart of this philosophy lies the idea that people will tend to stick with the defaults except when they find them significantly unpalatable and that then and only then will they make a change. The government is able to nudge individuals in one direction or another without giving them a hard shove.

This might seem surprising as a regulatory philosophy, but such a strategy has been observed in practice. One example comes from the state of Virginia's Retirement System, or VRS for short. In 1997, the VRS set up a new benefit program for employees covered under the state's public employee retirement system called the "cash match" benefit program. Under this program, the state matched dollar-for-dollar the contributions of its employees on a pretax basis. For example, if an employee's marginal tax rate is 30 percent, and she contributed $10 to her retirement fund, the state contributed another $10 on her behalf, so she essentially received a $20 contribution for an out-of-pocket cost of $7—a pretty favorable exchange of money now for retirement assets later.

Shockingly, most employees did not take advantage of this deal; in fact, less than 20 percent of new employees joined the program. VRS chalked this up to the status quo effect—that is, not entering the program was the default option, and new employees were loath to change away from it unless they were sure it was better to do so.

So, the VRS Board changed the default option to the maximum cash match option. Sure enough, going forward, 91 percent of new employees took that option. When presented with the options with no action resulting in maximum cash match, only 9 percent of new employees ended up not in the program.

---

[11] William Samuelson and Richard Zeckhauser, "Status Quo Bias in Decision Making," *Journal of Risk and Uncertainty* 1, no. 1 (1988): 7–59.

[12] Richard Thaler and Cass Sunstein, *Nudge: Improving Decisions About Health, Wealth and Happiness* (New York: Penguin, 2008).

In the same way that it helped explain the endowment effect, prospect theory can help explain the status quo bias as well. Many individuals might consider the default option as their reference point, considering losses and gains from that point in making their decisions. If there is uncertainty around the various options, they might feel that switching could result in a potential gain but could also result in a potential loss from the reference point, and the potential for losses will weigh heavier than the potential benefit from gains due to loss aversion.

Sticking with the default option also helps avoid regret, which prospect theory itself cannot explain.[13] If actively choosing away from the default option terminates in a poor outcome for the individual, it would be hard to argue that they did not make a mistake and hence the feeling of regret would be hard to avoid. However, if they were simply passive and never committed to an option themselves one way or another, it is easier to think that the government or even fate made the choice for them and hence it was not their fault that things went awry.[14] Consequently, these individuals may feel safer sticking with the default choice unless they are relatively certain that moving away from it is the best option.

■ Disposition Effect

Another effect, closely related to the endowment effect and status quo bias listed earlier as well as the sunk-cost bias discussed in Chapter 43, is the *disposition effect*. Consider the example from the Sunk-Cost Bias section of Chapter 43. You have paid $200 for a ticket to an event you no longer think you will enjoy and have been unable to sell the ticket thus far. Do you attend the event simply because you paid $200 for the right to go? Many people would do just that, even though traditional economic theory would frame this behavior as irrational. In that light, the $200 you paid has been sunk and cannot be recovered, so the only relevant question is whether the event is worth the transportation cost to go and the opportunity cost of the time spent there.

However, most individuals make decisions based on *mental accounting*. In a sense, one has a mental account set up related to this event, and thus far the event has cost $200 on one side of the balance sheet with the corresponding right to attend appearing on the other side. If one were to close the account without going to the event, he or she would be locking in a loss, which is an unpleasant feeling for most people. By attending, the individual could assign some sort of value to the other side of the balance sheet, which is a better feeling—even if the expected value of the event net of transportation and time costs is actually negative.[15]

A similar effect occurs prominently in investing behavior, with important consequences for financial markets. When liquidating investments in order to obtain cash for other uses, investors routinely liquidate stocks that hold paper gains before liquidating stocks that at current prices have lost them money. This is true regardless of the perceived future investment prospects of each stock.

---

[13] A point that Kahneman sees as an important weakness of prospect theory. See Kahneman, 287–288.

[14] See Chapter 42 for a broader discussion of prospect theory and regret.

[15] Kahneman, 243.

As an example, consider two stocks into each of which an individual had initially invested $10,000, currently facing the following prospects:

- Stock 1 currently has a gain of −$2,000 (i.e., a loss), and going forward has a 50 percent chance of going down $1,000 and a 50 percent chance of going up $2,500.
- Stock 2 currently has a gain of $2,000, and going forward has a 40 percent chance of going down $1,000 and a 60 percent chance of going up $2,500.

The individual needs to close out one position to pay off other debts. Which is he or she more likely to choose? From an investment standpoint, the current gain or loss is irrelevant—the goal is to maximize the expected return from this point forward, and hence all that matters is the future probability of returns. However, in practice, many close out the winning stock so that they can close that mental account out as a gain, hoping the losing stock will come back up as well, which it has a 50 percent chance of doing, so that they can close that account out as a gain in the future.

This is true despite the tax benefits of closing out losing stocks.[16] The majority of the time, investors close out winners before closing out losers, in every month of the year except one, December, when the tax implications are more on the investors' minds due to saliency.[17] Otherwise, investors are significantly more apt to sell winning stocks than losing ones, even if the winning stocks have better future potential.

Prospect theory provides a clear rationale behind this behavior. The idea of closing out an account and locking in a loss weighs heavily on an investor's mind—so heavy that it often feels better to close out a winner and lock in a gain, even despite the tax benefits, and even if the loser is likely to become an even bigger loser. Losses invoke such a negative emotion that this force outweighs the motivation to invest in such a way as to maximize the expected return.

■ Conclusion

Humans naturally have a tendency to stick with the conditions of their current situations, even in the light of strong motivations to do otherwise. When we are given items that have a potential use to us other than for trade, we place a significantly higher value on these items than we do if we are given currency and asked to buy those items instead. We also have a strong tendency to stick with the default option in a list of options, regardless of which option is labeled as such.

Prospect theory provides an explanation for these behaviors. When we are endowed with an item to start, we adjust our reference point to that particular endowment and feel that giving up the item we were endowed with would entail a loss for us. As prospect theory explains, it would take a higher-than-commensurate gain for us to feel compensated for such a loss due to loss aversion. Similarly, we tend not to

---

[16] In the United States, under certain conditions (e.g., the sale is not a wash sale, etc.), investors can write off losses from an investment sale on their tax returns, paying lower taxes overall.

[17] See Chapter 43 for a more extensive discussion of saliency and its effect on behavior.

move away from a default option, because we think of that option as our reference point, and hence moving away from it carries with it a risk of loss that we often do not feel comfortable bearing.

Prospect theory also provides an explanation for the so-called disposition effect, that investors are more likely to lock in a win by selling a winning stock than they are to sell a losing stock for cash, even if the prospects for the losing stock are less attractive. In our minds, we keep mental accounts of our paper positions; locking in a paper position as a loss carries with it such a negative feeling that it can outweigh the strong incentive we have to maximize our overall portfolio return.

CHAPTER 45

Relative Strength Strategies for Investing

From Mebane T. Faber, "Relative Strength Strategies for Investing" (El Segundo, CA: Cambria Investment Management, 2010).

■ Abstract

The purpose of this chapter is to present simple quantitative methods that improve risk-adjusted returns for investing in US equity sector and global asset class portfolios. A relative strength model is tested on the French-Fama US equity sector data back to the 1920s that results in increased absolute returns with equity-like risk. The relative strength portfolios outperform the buy and hold benchmark in approximately 70% of all years, and returns are persistent across time. The addition of a trend-following parameter to dynamically hedge the portfolio decreases both volatility and drawdown. The relative strength model is then tested across a portfolio of global asset classes with supporting results.

■ Momentum

Momentum-based strategies, in which we group both trend-following and relative strength techniques, have been applied as investment strategies for over a century. Momentum has been one of the most widely discussed and researched investment strategies (some academics would prefer the term "anomaly").

This chapter is not an attempt to summarize the momentum literature. There are numerous sources that have done a fine job on that front already including:

On the Nature and Origins of Trendfollowing–Stig Ostgaard
The Case for Momentum Investing–AQR Website

Bringing Real World Testing to Relative Strength—John Lewis
Global Investment Returns Yearbook—Dimson, Marsh, Staunton
Appendix in Smarter Investing in Any Economy—Michael Carr
Trendfollowing—Michael Covel
The Capitalism Distribution—BlackStar Funds
Annotated Bibliography of Selected Momentum Research Papers—AQR Website

Nor is this chapter an attempt to publish an original and unique method for momentum investing. Similar systems and techniques to those that follow in this chapter have been utilized for decades. Rather, our intent is to describe some simple methods that an everyday investor can use to implement momentum models in trading. The focus is on the practitioner with real-world applicability.

■ Data

This research report utilizes the French-Fama CRSP Data Library since it has the longest history and is widely relied upon and accepted in the research community. Specifically, we are using the 10 Industry Portfolios with monthly returns from July 1926 through December 2009, encompassing over eight decades of US equity sector returns. Our study begins in 1928 since a year is needed for a ranking period. We utilize the value weighted groupings rather than the less realistic equal weighted portfolios, and the sectors are described below:

Consumer Non-Durables—Food, Tobacco, Textiles, Apparel, Leather, Toys
Consumer Durables—Cars, TVs, Furniture, Household Appliances
Manufacturing—Machinery, Trucks, Planes, Chemicals, Office Furniture, Paper, Commercial Printing
Energy—Oil, Gas, and Coal Extraction and Products
Technology—Computers, Software, and Electronic Equipment
Telecommunications—Telephone and Television Transmission
Shops—Wholesale, Retail, and Some Services (Laundries, Repair Shops)
Health—Healthcare, Medical Equipment, and Drugs
Utilities
Other—Mines, Construction, Transportation, Hotels, Business Services, Entertainment, Finance

Data for the global asset classes are obtained from Global Financial Data and described in the Appendix, below.

■ Sector Returns

In the United States the 20th century experienced strong returns for an equity investor (Table 45.1 and Figure 45.1).

For comparison we have included a portfolio that is equal weighted among the ten sectors, rebalanced monthly, as well as the S&P 500 (Table 45.2).

Investors received strong returns for equities, but they were not without risk. Volatility and massive drawdowns were commonplace. Below we will examine a method for momentum investing, specifically relative strength. Below are the buy and sell rules for the system.

FIGURE 45.1   US Equity Sector Total Returns, 1928–2009.

TABLE 45.1	US Equity Sector Total Returns, 1928–2009				
Buy and Hold	**Non-Durab**	**Durab**	**Manuf**	**Energy**	**Tech**
Cagr	10.35%	9.04%	9.74%	11.30%	9.71%
Stdev	16.38%	27.06%	22.25%	20.95%	25.94%
Sharpe (3.81%)	0.40	0.19	0.27	0.36	0.23
Maxdd	(65.88%)	(90.07%)	(88.66%)	(75.66%)	(91.06%)
Buy and Hold	**Telecom**	**Shops**	**Health**	**Utilities**	**Other**
Cagr	8.66%	9.66%	11.03%	8.58%	8.20%
Stdev	16.22%	20.46%	20.11%	19.79%	22.88%
Sharpe (3.81%)	0.30	0.29	0.36	0.24	0.19
Maxdd	(71.89%)	(84.14%)	(74.94%)	(85.90%)	(90.28%)

TABLE 45.2	US Equity Total Returns, 1928–2009	
Buy and Hold	**S&P500**	**Equal Weight**
Cagr	9.39%	10.28%
Stdev	19.39%	18.38%
Sharpe (3.81%)	0.29%	0.35
Maxdd	(83.66%)	(81.67%)

RANKING

Each month the ten sectors are ranked on trailing total return including dividends. We use varying periods of measurement ranging from one to twelve months, as well as a combination of multiple months.

For example: If we are examining relative strength at the one-month interval on December 31, 2009, we would simply sort the ten sectors by their prior month (December 2009) total returns including dividends. For the three-month period, we would sort the ten sectors by their three-month (October 2009–December 2009) total returns including dividends.

■ BUY RULE

The system invests in the top X sectors. For Top 1, the system is 100% invested in the top ranked sector. For Top 2, the system is 50% invested in each of the top two sectors. For Top 3, the system is 33% invested in each of the top three sectors.

■ SELL RULE

Since the system is a simple ranking, the top X sectors are held, and if a sector falls out of the top X sectors it is sold at the monthly rebalance and replaced with the sector in the top X.

1. All entry and exit prices are on the day of the signal at the close. The model is only updated once a month on the last day of the month. Price fluctuations during the rest of the month are ignored.
2. All data series are total return series including dividends, updated monthly.
3. Taxes, commissions, and slippage are excluded (see the Real-World Implementation section later in the chapter).

Tables 45.3 through 45.8 are summaries of the various ranking periods and returns for the portfolios. The 1-, 3-, 6-, 9-, and 12-month combination simply takes an average of the five rolling returns for each sector every month to sort the 10 sectors.

TABLE 45.3 **1-Month Relative Strength Portfolios, 1928-2009**

	Top1	Top2	Top3	Top4	Top5	Top6	Top7	Top8	Top9	EQ-Weight
CAGR	12.63%	13.74%	14.33%	13.88%	12.91%	12.47%	12.01%	11.85%	11.22%	10.28%
STDEV	23.00%	20.46%	19.79%	19.17%	18.81%	18.80%	18.62%	18.51%	18.43%	18.38%
SHARPE (3.81%)	0.38	0.49	0.54	0.53	0.48	0.46	0.44%	0.43	0.40	0.35
MAXDD	(81.69%)	(74.21%)	(74.65%)	(76.36%)	(76.53%)	(78.31%)	(78.66%)	(79.49%)	(80.62%)	(81.67%)

TABLE 45.4 **3-Month Relative Strength Portfolios, 1928-2009**

	Top1	Top2	Top3	Top4	Top5	Top6	Top7	Top8	Top9	EQ-Weight
CAGR	13.32%	13.83%	13.44%	13.08%	12.43%	11.79&	11.40%	10.84%	10.62%	10.28%
STDEV	20.79%	19.52%	18.55%	18.40%	18.29%	18.07%	18.14%	18.15%	18.38%	18.38%
SHARPE (3.81%)	0.46	0.51	0.52	0.50	0.47	0.44	0.42	0.39	0.37	0.35
MAXDD	(64.50%)	(70.20%)	(73.92%)	(75.80%)	(77.52%)	(79.23%)	(79.92%)	(80.29%)	(80.57%)	(81.67%)

| TABLE 45.5 | 6-Month Relative Strength Portfolios, 1928-2009 | | | | | | | | | |

	Top1	Top2	Top3	Top4	Top5	Top6	Top7	Top8	Top9	EQ-Weight
CAGR	12.86%	14.10%	13.18%	12.60%	12.51%	11.72%	11.62%	11.01%	10.71%	10.28%
STDEV	21.60%	19.20%	18.29%	18.02%	17.87%	17.77%	17.87%	18.01%	18.24%	18.38%
SHARPE (3.81%)	0.42	0.54	0.51	0.49	0.49	0.45	0.44	0.40	0.38	0.35
MAXDD	(90.53%)	(84.30%)	(80.97%)	(76.81%)	(76.19%)	(77.68%)	(77.87%)	(78.86%)	(80.41%)	(81.67%)

| TABLE 45.6 | 9-Month Relative Strength Portfolios, 1928-2009 | | | | | | | | | |

	Top1	Top2	Top3	Top4	Top5	Top6	Top7	Top8	Top9	EQ-Weight
CAGR	14.80%	14.17%	12.60%	12.28%	12.07	11.80%	11.48%	11.13%	10.74%	10.28%
STDEV	22.21%	19.70%	19.00%	18.59%	18.36%	18.29%	18.06%	18.14%	18.22%	18.38%
SHARPE (3.81%)	0.50	0.53	0.46	0.46	0.45	0.44	0.42	0.40	0.38	0.35
MAXDD	(83.52%)	(75.94%)	(72.53%)	(75.26%)	(76.35%)	(76.86%)	(77.56%)	(79.10%)	(81.35%)	(81.67%)

| TABLE 45.7 | 12-Month Relative Strength Portfolios, 1928-2009 | | | | | | | | | |

	Top1	Top2	Top3	Top4	Top5	Top6	Top7	Top8	Top9	EQ-Weight
CAGR	16.05%	14.75%	13.94%	13.41%	12.96%	12.50%	11.67%	11.48%	10.82%	10.28%
STDEV	21.79%	19.57%	18.38%	18.18%	17.92%	17.87%	17.94%	18.16%	18.23%	18.38%
SHARPE (3.81%)	0.56	0.56	0.55	0.53	0.51	0.49	0.44	0.42	0.39	0.35
MAXDD	(76.91%)	(76.27%)	(71.29%)	(74.01%)	(74.18%)	(74.23%)	(77.70%)	(79.72%)	(81.07%)	(81.67%)

| TABLE 45.8 | Combination 1-, 3-, 6-, 9- and 12-Month Relative Strength Portfolios, 1928-2009 | | | | | | | | | |

	Top1	Top2	Top3	Top4	Top5	Top6	Top7	Top8	Top9	EQ-Weight
CAGR	16.13%	14.87%	13.75%	13.08%	12.68%	12.47%	12.19%	11.47%	10.78%	10.28%
STDEV	21.74%	19.16%	18.45%	18.17%	18.14%	18.22%	18.30%	18.18%	18.31%	18.38%
SHARPE (3.81%)	0.57	0.58	0.54	0.51	0.49	0.48	0.46	0.42	0.38	0.35
MAXDD	(77.21%)	(77.96%)	(72.65%)	(73.26%)	(75.63%)	(75.82%)	(76.78%)	(79.54%)	(81.07%)	(81.67%)
BESTYEAR	95.33%	105.28%	89.18%	65.50%	60.65%	62.53%	65.98%	55.96%	57.89%	53.38%
WORSTYEAR	(31.64%)	(31.30%)	(31.73%)	(30.70%)	(30.47%)	(30.14%)	(32.83%)	(35.01%)	(36.70%)	(38.21%)
%YEARS OUT	73.17%	70.73%	97.07%	71.95%	75.61%	73.17%	76.83%	74.39%	67.07%	-
TURNOVER	378%	331%	281%	235%	190%	197%	150%	119%	86%	0%

FIGURE 45.2   Relative Strength Portfolios, 1928–2009.

From these tables it is apparent that the relative strength method works on all of the measurement periods from one month to twelve months, as well as a combination of the 1-, 3-, 6-, 9-, and 12-month time periods. More interesting is that the system outperforms buy and hold in roughly 70% of all years. Figure 45.2 shows an equity curve for the combination measurement system. A rough estimate of 300–600 basis points of outperformance per year is reasonable.

Table 45.9 shows the outperformance by decade for the relative strength strategy on a yearly compounded basis. For example, the Top 1 beat the buy and hold portfolio by 2.68% a year in the 1930s.

TABLE 45.9	Relative Strength Portfolios, CAGR Outperformance by Decade 1928–2009		
	Top1	Top2	Top3
1930s	2.68%	2.61%	4.12%
1940s	5.61%	3.21%	2.00%
1950s	11.29%	9.77%	7.06%
1960s	8.11%	5.68%	4.19%
1970s	5.16%	2.29%	1.94%
1980s	2.27%	0.82%	1.14%
1990s	6.50%	6.65%	3.74%
2000s	3.85%	4.86%	1.76%
Average	5.68%	4.48%	3.24%

■ Solutions to the Drawbacks of Relative Strength Systems

The biggest drawback of a relative strength system is that the portfolio is long-only and fully invested, thus leaving the portfolio exposed to the risks of that particular asset beta. In this case the investor is exposed primarily to US stock risk. This detail can be seen in the volatility and drawdowns of all of the portfolios. There are two possible solutions to control for the losses and drawdowns while using a relative strength rotation system: (1) hedging and, (2) adding non-correlated asset classes.

Solution 1: Hedging (either moving to cash or hedging with shorts). Hedging can be done on a sector basis or on a portfolio wide asset class basis. An investor could utilize a static hedge that always hedges a percentage of the portfolio, or possibly the entire portfolio (market neutral). This hedging technique has the drawback of hedging the portfolio when the market is appreciating, but also protects against all declines and shocks. An investor could also use options to gain short exposure (essentially acting as insurance), with a cost, to the portfolio.

Another hedging option is a dynamic hedging technique that attempts to hedge when conditions are more favorable to market declines. Consistent with research we published in "A Quantitative Approach to Tactical Asset Allocation," using a long term moving average to hedge a portfolio results in a reduction in volatility and drawdown versus buy and hold. This approach can be seen in this research piece we published on trading Fidelity Sector Funds, "Combining Rotation and Timing Systems." In Table 45.10 we examine the combination of the 1-, 3-, 6-, 9-, and 12-month sector rotation portfolios when they are dynamically hedged. The portfolios move entirely to 100% cash (T-Bills) when the S&P 500 is below its 10-month Simple Moving Average (SMA). (Note: This system could also be run individually on the sectors with similar results.)

By adding the dynamic hedge, most portfolios preserve their returns (although the Top 1 takes a 150 basis point hit), but have the added benefit of reduced volatility and drawdowns. While an approximate 40–50% drawdown is still large, it is more tolerable than a 70–80% drawdown

Solution 2: Addition of non-correlated asset classes. The second possible solution to the drawback of single asset class exposure inherent in the US sector rotation strategy is to add non-correlated global asset classes to the portfolio. Just as we

TABLE 45.10	Dynamically Hedged Combination 1-, 3-, 6-, 9- and 12-Month Relative Strength Portfolios, 1928-2009								
	Top1	Top2	Top3	Top4	Top5	Top6	Top7	Top8	Top9	EQ-Weight
CAGR	14.67%	14.42%	13.28%	12.53%	12.38%	11.94%	11.61%	11.10%	10.75%	10.40%
STDEV	17.94%	15.32%	14.26%	15.21%	13.48%	13.02%	12.77%	12.51%	12.32%	12.14%
SHARPE (3.81%)	0.61	0.69	0.66	0.57	0.64	0.63	0.61	0.58	0.56	0.54
MAXDD	(54.69%)	(51.36%)	(49.42%)	(54.65%)	(48.55%)	(45.74%)	(43.69%)	(43.29%)	(42.20%)	(42.27%)

TABLE 45.11	Global Asset Class Total Returns, 1973-2009					
	Buy & Hold	**S&P 500**	**EAFE**	**10 YR**	**GSCI**	**NAREIT**
CAGR	10.01%	9.69%	9.62%	8.16%	8.82%	9.02%
STDEV	10.15%	15.75%	17.45%	9.07%	20.57%	18.23%
SHARPE (5.9%)	0.41	0.24	0.21	0.25	0.14	0.17
MAXDD	(46.02%)	(50.77%)	(56.40%)	(18.79%)	(67.64%)	(67.88%)

have demonstrated above that a momentum strategy works in US equity sectors, so too does momentum work across global asset classes. We detailed this method in our book *The Ivy Portfolio* with a global rotation system that adds foreign stocks, bonds, REITs, and commodities to the portfolio. Other asset classes and spreads could be included to further diversify the portfolio, but examining this simple five asset class portfolio is instructive.

Table 45.11 and Figure 45.3 illustrate the returns of the five asset classes we examine in this chapter since 1973. The buy and hold benchmark is an equal-weighted portfolio of the five asset classes, rebalanced monthly.

Tables 45.12 through 45.17 are summaries of the various ranking periods and returns for the portfolios.

From these tables it is apparent that the relative strength method works on all of the measurement periods from one month to twelve months, as well as a combination of time periods. More interesting is that the system outperforms buy and hold in roughly 70% of all years. A rough estimate of 300–600 basis points of outperformance per year is reasonable. Figure 45.4 is an equity curve.

FIGURE 45.3 Global Asset Class Total Returns, 1973-2009.

TABLE 45.12 1-Month Relative Strength Portfolios, 1973-2009

	Top1	Top2	Top3	Top4	Buy & Hold
CAGR	17.01%	14.79%	12.74%	10.93%	10.02%
STDEV	17.19%	12.26%	10.92%	10.60%	10.15%
SHARPE (3.81%)	0.65	0.72	0.63	0.47	0.41
MAXDD	(22.41%)	(29.39%)	(33.15%)	(44.04%)	(46.02%)

TABLE 45.13 3-Month Relative Strength Portfolios, 1973-2009

	Top1	Top2	Top3	Top4	Buy & Hold
CAGR	14.27%	13.23%	13.01%	10.72%	10.02%
STDEV	18.97%	12.75%	10.75%	10.40%	10.16%
SHARPE (5.9%)	0.44	0.58	0.66	0.46	0.41
MAXDD	(43.02%)	(31.46%)	(38.67%)	(41.85%)	(46.02%)

TABLE 45.14 6-Month Relative Strength Portfolios, 1973-2009

	Top1	Top2	Top3	Top4	Buy & Hold
CAGR	13.55%	16.13%	12.92%	10.87%	10.02%
STDEV	19.08%	12.29%	10.91%	10.28%	10.16%
SHARPE (5.9%)	0.40	0.83	0.64	0.48	0.41
MAXDD	(50.19%)	(34.22)	(40.22%)	(43.63%)	(46.02%)

TABLE 45.15 9-Month Relative Strength Portfolios, 1973-2009

	Top1	Top2	Top3	Top4	Buy & Hold
CAGR	15.31%	15.00%	14.31%	11.20%	10.02%
STDEV	18.73%	12.77%	10.93%	10.57%	10.16%
SHARPE (5.9%)	0.50	0.71	0.77	0.50	0.41
MAXDD	(38.91%)	(35.14%)	(39.84%)	(43.34%)	(46.02%)

TABLE 45.16 12-Month Relative Strength Portfolios, 1973-2009

	Top1	Top2	Top3	Top4	Buy & Hold
CAGR	15.41%	14.83%	13.32%	11.48%	10.02%
STDEV	18.89%	12.64%	11.05%	10.70%	10.15%
SHARPE (5.9%)	0.50	0.71	0.67	0.52	0.41
MAXDD	(48.74%)	(39.65%)	(43.56%)	(46.82%)	(46.02%)

TABLE 45.17 **Combination 1-, 3-, 6-, 9-, and 12-Month Relative Strength Portfolios, 1973–2009**

	Top1	Top2	Top3	Top4	Buy & Hold
CAGR	16.30%	16.47%	14.49%	11.06%	10.02%
STDEV	18.58%	12.62%	11.00%	10.47%	10.15%
SHARPE (5.9%)	0.56	0.84	0.78	0.49	0.41
MAXDD	(30.87%)	(33.38%)	(39.84%)	(47.20%)	(46.02%)
BEST YEAR	74.96%	37.89%	36.08%	32.46%	26.58%
WORST YEAR	(15.18%)	(8.63%)	(22.26%)	(31.07%)	(30.09%)
%YEARS OUT	70.27%	70.27%	78.38%	59.46%	—

Table 45.18 shows the outperformance by decade for the relative strength strategy on a yearly compounded basis. For example, the Top 1 beat the buy and hold portfolio by 6% a year in the 1990s.

What about combination both solutions? In Table 45.19 we report the results of rotation among global asset classes but only investing in the asset class if it is trading above its 10-month SMA (otherwise that portion is invested in T-Bills).

The results are slightly improved Sharpe Ratios and similar absolute returns, but with marked reductions in drawdown. The effect is most seen in the portfolios that utilized more asset classes.

FIGURE 45.4 Combination 1-, 3-, 6-, 9-, and 12-Month Relative Strength Portfolios, 1973–2009.

TABLE 45.18 Combination 1-, 3-, 6-, 9-, and 12-Month Relative Strength Portfolios, CAGR Outperformance by Decade 1973-2009

	Top1	Top2	Top3
1970s	11.98%	12.94%	5.94%
1980s	4.70%	1.46%	3.04%
1990s	5.75%	4.96%	5.00%
2000s	4.46%	8.28%	4.29%
AVERAGE	6.72%	6.91%	4.57%

TABLE 45.19 Combination 1-, 3-, 6-, 9-, and 12-Month Relative Strength Portfolios, 1973-2009

	Top1	Top2	Top3	Top4	Buy & Hold
CAGR	15.97%	16.50%	15.00%	12.94%	10.02%
STDEV	18.40%	11.94%	9.60%	8.14%	10.15%
SHARPE (5.9%)	0.55	0.89	0.95	0.86	0.41
MAXDD	(31.17%)	(21.67%)	(12.95%)	(12.46%)	(46.02%)
BEST YEAR	74.96%	38.04%	36.08%	32.46%	26.58%
WORST YEAR	(15.18%)	(1.21%)	(3.49%)	(1.10%)	(30.09%)
%YEARS OUT	72.97%	72.97%	78.38%	64.86%	—

■ Real-World Implementation

While this chapter is meant to be an instructive base case scenario, care must be observed when translating theory into real-world trading. While most industries over the period examined were represented by a robust amount of underlying companies, a few (Telecom and Health specifically) had less than twenty companies until the 1950s. The persistence of the momentum strategy by decade goes to show that this was not simply a property of markets 80 years ago, but continues to work today.

Obviously US sector funds did not exist in the 1920s. Attempting to transact in shares of the underlying companies would have been far too expensive to actively manage the portfolio in the early part of the 20th century as turnover of 100% to 400% is very high for transactions in exchange traded securities. However, even assuming a round trip cost of 1% to the portfolio would still allow for excess momentum profits to the portfolios.

The practitioner today can choose from thousands of mutual funds, ETFs, and closed-end funds. Many of these funds can be traded for $8 a trade or less, and many mutual funds and ETFs are now commission free at some online brokers. Mutual funds also avoid any bid ask spread and market impact costs, but also typically have higher management fees than ETFs and can be subject to redemption fees if held for short periods of time (many Fidelity funds require a holding period of 30 days). Some ETFs can be painfully illiquid so care must be taken when selecting funds.

To reduce trading frequency and possible transaction costs an investor could implement a sell filter. Assuming a universe of ten funds, the investor could buy the top three funds and sell them when the funds drop out of the top five funds. This approach would lower the turnover to sub-100% levels.

As with any strategy, taxes are a very real consideration and the strategy should be traded in a tax deferred account. It is difficult to estimate the impact an investor would experience due to varying tax rates by income bracket and over time, but an increase from 5–20% turnover to 70–100% turnover could result in an increase in taxes of 50–150 bps.

■ Conclusion

The purpose of this chapter was to demonstrate a simple-to-follow method for utilizing relative strength in investing in US equities and global asset classes. The results showed robust performance across measurement periods as well as over the past eight decades. While absolute returns were improved, volatility and drawdown remained high. Various methods were examined that could be used as solutions to a long only rotation system including hedging and adding non-correlated asset classes.

■ Appendix A—Data Sources

From the French-Fama website:

Detail for 10 Industry Portfolios	
Daily Returns:	July 1, 1963–December 31, 2009
Monthly Returns:	July 1926–December 2009
Annual Returns:	1927–2009
Portfolios:	Download industry definitions

We assign each NYSE, AMEX, and NASDAQ stock to an industry portfolio at the end of June of year t based on its four-digit SIC code at that time. (We use Compustat SIC codes for the fiscal year ending in calendar year t-1. Whenever Compustat SIC codes are not available, we use CRSP SIC codes for June of year t.) We then compute returns from July of t to June of t+1.

Fama and French update the research data at least once a year, but we may update them at other times. Unlike the benchmark portfolios, (1) we reform almost all these portfolios annually (UMD is formed monthly), (2) we do not include a hold range, and (3) we ignore transaction costs. In addition, we reconstruct the full history of returns each time we update the portfolios. (Historical returns can change, for example, if CRSP revises its database.) Although the portfolios include all NYSE, AMEX, and NASDAQ firms with the necessary data, the breakpoints use only NYSE firms.

S&P 500 Index–A capitalization-weighted index of 500 stocks that is designed to mirror the performance of the United States economy. Total return series is provided by Global Financial Data and results pre-1971 are constructed by GFD. Data from 1900–1971 uses the S&P Composite Price Index and dividend yields supplied by the Cowles Commission and from S&P itself.

MSCI EAFE Index (Europe, Australasia, Far East)—A free float-adjusted market capitalization index that is designed to measure the equity market performance of developed markets, excluding the US and Canada. As of June 2007 the MSCI EAFE Index consisted of the following 21 developed market country indices: Australia, Austria, Belgium, Denmark, Finland, France, Germany, Greece, Hong Kong, Ireland, Italy, Japan, the Netherlands, New Zealand, Norway, Portugal, Singapore, Spain, Sweden, Switzerland, and the United Kingdom. Total return series is provided by Morgan Stanley.

U.S. Government 10-Year Bonds—Total return series is provided by Global Financial Data.

Goldman Sachs Commodity Index (GSCI)—Represents a diversified basket of commodity futures that is unlevered and long only. Total return series is provided by Goldman Sachs.

National Association of Real Estate Investment Trusts (NAREIT)—An index that reflects the performance of publicly traded REITs. Total return series is provided by the NAREIT.

CHAPTER 46

Risk Control

From Perry J. Kaufman, *Trading Systems and Methods, +Website,* 5th Edition (Hoboken, New Jersey: John Wiley & Sons, 2013), Chapter 23.

Every trading style has losing streaks that will ruin an investor who begins trading at the wrong time or is undercapitalized; therefore, the size of the position, the markets to trade, and when to increase or decrease leverage become important for financial survival. Some risks, called *systematic risk,* can be controlled or reduced while *market risk,* which can take the form of a price shock, can never be eliminated.

This chapter covers a broad range of topics related to risk, including individual trade risk, collective risk, leverage, and a continuation of the effects of price shocks and catastrophic risk. It is not possible to say that one is more important than another. In a specific situation, any one of the areas discussed may be the answer to preventing a substantial loss. The first part of this chapter discusses capitalization and shows why many traders are successful for months and then lose everything in only a few days. It explains the choices in dynamic leveraging and offers alternatives of less risk. Profit-taking and stops, the two most common ways to control risk, are shown to apply to specific types of trading, rather than used as a generalized solution. The last section tries to distinguish between a system that is temporarily performing properly and when it has failed to live up to expectations of it.

■ Mistaking Luck for Skill

Embracing risk is more important than measuring risk. Understanding and accepting each day's losses and series of losses is essential for survival. Risk cannot be eliminated, as much as traders try to make each trade a profit or engineer systems to minimize losses. You can move the profits and losses around, but you cannot eliminate them or make them so small that they are meaningless. And measuring risk as a 10% chance of losing 20% of your equity is not as sobering as actually losing 20%. It is even devastating when you thought you could only lose 5%.

Daily market volatility gives a good approximation of short-term risk, and volatility of the actual profits and losses of a trading method provides a way to estimate how much risk must be absorbed to achieve the expected profits. Price shocks are the fly in the ointment. They add an unpredictable aspect to risk, coming at unexpected times, and cause losses that are larger than anything seen in the past. The previous chapter continued a discussion of some practical aspects of price shocks, with examples of how to manage both profits and losses caused by these large moves. This review only serves as a reminder of a very important problem.

A price shock represents the greatest risk for traders. In most cases, a price shock causes a loss, but when it is a windfall profit it can be disarming.[1] A price shock, such as 9/11, cannot be anticipated, and any profit that might have been gained is the result of luck, not skill. Traders must realize that the profit could have been a loss; they should assess how their account would have survived a drop of the same magnitude. Mistaking luck for skill ignores the risk and exposes the trader to future risk for which he or she is now unprepared. Long-Term Capital Management, a home for some of the smartest financial minds, believed they could engineer the risk out of each trade by explaining away all of the previous price shocks, then failed to survive the next price shock. Without including these larger, infrequent losses in the performance profile, trading accounts are likely to be undercapitalized.

The only way to reduce the possibility of loss from a price shock is to be out of the market as much as possible. This translates into two practical trading rules:

1. *Do not hold a position longer than necessary.* Choose a strategy that has good entry timing and has many opportunities for exiting the trade. It is best to be in the market when prices are moving and out when volatility drops and prices are no longer active. A trading method that is in the market only 40% of the time has a 60% chance of avoiding a price shock. A strategy that is always in the market will be exposed to all price shocks.

2. *Try to earn as much as possible while investing as little as possible.* The less you have invested, the less you have at risk. Futures and options offer an opportunity to leverage price moves by as much as 20:1; however, that works against you when a price shock causes a large loss. A fully leveraged trading program that has a theoretical return of 200% per annum will also be a total loss after an adverse price shock. A deleveraged program may return only 20% but is 10 times more likely to survive a price shock, a much better long-term alternative. A small reduction in returns for a larger reduction in exposure is a good trade-off.

■ Risk Aversion

Traders react differently to risk, and most are risk-averse. A primary reason for the popularity of trend systems is that they provide some degree of *conservation of capital*.

---

[1] A book entirely devoted to price shocks and the "black swan" is Nassim Nicholas Taleb, *Fooled by Randomness* (Texere, 2001). Taleb has popularized the phrase "mistaking luck for skill."

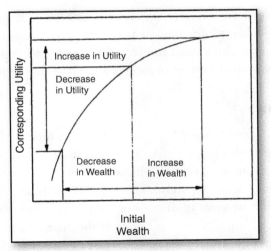

FIGURE 46.1 Changes in Utility versus Changes in Wealth.

Source: Peter Bernstein, *The Portable MBA in Investment* (New York: John Wiley & Sons, 1995), 38. © 1995 Peter Bernstein. Reprinted by permission of John Wiley & Sons, Inc.

They take small losses when prices move the wrong way, and hold a trade for much longer when it shows a profit. By taking small losses, the investor can wait until a sustained trend comes along. This gives the trending system its familiar profile of a large number of small losses offset by a few large profits. But each trader has her personal tolerance level for risk and not all of them find conservation of capital appealing. Some are risk seeking.

Daniel Bernoulli, a famous mathematician, proposed a theory of utility in 1738 that distinguished between price and value, where price is the same for everyone but value (utility) depends on the personal circumstances of the individual making the estimate.[2] Bernoulli's approach defined a concept of *diminishing marginal utility,* shown in Figure 46.1, which indicates that as wealth becomes greater, the preference for more wealth diminishes (unlike the concept of power). In the lower left part of the chart, where the investor has a small net worth, the likelihood of accepting risk is much higher, although the magnitude of the risk is still small. When risk becomes greater, even proportional to reward, all investors become cautious. Bernoulli's graph shows the curve beginning at zero and moving up and to the right in a perfect quarter-circle, ending horizontally where risk is no longer attractive. This implies that people are risk-averse. Most people are not interested in an even chance of gaining or losing an equal amount. Other theories that have been proposed are that the market maximizes the amount of money lost and the market maximizes the number of losing participants. All of these concepts appear to be true and are significant in developing an understanding of how the market functions.

---

[2] Peter L. Bernstein, ed., *The Portable MBA in Investment* (New York: John Wiley & Sons, 1995), 37.

Naturally, there are exceptions to most rules. People will spend small amounts to have a very small chance of winning a very large amount, as with various state lotteries. Young people with a small amount of money are willing to take greater risks, rationalizing that a small amount of savings is not significant for their future.

Risk Preference

The Bernoulli theory of utility recognizes that each investor has his or her unique objectives and attitudes toward risk. Some investors would like to keep risks low and returns steady; more speculative investors would risk a sizable amount of their capital for a chance at the big move. This trait is called the investor's *risk preference*. The *risk preference, P,* or *utility* of an investor for a specific venture (in this case a trade) can be found by adding the expected value of the investor's utilities or preferences, p_i, for the various outcomes of that event,

$$P = w_1 p_1 + w_2 p_2 + \cdots + w_n p_n$$

where $\sum w_i = 1$
$n =$ possible outcomes

The weighting factors may be the results of personal bias or may be the calculated probabilities of each outcome. For example, consider a gold trade that has a likely profit of $4,000 and a risk of $1,500. For convenience, adjust the reward values by dividing by 1,000. If the probability of success is 60%, the total utility of the trade is:

$$P(\text{trade}) = 0.60 \times 4 + 0.40 \times (-1.5) = 1.8$$

If the probability of success were increased, the utility P would increase linearly. But investors do not feel the same about different rewards. Given a scale of 0 to 100 (negative to positive reaction), an investor may rank a 60% chance of a $4,000 profit and a 40% chance of a $1,500 loss both as a 65. If the reward is increased to $8,000 while the risk remains at $1,500, the investor might only raise the preference of the trade to 80, although the utility would be 4.2, more than twice as large.

The various curves drawn through the computed utilities represent the risk preference of the individual. Figure 46.2 shows these curves progressing from extreme risk aversion to extreme risk seeking. As the risk increases in (1), the trader is risk-averse and less likely to participate in the trade; in (3), there is equal chance of taking the trade at all risk levels; and in (5), the trader is risk seeking and is more likely to enter a trade that has higher risk.

The Efficient Frontier

There are a large number of performance profiles that result from combining trading strategies, a diverse selection of stocks, futures, ETF, and funds, and the amount of leverage used. Each of these investments can be described in terms of its annualized rate of return and its annualized risk. Risk is most often the standard deviation of the annual returns; however, other measurements will be discussed in the next sections.

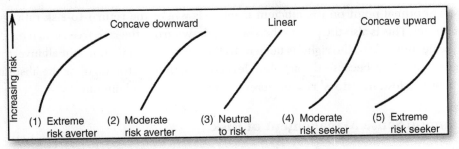

FIGURE 46.2 **Investor Utility Curves.**

Source: R. J. Teweles, C. V. Harlow, and H. L. Stone, *The Commodity Futures Game: Who Wins, Who Loses, Why?* (New York: McGraw-Hill, 1974), 133. © 1974. Reprinted with permission of The McGraw-Hill Companies.

The *efficient frontier* is a way of visualizing which choices would be made by any rational investor. Suppose there were 8 different investment programs, and all of them reported their annualized rate of return and the annualized risk. These could then be plotted in Figure 46.3. Let us also assume that these investments represented a good sample of all risk and return combinations.

A *rational investor* is one who wants the highest return for the lowest risk. Therefore, given a choice between investment *D* and investment *C,* we would choose *C* because it had the same risk but a substantially higher return. Similarly, if we were given a choice between investment *D* and investment *A,* we would choose investment *A* because it has the same return with a much lower risk. Given a choice of any two investments, displayed on a chart of risk and return, a rational investor will always choose the one that is higher and to the left.

The efficient frontier is a curve plotted through those investment alternatives that have the highest returns for a given risk, or the lowest risk for a given return. An investor seeking greater returns with a higher tolerance for risk will choose an investment further to the right on the curve; one with a lower risk tolerance must select a program farther to the left and lower, with less return.

FIGURE 46.3 **The Efficient Frontier.** The line drawn From *R,* the risk-free return, touches the efficient frontier at the point of best return to risk ratio, *B.*

The optimal point on the efficient frontier is where the return-to-risk ratio is a maximum. This is also the point where a line, drawn from the risk-free return on the left scale upwards to the right, is tangent to the curve. Nevertheless, not all investors choose this point because the absolute level of risk may be too high, or the absolute returns too low. Investors' risk preferences are personal and unique.

Common Sense Management of Risk

Risk control is as much an issue of common sense as it is complex rules and mathematics. Most of this chapter shows how various rules, measurements, and leveraging techniques can reduce risk for both discretionary and algorithmic trading; however, successful traders have applied common sense, without complex formulas, for a long time. Some of these successful principles are:

1. *Only risk a small amount of total capital on any one trade.* The total amount risked should allow you to comfortably survive a number of losses in a row. No trade should ever risk more than 5% of the invested capital.
2. *Know your exit conditions in advance.* There should be a clear exit criterion for every trade, even if the exact loss cannot be known in advance.
3. *Large profits mean large risk.* If the average profits or average losses are too large relative to the investment, then smaller positions should be taken.
4. *Exit a trade quickly.* Exit a trade as soon as you recognize that it has gone wrong. Don't try to manage the loss. Many floor traders believe that the smartest trader is the first one out.
5. *Don't meet margin calls.* Experienced traders believe that a margin call is an objective statement of a trade that's gone wrong, or a system that is not meeting expectations. It is a time to review trading performance rather than invest more.
6. *Liquidate your worst position first when lightening up.* The profitable trades have proved that they are trending or performing properly; the losing ones have proved they are not. Stay with the good positions and liquidate the worst.
7. *Be consistent with your trading philosophy.* If you are a trend follower, then keep losses small and let profits run. You cannot be a trend follower by taking profits whenever they occur.
8. *Be sure the trading profile is compatible with your risk preference.* You cannot follow a strategy that takes risks that are uncomfortably large. Be sure that profile is agreeable to you.
9. *Plan for contingencies.* Nothing ever goes as planned, and you must be prepared for infrequent but important exceptions, such as a price shock. Do not be undercapitalized.

■ Liquidity

The ability to implement any trading program is directly related to the liquidity of the market. Even though liquidity can have more than one meaning, lack of liquidity has only one trading result—poor execution. A *liquid* market does not necessarily mean good fills, but an *illiquid* market assures bad ones. Two types of illiquidity most often encountered in the markets are:

1. *Fast markets,* in which there are mostly buyers or sellers, and few traders willing to take the other side of the position.
2. *Inactive markets,* usually the smaller cap stocks, deferred futures contracts, and many ETFs, where there is less commercial or institutional interest.

The fast market is the result of developing news or an economic report where everyone has the same interpretation of the direction that prices should move. In futures this may be combined with a supply/demand imbalance or a perceived imbalance. Once a large number of buy orders flood the market, specialists, market makers, and locals all stand aside (or widen the bid-asked spread and offer very small quantity) rather than be run over. The few arbitrageurs, hedgers, and risk-seeking traders willing to take the opposite position do little to offset the vast number of orders that continue to push prices in one direction. In the inactive market, a large premium must be paid to attract another trader to take the opposite side. This only succeeds when the bid or offered price clearly appears to give the other trader a guaranteed short-term profit.

An illiquid market causes poor executions, which is the largest part of transaction costs and is sometimes too large to overcome. Ginter and Richie[3] have described this as a function of the order size, volume, and the speed of the market, in a single formula that applies to the futures markets, but could be adapted to individual equities:

$$C = K \times \frac{Q \times V}{L_c \times L_o}$$

where
- C = cost of execution due to liquidity
- Q = size of the order entered
- V = volatility of the market
- L_c = volume of the market (all contract months for futures or possibly the combined volume of highly correlated equities)
- L_o = volume of the specific delivery month or individual equity
- K = constant factor

The volatility V might be the daily price range, annualized volatility, or implied volatility. This provides a way to measure how much volume would move the market a specified number of points. The total volume (liquidity) L_c is important because it implies liquidity due to interdelivery spreading in futures. If applied to stocks, added liquidity may come from activity in a closely correlated industrial group. Volume also serves as a measurement of the general interest in the product or in the related stock group. Increased trading in other futures market delivery months, or in similar stocks, is a sign of growing interest.

---

[3] G. Ginter and J. Richie, "Data Errors and Price Distortions," in Perry J. Kaufman, ed., *Technical Analysis in Commodities* (New York: John Wiley & Sons, 1980).

The constant factor K varies according to the type of the execution order being placed and the current direction of the price with regard to that order. If prices are moving higher and a buy order is placed, K will be large; if prices are moving higher and a sell order is placed, K will be smaller. The investor can see that transaction costs, including commissions and execution slippage, will have considerably greater impact on systems that trade more often, have smaller average profits, and trade in the direction of the trend. Given a choice between systems of equal gross profits, the investor should favor the method of fewest trades in the most liquid markets.

■ Measuring Return and Risk

Risk and return are the two most important criteria for measuring performance and for determining that one trading method is better than another. Looking at only returns is not enough. However, the ways in which these and other measures can be combined to express the quality of performance varies considerably. For example, returns are often the annualized rate of return, but they can also be expressed as the slope of a straight line drawn through the daily or monthly returns. Risk has many more variations from the annualized standard deviation of returns to measurements of drawdown and time to recovery. The following section gives an overview of these techniques.

Risk Characteristics of a Trading Model

Before either risk or returns can be measured, it is necessary to have a strategy that has produced historic results, whether real or theoretical. The use of actual trading results is always better because it will show larger equity swings than hypothetical performance, regardless of how conscientiously you have performed the development and testing. Hypothetical results are always optimistic. In some cases, techniques such as analyzing trends in returns do not work with theoretical results but can be a great benefit in real trading.

Suppose there is a choice of systems to trade, and the daily equity of each is available. If only one can be selected, which should it be? There are some characteristics of performance that are normally considered better:

1. Larger profits rather than smaller profits because it leaves more room for execution error.
2. Upwards equity surges (profits) over downward surges (losses).
3. A shorter time-to-recovery rather than prolonged drawdowns.
4. Less time in the market because it avoids price shocks.

Results are always relative. If your choice is between a buy-and-hold portfolio in stocks with a return of 8% and risk of 11%, compared to a simple moving average system of S&P futures with 12% returns and 13% risk, then the moving average system is clearly better, although far from being a money machine. To find the best choice always include a benchmark. Most often this is the result of a theoretical portfolio of 60% stocks (using the S&P) and 40% Treasury bonds (using the Lehman Brothers Treasury Index).

The Sharpe Ratio and Information Ratio

The classic measurement of performance is the *Sharpe ratio* (SR), expressed as

$$SR = \frac{E - I}{\sigma}$$

where E = the expected return (the annualized rate of return)
   I = the risk-free interest rate (usually the 3-month rate)
   σ = the standard deviation, or fluctuation, of the periodic returns (the annualized volatility)

In calculations for the annualized rate of return and annualized volatility, for practical purposes, I is often omitted, with the simplified form called the *information ratio*, the most common performance statistic. The risk-free return, I, cannot be omitted when there is interest income on unused capital, or on some part of the account balance, that has been imbedded in the performance. For futures trading, interest can be earned daily on a large part of the market-to-market value of the account. For a comparison of different investments, it is necessary to specifically identify which returns include interest income. In the world of Commodity Trading Advisors (CTAs), there may be a performance hurdle, such as the yield on the 3-month Treasury bill, before any incentive is paid.

The Sharpe and information ratios satisfy the first universal criterion of system selection, that all else being equal (primarily risk), higher profits are better. It does not satisfy either of the other criteria illustrated in Figure 46.4 because it cannot distinguish between:

1. Consecutive small losses (System B) and alternating small losses (System A), shown in Figure 46.4a.
2. Large surges of profits and large losses, shown in Figure 46.4b.

Clearly, System *A* is best in both cases. Also note that performance of monthly returns is always better than results based on daily returns because it is inherently smoothed. It is unlikely that the end-of-month net asset value (NAV) will be either the lowest or highest of the month, although highest is more likely than lowest.

Treynor Ratio   An additional measure of return to risk is the *Treynor ratio* (TR), the annualized return less the risk-free return, all divided by beta, the relative volatility of the current portfolio compared to a benchmark, usually the S&P

$$TR_t = \frac{AROR_t - I}{\beta_t}$$

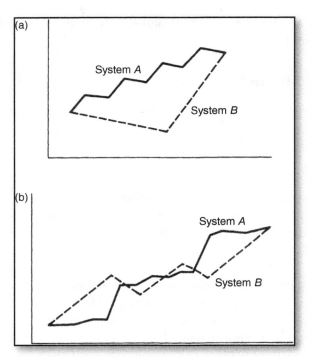

FIGURE 46.4 Two Cases in Which the Sharpe Ratio Falls Short. (a) The order in which profits and losses occur. (b) Surges in profits versus evenly distributed losses.

Average Maximum Retracement

Schwager[4] has presented a comprehensive study of risk and return evaluation techniques. Although each method may emphasize a particular equity trait, he seems to favor the *Average Maximum Retracement* (AMR). This method finds the average equity drawdown, the difference between the current value in the account and the highest past value, by ignoring all days when equity was on new highs.

$$AMR_t = \frac{1}{n} \sum_{i=t-n+1}^{t} POS\left(MCE_i - TE_i\right)$$

where $POS(X) = \begin{cases} x & \text{if } x > 0 \\ 0 & \text{if } x < 0 \end{cases}$

and MCE = closed-out equity (realized profits) on any trade entry date prior to i

TE_i = total equity on day i

n = total number of days of equity data or the calculation period

---

[4] Jack D. Schwager, *A Complete Guide to the Futures Markets* (New York: John Wiley & Sons, 1984).

When $TE_i > MCE_i$, then equity is on a new high and all traders will have a profit on day i, regardless of when they began. Schwager suggests that a much simpler computation would use only the low equity day of each month; it would give a rough but good approximation.

Measuring only the drawdowns is a concept similar to *semivariance* and is valuable because the distribution of profitable returns compared to losing returns is not symmetric; therefore, the standard deviation does not express it correctly and may bias the results in favor of profitable days, giving you an understated picture of risk.

Largest Loss and the Calmar Ratio

Measurements such as Schwager's AMR, and even the basic standard deviation, are good for comparing the long-term performance of one system against another; however, they lack a certain reality of simply looking at the largest loss seen over the test period. John Sweeney calls this the *maximum adverse excursion,*[5] advocating that traders should minimize the size of their largest loss.

Consider the standard deviation of equity changes, showing that in any month there is a 68% chance that your returns will be between 15% and −5% (a mean of 5% and a standard deviation of 10%). There is only a 2.5% chance that you will lose more than 15% in one month (2 standard deviations, one sided); therefore, there is a 50% chance you will lose that 15% in one of the first 20 months (20 ÷ 2.5). Yet probability shows that you should lose more if you keep trading or less if you stop sooner.

The largest historic loss, called the *maximum drawdown,* is a practical alternative. It simply states that the trading program *did* lose 15% during one month of a 3-year test. While it is possible, and even likely, that the program will have a larger loss in the future, you must be prepared for a 15% loss in a single month. The relationship of the drawdown to the returns are expressed as the *Calmar ratio*

$$Calmar\ ratio_t = \frac{AROR_t}{Max\ drawdown_t}$$

where *max drawdown* as of day t is the largest historic drawdown, peak to valley, from the beginning of the data to today.

Using the historic drawdown is practical but not without problems. In the previous chapter on testing, there were many cases where final system profile benefitted from unintentional overfitting. Even when parameters were chosen from a robust section of the test surface, they might all have looked good because the timing avoided a particularly bad price shock. Then the theoretical maximum drawdown might be understated. Even if not overfitted, then the future always brings larger profits and especially larger drawdowns.

---

[5] John Sweeney, "Maximum Adverse Excursions for Stops," *Technical Analysis of Stocks & Commodities* (April 1987).

Sortino Ratio

A variation on both the Sharpe ratio and semivariance, the *Sortino ratio* includes only the downside risk in the denominator and replaces the risk-free threshold with a minimum acceptable return (MAR) in the numerator. Then the Sortino ratio is calculated as

$$SR_t = \frac{AROR_t - MAR}{\sigma(PE_t - E_t)}$$

MAR may be the risk-free rate of return or any other threshold set by the investor. The denominator is the standard deviation of all the negative equity excursions, the difference between the peak equity (*PE*) and the current equity (*E*), not equal to zero, on each day during the calculation period.

Ulcer Index

Investors have increased anxiety as current returns drop farther below the highest returns previously achieved. This can be measured by the *Ulcer Index (UI)*[6] a form of semivariance, similar to Schwager's *Average Maximum Retracement*, that produces a statistical measure of relative declines on all days that were not new high returns.

$$UI_t = \sqrt{\frac{\sum_{i=t-n+1}^{t} D_i^2}{n}}$$

where D = the difference between the highest equity as of day *i* and the actual equity on day *i*

n = the number of days in the equity stream

If the equity on day *i* is a new high equity, then $D_i = 0$. As *UI* increases, investors are more anxious about performance.

Potential Risk

Risk is never a single value; it is a probability, and the standard deviation is the tool most often used for finding that relationship. Even if a drawdown has occurred that is larger than the previous maximum drawdown, there is still a small chance that another, even larger drawdown will occur. It is unreasonable to think that all future losses will be smaller than the maximum already experienced. This *potential for loss* can be expressed as a probability with two different measurements over *n* days:

---

[6] Created by Peter Martin in 1987, it appeared in a book by Peter Martin and Byron McCann, *The Investor's Guide to Fidelity Funds* (New York: John Wiley & Sons, 1989).

1. *Probability of a drawdown* (DP). This is essentially the method used by Schwager and the Ulcer Index. Calculate the standard deviation of all daily drawdowns, D_i, measured from the most recent equity high to today's equity value. When today's equity is also a new high equity, the value used is zero.

$$DP = stdev(D_i)$$

where $i = 1, n$, and n is only those days where a drawdown existed, that is $D_i \neq 0$.

2. *Semivariance (SV)*. Calculate the linear regression of the equity stream or *NAV*, then find the standard deviation of all drawdowns, D_i, below the corresponding value of the straight line fit, p'_i. Semivariance will produce a smaller value than DP because the values on the straight line will be lower than the peak equity.

DP is a more conservative version of both Schwager and the Ulcer Index because it omits those days on which the equity made a new high. The standard deviation will be increased in proportion to the number of days omitted. With either measure, DP and SV represent the value of 1 standard deviation. Therefore, there is a 16% chance that there will be a drawdown greater than DP or SV over the next n days. There is only a 2.5% chance of a drawdown of twice that amount over the next n days.

Either of these measurements can be used to form a ratio of return to risk, called a *drawdown ratio* (DR):

$$DR_t = AROR_t / DP_t$$

or

$$DR_t = AROR_t / SV_t$$

where $AROR_t$ = the annualized return on investment on day t.

These ratios satisfy all three of the original criteria: higher profits are favored because the rate of return is in the numerator, the order of profits and losses will result in larger and smaller net equity drops, and large gains are not penalized because only the drawdowns are used to measure risk.

Conservative investors may want to include some additional simple considerations of potential risk. All else being equal, systems will have greater risk if:

1. They are tested with smaller samples.
2. They have few historic equity drops (also likely to be a poor sample).
3. They concentrate on fewer product groups (not well diversified).
4. They compound positions.

Annualized Volatility The *annualized volatility* is mentioned separately because is it the most common way to express risk. It is simply the annualized standard deviation.

$$V_t = \sigma(r_i) \times \sqrt{252}, \ i = t - n + 1, \ t$$

where r represents the returns for the past n days and 252 is the number of trading days in the year. Analysts simply call this *volatility*. Even though we know that returns are not symmetric, this remains the most common measurement of risk. In portfolio analysis, this will be used to determine the *target volatility*.

Value at Risk   *Value at Risk* (VaR) is used in most companies to assess whether the current market positions are likely to produce a loss that is unacceptably large over the next few days. It is different from volatility given in the previous section because it attempts to *anticipate risk*, even though it is done using historic risk. This is done by finding the probability of loss of the current market positions based on past market movement. For example, Bank Two holds large short positions in fixed income futures to protect loan commitments at current levels. They also hold a wide variety of foreign currencies, of which 50% are hedged with forward contracts. If interest rates drop or the U.S. dollar strengthens, they could show large losses in their futures positions. According to bank policy, the loss allowed in a single day must be kept to under 0.5% of cash value of these commitments. If there is a potential risk exceeding that amount, the futures position must be immediately reduced.

VaR is a combination of cross-correlations between markets for which there is exposure, the position sizes, the volatility of those markets, the projected time period over which the risk will be forecast, and a confidence interval to determine the risk tolerance. Using the return series for the interest rate and FX exposure held by Bank Two, the *variance-covariance* solution for VaR can be calculated as[7]

$$VaR = \sqrt{\sigma_{IR}^2 + \sigma_{FX}^2 + (2 \times \rho_{IR,FX} \times \sigma_{IR} \times \sigma_{FX})}$$

where σ = the standard deviation of the return series for the individual markets
   p = the cross-correlation between the two return series

In this example, the return series reflects the position size and volatility of the exposure. This formula implies a VaR projected period of 1 day.

For example, Bank Two holds 1 million in EURUSD, which have a daily standard deviation of 0.565%. If the current EURUSD rate is 1.25, then the market value of the position is USD 1.25 million. It also holds a EUR 1 million position in 10-year Eurobond, which show a standard deviation of 0.605% and a market value of USD 1.25 million. Using 1.65 standard deviations to represent the 95% confidence level, and making the assumption that r_i/σ_i is normally distributed, and the EURUSD exchange rate should not drop more than $0.565 \times 1.65 = 0.932\%$ (less than 1%) on a single day, 95% of the time. The Eurobond should drop less than $0.605 \times 1.65 = 0.998\%$ on a single day. We could then expect the approximate risk of the FX position to be USD 1.25 million $\times 0.932\% =$ USD 11,650 and the risk of the Eurobund position to be \$1.25 million $\times 0.998\% =$ USD 12,475 over the next 24 hours.

[7] Jacques Longerstaey, *RiskMetrics*™ *Technical Document*, 4th ed. (Morgan Guaranty Trust Company, riskmetrics@jpmorgan.com).

The total risk of the FX and Eurobund positions is not the sum of the two risks, because correlations between the two markets may show that price movement of one market is partially offset by opposite movement in the other market. In this example, the correlation of the returns of two markets is -0.27, showing that there is a noticeable offsetting effect. Applying these values to the previous formula gives

$$VaR_t = \sqrt{12475^2 + 11650^2 + \left(2 \times -0.27 \times 12475 \times 11650\right)}$$

$$VaR_t = \text{USD } 17,068$$

The value at risk for the next 24 hours is far less than the sum of the two individual market risks because their price movements tend to offset each other.

A more general calculation of VaR uses separate values for the underlying prices, the position size, the time period, and the confidence interval. For three assets, this is

$$VaR_i = CI \times \sqrt{P}$$

$$\times \sqrt{w_1^2 x_1^2 \sigma_1^2 + w_2^2 x_2^2 \sigma_2^2 + w_3^2 x_3^2 \sigma_3^2 + 2w_1 w_2 x_1 x_2 \sigma_1 \sigma_2 r_{12} + 2w_1 w_3 x_1 x_3 \sigma_1 \sigma_3 r_{13} + 2w_2 w_3 x_2 x_3 \sigma_2 \sigma_3 r_{23}}$$

where CI = the confidence interval (expressed as 1.65 standard deviations for a 5% probability)

P = the VaR calculation period (5 is a projected period of 5 days)

w_i = the weighting factor, or relative position size

x_t = the current value or price of the asset on the current day t

σ_i = the annualized volatility, shown below

r_{ij} = the cross-correlation between market i and market j

The volatility, σ_i, is calculated using the prices, x_i, over n days, as the standard deviation of the price changes, annualized:

$$\sigma_i = \sqrt{252} \times stdev(d_i)$$

$$d_i = \frac{x_t - x_{t-1}}{x_{t-1}} \text{ over the past } n \text{ days}$$

The square root of 252 is used to annualize the daily values.

In the practical implementation of risk control, VaR would be calculated before the close of trading and, if its value exceeds the threshold amount, action can be taken to reduce the exposure on the same day.

Generalized VaR Calculation   The probability of loss at the end of a forecast period, P_E, is calculated as the difference between the cumulative percentage loss over that period and the cumulative expected return, dividing this value by the cumulative standard deviation, and applying the standard deviation of a normal distribution to give a probability estimate.[8]

---

[8] Mark Kritzman and Don Rich, "The Mismeasurement of Risk," *Financial Analysts Journal* (May/June 2002). This entire section uses material from the Kritzman and Rich article.

$$P_E = N\left[\frac{\ln(1+L) - \mu T}{\sigma\sqrt{T}}\right]$$

where $N[\ ]$ = the cumulative normal distribution function
         L = the cumulative percentage loss in periodic units
         μ = the annualized expected return in continuous units
         T = the number of years in the horizon, where 1 day is $\frac{1}{252}$
         σ = the standard deviation of continuous units

In this process, the compounding of periodic returns results in a lognormal distribution, while the continuous returns and standard deviation are normally distributed. To calculate VaR, this calculation is changed to specify the probability, Z, and solve for the size of the threshold loss.

$$VaR = -(e^{\mu T - Z\sigma\sqrt{T}} - 1)W$$

where   e = the base of the natural logarithm (2.7128)
         Z = the chosen probability deviate (for example, 5% is 1.65)
         W = the initial value of the asset

The result of this calculation gives the probability of loss at the end of the period, T, and does not reflect any losses that might have occurred during the period (if T is greater than 1 day). Losses during the period will always be at least as large as the loss at the end of the period.

A Simpler Value at Risk   There are three calculation methods associated with Value at Risk: variance-covariance, historical, and Monte Carlo. The section above discussed the classic variance-covariance approach, but most analysts will find the historical method easier to implement and intuitively simpler. In essence, to calculate the VaR for today, take today's market positions and apply them to the data from the past, say, 1 year (252 days). Specifically,[9]

1. Given n markets or assets, each with positions (contracts or shares) $w_1, w_2, \ldots, w_n$.
2. Calculate the returns for the past k days ($k = 252$) as $r_i = p_i/p_{i-1} - 1$, $i = t - k + 1, t$.
3. Calculate the total returns for day i as $R_i = w_1 r_{1i} + w_2 r_{2i} + \ldots + w_n r_{2i}$. Include the forex and conversion factors (for futures) if applicable so that the total returns are all in USD, euros, or any single currency.
4. Find the average, $\overline{R}$, and standard deviation, s, of R over the k days.
5. Given a confidence level specified in standard deviations (e.g., 99% = 2.33), the VaR for the current day, t, is $\overline{R} - 2.33s$. VaR is always expressed as a negative number.

---

[9] Thanks to Robert Ehbar, Mizuho Alternative Investments, for his help in this section.

Price Shocks and Realistic Distributions   Value at risk is a good indication of risk under most market conditions, but is known to be a poor measurement during extreme, highly correlated price moves across market sectors. It has been said that VaR works _except_ when you need it the most—when the risk is greatest. A _stress test_ is used to find out how VaR performs under extreme cases. This isolates specific market periods, such as price shocks, or can use simulated data in which all prices reverse direction and make a 2-to-3 standard deviation move with very high correlation, as in the subprime collapse in late 2008.

The assumption of a normal distribution in either returns or price movement is not realistic, an opinion held by Benoit Mandelbrot, among others, who maintained that using the standard deviation of equity changes underestimates the real risk of the financial markets.[10] Most return distributions are skewed and have a fat tail due to the application of conservation of capital and the unusually long, nonrandom distribution of runs. A log distribution could be substituted for a normal distribution, but this tends to be more extreme than necessary. The degree of fat tail present in the distribution can be measured using _kurtosis_,

$$k = \frac{\sum_{i}^{n} r_i^4}{n\sigma^4}$$

where r_i = the return on day i
σ^2 = the variance
n = the number of days

A normal distribution has a kurtosis of 3, but the actual returns series might have a kurtosis as large as 25, indicating a significant fat tail. Although the non-normal distribution can be identified, there does not seem to be a simple solution for the form of the distribution that can be applied to VaR. When extreme distributions exist, the practical solution is to perform stress tests to recognize the potential risk during extreme cases and treat these as exceptions in the same way that crisis management might be used during a price shock. Advanced work with VaR focuses primarily on alternative distributions and unexpected, extreme risk.

Hindenburg Omen   The _Hindenburg Omen_[11] is a price pattern that attempts to forecast a stock market crash. It is named after the famous Hindenburg disaster of May 6, 1937, during which the German Zeppelin _Hindenburg_ exploded and burned. The basis for the calculation is Norman Fosback's _High Low Logic Index_ (HLLI), which is the lesser of the NYSE new highs or new lows divided by the number of NYSE issues traded, then smoothed using an exponential moving average. The premise is that, under normal conditions, a large number of stocks either make new highs or new lows, but not both at the same time. The existence of both indicates a specific case of potential volatility. Specifically, on a given day,

---

[10] B. B. Mandelbrot, "A Multifractional Walk Down Wall Street," _Scientific American_ (February 1999).

[11] According to Wikipedia, the Hindenburg Omen originated with Jim Miekka, and the name was suggested by the late Kennedy Gammage.

- The number of NYSE new 52-week highs and the number of new 52-week lows are greater than or equal to 2.8% of the total issue that advance or decline that day. Note that the percentage 2.8, was raised from a previous level of 2.5 as overall market volatility has increased.

- The NYSE index is greater than it was 50 trading days ago.

- The McClellan Oscillator is negative.

- The new 52-week highs cannot be more than twice the 52-week lows, although the new lows may exceed the new highs by any amount.

- The combination of events must occur on 3 consecutive days.

Once the signal has occurred, a stock market crash is expected within 30 trading days, but only when the McClellan Oscillator is negative.

Depending on your definition of a "crash," a drop between 5% and 50%, you could expect the Hindenburg Omen to be successful about 25% of the time. Most recently, these included August 12, 20, 24, 25, and 31, 2010.

Risk Characteristics of Systems

Every trading method has its unique risk and return pattern. In general, a trend system has many smaller losses and fewer larger profits. A mean-reverting system has the opposite; many smaller profits and fewer larger losses. This is similar to the choices available with gambling strategies.

Even among trending systems there are enormous differences in trading risk. A typical moving average system, which qualifies under *conservation of capital,* keeps individual trade losses small compared to individual profits, but may have a series of losses that when combined, add up to one very large loss. In addition, trend systems fail when they encounter a sideways period, and frequently reverse from long to short and back again until prices finally pick a direction. Tests show that the number of trend trades cannot be reduced below a threshold level, even if the trend calculation period is very long. All trends seem to get caught in a sideways price pattern that generates a series of small losses.

A breakout system, the other very popular trending technique, exchanges a much larger risk for much greater reliability than moving average or exponential smoothing. When a new long position is entered at a new high price for a specific time period, the risk is defined as the price needed to make a new low for the same period. Therefore, the trade risk at the time of entry is the difference between the highest and lowest closing prices, or the highest high and lowest low for the period, n,

$$Trade\ risk = max(High, n) - min(Low, n)$$

Risk-Adjusted Returns   In order to choose one trading method over another, it is necessary to test them over the same time period and risk-adjust the returns. For example, if system A had an annualized return of 15% and an annualized risk of 10%, while system B had returns of 25% and a risk of 16%, we would multiply the returns of system *A* by 16/10 or 1.6 to get an adjusted return of 24%. Then system *B* would be slightly better. If you are not interested in the size of the returns then finding the information ratio, dividing the returns by the corresponding risk, 1.5 for system *A*, and 1.56 for system *B*, would give you the normalized relationships.

Time to Recovery A trading program that recovers quickly from losses is more desirable than a program that lingers at its lowest level of loss. The fact that a program recovers quickly does not change its level of absolute risk (maximum drawdown), but it will change the annualized volatility, measured using a standard deviation, or any statistic that averages the daily negative excursions.

Stability of Returns The most common calculation of returns is the average of the individual annualized returns; therefore, if a trading program returned 24%, 18%, 20%, 15%, and 19% in 5 consecutive years, most investors would see this as an average return of 19.2%. Another equally valid method is to find the slope of a straight line through the cumulative returns, 24%, 42%, 62%, 77%, and 96%. This gives the annualized returns as 17.9% because it reflects the slight tendency for returns to decline.

A systematic way of determining if your system worked better in the past but has been struggling in more recent markets is to find the slope through the annualized returns (monthly returns if much less data). If the slope is rising or sideways, then the system is performing well. If the slope is noticeably declining, then performance is decaying; it is not adjusting to current or changing markets.

How Much Bigger Could the Risk Really Be? Many of the risk measurements described in this section attempt to express the probability of a future loss. Within reason, many of them succeed, with VaR being the most likely. An investor must distinguish between the calculated probability and the effects of a real loss. If there was only a 1% chance of a 50% loss in a single month, then by the 50th month there would have been a 50% chance of a 50% loss. There is also a large error factor in most of these calculations because the amount of data used to find the statistics was too small. If 100 cases were used, there is a 10% chance of error in the results. The value of the measurement is also dependent upon the period in the market that was used to create these values; the risk in crude oil was exceptionally high during the Gulf War and then again in 2007. If those periods are not included, based on the assumption that they were outliers, the results will not reflect the future risk of trading crude oil.

It's Not the Markets, It's the Money

At the risk of repeating this too many times, market trends and market shocks are caused by institutions and investors moving money. When all markets move together it is not the fundamentals, it is simply panic. Under stress, investors withdraw money from every type of investment, causing them all to reverse and the correlations to go to 1.

Money seeks a safer place during times of extreme uncertainty, and this is seen as stock prices drop on widespread selling and bond prices rise on widespread buying. In 2011 and 2012, short-term rates went negative—investors were willing to pay the government to hold their money just to gain safety. No amount of correlation analysis or diversification will protect an investment from a price shock in which all markets move the same way based on a flight to safety. No amount of insightful analysis would have allowed for interest rates to go negative.

■ Leverage

Leverage is controlling an asset using less money than the face value of that asset (also called the *exposure*). If you bought a gold futures contract on 10% margin, then you are depositing only $16,000 to control the value of an asset worth $160,000, 100 ounces of gold at $1600/ounce. Then every price changing in gold, up or down, is magnified 10 times. If gold drops $10/ounce, then you make or lose $10 × 100 ounces = $1000. In the current volatile environment, gold can easily move $25 each day, or $2500, over 15% of your deposit. That is great when it's a profit, and horrible when it's a loss.

The consequences of leverage are readily seen by measuring the volatility of returns, and the consequences of high and low leverage will be discussed; however, leverage also plays a crucial role in both the trading strategy and the portfolio structure. Futures and options markets offer exceptionally high leverage opportunities, and some traders and analysts act as though they are obligated to take advantage of the maximum allowable. Without leverage, many futures prices show less risk than stocks. In stocks, leverage is only achieved by borrowing up to 50% of the face value of the stock, and that works best when interest rates are low. For the most part, the discussion in this chapter applies to futures. Leverage also allows you the flexibility to balance the risk of a portfolio.

Rules for Trading on Margin   A few rules should be understood at the beginning. Trading in futures is highly risky because of the leverage. Each exchange sets the *minimum margin* based on price volatility, but the investment house, or broker, often sets that number higher for their smaller customers. In addition, they may require a minimum deposit. They need to protect themselves in the event that a price shock wipes out the entire value of their customer's account and they are left making up the loss.

Commercials, those businesses dealing in commodities, can often put up only 5% rather than 10%. In some cases they substitute a letter of credit rather than any cash. In addition, they *sweep the account* each evening, removing any excess profits and replenishing any losses. There is no audit of how the positions taken by commercials offset business risk, so it is very common for these businesses to speculate under the guise of hedging. When the CFTC publishes its Commitment of Traders report, separating the open interest into speculators and commercials, those who believe that the hedge positions are offsetting physical exposure might be surprised.

Margin Rules and Volatility The rules of brokerage houses require that an investor replenish the amount in his or her account back to the full amount if the loss on any futures position exceeds 25% of the initial margin. If you were required to put up $16,000 for one gold contract, and gold fell $40, you would get a margin call that required another $4,000 deposited by the next day. If you capitalized the account at more than the initial margin, which is the usual process, then that $4,000 can be taken from the excess in the account. Because $40 is a move of only 2.5%, it is very impractical to have only $25,000 in an account that trades 1 contract of gold. If you started with $50,000, then your leverage is not really 10:1, based on margin, but only about 3:1, based on the entire investment. The minimum funds required by your broker is negotiable, based on your financial solvency and the size of the positions you trade, but can never be less than the minimum exchange margin.

Volatility will vary across markets, and the margin does not always reflect the difference in risk. Exchanges do not change the margin requirements often, and volatility must increase or decrease substantially, and remain at that level, before the exchange governors meet for their review.

Reserves and Targeted Risk Levels

How much do you really need in your trading account to be "safe" and still leverage your returns? During the past 10 years, the hedge fund managers and CTAs have gotten much more conscientious about identifying risk and figuring out the leverage needed to target a particular level of risk. Using the daily profits and losses from a simulated trading history, the process goes as follows:

1. Record the daily profits and losses.
2. Calculate the standard deviation of those profits and losses.
3. Decide your *target volatility*. That is the amount of risk you are willing to take, expressed as annualized volatility. Typically, this is about 15%.
4. Divide the standard deviation of returns (2) by the target volatility to get the investment size needed to achieve that volatility. If the investment is too big by say 25%, then your positions sizes are too big for the investment. Reduce the size of all your positions by 25%.

As an example, Table 46.1 shows a segment of daily returns. Column 2 (P/L) shows the daily profits and losses trading 1 contract of EURUSD futures using a trend system. At the bottom on column 2 is the annualized standard deviation (the standard deviation $\times$ $\sqrt{252}$). Using a target volatility of 15%, we divide the annualized standard deviation by 0.15 to get the initial investment needed for that volatility, $266,592, which starts column 3. Each P/L change is then added to the initial equity to get the running equity totals. The returns, in column 4, are the P/Ls in column 2 divided by the previous equity value, so that a P/L on 7/26/2011 uses the equity from 7/25/2011. Finally, the NAVs are calculated using $NAV_t = NAV_{t-1} \times (1 + r_t)$. When the annualized standard deviation of the returns is calculated at the bottom of column 4, it comes very close to the target of 15%.

TABLE 46.1 Calculating the Investment Size Based on Target Volatility

Date	P/L	Equity	Returns	NAV
7/19/2011	0	266592		100.00
7/20/2011	−486	266107	−0.0018	99.82
7/21/2011	−1155	264952	−0.0043	99.38
7/22/2011	1692	266643	0.0064	100.02
7/25/2011	1248	267892	0.0047	100.49
7/26/2011	537	268428	0.0020	100.69
7/27/2011	−198	268230	−0.0007	100.61
7/28/2011	−198	268032	−0.0007	100.54
7/29/2011	1750	269782	0.0065	101.20
8/1/2011	−1108	268673	−0.0041	100.78
8/2/2011	2648	271322	0.0099	101.77
8/3/2011	2544	273865	0.0094	102.73
8/4/2011	−863	273002	−0.0032	102.40
8/5/2011	−852	272150	−0.0031	102.08
8/8/2011	7164	279314	0.0263	104.77
8/9/2011	3477	282791	0.0124	106.08
8/10/2011	4819	287609	0.0170	107.88
8/11/2011	−3827	283782	−0.0133	106.45
8/12/2011	−1038	282744	−0.0037	106.06
8/15/2011	1797	284541	0.0064	106.73
Ann StDev	39989		14.5%	
Target Vol	15%			
Investment	266592			

It may seem surprising that an average daily P/L of $1968 requires an investment as large as $266,592, 135 times the average, but one standard deviation of this sample is nearly $40,000, and we can expect to lose at least 2 or 2.5 standard deviations over time, or $100,000. That would be 37% of the initial investment. Then 15% volatility is an aggressive target.

Reserves are the excess funds in the account not used for margin or committed for other purposes. Reserves are needed to cover losses and continue to trade at the targeted level of volatility. Reserves will vary as the position sizes are adjusted in order to keep volatility stable. Most investors, as well as professional managed accounts, set a maximum risk, at which point the positions are liquidated. The maximum level of risk is usually 50%, but it can be as low as 10%. In the previous paragraph, 2.5 standard deviations of the volatility gave a 2.5% chance of a loss greater than 37%, which would be reasonable with a maximum drawdown of 50%. However, a 10% maximum would be equivalent to a target volatility of $\frac{1}{5}$ of 15%, or 3%, which would also reduce the expected returns by 80%. In the real world, the lowest practical volatility target is 6%, more often 8%.

Leverage Based on Exposure

The traditional way to measure leverage uses *exposure*, the actual value of goods purchased. For example, the margin for 1 gold futures contract was raised to $9,450 on August 24, 2011, when gold was trading at about $1,800. That is 5.25% of the contract value, or leverage of 19:1. As mentioned before, a brokerage firm would never allow a customer to open a futures account with $10,000 to buy or sell 1 gold contract. A move of $25, only 1.4%, which happens often, would create a gain or loss of $2,500. If a loss, then the account value would fall to $7,500, generating a margin call and requiring replenishing the account by the next day. Each brokerage firm decides on the minimum account value based on what will be traded, as well as some assessment of the experience and credit history of the trader. For 1 contract of gold, it is likely that the broker will require $50,000, reducing the leverage to 3.6:1, a more likely scenario.

In Europe, some registered funds have leverage limits set by the government. Typically, this can be 2.5 times the current account value. Compared to U.S. regulation, this is very severe. For the gold contract valued at $180,000, the account must set aside $72,000. The biggest problem is with interest rate futures, which are also assessed at face value, although the risk is actually a function of the yield, which goes in the opposite direction. Then when Eurodollar rates are trading at 99.50, yielding only ½% interest, the regulatory authorities require $0.9950 \times \$1,000,000$ (face value), or $995,000 to trade one contract. That essentially eliminates trading Eurodollars in a small investment account because, as we will see in the next section on the calculation of position size, the current low volatility of Eurodollars requires a large position compared to other markets in a diversified portfolio. This risk calculation also causes most funds to choose a different method for calculating risk, such as VaR, which is permitted by European regulators.

Individual Trade Risk

Risk control begins at the moment a position is entered. There are two distinct issues at that time, the strategic element of the trade, for example, the risk and reward of a single share or contract, and the total exposure of that trade relative to the investment amount. We will look at the second one first.

Position Sizing

The traditional way of deciding how many shares to trade in a stock is to divide the total investment by the number of stocks in the portfolio, then divide that portion of the investment by the share price. Then each stock has the same invested amount, but not the same risk. For example, if we were trading four stocks, Apple, Amazon, Microsoft, and Bank of America where each stock had a nominal risk amount of $10,000 on October 7, 2011, the position sizes (line 2 in Table 46.2) could be found as $10,000 divided by the share prices (line 1). Then Bank of America has a very large position, 1695 shares, compared to the other stocks. But it turns out that BAC, trading at a low price, is relatively more volatile than the other stocks and this position size focuses all the risk on BAC.

TABLE 46.2	Comparison of Position Sizes Based on Three Methods			
7-Oct-11	AAPL	AMZN	BAC	MSFT
Close	369.80	224.74	5.90	26.25
10000	27	44	1695	381
Ann Vol	424	246	134	345
AvgTR	71	66	1400	2033
	AAPL	AMZN	BAC	MSFT
10000	62.7	38.1	1.0	4.4
Ann Vol	1.0	1.6	62.7	14.1
AvgTR	1.1	1.0	21.1	30.6

There are three basic ways to calculate the position size of any trade in stocks, given $10,000 to invest:

1. $10,000 divided by the share price
2. $10,000 divided by the dollar value of 100 × annualized volatility
3. $10,000 divided by the average true range × $\sqrt{252}$

Table 46.2 shows the considerable variation in the position size using these three methods. The upper part of the table gives the number of shares, and the lower part normalizes the shares by dividing each value on that row by the lowest value on the row. Then method 1 ("10000") shows that the low price of Bank of America results in a position size 62 times the size of the Apple position. In method 2, the annualized volatility, the results of Bank of America are reversed because the percentage returns of a volatile stock trading at a low price are unusually high. Instead of having the largest position, as in method 1, it has the smallest. Method 3 uses the highs and lows to find the average daily risk, then annualizes the value. This time Amazon has the highest risk and Microsoft the lowest. The three methods produce astonishingly different results.

The problem with calculating size for equities using a method other than (1) is that dividing the funds equally among the stocks does not work. Using method 1, the maximum number of shares for AAPL would be 27, so that there would not be enough money to buy 424 shares required by method 2, or 71 shares for method 3. It will be necessary to pool all of the money and redistribute it in proportion to the number of shares needed. For example, part 1 of Table 46.3 shows the dollar value needed to trade each of the stocks in each method given by Table 46.2. On the far right is the multiplication factor needed to reduce the totals of methods 2 and 3 to the $40,000 available. Part 2 multiplies the values in part 1 by the factor on the respective line, so that the investment required for each method comes to the same $40,000. Part 3 then divides the respective investment amounts from part 2 by the share price to get the actual shares traded.

Methods 2 and 3 in part 3 are fully risk-adjusted, but show a significant difference in the allocations. In method 2, there would be very low exposure to BAC, more to AAPL, and less to MSFT, while method 3 is very different. Which is better? The true

TABLE 46.3 **Adjusting the Shares Traded for Each Method of Position Sizing**

1   Investment amount needed to trade each method

Method	AAPL	AMZN	BAC	MSFT	Total	Factor
10000	10000	10000	10000	10000	40000	1.000
Ann Vol	156784	55331	793	9048	221956	0.180
AvgTR	26241	14922	8262	53357	102782	0.389

2   Total investment redistributed among stocks according to method

Method	AAPL	AMZN	BAC	MSFT	Total
10000	10000	10000	10000	10000	40000
Ann Vol	28255	9972	143	1631	40000
AvgTR	10212	5807	3215	20765	40000

3   Shares actually traded after redistribution of investment

Method	AAPL	AMZN	BAC	MSFT
10000	27	44	1695	381
Ann Vol	76	44	24	62
AvgTR	28	26	545	791

range method is considered a better measure of risk; however, it would be best to test each method over a wide range of stocks and futures and use the average information ratio to draw your own conclusions.

As an example, we will compare the traditional method 1 with method 3 using BAC because it had the greatest variability, and apply a 200-day moving average strategy over the past 20 years. Before discussing the results, it is important to understand that a single test cannot be conclusive because the best method should work regardless of the calculation period or the strategy. First, the total P/L, shown in Figure 46.5, indicates that BAC is not a successful candidate for trend trading, but the average true range method shows far less volatility, 27% lower, than trading

FIGURE 46.5   Total PL for BAC Using Methods 1 and 3, for 20 Years.

FIGURE 46.6 Number of Shares Traded in BAC Using the True Range
Method.

the same shares for each trade (this test used 2201, which was the average shares
traded using the true range method). Figure 46.6 shows a history of the number of
shares traded, with exposure dropping sharply from 1994 to 1996 while prices were
moving steadily higher (see Figure 46.7). Position sizes dropped from about 6000
shares to 1000 shares. The exceptional volatility in 2008 did not cause as much of a
reduction in position size, falling from about 1500 shares to 500 shares. Be reminded
that varying the number of shares based on volatility constantly changes the amount
needed as an investment, so that a rigorous test would need to define the investment
size as the largest amount needed over time.

Even with all the qualifications and calculations, adjusting the position size to
target the same risk on each trade gives each trade an equal chance to participate in
the results. Unless you can select which trades are most likely to be better than another, equal risk is the most conservative approach. Reducing the position size when
the market gets more volatility also prevents the volatility of returns from varying

FIGURE 46.7 Bank of America, Monthly from 1992 Through September 2011.

wildly. The price swings of the past 3 years would easily have resulted in portfolio volatility ranging from very low at 6% to as high as 25% if no attention was paid to position size.

Initial Position Risk

The entry point of a trade is the time of greatest uncertainty. Systematic strategies identify the critical point where the trend should change, but when the calculation uses a large number of days, the lag may cause a delayed reaction. In the case of a moving average system, the trend will converge on current prices during a sideways pattern, at which point the trend direction may flop back and forth until prices move out of the range. The period of greatest trend uncertainty is the point at which it changes direction.

For mean reversion traders, the greatest profits are in anticipating the change in direction of prices. They must buy when prices are falling, clearly an uncertain time. They count on the likelihood that certain moves cannot be sustained for more than a few days or that large moves are overblown. There is considerable uncertainty at the point of entry.

Each trading style has its own intrinsic risk associated with initial entries. The trend philosophy is known for its tenacity, entering a long position whenever prices turn up, taking a small loss if prices then turn down, and reentering the next time they turn up. The breakout technique will limit losses to the size of the current trading range and any attempt to reduce this loss, which can be large in a volatile market, conflicts with the essence of the method. Mean reversion systems must take large losses in exchange for a high percentage of smaller, profitable trades. If losses are limited using stops, then the percentage of profitable trades is reduced, and the profit/loss balance is upset.

Stop-Losses

Stops provide the ability to control risk on individual trades. A *sell stop* is placed below the current price and becomes a *Market Order* to sell once that price is touched. Stops do not guarantee that you are filled at the stop price because opening gaps, fast markets (after an economic report), and low volume can result in large slippage. If the market gaps lower on the open, below your stop order to sell, the order gets filled at the market price. Stops placed close to the price currently being traded are hit frequently. Because of the nature of price movement, the farther away you place a stop, the less often it is hit. The pattern is very similar to a normal distribution. Using random numbers, the number of times reached multiplied by the size of the stop will always be constant. Then a stop must be better than a random event to be a good trading rule.

The beginning trader may decide that no trade should lose more than $500, and place a stop at that point. Some more experienced traders believe that you should never lose more than 3% of your total investment on a single trade. On some level, it makes sense to scale your losses to the amount of money at risk, but stops are more sensible if they relate to the nature of the system, the timing of the trade, the market volatility, or a chart pattern. Some worthwhile possibilities that change with market conditions are:[12]

1. Advance the stop by a percentage of the price change, as in Wilder's parabolic system.
2. Use a swing high or low point, based on a percentage minimum swing.
3. Use the highest high or lowest low of the recent n periods.
4. Apply a method such as Kaufman's *Adaptive Moving Average* (KAMA) as a stop.
5. Adjust the stop by the volatility, such as 3 times the current 10-day average true range.

Initial Stop   Because the greatest period of uncertainty is at the point of the trade entry, a stop can be placed at that time and never moved. But trend systems already cut losses quickly, and mean reversion systems need a high percentage of profitable trades, the result of holding trades that initially go the wrong way, so it is not clear that any stop-loss would improve those profiles. Under highly volatile situations, they may be a benefit, but that would need to be tested for specific strategies, and the frequency of occurrence would be small.

Trailing Stops   A *trailing stop* is one that captures an increasing part of the profits as prices move in a favorable direction. Some trailing stops advance, but never retreat, as in Wilder's *Parabolic*; others, based on volatility and price changes, may retreat. Trailing stops are usually constructed in one of the following ways:

1. *Fixed percentage.* A long position was entered in IBM at $75 using a moving average. A trailing stop of 3% is calculated based on the highest prior close. The trade is liquidated if either the trend changes or prices fall by 3% from the high point of the trade, whichever comes first. Alternatively, a stop may be a percentage of the trend value and placed at the trendline minus 3% of the trendline, forming a smooth band.
2. *Volatility.* Because price volatility changes, a trailing stop may be calculated using any of the volatility measures discussed earlier, preferably annualized volatility or average true range, and placed below the highest high of the current price move. This method is more adaptable than the fixed percentage; however, when volatility increases, today's stop may move farther away than on the previous day. ISAM has suggested that a generic stop is $12 \times$ *average true range* calculated over the past 252 days; however, this conflicts with the idea that the multiplier should vary based on the calculation period of the trend.
3. *Percentage of profits.* Placing a stop at a point that captures 50% of the profits is a sensible technique except at the beginning of the trade. When there are only small profits, the stop would be too close; therefore, this method can only be used after some profits have already been accumulated in the trade, a *trigger* value. Prior to that, an initial stop would be based on price volatility. Once the profit stop is triggered, the closer of the two stops would be used.

---

[12] Tushar Chande and Stanley Kroll, *The New Technical Trader* (New York: John Wiley & Sons, 1994).

Standard Deviation Stop The standard deviation is the basis for traditional risk assessment, and it can be used to determine stop-loss levels.[13] In her *Dev-stop*, Cynthia Kase uses the following steps to create stop-loss levels for both long and short positions:

1. Calculate the *true range* (TR) of the past two trading days using the highest high and lowest low of the 2-day period.
2. Calculate the rolling *average true range* (ATR) of TR (in Step 1), using 30 periods for intraday charts and 20 periods for daily charts. Note that each period combines 2 days.
3. Calculate the standard deviations (STDEV) of the true ranges in Step 1 using the same 20- and 30-day period as in Step 2.
4. The stop-loss values are $DDEV = ATR + (f \times STDEV)$, where $f = 1$, 2.06 to 2.25, and 3.20 to 3.50, where the larger values of the pairs correct for skew and allow for greater risk.
5. The *dev-stop* for long positions is *trade high* − *DDEV*; the dev-stop for short positions is *trade low* + *DDEV*. *Trade high* and *trade low* are the prices corresponding to the greatest profit in the long and short trades.

This method adjusts for volatility using a standard statistical measurement and is applied to the extreme profit of a trade, in the manner of a trailing stop. In Figure 46.8, an 80-day moving average, the smooth, heavier line, is shown with 30-year bonds. The two other lines above and below prices are the standard deviation stops based on the 80-day price differences and a multiplication factor of 8. That value is then subtracted from the highest price of a long position or added to the lowest price of a short sale. The chart shows that the trend change from long to short, which occurred about December 1, 2010, would have been stopped out at least 15 days earlier. In

FIGURE 46.8 **30-Year Bonds with an 80-Day Moving Average and an 80-Period Standard Deviation with a Factor of 8 Measured from the High or Low of the Trade.**

---

[13] Cynthia Kase, "Redefining Volatility and Position Risk," *Technical Analysis of Stocks & Commodities* (October 1993).

the following short position, the daily high penetrates the stop, but the stop is only activated if prices close above that level. In the most recent long position, the stop is closer to prices than the moving average but manages to stay clear of being hit because it adapts to the price volatility.

Profit Targets   Profit targets are points at which the system captures a profit expected to be larger than the return at the end of the trade, or a short-term windfall, such as a favorable price shock. "Profit taking" may actually net a loss on the trade if a sudden partial recovery from a larger loss looks attractive. Profit targets are essential in short-term trading, where the price noise makes it likely that any favorable move will reverse soon. They are more difficult to incorporate into a longer-term trend-following system because they risk missing the bigger profit (from the fat tail) in exchange for smaller but more frequent profits. As a trend-follower, once you take profits but the trend direction is still intact, you need to find a way to reenter that trade to avoid missing the rare, but very large price move.

Profit-taking is best when it is based on price volatility (V), and is most often calculated as

1. For longs, a multiple of the average true range or annualized volatility added to the system entry point (not the actual fill), $E + f \times V$.
2. A favorable move of $f \times V$ on any single day, or combination of successive days, where f is a multiplication factor.

While any profit target assumes that prices will not continue in the same direction, method 2 may not net a profit on the trade. A large, favorable move may occur after an initial trade loss, and the net return may still be a loss. However, if the extreme move cannot be sustained, then taking a small loss is preferable over a larger loss.

The factors used for the net size of the profit-taking level are usually arrived at by data mining. Not to be outdone, we will look at the various levels of profit-taking applied to a short-term and longer-term moving average system for 60-minute euro currency futures.

In Table 46.4 the 60-minute euro futures are shown with an 80-bar and a 5-bar moving average system where profit-taking has been applied using a factor (shown on the left) multiplied by the average true range over a 20-bar period. Once the profit target has been hit, the system waits for the next trend trade. It cannot reenter the same trend. The top line shows the results with no profit-taking. The longer 80-bar average has the smallest profits but the highest percentage of profitable trades when the profit target is smallest. As the target gets larger, profits get larger. The no-profit case at the top shows that returns were best if there was no profit-taking.

The faster trend on the right shows that profit-taking turned a losing strategy into a profitable one for factors from 5.50 to 9.0. They were not large profits, but because of the higher level of noise in 5-minute bars, profit-taking can take advantage of short-lived price moves. Because longer calculation periods emphasize the trending nature of prices, taking profits prevents the system from realizing all of the trend.

TABLE 46.4   Profit-Taking Tests Using the Euro Currency Futures, 2002–2010

	80-Bar Moving Average				5-Bar Moving Average			
PT Factor	Net Profit	% Profitable Trades	Avg Trade	Profit Factor	Net Profit	% Profitable Trades	Avg Trade	Profit Factor
None	121655	45	1580	2.738	−3278	32	−7	0.991
10.00	94405	45	1226	2.348	−3278	32	−7	0.991
9.50	85693	45	1113	2.224	−3278	32	−7	0.991
9.00	90880	45	1180	2.298	4723	32	11	1.013
8.50	86030	45	1117	2.229	4160	32	9	1.012
8.00	81630	45	1060	2.166	6498	32	14	1.018
7.50	75543	45	981	2.079	19098	32	43	1.053
7.00	68168	45	885	1.974	11485	32	26	1.032
6.50	71483	46	916	2.021	6635	32	15	1.019
6.00	63583	46	815	1.908	4448	32	10	1.012
5.50	53945	46	692	1.771	523	32	1	1.001
4.50	35533	46	456	1.508	−11915	32	−27	0.967
4.25	30608	46	392	1.437	2785	32	6	1.008
4.00	26345	46	338	1.376	−8728	32	−19	0.976
3.50	17583	46	225	1.251	−14153	32	−32	0.960
3.00	25383	49	325	1.385	−27478	32	−61	0.923
2.50	21033	51	270	1.324	−29538	32	−66	0.917
2.00	22208	54	285	1.363	−31050	34	−69	0.911
1.50	13658	56	175	1.233	−24525	38	−55	0.927
1.00	18220	62	234	1.448	−40113	43	−89	0.873
0.50	11308	69	145	1.306	−37775	54	−84	0.862

Multiple Target Levels, Scaling Out of a Trade   Floor traders instinctively know how to reduce risk and give themselves the best opportunity for profit.[14] One technique that stands out is the way they take profits. Because they are dealing with trades that may last from minutes to hours, they are sensitive to market noise and realize that the size of the price move is very unpredictable. Instead of targeting a single price level as an exit point, they will often exit in three parts. For example, if you bought the emini S&P at 1125 and with an average daily volatility of 15 points, you might expect to target an exit of 1133. But what if the price reached 1132? Floor traders cannot count on being rigid about a target, so they are more likely to set three targets 1130, 1133, and 1135 to cover a wider range. If the first target is hit, they have reduced their risk considerably. If the second target is hit, they will never turn a profit into a loss. Then multiple targets, especially where the average is the same as your original target level, reduce your risk as the market goes yours way, and still give you a reasonable chance to capture the same total profit.

---

[14] Courtesy of Barbara Diamond, the first woman trader on the floor of the Chicago Mercantile Exchange.

Kaufman on Stops and Profit-Taking

Both profit-taking and stop-losses are a duel with price noise. If volatility causes a sharp drop followed by a recovery, then hitting a stop captures the worst exit. On the other hand, if volatility gives you a windfall profit, then exiting that position will be a good move. Because there is so much market noise, stop-loss orders are usually based on the closing price, or, if they are triggered by intraday price moves, the actual exit is still on the close to take advantage of a pullback. The opposite would be true of profit-taking. You would want to exit at the time of the intraday spike rather than waiting for the end of day.

There is a lot of debate about whether a stop-loss improves results or simply seems to be a good idea but does not actually result in better performance. Every trader can tell a story of how a stop order was executed at the worst price of the day, or how it saved him from a devastating loss. In fast markets, you are lucky if your stop is executed near your price. Often it gets filled at the extreme of the move, where all the buyers and sellers cluster. But that does not mean that stops do not work. Some work, and some do not work. The ones that are most likely to work must adapt to volatility, such as the standard deviation stop, rather than a fixed dollar amount or a percentage of price. And trailing stops are more practical than initial stops.

As an example, a test was run on U.S. 30-year bonds from 2000 to 2011, using a moving average trend strategy with calculation periods from 10 to 100 in increments of 10 days, and a standard deviation stop based on a fixed calculation period of 40 days but varying the factor from 2 to 10 in increments of 2. This produced 50 tests. Of course, we could have varied the calculation period for the stop and made the increments smaller, but then you would expand the number of tests considerably. This is only to give us the big picture.

Table 46.5 is a *heat map* arranged to see the continuous patterns. Although the tones may not be clear here, you can create the same chart using the *conditional formatting* option in Excel. The left scale is the moving average period, and the top

| TABLE 46.5 | Stop-Loss Test of 30-Year Bonds, 2000–2011, Applied to a Moving Average Strategy and Displayed as a Heat Map |

	Stop-Loss Factor						
MA Period	10	8	6	4	2	Average	No Stop
100	−11594	−6969	8625	11594	−6313	−931	−27875
90	10063	12250	35781	47594	35438	28225	688
80	11625	13063	33594	44688	21688	24931	4813
70	26063	32219	42406	41406	34063	35231	8531
60	1688	7844	13813	14250	16906	10900	6281
50	−10281	−1156	12750	22313	−344	4656	−8000
40	5906	13375	21375	30906	20156	18344	−3781
30	−19000	−13531	−3344	6781	7125	−4394	6938
20	33938	36156	34125	52500	44688	40281	36375
10	−1594	−813	1094	−188	17438	3188	−813
Average	4681	9244	20022	27184	19084	16043	2316

is the stop-loss factor. The upper left has the slowing moving average and the largest stop, and the bottom right is the most sensitive. The right-most column gives the profits of the same moving average strategy with no stop. There are also averages of the columns and rows. In comparing the two columns on the right, every stop-loss average except one was better than the corresponding strategy with no stop-loss. On the bottom, every stop-loss factor was better than the average of all trends with no stop loss. By any standard, we would consider this a robust improvement. Keep in mind that this is a test of only one market and over one selected time period. Interest rate markets are well known to have trends, so that results might be very different applied to equity index markets that are typically noisy.

Risk Protection or False Hope? Stops are normally *resting orders,* that is, they are held by the floor broker or in the electronic queue, to be executed as a *market order* when the price is touched. When a price shock occurs and the market jumps through your stop order, it is very likely that you will get filled at the worst price of the fast move. So stops work as you planned most of the time, except when you need them most. It is very similar to other financial phenomena, such as correlation, where a portfolio normally benefits from diversification except during times of extreme stress.

Market Noise, Trends, and the Frequency of Stops Because of market noise, stops that are close to the market price will get hit more often. As discussed briefly before, if we were dealing with random price data, the number of times that a stop is hit, times the distance of the stop from the market, will always be constant. Then a stop that is 100 points away may get hit 10 times for a total loss of 1000 points, and a stop that is 200 points away will get hit 5 times, also for a total of 1000 points. However, price data is not random, and the distribution implies that larger moves are more likely to change the direction of the trend. As you filter out more of the noise, those remaining events have a greater likelihood of being significant.

Proximity Risk When many stop orders cluster around the same point, there is *proximity risk.* One way this can be seen is in a gap as price breaks through a key resistance level. Given the large number of trend-following systems, it would not be surprising to find that many of them are generating the same orders on the close, especially following a very volatile price move.

Large macro trend systems, those with substantial assets under management, may take up to 3 days to enter a trade. The likelihood of proximity risk is greatly increased, and the cost of execution could be significant.

Managing Risk without Stops

A stop-loss is not the only way to reduce risk. An alternative is to reduce the size of your positions as volatility increases. This can be done at different places within the trading process. At the beginning of this chapter, we showed how to calculate the position size based on price volatility. The greater the volatility, the smaller the position. You can also rebalance those positions' sizes as the volatility changes, although you must consider the added switching costs. That could be done using a testing platform as long as you correctly estimate and include the commissions and slippage each time you change position size.

Risk Control Overlay   Some traders include stop-loss orders based on factors other than the price or volatility of the specific market traded. They generally take one of the following three approaches:

1. *A percentage of initial margin,* for example, 50% to 70% of initial margin. This is loosely related to long-term volatility but lags considerably.[15] An estimate of long-term volatility may be a more satisfactory alternative.
2. *A percentage of the portfolio value or total account value,* for example, 1.0% to 2.5%. This concept of equalized risk (and perhaps reward) across all markets is very popular; however, it is not sensitive to individual markets, and as with many stops, it imposes artificial overrides. If the volatility of one market increases or decreases faster than others, then this risk level would need to be adjusted to individual markets; otherwise, it could be reached on every trade or not reached at all.
3. *The maximum adverse excursion* determined by historic evaluation.[16] A stop is placed just beyond the maximum adverse excursion for each trade, or 2.5% of the price, whichever is smaller.

■ Ranking of Markets for Selection

Knowing which market to trade at the right time would clearly improve performance. To accomplish this, there are a number of ways to measure the *trendiness* of a market, from standard statistical techniques to more complex rules. Each method will measure some special characteristic of price movement. To take advantage of this, it is necessary to trade using a system that targets this type of price pattern. For example, if you use a correlation coefficient, r^2, to rank the trend over 20 days, then the highest-ranking markets may do best using a linear regression for the trend-following system, with a period no greater than 20 days. If the correlation is low then mean reversion would be favored.

To prove that ranking methods result in better performance, we would need to record their values in a table over various time periods.[17] For example, the five measurements below can be calculated for periods of 5, 10, 20, and 40 days.

1. Correlation coefficient, but only for values greater than 0.25.
2. Sum of the net moves, in dollars, over n, $2 \times n$, and $4 \times n$ days.
3. Slope of an n-day regression converted to a 1-day dollar-value change.
4. Wilder's Average Directional Movement Index (ADX), but only for values greater than 0.20.
5. Average of the absolute value of price changes.

---

[15] Tushar Chande and Stanley Kroll, *The New Technical Trader* (New York: John Wiley & Sons, 1994).

[16] John Sweeney, *Campaign Trading* (New York: John Wiley & Sons, 1997).

[17] Based on an idea suggested in Chande and Kroll, *The New Technical Trader* (New York: John Wiley & Sons, 1994).

Each measurement will need to have threshold values that determine when they represent significant trends. For the correlation coefficient, anything below 0.25 is most likely to be a sideways market; similarly, Wilder's ADX would need to be above 0.20 to indicate a trend. If the results are erratic, it may be necessary to smooth the last 3 days of each value. In the case of item 5, higher volatility is often associated with greater profits and greater risk for a trend-following system; therefore, it is necessary to take a careful look at how this ranking affects performance.

Commodity Selection Index

Among Wilder's trading tools is the *Commodity Selection Index* (CSI),[18] a calculation for determining which products are most likely to make the greatest move for each dollar invested. In this case, the movement measured is *directional* and, therefore, should apply directly to trending models. The CSI combines directional movement, volatility, margin requirements, and commission costs into an index that allows for comparison and selection. It is the result of the following calculations.

Directional Movement

The trending quality of the market, as defined by Wilder, begins with *directional movement,* the greater of either:

1. Plus DM (PDM), today's high minus yesterday's high, $H_t - H_{t-1}$.
2. Minus DM (MDM), today's low minus yesterday's low, $L_t - L_{t-1}$.

Note that *plus DM* and *minus DM* are often written as $+DM$ and $-DM$; however, to avoid confusion in the following calculations, they will be shown as *PDM* and *MDM*.

The directional movement is either up or down, whichever is larger of PDM and MDM. It is the largest part of today's range that is *outside* yesterday's range. The value that is not used is set to zero. When an inside day occurs, both PDM and MDM are zero, and the directional movement is zero (Figure 46.9).

In the calculation of PDM and MDM, DM is expressed relative to today's *true range* (TR1), $\max(H_t - L_t, H_t - C_{t-1}, C_t - L_{t-1})$. The true range is always positive.

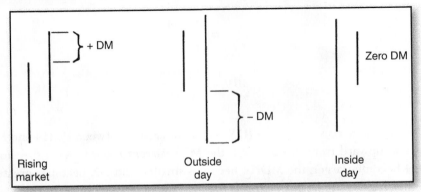

FIGURE 46.9   Defining the DM.

---

[18] J. Welles Wilder, "Selection and Direction" in Perry J. Kaufman, ed., *Technical Analysis in Commodities* (New York: John Wiley & Sons, 1980).

The relationship of the price direction to the true range is called the *Directional Movement* (DM). Today's directional movement is calculated using either the PDM or the MDM, whichever is greater. The notation "14" refers to the period over which the values are smoothed.

$$PDM14 = +\frac{DM14}{TR14} \quad or \quad MDM14 = -\frac{DM14}{TR14}$$

Once the first DM14 is calculated, using 14 days of price movement, an *average-off* technique is used to find each successive DM14 as follows:

$$PDM14_t = PDM14_{t-1} - \frac{PDM14_{t-1}}{14} + PDM14_t$$

$$MDM14_t = MDM14_{t-1} - \frac{MDM14_{t-1}}{14} + MDM14_t$$

The same procedure is followed for the true range:

$$TR14_t = TR14_{t-1} - \frac{TR14_{t-1}}{14} + TR14_t$$

These results can also be produced using a smoothing constant of 0.071, which is an approximation of the fraction $\frac{1}{14}$, where t is today's value:

$$PDM14_t = 0.071 \times PDM14_{t-1} + PDM14_t$$

$$MDM14_t = 0.071 \times MDM14_{t-1} + MDM14_t$$

$$TR14_t = 0.071 \times TR14_{t-1} + TR14_t$$

At this point, the Directional Movement components can be used as trading indicators; however, Wilder's interest was to use this in a more complete concept, shown in the following sections.

Directional Indicator and True Directional Movement Once the PDM14, MDM14, and the TR14 are calculated, the *directional indicators,* PDI14 and MDI14 follow,

$$PDI_t = \frac{PDM14_t}{TR14_t}$$

$$MDI_t = \frac{MDM14_t}{TR14_t}$$

and the *True Directional Movement* (DX) is the difference between PDI14 and MDI14. When an upward trend is sustained, the MDI current value is zero; therefore, the PDI14 becomes larger, the MDI14 becomes smaller, and DX becomes greater. This is then *normalized* in order to express the final value between 0 and 100.

$$DX_t = 100 \times \frac{|PDI14_t - MDI14_t|}{PDI14_t + MDI14_t}$$

where multiplying by 100 converts the percentage to a whole number, and the absolute value prevents DX from becoming negative. At the same time, the absolute value causes DX to lose the information about which direction prices are moving.

Average Directional Movement Index (ADX) The DX is then smoothed using the equivalent of a 14-day average (a 0.133 smoothing constant), and is called the *Average Directional Movement Index* (ADX).

$$ADX_t = ADX_{t-1} + 0.133 \times (DX_t - ADX_{t-1})$$

The ADX, the PDM, and the MDM are shown for NASDAQ 100 continuous futures in Figure 46.10. The heavier ADX line moves higher as the price trend becomes clear. The individual components, the PDM (shown as the thinnest line) and the MDM (the medium-weight line), indicate the relative strength of the upwards and downwards moves within the trend. As NASDAQ prices decline, the MDM remains above the PDM, which is shown along the bottom of the lower panel.

One last adjustment is made to the extreme variance of the ADX by taking the average of the current value and the value of the ADX 14 days ago. This final value is called the *Average Directional Movement Index Rating* (ADXR),

$$ADXR_t = \frac{ADX_t + ADX_{t-14}}{2}$$

The ADX and ADXR are shown plotted together in Figure 46.11. The ADX is seen to oscillate about the ADXR. Measuring the distance of the ADX from the zero line, a higher amplitude means higher directional movement and a stronger trend,

FIGURE 46.10 The 14-Day ADX, PDM, and MDM, Applied to NASDAQ 100 Continuous Futures Prices, February to August 2002.

FIGURE 46.11 The ADX and ADXR.

whether up or down. The peaks are always the extremes. The distance between the ADX and ADXR is used to measure the overbought and oversold condition of the trend. The larger the value, the greater the reactions to the trend.

Using the ADX as a Trending Indicator. The ADX has become a popular tool. Ruggiero[19] uses it to determine the trend with the following rules:

1. If ADX crosses above 25, the market is trending.
2. If ADX crosses below 20, the market is consolidating.
3. If ADX crosses below 45 after being higher, the market is consolidating.
4. If ADX rises above 10 on 3 of 4 days after being lower, the market will start to trend.
5. A trend based on rule 4 remains in effect until the 5-day difference in the ADX is less than 0.

Commodity Selection Index The creation of the Directional Movement Indicator, the different components, and finally the ADX leads to the *Commodity Selection Index* (CSI), which is calculated as:

$$CSI_t = ADXR_t \times ATR14_t \times \left[100 \times \frac{V}{M} \times \frac{1}{150 + C} \right]$$

where $ADXR$ = average directional movement index rating
$ATR14$ = 14-day average true range
V = conversion factor; value of a 1¢ move for a futures market (in dollars)
M = margin (in dollars)
C = commissions (in dollars)

The CSI can be applied to equities by setting $V = 1$ and M to the total share value of the investment. Note that for a particular futures market, or for equities, the value inside the bracket does not change. By calculating it once and calling that value K, the CSI can be expressed as:

$$CSI_t = ADXR_t \times ATR14_t \times K$$

[19] Murray A. Ruggiero, Jr., *Cybernetic Trading Strategies* (New York: John Wiley & Sons, 1997).

A portfolio allocation can be chosen by calculating the CSI daily or weekly for each market. Simply select those products to trade that have the highest CSI or allocate position size in proportion to their CSI value.

Retesting Directional Movement

When these indicators were published in 1978, they were all based on a 14-day calculation period, which is why all of the notations include the number 14.[20] With the ability to test these indicators over different calculation periods, the "14" was dropped from the notation. The first study to use PDI and MDI, the directional indicators, in a trading strategy was by Hochheimer, known for his other studies of moving averages, crossovers, and channels. He defined the rules of a *Directional Movement System* in two ways.[21] The first set of rules is:

1. a. *Enter a new long position and close out any short sales* if the PDI crosses above the MDI. Enter a *buy stop* on the next day using today's high price. This order remains as long as it is not executed and PDI remains higher than MDI.

   b. *Enter a new short sale and close out any long positions* if the PDI crosses below the MDI. Enter a *sell stop* on the next day using today's low price. Maintain this order until it is executed and while PDI remains below MDI.

Hochheimer calls the first case "directional movement with delay." The second case is an immediate market entry following the crossing of the directional indicators:

2. a. *Enter a new long position and close out any short sales on the open of the next day* if the PDI crosses above the MDI.

   b. *Enter a new short sale and close out any long positions on the open of the next day* if the MDI crosses below the PDI.

In both cases the system is always in the market. Before seeing the actual results, it is possible to generalize the expected performance.

1. Rule 2 must have more trades than Rule 1 because it always takes a position when a crossing occurs, while the first set of rules requires a confirmation.
2. Because there is no commitment to stay in the trade once entered (for example, no price channel), there could be frequent whipsaws using Rule 2.
3. Because Rule 1 uses the high and low of the prior day, its entry prices will always be equal to or worse than those of Rule 2.
4. If the Directional Indicator gives a highly reliable signal, it would be better to enter immediately, as in Rule 2.

In Hochheimer's tests, the following parameter ranges were used:

1. The PDM varied from 7 to 20 days.

---

[20] For a general discussion of this topic, see Perry J. Kaufman, *Trading Systems and Methods, +Website*, 5th Edition (Hoboken, New Jersey: John Wiley & Sons, 2013), Chapter 21.

[21] Frank L. Hochheimer, *Computerized Trading Techniques 1982* (New York: Merrill Lynch Commodities, 1982).

2. The MDM varied from 5 above to 5 below the PDM value.
3. Two *true ranges* (TR) were calculated, the first using the parameter value of the PDM, the other using the parameter value of the MDM.

The test data covered a wide range of those futures markets available from 1970 to 1981.

Rather than show the detail of those tests, which would be considered out of date with current markets and conditions, we ran a simpler test on directional movement using the first set of rules, varying only the basic calculation period. Tests include five most popular markets, one from each sector, and covered from 2000 through 2011. Results are shown in Table 46.6. The calculation periods were from 4 days to 80 days in increments of 4 days. While each market has areas of good profit, there was little consistency. The best period for bonds was 4, the DAX 54, EURUSD 28, crude 20, and copper 60. This alone does not satisfy our conditions for a robust system.

Trading Rules Combining PDM, MDM, and ADX Most often, the three indicators, PDM, MDM, and ADX, are used to complement a trending strategy by improving the entry or exit timing. However, Colby[22] has found that using a 2-day calculation period and the following rules, the Dow Jones Industrial Averages were profitable for 72 years from 1928 to 2000:

TABLE 46.6	Profits or Losses from the Directional Movement Test, 2000–2011				
Period	U.S. Bonds	DAX	EURUSD	Crude	Copper
4	21969	−106738	30688	28350	25800
8	−13500	−22063	21250	9990	29100
12	15250	−23500	58475	−11010	17275
16	10156	−36188	15775	−3880	72188
20	13813	−75563	50625	66400	23938
24	−37281	−5038	68425	54780	37288
28	−14688	−33000	90925	−5870	85525
32	−48250	19075	86150	−10310	107213
36	−55281	−8863	61000	48230	56525
40	−54531	−45413	56350	−12370	963
44	−43844	97775	59350	−20800	38863
48	−37438	79625	37925	−28960	103575
52	−42281	−2300	37175	−81440	99600
56	−23094	129625	14125	−102380	93425
60	−32719	130600	29738	−97750	116225
64	−33031	98588	19425	−104220	68075
68	−48313	88563	−12513	−132010	98300
72	−56938	71863	−56538	−118340	95488
76	−47281	66638	6938	−63060	44650
80	−46156	35688	11450	−34950	52325

---

[22] Robert W. Colby, *The Encyclopedia of Technical Market Indicators,* 2nd ed. (New York: McGraw-Hill, 2003).

Enter a new long position when the 2-day PDI > the 2-day MDI *or* the 2-day ADX > the 2-day smoothing of the ADX.

Close out a long position when the 2-day PDI < the 2-day MDI *or* the 2-day ADX < the 2-day smoothing of the ADX.

Entering a new short sale and exiting a short sale (buying to cover) are the opposite rules. All orders are executed on the close. The results show that a $100 investment would have returned $9,988 after profits were reinvested, which was better than a buy-and-hold strategy by 118%. Because of the strong bull market of the 1990s, this strategy would have lost money on its short sales during that period.

Ranking Trends Using Prices

Chande also created his own trend ranking based on a rolling period of 50 or 100 days.[23] His *trend strength* is calculated as

$$S_t = \frac{\ln \dfrac{P_t}{P_{t-n}}}{\sigma\left(\ln \dfrac{P_t}{P_{t-1}}, n\right) \times \sqrt{n}}$$

Where $\sigma(\ )$ is the standard deviation of the 1-period returns over n periods. The numerator is the net return over n days, divided by a volatility function. In this case, S_t can be either positive or negative to show the trend direction.

Kaufman's Strategy Selection Indicator

A market's *characteristic* is reflected in its price patterns. Some markets, such as the S&P 500 index, are very volatile with gradual upward moves and fast, sharp drops. In contrast, Eurodollar interest rates are very steady, often trading high volume at the same price. Qualifying markets by their underlying level of *noise* allows you to decide which trading strategy is most likely to be successful. Less noise favors trending systems and high noise makes mean-reverting techniques more appropriate.

The concept of *noise* is of great value when choosing which system to apply to a market and identifying when a market is best treated as trending. In essence, noise is market movement that has no direction or price movement in which the amount of direction is overwhelmed by erratic up and down movement. As a simple reminder, noise is defined using the *efficiency ratio, ER,* the absolute value of the net price change divided by the sum of the individual price changes taken as positive values, over the same time interval. Closing prices are used.

$$ER_t = \frac{|C_t - C_{t-n}|}{\sum_{i=t-n+1}^{t} |C_i - C_{i-1}|}$$

[23] Tushar Chande, "Which Trends (and Markets) Are Best?" *Futures* (May 1997).

ER is not the same as volatility and indicates that noise increases as *ER* gets closer to zero because the divisor increases with the amount of noise. Emerging markets have less noise and more trend because there are fewer participants and those that are active seem to have the same view of the direction of the market, or the lack of liquidity drives prices further in one direction than would be seen in a highly liquid market. But equity index markets could be a special case. To see if this process can be generalized, we compare the returns from a 65-day simple moving average system with the 65-day (quarterly) average noise.

Results of Efficiency Ratio Selection   The results of calculating the average value of the efficiency ratio and the corresponding profit factor for a wide range of markets is shown in Figure 46.12 and Table 46.7. Data included 1990 through mid-2011, or whenever the data started. The left scale of Figure 46.12 shows the profit factor, the gross profits divided by the gross losses (a measure of return to risk) and along the bottom the efficiency ratio. Note that the range in the efficiency ratio is small because the calculation period of 65 days is long. It is not necessary to use more days than the longest daily run of upward or downward price moves. Including more days only compresses the values, but 65 days was used for consistency. Results show that there is a pattern going from the bottom left to the upper right, consistent with lower returns when the efficiency ratio is small (indicating more noise) and higher returns when the ratio moves toward 1.

Table 46.7 gives the numbers used in Figure 46.12. The highest efficiency ratio and largest profit factors are for the short-term interest rates and Apple stock, which has had a spectacular move during the past 10 years. The interest rates tend to have strong trends based on the way monetary policy is implemented, and the short maturities track the government rates more closely than the long maturities, which include a greater degree of speculation about future policy.

At the bottom of the table are most of the other stocks as well as the most active equity index markets and grains. Index markets have greater noise than other sectors, and the grains have less long-term direction because of seasonality and their response to changes in the U.S. dollar.

FIGURE 46.12   Scatter Diagram of the Profit Factor Versus the Efficiency Ratio for a Wide Range of Futures and Equities, 1990 through Mid-2011.

TABLE 46.7 Values of the Efficiency Ratio (Noise) and Corresponding Profit Factor Sorted Highest to Lowest Average Noise

Market	Average Noise	Profit Factor
Eurodollar	0.1816	2.43
Sht Sterling	0.1620	1.65
AAPL	0.1520	2.28
Eurobund	0.1482	1.91
Nat gas	0.1476	1.52
Euro	0.1429	1.62
U.S. 10-year	0.1429	1.48
Japan	0.1399	1.56
IBM	0.1396	0.90
Copper	0.1389	1.70
AMZN	0.1387	1.01
DAX	0.1379	1.58
Crude	0.1377	2.12
MRK	0.1333	0.71
US bonds	0.1331	1.27
NASDAQ	0.1327	1.42
Cotton	0.1325	1.52
Gold	0.1296	0.94
Canada	0.1292	1.15
HO	0.1277	1.69
Soybeans	0.1277	0.87
MSFT	0.1269	0.88
Wheat	0.1248	0.99
GE	0.1208	0.88
CAC	0.1206	1.03
S&P	0.1203	1.16

Figure 46.12 is consistent with the results. Those markets with profit factors below 1.0 have net losses and are not good candidates for trend systems but may be best with mean-reversion strategies. Those farthest up and to the right are highly trending markets. When choosing markets to include in a diversified trading program, it is not necessary to include those that conflict with the nature of the strategy.

■ Probability of Success and Ruin

The relative size of trading profits and losses, the frequency of the losses, and the sequence in which they occur, combine to form an equity profile. This can apply equally to the returns of individual discretionary traders or fully automated trading systems. The profile can be used to determine the capitalization necessary to maintain trading during the losing periods and allow the system to continue uninterrupted trading. In investment terminology and probability theory, the level at which there is no longer enough money to continue trading is called the *point of ruin,* and the likelihood of getting there is the *risk of ruin.* The probability of the *risk of ruin* is expressed as

$$R = \left[\frac{1-A}{1+A} \right]^c$$

where $0 \le R \le 1$, and where 0 indicates no risk, and 1 is certain ruin
   $A = P - (1 - P)$; P is the proportion of winning trades, also called the *trader's advantage*
   c = the beginning units of trading capital (subsequent units can be expressed in fractional increments)

A trading system that has 60% profitable trades and trading capital in $10,000 units will have a risk of ruin calculated as follows:

$$A = 0.60 - (1 - .060) = 0.20$$

$$R = \left(\frac{1-0.20}{1+0.20} \right)^c = \left(\frac{0.80}{1.20} \right)^c = \left(\frac{1}{3} \right)^c$$

When $c = 1$ unit, and the initial investment is $10,000, the risk of ruin $R = 0.33$, or 33%. When $c = 2$ units and the initial investment is $20,000, $R = 0.11$, or 11%. Therefore, the greater the trader's advantage or the greater the capital, the smaller the risk of ruin (Figure 46.13).

When using profit goals, the point at which trading would stop if the goal was achieved, the chance of ruin should decrease as the goal becomes closer. The relationship would be expressed as:

$$R = \frac{[(1+A)/(1-A)]^G - 1}{[(1+A)/(1-A)]^{c+G} - 1}, \quad 0 \le R \le 1$$

where all terms are the same as above, and G is the goal in units of trading capital.

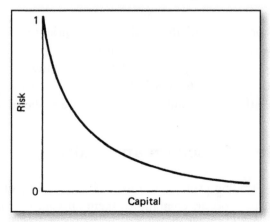

FIGURE 46.13   Risk of Ruin Based on Invested Capital.

Wins Not Equal to Losses

The basic equations in the previous section are generally applied to gambling situations, where the size of profits and losses are the same. This requires that the percentage of winning events exceed the losing events in order to avoid ruin. Trading, however, often results in more losing trades than profitable ones and must therefore return much *larger* average profits than losses. This pattern is common to all conservation-of-capital systems, such as trend following. The risk of ruin of unequal profits and losses, including an unequal chance of a profit or loss, can be found as:[24]

C_T = the total capital available for trading (in units)
C_R = the cutoff point, where level of ruin is reached $(C_R < C_T)$
$C_A = C_T - C_R$, capital available to be risked
E = the expected mean return per trade, the probability-weighted sum of values
     that a trade might take

$$E = \sum_{i=1}^{N} (PL_i \times p_i)$$

where PL_i = the possible profit or loss value
     p_i = the probability of PL_i occurring $(0 < p_i < 1)$
     N = the number of trades

E_2 is the expected squared mean return per trade, the probability-weighted sum of all the squared values of a trade,

$$E_2 = \sum_{i=1}^{N} (PL_i^2 \times p_i)$$

where PL_i and p_i are defined above.

$$D = C_A / \sqrt{E_2}$$

$$P = 0.5 + E / \left(2\sqrt{E_2}\right)$$

The risk of ruin is then

$$R = \left(\frac{1-P}{P}\right)^D$$

Introducing an objective and a desired level of capital L, the risk of ruin R becomes

$$R = 1 - \frac{[(1-P)/P]^D - 1}{[(1-P)/P]^G - 1}$$

where

$$G = 1 / \sqrt{E_2}$$

---

[24] Fred Gehm, *Quantitative Trading & Money Management*, rev. ed. (Chicago: Irwin, 1995).

As in the first situation, using equal profits and losses, the risk increases as the objective L increases.

Ralph Vince[25] derived similar results from Griffin's work,[26] which claims to provide a "fair approximation" of risk. Vince's approach has been modified here for convenience and given in a way that allows a spreadsheet solution:

```
Risk of Ruin = ((1 - P)/P)^(MaxRisk/A)
```

where the following terms are defined in the order needed for calculation:

AvgWin is the average winning trade (e.g., $400)
AvgLoss is the average losing trade (e.g., $200)
Investment is the amount invested (e.g., $10,000)
ProbWin is the probability (percentage) of a winning trade (e.g., 0.40)
ProbLoss is the probability (percentage) of a losing trade (e.g., 0.60)
MaxRisk is the maximum part of the investment that can be lost, in percent (e.g., 0.25)
AvgWin% is ABS(*AvgWin/Investment*)
AvgLoss% is ABS(*AvgLoss/Investment*)
Z is the difference of possible events, (*ProbWin* $\times$ *AvgWin%*) $-$ (*ProbLoss* $\times$ *AvgLoss%*)
A is the square root of the sum of the squares of possible events, $((ProbWin \times AvgWin\%)^2 + (ProbLoss \times AvgLoss\%)^2)^{(1/2)}$
P is $0.5 \times (1 + (Z/A))$

Table 46.8 gives the risk of ruin for a few cases. Case 1 is the basic configuration using a $10,000 investment, a $400 average win, and a $200 average loss. The

TABLE 46.8 Examples of Risk of Ruin with Unequal Wins and Losses

	Case 1	Case 2	Case 3	Case 4	Case 5	Case 6
AvgWin	400	400	400	350	325	325
AvgLoss	200	200	200	200	200	200
Investment	10000	5000	2500	10000	10000	10000
ProbWin	0.4	0.4	0.4	0.4	0.4	0.4
ProbLoss	0.6	0.6	0.6	0.6	0.6	0.6
MaxRisk	0.25	0.25	0.25	0.25	0.25	0.15
AvgWin%	0.04	0.08	0.16	0.035	0.0325	0.0325
AvgLoss%	0.02	0.04	0.08	0.02	0.02	0.02
Z	0.004	0.008	0.016	0.002	0.001	0.001
A	0.0200	0.0400	0.0800	0.0184	0.0177	0.0177
Z/A	0.2	0.2	0.2	0.1085	0.0565	0.0565
P	0.6	0.6	0.6	0.5542	0.5283	0.5283
Risk of Ruin	0.63%	7.93%	28.17%	5.22%	20.21%	38.31%

[25] Ralph Vince, *Portfolio Management Formulas* (New York: John Wiley & Sons, 1990).
[26] Peter A. Griffin, *The Theory of Blackjack: The Compleat Card Counter's Guide to the Casino Game of 21*, 6th ed. (Las Vegas: Gamblers Press, 1999).

probability of a win or loss is 40% and 60% respectively, and the maximum loss in the account is set at 25%. That gives a risk of ruin less than 1%, shown at the bottom of the Case 1 column. In Cases 2 and 3, the size of the investment is halved, and the risk of ruin increases to 7.9% and 28.1%. The risk of ruin goes up faster than the decrease in the investment size. In Cases 4 and 5 the *AvgWin* is reduced from $400 to $350 and $325 and the risk of ruin also increases rapidly. In the last Case 5, the *AvgWin* is held at $325 but the *MaxRisk* drops from 25% to 15% causing the risk of ruin to jump to 38.3%.[27]

■ Entering a Position

In the equities market, most people with retirement programs choose to add to their stock portfolio as money is available, and to reinvest profits. Over the long run, if the stock market continues to rise, that method is good. On the other hand, if a systematic trader gets an entry signal, they have only a few choices:

- Buy the entire amount at the time of the signal.

- Average into the position (or some weighted average).

- Wait for a better price.

We will compare these three choices, although the third, waiting for a better price, can be done at *any* better price or by applying some timing tool.

Averaging into a Position

It is not possible to cover all the different trading methods, but we can look at trend following as a popular example. We will take a small sample of markets, U.S. 30-year bonds, the emini S&P, and gold, to represent a trending, noisy, and popular market. We apply an 80-day moving average from 1990 through mid-2011 as the benchmark case.

First, consider the results if entry points are randomly distributed. That is, if there is no significance in the point at which a trend changes direction, then over time the technique of averaging into a trade should give the same results as simply entering the entire position at the point of the initial trend change.

The test will look at always entering 5 contracts (or in equities, 5 shares), spaced from 1 to 5 days apart. That is, the first case will enter 1 contract each day for 5 days, the next case 1 contract every 2 days for 10 days, and so on. The slowest will average every 5 days over 21 days (days 1, 6, 11, 16, and 21). The maximum range of 21 days would be too long for a fast trend system, so it is likely that the number of days used to average into a trade will depend on the average holding period of the trend system. This study simply looks at one trend period, 80 days.

---

[27] A full discussion of risk of ruin can be found in Ralph Vince, *The Handbook of Portfolio Mathematics* (Hoboken, NJ: John Wiley & Sons, 2007), Chapter 12.

When averaging into a trade, if the trend changes direction before the full position is set, then the loss on the trade will be less than if you had entered all contracts on day 1. On the other hand, if prices were to move steadily higher after a new long signal, then the average entry price will be worse than day 1, the point where the trend first changed.

Table 46.9 shows the results. The first column of values, *MA80*, is the benchmark 80-day moving average where the entire position of 5 contracts is set at the time of initial entry. The next column gives the results of setting 1 contract on each of the first 5 days beginning on the day of the initial entry. The next column, 5 × 2, sets 1 contract on the initial day, the next four on days 3, 5, 7, and 9 (spaced every 2 days). The remaining columns space the entries every 3, 4, and 5 days, respectively. Then the final column takes 21 days to enter a trade, days 1, 6, 11, 16, and 21. The first row for each market is the annualized volatility of the daily profits and losses. The second row is the first row divided by 15%, which gives an estimate of the investment size needed if the target volatility of the portfolio is 15%. This allows a comparison across markets. The third row is the total profit from the 20-year test, and the fourth row is the ratio of the total profit divided by the investment (row 3, Table 46.8). The ratio gives a simple way to compare all results.

Bonds are a trending market, so it would not be clear if waiting to enter is better than entering immediately; however, results improve to their best point by waiting 2 days between entries. With the emini S&P, which represents a highly noisy market, results continue to improve as entries are spaced out. The waiting process turns results from negative to position. For gold, waiting is also an improvement but results seem to stabilize after 2 days. If we chose to wait 2 days between each of the entry orders, all three of the markets would show improvements.

TABLE 46.9 **Results of Averaging into a New Position Based on an 80-Day Moving Average System. The Notation "5x2" Heading the Column Means 5 Total Contracts Entered 2 Days Apart.**

		Total PL					
		MA80	5 × 1	5 × 2	5 × 3	5 × 4	5 × 5
U.S. Bonds	Volatility	53047	51559	50482	49487	48626	47765
	@15%	353646	343728	336548	329913	324173	318435
	Total PL	454375	440688	461719	429000	399844	358625
	Ratio	**1.28**	**1.28**	**1.37**	**1.30**	**1.23**	**1.13**
emini S&P	Volatility	241349	10128	46535	45284	44193	43290
	@15%	1608997	67522	310231	301892	294618	288597
	Total PL	−212375	−35175	−2950	30775	40825	51362.5
	Ratio	**−0.13**	**−0.52**	**−0.01**	**0.10**	**0.14**	**0.18**
Gold	Volatility	60732	58617	57227	56184	55289	54546
	@15%	404879	390780	381516	374558	368593	363638
	Total PL	117000	161260	179890	173950	172240	166750
	Ratio	**0.29**	**0.41**	**0.47**	**0.46**	**0.47**	**0.46**

It will be very difficult to generalize these results to all systems, even all trend systems, because the delayed entry must depend on the speed of the trend. If we had used a 10-day moving average instead of 80 days, then entering over 21 days does not make any sense. The total time to enter should be proportional to the speed of the trend or the average holding period of the trade. It is also not clear how a mean-reverting strategy would fare by averaging in, but it might also improve. Averaging into a trade removes the uncertainty of a single entry and replaces it with a more stable value. In doing that, there seems to be an overall improvement in trend-following results.

Waiting for a Better Price

A simple way to improve an entry is to wait for a price that is better than the system signal. The obvious problem is when prices give a new signal and keep going and there is never a chance to enter at a better price. Statistically, it is possible that many small improvements will offset the occasional time when a trade is missed completely. To avoid the worst-case scenario of missing the biggest profit, we can enter at the close if no opportunity has occurred within 5 days, with the results shown in Table 46.10. If no opportunity occurred, the trade was entered on close of the fifth day. There is one explanation needed. The test platform used does not post the open position profit or loss on the last trade. For fast systems, where the trades have a short holding period, that makes little difference. For the 80-day moving average, which was the basis of this test, the last trade may have lasted for many months, as it did with gold. Had the last trade been included, as it was in the previous study, gold would show a large net profit. That does not change the effect of this rule, but should explain any inconsistencies between the results of the benchmark case here and in the previous example.

We see that waiting, even for a minimum move pullback after the initial signal, results in a significant improvement in performance for the three markets during the period from 1990 through mid-2011. However, a different range of thresholds was used for each market because the threshold is defined as a point value. It may be worth trying this with a percentage, but back-adjusted futures prices can be distorted when the data goes back many years, so you need to be careful about using percentages.

The minimum threshold, shown in the second row of values, cut the number of trades by about 40% in all three markets. This shows that there are many trend trades that lasted only a few days, and, because of waiting for a better price, the trend turned back in the previous direction, and the false signal was not taken. The minimum threshold also turned the gold results from a loss to a profit, while it cut the S&P losses in half. It had the least improvement in bonds, which has the strongest trend. We would expect markets with a large noise component to work well with this rule, so that the S&P had the biggest improvement even though it never showed a profit. A secondary benefit is that the profits per trade improved significantly.

The need for a maximum number of days in which this rules is applied is a critical element for its success. While these results show improvements, it is possible that

TABLE 46.10 Results Based on Waiting for a Better Price after the Initial Entry Signal

U.S. 30-Year Bonds					emini S&P					Gold				
Threshold	Total PL	Trades	% ProfTR	Prof/TR	Threshold	Total PL	Trades	% ProfTR	Prof/TR	Threshold	Total PL	Trades	% ProfTR	Prof/TR
None	61468	188	36.1	327	None	-44162	263	30.4	-168	None	-1580	246	32.9	-6
Min	72781	113	41.5	644	Min	-22337	155	26.4	-144	Min	12170	147	37.4	83
0.03125	71469	112	42.0	638	0.5	-22575	155	27.7	-146	1	10990	130	33.8	85
0.06250	69656	110	42.7	633	1.0	-21850	153	28.1	-143	2	14630	121	33.1	121
0.09375	69469	108	44.4	643	1.5	-22475	151	27.2	-149	3	14990	116	32.8	129
0.12500	69594	108	44.4	644	2.0	-20588	149	28.9	-138	4	14260	112	31.3	127
0.15625	68219	108	42.6	632	2.5	-22063	148	29.1	-149	5	15010	112	31.3	134
0.18750	69188	102	43.1	678	3.0	-20438	146	29.5	-140	6	15070	112	31.3	135
0.21875	70156	101	43.6	695	3.5	-18163	143	30.1	-127	7	14910	111	31.5	134
0.25000	73281	100	46.0	733	4.0	-14575	140	30.0	-104	8	15930	110	31.8	145
0.28125	71313	100	46.0	713	4.5	-14238	140	30.7	-102	9	16600	109	32.1	152
0.31250	71406	99	45.5	721	5.0	-13888	139	30.9	-100	10	12560	109	33.0	115
0.34375	72594	98	45.9	741	5.5	-11588	137	31.4	-85	11	13700	108	33.3	127
0.37500	70750	97	46.4	729	6.0	-11713	136	31.6	-86	12	13700	108	33.3	127
0.40625	67938	97	45.4	700	6.5	-11713	136	31.6	-86	13	13700	108	33.3	127
0.43750	69938	94	46.8	744	7.0	-11550	135	31.9	-86	14	14800	107	33.6	138
0.46875	69313	93	47.3	745	7.5	-10125	134	32.1	-76	15	15810	107	33.6	148
0.50000	70594	93	48.4	759	8.0	-9275	134	32.1	-69	16	19000	105	34.3	181
					8.5	-9175	134	32.1	-68	17	20890	103	34.0	203
					9.0	-9588	133	32.3	-72	18	20890	103	34.0	203
					9.5	-10250	131	32.1	-78	19	22420	103	34.0	218
					10.0	-9700	131	32.1	-74	20	22420	103	34.0	218

Market	Total PL	Trades	% Prof Trades	Profit / Trade
Bonds	65750	90	47.7	731
S&P	−10550	124	34.6	−85
Gold	22180	105	34.2	211

without the 5-day window, one exceptionally profitable trade would be missed. Even though it does not show in the tests, the possibility of that problem makes using a window necessary.

Using Timing for a Better Price

The last study applies a momentum indicator to find one better entry point after the initial trend signal. Linda Raschke's *First Cross* system used this as a primary rule for short-term trading. In this case, we will continue to use the 80-day moving average as a benchmark, and the popular RSI as a timing indicator. Long positions will be entered after the initial signal, or at the time of the initial signal, if the RSI is below a threshold level set at 30. The threshold for selling was 70. Again, a maximum window will be used to avoid missing a trade. The RSI will be 8 days rather than the default 14 days in order to find more opportunities within the window.

Table 46.11 shows results similar to the previous tests but with fewer trades. Even an 8-day RSI does not generate as many timing signals as the other studies, so that the trends reverse more often within the 5-day window without an entry occurring.

From the three studies, we can conclude that these three markets, and hopefully markets in general, benefit from entry timing. These techniques were very specific, using a long-term trend as a benchmark, but the same concept should apply across a reasonably broad set of trend calculation periods until we get to short-term trading. When trades are held for only a few days, the application may require using hourly data to time the entry instead of daily data. Still, prices do not go only one way, and market noise should allow us a better place to enter a trade.

■ Compounding a Position

At some point, most traders find themselves adding to, or compounding, their position (or seriously considering it). Some view this as a means of concentrating their resources on those markets that have more potential. There are two lines of thinking. When a trade becomes more profitable, it is confirming its move and is thought to deserve more of a commitment than a trade that has not become profitable. The alternative, when prices move against you, is *scaled-down buying,* or *averaging down,* popular in the securities industry. In pension programs, where new money is added at regular intervals, regardless of market movement, the timing is arbitrary, and profits are entirely dependent on whether the stock market as a whole, or the fund in which you are invested, is higher in the long run. But that is not trading. If positions are not added specifically based on profits, losses, or some timing method, then it is the same as averaging into a position.

The types of compounding are illustrated in Figure 46.14. Part a shows smaller positions added, with the added size on the left and the total position on the right. Part b shows equal positions added, and part c shows adding then removing positions. Systematic traders may use a number of conditions for entering addition size, ideally,

- A sustained basing formation

- Expectation of substantial additional profits

- A clear risk level

They expect profits to accumulate soon after adding positions

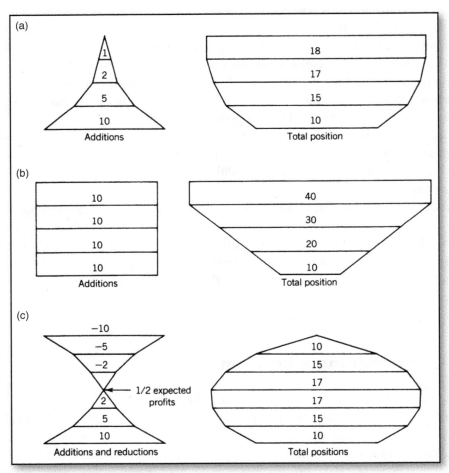

FIGURE 46.14 Compounding Structures. (a) Scaled-down size (upright pyramid) offers a small amount of compounding. (b) Adding equal amounts (inverted pyramid) gives maximum leverage. (c) Reflecting pyramid combines leverage and profit-taking.

No matter how well each entry is chosen, compounding will result in the largest holdings at the highest (or lowest) price; when the market reverses, losses occur on a larger base, and profits can disappear quickly. A compounded position can be very fragile and top-heavy; prices must be watched carefully for a change of direction. If you continue to leverage up with all available funds, then risk will become unmanageable.

Now consider building a position, similar to averaging in, rather than leveraging. If you plan to buy 1000 shares of Apple or 10 contracts of S&P, then you can start with 200 shares or 2 contracts and add the same amount at regular intervals, but only if you have new high profits. If prices go the wrong way, then you wait. If the trend reverses, the loss will be smaller if the maximum position was not set. Results could be similar to the previous study on averaging into a trade.

Adding on profits is not the same as waiting for enough profit and using those profits to add size. With both stocks and futures, the amount of profit would need to be very large to have enough to add, so the opportunities are small. For this method, there must be adequate funds set aside to carry the full position.

In the rest of this section, we will look at a few limited cases of entering a position in parts based on market conditions:

- Adding equal amounts on new high profits with a minimum number of days separating the entries

- Adding half the previous size with the same conditions as above

- Adding equal amounts on new losses with a minimum number of days between entries.

Intuitively, the last method should give a better entry price but might miss the move. In addition, if trend-following works, then we want the entire position set during those trades that capture the fat tail.

Adding on Profits

As with the previous studies, it is necessary to choose a trading system, and again we will use a simple moving average, but with a calculation period of 60 days. We will look at four markets, Apple (AAPL), Amazon (AMZN), 10-year Treasury notes (TY), and the emini S&P (ES). Both Apple and Amazon are popular stocks and have made big moves, 10-year notes are very trending, and the S&P is noisy, which gives us a somewhat varied sample. The data covers the past 20 years. The rules will be

1. Enter 1 unit on the new trend signal.
2. Enter another unit after n days only if the trade is on new high profits.
3. Stop entering after five units have been added.

Looking first at Apple, the first entry in Table 46.12, the largest total profits occur with the simple 60-day moving average without additional entries; however, the *Profit Factor* (gross profits divided by gross losses) improves steadily as the gap

TABLE 46.12	Building a Position on New High Profits					
	Method	Total PL	Prof Factor	Trades	Profits/Trade	Units Entered
Apple	MA 60	430.35	2.79	238	1.810	5.00
	1 Day	389.34	3.42	624	0.624	2.62
	3 Days	374.54	4.18	501	0.748	2.11
	5 Days	350.82	4.34	473	0.742	1.99
	10 Days	305.34	4.33	425	0.718	1.79
Amazon	MA 60	153.08	1.45	172	0.890	5.00
	1 Day	96.98	1.43	425	0.228	2.47
	3 Days	76.90	1.36	389	0.198	2.26
	5 Days	71.74	1.36	348	0.206	2.02
	10 Days	56.72	1.35	307	0.185	1.78
Notes	MA 60	13734	1.11	292	47.04	5.00
	1 Day	29825	1.42	647	46.08	2.22
	3 Days	30791	1.49	569	54.10	1.95
	5 Days	27700	1.48	519	53.36	1.78
	10 Days	17828	1.34	464	38.42	1.59
S&P	MA 60	22162	1.14	301	73.00	5.00
	1 Day	28875	1.28	719	40.16	2.39
	3 Days	28225	1.3	626	45.08	2.08
	5 Days	34463	1.43	564	61.10	1.87
	10 Days	30728	1.46	484	63.48	1.61

between entries increases. At the same time, the average return per share (*Profits/Trade*) will decline because the average entry price will increase for longs and decrease for short sales. On the far right, the *Units Entered* give us an idea of how many units were traded on average. For example, for the 1-day wait, 2.62 units indicates that the average trade had 2.62 shares while the 60-day moving average would always have 5 shares. Amazon, the second set, is the exception, showing a decline in the profit factor.

The two futures markets both show improved total profits as well as higher profit factors as trades are entered over time; 10-year notes peak with a 3-day wait while the emini S&P peaks at 5 days for profits and 10 days for the profit factor. Overall, entering as profits accumulate rather than entering all at one time gives much better results for the two futures markets and reasonably good results for the two stocks.

There are many combinations that could have been tested, a wide range of trend speeds, a mean reversion system, and different ways of adding to the trade. Analysts will always need to study these techniques in a conceptual framework as well as how it applies specifically to their set of trading systems.

Averaging Down

Because the practice of averaging down is pervasive in the equities markets, we would be remiss if we did not run the same test as *Adding on Profits* but reverse the logic so that we are *adding on losses*. Equal positions were added after at least *n* days provided that the open position was making new losses greater than remaining at the previous loss. There was an additional weaker test that allowed new positions to be entered as long as the trader showed a loss every *n* days, but those results were actually worse than this study.

Table 46.13 shows that Apple was the only market in which averaging down improved long-term performance, both in total profits and profit factor. The other three test markets produced noticeably worse results for all combinations of delay, given the same trend period of 60 days. Of course, other trend periods might have given different results, but a 60-day moving average is representative of the faster end of the macrotrend space and generally a conservative choice. Although a brief test, we would expect that any of the other methods, averaging in or adding on profits, are likely to yield better results.

	Method	Total PL	Prof Factor	Trades	Profits/Trade	Units Entered
TABLE 46.13	**Averaging Down by Adding Equal Amounts Whenever There Was a New Low Separated by a Minimum Number of Days**					
Apple	MA 60	430.35	2.79	238	1.810	
	1 Day	877.4	3.36	377	2.330	1.58
	3 Days	672.07	3.32	308	2.180	1.29
	5 Days	505.64	2.81	284	1.780	1.19
	10 Days	502.1	2.91	263	1.910	1.11
Amazon	MA 60	153.08	1.45	172	0.890	
	1 Day	−19.55	0.97	278	−0.070	1.62
	3 Days	65.83	1.13	226	0.290	1.31
	5 Days	70.13	1.16	207	0.340	1.20
	10 Days	102.42	1.26	191	0.540	1.11
Notes	MA 60	13734	1.11	292	47.04	
	1 Day	−7234	0.97	455	−15.90	1.56
	3 Days	7171	1.04	377	19.02	1.29
	5 Days	7000	1.04	357	19.61	1.22
	10 Days	8015	1.05	323	24.82	1.11
S&P	MA 60	22162	1.14	301	73.00	
	1 Day	−2475	0.99	456	−5.43	1.51
	3 Days	5437	1.03	378	14.38	1.26
	5 Days	10737	1.06	351	30.59	1.17
	10 Days	23712	1.14	324	73.19	1.08

◼ Equity Trends

Every system has profit and loss patterns that can be seen clearly by plotting its daily or weekly returns. Long-term trending techniques show that once or twice each year, there are major increases in profits corresponding to a trending market; at other times, returns show a steady decline or a stabilizing pattern.

Increasing position size as equity increases during a trending period always results in being fully invested at the top of the cycle, when losses begin. Losses will be on a larger base than profits, and equity will drop much faster than it increased. Decreasing size as profits increase will reduce risk but lose the advantage of capturing the fat tail. Similar changes can occur at the bottom of an equity cycle after a nontrending market period. A sustained losing streak may cause a speculator to reduce the investment in proportion to dwindling capital. If this happens, the result will be entering into a profitable period with a smaller investment than the prior losing period. The system must have disproportionately larger profits to recover the losses and achieve a net gain.

A classic example of a pattern in returns is one where there is a 100% gain for each profitable period, followed by an interval where there is a 50% loss. If this cycle is repeated twice each year then each year will have the following equity pattern:

	Change in Equity	Total Equity	
Original Investment		$10,000	
Gain of 100%	+10,000	20,000	First 6 months
Loss of 50%	−10,000	10,000	
Gain of 100%	+10,000	20,000	Second 6 months
Loss of 50%	−10,000	10,000	

Trading would be a great deal of effort for no return.

Some investors choose not to compound their returns, but let profits accumulate as *reserves*, also called *account excess*. Given the same profit/loss cycle as above, but holding the investment constant results in a very different equity pattern. The management of the reserves is the key to successful management. Starting with margin and reserves equal, reserves increase during profitable periods and decrease during losing ones. Proportionately more of the total equity is traded during losing phases. The results are:

	Change in Equity	Margin	Reserves	Total Equity	Reserves/ Equity
Original investment		10,000	10,000	20,000	50%
Gain of 100%	+10,000	10,000	20,000	30,000	67%
Loss of 50%	−5,000	10,000	15,000	25,000	60%
Gain of 100%	+10,000	10,000	25,000	35,000	71%
Loss of 50%	−5,000	10,000	20,000	30,000	67%

Using the natural pattern of trading returns, hold the number of positions the same and allow the reserve to increase during profitable periods; maintain the same position size through the beginning of the next losing period. When the drawdown has slowed or stabilized, the total account value can be redistributed into margin and excess according to the original 50% formula. In the next example, the total account value of $25,000 is distributed 40% to margin and 60% to reserve at the end of the first cycle. It is redistributed so that the next profit phase will be entered with a larger base than the previous losing cycle. The result is a gradual increase in profits:

	Change in Equity	Margin	Reserves	Total Equity	Reserves/ Equity
Original investment		10,000	10,000	20,000	50%
Gain of 100%	+ 10,000	10,000	20,000	30,000	67%
Loss of 50%	−5,000	10,000	15,000	25,000	60%
Redistribute		12,500	12,500	25,000	50%
Gain of 100%	+10,000	12,500	25,000	37,500	67%
Loss of 50%	−5,000	12,500	18,750	31,250	60%
Redistribute		15,625	15,625	31,250	50%

Trading on Equity Trends

It seems reasonable to think that the equity stream generated from a trend-following system, especially a long-term macrotrend system, would also trend. We would expect prices to move in a favorable direction the majority of the time, producing a chart with reasonably smooth swings. By applying a simple moving average to the accumulated profits and losses, we could exit positions when the trend of equity is down.

Using the results from an 80-day moving average applied to the same futures markets used earlier, 30-year bonds, the emini S&P, and gold, we applied both a 10-day and 60-day moving average to the cumulative profits over 20 years. When the trend of the equity was up on day t compared to $t - 1$, we used the returns on day $t + 1$; otherwise, we used a return of zero. While this is only one calculation period, 80 days represents the heart of the macrotrend system. For simplicity, only 1 contract was traded on each signal rather than a risk-adjusted position size. The results are shown in Figures 46.15a–c.

None of the three cases show consistency, even though there were improvements for the S&P and gold using both the 10-day and 60-day equity trends. Bonds, the market with the most trend, show a significant deterioration using this method. The equity trend method also did not include any switching costs, which would be more significant for the 10-day equity trend. We can infer that this method would perform poorly on a diversified portfolio, which should have shorter periods of negative movement. Of course, this does not mean that a solution cannot be found, only that a simple approach to finding trends in systematic equity patterns is not going to be easy.

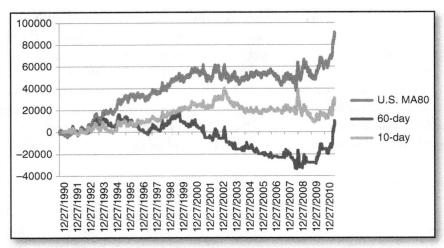

FIGURE 46.15a 30-Year Bonds Cumulative Profits Shown with a 10-Day and 60-Day Equity Trend Calculation.

FIGURE 46.15b The *e*mini S&P Cumulative Profits Shown with a 10-Day and 60-Day Equity Trend Calculation.

In pursuing this, you should first find out if the returns are positively autocorrelated, meaning that there is persistence in either positive or negative returns. You must also consider that applying this to hypothetical equity patterns is not likely to work because hypothetical results are always better than actual trading results.

■ Investing and Reinvesting: Optimal *f*

Optimal f is the optimal fixed fraction of an account that should be invested at any one time, or the size of the bet to place on any one trade. The amount to be risked is measured as a percentage of the portfolio size. The objective is to maximize the amount invested (put at risk) yet avoid the possibility of a loss greater than some target amount. Trading a very small part of assets can be a poor use of capital,

THEORY AND ANALYSIS

FIGURE 46.15c Gold Cumulative Profits Shown with a 10-Day and 60-Day Equity Trend Calculation.

while trading too much guarantees bankruptcy or ruin. Optimal f is the ideal portion of an investment that should be placed at risk at any one time.

Investing generally has a 2-level optimal f: (1) the part of the total portfolio put at risk compared to that part held in cash equivalents, and (2) the individual size of the commitment to each stock or futures contract within that portfolio. This is particularly important for futures, where the high leverage of individual markets makes it very easy to risk too much on each trade.

Risk Assessment

Then, how much should be invested? The optimal amount is difficult to pinpoint because you would have to know what risks lie ahead, and, of course, that's not possible.

The most extreme situation can be found by using the calculation for *risk of ruin* in a previous section of this chapter, most often applied to gambling situations in which the bet sizes, payout, and odds are well defined. When there are enough test data and trades, this technique has been applied to trading systems (see the section "Wins Not Equal to Losses"). All this depends on using historic data, which is often not a reliable indication of future price movement, which seems to get more correlated and more volatile.

Some analysts have tried to deal with the uncertainties of price movements by using a *Monte Carlo* technique in testing, which moves blocks of data, or sequences of returns, using a random process. This results in a distribution of possible risk combinations from which you can assign the probability of loss. Monte Carlo risk analysis is considered unusually severe because many of the worst combinations happen because the return series is identified without regard to possible cause-and-effect relationships. For example, a long-term trend-following technique expects to capture moves that are based on economic or government policy; therefore, sustained profits are most often followed by a reversal before the trade is ended. In fact, the size of the change of direction at the end of a trend is directly related to magnitude of the prior trend because of the lag. To move this data around so that the loss at the end of the trend comes at a different time may create a large loss without the preceding profit, a situation that is unfair to the trading strategy. Yet even an analysis of real performance is likely to understate the size of the future risk.

For an initial investment, optimal f is simply the maximum part of that portfolio that can safely be traded without any significant risk of ruin. For those investors who withdraw profits as they occur and continue to trade based on the same assumed initial investment, nothing need be changed unless exceptionally high risk requires a decrease in the amount of leverage. However, it is more common—and more complicated—for the investor to vary the amount committed to the market by either increasing or decreasing leverage. This involves (1) determining the right time to change the leverage, (2) calculating the amount to increase the investment when there are profits, and (3) figuring the size of the reduction when there are losses exceeding some designated amount. These are issues that are addressed by optimal f.

Finding Optimal f

Ralph Vince, in his popular book *Portfolio Management Formulas*,[28] focuses on optimal f, risk of ruin, and other practical items. The significance of this approach is the need to maximize the amount invested yet avoid the risk of ruin. Optimal f is the ideal amount of an investment that should be put at risk at any one time. First, we need to know what percentage gain is required to recover a percentage loss.

$$Required\ gain = \frac{1}{1 - Percent\ loss} - 1$$

That is, a 50% loss requires a 100% gain to restore the original value. Because the amount risked on each trade depends on our expectations of loss, the results obtained from the optimal f calculation will be the size of the bet, the invested amount, or the number of futures contracts to be traded, as a percentage of the maximum loss. The value used as a maximum loss will be an estimate, because losses can always be greater than those already experienced in the market, or those found by historic testing. In addition, the optimal f will be different for each system, depending upon its performance profile.

The mathematics needed to determine optimal f is based on the Kelly Betting System.[29] Kelly states that the optimum bet is the one that maximizes the growth function $G(f)$:

---

[28] Ralph Vince, *Portfolio Management Formulas* (New York: John Wiley & Sons, 1990), 79–86. Also see Ralph Vince, *The Handbook of Portfolio Mathematics* (Hoboken, NJ: John Wiley & Sons, 2007), Chapters 4 and 5.

[29] John L. Kelly, Jr., "Kelly Betting System," *Bell System Technical Journal* (July 1956). Kelly's own method began with the optimal bet size based on unequal payouts as $p - (1 - p)/r$, where p is the probability of winning and r is the win/loss payout ratio.

$$G(f) = P \times \ln(1 + B \times f) + (1 - P) \times \ln(1 - f)$$

where f = the optimum fixed fraction
P = the probability of a winning bet or trade
B = the ratio of the average winning return to the average losing return
$\ln$ = the natural log function

The solution for finding the optimal fixed fraction to invest uses the geometric product and geometric mean, which represent the way in which profits and losses accrue.

$$Optimal\ f = \max\left[\prod_{i=1}^{n}\left(1 + \frac{f \times (-R_i)}{Largest\ loss}\right)\right]^{1/n}, \quad for\ f = 0.01\ to\ 1.0$$

where   max = the function that returns the maximum value
$\prod$ = the product function
R_i = the series of individual trade returns
n = the number of trades

By testing values of f between 0.01 and 1.0, and finding the geometric mean of all trades (each percentage profit or loss applied to the account value before the current trade), the value of f is found that gives the best return. That f-value is the optimal f, the percentage of the total account that should be invested for each trade. Another way of expressing optimal f, is given as[30]

$$f = [p \times (PLR + 1) - 1]/PLR$$

where   PLR = the ratio of average profit to average loss
p = the probability of a winning trade

Therefore, if $p = 0.50$, there is an equal chance of a profit or a loss, and the average profit is \$400 while the average loss is \$200 (giving $PLR = 2.0$), then $f = (0.50(2 + 1) - 1)/2 = 0.5/2 = 0.25$ or 25% of the available capital. Given an equal chance of a profit or a loss, it is not likely that there would be 4 losses in a row, each of 25%; however, the theory of runs shows that, out of every 100 trades, there should be one run of 6. Eventually, there will be a run of 4 or 5 losses in a row. Optimal f, however, invests a fraction of the current equity; therefore, after a loss of 25%, the next investment is 25% of the balance, or 18.75% of the initial equity. If there are further losses, that amount drops to 14.06%. After three losses in a row, instead of having lost 75% of the initial equity, the investment has only dropped by 57.81%. Over time, with profits twice as large as losses, and winning trades alternating normally with losing trades, the losses will be recovered.

[30] Robert P. Rotella, *The Elements of Successful Trading* (New York: The New York Institute of Finance, 1992), 549–550.

Observations of Optimal f

According to Alex Elder,[31] there are some difficulties in using optimal f. Because the value is based on every historic trade, the ideal amount to invest on the next trade will keep changing. In addition, if you trade a position larger than determined by optimal f, and get average results, you can expect to go broke eventually because you are overinvesting. On the other hand, if you invest less than the optimal amount, then your risk decreases arithmetically, but your profits decrease geometrically, which is another bad scenario. Because this is too complicated for most investors, the simple solution is to keep trading the same amount, with a reserve sufficiently large to absorb most extreme, adverse price moves.

On the positive side, Dr. Elder concludes that the most useful result of optimal f is that it shows the trader to:

- Never average down.

- Never meet margin calls.

- Liquidate the worst position first.

The application of optimal f uses the end value of individual trades, somewhat similar to the payout of a bet, while trades are comprised of many days of individual returns. The drawdown during a trade could be much larger than the final outcome of that trade. Then there is more risk than can be seen using only the final trader result.

Markowitz also took a look at this problem in 1959, with the following approximation:

$$Expected\ log\ return = Expected\ return - \frac{1}{2}\ Variance\ of\ returns$$

Using an amount of leverage M, the log returns becomes:

$$Expected\ leveraged\ log\ returns = M \times Expected\ return - \frac{1}{2}\ M^2\ Variance\ of\ returns$$

then

$$Optimal\ leverage = Returns/Variance = \mu/\sigma^2$$

As with other methods, this depends on the future being the same as the past. Because of the uncertainty, it may be best to consider using these methods only to reduce leverage, not increase it. Traders should measure success in terms of a return-to-risk ratio; therefore, this method of leveraging should be compared to other volatility stabilization approaches.

■ Comparing Expected and Actual Results

In the development of an economic model or trading system, the final selection, as well as the choices made along the way, are based on comparing the results of one method with another. Often the results are given in terms of information ratios,

---

[31] Dr. Alexander Elder, *Trading for a Living* (New York: John Wiley & Sons, 1995).

profit/loss ratios, annualized percentage profits, expected reliability, and drawdown ratios. Although these statistics are common, their predictive qualities and sometimes their accuracy are not known. On occasion, these results are generated by a sample that is too small; usually they are not the results of actual performance but an historic test. This does not mean that the model will be unsuccessful, but that the pattern of success might vary far from expectations. In actual trading, everyone experiences a series of losses far exceeding the maximum level that was expected; at that point, it is best to know whether this situation could occur within the realm of the system's profile or whether the system has failed. For example, a moving-average system is expected to have about 33% profitable trades with an average profit to average loss ratio of 4:1. But the first 10 trades of the system are losers. Should trading be stopped?

Binomial Probability

Consider the application of a random-number sequence to the trading model. What is the probability of l losses in n trades when the probability of a loss is p? Most of the work in this area of probability is credited to Bernoulli, whose study of a random walk is called a *Bernoulli process*. A clear representation of a random walk is shown by Pascal's triangle (Figure 46.16), where each box represents the probability of being in a particular position at a specific time in a forward random walk. The result of this process is called a *binomial distribution*.

The forward random walk has an analogy to price movement, with the far edges of Pascal's triangle showing the probability of a continuous sequence of wins or losses using random numbers. The sequence $\frac{1}{2}, \frac{1}{4}, \frac{1}{8}, \dots, (\frac{1}{2})^n$ is exactly the same as in the discussion of the Theory of Runs. The probability of successive losses can be calculated as the likelihood of a run of the same length, $(\frac{1}{2})^n + 2$.

A binomial distribution is useful in considering the total number of losses that can occur in any order within a sequence of trades; it is the probability of getting to a specific point at the base of Pascal's triangle when there is a high probability of moving to the left (losses) rather than the right (profits). The formula for the binomial probability is:

$$B(l : p, n) = \frac{n!}{l!(n-l)!} p^l (1-p)^{n-l}$$

					1					
			½		0		½			
		¼		0		¾		0	¼	
	⅛		0		⅜		0		⅜	0	⅛
¹⁄₁₆		0		⁴⁄₁₆		0		⁶⁄₁₆		0	⁴⁄₁₆	0	¹⁄₁₆

FIGURE 46.16 Pascal's Triangle.

where 　　l = the number of losses

　　　　n = the total number of tries

　　　　p = the probability of a loss

and the symbol "!" is the *factorial* (e.g., 5! = 5 × 4 × 3 × 2 × 1).

Consider the first 5 trades of a system with a probability of success of 1/3. How many losses should be expected? To answer the question, it must be phrased differently. In this case, what is the probability of having 4 losses out of the first 5 trades? Let $l = 4$ and find the binomial probability B for all possibilities based on a normal distribution function. Then,

$$B(4:0.667,5) \frac{5!}{4!1!} \times (0.667)^4 \times (0.333)^1$$

$$= \frac{120}{24} \times (0.19792) \times (0.333)$$

$$= 5 \times 0.659 = 0.32954$$

The binomial probability of having 4 losses out of the first 5 trades is about 33%. Table 46.14 shows the probability of loss for the first 5, 10, and 15 trades of a system

TABLE 46.14　The Probability of a Specific Number of Losses

5 Trades		10 Trades		15 Trades	
Losses	Probability (%)	Losses	Probability (%)	Losses	Probability (%)
0	1	0	0	0	0
1	4	1	0	1	0
2	16	2	0	2	0
3	33	3	2	3	0
4	33	4	5	4	0
5	13	5	14	5	1
		6	23	6	2
		7	26	7	6
		8	19	8	11
		9	9	9	18
		10	2	10	21
				11	20
				12	13
				13	6
				14	2
				15	0

m = 3⅓	m = 6⅔	m = 10
sd = 1.05	sd = 1.5	sd = 1.825

m = Mean.

sd = Standard deviation.

with a ⅓ predicted reliability. Results show the highest probability of loss is at the ⅔ point (mean) for each sequence, but the standard deviation gives the range of variance about the mean, so that from 2.3 to 4.4 losses are expected in every 5 trades, 5.2 to 8.2 in 10 trades, and 8.2 to 11.8 losses in 15 trades.

Note that in the 5-trade example, the chance of no loss is only 1% and there is a 13% chance of all losses. For the purpose of evaluation, it is easier to look at the maximum rather than the minimum number of losses. For 15 trades, there is an 8% chance of 13 or more losses; if the system has produced more than 12 losses in that period, there may be something wrong with the trading method.

Instead of the Pascal distribution, which is normal, the Poisson and various skewed distribution functions will be more appropriate for trading performance. It is well known that price changes and their returns have a skewed distribution with a fat tail.

χ^2—Chi-Square Test

Once a system has been traded and there is enough data to give a performance profile, a simple correlation between these actual results and the expected results can be found using the *chi-square test*. The sample error, $1/\sqrt{N}$, will tell you if there is enough data.

Assume that the real trading results show a reliability of 20% (1 out of 5 profitable trades) as compared to the expected reliability of 35%. What are the chances of getting the expected results? The chi-square test is

$$\chi^2 = \frac{(O-E)^2}{E}$$

where O = the observed or actual result
         E = the expected or theoretical result.

then,

$$\chi^2 = \frac{(20-35)^2}{35} + \frac{(80-65)^2}{65}$$

$$= \frac{(-15)^2}{35} + \frac{(-15)^2}{65}$$

$$= \frac{225}{35} + \frac{225}{65} = 6.428 + 3.46$$

$$= 9.89$$

The percentage of actual winning trades is compared with the anticipated winning trades and the losing trades with the expected losing trades. The answer must be found in the first row of Table 46.15, which gives the distribution of χ^2.

The probability is distributed unequally in the table because the results are only significant if the probability is small, showing less likelihood of the results occurring by chance. For this simple 2-element test, the result P is classified as

TABLE 46.15 Distribution of χ^2

Cases Less	.70	.50	.30	.20	.10	.05	.02	.01	.001
1	.15	.46	1.07	1.64	2.71	3.84	5.41	6.64	10.83
2	.71	1.39	2.41	3.22	4.61	5.99	7.82	9.21	13.82
3	1.42	2.37	3.67	4.64	6.25	7.82	9.84	11.34	16.27
4	2.20	3.36	4.88	5.99	7.78	9.49	11.67	13.28	18.47
5	3.00	4.35	6.06	7.29	9.24	11.07	13.39	15.09	20.52
6	3.83	5.35	7.23	8.56	10.65	12.59	15.03	16.81	22.46
7	4.67	6.35	8.38	9.80	12.02	14.07	16.62	18.48	24.32
8	5.53	7.34	9.52	11.03	13.36	15.51	18.17	20.09	26.13
9	6.39	8.34	10.66	12.24	14.68	16.92	19.68	21.67	27.88
10	7.27	9.34	11.78	13.44	15.99	18.31	21.16	23.21	29.59

(The top row header reads "Probability of Occurring by Chance"; first data column header row: 1)

Highly significant — if $P \geq 10.83$ (0.1% or 1/1000)
Significant — if $P \geq 6.64$ (1% or 1/100)
Probably significant — if $P \geq 3.84$ (5% or 1/20)

The answer $\chi^2 = 9.89$ is between 0.1% and 1.0%, which shows *significance*. For a large sample, the actual reliability should not have been 20% when 35% was expected.

The chi-square test can be used to compare actual price movement with random patterns to see whether there is appreciable variation. Based on the expected number of runs, Table 46.16 shows the difference between the expected runs of a random series compared to the actual runs of a price series.

Applying the actual data for runs of 1 through 8 against a random distribution, based on Table 46.16,

TABLE 46.16 Results from Analysis of Runs

Expected Length of Run	Actual Results (E)	Results (O)
1	1225	1214
2	612	620
3	306	311
4	153	167
5	77	67
6	38	41
7	19	16
8	10	5
9	5	3
≥ 10	4	5
$\geq 8*$	19	13

*The last groups were combined in order not to distort the results based on a small sample.

$$\chi^2 = \sum_{i=1}^{8} \frac{(O_i - E_i)^2}{E_i}$$

$$= \frac{(1214 - 1225)^2}{1225} + \frac{(620 - 612)^2}{612} + \frac{(311 - 306)^2}{306} + \frac{(167 - 153)^2}{152}$$

$$+ \frac{(67 - 77)^2}{77} + \frac{(41 - 38)^2}{38} + \frac{(16 - 19)^2}{19} + \frac{(13 - 19)^2}{19}$$

$$\overset{(1)}{= 0.09877} + \overset{(2)}{0.10457} + \overset{(3)}{0.08169} + \overset{(4)}{1.2810} + \overset{(5)}{1.2987}$$

$$\overset{(6)}{+ 0.23684} + \overset{(7)}{0.47368} + \overset{(8)}{1.8947}$$

$$= 5.470$$

From Table 46.15, the probability can be found in row 7 to be between 50% and 70% for 8 cases. These results are not significant; the Theory of Runs shows that all cases taken together give the same patterns as chance movement. Individual runs or sets of 2 or 3 adjacent runs can be inspected for distortion. In both cases, the results are further from normal but not mathematically significant. The two runs that differed the most were 4 to 5 days, which showed an 11% probability of occurring by chance.

Highly significant price runs can be found in the occurrence of extended runs, for example, 20 days, which is found occasionally in trending markets. By looking at the *asymmetry* of price movement, where a reverse run of 1 day is of negligible value, the significance of these runs will dramatically increase. Price movement is not a simple matter of random runs and equal payout.

Yates Correction Frank Yates, an English statistician, determined that the chi-square test often overestimates the significance for small amounts of data (under 5 data points). This can be corrected by subtracting 0.5 from the difference between each observed value and the expected value,

$$\chi^2_{Yates} = \sum_{i=1}^{N} \frac{(|O_i - E_i| - 0.5)^2}{E_i}$$

It should be noted that using a small number of data points is unreliable at best.